AGING AND MENTAL HEALTH

positive psychosocial
and biomedical approaches

The great Russian novelist and teacher Leo Tolstoi telling stories to his grandchildren.
Tolstoi's creative work has extended understanding
of the nature and flow of human life from childhood to old age.
Family life, faith, war and peace, human liberty, poverty and power,
love and death were among his great literary themes.

AGING & MENTAL HEALTH

positive psychosocial and biomedical approaches

ROBERT N. BUTLER, M.D.

Director, National Institute on Aging, National
Institutes of Health, Bethesda, Maryland

MYRNA I. LEWIS, ACSW

Social Worker, Psychotherapist and Gerontologist
in Private Practice, Washington, D.C.

THIRD EDITION

with 53 illustrations

The C. V. Mosby Company

ST. LOUIS • TORONTO • LONDON   1982

MOSBY

1906 **75** 1981
YEARS

A TRADITION OF PUBLISHING EXCELLENCE

Editor: Diane L. Bowen
Assistant editor: Susan Dust Schapper
Manuscript editor: Terry Young
Design: Diane Beasley
Production: Jeanne Gulledge

THIRD EDITION

The C.V. Mosby Company
11830 Westline Industrial Drive, St. Louis, Missouri 63141

Library of Congress Cataloging in Publication Data

Butler, Robert N.
    Aging and mental health.

    Includes bibliographies and index.
        1.   Aged—United States—Mental health services.
2.   Aged—United States—Services for.   3.   Geriatric
psychiatry—United States.   4.   Aged—Mental health.
I.   Lewis, Myrna I.   II.   Title.   [DNLM: 1.   Aged—
Psychology.   2.   Mental disorders—In old age.
WT 150 B986a]
RC451.4.A5B87   1981   362.2′0880565   81-14071
ISBN 0-8016-0924-0   AACR2

GW/VH/VH   9   8   7   6   5   4   3   2   1   02/D/227

To our
grandparents

Also by

Robert N. Butler and **Myrna I. Lewis**

Sex After Sixty

Love and Sex After Sixty (paperback title)

by

Robert N. Butler

Why Survive? Being Old in America

Human Aging (co-author)

Foreword

Many older persons are already deeply indebted to Dr. Butler for the significant contributions he has made to the field of aging. The number of indebted persons will increase sharply as the result of the decision by Dr. Butler and Ms. Lewis to author *Aging and Mental Health: Positive Psychosocial and Biomedical Approaches*.

Physicians, clergymen, social workers, nursing home personnel, and all others who deal with emotional crises that confront older persons will benefit from reading this discussion. Hopefully, many older persons who are not working in the field of aging will also read the book. From it, they can derive knowledge and insights that, if heeded, can contribute to the prevention of mental illness in the latter years of life.

As I have had the privilege of meeting with thousands of older persons in the last 2 years I have identified, among others, the following three messages that they are endeavoring to convey to society:

1. We want to make our own decisions regarding our own lives; we don't want other persons to make the decisions for us.
2. We want to continue to be involved in life; we don't want to be put on the shelf.
3. We want to be treated with dignity.

This affirmative approach to old age is the theme that runs throughout *Aging and Mental Health: Positive Psychosocial and Biomedical Approaches*. The "losses" that older persons experience are confronted in a frank and realistic manner. At the same time the authors demonstrate how these losses can contribute to the strengthening rather than the deterioration of mental health in old age.

Older persons want to approach life affirmatively. The chief obstacle to such an approach is the impact of ageism, which the authors so effectively identify and analyze. Those who give expression to ageism assume that growing old consists of a series of defeats. The authors believe that society has the capability, by rejecting ageism, of making it possible for the aging process to be characterized by a series of victories.

Far too often, for example, it is assumed that when an older person enters a nursing home he does so in preparation for death. It is clear, however, that many can be rehabilitated, both physically and mentally, if their care is approached with that objective in mind. Then it becomes possible for them to return to their own homes, often to become involved in constructive activity on behalf of society, and to experience the satisfaction that comes from a realization that the last days of life are indeed proving, in many respects, to be the best days.

The emphasis these authors place on the importance, both for the older person and for society, of continued involvement in life is one that needs to be underlined. Unfortunately, the trend in our nation is in the direction of more and more institutions' requiring retirement at a given age. In addition there is a trend in the direction of lowering the age for compulsory retirement. This means that our society must provide counseling, training, and placement services that will enable those who will be or have been forced to retire to have an opportunity for systematic, meaningful involvement in, for example, community service activities. Noninvolvement leads to rapid mental and physical deterioration. Noninvolvement deprives society of services that older persons are uniquely equipped to render.

It is hoped that the leadership provided by the authors of this book, as well as other leaders in the field of aging, will lead to a decision on the part of many educational institutions to help prepare persons to work in the field of aging. Far too many physicians and clergymen, for example, try to avoid ministering to the needs of older persons. Many medical and theological schools, by ignoring the importance of studies in the area of aging, share responsibility for such attitudes—attitudes that are in direct conflict with the concept of the dignity and worth of each individual irrespective of age.

I believe that Dr. Butler and Ms. Lewis have made a contribution that will lead to replacing despair with hope in the lives of many older persons.

Arthur S. Flemming

Chairman, 1971
White House Conference on Aging
(Foreword prepared 1973)

Postscript to foreword–1980

I am delighted that a new edition of this outstanding contribution to the field of aging is to be published. As I have continued to work in the field of aging first as U.S. Commissioner on Aging and now as Chairman of the U.S. Commission on Civil Rights, I have become increasingly aware of the opportunities for service to older persons that confront those who are trained in the field of mental health. Hearings conducted by our Commission make it clear, however, that the widespread prevalence of ageism means that many older persons are denied access to mental health services. I know that those trained in the field of mental health who read this book will be challenged, inspired, and helped to respond to the needs that older persons have for their help and assistance. I am likewise confident that those who work with or are associated with older workers in any capacity who read the book will be better equipped to help those older persons achieve the goal of the last days of life being the best days.

Arthur S. Flemming

Chairman,
U.S. Commission on Civil Rights (1981)

Preface to third edition

The extent of revision in a new edition varies with the rate of change in a field. This third edition reflects some fairly marked progress in mental health care for older people as we shall describe. New demographical and biometrical data, developments in the neurosciences, and the growth of information in the psychopharmacology of old age have been added to the present edition, as well as discussion of the impact of the newest classification of mental disorders (DSM-III). Because of the timing of this edition, 1980 Census material was not yet available; instead we have supplied the latest projections provided by the U.S. Census Bureau, based on the previous census and current population studies. Information on minority elderly has been expanded, as well as material on new legislation affecting the age of retirement, age discrimination, pensions, nursing home regulations, and legal service. The importance of patient education and self-care has been stressed.

The title of *Aging and Mental Health* has been expanded in this edition to include not only positive psychosocial approaches but also positive biomedical approaches in order to present new biomedical findings that are becoming incorporated into treatment and to give more emphasis to the roles of nurses, primary physicians, and other medical personnel involved in the mental health care of older persons. We have been particularly impressed by the pioneering part played by the nursing profession in caring for older people, both physically and emotionally, and have described this in some detail.

We have summarized here some of the more exciting recent developments affecting mental health in later life, all of which are described in greater detail in this edition:

1. Major developments in the neurosciences.
    a. New knowledge about the operation of the central nervous system and the 25 or so neurochemicals that play a role in regulating brain function (including the chemical conduction of messages to the brain). The development of positron emission transverse tomography (PETT) is an important experimental diagnostic tool for the precise measurement of central nervous system physiology.
    b. Further exploration of the character of the blood-brain barrier, the functional screen that separates and controls the admittance of certain chemicals from the general circulation into the cerebral circulation.
    c. An increased understanding of the biochemical concomitants of depression, including the mode of action of and the nature of brain receptors to antidepressant agents. This is leading to more effective treatment combining careful use of drugs with relatively short-term psychotherapy.
2. New developments in the medical and re-

habilitative care of older people, especially in those conditions like stroke and hearing and visual impairment that are notorious for producing profound psychological trauma and symptoms. To illustrate, the use of aspirin presents possibilities of prevention of stroke in men (but not in women, for reasons not yet understood). New surgical approaches and stroke rehabilitation techniques are improving as well. Also for the first time there will be scientific studies of the indications and contraindications of the use of active treatment by antihypertensive medications of isolated systolic hypertension among older people.

As another example, efforts have been begun, led by the National Institute on Aging and the National Institute of Neurological Communicative Disorders and Stroke, to understand deafness in old age, from fundamental mechanisms of presbycusis to studies of more effective prosthetic technology.

3. New diagnostic and treatment procedures are developing to deal with the sexual problems of both older men and women, as well as a new climate of acceptance of later life sexuality (including both hetero- and homosexuality).

4. Greater efforts to identify and capitalize on the treatment possibilities of mental impairments in older people in the early stages of their illnesses. This involves the education of the "gate keepers"—those doctors, nurses, social workers, and psychologists who first have contact with older people in distress—to recognize types of delirium (psychiatric emergencies which used to be called acute brain syndromes), many of which are reversible if correctly diagnosed and promptly treated.

5. A multiplying of efforts to understand and treat senile dementia of the Alzheimer type, perhaps the most personally devastating and socially costly of the physical afflictions of

later life. The National Institute on Aging, the National Institute of Neurological and Communicative Disorders and Stroke, and the National Institute of Mental Health have all been devoting increasing resources to understanding this condition or conditions. Promising leads in finding out the causes of senile dementia include a deficiency in the cholinergic system (one of the neurochemical systems), the possible role of slow viruses, the presence of antibrain antibodies, an increased concentration of aluminum in the central nervous system cells, and the possible role of genetics. Even if none of these proves to be a critical factor, all are enticing scientists into the challenge of finding the causes and cure or prevention of senile dementia.

The actual delivery of mental health services has lagged behind the development of new knowledge. But there have been promising steps in the service areas as well:

- A President's Commission on Mental Health identified older people as one of the "underserved groups," bringing greater visibility to the problems of later life.

- The 1980 White House Conference on Families drew some attention to the issues faced by older people and their families.

- The 1981 White House Conference on Aging activities provided still another opportunity to acquaint the American public, older people themselves, their families, and health and social service providers with the realities of age and a look at the many great contributions old people make to their community and civic and national life if given opportunities for basic financial, social, and medical support.

- The United Nations World Assembly on Aging will take place in 1982, calling worldwide attention to the growing populations of older people everywhere and launching an international action program aimed at guaranteeing economic and social security to older persons, as well as opportunities to contribute to national development.

- The U.S. Civil Rights Commission (under Arthur S. Flemming) has documented the bias against and neglect of older people in mental health services, leading to a need for adequate implementation of the law against age discrimination.
- The hospice movement for the physical and emotional care of the terminally ill has become a growing force in the American health care system.
- Rigid retirement practices that have brought psychological problems for so many have been ended. Mandatory retirement has ceased in the federal job sector, with an elevation of retirement age to 70 in the private sector (in large measure due to the efforts of Congressman Claude Pepper).
- Increasing attention is being drawn to the widespread problems of alcoholism through the efforts of former Congressman Wilbur Mills.
- A surge of interest is developing in the special problems of older women. Many of the issues of later life are largely the issues of those vast numbers of older women who are outliving men in greater and greater numbers. It can reasonably be said that aging, especially among the very old, is mostly a woman's problem, both in the developed and developing nations.
- Some new efforts have been started to help older people stay in their homes through expansion of at-home services as well as day-care and nutritional programs.
- Some improvement has occurred in the economic lot of at least those older persons who are now coming into old age and have the advantage of Social Security coverage. The Employee Retirement Income Security Act (ERISA) has brought some pension reform.

- The Department of Health and Human Services (formerly the Department of Health, Education and Welfare) has undertaken a significant examination of long-term care and various alternatives to institutionalization of the sick elderly.
- The psychotherapeutic value of reminiscence for older people has become increasingly recognized. The study of reminiscence and the use of it in outpatient and institutional settings are becoming more common.
- A Center on Mental Health and Aging has been formed at the National Institute of Mental Health.
- The National Institute on Aging, the newest (1976) of the 11 National Institutes of Health, has focused attention on basic research on old age. Its priorities include the study of geriatric medicine (and geriatric psychiatry), senile dementia, pharmacology, nutrition, endocrinology, immunology, and family life (for example, the effects of bereavement).
- Professional schools and other training institutions are beginning to introduce studies pertaining to old age into their curricula. Some 3000 institutions of higher education now have at least one course or more in gerontology.
- Professional organizations are starting to form around the issues of aging and mental health, for example, the American Association of Geriatric Psychiatry.

We will also briefly catalogue some of the current major problems, both in bringing quality mental health care to older people and in creating an environment that promotes mental health:

1. Just as new gains are being made in the scientific knowledge base for diagnosing and treating the mental and emotional disorders of later life, the nation is confronted with a reduction in national resources and a move to cut back both research and services.

2. Basic research in aging was meagerly funded even before the current national economic crisis. For example, less than 2% of the total funds for the National Institutes of Health in 1980 went to aging research, and less than 0.001% of all of the health costs associated with aging were directed toward research in aging.

3. The United States has not been able to gain control over costs for long-term care. Nursing home costs have risen from $10 billion in 1976 to over $21 billion in 1980, with a projected $75 billion or more by 1990. This creates a mood of despair and negativism toward new service programs and the improvement of existing mental health services. Finding a suitable method of financing long-term care is a priority issue. An even greater priority is prevention of institutionalization altogether through research that will lead to the elimination of the diseases of later life.

4. Remembering that economic security is a basic underpinning for emotional health, it is shocking to realize that the median income of an individual older person in 1979 was $83 per week, with double digit inflation hitting hardest at those with fixed incomes. Older women are still the poorest of the poor in both white and minority cultures. But the minority elderly of both sexes, especially Latino, black, and American Indian, suffer disproportionately compared to whites of both sexes.

5. Increasing crime and fear of crime have made many older persons prisoners in their own homes and defeat the potential for an improved quality of life.

6. "Deinstitutionalization"—the program designed to move people out of mental hospitals into the community—has resulted in shifting the chronically mentally ill and the elderly from one set of institutions to another. In 1955 about 47% of all mental patients were in nursing homes; in 1975 it was 75%: Nursing homes have become psychiatric holding-zones, without treatment facilities and personnel to treat the mentally ill. The Mental Health Systems Act introduced in 1979 was an effort in part to address the problem of "deinstitutionalization," to improve the community mental health centers, and to give priority to "underserved groups" in special programs, namely the aged, racial and ethnic minorities, and children.

7. The community mental health movement has yet to demonstrate any real commitment to the mental health care of the old.

8. Despite the intuitively understood importance of the "talking therapies" (psychotherapies), through which older people have a hearing for their emotional concerns as well as help with serious psychopathology, there are not yet well-designed, sophisticated scientific studies that demonstrate the effectiveness of such therapies. As a result, reimbursement for psychotherapy is at risk of being eliminated from or markedly reduced in federal Medicare and Medicaid and private insurance programs.

9. Although improvements have been made in the treatment of depression, the suicide rate in old age remains high, essentially as high as it was some years earlier.

10. Despite new leads in research and new knowledge of the central nervous system, the causes and therefore the treatment or prevention of the profoundly destructive organic brain diseases remain a mystery. Furthermore, there are not yet reliable, comprehensive, and clinically usable methods of measuring mental status and central nervous system function.

11. The understanding of how psychopharmacological drugs function in older persons is still limited.

12. Although spectacular advances have been made in molecular and cell biology, there is as yet no clear, testable set of hypotheses that would contribute to the understanding of the mechanisms of biological aging.

13. Technology developed for other uses, for example, in the space program, has not yet been redesigned and translated for use by those handicapped older persons with sensory, mobility, and communicative defects, even though this would be a logical and cost-effective redirection of such technology.

14. Unfortunately, interest in working with older people is still relatively slight among many of the helping professions—social work, psychology, medicine, etc. (Over 50% of older people receive their primary mental health care, such as it is, from primary care physicians.) Ageism has hardly been reversed in the training programs of professional schools and in institutions serving the old. Even nurses, traditionally the most involved with the old, show a reluctance to become too committed to work with the aging. Only 56,000 registered nurses work in 18,000 nursing homes, far fewer than are needed (reflecting partly, of course, the general shortage of nurses and the poor working conditions in many nursing homes).

15. The American family, always the major source of support of every kind for older people, has been undergoing critical changes, including a dramatic rise in the number of multigeneration families, a decreasing birth rate, and the sheer growth in numbers of older people. All of this places older people (especially older women since they outlive men) in critical jeopardy, with fewer younger family members on whom they can rely. Furthermore, with more middle-aged women entering the paid work force, there are less women to play the customary role of caregiver to older family members.

We have discussed all of these problems in this edition, along with current ideas for resolving them. The extraordinary triumph of greater survivorship to old age in the United States and the developed countries and to a growing extent around the globe has meant that for the first time a newborn infant has an excellent chance of living a full life-span. Our interest, and that of many others, is in helping to ensure the quality of that long life.

Robert N. Butler
Myrna I. Lewis
January 1981

Preface to first and second editions

Much about old age is not known, but infinitely more is known than is applied. This text is being written at a time of some progress in the struggle for quality mental health care of older persons. Isolated instances of fine care can be found in mental hospitals, medical centers, community mental health centers, nonprofit homes for the aged, and even commercial homes. But progress is still inadequate in most parts of our country. Little basic education on the nature of old age and its problems is offered in the professions of medicine, nursing, social work, and the varied mental health specialties.

Students who are otherwise humane and interested in people are likely to be uninterested, repulsed, or frightened by the thought of working with older persons. Educators, professionals, and lay people alike react in a similar manner. Why? Part of the answer lies in a familiar national prejudice we have called *ageism*. Ageism is a systematic stereotyping of and discrimination against people because they are old, just as racism and sexism accomplish this in relation to skin color and gender. Older people are categorized as senile, rigid in thought and manner, garrulous, and old-fashioned in morality and skills; and a multitude of other labels are applied. Ageism allows the younger generations to see older people as different from themselves; thus they subtly cease to identify with their elders as human beings. Men-

tal and physical health problems can be more easily ignored, as can the frequently poor social and economic plight of older people. However, an added factor in ageism causes uneasiness. Unlike racists and sexists, who never need fear change in their skin color or gender, ageists are at least dimly aware that if they live long enough they too will end up being ''old''—the object of their own prejudice—and the ageists' attitudes turn into self-hatred. Where does ageism come from? There are many cultural influences, ranging from a productivity-minded society that places little value on the nonproducers to a thinly disguised attempt to avoid the personal realities of human aging and death. The traditional buffers of religious beliefs are in a process of challenge and change. No generally accepted ethical or philosophical system has yet evolved to deal with human life and death as a whole. So the individual fills the frightening vacuum with a self-protective prejudice that makes older people its victims. As is often the case with prejudice, the victims tend to believe the negative definition of themselves, and old people may accept and expect the treatment they receive—hardly a condition for sound mental health.

Ageism plays an important role in the generally negative opinion about mental health care in old age. In this text we hope to dispel some of the traditional diagnostic and treatment myths. We shall be discussing normal healthy aging versus mental illness in old age, age-related problems versus lifelong problems, and endogenous (inside —that is, personality) versus exogenous (outside—that is, environmental) problems. Contrary to popular belief older people can change, they can use treatment, and they often do improve as a result of care. Individual and group psychotherapy should always be considered rather than automatically ruled out. ''Senility'' is an overused and inaccurate term that locks the old into a hopeless category. Older people need freedom—encouragement to move in new directions; autonomy and independence are precious commodities for them. ''Identity'' needs to be flexible so that individuals are not trapped in a fixed role or view of themselves. In summary, the physical, social, cultural, and economic aspects of people's lives are all intricately woven into their psychological well-being.

In providing information about old age, we do not espouse such fields as geriatric psychiatry, geriatric psychology, and geriatric social work. Mental health specialties must of course include the significant emotional aspects of old age, but we believe this information should be part of a core therapy of the life cycle of human beings rather than a separate entity. Some specialization is inevitable; some research foci are desirable, but excessive specialization is fragmentation, pure and simple, and more comfortable for the provider of mental health care than for those receiving services. Mental health specialists should be responsible for persons of all ages, races, socioeconomic classes, and diagnostic categories if they are to function in a flexible, useful manner. The swing toward specialization has focused attention on particular problem areas, but now we see the need for a gathering together: a focusing on the individual from birth through death in a coherent manner. Older people are first of all people, like everyone else, with old age being a developmental stage of their ongoing lives. We seem to forget that people in their later years are still alive, with human needs and feelings, until the very moment of death.

The mental health specialists we will be referring to include all the people who contribute to the mental health care of older people in various settings. Nurses' aides, nursing assistants, technicians, and paraprofessionals are as vital to care as psychiatrists, social workers, family doctors, psychologists, and registered nurses. All function interdependently and even in some cases interchangeably. Homemakers and community aides and physical, recreational, and occupational therapists are included, as well as administrators and the nonpsychiatric staff of treatment institutions. Members of the clergy, police officers, and lawyers are surprisingly involved in the lives of mentally ill old people. Older people receive psychiatric care in public clinics and hospitals, foster care homes, nursing homes, and health maintenance facilities. If they can afford it, they go to private practitioners, private hospitals, and counseling agencies. A myriad of services closely affect the mental health of older people—welfare agencies, food stamp programs, Social Security and Medicare, health insurance companies, churches, public transportation, police protection, and pharmacists. The absence, presence, and style of functioning of any of these can greatly influence emotional well-being or cause stress.

We are particularly concerned about the training institutions and programs that produce mental health specialists—schools of medicine, social work, or nursing, departments of psychology, and mental health training courses. Negative predilections about older people may become solidified as students see the problems of old age given short shrift in classroom curricula. We have heard and seen grossly inaccurate material presented by otherwise well-trained educators. Relatively few students want the field work placements in old age homes or training duty on geriatric wards. Older people are written off as untreatable and depressing. Research, when it is done, is too often aimed at lengthening life rather than making life satisfying, dignified, or at least bearable. In our view, the study of late life is a natural and valuable part of an understanding of human beings.

Treatment of mental health problems of older people is not only mandatory but often productive.

In this revision we have adopted the policy of compiling footnoted and end-of-the-chapter basic references rather than simply up-to-date ones, except when new ground is explored and new contributions have been made. In our judgment there has been a surprising lack of historical emphasis in many gerontological writings, with a "rediscovering the wheel" result and a failure to give credit to earlier work. Our aim is to provide students of gerontology with a sense of the historical growth of the field.

In our writing, we have aimed for a down-to-earth, practical approach that nonetheless, points to an ideal not yet attained. We have made a deliberate effort to write in a straightforward style, avoiding jargon while at the same time introducing the basic terminology of the field. We hope that both professional and lay readers will find the book useful in their understanding of older people.

We acknowledge first the many older people with whom we have collaborated in care and research. Through their questions, and those of medical, social work, and nursing students, as well as allied health professionals, we have been forced to think through our understanding of the nature of older people and their problems.

Certain people have directly contributed to this book. Jean Jones, Librarian of the American Psychiatric Association, was a great aid to us. Helen Zeidler has served as research assistant. Monte Vanness, Cindy Hamilton, and Nancy Schwartz have typed the manuscript.

We are especially indebted to Dr. William A. Reid and to Shirley Ford, Magnolia Burton, and Irving Williams, of the Parkside-Arthur Capper Community Mental Health Team in Washington, D.C.

Drs. Dexter Bullard, Marvin L. Adland, and Otto A. Will provided one of us (R.N.B.) the opportunity to create an experimental unit for psychotherapy of older people in 1958.

We wish to give special recognition to the contributions of the Committee on Aging of the Group for the Advancement of Psychiatry: Drs. Charles M. Gaitz, Alvin I. Goldfarb, Lawrence F. Greenleigh, Maurice E. Linden, Prescott W. Thompson, Montague Ullman, and Jack Weinberg.

We very much appreciate the help of Dr. Leslie S. Libow, Chief, Geriatric Medicine, Jewish Institute for Geriatric Care, New Hyde Park, New York.

We are grateful to our critical readers: Frances M. Carp, Ph.D., Institute of Urban and Regional Development, Berkeley, California; James Carter, M.D., Department of Psychiatry, Duke University Medical Center, Durham, North Carolina; Arlene Hynes, Librarian, St. Elizabeths Hospital, Washington, D.C.; Hobart C. Jackson, M.S.S., Administrator, Steven Smith Home for the Aged, Philadelphia, Pennsylvania, and Chairman, National Caucus on the Black Aged; Jean Jones, Librarian, American Psychiatric Association, Washington, D.C.; Marjorie F. Lowenthal, Professor and Director, Adult Development Research Program, Langley Porter Neuropsychiatric Institute, San Francisco, California; Robert Morris, Ph.D., Professor of Social Planning, Florence Heller Graduate School, Brandeis University, Walthan, Massachusetts; Dorothy V. Moses, R.N., Professor of Nursing, San Diego State College School of Nursing, San Diego, California; Bernice L. Neugarten, Ph.D., Professor and Chairman, Committee on Human Development, University of Chicago, Chicago, Illinois; Helen Padula, ACSW, State of Maryland Department of Mental Hygiene, Baltimore, Maryland; Ollie A. Randall, Ph.D., Social Work, New York, New York; William A. Reid, M.D., Psychiatrist and Director, Parkside-Arthur Capper Community Mental Health Team, Washington, D.C.; George Roby, M.S.W., Division Chief, Adult Services, Washington, D.C.; Sheldon S. Tobin, Ph.D., University of Chicago School of Social Work, Chicago, Illinois; Montague Ullman, M.D., Director, Community Mental Health Center, Maimonides Medical Center, Brooklyn, New York; Arthur Waldman, M.A., Administrator, Philadelphia Geriatric Center, Philadelphia, Pennsylvania; Jack

Weinberg, M.D., Clinical Director, Illinois State Psychiatric Institute, Chicago, Illinois; and George Wolfe, M.S., Social Work, Takoma Park, Maryland.

Robert N. Butler
Myrna I. Lewis

1973

Contents

Appendixes

Glossaries

ONE

THE NATURE AND PROBLEMS
OF OLD AGE

1

Who are the elderly?

How do older people first come to the attention of mental health workers? We will give a few typical examples of situations that are likely to propel older people into the hands of those who offer mental health services.

■ Mr. K is a black man, age 66. He has come to a psychiatric hospital on his own, stating that he is depressed and has recently felt almost uncontrollable impulses to harm others. Occasionally he worries that he is being followed, his phone tapped, his food tampered with. He appears in poor health and underweight, although dressed neatly and appropriately. He lives with a 68-year-old widowed sister in two rented rooms; he was married and separated years ago and has no children. He has been employed regularly all his life in a variety of jobs, from service station attendant to cook in a hamburger shop. Two years ago he was forced to stop work because of ill health, but his sister is still employed as a housekeeper. Income is minimal. He responds to a black nursing assistant at the hospital with an outpouring of his feelings of anger and bewilderment but becomes passive and vague in the presence of both black and white male resident physicians.

Are Mr. K's psychiatric symptoms a result of his personality characteristics and early history? Or could a physical disease condition be affecting his personality? What part may be played by malnutrition? Is he underweight because he is either physically sick or psychologically unable to care for himself, or is it because he has almost no money for food from month to month? Is his depression an acute reaction to physical illness or a lifelong response to social conditions? Why does he speak to the nursing assistant but turn silent at the sight of doctors? Why does he seem to have so little retirement income?

■ Mrs. P, white, age 88, has become disoriented and wanders out on the streets at night. After neighbors called the Community Mental Health Center, a psychiatrist–social worker team made a home visit. Mrs. P's husband died 15 years previously, and she has been living alone in a home they purchased 50 years ago in the central part of the city. Her income is higher than that of most widows. The home is orderly but badly in need of repair. The heat has been turned off by the gas company. Mrs. P's hearing has deteriorated. She expresses a terror of intruders and has armed herself with a stick and a kitchen knife. She determinedly announces she will never leave her home.

Why is she living alone in a big house and why has she allowed the home to deteriorate and the gas to be shut off? Is her disorientation caused by poor health, isolation resulting from hearing loss, or lack of a proper diet? Is her fear of intruders exaggerated or realistic in her neighborhood? What has she been doing with her money, since she appears to have very little food? Should she be moved forcibly to a nursing institution, or is there some way to help her remain at home?

■ Mr. H is a white man, age 70. He has contacted a private psychiatrist because he is feeling suicidal. He is well off financially, lives with his wife, but feels increasingly upset and self-destructive. He retired as a college professor earlier in the year. His health is good but recently he has panicked because he feels his memory is failing.

Is Mr. H overreacting to a minor memory change? If so, why is this so upsetting to him? Or does he perhaps have an undiagnosed brain disease? Are suicidal thoughts rare for a man his age?

■ Mrs. F is a 79-year-old Spanish-speaking woman who is progressively disoriented and confused. She becomes agitated at night and has been returned home by neighbors and police after being found confused, walking the streets. She has been incontinent of urine and feces but has not shown neurological symptoms. Is she suffering from senile dementia of the Alzheimer type? If so, can she be cared for at home? Is the disease treatable?

Each of these older persons came to the attention of mental health personnel because of psychiatric symptoms. But, as is obvious, evaluation of the symptoms requires an understanding of the person's entire life situation—physical status, personality, family history, racial background, income, housing, social status, educational level. Realistic and appropriate treatment is greatly facilitated by a fairly sophisticated understanding of social, psychological, and medical phenomena.

What is old age?

Photo by David Spilver.

We shall therefore in this chapter give an overview of the environmental realities of older persons in order to provide a general background for our later discussion of the more specific aspects of mental health care of older people.

WHAT AGE IS CONSIDERED "OLDER"?

Aging, of course, begins with conception.[1] The selection of age 65 for use as the demarcation between middle and old age is an arbitrary one, patterned after the social legislation of Chancellor Otto von Bismarck in Germany in the 1880s. (Actually, 70 was the original age selected by Bismarck.) This definition of old age has been adhered to for social purposes—as a means for determining the point of retirement or the point of eligibility for various services available to older persons. But the age of 65 has somewhat limited relevance in describing other aspects of functioning such as general health, mental capacity, psychological or physical endurance, or creativity. Gerontologists have attempted to deal with this unreliable concept of "oldness" after 65 by dividing old age into two groups: early old age, 65 to 74 years, and advanced old age, 75 and above. But the obvious point is that age is a convenient yet frequently inaccurate indicator of a person's physical and mental status and must not be relied on too heavily for evidence about human beings.

NUMBER OF OLDER PERSONS IN THE UNITED STATES[2]
Total older population

In the United States at the end of 1981 there were an estimated 25.6 million people who were age 65 or over—just over 11% of the population.[2a]

In mid-1979 most older people were under 75 (61.9%), over half were under 73, more than a third (35.2%) were under 70, and about 9% (2.3 million) were over 85 years of age. The 75-plus and 85-plus age groups are the fastest growing age segments of the U.S. population. This is of great social, economic, and medical importance because of the dramatic increase in the need for care in the 75-plus and especially the 85-plus age groups. For example, 40% of nursing home residents are over 85.

We do not have accurate information on the number of centenarians. At the end of 1976, about 10,700 persons produced some "proof of age" of over 100 years and were receiving Social Security benefits.[3] It is interesting that more than 106,000 persons reported themselves as over 100 years of age in the 1970 U.S. Census.[4] This is probably an exaggeration and illustrates pride in extreme old age—the U.S. Office of Population Estimates has concluded that some 100,000 of these self-reported centenarians were not actually that old.

In all nations—including the developing nations—there is an increase in the absolute numbers of older people because of major improvements in maternal, childhood, and infant mortality as well as in middle- and late-life mortality from heart disease and stroke. In the developed nations there is also a significant increase in the relative proportions of older versus younger persons.

The age composition of the United States is undergoing extraordinary change. In 1900 the average life expectancy was 47 years and only 4% of the population was 65 and older. The high rates of maternal, childhood, and infant mortality contributed to the low life expectancy. Social, economic, and health progress have made a vast dif-

---

[1] Strictly speaking, aging begins before conception. A female is born with all her ova (eggs) and they age as she ages. There are no new eggs. Because of this fact, there is an increased incidence of Down's syndrome, causing mental retardation, in children born to older women.

[2] 1980 Census data were not yet available for analysis during the preparation of this third edition. We have used the latest available census material and are greatly indebted to the work of Herman Brotman, consulting gerontologist.

[2a] Of Americans, 5,000 become 65 every day. Thirty-four hundred people 65 and over die every day. Thus, there is a daily gain in the 65-plus population of 1,600. This is referred to as the "turnover rate."

[3] Social Security Administration: Research and statistics note no. 19, Oct. 5, 1976.

[4] U.S. Bureau of the Census: General population characteristics, U.S., 1970, pp. I-265.

ference. By 1979 the average life expectancy at birth was nearly 73.[5]

By present projections—between the years 2020 and 2030—when the post–World War II baby boom grows old, about 20% or 1 of 5 Americans could be over 65. (See Figs. 1 and 2.) So far in the twentieth century, all projections of the numbers of older people have turned out to be underestimations. This is partly because of the unprecedented drops in mortality in the middle and later years from heart disease and stroke and partly because of a drop in the birthrate, bringing it *below* zero population growth. With new medical discoveries, improved health care, and a persisting low birthrate, the population of older persons may increase even more dramatically.

This "demographic revolution" should be seen

as a triumph of survivorship rather than as a cause for despair. What it means is that more and more people have the opportunity to live out a full life course.[6] This revolution or triumph will increase the median age of the population from 27.9 in 1970 and 29 in 1976 to 37.6 in 2025[7]—hardly an "aging" or "graying" society but certainly one with a different blend of age groups and generations. The age distribution of the total population in 1975 compared to 2025 provides a clearer overall picture of our future society than either the per-

---

[5] The sharp increase in survival has had many profound social consequences; for example, when marriage was made a sacrament in the ninth century A.D., the prospect of marriage lasting into the couple's forties was small. The concepts of retirement and late-life leisure were rudimentary at best.

[6] The twentieth century has seen increased life expectancy—but not increased natural or maximal life-span. It is most important to distinguish between "life expectancy," the actuarial projection of probable years of life from a base year such as birth or age 65, and "life-span," the inherent, maximal length of life of a species.

[7] See U.S. Bureau of the Census: Projections of the population of the United States: 1977 to 2050, Current Population Reports, Series P-25, No. 704, Washington, D.C., 1977, U.S. Government Printing Office.

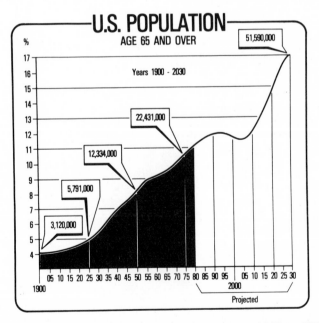

Fig. 1. Percentage of American population 65 and older from 1900 to 1975, with predictions for 1980 to 2030.

U.S. Bureau of the Census. 1978.

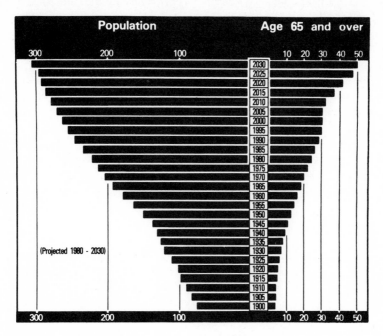

Fig. 2. Bars show number of persons age 65 and older compared with total population from 1900. The chart extends to the year 2030.

U.S. Bureau of the Census, 1978.

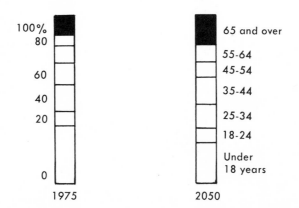

Fig. 3. Age distribution of total population in 1975 compared to projections for the year 2050.

Based on U.S. Bureau of the Census figures, and reprinted with permission from Rhine, S.: Older workers and retirement, Conference Board Research Report No. 738, New York, 1978, The Conference Board, Inc.

centage of persons over 65 or the median age (see Fig. 3).

A word should be said here about the considerable concern of policy makers and the public over what is known as the "dependency ratio"—the income maintenance and health costs of the burgeoning older population. In truth, the proportional financial "burden" on the middle working generations has not changed much because there are also fewer children and youths for these people to support (see Table 1-1).

Of the present older population, 15% were born somewhere other than in the United States (see

Table 1-1. "Dependency ratio": comparison of numbers of persons under 18 and over 65 (the "dependents") to the middle generations (the "workers")

Year	Number of persons under age 18 per 100 persons age 18 to 64	Number of persons age 65+ per 100 persons age 18 to 64	Total number of "dependents" per 100 "workers"
1970	61.1	17.6	78.7
1977	49.7	18.2	67.9
2000	43.2	20.0	63.2
2025	42.1	29.6	71.7
2050	41.7	30.2	71.9

From Brotman, H.B.: Every ninth American, p. 28. In U.S. Senate Special Committee on Aging: Developments in aging, 1978, Washington, D.C., 1979, U.S. Government Printing Office (revised June 1980).

Table 1-2. The number and percentage of Americans over 65 who are foreign born,* 1970

No. of population†	20,087,000
No. of foreign born‡	3,010,103
Percentage of foreign born	15

*The foreign born include those who have not become U.S. citizens.
†U.S. Bureau of the Census: Population estimates and projections, Current Population Reports, Series P-25, No. 721, Washington, D.C., U.S. Government Printing Office.
‡U.S. Bureau of the Census: National origins and languages, 1970 Census, Subject Report PC(2)-1A.

Table 1-2). Many immigrated in their youth with the great migrations from Europe. Others came later from countries like Mexico and Cuba. Not all are citizens of the United States, not all speak English, and many still carry the customs and cultural pattern of their mother countries in adapting to old age. This adds to the richness and uniqueness of the older population but makes the provision of services in later life more complicated.

Men versus women

This is not only the century of increasing proportions of older people but of older women. A marked difference exists between the life expectancies of men and women (see Table 1-3). In the United States women live 7.8 years longer from birth and 4.4 years longer from age 65. Older women numbered more than 14.6 million in mid-1979 compared to 10 million men. Women outlive men every place in the world where women no longer perform backbreaking physical labor and where adequate sanitation and a reduced maternal mortality are present.

In the United States women outlive men because of the higher male mortality from arteriosclerotic heart disease, lung cancer and emphysema (associated with tobacco intake), industrial accidents and toxicity, motor vehicle and other accidents, suicide, cirrhosis of the liver (associated with alcoholism), etc. These account for three quarters of the sex differential in mortality—the other one quarter is still unclear.[8] Life-style, life

[8] Waldrom, I., and Johnston, S.: Why do women live longer than men? Journal of Human Stress, **2**(pt. 1):2-13, 1976; **2**(pt. 2):19-30, 1976.

Table 1-3. Life expectancy of males and females, 1978

	Male	Female	Both sexes
At birth	69.3	77.1	73.2
65 years	13.9	18.3	16.3

Data from U.S. Bureau of the Census, 1978.

stress, hormonal differences, genetic differences in immune resistance, and other possible differences between the sexes must be further studied.[9] For every 100 men over 65 years there are 146 women. The ratio changes from about 130 women per 100 men for ages 65 and 74 to more than 224 women per 100 men at age 85 and over.

In the United States in 1979 there were 105.5 females per 100 males in the total population. More boy babies were born than girl, and boys continue to outnumber girls until age 18. At this point a shift occurs in the opposite direction, becoming most pronounced in the older generations.

---

[9]Fears that American women will lose their long-living capacity as they move into the labor force (the proportion of women in the labor force increased from 28% in 1950 to 42% in 1978; most were married women) have so far been unsubstantiated. For example an 8-year study of 352 housewives, 387 working women, and 580 men involved in the Framingham Heart Study found that working women did not have a significantly higher incidence of coronary heart disease (CHD) than housewives (7.8% versus 5.4%) and, in fact, those women working the longest period of time, for example, single women, had the lowest rate of CHD. (A factor here could be that relatively healthy women are the most likely to join the labor force, leaving less healthy women at home.) However, working women who had ever been married, had raised three or more children, and had been employed in clerical work had a higher risk of CHD, suggesting that clerical work is a particularly stressful occupation, especially when combined with the demands of raising a family and/or that women with personalities prone to develop stress diseases select clerical work when they become employed. See Haynes, S.G., and Feinlieb, M.: Women, work and coronary heart disease: prospective findings from the Framingham Heart Study, paper presented at the 86th Annual Meeting of the American Psychological Association, Toronto, Canada, Aug. 1978.

The life expectancy of a baby boy born in the United States in 1977 is 69.3 years and that of a baby girl is 77.1 years, almost 8 years longer. In 1977, for people who were already 65 years old, life expectancy was 16.3 additional years, again with a differential between men (13.9 years) and women (18.3 years).

Nonwhite versus white

The survival pattern for the white U.S. population has always been better than that of the nonwhite races.[10] However, the difference in life expectancy between whites and nonwhites is narrowing. Life expectancy at birth for whites was 15.9 years higher in 1900-1902 and decreased to a 5.2 year difference in 1976, a 67% decrease. Similarly, life expectancy at age 65 for whites was 1 year higher than for nonwhites in 1900-1902 and dropped to a 0.3 year difference in 1976, a 70% drop (see Table 1-4).

The number of black older persons has risen from 1.2 million in 1960 to 1.8 million in 1977.

---

[10]This is with the exception of Asian-Americans of all ages, who generally fared better than did whites in the mortality statistics. Asian-Americans had the highest levels of income and education and the lowest death rates, while blacks had the lowest income and educational levels and the highest death rates. The death rates for blacks as well as for American Indian and Alaskan natives are particularly high in the younger and middle age groups. Deaths among black infants are twice as high as those of white infants. The death rate for blacks age 24 to 44 is nearly 2.5 times as high as the rate for whites of that age group, with violent causes of death—accidents and homicides—especially high. See U.S. health called 'never better,' but blacks continue to lag, Washington Star, Dec. 6, 1975, p. A-5.

Table 1-4. Life expectancy by race

	White		Nonwhite	
	At birth	**Age 65**	**At birth**	**Age 65**
1900-1902	49.7 years	11.9 years	33.8 years	10.9 years
1976	73.5 years	16.1 years	68.3 years	15.8 years

From Siegel, J.S.: Recent and prospective demographic trends for the elderly population and some implications for health care, U.S. Bureau of the Census, Washington, D.C., 1977, U.S. Government Printing Office.

An older black inner-city resident.

Photo courtesy of Harold Grandy of the New Thing
Art and Architecture Center, Washington, D.C.

They now constitute 7.2% of the total black popu-lation of 25 million. Their lower life expectancy results, we can safely assume, from the generally lower socioeconomic status accorded to blacks in the United States. However at a certain point a re-versal occurs in which blacks begin to show a greater survival rate than whites. This "cross-over" was first reported in 1968.[11] In 1976 the cross-over in life expectancy occurred at age 65 for men and age 72 for women. The explanation for the cross-over is unclear, but it appears to be a "survival of the strongest" phenomenon in which the weak die early and only the strongest blacks survive. It is postulated that aged whites can afford better care and thus more of the weak survive, to die at a greater rate later on.

Although they comprise more than 11% of the total population, black people make up only 8% of the older age group. The effects of institutional-ized racism fall most heavily on black men—their life expectancy in 1976 of 64.1 years was 5 years less than that of white men, who could expect to live 68.9 years. White and black women had life expectancies of 76.6 and 72.6 respectively, with over a 4-year difference between them (see Table 1-5).

[11] Thornton, R., and Nam, C.: The lower mortality rates of nonwhites at the older ages: an enigma in demographic analysis, Research Reports in the Social Sciences **11**:1-8, 1968.

Table 1-5. Life expectancy (years) at birth and at age 65 by race and sex, 1976

	Whites		Nonwhites		
	Male	Female	Male	Female	All classes
At birth	69.7	77.3	64.1	72.6	72.8
65 years	13.7	18.1	13.8	17.6	16.0

Data from U.S. Department of Health, Education and Welfare, Public Health Service: Monthly vital statistics report **26**(12):supp. 2, March 1978.

Black older women outlive black men to an increasing degree, as do their white counterparts. The ratio of black women per 100 black men has increased from 115 in 1960 to 131 in 1970, and black females make up 56.7% of the total black aged population.

The impact of socioeconomic class on survivorship[12]

One's class definitely affects one's life expectancy. Demographic data show conclusively that an increasing life expectancy follows in the wake of increasing income and status. Professional and white-collar workers have lower mortality than blue-collar workers. In fact, the impact of social class may be even greater than is currently evident. Mortality studies are usually done by demographers and epidemiologists rather than by economists and thus most studies fail to take note of wealth beyond yearly income. Yet such wealth enormously affects the capacity to maintain health (through greater opportunities for rest, good nutrition, recreation, emotional security, and status) and to treat illness (through greater access to the finest acute and chronic care).

[12] See the work of Dr. Evelyn Kitagawa, Professor of Sociology at the University of Chicago and a past president of the Population Association of America. Her book, co-authored with Dr. Philip M. Hauser, entitled *Differential Mortality in the United States: A Study in Socioeconomic Epidemiology* (1973), summarizes the major findings to date on the relationships between socioeconomic status and life expectancy (mortality).

Table 1-6. Distribution of older persons by marital status, 1900 and 1978

Status	1978		1900	
	Men	Women	Men	Women
Married	75	37	67.3	34.3
Widowed	14	52	26.5	59.5
Other				
Divorced	6	5	0.5	0.3
Never married	5	6	5.8	6.0
TOTAL	100.0	100.0	100.0	100.0

Data from U.S. Department of Health, Education and Welfare: Facts about older Americans, Pub. No. (OHD) 75-20006, Washington, D.C., 1975, U.S. Government Printing Office; and U.S. Department of Commerce, Bureau of the Census: Social and economic characteristics of the older population, Washington, D.C., 1978, U.S. Government Printing Office, p. 3.

MARITAL STATUS

In looking at the marital situation of older people, one fact becomes strikingly clear. Most older men are married (77% in 1979); most older women are widows. One finds at least three times as many widows as widowers. Fifty-two percent of all older women are widows. This imbalance of women versus men, resulting from a combination of the greater female life expectancy and the fact that most women are younger than their husbands to begin with, represents one of the most poignant problems of the aged. Older men, if they survive, have greater options maritally. Chances are their wives are younger and will outlive them. But if not, the man can quite freely find a second wife. The odds are with him. There are many women from which to choose. It is socially acceptable for a man to find a wife in either his own age group or any of the younger age groups. An older woman, however, is looked on with disdain if she marries someone much younger. In 1976 some 38,820 older men married, while for women the comparable figure was only 21,180, even though women in the age group outnumbered men by 4.6 million (see also Table 1-6).

There is a larger number of older blacks than whites who do not live with their spouses. This has been attributed to the greater economic pressures on families, including unemployment and public welfare laws that encourage black men to leave home early in life. The shorter life expectancy of black men also is an important factor, leaving a black woman widowed much earlier than a white woman.

HOUSING STATUS
With whom do older persons live?

One of the more prevalent myths about older people is that large numbers of them live in institutions: chronic disease hospitals, homes for the aged, nursing homes, mental institutions, foster homes, etc. If one asks any group of ordinary citizens—or for that matter a group of medical, nursing, or social work students—what percentage of older people live in such settings, the answers will range all the way up to 50%. The reality is that at one time only 5% of all older people are in such institutions.[13] This is, of course, a substantial number of people and rightly deserves serious attention. But it is important to remember that 95% of the aged are on their own in the community, living either by themselves or (more often) with a spouse, family, or friends. Out of every 10 older Americans, 7 live in families. Approximately one fourth live alone or with nonrelatives. Again the situation differs with regard to men and women. Men, because of their shorter life-span, usually live with a spouse and/or family. But only one third of women do so. Women are three times more likely to live alone or with nonrelatives.

In reference to the black older population, another widely held idea bears a more thoughtful look. It has been frequently stated that older black people are more likely to live in extended families than are older whites. Yet in 1960, 50.2% of black people 60 years of age and above lived alone or with only one other person, relative or nonrelative; 16% lived entirely alone. One study found that 11 of every 100 older blacks had no living relatives, compared to 6 out of 100 whites with no relatives. It is true that the black older persons are more likely than white to have people other than spouses living with them: 20% of blacks, as compared to 12.5% of whites, had others in their households besides a husband and wife. We can surmise that this is a result of economic necessity or convenience, which solidified in a cultural style of living earlier in the life cycle. Data contrasting men and women show that half of all black older men live with their wives but, again because of a longer life-span, only one fifth of black older women live with their husbands.

GEOGRAPHICAL DISTRIBUTION

Older people, both black and white, live most frequently in central parts of cities and in rural locations.[14] The Midwest and upper New England areas have concentrations of older people because many of the young have left the farms. Older people have the lowest migration rates of all age groups; those older persons who do migrate tend to be the most affluent. Florida has the highest proportion of elderly, with 18.1% of its population comprised of older residents. Almost a quarter of the older people in the United States live in three states: California, New York, and Florida. Half of the nation's aged live in eight states, adding Pennsylvania, Texas, Illinois, Ohio, and Michigan. Arkansas, Iowa, Kansas, Maine, Massachusetts, Missouri, Nebraska, New Hampshire, North and South Dakota, Oklahoma, and Vermont all have greater than the national average of older people. New York State and California each have more than 2 million older residents, while Illinois, Florida, Ohio, Texas, and Pennsylvania have more than 1 million older persons, or one twentieth of the country's entire older population. The highest growth in percentage since 1970 is in Arizona, Florida, Hawaii, Nevada, and New Mexico—all states with warm climates and low industrialization, which older people find appealing.

---

[13] Although only 5% of older people are in institutions at any one time, 20% of all older persons at some time in their lives will receive nursing home care.

[14] There are increasing numbers of suburban older residents; it is projected that 15 years from now the suburbs may be predominately older persons.

The extent of poverty in old age.

Photo by David Spilver.

Older black persons again show a somewhat different configuration than older people as a whole. Three fifths still reside in the South, many in rural areas. But because large numbers moved to urban areas in the black rural-to-urban migrations of the early 1900s, older black persons are now also concentrated in central cities, primarily in those areas with the worst housing. Indeed, by 1970 1 of 2 older blacks lived in central city locations. Many are trapped there under the dual influence of economic hardship and a continuing racism that tends to preserve the suburban areas for whites. One

must add that the suburbs often welcome only whites with adequate finances and acceptable credentials. Public housing and housing for older persons, the mentally ill, or addicted whites are fought with the same vehemence as black or integrated housing. Older blacks increasingly share the inner city with younger blacks and those older whites who cannot afford to leave (although this pattern may change if continuing increases in oil prices make suburban commuting undesirable). The District of Columbia is an example of this phenomenon, with a population which in 1970 was

71.8% black. Older black people accounted for 11% of this total black population. Of the approximately 70,000 older persons in the nation's capital in 1971, 57% were white and 43% black, obviously a complete reversal from the younger population, which contains proportionately many more blacks. Younger whites have tended to move to the surrounding suburbs.

Standards of housing

It has been estimated that up to 30% of older persons in the United States live in substandard housing. This is largely a result of outright poverty or marginal income. Two thirds of all older people own their own homes. However, most of these homes were purchased in early adulthood 40 to 50 years before, and many have become substandard. The cost of maintenance, utilities (especially fuel), and property taxes has so skyrocketed that upkeep and needed improvements become impossible for older people on fixed incomes. The remaining one third of older persons live, either alone or with relatives or friends, in retirement villages, rented tenements, retirement hotels, low- and middle-class government-subsidized housing, or housing sponsored by unions, churches, and benevolent associations. Some older people live in public housing, which is often seen by them as a highly desirable resource in view of the wretched alternatives available. Finally, many older people are so poor they cannot afford even public housing.

An example of this is the situation that came to light in the Washington, D.C., newspapers in 1970 when several people (one of them elderly) were found to be living in a shelter made of cardboard and scraps. They had been living there for months, in sight of the Capitol.

An essential concern for people on fixed income is the percentage that they must use for housing. Many of the 1 million older people in New York City were surviving because of rent controls that maintained rents at a fixed rate until a tenant moved. In 1971 the state government removed rent control, leaving older persons stranded with increasing rents.

INCOME
Extent of poverty

Poverty, like substandard housing, is typically associated with old age. People who were poor all their lives can expect to become poorer in old age. But they are joined by a multitude of people who become poor only after becoming old (see Table 1-7). About 14% (3.2 million) of older people were below the official poverty level in 1978.[15] (The unrealistically low annual income levels of $3,116 and $3,917 for a single person and a couple, respectively, were used.) In our opinion this is a gross underestimation of poverty. We believe 25% of older persons are poor by more realistic standards such as economist Leon Keyserling's Deprivation Index.[16] Although older people represent only 11% of the total population, they constitute 20% of the poor in America. Of the older poor, 85% are white.[17] There are clearly many more poor whites in actual numbers than poor blacks. However, a greater proportion of the black aged are poor and their poverty is more profound. Hispanic-American, Indian American, and certain Asian- and Pacific Island–American older persons are also especially disadvantaged, as are women of all ethnic and racial groups.

Older persons receive half the income of younger persons. In 1978, half of the families headed

[15] The poverty index was adopted by a federal interagency committee in 1969. The index is based on the Agriculture Department's 1961 Economy Food Plan and reflects the different consumption requirements of families based on their size and composition, sex and age of the family head, and farm-nonfarm residence. For example, it was determined that families of three or more persons spend about a third of their income on food. As a result, the poverty level of these families was set at about three times the cost of the economy food plan. "Income" refers only to money income and does not reflect nonmoney transfers such as food stamps, health benefits, and subsidized housing.

[16] See Butler, R.N.: Why survive? Being old in America, New York, 1975, Harper & Row, Publishers, Inc., p. 28.

[17] A little-known example of poverty among whites is that found among the Jewish elderly. In Los Angeles alone a recent study found 8,000 older Jewish poor on public assistance and another 10,000 eligible who had not applied. See also the account of elderly Jews in Venice, California, by anthropologist B. Myerhoff: Number our days, New York, 1979, E.P. Dutton & Co., Inc.

Table 1-7. Aggregate income in 1977 for persons 50 years old and over, by age and sex (numbers in thousands; population as of March 1978)

Subject	All ages	Age (years)				
		50 to 54	55 to 59	60 to 64	65 to 69	70 and over
Both sexes						
Total with income	139,422	9,824	9,196	8,368	7,825	13,641
Median income (dollars)	6,429	10,065	9,384	6,713	4,295	3,712
Mean income (dollars)	8,886	12,368	12,041	9,620	6,596	5,427
Aggregate income (billions of dollars)	1,239	122	111	81	52	74
Male						
Total with income	74,015	5,586	5,196	4,494	3,535	5,610
Median income (dollars)	10,123	14,842	13,612	10,511	6,516	5,007
Mean income (dollars)	12,063	16,714	16,279	13,295	9,357	7,202
Aggregate income (billions of dollars)	893	93	85	60	33	40
Female						
Total with income	65,407	4,238	4,001	3,874	4,290	8,032
Median income (dollars)	3,941	5,628	5,398	3,769	3,040	3,108
Mean income (dollars)	5,291	6,641	6,539	5,356	4,321	4,187
Aggregate income (billions of dollars)	346	28	26	21	19	34

Data from U.S. Bureau of the Census: March 1978 current population survey.
Note: While it demonstrates the decline in income as people age, this table also illustrates the considerable collective purchasing power of persons over 60: an aggregate money income of $207 billion in 1977 out of the total of $1,239 billion for the entire population.

by an older person had incomes of less than $10,141, as compared with $19,310 for families with heads under 65. The median income of an older person living alone or with nonrelatives was $4,303, compared with $8,530 for those under 65. That is about $83 per week, compared to about $164 per week.

Without Social Security the economic picture for older people would be even more bleak. The average monthly Social Security payment to the retired worker in 1979 was $293.39, to their wives or husbands $148.03, and to their children $118.90. Almost 60% of all retired workers are receiving "reduced benefits" because they started to draw benefits before reaching age 65. Some did so out of choice, but others were forced to because of poor health or unemployment. In 1979 nearly 2 million, or one twelfth of older people, received Supplemental Security Income (SSI).

Most income must go for food, shelter, and medical expenses—the essentials of existence. Thus the shortage of money has given rise to the myth that the aged can live on less because they do not need as much for clothing, transportation, entertainment, recreation, or education as the young. The truth is simply that older persons are not able to afford these items, which for younger people are considered necessary for mental health, social status, avoidance of isolation, and growth of the individual.

Middle and upper incomes

There are, of course, some middle- and upper-class older persons. Not all the old are poor. But, as we have seen, the gay rich widow is rare. In 1978 there were 8.5 million families headed by persons over 65; of these, half had incomes in excess of $10,000 per year.

Approximately 15% of the income of the older persons derives from accumulated assets. Those who clip coupons or collect rents are not penalized by offsetting reductions in Social Security. Of families with heads of household over 65, 1,538,000 have incomes over $20,000, and 168,000 of these had incomes over $50,000.

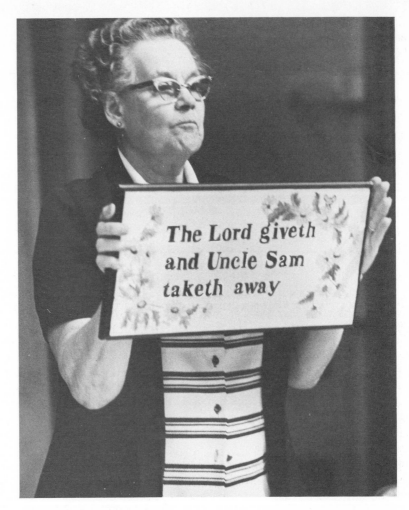

Citizen protest against proposed cut in retirement benefits.

Photo by Patricia and William Oriol.

Sources of income

Older people earn 29% of their aggregate income from continuing employment, while 46% comes from retirement, 4% from public assistance programs, and the remainder from investments (15%), veterans benefits (3%), and contributions from relatives (3%). It is commonly believed that older persons are adequately provided for by Social Security and Medicare, but these programs have not met their needs. By 1978, the average monthly Social Security benefits amounted to $261 for an individual. Many unskilled jobs, held primarily by blacks and women, were not covered until recently. Even now, some employees (for example, many domestic workers) are not covered. Medicare, too, needs improvements. Only 38% of the health expenses of older persons are met; the rest must be paid for out of their incomes. Hearing aids, glasses, dental care, podiatry, and various drugstore supplies, which are not covered under Medicare, are among items of obvious importance to older people.

EMPLOYMENT

Employment should ideally be a matter of choice after age 65. Indeed older people do earn 29% of their income. But their ability to work is hampered by two major factors: the Social Security ceiling on earnings (which says in effect that an older person is allowed only a small amount of earnings, for if more is earned, the Social Security check is reduced) and age discrimination in employment (both arbitrary retirement at 70[18] and bias against hiring older people). In addition, educational and technological obsolescence and the possible physical limitations of older persons combine to squeeze them out of the job market. Most of their work is concentrated in three low-earning categories: agricultural work, part-time work, and self-employment. Since 1900 the number of older men in the labor force has dropped from two thirds to one fifth. On the other hand, the percentage of women workers has remained at about 8%.

Black older men participate in the labor force in the same proportions as whites; but they earn less, do harder physical work, and are in poorer health (again remember that they die an average of 7.5 years sooner than white men). Older black women are more likely to work than white women, indicating their greater need to support themselves or supplement their husband's earnings. They, like black men, earn less, usually doing domestic and service work. Retirement by choice is less of an option because blacks' retirement benefits are often meager, in line with their previous low earnings. Indeed there may be no benefits at all. When they can no longer work, older blacks are simply mustered out of the labor market. They frequently must turn to SSI as the only income source available. Thus SSI programs have a disproportionate number of older blacks on their rolls, compared to whites, and it is important to understand why.

[18] Mandatory retirement has ended for federal employees.

HEALTH

It is obvious that old people get sick more frequently than the young. Yet 81% move about on their own legs, and only 5% are confined to institutions for physical or emotional care. In 86% there are chronic health problems of one kind or another that require more frequent doctors' visits, more and longer hospital stays (an average of 14 days a year), as well as more periods of illness at home, and result in more physical and emotional disability. In 1968 the annual per capita expenditure by older persons for health care was $590, considerably greater than that required by the average person in the United States. By 1977 the expenditure had risen to $1,745.

The mental health needs of older persons are substantial. Emotional and mental illnesses escalate over the course of the life cycle. Depression in particular rises with age, and suicide attains its peak in white men in their eighties. The suicide curves of white women and black men and women rise in the middle years and then decline. Depression and hypochondriasis commonly accompany the many physical ailments of old age, which range from cardiovascular disease to arthritis and hearing loss.

Organic brain disorders show increased incidence in old age. Older persons used to make up as much as 25% of all public mental hospital admissions, prior to recent efforts—at times precipitous and unfortunate—to reduce admissions.

EDUCATION

In a society in which formal schooling is the key to power and status, most older people cannot compete with the young. Only 8% are college graduates, while 2.1 million or 9% are functionally illiterate, with either no schooling or less than 5 years. No more than one half have completed elementary school. (Of the cohort generation born in 1880, 6% graduated from high school; 82% of the cohort generation born from 1945 to 1949 did so.) Blacks have greater illiteracy than whites but the problem of little formal education is a shared one. Our society pays little heed to experience, the "school of hard knocks," or informal education. Thus older persons are left with their accrued body of knowledge and understanding locked within themselves, unsought and unavailable to others.

POLITICAL POTENTIAL

The political strength of older persons is growing and will prove to be one of the "sleeper" surprises of future politics. Almost 90% of older people are registered to vote and two thirds vote regularly, many more than in any other age group. Older people are organizing themselves for political action and influence. There is growing restlessness and militancy among the elderly for "senior power." Along with political strength will come a new sense of self-respect and a respect from others that will not be dependent on solicitude but rather on a sober recognition of power at the ballot box on public issues.

HISPANIC OR LATINO OLDER PERSONS

Not enough is known about our second largest minority, the Latino[19] population, which in fact may be the largest racial/ethnic group in the United States by the year 2000.[20] Census figures for 1978 report the total Latino population at 12 million people.[21] This includes 10.5 million persons of Cuban, Central or South American, Mexican, or Puerto Rican origin and 1.5 million "other Spanish," many of whom are of European-Spanish background. The population of 12 million does not include the 2.8 million Spanish-speaking persons in Puerto Rico and a possible 8 million Spanish-speaking illegal aliens now living in the United States. Approximately 6 to 7 million of the 12 million Latino-Americans are of Mexican extraction, and about 80% of those live in urban areas, primarily in five Southwestern states: Arizona, California, Colorado, New Mexico, and Texas. Older persons make up an estimated 4% of the Latino population.[22]

Life expectancy is low. For example, in Colorado the life-span of the Mexican-American is 56.7 years in comparison to 67.5 for other Colorado residents. This is much lower than that for non-Mexican-American whites and even substantially lower than blacks'. In addition to poverty, poor housing, and lack of medical care and education, which have become our historical gift to minority citizens, older Latinos face the turmoil of drastic changes in their traditional life-styles. The young are breaking rapidly with their past, the extended family is shrinking into the nuclear family, and the

---

[19] A great difficulty in talking about the so-called Hispanic-American population is in simply defining that population. The various names used to describe parts or all of the group are in themselves confusing, for example, Chicanos, Boricuas, Mexican-Americans, Latinos, Puerto Ricans, Spanish-Americans, Razas, Latin-Americans, Hispanics, "persons of Spanish origin," and "persons with Spanish surnames." Researchers and demographers have used various measures like Spanish surname, Spanish-speaking, birthplace of the individual or his/her parents, Spanish-origin (self-identification of descent), and race (Indian, white [Spanish], black, or mestizo [mixture of Indian and Spanish]) to try to clarify populations under study but no single method of "naming" has yet been generally successful. Race and class bias are built into most descriptions. Until a better term is developed, we shall use "Latino," a term that seems the least objectionable and yet is recognizable to the U.S. public. See Hayes-Bautista, D.E.: Identifying 'Hispanic' populations: the influence of research methodology upon public policy, American Journal of Public Health **70**(4):353-356, 1980.

The U.S. Bureau of the Census directly measured the "Spanish origin" (the Census Bureau term) population in the 1980 Census, in contrast to the past when the Bureau took limited samplings of the group, using different identifiers (language, surname, national origin) in different states. Partly because of fear and distrust, members of the Latino community have avoided the census taker. Thus there is probably an undercount, affecting federal funding to assist Latino-Americans in need. Latino leaders believe the Latino population is 16 million rather than 12 million, without counting the estimated 4 to 8 million illegal aliens (also called undocumented workers).

[20] Macras, R.F.: U.S. Hispanics in 2000 A.D.—projecting the number, Agenda Magazine, May-June 1977, p. 16.

[21] U.S. Bureau of the Census: Persons of Hispanic origin in the United States, Current Population Reports, Series P-20, No. 328, Washington, D.C., 1978, U.S. Government Printing Office.

[22] Except for the Cuban population, with 8.6% over 65 years.

aged tend to be cut adrift from their rich culture and tradition. A sense of personal privacy and pride make it difficult for older persons to ask for and accept financial or medical aid. The government's SSI is not popular and often is unused. In addition, Spanish-speaking older persons face a language barrier and are too frequently expected to adapt to English, with no instruction, rather than receiving the courtesy of translations or Spanish-speaking and Spanish-oriented services.

AMERICAN INDIAN (NATIVE AMERICAN) OLDER PERSONS

As with the Latino-Americans, no one really knows how many American Indians there are—an ironic comment in a nation preoccupied with statistics. The 1970 census counted 792,730.[23] About 45% live in urban areas (20% of these are in central cities, with 25% in suburbs or small towns), while 30% live in rural areas, primarily reservations that are relatively isolated and inaccessible to the outside world. Nearly half of all Indians live in the West, primarily in Oklahoma, Arizona, California, and New Mexico, in that order of population density. There are no reliable estimates as to the number of older persons. But with an average life expectancy of 47 years,[24] one third shorter than the national average, it seems a wonder that any Indians survive to age 65.

Indians are the poorest people in the land. In 1971 one half of the families had incomes of less than $4,000 a year. Unemployment in 1972 reached 45% compared with 5.8% for non-Indians. Hunger and malnutrition are constant problems. If such poverty is the rule, we can be certain older Indians are even poorer. The traditional kinship support of the family is infeasible when the family itself has no resources. Older persons are left impoverished—particularly if their children leave the reservation.

[23] Criteria include at least one fourth Indian blood and registration on a recognized and approved tribal roll.

[24] Margolis, R.J.: Indians: a long list of grievances, The New York Times, Nov. 12, 1972. (Interestingly, the Indian Health Service placed life expectancy at 64 years in 1967, but this included only those Indians on or near a reservation.)

The medical care provided by the U.S. Public Health Service is considered totally inadequate to care for the Indian population. It is said that service for the most part is provided only for those who manage to make it to a hospital alive. The Public Health Service has no outreach program or preventive care. Thus older persons, along with the poor, the young, and the very sick, are at a terrible disadvantage in terms of survival on the desperate trek to the nearest medical facility.

Through all this, some Indians do manage to survive to old age, imbued with a fierce sense of reverence for their land. To older Indians the physical aspect of land is an essential element in their identity and sense of belonging—this in spite of the deprivation they experience in tenaciously holding on to that land.

The beginnings of descriptive studies of the characteristics and the lives of minority older persons in New Mexico,[25] Miami,[26] and the San Diego area[27] may be of further interest.

Because of their physical remoteness, the Eskimo and Aleut populations in Alaska are seldom noted in discussions of American older persons. The Aleuts have a greater life expectancy than the Eskimos, perhaps because the latter live in the more demanding environments of northern Alaska and Greenland. The perilousness of the environment is demonstrated in the fact that accidents are the leading cause of death for older Alaskan natives and American Indians.

[25] Rogers, C.J., and Gallion, T.E.: Characteristics of elderly Pueblo Indians in New Mexico, The Gerontologist **18**:482-487, 1978.

[26] Reys, M.J.: Elderly Cubans in exile: a working paper, report prepared for U.S. Senate Special Committee on Aging, Nov., 1971, Washington, D.C., 1971, U.S. Government Printing Office.

[27] Valle, R., editor and project director: A cross-cultural study of minority elders in San Diego, San Diego, 1978, The Campanile Press, San Diego State University. This study includes the following minority elders: F.D. Kepon, the elder American Indian; E.P. Stanford, the elder black; E. Cheng, the elder Chinese; W.H. Ishikawa, the elder Guamanian; K.C. Ishizuka, the elder Japanese; R. Walle and L. Mendoza, the elder Latino; R. Peterson, the elder Filipino; and W.H. Ishikawa, the elder Samoan.

ASIAN-AMERICAN AND PACIFIC ISLAND–AMERICAN OLDER PERSONS

As a combined minority group, the 2 million Asian-Americans[28] (primarily Chinese, Pilipino,[29] Japanese, Korean, and Samoan) make up about 1% of the U.S. population. By 1980 the Pilipinos were the largest Asian-American minority group, surpassing the Japanese, who have been the largest group since 1910.

More than 90% of Asian-Americans are located in metropolitan areas. The majority live in California and Hawaii as a result of immigration directly to those areas. Immigration policies have profoundly affected the lives of older Asian-Americans, particularly with regard to family life and male-female sex ratios. In the 1970 U.S. Census there were 26,856 Chinese over 65 years of age, about 6% of the total Chinese-American population. (However these figures are unreliable, since large numbers of people go unreported because of their illegal immigrant status.) Older males outnumber females (15,244 men to 11,612 women), reflecting pre–World War II immigration laws that prohibited women and children from accompanying men to the United States. Only 27% of the older Asian-Americans live with a spouse, compared to 43% for the general population of older persons. About 95% live in cities and two thirds have settled in San Francisco alone.[30] One study of older persons in San Francisco's Chinatown found half subsisting below the poverty line. About 80% live in households with annual incomes of less than $4,000 and 31% had less than $2,000.[31] Nationally the 1970 Census figures show 28% of all Chinese older persons are poor (according to the official poverty index). In New York City the rate was 40%. Traditional patterns of kinship and community responsibility have been damaged by the experiences of immigration and forced disruption of normal family life. Many of the older people speak little English—and can neither read nor write English or Chinese—thus increasing their difficulties in an alien culture.

In 1970, 47,159 Japanese-Americans (26,654 women and 20,505 men), or 8% of the total Japanese-American population, were over 65 years of age. Japanese-Americans appear to have been able to provide their older persons with greater family support and economic security, since they were not so severely restricted from bringing their families with them when immigrating. Yet one fifth of these older Japanese are poor, especially in areas outside California and Hawaii. Over half (58%) live alone, and the majority of these are widowed females. Older Japanese men usually speak at least broken English, but older women tend to speak only Japanese. Health surveys have found that many of these older persons are physically healthy and long-lived.

Older Pilipino-Americans are a smaller group, with 21,249 persons over 65 in 1970, representing almost 7% of the total Pilipino-American population. Eighty-one percent are male; however, 30% of these men live with a spouse as a result of interracial marriages. Two thirds reside in urban areas. (See Chapter 6 for further discussion.)

[28] Kalish, R.A., and Yuen, S.: Americans of East Asian ancestry: aging and the aged. The Gerontologist **2:**36-47; Asian-American elderly, Report on Special Concerns, The White House Conference on Aging, 1971, Washington, D.C. Additional data are from the 1970 Census and from a study supported by the Office of Special Concerns: A study of selected socio-economic characteristics of ethnic minorities based on the 1970 census, vol. 2, Asian-Americans. Life expectancy figures for Asian-American groups do not exist as of Spring 1976, since they are included in the category of "Negro and other races" in the life expectancy tables of the National Center for Health Statistics, Department of Health, Education and Welfare. In addition, national data on the extent of poverty for Koreans and Samoans do not exist. Demographic and poverty statistics on the Chinese in New York, the Pilipinos in San Francisco, and the Japanese, Koreans, and Samoans in Los Angeles were accumulated in 1976.

[29] The term "Filipino" was used in the 1970 Census. However the term "Pilipino" is preferred by the Pilipino community since their native language has no "f" sound.

[30] Nee, V.G., and de Bary, B.: Longtime Californ': a documentary study of an American Chinatown, New York, 1973, Pantheon Books.

[31] Carp, F.M., and Kataoka, E.: Health care problems of the elderly of San Francisco's Chinatown, The Gerontologist **16:**30-38, 1976.

RURAL OLDER PERSONS[32]

Although 40% of older persons lived in nonmetropolitan areas by 1981, only 5% actually live on farms. The remaining 35% reside in small towns. The benefits of rural and semirural life are many: fresh air and sunshine, opportunity to play and work out of doors, a leisurely life-style, lack of congestion, and friends and neighbors of long acquaintance. But there are also unfavorable features: transportation for older people can be especially difficult because of poor roads, lack of public transport, and the need to maintain private cars or rely on someone else. Medical facilities are generally inadequate, since most health care and medical services are urban-based. Many communities are without a doctor or nurse. Income levels are low; few rural people are covered by private pension plans. Social Security, employment, savings, and welfare are the usual income sources, but Social Security benefits are lower in rural areas because agricultural workers and the self-employed have only recently been covered. There is a shrinking tax base, and increasing scarcity of services and loss of family members are caused by the migration of young people to cities in search of work. Rural older persons are left with rising property taxes and sales taxes to maintain communities and services. A shortage of paid jobs hampers older people in their attempts to supplement their income, and present federal programs do little to help—although half of all older people live in rural areas, most federal programs primarily address the needs of urban older persons.

• • •

We have tried to acquaint you with a general profile of America's older population as well as to detail some specifics about the more disadvantaged minorities. Successful intervention in meeting the mental health needs of older people depends on preserving a basic awareness of the general facets of their lives while focusing attention on the unique individual and his or her social, economic, and familial context.

[32] See Wilkinson, C.W.: Comprehensive annotated bibliography on the rural aged, 1975-1978. This is the first in a series of occasional papers on the rural aged prepared by the Gerontology Center, 709 Allen Hall, West Virginia University, Morgantown, W. Va. 26506. A subject guide and author index are included for the 167 critically annotated publications.

REFERENCES

Benedict, R.: A profile of Indian aged. In Minority aged in America, Ann Arbor, 1972, University of Michigan.

Birren, J.E.: Handbook of aging and the individual, Chicago, 1959, University of Chicago Press.

Brotman, H.B.: Every ninth American. In U.S. Senate Special Committee on Aging: Developments in aging, 1978, Washington, D.C., 1979, U.S. Government Printing Office (revised June 1980).

Brotman, H.B.: Facts and figures on older Americans, Washington, D.C., 1971, U.S. Department of Health, Education and Welfare.

Butler, R.N.: Toward a psychiatry of the life cycle: implications of socio-psychologic studies of the aging process for the psychotherapeutic situation. In Simon, A., and Epstein, L.J., editors: Aging in modern society, Washington, D.C., 1968, American Psychiatric Association.

Butler, R.N.: Why survive? Being old in America, New York, 1975, Harper & Row, Publishers, Inc.

Comfort, A.: Aging, the biology of senescence, ed. 3, New York, 1979, Elsevier North-Holland.

Doherty, R.P.: Growing old in Indian country. In Employment prospects of aged blacks, Chicanos, and Indians, Washington, D.C., 1971, National Council on the Aging.

Doherty, R.P.: Mexican-Americans . . . growing old in the barrio. In Employment prospects of aged blacks, Chicanos, and Indians, Washington, D.C., 1971, National Council on the Aging.

Fujii, S.: Older Asian Americans, Civil Rights Digest **9**(1): 22-25, 1976.

Group for the Advancement of Psychiatry: Toward a public policy on mental health care of the elderly, Report No. 79, 1970.

Hill, R.: A demographic profile of the black elder, Aging, Nos. 287-288, Sept.-Oct. 1978, pp. 2-9.

Jackson, J.J.: Some useful information about black aged, preliminary draft prepared for the National Caucus on the Black Aged, 1971.

Kitagawa, E.M., and Hauser, P.M.: Differential mortality in the United States: a study in socioeconomic epidemiology, Cambridge, Mass., 1973, Harvard University Press.

Kovar, M.G.: Elderly people: the population 65 years and over. In Department of Health, Education and Welfare, National Center for Health Statistics: Health, United States 1976-1977, Pub. No. (HRA) 77-1232, Washington, D.C., 1977, U.S. Government Printing Office, pp. 3-26.

Maldonado, D., Jr.: The Chicano aged, Social Work **20**:213-216, 1975.

Neugarten, B.L., editor: Middle age and aging: a reader in social psychology, Chicago, 1968, University of Chicago Press.

Shanas, E., and Streib, G.F.: Social structure and the family. Generational relations, Englewood Cliffs, N.J., 1965, Prentice-Hall, Inc.

Siegel, J.S.: Demographic aspects of aging and the older population in the United States, Current Population Reports: Special Studies, Series P-23, No. 59, U.S. Bureau of the Census, Washington, D.C., 1976, U.S. Government printing office (revised Jan. 1978).

Taskforce, U.S. Senate Special Committee on Aging: Economics of aging: toward a full share in abundance, Washington, D.C., 1969, U.S. Government Printing Office.

Uhlenberg, F.: Changing structure of the older population of the U.S.A. during the twentieth century, The Gerontologist **17:**197-202, 1977.

U.S. Bureau of the Census: Projections of the population of the United States, 1979 to 2050; Current Population Reports, Series P-25, No. 704, Washington, D.C., 1977, U.S. Government Printing Office.

U.S. Bureau of the Census: Social and economic characteristics of the older population: 1978, Current Population Reports, Series P-23, No. 85, Washington, D.C., 1979, U.S. Government Printing Office, prepared with the support of the National Institute on Aging.

U.S. Department of Health, Education and Welfare: Our future selves: a research plan toward understanding aging, DHEW Pub. No. 77-1096, Washington, D.C., 1977, U.S. Government Printing Office.

U.S. Department of Health, Education and Welfare: Our future selves: a research plan toward understanding aging, report of the panel on biomedical research, DHEW Pub. No. (NIH) 78-1445, Washington, D.C., 1978, U.S. Government Printing Office.

U.S. Department of Health, Education and Welfare: Our future selves: a research plan toward understanding aging, report of the panel on behavioral and social science research, DHEW Pub. No. (NIH) 78-1444, Washington, D.C., 1978, U.S. Government Printing Office.

U.S. Senate Special Committee on Aging: The multiple hazards of age and race: the situation of aged blacks in the United States, working paper prepared by Inabel B. Lindsay, DSW, Consultant, Washington, D.C., Sept. 1971, U.S. Government Printing Office.

Yarrow, M., Blank, P., Quinn, O.W., Youmans, E.G., and Stein, J.: Social psychological characteristics of old age. In Birren, J.E., Butler, R.N., Greenhouse, S.W., Sokoloff, L., and Yarrow, M.R.: Human aging: a biological and behavioral study, Pub. No. (PHS) 986, Washington, D.C., 1963, U.S. Government Printing Office (reprinted as Pub. No. [HSM] 71-9051, 1971, 1974).

Youmans, E.G.: Older rural Americans, Lexington, 1967, University of Kentucky Press.

2

Healthy, successful old age

Old age can be an emotionally healthy and satisfying time of life with a minimum of physical and mental impairment.

■ Mr. S, a 76-year-old retired businessman, is spontaneous, talkative, and relevant. He has appropriate and varied affect and no sign of psychomotor retardation. When interviewed, he spoke in a frank and integrated manner about his achievements. Although some general forgetfulness is noted on his history, there is no sign of a marked intellectual decline and no memory impairments were found on the mental status examination.

He was born on a farm in central Europe, the oldest of 10 children. He was already employed at age 9 and left home at age 13. He describes his parents as having some problems, and he states that he felt closer to his mother but attained a greater understanding of his father as years went by. At age 23 he married and emigrated to the United States. His marriage is viewed by him as an excellent one, and his wife is in good health. Mr. S has experienced a modest decrease in sexual desire and continues sex relations on a less frequent basis. His relationship with children and grandchildren is satisfying, with moderate interaction. He remembers that his children's adolescent rebellions gave him a chance to look anew at his own early years.

Mr. S had made plans for his older years and continues to plan optimistically for the future. He feels concerned about death and hopes he will have a sudden death or die in his sleep. He feels some interest in religion but denies any marked change since youth. He has made out a will and has arranged for a burial site.

In viewing his aging condition he shows a reasonable recognition of his capacities and limitations, with no obvious denial. He appears to have accepted his physical changes. He is no longer very active but takes walks and moves about the house and yard with regularity. He shows no history of lifelong psychopathology, and there is no evidence of new psychopathology as he ages. There is no psychological isolation, and it is deemed unlikely that he will in the future have a functional breakdown.

Mr. S is an example of an older person who has adapted to old age with minimal stress and a high level of morale. With old age, just as with any other age, one can learn much about pathological conditions by understanding healthy developmental processes. Unfortunately Mr. S and other healthy older people are rarely the subjects of research investigation or theoretical constructs. The study of ''normal'' development has seldom gone beyond early adult years, and the greatest emphasis has been on childhood. The healthy aged tend to be invisible in the psychology of human development, and this is in accord with the general public avoidance of the issues of human aging.

NEGATIVE STEREOTYPE OF OLD AGE

Few people in the United States can think of old age as a time of potential health and growth. This is partly a realistic reflection, considering the lot of many older people who have been cast aside, becoming lonely, bitter, poor, and emotionally or physically ill. American society has not been generous or supportive of the unproductive—in this case persons who have reached retirement age. But in a larger sense the negative view of old age is a problem of Western civilization. The Western concept of the life cycle is decidedly different from that of the Far East, since they derive from two opposing views of what "self" means and what life is all about. Eastern philosophy places the individual's self, life, and death *within* the process of the human experience. Life and death are familiar and equally acceptable parts of what self means. Death is characteristically seen as a welcome relief from suffering and/or, as in Japanese ancestor worship, a step upward in social mobility

to join the revered ancestors.[1] In Buddhism, death is merely a passage to another reincarnation unless the person achieves an enlightenment that releases him or her from the eternal cycle.

In the West, death is considered as *outside* of the self. To be a self (a person) one must be alive, in control, and aware of what is happening. The greater and more narcissistic Western emphasis on individuality and control makes death an outrage, a

[1] There appears to be a relative absence of fear of death. For a discussion of psychological attitudes toward death among older Japanese-Americans, see Osako, M.: Aging, social isolation and kinship ties among Japanese-Americans. In Project Report to the Administration on Aging, Washington, D.C., 1980, The Administration on Aging, pp. 116-120.

Triumphant old age.

Photo by Russell Lewis.

tremendous affront to humans rather than the logical and necessary process of old life making way for new.

The opposite cultural views of East and West evolved to support two very different ways of life, each with its own merits; but the Western predilection for "progress," conquest over nature, and personal self-realization has produced difficult problems for older persons and for those preparing for old age. This is particularly so when the national spirit of the United States and the spirit of this period in time have emphasized and expanded the notion of measuring human worth in terms of individual productivity and power. Older people are led to see themselves as "beginning to fail" as they age, a phrase that refers as much to self-worth as it does to physical strength. Religion has been the traditional solace by promising another world wherein the self again springs to life, never to be further threatened by loss of its own integrity. Thus the consummate dream of immortality for Westerners is fulfilled by religion, yet the integration of the aging experience into their life process remains incomplete. To make matters more complicated, increasing secularization produces a frightening void around the subject of death itself, which frequently is met by avoiding and denying the thought of one's own decline and death and by forming self-protective prejudices against the old.

Medicine and the behavioral sciences have mirrored societal attitudes by presenting old age as a grim litany of physical and emotional ills. *Decline* of the individual has been the key concept and *neglect* the major treatment technique. Until 1960 most of the medical, psychological, psychiatric, and social work literature on the aged was based on experience with the sick and the institutionalized even though only 5% of the older people were confined to institutions. A few research studies that have concentrated on the healthy aged give indications of positive potential for the entire age group. But the general almost phobic dislike of aging remains the norm, with healthy older people being ignored and the chronically ill receiving half-hearted custodial care. Only those older persons who happen to have exotic or "interesting" diseases and emotional problems or substantial financial resources tend to receive the research and treatment attentions of the medical and psychotherapeutic professions.

WHAT IS A HEALTHY OLD AGE?

In thinking about health, one is led to the understanding that, in addition to the general lack of interest in older persons, science and medicine have historically been more concerned with treating "what went wrong" than with clarifying the complex, interwoven elements necessary to produce and support health. Typical of this is the treating of coronary attacks after the fact rather than prescribing a preventive program of diet, exercise, protection from stress, and absence of smoking. Most of the major diseases of older people could be cited as examples of this same phenomenon. The tedious and less dramatic process of prevention requires an understanding of what supports or what interferes with healthy development throughout the course of the life cycle.

The World Health Organization has defined health as "a state of complete physical, mental and social well-being and not merely the absence of disease or infirmity" (WHO, 1946). This, of course, represents an ideal with many possible interpretations. But the broad elements of health— physical, emotional, and social—are the framework in which one can begin to analyze what is going well in addition to what is going wrong. The attempt must be made to locate those conditions that enable humans to thrive, not merely survive.

Old age does involve unique developmental work. Childhood might be defined as a period of gathering and enlarging strength and experience, whereas a major developmental task in old age is to clarify, deepen, and find use for what one has already attained in a lifetime of learning and adapting. Older people must teach themselves to conserve their strength and resources when necessary and to adjust in the best sense to those changes and losses that occur as part of the aging experi-

A healthy and vigorous older man.

Courtesy Easter Schattner.

ence. The ability of the older person to adapt and thrive is contingent on physical health, personality, earlier life experiences, and on the societal supports he or she receives: adequate finances, shelter, medical care, social roles, recreation, and the like. An important point to emphasize is that, as true for children, adolescents, and the middle-aged, it is imperative that older people continue to develop and change in a flexible manner if health is to be promoted and maintained. Failure of adaptation at any age or under any circumstance can result in physical or emotional illness. Optimal growth and adaptation can occur throughout the life cycle when the individual's strengths and potentials are recognized, reinforced, and encouraged by the environment in which he or she lives.

Popular ideas of human development need revision to encompass the experience of older persons. They should not have to view themselves as "failing" or "finished" because one or another element of life is changing or declining. For example,

a loss in physical health or the loss of a loved one is indeed a serious blow, but the potential for continuing adjustment and growth needs therefore to be even more carefully exploited than under less critical circumstances. In our too-quick assumption that old age is a relentless downhill course we ignore the lifetime-gathered potential of older persons for strength as well as for a richer emotional, spiritual, and even intellectual and social life than may be possible for the young. Youth must concentrate on the piece-by-piece accumulation of personality and experience. Old age, in its best sense, can mean enjoyment of the finished product—a completed human being.

BECOMING "OLD"

To attempt to clarify and disentangle what "old" means, we must emphasize that the concern here is not with those characteristics of old people that are the result of preexistent personality factors. The kind of personality one carries into old

A couple married 50 years and in excellent physical and emotional health.

Photo by Myrna Lewis.

age is a crucial factor in how one will respond to the experience of being older; personality traits produce individual ways of being old. However, we wish to deal with the more general characteristics of old age and the changes that are fairly uniformly common to the aging population in the United States.

Physical changes

Some of the outward alterations experienced by older persons are graying of hair, loss of hair and teeth, elongation of ears and nose, losses of subcutaneous fat, particularly around the face, wrinkling of skin, fading of eyesight and hearing, postural changes, and a progressive structural decline that may result in a shortened trunk with comparatively long arms and legs. Not all of these changes happen to everyone—nor at the same rate. A person can be a ''young'' 90-year-old in a physical sense or an ''old'' 60-year-old. Little is known about the onset and progress of many of these changes, since they were long thought to be simply the inescapable and universal consequences of growing old. But recent research has revealed that some, or perhaps many, are results of disease states that occur with greater frequency in late life and may be treatable—possibly preventable and probably retardable. Atherosclerosis and osteoporosis are cases in point. Even heart disease and cancer will someday be conquered, although not many years ago someone dying of cancer was said to be dying of ''old age.'' Other reasons for bodily changes have been identified as results of unusual amounts of exposure to some pathogenic element—too much sun (causing skin wrinkles), cigarette smoke, and air pollution, to name a few. Genetic traits can be responsible for changes like graying hair and loss of hair. Yet in the best of all future worlds, with acute and chronic disease states identified and eliminated, undesirable genetic traits nullified, and pathogenic environmental conditions removed, a process called aging will still occur.

The potential for life can be lengthened and enhanced, but the mysterious flow of human existence from birth through death will prevail. As many older people realize more calmly than the young, aging and death must be accepted as part of human experience.

The overall physical health of the body plays a critical role in determining the energies and adaptive capacities available to older people. They experience a good deal more acute and chronic disease than the younger population. Specific physical disabilities and diseases such as cardiovascular and locomotor afflictions are particularly debilitating, especially when they affect the integrative systems of the body—the endocrine, vascular, and central nervous systems. Severe or even mild organic brain disease can interfere markedly with functioning. Perceptual losses of eyesight and hearing can deplete energy and cause social isolation. However, although 86% of older persons have one or more chronic health problems, 95% are able to live in the community. Their conditions are mild enough to enable 81% of older persons to get around with no outside assistance. If significant breakthroughs occur in research and treatment of diseases of the aged (heart disease, cancer, arthritis, arteriosclerosis, and acute and chronic brain syndromes), one can envision a very different kind of old age. Assuming adequate environmental supports, including proper nutrition, old age could become a time of lengthy good health with a more gentle and predictable decline. Older persons would not have to battle the ravages of disease, and a fuller measure of their physical strength could be available for other uses. Already today one can see the possibilities in those older people who are disease-free. They can more vigorously cope with the emotional and social changes specific to their age group and in so doing have the opportunity for a successful and satisfying later life.

Emotional changes

Older people are often described as slow thinkers, forgetful, rigid, mean-tempered, irritable, dependent, and querulous. They may suffer from anxiety, grief, depression, and paranoid states. One must separate out the personality traits demonstrated in earlier life, realistic responses to actual loss of friends and loved ones, personal reactions to the idea of one's own aging and death, and the predictable emotional responses of human beings at any age to physical illness or social loss. The emotional aspects of aging are more fully discussed in Chapter 3.

Intellectual changes

The effects of aging on intellectual functioning have been studied since the post–World War I era. The earliest assumptions were that intelligence declined progressively with age. The Army Alpha Test of World War I on officers and recruits 18 to 60 years of age and older seemed to confirm the idea of intellectual decline, since lower and lower test scores were found as age increased. In 1931 Miles and Miles[2] reported much the same results with 823 subjects ranging from age 5 to 94. Intelligence scores were shown to increase until age 18 and then begin a long decline. Jones and Conrad[3] in 1933 produced similar general results with 1,191 subjects age 10 to 60, including children, parents, and grandparents. In 1955 Wechsler featured an IQ test adjusted for each age group, which artificially gave older people a boost in their otherwise declining raw test scores.

All the above studies were cross-sectional, with each subject interviewed once. This methodology produced inherent biases favoring the better-educated young and reflecting historical and environmental differences between the generations. On the other hand, longitudinal studies on the same individual over a period of time were also being done, making it possible to measure actual intelligence changes over the life cycle while avoiding

[2]Miles, C.C., and Miles, W.R.: The correlation of intelligence scores and chronological age from early to late maturity, American Journal of Psychology **44:**44-78, 1932.

[3]Jones, H.E., and Conrad, H.S.: The growth and decline of intelligence. A study of a homogeneous group between the ages of ten and sixty, Genetic Psychological Monograph **13:** 223-298, 1933.

the pitfalls of cross-sectional research.[4] In the 1920s both Bayley[5] and Bradway conducted longitudinal studies that are still continuing today, in which they have tested and retested persons (now in later life) beginning with childhood. They found IQ scores increasing until the twenties and then eventually leveling off, remaining unchanged until late in life. There was no overall decline with age. The work of Owens[6] and others corroborated these findings.

Lorge[7] meanwhile tested the assumption that one aspect of intelligence—speed of reaction—may indeed decrease with age. (Reaction time studies, such as those by Birren, demonstrate a loss in speed of response in the central nervous system with age.) He concluded that, generally speaking, if older persons were given enough time on tests, they functioned as accurately as those who were younger. The health factor in later life has also been evaluated for its effect on intelli-

gence and other psychometric tests. Even minimal poor health can adversely affect test scores.[8] Jarvik and others[9] found a drop in intellectual measures just before death.

Eisdorfer[9a] and others believe that the over-arousal of the autonomic nervous system during stress affects the verbal learning abilities of older people. Therefore, by giving an adrenergic blocking agent to one group and a placebo to another they found fewer errors as well as lower pre–fatty acid levels (a reflection of stress). In general, with good physical and mental health, adequate educational levels, and intellectual stimulation, it appears that there is not the amount of decline in intellectual abilities with age as previously thought.[10] Some abilities may, in fact, increase, such as judgment, accuracy, and general knowledge.

However, if one lives long enough there are decrements in important abilities of intelligence that are not yet readily accounted for by disease.[11]

---

[4] Longitudinal research presents methodological problems of its own, as described by Greenhouse et al. and Schaie. When a sample is studied over a span of time, differentiating intrinsic changes from those caused by environment becomes difficult and it is impossible to rule out the bias of survivorship itself. See Greenhouse, S.W., and Morrison, D.F.: Statistical methodology. In Birren, J.E., Butler, R.N., Greenhouse, S.W., Sokoloff, L., and Yarrow, M.R., editors: Human aging: a biological and behavioral study, Pub. No. (PHS) 986, Washington, D.C., 1963, U.S. Government Printing Office (reprinted as Pub. No. [HSM] 71-9051, 1971, 1974); and Schaie, K.W.: A general model for the study of developmental problems, Psychological Bulletin **64:**92-107, 1965. See also Baltes, P.B.: Longitudinal and cross-sectional sequences in the study of age and generation effects, Human Development **11:**145-171, 1968.

[5] Bayley, N., and Oden, M.H.A.B.: The maintenance of intellectual ability in gifted adults, Journal of Gerontology **10:** 91-107, 1955.

[6] Owens, W.A.: Age and mental abilities: a second adult follow-up, Journal of Educational Psychology **57:**316-325, 1966.

[7] Lorge, I.: The influence of the test upon the nature of mental decline as a function of age, Journal of Educational Psychology **32:**100-110, 1936.

[8] Botwinick, J., and Birren, J.E.: Mental abilities and psychomotor responses in healthy aged men. In Birren, J.E., Butler, R.N., Greenhouse, S.W., Sokoloff, L., and Yarrow, M.R., editors: Human aging: a biological and behavioral study, Pub. No. (PHS) 986, Washington, D.C., 1963, U.S. Government Printing Office (reprinted as Pub. No. [HSM] 71-9051, 1971, 1974).

ing Office (reprinted as Pub. No. [HSM] 71-9051, 1971, 1974).

[9] Jarvik, L.F., Eisdorfer, C., and Blum, J.E., editors: Intellectual functioning in adults, New York, 1975, Springer Verlag.

[9a] Eisdorfer, C.: Autonomic changes in aging. In Gaitz, C.M., editor: Aging and the brain, New York, 1972, Plenum Publishing Corp.

[10] Schaie, K.W., and Labouvie-Vief, G.: Generational versus ontogenetic components of change in adult cognitive behavior: a fourteen-year cross-sequential study, Developmental Psychology **10:**105-320, 1974. See also Baltes, P.B., and Schaie, W.E.: The myth of the twilight years (debate), Psychology Today **7:**35-40, 1974.

[11] Horn, J.L., and Donaldson, G.: On the myth of intellectual decline in adulthood, American Psychologist **31**(10):701-719, 1976. See also Siegler and Botwinick's findings regarding the impact of selective subject attrition on valid conclusions in relation to changes in intellectual abilities in older persons in Siegler, I.C., and Botwinick, J.: A long-term longitudinal study of intellectual ability of older adults: the matter of selective subject attrition, Journal of Gerontology **34:**242-245, 1979. Finally, note the work of Arenberg on verbal learning, memory, and problem solving, derived from his work in the Baltimore Longitudinal Study on Aging (National Institute on Aging), in Arenberg, D.: Cognition and aging: verbal learning, memory, problem solving and aging. In Eisdorfer, C., and Lawton, M.P., editors: The psychology of adult development and aging; and Arenberg, D.: A longitudinal study of problem solving in adults, Journal of Gerontology **29:**650-658, 1974.

There appear to be losses in brain cells through-out life,[12] for example, and brain cells do not continue to replace themselves. Nonetheless, the significance of the cell loss, since there is a redundancy of cells, is not established. There are also changes in the nerve cell (neuron) itself, especially the dendrites, which participate in neurotransmission.[13]

Social changes

It is in the social realm of an older person's life that the most clearly age-specific patterns can presently be seen. The nature of families and societies in the course of the life cycle decrees certain conditions that can be described as "natural" for older people. They find themselves the eldest group in the population with two, three, or even four generations below them. Many have grown children and grandchildren with whom they are involved. Grandparentage becomes a new social role. The older husband and wife each face prospects of widowhood and membership in a peer group with a large proportion of widowed contemporaries. There are increasing numbers of women compared to men as they age. Many older persons are less involved than previously in work and income-related activities and thus have more time available for their own use.

Beyond these certain basic social conditions, older people experience wide variations from culture to culture.[14] They may be venerated or scorned, treated oversentimentally or rejected, protected or abandoned. At times they are arbitrarily respected for great wisdom and counsel or at other times, paradoxically, seen as burdens that waste their society's strength and resources.

The older person's relative position in any society tends to be favorably influenced by several institutional factors:

1. Ownership of property and control over the opportunities of the young
2. Command of strategic knowledge and skills
3. Strong religious and sacred traditions
4. Strong kinship and extended family bonds
5. A less product-oriented society
6. High mutual dependence and reciprocal aids among society members

In the United States the overwhelming majority of older people face a prevailing sense of being put on the shelf and forgotten after age 65. A split and contradictory set of roles exists for older men, since some of them remain active in government, political parties, religious affairs, and business life. They may have strong executive and administrative responsibilities. In the United States Supreme Court, 85% of all service has been supplied by men over 65. Such opportunities exist for relatively few older men, however; and older women, because of their cultural roles as homemakers, have almost no positions of public power and status.

The feelings of social loss among the aged are tremendous. Mandatory retirement and Social Security regulations put them out of the work force when many would prefer employment. Income becomes drastically reduced, in many cases to outright poverty. The mobile nuclear family system may leave an isolated situation for households of older persons, of whom 26% live alone and 32% with just a spouse. Children and grandchildren may live miles away and maintain infrequent contacts.[15] Older men find themselves unprepared for finding life meaningful after retirement. Older women, after a lifetime of being wives and mothers, can be emotionally traumatized in widowhood. Society provides few supports and little

[12] Brody, H.: Organization of the cerebral cortex. III. A study of aging in the human cerebral cortex, Journal of Comparative Neurology **102:**511-556, 1955.

[13] Scheibel, M.E., Lindsay, R.D., Tomiya, V., and Scheibel, A.B.: Progressive dendritic changes in aging human cortex, Experimental Neurology **47:**392-403, 1975.

[14] Cross-cultural studies in the psychology of later life give insights concerning universal features of aging and offer opportunities for borrowing new social and cultural arrangements.

[15] It must be added, however, that outright neglect or isolation from families is *not* the norm, except when geographical distances are a factor. Even though they may live in separate households, which both generations may prefer, many families are deeply supportive of their older members.

encouragement; individual older people must forge their own roles—when and where they can.

Old age, then, is a multiply determined experience that depends on an intricate balance of physical, emotional, and social forces, any one of which can upset or involve the others. An older person who is socially lonely may not eat well and therefore may develop physical symptoms of malnourishment, which in turn cloud intellectual functioning. Hearing loss can lead to a suspiciousness that irritates people and causes them to shun the person's company, leaving him or her isolated. A widower, grieving the loss of his wife, may develop psychosomatic symptoms and lose his job. It is evident that much suffering could be eliminated by application of knowledge and skills already available. People need to be fed and sheltered decently; they must have medical and psychiatric care; they need loving and supportive personal contacts; and finally they require meaningful social roles. Health is not really an elusive concept, but it does require that we make commitments *as* human beings *to* human beings.

HISTORICAL FACTORS IN ADAPTATION

People are shaped not only by their own personal history, family environment, and inherent personality characteristics but also by the larger world around them. So in understanding the aged it is useful to consider those factors in local, national, and world history that may have influenced them as they grew from infancy to old age.[16]

The median time of birth of the present 65-plus population was around 1905, at a time when Herbert Spencer's social Darwinism or "survival of the fittest" was the popular social theory. Huge fortunes were amassed by families with names like Gould, Morgan, Rockefeller, and Carnegie, while poorly paid immigrant workers provided labor. The Protestant ethic, inspired by Calvin's philosophy of success through hard work and self-sacri-

---

[16] For an overview of the experience of today's older persons it is useful to read Barbara Tuchman's *The Proud Tower* and Frederick Lewis Allen's *The Big Change*.

fice, was the dominant religious influence. The labor movement and women's suffrage and child labor laws were evolving as protection against exploitation. Thus the nation had reached a crossroads between accepting the notion of survival of the strongest and attempting the protection of all, including the weak.

This raw dichotomy was the earliest societal experience of the now-older population. Many of them still feel the tug of these forces in their personal lives and insist on being independent in the face of real personal limitations. They often berate themselves for not being allowed or able to work, since they were taught as children that leisure and idleness are sinful. They may accept their difficult economic and social conditions as evidence that they are not among the elite, or "fittest," and thus do not deserve better. They are not as comfortable as their children and grandchildren with the notion that government and social policies must be designed to serve them, and they tend to be somewhat ambivalent about Social Security and Medicare. The massive depression of the 1930s served to propel scores of "rugged individualists" into reluctant acceptance of governmental intervention in their lives, but many emotionally felt such intervention to be evidence of personal failure rather than overwhelming social forces. Two world wars, a Korean war, and the war in Southeast Asia have made the lives of older persons a time of frequent preparation for, participation in, or recovery from war. Many have lost children and grandchildren. They have contended with the tumultuous concept of progress through industrialization and automation and with the technological notion of human obsolescence. This has served to increase their sense of uselessness as their own skills are performed by machines and they themselves are seen as burdens.

POPULAR MYTHS ABOUT AGING

The dominance of *chronological aging* is a myth, and a more apt measure of actual age might be that old maxim "You're as old as you feel." Young 80-year-olds can look very different from old 80-year-olds. It is well established that large disparities often exist between physiological, psychological, chronological, and social ages. People age at such different rates that physiological indicators show a greater range from the mean in old age than in any other age group, and people may become more diverse rather than similar as they age.[17] Of course certain diseases have a leveling effect that causes a look-alike appearance from person to person. Massive organic brain damage and the major illnesses can so damage body and brain that their victims may react and behave very much like each other, as do invalids of all age groups. Poverty and illiteracy also tend to obscure individual uniqueness and variation.

Another widespread myth surrounding aging is the conviction that all old people are "senile." *Senility,* although not an actual medical term, is excessively used by doctors and lay people alike to explain the behavior and condition of older people. Many of the reactive emotional responses of older people, such as depression, grief, and anxiety, are labeled senile and thus considered chronic, untreatable states. Senility is an especially convenient tag put on older women by doctors who do not wish to spend the time and effort necessary to diagnose and treat their complaints. The popular medical school term for older people is "crocks"; thus attitudes are formed that affect future practice. To be sure, brain damage from cerebral arteriosclerosis and senile brain disease is a realistic problem, probably causing 50% of cases of mental disorder in old age. But even with brain disease there can be overlays of depression, anxiety, and psychosomatic disorders that are responsive to medical and psychotherapeutic intervention.

A third myth, the *tranquility myth,* presents a strange and contradictory position, considering the general public disdain and neglect of older persons. This myth sets forth the sugar-coated "Grandma-with-her-goodies" vision of old age as a time of idyllic serenity and tranquility when

older persons enjoy the fruits of their labors. A combination of wishful thinking about their own future old age and denial of the realities that presently exist is evident in the younger generation's image of happy-go-lucky older people.

■ Mrs. G and her husband retired with an estate of a quarter of a million dollars. He had been a successful doctor in a Midwestern city. Dr. G was 69 when he chose to retire and his wife was 4 years younger. Only 2 years later he was dead. Their son, age 44, died of a coronary a year afterward. Mrs. G paid many of the expenses of her son's terminal illness and also helped her daughter-in-law meet the college expenses of her grandchildren. Ten years later at 77 years of age Mrs. G, the respected and wealthy physician's wife, was herself impoverished and enfeebled. Her money had run out.

We cite this example to illustrate how people who may have entered old age in the most favorable circumstances can nonetheless be subject to major and continuing emotional and financial crises.

There is the *myth of unproductivity* associated with old age. It is assumed that older people can no longer produce in a job or be active socially and creatively. They are presumed to be disengaged from life, declining and disinterested. But in the absence of disease and social adversity, this does not happen. Older people tend to remain actively concerned about their personal and community relationships. Many are still employed. Numbers of others do "bootleg work" to avoid reporting their earnings, because of Social Security income ceilings.

The *myth of resistance to change* is equally as suspect as all the others. It is true that adult character structure is remarkably stable, but ability to change depends more on previous and lifelong personality traits than on anything inherent in old age. Often when conservatism occurs, it derives not from aging but from socioeconomic pressures. An example might be the decision of older people to vote against school loans because of the increase those loans would mean in their personal property taxes.

---

[17] See the National Institute of Mental Health's *Human Aging* studies (Birren et al.) and the work of Heron and Chown.

NEW INTERPRETATIONS OF AGING FROM RESEARCH

In attempting to gain a more realistic picture of aging, a few investigators responding to the paucity of information in this area began studying healthy older people. Community-resident and socially autonomous older people were examined from a wide range of research perspectives in studies beginning in the late 1950s and early 1960s. Busse was responsible for some of the first work and Shock studied some 600 men longitudinally every 18 months. The National Institute of Mental Health (Birren et al.) undertook collaborative studies involving separate academic disciplines and medical specialties over a period of 11 years. The NIMH findings were surprisingly optimistic and in general reinforced the hypothesis that much of what has been called aging is really disease.

Decreased cerebral (brain) blood flow and oxygen consumption were found to be probable results of arteriosclerosis rather than an inevitable companion of aging. Healthy older men with an average age of 71 presented cerebral physiological and intellectual functions that compared favorably with those in a younger control group with an average age of 21. Some evidence of slowing in speed and response was found, but this correlated with environmental deprivation and depression as well as physical decline.

Older persons were found to have the same psychiatric disorders as the young with similar genesis and structure. Adaptation and survival appeared to be associated with the individual's self-view and sense of ongoing usefulness as well as continuing good physical health. Current environmental satisfaction and support were found to be of critical import to psychological stability. Individuals who were "self-starters" and could structure and carry out new contacts, activities, and involvements were found to have the least disease and the longest survival rates. The interrelating between sound health and adaptability was validated by the sensitivity of psychometric test results to even minimal disease. In general the healthy aged were characterized by flexibility, resourcefulness, and optimism, whereas manifestations of mental illness were attributed to medical illness, personality factors, and sociocultural effects rather than the aging process.

See Table 2-1 for illustrative longitudinal studies involving older people. Such studies are important to our understanding of human change over time.

PSYCHOSOCIAL THEORIES OF AGING

The controversial "disengagement theory" in gerontology evolved from the Kansas City aging studies conducted by the University of Chicago

Table 2-1. Illustrative longitudinal studies involving older people

Study	Year began	Sex studied
Berkeley/Oakland Human Development Studies (National Institute of Child and Human Development/National Institute on Aging)	1928/1932	Male and female
Adaptation to Life (Harvard Medical School)	1937	Male
Thousand Aviators (U.S. Navy)	1940	Male
Framingham Study (National Heart Lung and Blood Institute and National Eye Institute)	1950	Male and female
Duke University I and II (National Institute on Aging—supported)	1955	Male and female
National Institute of Mental Health of the National Institutes of Health	1955	Male
Baltimore Longitudinal Study (National Institute on Aging—intramural)	1958	Male and female
Langley-Porter/University of California, San Francisco (National Institute of Child and Human Development/National Institute on Aging)	1958	Male and female
Veterans Administration Normative Study	1958	Male

Committee on Human Development in the late 1950s.[18] This theory postulated that older people and society mutually withdraw from each other as part of normal aging, and that this withdrawal is characterized by psychological well-being on the part of the older person.

Later the disengagement theory was modified by Havighurst et al.[19] in a series of papers beginning in 1963, using the same original Kansas City data. Disengagement was redefined by them as simply a process rather than a theory of optimum aging and as only one of many possible patterns of aging. Of 88 subjects studied, all but 18 fell into the following groups: (1) the integrated, who were high on most positive personality variables; (2) the "defended" group, aggressive and full of energy; (3) the passive-dependent group; and (4) the unintegrated group, low on almost all personality measures. These four categories were common to both men and women. There were two further groups of men: One group was characterized as introspective, timid, stable, and high on super-ego control but lacking in internalization of institutional values. The other group was fearful of failure and of becoming dependent on others. One group of women had feelings of inferiority and self-doubt and was overcontrolled and dissatisfied. Another group of women similarly was self-doubting but very aggressive and competitive.

Reichard et al.[20] interviewed 87 men, 55 to 84 years of age, in California. They found 64 of these subjects fit into 5 groups. Three of these groups were accepting of aging: (1) the mature, philosophical men, (2) the rocking chair men who seemed glad to have time to relax, and (3) the armored men who tried to keep active at all costs and used this as a defense against old age and death. Group 4 was labeled aggressive and seemed to blame others for its disappointments and frustrations. Those in group 5 were intrapunitive, depressed, and gloomy. Of the 87 men, 23 did not fit neatly into any of these categories.

Carp's[21] study of residents in a home for the aging in Texas produced evidence that in a positive environment older people generally moved toward activity and informal social contacts, rather than disengagement. She raised the possibility that so-called age-related behavior such as disengagement may be the result of the environmental conditions that so often accompany old age. Carp also observed that rigidity was not intrinsic to the aging personality. Rigid behavior could be brought on by difficult social or physical situations; but once the difficulties were alleviated, the rigidity disappeared.

Rosow (in *The Social Integration of the Aged*) showed that older people who live among other older people make more friends than those who live among the young, refuting a conclusion of the disengagement theory. His sample included 1,200 older people living in three kinds of housing—one with a mix of ages, one with a number of older people, that is, "age concentrated," and one almost totally aged, that is, "age dense." Hochschild (in *The Unexpected Community*) also found in her intensive study of 43 older people residing in a small apartment building that "age dense" housing arrangements expand the potential circle of friends for older people.

An "exchange" theory pertaining to imbalances in social exchange and their relationship to rewards and power has been posited as an explanation for the disengaging behavior seen in some older persons.[22] Martin and Dowd, in particular, have ad-

[18] Cummings, E., and Henry, W.E.: Growing old: the process of disengagement, New York, 1961, Basic Books Inc., Publishers.

[19] Havighurst, R.J., Neugarten, B.L., and Tobin, S.S.: Disengagement and patterns of aging. In Neugarten, B.L., editor: Middle age and aging, Chicago, 1968, University of Chicago Press.

[20] Reichard, S., Livson, F., and Peterson, P.G.: Aging and personality, New York, 1962, John Wiley & Sons, Inc.

[21] Carp, F.M.: A future for the aged: Victoria Plaza and its residents, Austin, 1966, University of Texas Press.

[22] Homans, G.: Social behavior: its elementary forms, New York, 1961, Harcourt, Brace and World; and Blau, P.: Exchange and power in social life, New York, 1964, John Wiley and Sons, Inc.

vanced the notion that the more one values rewards, the more one loses power.[23]

Havighurst and colleagues[24] from Holland, Italy, Germany, and the United States conducted a cross-national study of steelworkers and retired teachers in order to test and expand on the findings of the Kansas City studies.

Out of all of this has come the current and prevailing view that activity rather than disengagement produces the most agreeable psychological climate for older people.[25] The "activity theory" maintains that older people should remain active as long as they possibly can. When certain activities and associations must be given up, for example, employment, substitutes should be found. The older person's personality is a key element in shaping reactions to biological and social changes —an active rather than a passive role is important for mental health and satisfaction.

Lowenthal and associates[26] studied 216 adults at four points in their lives, beginning with high school seniors and ending with men and women about to retire. They compared life-styles, adaptation, and attitudes and examined concepts such as intimacy, mutuality, and time orientation. They identified ways in which adults cope with changes and compared the socialization and response to

stress and change in women versus men. Differences between the sexes were more significant than between the old and the young. The authors found that the old were no more rigid psychologically than the young and that an individual's point of view, values, and outlook depended on how well one had managed to adapt to one's particular life stage.

Neugarten and Guttman[27] have advanced the interesting conclusion that men and women, somewhere in their mid-fifties, begin to reverse roles in terms of authority within the family structure. Their study finds men becoming more nurturing and women more aggressive and assertive. (Jung described this as the emergence of animus or the masculine component in women, and anima or the feminine component in men.)

In spite of the work already done, Schaie and Marquette[28] rightly conclude that study of the effects of age and other elements on personality development in later life is just beginning. The more obvious problems at this point are the measurement of generational differences and the lack of adequate norms against which to measure behavior. There is growing attention to what has been called "life-span developmental psychology"—the attempt to study development as a lifelong process.[29]

[23] Martin, J.D.: Power, dependence and the complaints of the elderly. A social exchange perspective, Aging and Human Development **2**:108-112, 1971; and Dowd, J.J.: Aging as exchange: a preface to theory; Journal of Gerontology **30**: 584-594, 1975.

[24] Havighurst, R.J.: Successful aging. In Williams, R.H., Tibbitts, C., and Donahue, W., editors: Processes of aging, New York, 1963, Atherton Press.

[25] For discussions of the disengagement theory see Carp, F.M.: Some components of disengagement, Journal of Gerontology **23**:383-386, 1968; Hochschild, A.R.: Disengagement theory: a critique and proposal, American Sociology Review **40**: 553-569, 1975; Tallmer, M., and Kutner, B.: Disengagement and morale, The Gerontologist **110**:317-320, 1970; and Orbach, H.L.: Disengagement—activity controversy: underlying theoretical models of aging, The Gerontologist **13**:72, 1973.

[26] Lowenthal, M.F., et al.: Four stages of life: a comparative study of women and men facing transitions, San Francisco, 1975, Jossey-Bass, Inc.

[27] Neugarten, B., and Guttman, D.: Age-sex roles and personality in middle age: a thematic apperception study. In Neugarten, B.L., editor: Middle age and aging, Chicago, 1968, University of Chicago Press.

[28] Schaie, K.W., and Marquette, B.W.: Personality in maturity and old age. In Dreger, R.M., editor: Multivariate personality research: contributions to the understanding of personality in honor of R.B. Catell, Baton Rouge, La., 1971, Claitor.

[29] There have been four important books on life-span developmental psychology, all generated by West Virginia University and published in New York by Academic Press: Goulet, L.R., and Baltes, P., editors: The theory and status of life-span research, 1979; Nesselroade, J., and Reese, H.W., editors: Methodological issues, 1973; Baltes, P.B., and Schaie, K.W., editors: Life-span developmental psychology: personality and socialization, 1973; and Datan, N., and Ginsberg, L.H., editors: Life-span developmental psychology: normative life crises, 1975.

SOME SPECIAL CHARACTERISTICS OF OLDER PEOPLE

A number of characteristics that we have seen quite frequently in older people are connected with the unique sense of having lived a long time and having accepted the concept of life as a cycle from birth through death.

Desire to leave a legacy

Human beings have a need to leave something of themselves behind when they die. This legacy may be children and grandchildren, work or art, personal possessions, memories in the minds of others, even bodies or parts of them for use in medical training and research. Motivations for the tendency toward legacy are generally a combination of not wanting to be forgotten, of wanting to give of one's self magnanimously to those who survive, of wishing to remain in control in some way even after death (for example, through wills), of desiring to tidy up responsibly before death. Legacy provides a sense of continuity, giving the older person a feeling of being able to participate even after death.

The "elder" function

Closely connected with legacy, the "elder" function refers to the natural propensity of the old to share with the young the accumulated knowledge and experience they have collected. If unhampered and indeed encouraged, this "elder" function takes the form of counseling, guiding, and sponsoring those who are younger. It is tied to the development of an interconnectedness between

The "elder" function of the aged.

Photo courtesy Jerome Lewis.

the generations. It is important to a sense of self-esteem to be acknowledged by the young as an elder, to have one's life experience seen as interesting and valuable; on the other hand, it can be devastating to be shrugged off by seemingly uninterested younger people as old-fashioned and irrelevant. Not all older people, however, have a nurturant feeling toward the young. Some, because of their life experience, look on the young with envy and distrust.

Mental health personnel can learn much about how to help older people by respecting and benefiting from what the elderly have to teach. This occurs through listening to them with an open mind, reading the writings of older people, viewing their arts, hearing their music, and in general absorbing the culture created by them.

Attachment to familiar objects

An increasing emotional investment in the things surrounding their daily lives—home, pets, familiar objects, heirlooms, keepsakes, photo albums, scrapbooks, old letters—may be noticed. Such objects provide a sense of continuity, aid the memory, and provide comfort, security, and satisfaction. Fear of loss of possessions at death is a frequent preoccupation. Older people generally feel better if they can decide in an orderly manner how their belongings will be distributed and cared for. Younger family members or friends should take such concerns seriously, offering their help rather than denying that the older person will someday die. Possessions may have to be painfully given up before death as a result of moves from a house to an apartment, an institution, etc. Some institutions are now recognizing the value of encouraging people to bring some of their own familiar possessions with them.

Change in the sense of time

There may be a resolution of fears about time running out, with an end to time panics and to boredom, and the development of a more appropriate valuation of time. While the middle-aged begin to be concerned with the number of years they have left to live, older persons tend to experi-

ence a sense of immediacy, of here and now, of living in the moment. This could be called a sense of "presentness" or "elementality." The elemental things of life—children, plants, nature, human touching, physically and emotionally, color, shape—assume greater significance as people sort out the more important from the less important. Old age can be a time of emotional and sensory awareness and enjoyment.

Sense of the life cycle

Older people experience something that younger people cannot: a personal sense of the entire life

A sense of the life cycle.

Photo by David Spilver.

cycle. We discuss this further in Chapter 8. There may be a greater interest in philosophy and religion, in enduring art or literature. In Japan it is common for old men to write poetry, thus giving another expression of life and its meaning. A sense of historical perspective and a capacity to summarize and comment upon one's time as well as one's life sometimes develop.

Creativity, curiosity, and surprise

Creativity does not invariably decline with age. Many persons recognized as creative have continued their work far into old age—Cervantes, Voltaire, Goethe, Tolstoi, and Picasso—to name a few. It is of course easy to name persons of achievement who continue to be productive in late life. But less well known is the fact that *most* older people remain productive and active in the absence of disease and social problems. Many become creative for the first time in old age, and the list does not begin and end with Grandma Moses. Factors that impede or support creativity and activity must be studied.

Curiosity and an ability to be surprised are other qualities that have a strikingly adaptive quality. Such qualities are especially attractive to younger people, who take heart and hope in them for their own old age. This type of enthusiasm probably reflects lifelong personality traits and serves the individual well in old age. Such older people are described as lively, full of life, spry, bright-eyed, and zestful.

Sense of consummation or fulfillment in life

A feeling of satisfaction with one's life is more common than recognized but not as common as possible. It is a quality of "serenity" and "wisdom," which derives from resolution of personal conflicts, reviewing one's life and finding it acceptable and gratifying, and viewing death with equanimity. One's life does not have to be a "success" in the general sense of that word in order to result in serenity. The latter can come from a feel-

ing of having done one's best, from having met challenge and difficulty, and sometimes from simply having survived against terrible odds.

MIDDLE AGE AND THE TRANSITION TO OLD AGE

An understanding of old age requires consideration of the transition from the middle years. Neugarten and Lowenthal have contributed much to the study of mid-life. Middle age is usually regarded as the period from age 40 to 65, during which most people are engaged in providing the livelihood for a family and finishing the rearing of children. The middle-aged are the people in command in society in terms of power, influence, norms, and decisions. They make up roughly 40% of the population and carry much responsibility for the old and the young.

Two themes that predominate in mid-life are the growing awareness of personal aging (eventual

A sense of fullfillment.

death) and the changes in life patterns that occur as the middle-aged person's children grow up, his own parents grow old, and he assumes new roles personally and socially. People become aware of a different sense of time; they begin to think about how long they have left to live rather than about how long they have lived. Men are aware of the possibility of their own imminent death whereas women, who have a longer life-span and often are married to an older spouse, worry about the death of the husband. They may consciously or unconsciously prepare for widowhood.

A personal sense of death can no longer be easily denied and avoided. The death of parents leaves the middle-aged next in line. Friends and peers begin to die; unmistakable physical changes occur; one's own children reach adulthood. But the perception of death may be a matter-of-fact acceptance rather than negative fears and worries. It can lead to greater respect for and attention to one's physical health; Neugarten has called this "body monitoring": the activities undertaken to keep the body in physical condition and to care for any physical illnesses or chronic conditions that have developed. It also leads to a reassessment of one's life, a stock-taking in terms of marriage, career, personal relationships, values, and other commitments made earlier in youth. According to Neugarten, an increased "interiority" takes place. Career changes and divorces are not infrequent, and sometimes the whole way of life may be changed. Mid-life has been compared to a second adolescence—one in which people reassess, change, strike out in new directions. (A third such period may occur after retirement, when again one sees reevaluation, with new identities and directions emerging.) A conception of personal death must become consciously realized. At first this can be frightening and painful, but if favorably resolved, a mature resignation frees the person from fear. Mid-life and eventually old age can then be enjoyed but with a full awareness of death, which lies beyond. Appreciations of some of the elemental things that people tend to value more highly as they age—human love and affection,

insight, pleasures of the senses, nature, children—are probably a result of the restructuring and reformulation of concepts of time, self, and death.

Studies thus far seem to indicate that the majority of people adjust and adapt remarkably well to the demands and problems of middle life. But difficulties do occur and are sometimes called "mid-life crises." Middle-aged people may panic and attempt to recapture youth by adopting inappropriate dress, manners, and behavior. They may envy the young and feel inferior to them or, on the other hand, hate and disparage them. There can be an overexaggeration of body monitoring, which becomes hypochondriacal. There can be such a fear of change that people will remain in pressured or boring jobs and marriages or will leap into almost identical situations if they do decide to take action. There may be preoccupations with age and appearance and self-consciousness about how to act and relate. Depression and alcoholism tend to increase. Although the "empty nest" (when children have left home) and the menopause do not ordinarily cause serious problems for women (and indeed may bring a sense of freedom and spontaneity), both of these may become overemphasized. Sexual promiscuity in order to prove youth and attractiveness may develop, as well as increased religiosity that has a hollow and desperate ring to it. Men may be haunted by a need to "succeed." All of these represent unresolved fears of aging and attempts to deny it by trying to turn back the clock. One can see fixation, rigidity, fatalism, pessimism, or overexpansiveness.

Middle age can be and is for most people the prime of life. But it can be complicated by periods of genuine crises, ranging from the superficial and reversible to the profound and more pathological. The middle-aged person who truly wants to be young again is rare, but most would like to preserve the good health and energy of youth. In its best sense mid-life can become a time of increasing sensitivity, self-awareness, use of capacities and skills to the fullest, and separation of that which is valuable from the less valuable in order to use time wisely and enjoyably. It can in this sense become a healthy preparation for the transition to old age.[30]

THE CHANGING AWARENESS OF OLD AGE

A large aged population is a new phenomenon, with older people moving from a position of rarity to one of commonality. Older people have become more highly visible since the nineteenth century as greater life expectancy and various social and economic conditions have unfolded the life cycle, making its stages stand out in bolder relief. An example of the fast-changing nature of this age group is the fact that 70% of the present 65-plus population have joined that group since 1959. Each day there are 1,600 more older Americans; each year nearly 600,000 more. By the year 2020, older people could make up one fifth of the total population. As their numbers grow, older people have slowly begun to be of interest of American sociologists and psychologists. G. Stanley Hall was a pioneer, writing the first major American book on the psychology of old age in 1922. Politicians have begun to grasp the value of supporting programs to benefit older persons since they have become a major voting bloc. But the medical and psychotherapeutic professions, which come most closely in contact with older people, still have not made an active commitment to their special concerns and problems. Older people are beginning to challenge this by dint of their growing self-aware-

ness and sophisticated use of public opinion and public policy. Their increasing good health and survival rates may at last bring older people hope for a vital participation in a better future for themselves and all of us.

REFERENCES

Bengtson, V.L., and Cutler, N.E.: Generations and intergenerational relations: perspectives on age groups and social change. In Binstock, R., and Shanas, E., editors: Handbook of aging and the social sciences, New York, 1976, Van Nostrand Reinhold Co., pp. 130-159.

Binstock, R., and Shanas, E., editors: Handbook of aging and the social sciences, New York, 1976, Van Nostrand Reinhold Co.

Birren, J.E., Butler, R.N., Greenhouse, S.W., Sokoloff, L., and Yarrow, M.R., editors: Human aging: a biological and behavioral study, Pub. No. (PHS) 986, Washington, D.C., 1963, U.S. Government Printing Office (reprinted as Pub. No. [HSM] 71-9051, 1971, 1974).

Borkan, G.A., and Norris, A.H.: Assessment of biological age using a profile of physical parameters, Journal of Gerontology **35:**177-184, 1980.

Botwinick, J.: Aging and behavior, New York, 1973, Springer Publishing Co.

Botwinick, J., and Storandt, M.: Memory, related functions and age, Springfield, Ill., 1974, Charles C Thomas, Publisher.

Britton, J.H., and Britton, J.O.: Personality changes in aging: a longitudinal study of community residents, New York, 1972, Springer Publishing Co.

Bromley, D.B.: The psychology of human aging, ed. 2, Baltimore, 1974, Penguin Books, Inc.

Buhler, C.: The general structure of the human life. In Buhler, C., and Massarik, F., editors: The course of human life: a study of goals in the humanistic perspective, New York, 1968, Springer Publishing Co.

Busse, E.W.: Therapeutic implication of basic research with the aged, Strecker Monograph Series No. 4, The Institute of Pennsylvania Hospital, 1967.

Butler, R.N.: Myths and realities of clinical geriatrics, Image and Commentary **12:**26-29, 1970.

Butler, R.N.: Psychiatry and psychology of the middle-aged. In Freedman, A.M., Kaplan, H.I., and Saddock, B.J., editors: The comprehensive textbook of psychiatry, ed. 2, Baltimore, 1980, The Williams & Wilkins Co.

Cain, L.D.: Aging and the law. In Binstock, R., and Shanas, E., editors: Handbook of aging and the social sciences, New York, 1976, Van Nostrand Reinhold Co., pp. 342-368.

Califano, J.: The aging of America: questions for the four generation society, Annals of the American Academy of Political and the Social Sciences **438:**96-107, 1978.

Carp, F.M.: Senility or garden-variety maladjustment? Journal of Gerontology **24:**203-209, 1969.

---

[30] There have been two books of considerable theoretical interest about middle age, although limited only to men: Levinson, D.J., Darrow, C.M., Klein, E.B., Levinson, M.H., and McKee, B.: The seasons of a man's life, New York, 1978, Alfred A. Knopf; and Vaillant, G.E.: Adaptation to life, Boston, 1977, Little, Brown & Co. There is also Rubin's book on middle aged women: Rubin, L.S.: Women of a certain age: the midlife search for self, New York, 1979, Harper & Row, Publishers, Inc. This is an in-depth study of the psychological identity of 160 women. Rubin concludes that issues around the stages of life are not intrapsychic per se but rather directly connected with social events and trends. The future should bring increasing research attention to the middle life period of men and women.

Cummings, E., and Henry, W.E.: Growing old: the process of disengagement, New York, 1961, Basic Books, Inc., Publishers.

Eisdorfer, C., and Lawton, M.P., editors: Psychology of adult development and aging, Washington, D.C., 1973, American Psychological Association.

Elias, M.F., Elias, P.K., and Elias, J.W.: Basic processes in adult developmental psychology, St. Louis, 1977, The C.V. Mosby Co.

Granick, S., and Patterson, R.: Human aging. II. An eleven-year follow-up biomedical and behavioral study, National Institute of Mental Health, Pub. No. (HSM) 71-9037, 1971.

Greenhouse, S.W., and Morrison, D.F.: Statistical methodology. In Birren, J.E., Butler, R.N., Greenhouse, S.W., Sokoloff, L., and Yarrow, M.R., editors: Human aging: a biological and behavioral study, Pub. No. (PHS) 986, Washington, D.C., 1963, U.S. Government Printing Office (reprinted as Pub. No. [HSM] 71-9051, 1971, 1974).

Group for the Advancement of Psychiatry: Toward a public policy on mental health care of the elderly, Report No. 79, 1970.

Gruen, W.: Adult personality: an empirical study of Erikson's theory of age development. In Neugarten, B.L., et al., editors: Personality in middle and late life, New York, 1964, Atherton Press.

Guttman, D.L.: The country of old men: cross-cultural studies of the psychology of later life. In Occasional papers in gerontology, vol. 5, Institute of Gerontology, Ann Arbor, 1969, University of Michigan–Wayne State University Press.

Hall, G.S.: Senescence: the last half of life, New York, 1922, D. Appleton & Co.

Harris, L.: The myth and reality of aging in America, Washington, D.C., 1975, Council on the Aging, Inc.

Henretta, J., and Campbell, R.: Status attainment and status maintenance: a study of satisfaction in old age, American Sociology Review **41**:981-992, 1976.

Heron, A., and Chown, S.: Age and function, Boston, 1967, Little, Brown & Co.

Jacque, E.: Death and the midlife crisis, International Journal of Psychoanalysis **46**:502-514, 1965.

Jarvik, L.F., and Blum, J.E.: Cognitive declines as predictors of mortality in twin pairs: a twenty-year longitudinal study of aging. In Palmore, E., and Jeffers, F.C., editors: Prediction of life-span, Boston, 1971, D.C. Heath & Co.

Kimmel, D.C.: Adulthood and aging, New York, 1980, John Wiley & Sons, Inc.

Lowenthal, M.F., and Chiriboga, D.: Transition to the empty nest: crisis, challenge, or relief? Archives of General Psychiatry **26**:8-15, 1972.

Maddox, G.L.: Sociology of later life, Annual Review of Sociology **5**:113-135, 1979.

Neugarten, B.L.: Awareness of middle age. In Neugarten, B.L., editor: Middle age and aging, Chicago, 1968, University of Chicago Press.

Neugarten, B.L., Havighurst, R.J., and Tobin, S.S.: Personality and patterns of aging. In Neugarten, B.L., editor: Middle age and aging, Chicago, 1968, University of Chicago Press.

Palmore, E.: Normal aging: reports from the Duke longitudinal study, 1955-1969, Durham, N.C., 1970, Duke University Press.

Pressey, S.L., and Kuhlen, R.G.: Psychological development through the life cycle, New York, 1957, Harper & Row, Publishers, Inc.

Reichard, S., Livson, F., and Peterson, P.: Aging and personality: a study of eighty-seven older men, New York, 1962, John Wiley & Sons, Inc.

Riegel, K.F., and Riegel, R.M.: Development, drop and death, Developmental Psychology **6**:306-319, 1972.

Rosow, I.: Socialization to old age, Berkeley, 1975, University of California Press.

Rosow, I.: Status and role change through the lifespan. In Binstock, R., and Shanas, E., editors: Handbook of aging and the social sciences, New York, 1976, Van Nostrand Reinhold Co., pp. 457-482.

Schaie, K.W.: A general model for the study of developmental problems, Psychological Bulletin **64**:92-107, 1965.

Schaie, K.W., and Labouvie-Vief, G.: Generational versus ontogenetic components of change in adult cognitive behavior: a fourteen-year cross-sequential study, Developmental Psychology **10**:305-320, 1974.

Shanas, E.: The health of older people: a social survey, Cambridge, Mass., 1962, Harvard University Press.

Shanas, E., and Maddox, G.L.: Aging, health, and the organization of health resources. In Binstock, R., and Shanas, E., editors: Handbook of aging and the social sciences, New York, 1976, Van Nostrand Reinhold Co., pp. 592-618.

Spence, D.C., Feigenbaum, E.M., Fitzgerald, F., and Roth, J.: Medical student attitudes toward the geriatric patient, Journal of the American Geriatrics Society **16**:976-983, 1968.

Strehler, B.L.: Time, cells and aging, ed. 2, New York, 1978, Academic Press, Inc.

Thomae, H.: Patterns of aging: findings from the Bonn longitudinal study of aging, Basel, Switzerland, 1976, S. Karger.

World Health Organization: Constitution of the World Health Organization, Public Health Report **61**:1268-1277, 1946.

Zuckerman, H., and Merton, R.D.: Age, aging and age structure in science. In Riley, M.W., Johnson, M.E., and Foner, A., editors: Aging and society, vol. 3, A sociology of age stratification, New York, 1972, Russell Sage Foundation.

SELECTIVE READINGS IN THE SOCIOLOGY OF AGING

Atchley, R.C.: The social forces in later life, Belmont, Calif., 1972, Wadsworth Publishing Co., Inc.

Bennett, R., editor: Aging, isolation and resocialization, New York, 1980, Van Nostrand Reinhold Co.

Blau, Z.S.: Old age in a changing society, New York, 1973, Franklin Watts, Inc.

Brim, O., and Wheeler, S.: Socialization through the life cycle, New York, 1966, John Wiley & Sons, Inc.

Cowgill, D.O., and Holmes, M.P.: Aging and modernization, New York, 1972, Appleton-Century-Crofts.

Curtin, S.: Nobody ever died of old age, Boston, 1972, Atlantic Monthly Press.

Eisenstadt, S.: From generation to generation: age groups and social structure, New York, 1956, The Free Press.

Elder, G.H., Jr.: Children of the great depression, Chicago, 1974, University of Chicago Press.

Estes, C.: The aging enterprise, San Francisco, 1979, Jossey-Bass, Inc., Publishers.

Gubrium, J.: The myth of the golden years: a socio-environmental theory of aging, Springfield, Ill., 1973, Charles C Thomas, Publisher.

Hareven, T.K., editor: Transitions: the family and the life course in historical perspectives; New York, 1979, Academic Press, Inc.

Hess, B.B., and Watson, E.W.: Aging and old age: an introduction to social gerontology, New York, 1980, Macmillan Publishing Co., Inc.

Hochschild, A.R.: The unexpected community, Englewood Cliffs, N.J., 1973, Prentice-Hall, Inc.

Myerhoff, B.G.: Number our days, New York, 1979, E.P. Dutton & Co., Inc.

Myerhoff, B.G., and Simic, A., editors: Life's career—aging: cultural variations on growing old, Beverly Hills, Calif., 1978, Sage Publications, Inc.

Riley, M.W., editor: Aging from birth to death, Boulder, Colo., 1979, Westview Press, Inc.

Riley, M.W., Johnson, M.E., and Foner, A.: Age strata in society. In Riley, M.W., Johnson, M.E., and Foner, A., editors: Aging and society, vol. 3, A sociology of age stratification, New York, 1972, Russell Sage Foundation.

Ross, J.K.: Old people, new lives: community creation in a retirement residence, Chicago, 1977, University of Chicago Press.

Ryder, N.: The cohort as a concept in the study of social change, American Sociology Review **30:**843-861, 1965.

Ward, R.A.: The aging experience: an introduction to social gerontology, New York, 1979, J.B. Lippincott Co.

Watson, W.H.: Stress and old age, New Brunswick, N.J., 1980, Transaction Books.

3

Common emotional problems

Loss is a predominant theme in characterizing the emotional experiences of older people. The psychological treatment goal is obtaining insight and restitution possibilities within the limits of the life situation and individual personality. Losses in every aspect of late life compel older persons to expend enormous amounts of physical and emotional energy in grieving and resolving grief, adapting to the changes that result from loss, and recovering from the stresses inherent in these processes. Older people can be confronted by multiple losses, which may occur simultaneously: death of marital partner, older friends, colleagues, relatives; decline of physical health and coming to personal terms with death; loss of status, prestige, and participation in society; and, for large numbers of the older population, additional burdens of marginal living standards. Inevitable losses of aging and death are compounded by potentially ameliorable cultural devaluation and neglect.

In the complex of factors affecting subjective experience, overt behavior, and level of adaptation of the older persons any or all of the following may be significant.

Environmental or extrinsic factors
Personal losses or gains
  Marital partners; other loved and significant figures (friends, children)
Social forces (losses or gains)
  Status changes, prestige changes: in social groups other than family and as paterfamilias

Socioeconomic adversities: income drop, inflation
Unwanted retirement: arbitrary retirement policies
Cultural devaluation of older persons: sense of uselessness, therapeutic pessimism, forced isolation, forced segregation

Intrinsic factors
Nature of personality: character structure (defensive and integrative mechanisms), life history, survival characteristics
Physical diseases: disease of any organ system; perceptual decrements; sexual losses; disease of integrative systems (hormonal, vascular, and central nervous systems); brain damage; arteriosclerosis, senile dementia, etc.; physical limitations (such as arthritis)
Age-specific changes (largely obscure and mysterious, but inexorable with objective passage of time): losses of speed of processes and response; involutionary processes; others (heredity, survival qualities); changes in body size and appearance ("slipping" and "shrinkage")
Experience of bodily dissolution and approaching death (subjective passage of time)

Older people often are handicapped by their own bodies, which respond to challenge with less energy and strength than were formerly available, particularly if major illnesses have taken their toll. Emotionally, a rapid succession of losses can leave individuals with accumulated layers of unresolved grief along with fatigue and a sense of emptiness. There may be little societal support for grief and mourning as the rituals of religion and custom are increasingly questioned and discarded.

It is an odd distortion of reality when older persons are popularly depicted as weak, unassuming, gently tranquil people who passively wait out their last days. Becoming old, being old, and dying are active physical and emotional processes that test the mettle of each person. Reluctance to accord older people appropriate recognition for their strengths and capacities indicates a failure to understand what is required in being old. We have lost our naiveté about the carefree nature of childhood as we have developed our understanding of the difficult and frightening developmental work each child must do to grow up. But simplistic illusions about old age continue, with little conceptualization of the normative stages one must pass through in late life.[1] Certain dramatic events (for example, widowhood) have been more widely studied than others, but there is as yet no cohesive, reliable body of information against which one can measure adjustment patterns.

EMOTIONAL REACTIONS TO AGE-RELATED LIFE CRISES

Certain life crises occur in old age regardless of socioeconomic and cultural circumstances, as part of the current aging experience in the United States.

Widowhood

The loss of spouse represents a major psychological issue. The mourning process itself occurs at the same time as the need to make practical though emotion-laden decisions about where to live, what to do about the family home and posessions, how to dispose of the spouse's personal effects, what kind of contact to maintain with the spouse's relatives, and what to do about new social roles. Although research data are not available on the progress of couples (or of individuals, for that matter) through the entire life-span, one can observe the interdependence that results from years of living together. Birren et al. (1963) found that losses of significant persons were important factors where there were any evidences of deteriorated functioning in healthy aged men. Other investigations point toward associations between bereavement and increased medical and psychiatric morbidity.[2] Jacobs and Ostfeld estimate 25,000 excess deaths among survivors during the first year following the death of a close loved one, usually a spouse.[3] The widowed and their children may be ambivalent about the more involved roles that many grown children feel compelled to accept in relation to the remaining parent. Friends and associates tend to socially ostracize the widowed individual for varieties of reasons: pain over the reminder of the loss of a friend; anxieties and denial of their own aging; awkwardness in knowing how to comfort a grieving person; and uneasiness about accepting a single man or women into a cultural pattern of couples. Thus widows and widowers may be forced to seek out each other's companionship or fall back on their own resources.

Marital problems[4]

Couples who enter old age together find new situations awaiting them. There is a greater amount of close contact and free time for each other. With retirement, the older man spends most of his day at home for the first time in his adult life. Wives may complain of husbands being underfoot all day with nothing to do as the wives continue their ac-

---

[1] "Senescence" is a term that has been used to describe the developmental stages of later life. It is an analogue to pubescence and adolescence; no similar term has been formulated for middle age.

[2] The interdependence or mutual support of *some* older couples can become symbiotic to the extent that the remaining member may die shortly after the death of the other, even though he or she has been seemingly healthy. In other cases severe depression may ensue.

[3] Jacobs, S.C., and Ostfeld, A.M.: The effects of illness and death of one family member on other family members: a review with some recommendations for research and medical practice, commissioned by the National Institute on Aging, completed Sept. 1978.

[4] Very little data are available on old-age marital relationships. There have been no studies of husband and wife through the life-span; therefore we must largely theorize from clinical experience.

customed routines of housework. Some men actively pursue new interests but many encounter difficulties in finding a meaningful substitute for work. As one or the other becomes ill and requires nursing care, the healthy spouse is torn between the desire to provide such care for the sick person and a need to have a life of his or her own outside the sickroom. Typically, because of a shorter life expectancy and a tendency to be older than his wife at the time of marriage, it is the husband who becomes ill, often chronically so, and the wife nurses him until his death. If the illness is a long and draining one, the wife can be expected to feel some bitterness and sense of exploitation. This becomes a more serious problem when the wife denies her feelings and insists on the pretense that her husband is no burden. The husband, sensing his wife's frustrations, may react with hurt and anger, and a troubled marital relationship ensues wherein both need guidance and reassurance.

Discrepant rates of change, narcissism, fear of death, and the relationship to the children are among critical variables that seem pertinent to marital problems in late life and require study.

■ A daughter of a 78-year-old patient wrote concerning the present relationship of her parents: ''I might note here that when I was growing up, my father objected to even the words darned or damned. He now swears freely and will mutter Jesus Christ under his breath the minute he hears mother call. He seems to feel that both her present philosophical outlook and her physical inabilities could be improved if she 'had the guts.' He bitterly resents her balkings and her standard 'I can't answer.' His answer to her frequent plea 'love me' is 'give me something to love'. . . . He is crushed by her condition. She is crushed by his cruelty and intolerance.''

At times, underlying disease states may be misread by a spouse as emotional moods.

■ The wife of a 75-year-old patient bitterly complained of her husband's glum, depressed nature. He denied being as depressed as she insisted. He had the typical ''ironed-out'' facies of parkinsonism, although no other manifestations of this disorder were present. A medical examination revealed that he did indeed have parkinsonism.

Sexual problems

Sex relations, although tending to be diminished in frequency, are practiced by many older people; however, problems can arise physically and emotionally in relationship to aging and illness. Surgery requiring a colostomy, for example, can seriously deter sexual expression for esthetic and physical reasons. Physiological changes in females (for example, untreated ''senile'' vaginitis) and prostatic problems in males are some of the possible organic impediments to sexual intercourse. Older people, like the young, tend to react with anxiety and depression over threats to potency and sexual fulfillment. In addition, new fears can present themselves. One of the more common worries is fear of the effects of sexual exertion on the heart or circulatory system. Studies indicate that much of this fear is unwarranted. Other problems result from spending a long life together: one partner may begin to find the other less and less sexually attractive as they age or be simply bored by the routine of the same partner over a period of years. A widow has an especially difficult situation, since chances for remarriage are so slight. Older people are inclined to follow the strict sexual customs of their youth—no sex outside of marriage—and are therefore forced into celibacy regardless of personal inclination. (We discuss sex more fully in Chapter 6.)

Iatrogenicity (a physician's induction of pathological reactions) is pertinent to the discussion of sexual problems. By means that range from the injunction to ''take it easy,'' said to the active man now suffering from a cardiac disorder, to the failure to prepare the patient who is about to have a prostatectomy and orchidectomy, the physician may contribute to depressive reactions so common in older people.

■ A 76-year-old retired political scientist who was still active sexually required a prostatectomy and orchidectomy for malignancy. He was not psychologically prepared, developed extreme anxiety at the time of operation, and had a profound suicidal depression following the procedure. He put himself to bed, ate poorly, talked little, discouraged visitors, and died 8 months later. Autopsy revealed that metastases did not fully account for his death.

Retirement

Women enjoy a mixed blessing in relation to retirement. Many of the current generation of older women have never worked outside the home and therefore are not as subject as men to the generally arbitrary retirement policies of employers. The traditional housewife's job identity is threatened in mid-life as her children leave home but as she adjusts to caring for only herself and her husband, she has a definite pattern of work—at least until her husband dies. Even in her widowhood a woman continues to have the routines of homemaking available to her. For those women who do work outside the home, many carry the dual role of homemaker and career person, thus ameliorating the impact of retirement.

For men, retirement is a concern that can affect the very essence of their lives. A large number of men derive an almost single-minded identity from their work (some even becoming ''workaholics'' —addicted to work). Many develop no diversified interests outside their employment and are caught up in a narrow definition of who they are and what they are worth as people. Work and life become so interconnected that the loss of a job can demolish the reason for living.

■ Mr. J, a retired legal adjudicator, was diagnosed as having an adjustment reaction to old age—in this case, to retirement. He was irritable, sad, anxious, fearful, and perplexed. He described himself as always having been fidgety, but this trait had increased since his retirement. Time dragged heavily, and he missed feeling useful. He had voluntarily retired 4 years ago (at 66), having done little planning for his old age or the future. He tended to deny his aging state and felt frightened and depressed about the future. He had shown no previous adjustment or personality problems.

The syndrome of the restless and depressed retired person is common indeed, with little hope for wide-ranging solutions in the near future. There is both commonsense and research evidence that people adjust better if they can choose when and how completely they wish to retire, but such evidence is of little import in a youth- and production-oriented economic system. Eventually a redefinition

of work itself may bring a more satisfying retirement picture. Perhaps work, leisure, and study could be alternated throughout the life cycle instead of being parceled out according to age group.

Men should also be encouraged to take a more active part in other aspects of life—with more involvement in the care of children and home, a sharing of responsibility for financial support with the wife, more leisure time throughout life for rest and study, and active involvement in cultural and social activities. A call for male as well as female liberation is in order if men are to escape the crushing burden of overidentification with work and problems of stress, coronary disease, retirement shock, and shortened life expectancy that are associated with it.

Financial worries

There is considerable financial distress among older persons, as we have emphasized earlier. Poverty and the fear of poverty do of course influence mental health. Moreover, continuing public discussion of the integrity and unfunded liability of Social Security as well as public and private pension systems add to the worries of older people. Economic projections into the future have emphasized the declining number of workers to contribute to the support of older people. Frequently the fact that there is also a declining number of young people for the working generation to support is not emphasized. (See Table 1-1, Dependency Ratio.)

Sensory loss

Significant hearing loss, which affects men[5] more often than women (probably because of industrial noise), occurs in some 30% of all older people and is potentially the most problematical of the perceptual impairments.[6] It can reduce real-

---

[5] Butler, R.N., and Gastel, B.: Hearing and age, Annals of Otology, Rhinology and Laryngology **43:**676-682, 1979.

[6] Older people usually first notice hearing loss in the high-frequency range. This includes the consonants. To get a sense of what many older persons miss, write a sentence and remove the f's, s's, and th's.

Table 3-1. Relation of auditory acuity and depression to reaction time

Diagnostic category	Very healthy older men		Healthy older men	
	Number of subjects	Mean reaction time	Number of subjects	Mean reaction time
No decrease in auditory acuity; no depression	11	0.21	12	0.22
Decrease in auditory acuity; no depression	7	0.21	3	0.26
No decrease in auditory acuity; depression	8	0.24	2	0.30
Decrease in auditory acuity; depression	0	—	2	0.33
TOTAL	26		19	

From Butler, R.N., and Perlin, S. In Birren, J.E., Butler, R.N., Greenhouse, S.W., Sokoloff, S.W., and Yarrow, M.R.: Human aging: a biological and behavioral study, Pub. No. (PHS) 986, Washington, D.C., 1963, U.S. Government Printing Office, p. 300 (reprinted as Pub. No. [HSM] 71-9051, 1971, 1974).

ity testing and lead to marked suspiciousness, even paranoia.

From clinical observations it has long been thought that a relationship exists between hearing loss and depression. The National Institute of Mental Health (NIMH) study of older men provides evidence of such a relationship and its connection with reaction time. An analysis of variance (a statistical procedure) based on the data tabulated showed an interaction between depression and decreased auditory acuity, which was statistically highly significant.

Hearing loss causes greater social isolation than blindness because verbal communication is so vital to human interaction. Onlookers may mistake the hard-of-hearing as mentally abnormal or "senile." There is little social sympathy—older people who are deaf are often excluded from activities and become less and less well oriented. The loud or badly articulated speech associated with hearing loss can have a negative effect on others and the hard-of-hearing are given less consideration than the elderly blind, probably because their handicap is not so obvious to the onlooker.

Although most old people need glasses, poor vision is not as widespread as is usually thought. About 80% have fair to adequate visual acuity to age 90 and even beyond. Often one eye may continue to function, even if the other does not. Older persons find the possibility of cataracts, glaucoma, and other disorders frightening because of the iso-

lating and immobilizing effects. Visual loss can cause decreasing mobility, poor orientation, and frightening visual impressions that resemble hallucinations. Reading, television, and other visual pastimes are reduced or eliminated. Furthermore, older people feel more vulnerable to danger and crime when handicapped by sensory loss.

Smell also declines with age, and up to 30% of people who are over 80 years have difficulty identifying common substances by smell. Taste too is affected, since two thirds of taste sensations are dependent on the ability to smell; in addition, taste buds decrease sharply in number with age.[7] There is also a falloff of tactile response as both perception and motor expression decline in reaction to stimuli. However, the slowing of speed and response, which at first appears to be a characteristic of old age, was found in the NIMH studies to be also related to environmental deprivation and depression.

On a more positive note, Beard in 1967 studied 270 male and female centenarians (100 years old or more) and found only 5.2% blind and only 1.9% completely deaf. However, 58.5% had only fair to poor vision. Hearing disappeared more slowly than sight. Women lost more vision than the men, and men lost more hearing than did women.[8]

[7] In Shakespeare's *As You Like It,* old age is described as "sans teeth, sans eyes, sans taste, sans everything."

[8] Beard, B.B.: Social competence of centenarians, Athens, 1967, University of Georgia Printing Department.

Aging, disease, and pain

The chronic and acute illnesses and diseases in old age provide the fulcrum determining the physical functioning and energy levels that are available to older people. Just as loss and grief define the critical emotional variable for the old, so illness presents the prime physical variable. The Roman adage "mens sana in corpore sano," a sound mind in a sound body, recognizes the interrelationships between the two. There have been a few studies on stress and age.[9] Psychometric tests have proved to be unusually sensitive to even minimal disease. Physical illness frequently generates both appropriate and distorted emotional reactions, since it represents so much that is inherently frightening to human beings. For example, persons with diabetes, faced with the prospect of lifelong disease, possible blindness, a lowered life expectancy, and in some cases loss of sexual response, are under considerable emotional pressures that may influence the course of their disease—affecting metabolic homeostasis and causing diabetic complications.[10] Psychological attitudes and beliefs may also affect behavior toward prescribed treatment regimens.

Latent fear and anxiety about death grow real with illness. Feelings of helplessness and vulnerability buried deep within the individual are resurrected in the face of implacable illness and the aging process. Hope for cures from medicines, luck, or a supreme being diminishes in the light of the general knowledge most people now possess about aging and the current irreversibility of many chronic diseases. Older people's sense of pride in their own body's reliability is shaken when they experience greater susceptibility to communicable diseases, air pollution, dampness, cold weather, and exertion. Moreover, aging and disease threaten people's sense of who they are—their identities—as their bodies change "in front of their eyes." People report feelings of shock and disbelief at their mirror images, in reaction both to aging (is that old person me?) and to illnesses, which even more rapidly change the size, shape, and appearance of the body.

A common feature of old age, which begins in the middle years, is "body monitoring"—the need to concern oneself with the care of one's body and its functions in a more concerted way than before. Bodily processes that formerly took care of themselves or required minimal attention begin to demand more and more time as people age. Among older persons, 86% have some kind of chronic health problem requiring more visits to the doctor, added stays in the hospital, special diets, exercises, drugs, rehabilitative therapy, or additional provisions for daily life at home. With 81% of older people ambulatory and to a substantial degree responsible for their own self-care (only 5% are in institutions and, even there, many have some degree of self-care), it is apparent that body monitoring is a compelling preoccupation. Some older people welcome the relief from other anxieties, which occurs as they absorb themselves in their own care. But others are annoyed, wearied, or bored by the routines imposed on them by ill health and the decline of their bodies. The composer Stravinsky in his eighties wrote of his irritation at having to spend so much time on his body when he wanted to write music. One can assume that his complaint is echoed by many who wish to continue active, interesting lives.

Pain is another frequent preoccupation for the aged. The periodic aches and pains of rheumatism, the throbbing relentless pains of arthritis, the sharp distress of angina pectoris—these are examples of pain in some of its shapes and forms. Older persons deal with pain according to their life style, personality, and cultural background, as well as the nature and extent of the pain. (Individual pain thresholds vary from person to person and vary also in intensity at different times in the same individual.) For many persons, the use of drugs offers

---

[9] See Eisdorfer, C.: Stress, disease and cognitive change in the elderly. In Eisdorfer, C., and Friedel, R.O., editors: Clinical issues, Chicago, 1977, Year Book Medical Publishers; and Levi, L.: Society, stress and disease, Oxford, England, 1979, Oxford University Press.

[10] There are over 5 million diagnosed diabetic individuals in the United States, and many more who are undiagnosed.

the most consistent relief, yet drugs sometimes produce side effects that can be particularly devitalizing or disorganizing to older people—dizziness, loss of appetite, weakness, nausea, or dulling of consciousness. Twelve of the twenty-two most frequently prescribed drugs have a sedating effect. Older people often fear drugs on the basis of frightening past experiences, and at times clarity of consciousness and preservation of strength may be more important than absolute freedom from pain.

Hospitalization and surgery

Heart and circulatory diseases, digestive conditions, and disturbances of the nervous system are the primary causes of hospitalization after age 65. Hospitalization is drastic and dramatic proof that something is wrong or may be wrong. Fears become heightened and, since so many older persons now die in hospitals and nursing homes rather than at home, such institutions come to be viewed as places to die as well as places to regain health. There is still far too little attention paid to the emotional feelings of sick people, and this is especially the case with the aged. The emphasis on treating physical disease, the often cold and cheerless environment of hospitals, the generally efficient but overworked and impersonal medical staff, and too rigid visiting regulations combine to make the older person feel isolated, unprotected, lonely, and bored. There is little to do except watch television, a pastime that becomes limited if hearing or sight is impaired. Occupational and recreational therapies are usually minimal. Removal from the home environment (with consequent deprivation of adequate contact with family and friends, lack of responsibility, and restriction of mental and somatic activity) encourages anxiety, irritability, disorientation, and eventual regression.

Insufficient thought has been given to the side effects of various surgical procedures. An example is the "black patch" syndrome, which until relatively recently puzzled the medical profession. Following bilateral cataract surgery when patches were placed over both eyes, some older people became delirious and disoriented. It was observed that the syndrome did not occur when one eye was operated on at a time, leaving the sight in the other available to the patient. Finally, the conclusion was correctly drawn that the black patch reaction was simply the result of loss of contact with people and environment. Therefore, operating on one eye at a time and providing additional sensory stimuli will allow patients to maintain orientation. It seems logical that other undesirable side effects of surgery might be alleviated through just such careful thinking through of the problems.

Several organizations assist persons undergoing particular kinds of surgery. The Reach to Recovery program of the American Cancer Society is a rehabilitation program for women who have had breast surgery. The United Ostomy Clubs[11] offer information and counseling to those who have had colostomies and ileostomies.

Dying and death

Preparation for death involves a condition unknown in past or present experience, for one cannot truly imagine one's own nonexistence. Yet, strangely, although fear of death is part of human experience, older people tend to fear it less than the young do and often are more concerned about the death of those they love than about their own. Many can accept personal death with equanimity. In terminal illness it may even be welcomed as a release from pain and struggle. Reactions to death are closely related to a resolution of life's experiences and problems as well as a sense of one's contributions to others.[12] Profound religious and philosophical convictions facilitate acceptance. The process of working through one's feelings about death begins with a growing personal awareness of the eventual end of life and the implications of this for one's remaining time alive. For some people the process begins early; for others

---

[11] Central office—1111 Wilshire Blvd., Los Angeles, Calif. 90017, with 250 local chapters.

[12] The psychoanalytically influenced explanation of fear of death as "castration anxiety" suggests a denial of the reality of death on the part of psychoanalysts themselves.

the physical signs of aging occur before awareness is allowed to surface. Some few attempt to
deny death to the very end. A resolution of feelings about death may be responsible for those elusive qualities, seen in various old people, known
as ''wisdom'' and ''serenity.'' The German
philosopher Feurbach has written that ''anticipation of death is seen as the instrument of being—of
authentic existence.'' There are of course varying
degrees and levels of acceptance; perhaps the most
satisfying is that described by another philosopher,
Spinoza: ''The adult who sees death as completion of a pattern and who has spent life unfettered
by fears, living richly and productively, can integrate and accept the thought that life will stop.''

In the NIMH study, 55% of older people in
good health seemed to have resolved the problem
of their death, 30% manifested denial, and 15%
candidly expressed fear.

Few older persons today have the opportunity to
die at home as their parents and grandparents did.
More than 50% of all deaths take place in hospitals, and many in nursing homes. The process of
dying is made more difficult by this shift from
home to institutions, where the emphasis is on
physical rather than emotional concerns. Short and
inflexible visiting hours and lack of accommodations for intimate family contact encourage families and friends to withdraw from dying persons,
in anticipatory grief (working out feelings of grief
as though the person were already dead). Thus the
aged person, who may have resolved many of his
own difficult feelings about death itself, is left
without human comfort and warmth as death approaches. Older people often remark that their
greatest fear is of ''dying alone.''

There is an increasing interest in the subject of
death and dying, as evidenced by a growing body
of research and literature. One of the best-known
reports is the Kübler-Ross work (1970) on the
stages of dying, in which she suggests five more
or less distinct stages or levels of experience during the actual course of dying. The first stage is
denial of death, in which the person simply refuses to believe the evidence of his or her own

approaching demise. In the second stage, denial is
replaced by anger and rage at the injustice and
unfairness of life's ending. Third, the person
moves into a bargaining stage during which he or
she tries to make a deal with God or fate in return
for life (promises of being a better person, showing
more concern for others, etc.). When this is seen to
be futile, the person moves into a period of depression and preparatory grief over the loss of life and
loved ones. Finally, in the last stages, a level of
acceptance is reached—a quiet expectation of
death and a lessening of interest in the outer world,
including loved ones. In our experience and that
of others working with dying persons, these stages
seldom occur as neatly and orderly as described
here. Therefore, keeping the various stages in
mind can be very useful in understanding the
dying, as long as one does not depend on them too
rigidly.

COMMON EMOTIONAL REACTIONS AS EXPRESSED IN OLD AGE

Older persons experience human feelings that
are similar for people of every age, but as with
each age, there is a uniqueness in the character of
such feelings as they reflect the life events of old
people. Both the uniqueness and the similarities
bear examination if one is to clarify the distinctive
nature of old age.

Grief (mourning)

As has been previously discussed, grief as a result of loss is a predominate factor in aging. Loss
of the marital partner or other significant and loved
people can be profound, particularly since it is difficult in later life to find any kind of substitute for
such losses. This is illustrated in the tender and
grief-stricken passage by St. Augustine in his
Confessions:

> I pressed her eyes closed, and a huge wave of sorrow
> flooded my heart and flowed outward in tears. . . . What,
> then, was it which caused grevious pain within me, if
> not the fresh wound arising from the sudden breaking of
> a very sweet and cherished habit of living together?
> Since I was thus bereft of such great comfort from her,

my soul was wounded and it was as if life which had been made one from hers and mine was torn to shreds. . . . It was a relief to weep in Thy sight about her and for her, about myself and for myself.

The primary adaptive purpose of grief and mourning is to accept the reality of the loss and to begin to find ways of filling up the emptiness caused by the loss through identifying with a new style of life and new people. Parkes (1970), in his studies of London widows, describes the futile search for the lost love object in which the mourner is torn between the desire to recover or resurrect the dead person and the knowledge that this is irrational.[13] A cultural adaptation is found in the practice of ancestor worship in Shintoism and Buddhism, where the mourner believes the presence of a departed loved one remains (to be fed, prayed to, etc.) yet in a new spirit form that does not allow direct physical contact. Thus both the reality of death and the wishful recovery of the person are provided for, in a religious belief that gives structure to the grief process.

A typical grief reaction has an almost predictable pattern of onset, regardless of age—numbness and inability to accept the loss, followed by the shock of reality as it begins to penetrate. There are physical feelings of emptiness in the pit of the stomach, weak knees, perhaps a feeling of suffocation, shortness of breath, and a tendency to deep sighing. Emotionally the person experiences great distress. There may be a sense of unreality, including delusions and obsessive preoccupations with the image of the lost person and acting as though the deceased were still present. Generally feelings of guilt are present as well as anger and irritability, even toward friends and relatives. There is usually a disorganization of normal patterns of response, with the bereaved person wan-

dering about aimlessly, unable to work or take social initiative. Anxiety and longing alternate with depression and despair. Insomnia, digestive disturbances, and anorexia are common. Acute grief ordinarily lasts a month or two and then begins to lessen; on the average, grief may be largely over in 6 to 12 months, although further loss, stress, or some reminder can reactivate it.

Exaggerated grief reactions may occur:

■ A 66-year-old woman was as angry and depressed over the death of her husband 16 months after his death as she was in the immediate weeks. She had passed through the ''markers'' of a year—the anniversary of their marriage, Thanksgiving, Christmas, Valentine's Day, Easter, and summer vacation reminiscence. But she could not shake her oppressive depression. She was furious at her brother-in-law, who she felt would find ways to cheat her of her inheritance. She chastised her two sons for their neglect. It was only through open exploration of her anger, first with the help of her sophisticated clergyman and then with a psychiatrist, that her depression began to lift.

''Morbid'' grief reactions are distortions or prolongations of typical grief. Such reactions may take the form of delay, in which the grief is delayed for days, months, or even years, and in its extreme form is generally bound up with conscious or unconscious antagonism or ambivalence toward the deceased. Inhibited grief, according to Parkes, produces minimal mourning but other symptoms develop such as somatic illnesses, overactivity, or disturbed social interaction. Chronic grief, yet another of the morbid grief reactions, is the prolongation and intensification of normal grief over an extended or limited period of time.

We have observed a not infrequent form of grief reaction that we call ''enshrinement,'' in which the survivor attempts to keep things just as they were before the death of a loved one occurred. The dead person's possessions and even entire rooms may be kept intact as shrines to the person's memory. The survivor may surround himself or herself with photographs and memorabilia connected with the lost person and make regular and conscious attempts to evoke memories of the de-

---

[13] Studies indicate that some widowed people have hallucinations and delusions of contact with the lost spouse. These may last for years and are more likely to occur in individuals who had been happily married. The most common hallucination reported was feeling the dead spouse's presence; others thought they saw, heard, were touched by or spoken to by the spouse.

ceased. There may be frequent references to the dead person in conversation with others, as well as a deliberate avoidance of new contacts that might replace the role of the one who died. Much of this is a result of survival guilt and a misplaced fear of infidelity if one were to take an active role in getting life moving again. It can also be symptomatic of a "silent" and internal adult temper tantrum—a stubborn refusal to accept death.

Anticipatory grief is the process of mourning in advance, before an actual loss is sustained. This form of mourning can occur during long illnesses; for example, a wife caring for a sick husband may go through a grief reaction and may have reached some degree of acceptance before death occurs. Such grief is seen as a protective device that prepares the bereaved for their loss, but it can lead to problems if it causes loved ones to disengage themselves prematurely from the dying person, leaving him isolated and alone.

Interrelationships between grief and vulnerability to both physical and emotional illness have been the subject of a number of investigations. Bereavement as a loss is hypothesized to be the single most crucial factor in predicting decline or breakdown in functioning on a physical or emotional level. In addition, losses of health, money, possessions, employment, or social status or changes in appearance seem to be possible factors in precipitating decline or lowering resistance.

Guilt

Old age is a time of reflection and reminiscence that can evoke a resurgence of past conflicts and regrets. Guilt feelings may play a significant role as the older person reviews his life, attempting to consolidate a meaningful judgment as to the manner in which life has been lived and to prepare for death and cope with any fears of death. The sins of omission[14] and commission for which an individual blames himself weigh even more heavily in the light of approaching death and dissolu-

tion. If expiation and atonement are to occur, they must occur now; time for procrastination begins to run out. Individuals who have held grudges for a lifetime may decide to resolve their differences. Some may undertake a variety of reparations for the past. Others become more religiously active, in the hope of forgiveness. Such feelings should be dealt with seriously and not simply treated with facile reassurance. For many the resolution of guilt feelings is an essential part of final acceptance of their lives as worthwhile.

Other forms of guilt are the "death survival guilt"[15] from outliving others and "retirement guilt" from no longer being employed and working. The latter is especially hard on Horatio Alger types.

Loneliness

In infancy, being alone is a condition that provokes terror, anger, and disconsolation. A baby's early cries communicate the primitive drive for physical survival. But very early a new element is introduced. As the child alternately experiences the gratifying warmth and comfort of his family and the aloneness of his crib, he learns a new fear, the fear of not being able to get back to people— of being left alone. Thus there appear to be two elements in the early sense of loneliness: *aloneness,* or the fear for physical survival in a threatening uncertain world, and *loneliness,* the fear of emotional isolation, of being locked inside oneself and unable to obtain the warmth and comfort that one has learned is available from others if one can gain it. Growth and a refinement occur as children move outside of themselves and their isolation, not only toward other people but also toward an absorption in play, learning, work, and other creative efforts. That moment is significant when the child

---

[14] Surviving relatives, especially spouses, frequently feel guilty about things they believe they failed to do for the person who died.

[15] Chodoff especially has emphasized "survival guilt" as a result of concentration camp experiences. We have observed this also in older people who have outlived their peers and spouses, although of course many take pride in survival as well. See Chodoff, P.C.: Late effects of the concentration camp syndrome, Archives of General Psychiatry **9:**323-333, 1963. Thomas Mann in *The Magic Mountain* observes that "a man's dying is more the survivor's affair than his own."

first learns to escape his own aloneness or consciousness of himself and becomes totally involved in a task—a moment described as an escape from loneliness, which is not dependent on the presence of another person. (Paul Tillich describes this as a distinction between loneliness and solitude.)

The etiology of loneliness developmentally is significant in regard to older people, not in a simplistic sense of comparing them to children but in attempting to comprehend the special character of loneliness in old age. The primitive fears concerning physical survival and emotional isolation recede as human beings grow to adulthood and learn to successfully provide for their own physical sustenance and achieve emotional satisfactions through family, friends, and work. But with old age, the combination of harsh external forces and a diminishing self-mastery revives once again the latent threats. The old adage that we are born alone and we die alone reflects the experience that each of us encounters in the course of the life cycle. But, unlike the usual experience of children, the older person does not suffer so much from a fear of being unable to relate as from the reality of having no one to relate to. With the death of loved ones, there is a diminishing circle of significant people who are not readily replaceable. Former compensations of work may be gone. Children and grandchildren, if they exist, may live far away. The all too limited outlets of religion, hobbies, television, pets, and a few acquaintances, which form the daily existence of so many older persons, are not enough to satisfy emotional needs.

The American dream of self-reliance and independence can further isolate the older person within himself. At a time when increased human contact could be supportive, older people hold on to cultural notions that living alone and "doing for oneself" must be maintained. Familiarity with and determination to continue such patterns make communal living in hospitals, nursing homes, or group homes difficult in sheerly social terms. It has been observed that older people in more group-oriented societies, such as the rural kibbutzim in Israel, can enjoy the companionship and involvement inherent in a close living situation with others without the same loss of self-esteem and sense of dependency felt by "rugged individualists." Cultures that advocate societal and group responsibility for the individual are perhaps more in sympathy with the natural needs of older people.

Depression

Depressive reactions increase in degree and frequency with old age as a corollary to the increased loss of much that is emotionally valued by the older person. Unresolved grief, guilt, loneliness, and anger are expressed in mild to severe depressions with symptomatology including insomnia, despair, lethargy, anorexia, loss of interest, and somatic complaints. (See Chapter 4.)

Anxiety

The sense of free-floating anxiety intensifies in older people as illness and imminent death undermine illusions of invulnerability built up as protection during a lifetime. (A very powerful anxiety is the fear of becoming a pauper.) In addition, new modes of adaptation become necessary, creating additional anxieties in the face of constant change. Notice is seldom taken of the amount of new learning an older person must undergo to adapt to the accelerating changes in body, feelings, and environment. As with any new learning, anxiety develops in proportion to the task at hand, the resources available to master it, and the chances for and consequences of failure. Anxiety manifests itself in many forms: rigid thinking to protectively exclude external stimuli (a person may "hear" only what he wants to hear), fear of being alone, and suspiciousness to the point of paranoid states. It may also become somatized into physical illness. Frequently anxiety and its expressions are incorrectly diagnosed as "senility" and wrongly considered untreatable.

One type of anxiety derives from life history, the observations of older people during one's childhood. For example, the fear that they will have the diseases of old age that as children they observed in their grandparents or in other older people is one possible ingredient in the denial or projection seen in the aged.

■ A 70-year-old retired chemist who had been born when his mother was 40 years old had seen her develop severe parkinsonism and become increasingly helpless when he was 20 years old. He carried this image with him all his life, but after he retired, it became obsessional. He gradually convinced himself and his doctors that he did have the disease. If he did, it was clinically negligible.

Sense of impotence and helplessness

A significant reaction for older men, particularly those white men who as a group can be postulated to have once held the major power and influence in American society, is a sense of their present impotence and helplessness. The highest suicide rates occur among older white men in their eighties. The older black man and all women, black, white, or other races, are affected by loss of esteem and cultural status as they age but do not experience quite the same degree of loss of power and privilege. In fact, an interesting reversal can occur for older women within the traditional marital relationship. As their husbands decline, wives may assume more of the initiative, taking over financial management, nursing care, and household repairs; they may therefore feel more status and influence than at any previous point in their lives.

Rage

Another of the emotional manifestations of old age is a sense of rage at the seemingly uncontrollable forces that confront older persons, as well as the indignities and neglect of the society that once valued their productive capacities. The description of some older people as cantankerous, ornery, irritable, or querulous would be more realistically interpreted if one became sensitive to the degree of outrage older people feel, consciously or unconsciously, at viewing their situation. (Interestingly, grouchiness and pugnacity have been related to a longer life expectancy in one study.) Much of the

rage is an appropriate response to inhumane treatment. Some older people, of course, rage against the inevitable nature of aging and death, at least at some point in their coming to terms with these forces, but this too would seem to be a legitimate reaction. Dylan Thomas's words, "Do not go gently into that good night," express the desire of many to be alive to the end and to die with a sense of worth and purpose, if not righteous indignation at being obliged to leave life.

COMMON ADAPTIVE TECHNIQUES
Defense mechanisms[16]

Older persons have throughout their lifetimes acquired individual and characteristic methods of handling anxiety, aggressive impulses, resentments, and frustration. Such methods, known as defense mechanisms, are internal, automatic, unconscious processes whereby the personality protects itself by attempting to provide psychological stability in the midst of conflicting or overwhelming needs and stresses that are part of human existence. As people mature, some new defenses may be added and old ones discarded; but others persist throughout life, taking on different tones and colorations at different stages in the life cycle. Emphasis here will be on the defense mechanisms that most often appear in old age and on nuances that are characteristic of older people.

Denial

The denial of old age and death found in the young person's attitude of "This won't happen to me" may also occur in old age in the form of "This isn't happening to me." In one of its ex-

---

[16] "Nowhere in the literature is there a complete, dynamically meaningful analysis of defenses. Most writers have utilized lists which are incomplete, not logically ordered or mutually exclusive," according to Cohen, R.A., and Cohen, M.B.: Research in psychotherapy: a preliminary report, Psychiatry **24**:46-61, 1961. We would recommend the glossary of defenses in Eisler, R.S., et al.: The psychoanalytic study of the child, vol. 16, London, 1961, Hogarth Press, Ltd., pp. 62-71.

treme forms denial can manifest itself in a "Peter Pan" syndrome, with the older person pretending to be young and refusing to deal with the realities of aging. There may be a self-attribution of strength—claiming that one is still capable of everything. Not all denial is pathological. It is, in fact, a necessary and useful component for maintaining a sense of stability and equilibrium. But the usefulness of denial is eroded when it begins to seriously interfere with the developmental work of any particular age. In old age, an individual who denies that he or she is sick and refuses to take medicine or see a doctor is showing an example of denial that no longer accomplishes a life-protective purpose.

Denial, like other defenses, often responds to psychotherapy:

■ *Chief complaint:* "I can't catch my breath." This is the case of a man who was always in a hurry and had eventually to stop to catch his breath.

A 68-year-old, highly intelligent and intellectual sociologist developed a severe cough on his return from an extended and exciting journey abroad. An x-ray shadow increased the medical suspicion of malignancy. Without prior discussion and preparation the patient was inadvertently but directly told this by a secretary arranging his admission for surgery. The operation revealed a lung abscess and the patient responded well physically both to the operative procedure and in the recovery room period, with one exception: he could not catch his breath. His internist suggested an extended vacation, and later tranquilizers, and offered reassurance. After some months the doctor strongly recommended psychotherapy, as he realized the patient was becoming increasingly agitated and depressed without adequate medical explanation. The patient was extremely tense and restless. He appeared somewhat slovenly. His pants hung loose from his suspenders and his fly was partly open. In short, he gave the impression of having some organic mental disorder but he spoke clearly and well. Despite his obvious gloom, he managed some humor and clarity in giving his present and past history.

His situation was socially and personally favorable. He had a good relationship with a devoted wife. He had many good friends and professional colleagues. He was well regarded professionally. He was under no pressure to retire, and consultancies were open to him. He had a wide range of interests in addition to his professional field. His relationships with his brothers and sisters were good. With the exception of the chief complaint, his physical status was excellent. He believed his physician's report that there was no major organic disease; in other words, he was not suffering from a fear that he was being misled. But despite all of this he was tense and depressed. Recurrent dreams included one in which "a paper was due" and another in which he was "behind in an exam." He had never taken out any life insurance. He had made no conscious admission to himself that he might age. He had made nothing of birthdays. Nor did he have a very clear concept of the natural evolution of the life cycle. He did not have sense of stages and development of middle and later life. He had an enormous capacity for work and had kept busy all his life as though unaware of the passage of time. He had never been bored. He had great capacity for self-discipline and was not given to marked expression of either grief or anger but only to a narrow spectrum of affects, including fearfulness and pleasure. He was a kind of Peter Pan and he and his wife eventually concluded in the course of his psychotherapeutic work that he, and in some measure she, had imagined themselves as remaining in their twenties instead of in their late sixties. As he reviewed his life and the realities of aging and death, he became freer in his expression of more negative affects. His depression and tension improved and he remained well in a follow-up of some 6 months. He was no longer short of breath.

Projection

Some older persons attempt to allay anxieties by projecting feelings outward onto someone else. They may appear suspicious and fearful, with characteristic complaints of merchants cheating them, doctors ignoring them, their children neglecting them. They often become concerned about physical safety on the streets. Much of what is named projection may indeed be legitimate complaints and fears about situations that exist, either potentially or in actuality, and one runs the risk of denying reality by labeling them projection. But actual projection itself does occur, signifying internal stress (people with hearing losses are prime victims) and can reach paranoid proportions unless the stress is alleviated.

Fixation

Fixation is most often associated with old age as a carryover defense from earlier life, implying that the fixation point occurred somewhere in childhood. But if one views old age as having developmental work of its own, fixation is a useful concept in describing the older person who may reach a particular level of development and be unable to go further. An example might be the person who has adapted well to living alone, without a spouse, but cannot accept in an insightful manner the need for outside help as physical strength wanes. Such a person may unconsciously want to stop the action and refuse to accept a new change.

Regression[17]

Regression, or a return to an earlier level of adaptation, is an overused and catchall explanation for much behavior in old age. Familiar descriptions of older people as ''childlike,'' ''childish,'' or ''in second childhood'' imply a reverse slide back to earlier developmental stages with no cognizance of a lifetime of experience that unalterably separates them from their childhood patterns of coping. A pejorative connotation is given, with the notion that older people lose their ''adultness'' under stress of illness and age and begin to act like children. Regression implies a disruptive, deteriorative, nonadaptive retreat in which the personality is not up to facing the stress it must overcome; the weakness is internal. But in old age much of the stress is from external sources that strain the resources of even the most healthy personalities. The use of the concept of regression to describe the attempts of older people to adapt in such situations is similar to the popular use of ''paranoid'' to describe the reactions of black people to racism.

What appears to be something pathological may indeed be the normal and necessary patterns of behavior.

Displacement

The function of displacement is to disguise the real source of anxiety or discomfort for a person by placing it on some other object or circumstance. For example, a person whose body is drastically undergoing change may displace the cause of his or her problems by declaring that the world is going to ruin or that things are not the way they were when he was young.

Counterphobia

Counterphobia[18] is the compelling and sometimes risky tendency to look danger in the face in an attempt to convince oneself that it can be overcome. An older man with dizzy spells may insist on climbing a ladder to fix his own roof. Another, with a history of visual blackouts, may demand that he drive the family car just as before. A woman with heart trouble ignores her racing pulse as she continues to carry tubs of laundry from her basement. In each case the individual ignores a realistic appraisal of limitations and relies upon sheer force of will to undo the danger.

Idealization

One type of defense is the idealization of the lost object, be it person, place, life-style, or status. A person may, for instance, idolize a deceased mate, glorifying the past and the good old days. The purpose is to make one's life seem meaningful and not wasted.

Rigidity

There is little evidence that older people become rigid in personality as they age. Rather, when rigidity is seen, it is a defense against a general sense of threat or actual crises.

---

[17] Originally a neurological rather than a psychological concept, constructed by English neurologist Hughlings Jackson.

[18] See the original contribution of Frenichel, O.: The counterphobic attitude, International Journal of Psychoanalysis **20:** 263, 1939.

Other defensive behavior
Selective memory

The dulling of memory and the propensity to remember distant past events with greater clarity than events of the recent past have generally been attributed to arteriosclerotic and senile brain changes in old age. However, it appears that such memory characteristics can at times have a psychological base, in that the older person may be turning away from or tuning out the painfulness of the present to dwell on a more satisfying past.

Selective sensory reception

A process of "exclusion of stimuli" described by Weinberg (1956) has been observed in older people, by which they block off the sensorium that they feel unprepared to deal with. This is more often observed in people with hearing problems, who at times seem to hear what they want to hear. This may be the only way an older person can control the amount of input impinging upon him.

Exploitation of age and disability

Older people can use changes occurring in their lives to obtain secondary gains—that is, benefits which in and of themselves may be satisfying or desired. An example is shown by older persons who insist they must remain in a hospital or other care facility, even though they no longer need medical care, because they enjoy the extra attention and sense of importance accruing from the illness. Or an individual with a proclivity to control others can use illness or impending death to manipulate those around him. Examples are the tyrant on the sick bed who terrorizes family and friends through guilt, and the invalid who commandeers personal services from everyone through appearing totally helpless and passive. Exploitation of age and disability can also result in freedom from social expectation, with the older person not feeling bound by the social amenities and established patterns. In this sense, the defensive behavior may allow the person to try on a new identity or a new way of relating. Behavior that in youth might have been considered unacceptable or even bizarre can be viewed in old age as pleasantly idiosyncratic or at least harmless.

An interesting form of age exploitation is what we have called the "old man" or "old woman" act. This is the older person who, even when physically and mentally sound, puts on the act of being a tottering, frail, helpless "old" person. This phenomenon can occur as early as the fifties but may be used by older people at any age to avoid responsibility toward themselves and others and to evoke sympathy. Sometimes the older person uses this act very selectively on those who are most gullible, while appearing quite sound and capable to others.

The changing adaptive value of psychopathology

Related to adaptation is the changing adaptiveness found with psychopathology, which will be discussed in Chapter 9. Paranoid personality structures appear to become even less adaptive with age as the few persons in the paranoid's circle die, isolation hardens, and crises occur. On the other hand, the schizoid personality structure seems to insulate against loss. The obsessional and compulsive personality whose fussbudget behavior may have impaired effectiveness earlier in life may adjust well to the void of retirement or losses, through meticulous and ritualistic activities.

Restitution, replacement, or compensatory behavior

Numerous activities may be adopted to make up for a loss. These may include practical measures such as memory pads and reminders of all kinds to compensate for poor memory. Or they can take the form of finding new persons to replace lost ones. Attempted restitution is frequently seen, in which a person tries to give back or get back that which has been lost or taken away.

Use of activity or busyness

General busyness, known as "working off the blues," is a defense against depression, anxiety, and other conditions that are painful or unacceptable. It involves concentrating on activity of some kind, whether productive or nonproductive, with the purpose of warding off the unwanted feelings.

Insight as an adaptive technique

Successful adjustments to real life conditions are not optimally possible if feelings and behavior are unconsciously motivated and therefore not subject to conscious control. Similarly, it can prove non-adaptive to be unaware of the natural course of life: what to expect, what can be changed, and what cannot. Thus insight requires not only an inner sense of oneself and motivations but also an inner knowledge of the human life cycle—a realization of life and how it changes. The older individual who has a steady comprehension of the life process from birth to death is thereby assisted in his or her efforts to decide what to oppose and what to accept, when to struggle and when to acquiesce, and, ultimately, to understand the limits of what is possible. An example is what one of us (M.I.L.) calls "responsible dependency." This concept implies the realistic evaluation of when one begins to require help from others and an ability to accept that help with dignity and cooperativeness, rather than denying the need or abusing the opportunity to be dependent. Insight includes the willingness and ability to substitute available satisfactions for losses incurred. It is the most widely used and successful adaptation found in healthy older people.

Exercising rational control over one's life is a mature, effective concomitant of insight. The conscious suppression of problems ("sufficient unto the day is the evil thereof"), the mastery of feelings, the unanxious anticipation of events, seeking pleasures and avoiding pain, and sublimation of unacceptable feelings by more acceptable ones are illustrative. Moreover, deliberate altruism, the personal and social concern for others, is a sophisticated and enlightened form of self-interest.[19]

---

[19] Many of these qualities of mastery of one's environment and rational control of feelings are present among longliving people, for example, the Abkhasians in the U.S.S.R. and music conductors.

Positive emotions (humor, joy, etc.) as adaptive techniques

Norman Cousins writes about the healing power of humor from his own experience as a patient[20]:

"Any medical student," says Cousins, "can give you a horrendous catalogue of all the terrible things that happen to the body under the impact of negative emotions: fear, hate, rage, exasperations, frustration. You learn about constriction of the blood vessels, increase in blood pressure, excess flow of hydrochloric acid, adrenal depletion, indigestion, headaches.

But we haven't yet sufficiently recognized that the body does not operate only on one wave length. It just doesn't respond to negative emotions, it responds to the positive emotions. It's impossible to have one without having the other. But the salutary effect is not as well understood."

THE LIFE REVIEW

The tendency of older persons toward self-reflection and reminiscence used to be thought of as indicating a loss of recent memory and therefore a sign of aging. However, in 1961 one of us (R.N.B.) postulated that reminiscence in the aged was part of a normal life review process brought about by realization of approaching dissolution and death. It is characterized by the progressive return to consciousness of past experiences and particularly the resurgence of unresolved conflicts that can be looked at again and reintegrated. If the reintegration is successful, it can give new significance and meaning to one's life and prepare one for death, by mitigating fear and anxiety.

This is a process that is believed to occur universally in all persons in the final years of their lives, although they may not be totally aware of it and may in part defend themselves from realizing its presence. It is spontaneous, unselective, and seen in other age groups as well (adolescence, middle age); but the intensity and emphasis on putting one's life in order are most striking in old age. In late life, people have a particularly vivid

---

[20] Cousins, N.: Anatomy of an illness as perceived by the patient, New York, 1979, W.W. Norton & Co., Inc.

The life review.

Photo by Robert N. Butler, M.D.

imagination and memory for the past and can recall with sudden and remarkable clarity early life events. There is renewed ability to free-associate and bring up material from the unconscious. Individuals realize that their own personal myth of invulnerability and immortality can no longer be maintained. All of this results in reassessment of life, which brings depression, acceptance, or satisfaction.[21]

The life review can occur in a mild form through mild nostalgia, mild regret, a tendency to reminisce, story-telling, and the like. Often the person will give his life story to anyone who will listen. At other times it is conducted in monologue without another person hearing it. It is in many ways similar to the psychotherapeutic situation in which a person is reviewing his or her life in order to understand present circumstances.

As part of the life review one may experience a sense of regret that is increasingly painful. In severe forms it can yield anxiety, guilt, despair, and depression. And in extreme cases if a person is unable to resolve problems or accept them, terror, panic, and suicide can result. The most tragic life review is that in which a person decides life was a total waste.

Some of the positive results of reviewing one's life can be a righting of old wrongs, making up with enemies, coming to acceptance of mortal life, a sense of serenity, pride in accomplishment, and a feeling of having done one's best. It gives people an opportunity to decide what to do with the time left to them and work out emotional and material legacies. People become ready but are in no hurry to die. Possibly the qualities of serenity, philosophical development, and wisdom observable in some older people reflect a state of resolution of their life conflicts. A lively capacity to live in the present is usually associated, including the direct enjoyment of elemental pleasures such as nature, children, forms, colors, warmth, love, and humor. One may become more capable of mutuality with a comfortable acceptance of the life cycle, the universe, and the generations. Creative works may result such as memoirs, art, and music. People may put together family albums and scrapbooks and study their genealogies.

One of the greatest difficulties for younger persons (including mental health personnel) is to listen thoughtfully to the reminiscences of older people. (See Chapter 12 for a discussion on life review therapy.) We have been taught that this nostalgia represents living in the past and a preoccupation with self and that it is generally boring, meaningless, and time-consuming. Yet as a natural healing process it represents one of the underlying human capacities on which all psychotherapy depends. The life review as a necessary and healthy process should be recognized in daily life as well as used in the mental health care of older people.

---

[21]Coleman, P.G.: Measuring reminiscence characteristics from conversation and adaptive features of old age, International Journal of Aging and Human Development **5:**281-294, 1974.

REFERENCES

Birren, J.E., Butler, R.N., Greenhouse, S.W., Sokoloff, L., and Yarrow, M.R.: Summary and interpretations. In Birren, J.E., Butler, R.N., Greenhouse, S.W., Sokoloff, L., and Yarrow, M.R.: Human aging: a biological and behavioral study, Pub. No. (PHS) 986, Washington, D.C., 1963, U.S. Government Printing Office (reprinted as Pub. No. [HSM] 71-9051, 1971, 1974).

Butler, R.N.: The life review: an interpretation of reminiscence in the aged, Psychiatry **26**:65-76, 1963.

Butler, R.N.: Re-awakening interest, Nursing Homes **10**:8-19, 1961.

Butler, R.N., and Perlin, S.: Physiological-psychological-psychiatric interrelationships. In Birren, J.E., Butler, R.N., Greenhouse, S.W., Sokoloff, L., and Yarrow, M.R.: Human aging: a biological and behavioral study, Pub. No. (PHS) 986, Washington, D.C., 1963, U.S. Government Printing Office (reprinted as Pub. No. [HSM] 71-9051, 1971, 1974).

Gitelson, M.: The emotional problems of elderly people, Geriatrics **3**:135-150, 1948.

Glaser, B.G., and Strauss, A.C.: Awareness of dying, Chicago, 1965, Aldine Publishing Co.

Gorer, G.: Death, grief, and mourning, New York, 1965, Doubleday & Co., Inc.

Hinton, J.: Dying, Baltimore, 1967, Penguin Books, Inc.

Hollingshead, A.B., and Redlich, F.: Social class and mental illness, New York, 1958, John Wiley & Sons, Inc.

Kübler-Ross, E.: Five stages a dying patient goes through, Medical Economics **47**:272-292, 1970.

Lindemann, E.: Symptomatology and management of acute grief. In Parad, H.J., editor: Crisis intervention: selected readings, New York, 1965, Family Service Association of America.

Lopata, H.: Widowhood in an American city, Cambridge, Mass., 1973, Schenkman Publishing Co., Inc.

Marris, P.: Widows and their families, London, 1958, Routledge & Kegan Paul, Ltd.

Neugarten, B.L.: The awareness of middle age. In Owen, R., editor: Middle age, London, 1967, British Broadcasting Corp.

Parkes, C.M.: The first year of bereavement, Psychiatry **33**:444-467, 1970.

Parkes, C.M.: Seeking and finding a lost object, Social Science and Medicine **4**:187-201, 1970.

Perlin, S., and Butler, R.N.: Psychiatric aspects of adaptation to the aging experience. In Birren, J.E., Butler, R.N., Greenhouse, S.W., Sokoloff, L., and Yarrow, M.R.: Human aging: a biological and behavioral study, Pub. No. (PHS) 986, Washington, D.C., 1963, U.S. Government Printing Office (reprinted as Pub. No. [HSM] 71-9051, 1971, 1974).

Rossman, I., editor: Clinical geriatrics, ed. 2, Philadelphia, 1979, J.B. Lippincott Co.

Tolstoi, L.: The death of Ivan Ilych (1886), New York, 1960, Signet Classic Paperback.

Weinberg, J.: Personal and social adjustment. In Anderson, J.E., editor: Psychological aspects of aging, Washington, D.C., 1956, American Psychological Association.

Weisman, A.D., and Kastenbaum, R.: The psychological autopsy: a study of the terminal phase of life, Community Mental Health Journal, Monograph No. 4, New York, 1968, Behavioral Publications, Inc.

4

Functional disorders

OVERVIEW OF PSYCHOPATHOLOGY IN LATE LIFE

The mental disorders of old age have generally been divided into two kinds: the *organic disorders,* which have a known physical cause (Chapter 5), and the *functional disorders,* for which at present no physical cause has been found and for which the origins appear to be emotional—related to the personality and life experiences of people. The division between organic and functional disorders is breaking down, however. Social and psychological factors have been identified in the "organic" disorders and spectacular advances in the neurosciences reveal biochemical (physical) correlations with "functional" disorders.

The extent of mental disorders in old age is considerable. It has been estimated by the American Psychological Association[1] that at least 3 million, or 15%, of the older population need mental health services. We would consider this to be a conservative estimate. A million older people are at this moment in institutional settings for a variety of reasons. The effects of institutionalization itself ensure further emotional problems on top of those already existing. At least 2 million people living in the community have serious chronic disorders, predominantly physical but also mental. It is evi-

dent that the majority of people having chronic physical illness also have associated emotional reactions requiring attention. In addition are those persons who need treatment for primarily mental illnesses. As a further complication, older people tend to underreport their mental illnesses and many do not seek help. Most "epidemiological" studies have been based on rates of utilization of hospitals and community mental health centers. Since older people often are not admitted or are transferred out, the figures do not express the true incidence and prevalence of mental health problems among the older population.

Added to this list of those at risk are the some 7 million older persons who live below or near the official poverty level in conditions that are known to contribute to emotional breakdown or decline. Finally, the effects of lowered social status and self-esteem in old age take a toll on mental health. Thus, the true proportion of psychiatric need among older people has not been fully documented.

Institutional care

In 1976 there were 171,497 resident patients (of all ages) in state and county mental hospitals. Of that number, 28.7% were older persons (59.5% of the elderly were women).[1a] Figures for residence

---

[1] Eisdorfer, C., and Lawton, M.P., editors: The psychology of adult development and aging, Washington, D.C., 1973, American Psychological Association.

[1a] Division of Biometry and Epidemiology, National Institute of Mental Health, unpublished 1976 data.

of older persons in hospitals included these approximately 49,100 persons of age 65 and over in state and county mental hospitals (1976 figures), an additional 1,800 in private hospitals, and 5,800 in Veterans Administration hospitals (1973 figures —more recent data are not available). It is estimated that about one third to one half of older patients were admitted to hospitals as younger patients and the remainder were admitted at age 65 or older.

About 8,200 older people entered state and county mental hospitals in 1975 for the first time, representing 6.8% of all first admissions. More recent resident figures for private hospitals are unavailable, since the census from which these figures came was discontinued in 1972. However in 1972, 10,676 older people were admitted to private mental hospitals, 11.7% of those admitted. It is clear that older people make up a substantial number of the first admissions as well as the total residents. However, they have received little attention other than custodial care.

Furthermore, older patients are being increasingly pushed from inadequate mental institutions into other inadequate custodial facilities, known euphemistically as "the community." Since 1940, even before introduction of tranquilizing drugs, the resident hospital populations began a downward slope as attempts were made to shorten hospital stays. In the 1950s and 1960s, lower rates of admission began to be encouraged, along with the shorter hospitalizations. From the 1960s on, the emphasis was on transferring the older patients out of hospitals, wholesale. This was officially called "deinstitutionalization." Unofficially it was known as "dumping." The rhetorical reason given was that it was "better" for people; actually the real reason was a fiscal policy in which the states could save money by obtaining federal financial support for use of community facilities. See Table 4-1 for an example of the shift of older persons with mental disorders from mental hospitals to nursing homes in the 1960s. Between 1956 and 1975 the state and county mental hospital population declined from 559,000 to 191,391. The various nursing homes, personal care homes, and fos-

Table 4-1. Location of persons 65 years and over with mental disorders

	1963	1969
Percent in mental hospitals	47	25
Percent in nursing homes	53	75

Data from Psychiatric services and the changing institutional scene, research on disorders of the mind: progress and prospects, 100th Meeting of the National Advisory Mental Health Council, Washington, D.C., 1977, U.S. Department of Health, Education and Welfare, National Institute of Mental Health, p. 53.

ter care facilities to which older people were and still are being transferred, often indiscriminately, are frequently of dubious quality. Many are firetraps, offer poor nursing and medical care, give little or no psychiatric care, and are generally unsafe. Regulations and controls are inadequate and unenforced. Since 1965 and the enactment of Medicare and Medicaid amendments to the Social Security Act, there has been a proliferation of such facilities as the care of the aged has become profitable business. The controversial 1972 legislation regarding "intermediate care facilities" led to further transferring of older mental patients out of mental hospitals. As has been said, "The patient goes where the money flows."

We certainly support the growing trend toward *appropriate* care outside of hospitals when it is in the interest of patients. But the present transfer policy is unsound, medically, psychiatrically, and socially.[2] Data show that transfer of the very old increases morbidity and mortality. Many people have lived in hospitals for 20, 30, or more years and have made some kind of adjustment: Many have developed such a "hospitalitis" or "institutionalitis" that it is difficult for them to survive in a new and strange environment. Now suddenly— when they are 70, 80, or even 90 years old—they are being transferred, often without their consent, into largely underregulated and inadequate com-

[2]The American Federation of State, County and Municipal Employees (AFSCME) published its study of deinstitutionalization in several states (for example, Illinois and New York): *Out of Their Beds and Into the Streets,* by Henry Santiesteven, Washington, D.C., 1974, AFSCME.

munity facilities. Such transfers are obviously not for the patients' benefit. Instead, they represent political and financial arrangements between states, the federal government, and private enterprise.

Outpatient care

Older people are not seen as outpatients in psychiatric clinics, in community mental health centers, and in the offices of private psychiatrists or other therapists in proportion to their emotional and psychiatric needs. Only about 2% of persons seen in psychiatric clinics are over 60. About 4% to 5% of the people seen in community mental health centers are over 65. And only about 2% of private psychiatric time involves older persons. In all of these settings older persons are often not seen for treatment but, rather, for routine workups and rapid disposition.

Two major groups of older mental patients

It is important to bear in mind that older people in mental hospitals or in nursing homes and related facilities are from two groups. In the first are people who were admitted to mental hospitals early in life and who grew old there or who have been transferred to community settings. This tragic group reflects society's failure to provide adequate care so that their lives could be salvaged. Many of course became ill before the development of "modern" treatments such as electroshock therapy, various forms of individual and group therapy, and tranquilizers and antidepressant drugs. But this cannot explain why so many have been neglected for so long. They are the victims of prejudice toward the mentally ill and of inadequate, fluctuating state hospital budgets that have made sound diagnosis and good treatment impossible.

The second group of people are those who developed mental illness for the first time in late life. Many have chronic, organic, brain disorders; but a surprising number have reversible brain disorders as well as functional illnesses like depression and paranoid tendencies. The long-term and the recently admitted patients differ from each other in diagnosis and prognosis; therefore their treatment

should reflect these differences. At present they are often all misleadingly identified as geriatric patients, and even those who have reversible brain disorders are not singled out for treatment.

Drug problems

The oft-heralded "tranquilizer revolution" has produced abuses and misuses that lead one to believe that these drugs are too often employed more for the benefit of the therapist or the quiet serenity of institutions than in the best interest of patients. Patients may be kept on high dosages for years at a time, with minimal medical monitoring. Drug treatment is often the *only* treatment given. As noted previously, between 1956 and 1975 the state and county mental hospital population declined from 559,000 to 191,391. As a result, there are increased numbers of people in the community whose fundamental problems in living have not been solved but who are simply pacified. The side effects of prolonged tranquilizer use are tolerated more easily by physicians than by their patients. For example, tardive dyskinesia is a serious and irreversible syndrome resulting from phenothiazine therapy. It seems to be more common in the brain-damaged, such as older people with brain disorders. Yet many doctors discount the potential long-term effects of drugs, believing that the problems of older persons and the mentally ill are so incomprehensible that massive experimental drug usage is warranted.

Research on mental illness in community-resident aged

The Langley Porter Institute's Studies of Aging, under the general direction of Alexander Simon and Marjorie Fiske (Lowenthal), represent one of the first major attempts in the United States to explore the associated characteristics of mental illness among community-resident older people.[3] These studies examined 600 San Francisco residents over age 60 and 500 residents who were hospitalized for mental illness. Physical illness was

[3] Lowenthal, M.F., et al.: Aging and mental disorder in San Francisco—a social psychiatric study, San Francisco, 1967, Jossey-Bass, Inc., Publishers.

found to be unequivocally related to psychiatric complaint. In contrast, widowhood and retirement were demoralizing but not clearly causative of hospitalizable mental illness, according to their findings.

A study in Syracuse[4] was concerned with the more limited problem of "certifiability" for mental hospitalization, and the work *Five Hundred Over Sixty*[5] dealt with life problems and measures of psychological adjustment rather than mental illness. Three gerontological research programs— The Kansas City Study of Adult Life,[6] the National Institute of Mental Health work, and studies by the Center for the Study of Aging at Duke University—were based on volunteer samples within the range of "normal" patterns of personality and adjustment.

Gurland et al. undertook three major studies that form the basis for extensive data analysis and a series of reports: a cross-national survey of older persons residing in the community in New York and London; a study of the family relationships among older New Yorkers; and a cross-national survey of the costs, quality, and outcome of care of the institutionalized aged in New York and London.[7]

It is difficult to compare the results of these studies because of the different methodologies and notions of what constitutes mental illness. But all of them add valuable insights and information to this growing field.

There is immediate need for a community-based study of the incidence and prevalence of mental disorders in old age. The National Institute on Aging has committed intellectual and financial resources to provide for an oversampling of the population 65 years of age and older in a Yale study under Jerome Myers in New Haven, Connecticut, supported by the National Institute on Mental Health.

Diagnostic nomenclature

We are including abbreviated outlines of the American Psychiatric Association's *Diagnostic and Statistical Manual of Mental Disorders* (DSM-II and DSM-III) at the end of this chapter. The DSM-II outline includes psychotic and nonpsychotic organic brain syndromes, functional psychotic conditions, neuroses, personality disorders, psychophysiological disorders, and transient situational disturbances of late life.

This nomenclature left much to be desired in diagnosing conditions of older persons, particularly in the case of acute and chronic brain disorders. However, for hospital charts, insurance forms, and various other administrative purposes as well as for understanding the literature in the field of aging, it is still necessary to be familiar with the 1968 DSM-II nomenclature as well as the earlier terms used in DSM-I (1952). Fortunately, the 1980 DSM-III represents some improvements in the classification of the mental disorders of older persons. It features much more specific diagnostic criteria, an expanded description of disorders, and a multilevel or multiaxial approach to evaluation that takes into consideration the following 5 axes: (I) physical diseases, (II) current stresses in the patient's life, (III) recent changes in functioning, (IV) the degree of functional impairment, and (V) the course of the disorder (a description of the usual course is furnished for comparison purposes).

Assessment of the older person's functioning is critical. For example, an older person who is diagnosed as having severe brain damage (by sophisticated psychiatric examination and psychological test scores) may function quite well in a supportive milieu. Another person may have minimal brain damage but have no economic, personal, and social supports and thus have more trouble functioning— not because of any inherently serious mental condition, but because he or she has no environmental

[4]Gruenberg, E.M.: A mental health survey of older persons. In Hoch, P.H., and Zubin, J., editors: Epidemiology of mental disorders, New York, 1961, Grune & Stratton, Inc.

[5]Kutner, B., Fanshel, D., Togo, A.M., and Langner, T.S.: Five hundred over sixty: a community survey on aging, New York, 1956, Russell Sage Foundation.

[6]Williams, R.H., and Wirths, C.G.: Lives through the years, New York, 1965, Atherton Press.

[7]See Assessing the older person in the community—findings and experiences from a cross-national study, International Journal of Aging and Human Development (special issue) **8:** 1-92, 1977-1978, for the studies of Gurland et al.

supports. Thus diagnosis and treatment, as well as prevention, must go beyond the traditional psychiatric diagnostic evaluation to include the context in which symptoms develop and the healthy assets and resources of the personality.

We might add here that the use of insurance forms requiring a therapist to state the diagnosis of a patient creates a sticky, ethical problem. The patient's interest may be compromised if a diagnosis is given that can be later used irresponsibly. We have no assurances about the confidentiality of insurance records; and they do get lost, misplaced, and confused with other patients' records. On the other hand, a vague, general diagnosis can make the whole matter of insurance information irrelevant, especially when statistics are collected from these sources on the "mental illness" of policyholders. Many practitioners choose to protect their patients when possible. Diagnoses such as schizophrenia or antisocial personality may be down played. The nomenclature more commonly used includes such designations as anxiety, depression, and other terms that are nonrevealing.

FUNCTIONAL DISORDERS

For a long time mental illness in old age was thought to be related to brain damage. There were some nonpsychiatric writers who recognized and described depression in old age, such as Goethe in his novel *Wilhelm Meister's Lehrjahre*. By 1930 more and more investigators were cautioning clinicians not to misdiagnose arteriosclerosis or senile psychosis when in fact depression was the problem.[8] Studies in England by Post, Roth, and their colleagues emphasized the significant incidence of affective (referring to people's emotions or feelings) illnesses in old age. These workers developed methods for differentiating depression from organic illness through studies of outcome (for ex-

Table 4-2. Average annual incidence rates of psychoses (per 100,000 population of total psychoses, functional and organic, Texas, 1951-1952)

Age-group	Males	Females	Average
To 15 years	1	1	1
15 to 24 years	42	48	45
25 to 34 years	90	117	103
35 to 44 years	98	127	112
45 to 54 years	106	135	120
55 to 64 years	133	127	130
65 to 74 years	155	122	137
75 and over	274	183	228
TOTAL RATES	68	78	73

From Jaco, E.G.: The social epidemiology of mental disorders, New York, 1960, Russell Sage Foundation.

ample, discharge from hospitals, death) and psychological tests. Brief (and primitive) tests of orientation and memory such as the Mental Status Questionnaire (MSQ) of Kahn and Goldfarb[9] became helpful in establishing the organic diagnosis.

The incidence of mental illness increases as people age. Table 4-2 shows the average annual incidence rates of total psychoses (functional or organic) per 100,000 population for the state of Texas, 1951-1952. This table demonstrates also the markedly increasing incidence of psychopathology, decade by decade, with advancing age. The National Institute of Mental Health has presented data confirming the same generalizations (WHO, 1959). (It is unfortunate that we must present such dated information. We await community-based epidemiological studies such as those of Jacob Brody et al. [National Institute on Aging] in the NIMH-NIA New Haven study.)

Further investigation has shown that the increasing mental illness in old age is explained in large measure by the rising occurrence of depression and organic brain disorders. In the 1950s and 1960s in England and America, independent researchers

---

[8] There are differences in diagnostic procedures as well as findings between the United States and England. See Cooper, J.E., Kendell, R.E., Gurland, B.J., Sharpe, L., and Copeland, J.R.M.: Psychiatric diagnosis in New York and London: a comparative study of mental hospital admissions, Maudsley Monograph No. 20, Oxford, England, 1972, Oxford University Press.

[9] Kahn, R.C., Goldfarb, A.I., Pollack, M., and Peck, A.: Brief objective measures for the determination of mental status in the aged, American Journal of Psychiatry **117**:326-328, 1960.

simultaneously highlighted the importance of recognizing depressions. Estimates vary, but probably about 30% to 40% of major illness (that is, illness likely to lead to hospitalization) is composed of functional disorders.[10] However, the remaining 70% that are organic cases may contain as many as 50% reversible organic states, either isolated or superimposed on a chronic condition, because of such varied causes as malnutrition, congestive heart failure, drug reactions, and infections. Depression can be and often is an accompanying part of the organic conditions, and it too can be treated and possibly reversed along with the reversible brain disorders. (Again, "functional" and "organic" are not ideal terms; functional disorders such as depression may have biochemical causes or concomitants and patients with "organic" disorders may have life-style and other psychosocial determinants and consequences.)

Use of the term "psychosis"

Psychosis implies varying degrees of personality disintegration and of difficulty in testing and correctly evaluating external reality. Delusions and hallucinations are characteristic, as well as inappropriate behavior and attitudes and a diminished control of impulses. In contrast to DSM-II, DSM-III does not use the term "psychotic" to classify the nonorganic (functional) mental disorders. This is to avoid classifying the major affective disorders as psychotic since they often do not have psychotic features. When psychosis is present it is indicated as a subcategory of the major classification.

Schizophrenic disorders[11]

Schizophrenia is a severe emotional disorder marked by disturbances of thinking, mood, and behavior, but thought disorder is the primary feature. Hallucinations, delusions, and poor reality testing are characteristics.

In our experience it has been rare to see a newly developed schizophrenic disorder in an older person. "Senile schizophrenia," or "paraphrenia"[12] as it is called in England and on the Continent, may be equivalent to the diagnosis of so-called paranoid states in America. Kay and Roth state, "The relationship between paraphrenic, paranoid and schizophrenic illness has long been disputed, and no view at present commands general acceptance."[13] Late paraphrenia is used by European authors for cases with a paranoid symptom complex in which signs of organic dementia or sustained confusion are absent and the delusional and hallucinatory symptoms do not appear to be caused by a major affective disorder or by paranoia, in which delusions would be better systematized. However, in the course of time the illness changes features, which makes diagnosis uncertain. Social factors often include little human contact. Deafness is a common physical factor.

Many older people have developed types of schizophrenia in earlier years and carried them into old age.[14] These persons are often called "chronic schizophrenics." The classic age of onset is adolescence. One sees persons with schizophrenia who have been hospitalized as long as 50 or 60 years; many never received treatment and were simply "stored" out of sight in hospitals, beyond the mainstream of medicine and psychiatry. (Privately paying patients usually fared better: they

---

[10] Kay, D.W.K., Beamish, P., and Roth, M.: Old age mental disorders in Newcastle-upon-Tyne: a study of prevalence, British Journal of Psychiatry **465:**146-158, 1964.

[11] The DSM-III definition of schizophrenia is more restrictive than that of DSM-II, in an attempt to delineate a more homogeneous classification. In the past, schizophrenia was one of those "wastebasket" classifications into which a great variety of symptoms were thrown. One hopes that we are now moving toward more refined understanding and hence more precise diagnosis.

[12] Bridge, T.P., and Wyatt, R.J.: Paraphrenia: paranoid states of late life, I. European research, pp. 193-200; II. American research, pp. 201-205, Journal of the American Geriatrics Society **28**(5), 1980.

[13] Kay, D.W.K., and Roth, M.: Environmental and hereditary factors in the schizophrenias of old age ("late paraphrenia") and their bearing on the general problem of causation in schizophrenia, Journal of Mental Science **107:**649-685, 1961.

[14] For an investigation of changes over time in the manifestations of schizophrenia, including the theory that schizophrenic illness "burns out" as one ages, see Lawton, M.P.: Schizophrenia 45 years later, Journal of Genetic Psychology **121:**133-143, 1972.

were likely to be hospitalized on occasions of decompensation and then released to their homes where further care could be given as needed.) The following is an example of a chronic schizophrenic patient hospitalized for 40 years:

■ Mr. M is 67 years of age. The diagnosis in his case was schizophrenic reaction, chronic undifferentiated type, of moderate severity, with onset at approximately 21 years of age. He was also diagnosed as showing a moderate depressive reaction for the past 2 years.

Mr. M was hospitalized about 40 years ago and in the last 6 months has been moved to a foster care home. He has only minimal impairment of his recent memory and his level of intellectual functioning has not declined. His impairments of judgment and abstraction are interpreted as psychogenic and not organic. Psychiatric symptoms include hypochondriacal ideas, suspiciousness, depressive trend, illusions, obsessions, compulsions, phobias, nightmares, sexual maladaptation (he claims he never had sexual intercourse), and psychosomatic symptoms. There is a history of auditory hallucinations.

Since age 21, when he began feeling "hot, dizzy, unable to breathe and I've been no good since," he has been treated with tonics, sedatives, and electroconvulsive therapy. He began work at 12 and had a good work history until he became ill.

Developmental history includes the death of his father at age 15; immigration to the United States from Germany at that time, with mother, brother, and two sisters; financial difficulties; language problems and stuttering that impeded his school work. Neither he nor any of his siblings married. He was apparently inordinately close to his sisters and hated his brother. He wanted to spend his later years traveling with his sisters but they died.

Mr. M was moved to the foster care home where his blind brother had been placed earlier. He has become increasingly nervous and depressed ever since the transfer. His defense is to continue to be future-oriented. Although he sees himself as trapped in a home with a despised brother and deserted by the death of sisters, he holds out the hope that he "may find the answer" to a better life for himself.

In addition to his personality characteristics it seems clear that there was little basic understanding of the environmental stresses on Mr. M at the time of his breakdown and little treatment given, beyond minimal care. But 40 years later he is still "hoping" for a cure and a better future. One could say either that he is denying

reality or that in spite of everything he has refused to give up.

In the later years schizophrenia may coexist with an organic brain disorder as illustrated in the next summary:

■ Mrs. W was diagnosed as showing schizophrenic reaction, paranoid type, and chronic brain syndrome associated with arteriosclerosis and senile brain disease (mixed). The schizophrenia was regarded as chronic, severe, and of many years' duration, whereas the chronic brain syndrome is of recent origin.

She is 74 years old, her husband is dead, and she has been intermittently hospitalized since her early twenties. Her appearance is one of sadness, suspiciousness, and distance. Major psychiatric symptoms include depressive trend, grandiose ideas, auditory and visual hallucinations and illusions. The chronic brain syndrome is evidenced by difficulty in maintaining attention and set, irrelevance, fabrication, perseveration of ideas, shifts of mood, and inappropriate and shallow affect. It is difficult to differentiate between the two disorders. At first the brain syndrome is most evident, but as one talks with Mrs. W she seems to have less and less ability to integrate and suppress her delusional systems. At this point the schizophrenia becomes clearly obvious.

Paranoid disorders

Paranoid disorders are disorders with a delusion, usually persecutory or grandiose, as the main abnormality. From this delusion follow disturbances in mood, behavior, and thinking. Paranoid states are therefore different from the affective disorders and schizophrenias, in which mood and thought disorders are the essential problem. Intellectual functions are not impaired. Paranoid disorders are usually of short duration but are sometimes chronic, as in classic paranoia. They tend to occur under adverse conditions: imprisonment, deafness, isolation, disfigurement, infections, drunkenness, or blindness. Isolation from human contact and a hearing loss that results in misinterpretation of incoming stimuli are perhaps the primary precipitating factors. Women are affected more than men, although paranoid disorders are quite common in older persons of both sexes.

Actual classic paranoia itself is extremely rare,

marked by an elaborate, well-organized, paranoid system in which the person may consider himself or herself remarkably endowed with superior ability and powers. Allen and Clow describe four types of paranoid reactions generally seen in older people: "1) a type which may be called 'consistent' since it reveals the inevitable but overreactionary annoyances at the real physical and environmental limitations that are present to some extent in the lives of all those over 60; 2) a type characterized by episodic paranoid conditions with generally favorable prognosis; 3) the paranoid type of involutional psychosis in which the prognosis is frequently poor; and 4) a type displaying a paranoid trend associated with organic brain disease where the prognosis precludes complete recovery."[15]

Sometimes the paranoid symptoms may be very discrete or circumscribed. An older woman in her late seventies may seem free of major psychopathological symptoms, but at nighttime she thinks that the neighbor above is purposely taking a cane and pounding the ceiling or that fumes are being sent out from the radiators in the bathroom. However, study may uncover the fact that this is a discrete, circumscribed delusion related to fears, say, of being alone at night or lacking visual orientation in the dark. Such symptoms are, characteristically, isolated and may not influence everyday activities.

Folie à deux (called a "shared paranoid disorder" in DSM-III) is a mental disorder in which two persons who are intimately associated with each other develop the same delusions. One person is dominant. The submissive partner may be more shaky in his or her beliefs and when separated from the stronger personality may give up the delusional system. It is more frequent among people with similar backgrounds, such as siblings, parents, and children, but it can develop among unrelated (nonconsanguineous) persons, including husband and wife. Misperception may attain paranoid proportions.

---

[15] From Allen, E.B., and Clow, H.E.: Paranoid reactions in the aging, Geriatrics **5:**66-73, 1950.

■ The frightened voice of a woman begged me (R.N.B.) on the phone to see her and her mother because (and she lowered her voice) "mother wants to move again." Otherwise "they" will get her.

At the appointed hour a woman of 42 and of faded attractiveness arrives, with a frail, sharpfaced woman of 70. In the office they insist on my seeing them together, not separately. They describe the harassment they have received from two men living below. They mention the possibility that some wires are used to listen to them, perhaps in connection with their TV set or toaster. The older woman reveals excellent intellectual functioning, but she states that a man in the apartment above is shooting rays at her body, including "indecent places." He wants to kill her and she is powerless. He brings pains to her hands and knees, scorches parts of her body, and "stuns my consciousness." She refuses to see doctors, considers medications "harmful," and denies any illnesses (despite obvious malnutrition, manifestation of probable hypovitaminosis, arthritic changes, and a Meniere-like syndrome). She also insists that she has aged very little. Her unmarried daughter, deeply conflicted, nearly "believes" there are men responsible. Such quasi folies à deux are not rare.

Several theories have been offered to explain the genesis of paranoid disorders. Freud believed unconscious homosexuality was the basis and thus analyzed the famous Schreber case (Schreber was a German jurist). Most dispute this single-factor approach and instead conceptualize that paranoid behavior is the result of family and interpersonal forces of distortion and a basic, profound insecurity. The personality of the paranoid patient grown older is one that may have been marked by sullen quietness, sensitivy, disdain, and fearfulness about a frightening, inimical world. Some move through life with certain uncertainty or uncertain certainty, eccentric, and the object of public attention.

■ The slim bronzed white-haired man stalked the resort boardwalk during all the seasons. He often carried flowers in one hand and a transistor radio in the other. He would seem totally inattentive of others, muttering unintelligible sounds at various decibel levels.

Many, perhaps most, people with paranoid disorders go through life outside hospitals. They may be relatively harmless to others but are unable to experience intimacy and full psychological growth. They are seen as cranks, eccentrics, hard to get along with, touchy, angry. They are avoided, and what few human and other attachments they may have in life increasingly disappear with advancing age. Following is an example of the growing late-life isolation of a person suffering from a paranoid disorder.

■ Dr. J, a 72-year-old man, was diagnosed as having paranoid personality with obsessive features, chronic, severe, and of lifelong duration. His second diagnosis was depressive reaction, moderate, and of 2 or 3 years' duration. He compensated well in a suitable, supportive, and structured environment.

He was a dentist in semiretirement who was irritable, suspicious, depressed, and anxious. He was extremely intelligent and integrated very well during interviews. He was paranoid, belligerent, and self-centered; yet it was remarkable how he could put aside his belligerance and tell of his delusions.

He was in semiretirement because of a failing practice and not of his own choice. He applied for room in an old age home because he felt he was at the end of his rope. He saw his situation as resulting from the imperfections of the world and other people but at other times described his life adjustment as poor and said he hated himself.

He was born in Poland, came to the United States at 20, was unusually attached to his mother, and had "nothing in common" with his siblings. His father died when Dr. J was 12. He rebelled against education and did not enter dental school until he was 32. He married at 37 against his own desires, out of fear of an implied breach of promise suit, and was divorced 4 years later. He never considered remarriage. Marriage was his first and only sexual experience. He practiced dentistry in a poor neighborhood and had no close personal relationships. He distrusted others and thought that only his alertness saved him from being exploited by them.

As Dr. J grew older, his isolation became more complete and he developed an angry depression through which he despised himself and the world. He seemed unable to experience pleasure.

As Dr. J illustrates, such a person may paradoxically get along in the community by being isolated. No one bothers with him and he bothers no one. But eventually a problem will emerge in which the person no longer can care for himself and must obtain help in some way. This is frequently the paranoid person's path to the mental hospital or, as in Dr. J's case, to an old age home.

The older paranoid person can be dangerous. Paranoid rage and murderousness do occur.

■ A slight, 89-year-old man who needed a cane to walk killed his daughter, a librarian, with a hatchet. "I wanted to see her die before I do," he said.

The body of the daughter, 57, was found in her bed with deep wounds in her head and body. Her father, who notified police by telephone that he had slain his daughter, was booked on a murder charge.

"The devil prompted me to do this," he told police.

However, such extreme behavior is the exception. In general, the following rule of thumb can be followed in evaluating paranoid disorders: "Show me one truly paranoid person and I will show you ten who are truly persecuted." Much of what appears to be paranoid behavior is a reaction to extraordinary and unbearable stress—physical, emotional and environmental.

See Chapter 13 for a discussion of the treatment of paranoid disorders.

Use of the concept "neurotic disorders"

The major and most controversial change in DSM-III was to eliminate "neurotic disorders" as a separate category and, instead, to include them under affective, anxiety, somatoform, dissociative, and psychosexual disorders. In so doing, the meaning of the concept was also changed. Although traditionally "neurosis" has implied unconscious conflict as its cause, leading to the development of defense mechanisms that produce symptoms or personality disturbance, DSM-III avoids the question of etiology by using the term solely descriptively to simply indicate a painful symptom in a person with intact reality testing. The reason for this decision was the feeling that so many new theories about the etiology of neurotic disorders have developed, including social learning, cognitive, behavioral, and biological theories, that it is currently best to avoid any specific assumptions about how these disorders arise. We shall use the new DSM-

III terms while indicating the DSM-II terms in parentheses. Since the old DSM-II terms are included in the latest *International Classification of Diseases* (1979), it is still acceptable to use them as alternatives to the recommended DSM-III terms.

In spite of their clinical significance, neurotic disorders in old age are largely ignored in the literature. With neurosis there is neither gross distortion of reality nor profound personality disorganization, although thinking, judgment, and general functioning may be impaired. A chief characteristic is one or more symptoms that are distressing and unacceptable to the patient. Probably most older people who develop neurotic symptoms had similar difficulties earlier in life. Neuroses are not inevitable in old age, but they are extremely common.

Affective disorders

The affective disorders are distinguished from schizophrenia because they are primarily *mood* rather than thought disorders. Either extreme depression or elation (mania), or a mixture of the two, is characteristic and accounts for whatever loss of contact with the environment exists. Psychotic features (gross impairment of reality testing) may or may not be present. A psychological stress may set off the first episode, but recurrent episodes can occur apparently without a precipitating factor, although this is still debatable. For many other people, stressful events are *not* a necessary condition for the development of an affective disorder.

Bipolar disorders (manic-depressive illness)

Bipolar disorders are characterized as severe mood swings from depression to elation or the full or partial development of one or more manic episodes alone with a persistent elevated, expansive, or irritable mood.[16] Bipolar disorders typically occur before age 30 and are apparently found equally commonly in men and women. They can persist into old age, but the typical lifelong course is still not clear.

Major depression (unipolar) and other depression

Depression is the most common of the emotional illnesses found in older people and can occur at any time in life. We will discuss all types of depression together since there is increasing disagreement on categories of depression and their causes. The diagnosis of major depression in DSM-III is used to refer to a severe, persistent episode of depressed mood in which the person loses interest or pleasure in the usual activities of life.[17] (The only feature differentiating a major depression from the depression found in bipolar disorders is the lack of a manic episode associated with it.)

When a depression is less severe or prolonged it is called cycothymic (mood swings from depression to hypomania) or dysthymic (the DSM-II category of depressive neurosis). A differential diagnosis of depression is often difficult because many of the typical symptoms are similar whether the depression is classified as major, dysthymic, or simply grief or an adjustment disorder with a depressed mood. Table 4-3 gives some useful clues to diagnosis, if one remembers to translate the old DSM-II terms into DSM-III categories. (We have done this in brackets.) Depression varies all the way from transient "blues," which everyone experiences, to the extremes of psychotic withdrawal or suicide.

Depressive symptoms may be obvious and apparent or occult and hidden. Usual indicators of the presence of depression are feelings of helplessness, sadness, lack of vitality, frequent feelings of guilt, loneliness, boredom, constipation, sexual disinterest, and impotence. Insomnia, early morning fatigue, and marked loss of appetite may be seen. Hypochondriasis and somatic symptoms are common. Sleep is often disturbed in depression, with

---

[16] Since practically all manic episodes eventually culminate in depressive episodes, the diagnosis of "bipolar disorder" is given even when there has not yet been a depressive episode.

[17] DSM-II's category of "psychotic depressive reaction" is classified in DSM-III as "Major depression, single episode, with psychotic features," with coding of the severity of the psychosocial stressor.

Table 4-3. Differential diagnosis of depressions

Psychotic states	Criteria for evaluation		
	Loss of love object	**Self-esteem**	**Relationship to others**
Mourning	Real	Not impaired	Not disturbed
Neurosis [dysthymic depression]*	May be real or fancied	May be impaired	May be disturbed
Psychosis [major depression]	May be real or fancied	Shattered, with end point at suicidal stage	Chaotically disrupted

From Hall, B.: New faces of depression, Medical World News **19**(12):53, 1968.
*Bracketed material added by the authors.

the more depressed individuals, especially the agitated, typically sleeping less in the latter half of the night. Diagnostic criteria for depressive disorders follow[18]:

Pervasive affective disturbances

1. Depressed: sad, blue, downhearted
2. Tearful: have crying spells, feel like it

Physiological signs

1. Diurnal variation
2. Insomnia, middle and late
3. Decreased appetite
4. Decreased weight
5. Decreased libido
6. GI: constipation
7. CV: tachycardia
8. MS: fatigue

Psychomotor disturbances

1. Agitation
2. Retardation

Psychological symptoms

1. Confusion
2. Emptiness
3. Hopelessness
4. Indecisiveness
5. Irritability
6. Dissatisfaction
7. Personal devaluation
8. Suicidal rumination

It is currently often difficult or impossible to identify the exact cause of a particular depression.[19] The affective disorders are thought to be insufficiently explained by stressful life events or physical disorders, although a psychosocial stress may precipitate an attack. A number of chemicals in the brain that play a role in sending messages and in regulating nervous system activity have been identified. Two classes are particularly important to affective disorders: the catecholamines, which include dopamine and norepinephrine, and an indolamine, serotonin. The catecholamine hypothesis suggests that the functional turnover of catecholamines is increased at specific central synapses in mania and decreased in depression. The indolamine hypothesis posits a deficit of serotonin turnover in both mania and depression, with a greater decrease of serotonin in depression. In addition, cholinergic mechanisms may play a role in the causes of affective disorders. The most successful drug treatment of affective illnesses involves the use of drugs that trigger release of norepinephrine, a neurotransmitter of the catecholamines.

The psychosocial triggers and/or causes of de-

---

[18] Data from Zung, W.W.K., and Green, R.L., Jr.: Detection of affective disorders in the aged. In Eisdorfer, C., and Fann, W.E., editors: Psychopharmacology and aging, New York, 1973, Plenum Publishing Corp.

[19] Although the older population has usually been omitted from studies, those that do examine old age have found evidence of physiological concomitants of depression in the aged (Birren, J.E., Butler, R.N., Greenhouse, S.W., Sokoloff, L., and Yarrow, M.R.: Human aging: a biological and behavioral study, Pub No. [PHS] 986, Washington, D.C., 1963, U.S. Government Printing Office, [reprinted as Pub. No. (HSM) 71-9051, 1971, 1974]). Hormonal changes have been demonstrated in depression at younger ages by Bunney and others.

pression, when they are present, can be external (exogenous) or internal (endogenous). Exogenous depressions are explained by outside events in one's life. Endogenous depressions are internal and apparently not caused by immediate outside occurrences. They may be related to early developmental deprivations and losses. They may also be caused by the inner process known as the life review in older persons. It is often not possible to differentiate clearly between these types of depression.

Loss of love or a loved one, disappointments, criticism, and other threats, both real or imagined, are frequent paths leading to depression.

■ Mr. P is a 69-year-old insurance salesman who was diagnosed as having depressive neurosis, moderate, with an estimated duration of 15 years.

In 1941 he was in serious financial difficulties of his own making, and legal proceedings followed. He became depressed and made a serious suicidal attempt (opened his veins in the bathtub). He recovered and was then tried, convicted, and imprisoned for 6 months. He tells this with a stir of martyrdom and denies guilt or regret over it. He was able to recover his insurance license but thereafter suffered a declining career. He and his wife had basic disagreements, which were exacerbated by his semiretirement. He became more and more depressed and felt misunderstood and victimized. He evidences considerable anger toward his wife and gives a history of many extramarital affairs. He denies depression but obliquely indicates he *may* get depressed over not having done enough for others, such as children, but he would not be depressed *for himself.* He sleeps poorly and is afraid of death.

His early life was one of deprivation and poverty. He was underweight and sickly and was diagnosed as malnourished. At 11 he left his home, fanatically religious father, and "charitable" mother and developed his own moral code of independence ("don't like to be helped"). In truth he is extremely dependent on women (wife and mistresses) but scoffs at them as pitiful figures ("It is a curse to be a woman"). He handles his inadequate and depressed feelings by a kind of compensating grandiosity—a fantasy life in which he would make the world all right. When one thinks of his early losses and his more recent ones, it becomes apparent that this current depression is a reactivation of earlier depressed feelings.

Busse has emphasized decreased self-regard as much more important than guilt in the causation of depression in older people, and this has been repeatedly stressed in the psychiatric literature. However, we believe this is overstated. Older people are still capable of actions that produce guilt, even when they are on a death bed. Old age does not wipe out vindictiveness, anger, greed, or similar characteristics that are hurtful to others. Older persons also must deal with their guilt from the past, particularly during the life review process through which they examine past actions. As one older woman said, "That's the story of my life, doctor. I wish I were dead." And even recognizing that reduced self-regard is an important ingredient in depression does not gainsay the fact that the more guilty are more vulnerable. A prolonged depressive reaction following the death of someone close is often related to problems with the deceased person earlier in life. Thus the grief is burdened by guilt.

■ Mrs. P is an 85-year-old Southern gentlewoman of charm as well as so-called helplessness. She was admitted as a voluntary mental patient 8 years ago, just after the death of her husband. Following the retirement of her wealthy husband, she was said to have developed delusions of poverty, and she showed increasing bitterness toward him. After he had sustained a cerebrovascular accident, she pushed him in his wheelchair down a flight of stairs because he would not speak. On admission, she was described as complaining, being confused, and being extremely controlling. The psychological studies showed little or no intellectual deterioration but rather many superior intellectual capacities. She was tense and paranoid. Psychotherapy was strongly recommended but was refused by the patient.

She remains lively, cantankerous, and bitter. She expresses her anger with great determination and notable effect. To illustrate, she once urinated in church in the company of her one surviving son. She did not acknowledge any awareness of her anger toward her son and dismissed the episode by noting, "The young man next to me seemed embarrassed by the smell." She also coerced the staff to provide a commode in her room because "I can't get to the bathroom at night on time." And she fights the nurses by utilizing it unnecessarily during the day.

She is a voluntary patient. She is not overtly psychotic. She is in good physical health. She is monied. She is obviously full of life. She has *chosen* to live out her remaining years in comparative oblivion in a mental hospital rather than live in the outside world closer to her surviving family. She discourages visitors, including her favorite granddaughter. On the other hand, it is equally clear at times that she strains to be related. One might speculate that this self-imprisonment offers her the opportunity for expiration for past wrongs, a way of readying herself for Judgment Day.

Severe depressive reactions are often found associated with physical disease, especially with diseases that leave people incapacitated or in pain. Dovenmuehle and Verwoerdt[20] and others have demonstrated correlations between the two. Unfortunately the presence of physical or organic disorders tends to discourage practitioners from treating the depressions that accompany or are added to them. Family members may agree with nontreatment, believing that treatment would be too much for the person to handle. The following is an example (from case notes of R.N.B.) of a depressed man with an organic brain syndrome who was "protected" from treatment, even though it was thought he could have benefited:

■ I was asked to see a 76-year-old man who lived alone in a large apartment. His son had arranged for around-the-clock nursing because his father was confused, disoriented, and not able to take care of himself. I learned that his wife had been placed in a nursing home 8 months before because of increasing confusion and depression further complicated by serious heart disease. The husband became increasingly upset on his visits to see her. The wife had died 4 months earlier, and the son had decided to spare his father that "dreadful news." Therefore he was not taken to the funeral. The father had given up reading newspapers and so had not seen the obituary. Despite the father's worsening condition, a psychiatrist had not been called because "It is too late. He is simply senile. There is nothing that can be done." In the two visits that I made I did not succeed in making very profound contact with him. It was apparent that he was

severely depressed as well as suffering from organic damage. Among a number of suggestions I made to the family was that he be told of his wife's death. But the son did not agree to this.

The man's depressive illness had dated from his separation from his wife. It seemed likely that he was preoccupied by her situation and imagined her to be deeply suffering, both from her physical disease and their separation. Not knowing she was dead, he was in no position to make even the initial movements toward the resolution of grief. He may even have imagined her suffering to have been worse than it really was, especially since he may have seen through his son's efforts at deception and may have misinterpreted these efforts to mean that the son was covering up her suffering. He may have felt guilty over his own apparent inability to visit with his wife and regarded himself as a deserter who deserved punishment.

One might understandably say I am drawing an awful lot of conclusions from very little contact, only 2 hours. Perhaps his central nervous system was so diseased that he could not have understood the news of his wife's death anyway. And, if he was sufficiently able to grasp the message, why should he be subjected to grief under the circumstances? I strongly suspect that the son was quite correct when he concluded that his father would understand and would suffer. Where the son and I parted company was that he could not visualize that grief can be resolved and that some (but not all) of his father's symptomatology might have lifted as a consequence.

Another prominent cause of depression among older people is drug use. Drugs like tranquilizers, antihypertensive medications (for example, the Rauwolfia series, including reserpine, as well as other antihypertensive agents like methyldopa [Aldomet] and hydralazine [Apresoline]), the antiarrhythmic heart drug procainamide (Pronestyl), and the β-adrenergic blocking agent propranolol (Inderal) can all cause the whole range of depressions. Such depressions may mimic organic symptoms and confuse the diagnostician.

What is the course of depression in old age? Müller and Ciompi, at the University of Lausanne, have major studies now in progress on the late-life outcomes of patients hospitalized with a variety of psychiatric disorders before 65. The material on 555 cases of depression, for example, shows a

---

[20] Dovenmuehle, R.H., and Verwoerdt, A.: Physical illness and depression symptomatology, II. Factors of length and severity of illness and frequency of hospitalization, Journal of Gerontology **18**:260-266, 1963.

lessening intensity with age, greater tendency to somatization, etc. These studies on the natural history of psychiatric disorders inescapably provide insights concerning the life cycle. These particular studies, of course, do not concern the development and evolution of psychiatric disorders that occur for the first time in late life. More studies of both categories, along with longitudinal, psychodynamic, life cycle investigations of people who have not suffered psychiatric disorders before or after 65 are indicated. The "control group" of the natural courses of life events is the least examined.

Involutional melancholia—does it exist?

Originally the diagnosis of involutional melancholia referred to the appearance of depression in women who had reached or passed the age of menopause (the climacteric or involutional period). It had long been believed that physiological and psychological stresses during and after menopause caused an upsurge in depression. However, new research as well as reexamination of older research has failed to support this conclusion. Weissman and others[20a] find no evidence that the onset of depression in women correlates with menopause or that depression occurring in the involutional period is distinct from depression occurring at other stages of life. Therefore the diagnosis of "involutional melancholia" is no longer used and the category has been eliminated from DSM-III. Instead a depression in this age group of women would be called a "major depression, single episode, with melancholia or psychotic features." "Melancholia" is used, on a continuum of mild to severe, simply to indicate that a depression is severe.

The incidence of depression increases gradually with age in both men and women, with a higher incidence in women throughout the life cycle. The greater vulnerability of women is believed related to social roles.[21] Gore, at Vanderbilt University, found married women have higher rates of mental illness than married or single men, while single women have lower rates than men, whether single or married. This has been confirmed by other investigators. Weissman speculates that in addition to higher social status, men traditionally have had greater outlets for emotional frustrations and depression in work outside the home, alcohol, extramarital relationships, and companionship with other men. They also turn more frequently to suicide and crime.

The rise in depression with age in both men and women suggests a relationship to the emotion-laden life events in middle and later life—the children leaving home, the culmination of career possibilities, beginning signs of physical aging, the sense of time passing more quickly. The impact of these life events depends on the individual's personality, previous life experience, and contemporary circumstances.

Anxiety disorders

With anxiety disorders, anxiety is experienced directly by a person rather than controlled unconsciously by conversion, denial, or other psychological mechanisms. These disorders can either appear for the first time in old age or represent an increase in a previous history of anxiety. They may take the form of a nameless dread and sense of threat when no obvious danger is present, or they may be an exaggerated response to real trouble and danger. Also, like people of all ages, older people may be struggling to curb unconscious and unacceptable impulses, aggressive or sexual. Finally,

---

[20a] See Weissman, M.M.: Environmental factors in affective disorders, Hospital Practice **14**(4):103-109, 1979; and Weissman, M.M., and Klerman, G.: Sex differences and the epidemiology of depression, Archives of General Psychiatry **34**:98-110, 1977.

[21] There seems to be no correlation of depression and the menstrual cycle. Even though many women experience premenstrual tensions, clinical depression is not a part of this picture. An exception is the hormonal changes in pregnancy, when depression (the "baby blues" or postpartum depression) occurs in such a predictable pattern that these temporary depressions are considered "normal" and expected. See Weissman, M.M.: Environmental factors in affective disorders, Hospital Practice **14**(4):103-109, 1979; and Weissman, M.M., and Klerman, G.: Sex differences and the epidemiology of depression, Archives of General Psychiatry **34**:98-110, 1977.

anxiety symptoms may portend some oncoming physical disease or condition that is beginning to unfold.

"Anxiety states" ("anxiety neurosis" in DSM-II) include panic disorder and its lesser equivalent, generalized anxiety disorder, as well as obsessive compulsive disorder ("obsessive compulsive neurosis" in DSM-II). The latter is seen when unacceptable thoughts or actions occur, such as thoughts (obsessions) of violence or contamination or the need for repetitive, ritualistic behavior (compulsions) like endless handwashing or counting.

Phobic disorders ("phobic neurosis" in DSM-II) represent an intense, exaggerated fear of an object, activity, or situation, resulting in a persistent need to avoid this dreaded stimulus—for example, an intense fear of bridges, elevators, or public transportation.

Somatoform disorders

The somatoform disorders exhibit physical symptoms that suggest physical disorder, but on examination they appear to be psychologically rather than physically caused. These disorders include conversion disorder ("hysterical neurosis, conversion type" in DSM-II), an example of which is the person who cannot move an arm or leg although there is no physical reason for not doing so. Only the special senses or the voluntary nervous system are involved. The mechanism for causing this is unconscious, as opposed to the conscious manipulations of the malingerer. The autonomic nervous system is not involved and thus provides diagnostic differentiation from psychophysiological (psychosomatic) disorders. In older people with this tendency, symptoms or illnesses may be exaggerated, and in this way a "secondary gain" is achieved in the form of extra attention and help.

Hypochondriasis, another somatoform disorder, is an overconcern with one's physical and emotional health, accompanied by various bodily complaints for which there is no physical basis. However, this does not mean that the complaints are "imaginary." They have an emotional basis that

requires treatment. Hypochondriasis is commonly associated with depressive feelings, but it may stand alone. It has many meanings, one of which may be a symbolization of the older person's sense of defectiveness and deteriorarion (see self-drawings, pp. 243-244). It may be a means of communication and interaction with others—family members, doctors, nurses, social workers. It can be used to displace anxiety from areas of greater concern. It can include identification with a deceased loved one who had similar symptoms. And it can serve as punishment for guilt, as an inhibition of impulses, and as an aid in the desire to control others. Finally, Busse,[22] who contributed some of the earliest work on hypochondriasis among older persons, emphasized its role in avoiding problems by allowing escaping into the "sick" role. The following list summarizes the psychic functions of hypochondriasis in persons of all ages.

1. To symbolize and make concrete one's sense of defectiveness or deterioration
2. To serve as a ticket to interaction with caretakers (or punishers), doctors, nurses, etc.
3. To displace anxiety from areas of greater concern
4. To serve as part of identification with a deceased loved one through similar symptoms
5. To serve as punishment for guilt
6. To avoid or inhibit unwanted behavior or interactions
7. To punish others
8. To regulate (usually reduce) interpersonal intimacy[23]

Meyersberg's work[24] on "crocks" is an excellent study of hypochondriasis. He speaks of the typical withdrawal of the physician in the face of

---

[22] Busse, E.W.: The treatment of hypochondriasis, Tristate Medical Journal **2:**7-12, 1954.

[23] From Patterson, R.D., Freeman, L.C., and Butler, R.N.: Psychiatric aspects of adaptation, survival and death. In Granick, S., and Patterson, R.D., editors: Human aging, II, Pub. No. (HSM) 71-9037, Washington, D.C., 1971, U.S. Government Printing Office.

[24] Meyersberg, H.A., and colleagues, George Washington University Medical School, Washington, D.C., unpublished work, 1966.

treatment defeat, the voluminous clinic and hospital records for these patients, the expectation of patients that treatment personnel will magically alleviate their suffering. There is much overlap between depression and hypochondriasis. Most depressive individuals show some hypochondriacal preoccupations, and hypochondriasis has a gloomy and depressive mood associated with it. But whereas a basically depressed person will withdraw and not seek help, the hypochondriac sees his or her problems as physical and goes to the doctor, thus at least relieving the isolation. Meyersberg sees hypochondriasis as a prophylactic measure, in that the person may be taking steps that ward off more incapacitating mental illness. Thus medical help, although not curing the problem, may be a preventive measure, particularly if it can lead the patient to examine the real reasons he or she is seeking help. Even if it cannot, a service is being provided. Patients with hypochondriasis should be listened to and accepted. Of course, special difficulties arise if hypochondriasis is connected with a real organic condition. Then, diagnosis and treatment may be difficult.

Dissociative disorders

Dissociative disorders ("hysterical neurosis, dissociative type" in DSM-II) are seen when an older person's consciousness, identity, or motor behavior is suddenly and temporarily altered, resulting in fugue states, stupor, amnesia, and confusion. Sleep walking or night wandering is sometimes included in this category when there is no physical basis for such behavior. Psychotic features may be present.

Psychosexual disorders

We discuss some of these disorders in Chapter 6, but sexual exhibition, a charge often associated in the public's mind with older men, will be dealt with here. Sexual exhibitionism in older people is overestimated and overstated. Most such sexual pathology is related to young adulthood.[25] Sensa-

tionalism in court cases concerning children who have been "molested" has been misleading in many instances. The sexual element may have been less significant than the loneliness of the older person, who may have no children or grandchildren. Some older men have fantasies of rejuvenation in contact with young children,[26] rather than any direct sexual preoccupation. Children of course must be protected from any exploitation that may occur. But the older person needs sympathetic understanding rather than punishment, and efforts should be made to provide that which is lacking in their lives. In some cases, total misinterpretation occurs. We have known of older people who were supposedly molesting younger children and have been arrested for exhibitionism; actually they were confused, needed to urinate, and found the most convenient spot.

Personality disorders

Personality traits become personality disorders only when they are so inflexible and maladaptive that they cause serious problems for an individual. Personality disorders are separated from the other disorders in the DSM-III classification in order to avoid overlooking them. They are presented as the underlying personality of the individual. (See description of Axis II on p. 87.) In this broad group of disorders we see defects in personality development that are of lifelong nature. There is little sense of anxiety or distress associated with them. Maladaptive patterns of behavior are deeply ingrained.

Certain personality disorders serve different adaptive functions, depending on the stage in the life cycle. This phenomenon, the changing adaptive nature of psychopathology, was observed in the NIMH studies by Perlin and Butler. For example, a so-called schizoid or introspective personality may function somewhat better in old age. Such an individual tends to be insulated against the experiences of life and therefore may feel relatively more comfortable with some of the loneliness and

---

[25] Gebhard, P.H., Pomeroy, W.B., Christenson, C., and Gagnon, J.H.: Sex offenders: an analysis of types, New York, 1965, Harper & Row, Publishers, Inc.

[26] This idea is of a standard biblical conception. The elderly King David, for example, was advised to "lay" with young girls.

difficulties of old age. On the other hand, he or she may become even more of a recluse with almost no human contact. The person with a paranoid personality has perhaps the most problems in later life, as the individual loses what few friends and relationships he or she has and becomes increasingly isolated.[27] The inadequate, dependent person may welcome and enjoy the opportunity for greater dependence in old age and the freedom from work responsibilities. Obsessive compulsiveness can become useful in scrupulous caretaking of oneself and in keeping busy with many details; in fact this type of individual can create a whole life for himself by "taking care" of things—possessions, spouse, grandchildren, bodily ailments, etc. (as Mr. H has done).

■ Mr. H has been retired for 3 years. His obsessions and compulsions are useful mechanisms in filling the vacuum of a forced retirement. "My home is always in order," says Mr. H, as he putters around the house, arranging everything according to strict schedule in a careful, meticulous manner. He is thrifty and even hoarding of his possessions, not to mention his feelings.

He takes care of his health with religious fervor and follows the doctor's orders precisely. He has arranged for two grave sites (one in St. Louis and one in Florida) so he can be well taken care of in case he dies, whether at home or on vacation. He has checked actuarial tables to predict his death at age 88, leaving no stone unturned.

From a therapeutic perspective it is important to realize the possible adaptive qualities of personalities. A cyclothymic personality can be fostered by the therapist to help activate an individual psychologically. Persons with obsessions may be encouraged to make constructive use of ritual. The thera-

pist can help persons with hysterical neurosis keep alive their dramatic qualities and, at times, their childlike expectations.

The antisocial criminal activities of an antisocial personality are rare in late life. Violent crimes are seldom committed, although embezzlement and other less violent crimes do occur. Old "sociopaths" do fade away, it seems. Thus geriatric delinquency is not a problem to rouse one's keen interest.

Psychological factors affecting physical condition

The psychophysiological disorders (called "psychophysiologic disorders" in DSM-II or "psychosomatic disorders") are physical symptoms caused by emotional factors and involving an organ system under control of the autonomic nervous system. Anxiety leads to these chronic and exaggerated expressions of emotions characterized by effects on secretion, mobility, and vascularity in various tissue and organ systems. Alfred Adler, Flanders Dunbar, and Franz Alexander contributed much to our understanding of the interplay between physiological and psychological events.

It is important to differentiate psychosomatic disorders from conversion reactions and hypochondriasis. Following are signs of psychosomatic disorders.

1. The autonomic nervous system is involved, and not the voluntary musculature and sensory perceptive systems.
2. The disorder does not reduce anxiety, thus contrasting with the conversion reaction, in which the phenomenon of *la belle indifférence* (beautiful indifference) occurs.
3. There is a physiological rather than symbolic origin of symptoms.
4. There is a definite somatic threat because of structural change.

In older people some of the common psychophysiological reactions include skin reactions such as pruritus[28] ani and vulvae, psychogenic rheumatism, hyperventilation syndromes, irritable colon,

---

[27] Occasionally a folie à deux may result, involving the older person and someone close to him or her. One kind of "eccentricity" is observed when a mother and daughter, two brothers, or two sisters become recluses, living in a house that ages as they do—or, more precisely, deteriorates. It is usually the health department that becomes alerted for purposes of cleanup or eviction. Electricity may be off, plumbing and toilets may not function, there may have been small fires, human feces may be found on the bathroom floor, cat litter may be evident, window screens may be rusting, the house may need painting and repairs, the garden may be overgrown.

---

[28] Itchiness.

nocturia,[29] and cardiac neuroses with fear of sudden death. Constipation is a frequent complaint; in fact, preoccupations with bowel habits are common, perhaps less related to age than to cultural considerations. Laxatives, certain food habits, and theories of diseases in the early 1900s were very influential in the childhoods of contemporary older people: theories of ptomaine poisoning, focal infections, and fletcherism (the meticulous chewing of food) are all heritages of both the national and the medical culture.

In our experience some psychosomatic disorders—for example, ulcers—are less common in old age; other types—especially muscular, skeletal, genitourinary, and dermatological problems—are perhaps more common. Psychotherapy is helpful.

■ Mr. B visited to ask our help for a pruritic scalp condition on his essentially bald head; he "incidentally" told us of the recent death of his wife. He could not get himself to say Kaddish, the mourner's prayer in the Jewish faith. The scalp condition was similar to the rim of a skull cap, worn by men in the synogogue. We treated his already infected lesions and discussed his wife and the question of saying Kaddish. He later reported having said the prayer and of having a "clear" scalp. (He also reported newly growing hair!)

How important is diagnostic classification?

Strömgren has stated that classification of the psychiatric disorders of old age is complex and that they "very often have no clear-cut border lines. In many cases the onset is so insidious that it is impossible to state the time at which a person is passing from the 'healthy' group to the 'ill' group. In addition, the nosological entities in many cases are not sharply defined, with the result that frequently it may, in principle, be impossible to say definitely whether the case under consideration should be included in the group."[30]

We would warn against a rigid preoccupation with making a "correct" diagnosis. The diagnosis should be flexible and open to testing through careful, sensitive observation of the older person. If a particular treatment direction is not working, the therapist should back up, rethink the issue, and begin again in a new direction. Above all, the diagnostic task is to establish the basis for a functional, workable, useful treatment—just as much emphasis should be on determining what is remediable as in simply establishing what is wrong.

SOME SUBJECTS PERTINENT TO MENTAL BREAKDOWN
Lack of mourning rites

Older persons in the United States today do not receive necessary cultural support for grief and mourning. Learning how to mourn productively and restoratively requires models in ritual and custom as well as in personal experiences with others who mourn. Lack of such support can prolong depression and leave grief unresolved. Patterns of mourning for the dead are in disarray as many time-honored customs become discarded (wearing black clothing, abstaining from social events for a period of time) and others are practiced piecemeal (religious rituals, the rallying around of friends and family). Still other patterns are recent and psychologically suspect innovations (funeral directors or morticians who "console" the family, the use of barbiturates to calm nerves and deaden the feelings). Gorer (1965) remarks that, up to 1900, every society in the world had definitie rules for mourners to follow.[31] This is no longer true, and the picture might accurately be described as "every man or woman for himself/herself" as long as mourning does not bother anyone else. Our culture seems reluctant to acknowledge the pain of death and to bear the agony of experiencing it through to acceptance. Some churches and many individuals deny the existence of death, preferring to speak of it as "merely sleep" or "the beginning

---

[29] Frequency of urination at night.

[30] From Strömgren, E.: Epidemiology of old-age psychiatric disorders. In Williams, R.H., Tibbits, C., and Donahue, W., editors: Process of aging, vol. 2, New York, 1963, Atherton Press.

---

[31] Gorer, G.: Death, grief, and mourning, New York, 1965, Doubleday Anchor Press.

of life hereafter.'' This may reassure individuals but it does not help them resolve the pain of separation and the need to find new attachments.

In the United States people receive some support in the period of initial shock, from the time of the death to burial. But after the church services are over, the undertaker disappears with a sizable portion of the mourner's money and relatives and friends go home, taking away their casserole dishes and other gestures of help and support. But for the mourner the intense period of mourning is just beginning and it must usually be experienced alone. Onlookers will try to divert the mourner's attention to other things. Crying is considered indulgent and possibly harmful rather than a psychological necessity. Gorer compares our present attitudes toward death and mourning with the prudish attitudes toward sex in the past: death has become an obscenity—one should not discuss it in public, the feelings are ''bad,'' and any indulgence in mourning must be done in secret.

Gorer goes on to point out the maladaptive behavior that results. Exaggerated depression, aimless busyness, deification of the dead person, or callous denial of others' grief as well as one's own may occur. People may become excessively preoccupied with death or violence. Since death is an unavoidable crisis inherent in the human life cycle, it is peculiar that a society can so determinedly avoid the provisions of cultural custom and ritual that could make it easier to bear. However, such a coming to terms with death would require a coming to terms with the value of human life. This would mean some considerable reshuffling of values in American society.

Suicide in old age

The highest rate of suicide occurs in white men in their eighties. Suicide is one of the 10 leading causes of death in the United States. Older persons, about 11% of the population, accounted for roughly 25% of reported suicides—about 5,000 to 8,000 yearly—in 1970[32] and this is still roughly

[32] Resnik, H.L., and Cantor, J.M.: Suicide and aging, Journal of the American Geriatrics Society **18:**152-158, 1970.

Table 4-4. Suicides per 100,000 population by age and sex in 1977

Age	Male	Female
5 to 14	1.6	0.3
15 to 19	14.2	3.4
20 to 24	29.9	7.3
25 to 29	28.8	8.5
30 to 34	24.0	9.5
35 to 39	24.4	9.3
40 to 44	23.0	11.5
45 to 49	23.3	12.6
50 to 54	25.9	12.5
55 to 59	28.2	11.2
60 to 64	30.4	9.7
65 to 69	31.9	9.0
70 to 74	39.3	8.3
75 to 79	45.9	7.5
80 to 84	44.3	6.8
85-plus	45.8	4.2
ALL AGES	20.1	6.8

From Mortality Statistics Branch, Division of Vital Statistics, National Center for Health Statistics: Vital statistics of the United States, vol. 2, Mortality (published and unpublished data).

true today. The peak rate of suicide for white women occurs in middle age. However, throughout the world, suicide rates have been increasing for women, especially older women.[33] Rates for nonwhite men and women are lower, with a peak in the years 25 to 29. Table 4-4 shows suicides per 100,000 population by age and sex.[34] The increased suicide rate with age is found in all countries which keep reliable statistics.

■ The 75-year-old man suffocated after he tied a plastic bag over his head and pulled it tight with a pajama drawstring. He was despondent over ill health.

■ Police in Blaine, Minnesota, reported that an 85-year-old man, depressed over a painful illness, arranged for his own funeral, then drove to the mortuary and shot

[33] Weiss, J.M.A.: Suicide in the aged. In Resnik, H.C.P., editor: Suicidal behaviors, Boston, 1968, Little, Brown & Co.
[34] The actual rate of suicide is underreported because of shame and guilt. Some religious groups such as Catholics and Orthodox Jews have denied burial rites to persons who committed suicide. It is also underestimated because of deception to protect life insurance benefits.

himself in his car. Police said he telephoned the Wexler Funeral Home Sunday and inquired about the cost of cremation, telling an employee he would be over later. He wrote a note to his wife. Authorities found him dead in his car with a $300 check made out to the funeral home.

■ Rear Admiral B, 56, who retired from the Navy last year after 30 years of service, was found dead in a hotel room with a .22 caliber bullet wound in his head. A pistol was found near the body. Police ruled the death a suicide.

In the German language suicide means self-murder (Selbstmord). This etymology tells something of the motives of hatred of self or others that are present in many suicides. Freud in 1925 said that perhaps no one could find the psychic energy to kill himself unless in the first place he was thereby killing at the same time someone with whom he had identified himself. Meninger (1938) has written that the suicide victim wishes to die, to kill, and to be killed. Indeed, suicide is three times more common than homicide. Perhaps it is emotionally less threatening to consider killing oneself than others.

Other theoretical views concerning motivation for suicide include Durkheim's notion of *anomie* or *alienation*. Older white men commit suicide at greater rates than black men or women in general (after the different life expectancies of each group are accounted for). We surmise that the explanation lies in the severe loss of status (ageism) that affects white men, who as a group had held the greatest power and influence in society. Black men and most women have long been accustomed to a lesser status (through racism and sexism) and ironically do not have to suffer such a drastic fall in old age. In fact black people may enjoy a rise in social status as they age.[35]

Control is another motivational element. Seneca said, "Against all the injuries of life, I have the refuge of death"; and Nietzsche stated, "The thought of suicide gets one successfully through

many a bad night." Death itself is certain but its timing and its character are not. One can defy and control death by virtue of initiating the act of one's own death. Control also extends beyond the grave—survivors are deeply affected and a grim, unmistakable legacy of guilt, shame, and regret may be left for them to bear.

A *sacrificial romantic* quality can be present as in the double suicide pacts of lovers, old or young.

In death pacts between lovers we meet the age-old belief, found in myth and history, that two people who die together are united forever beyond the grave. This belief is also encountered in the German Romantic Period. In Japan it is known as *shinju*. It is but a step from such a belief towards symbolization of the grave as a bridal bed.[36]

A *rational* or *philosophical* decision to kill oneself is undoubtedly more common in old age as people perceive themselves to be failing. Older men, especially, may decide to kill themselves rather than leave their widows penniless from the cost of a long illness. Married couples may commit double suicide or a combination of mercy killing of one and suicide of the other.

Documents left by the married couples yield a typical picture of an aging man and woman, one or both suffering from grave illness, which is never absent from their thoughts. A deeply devoted pair, childless, in modest circumstances and with few interests and friends, they are deeply absorbed in their own small world. Prolonged insomnia speeds the decisive act. "We are at the end of our rope" is a phrase which repeatedly occurs. Here is a typical situation. A 56-year-old ex-miner, with impaired vision and an injured leg, underwent an operation for cancer of the bowel. The operation was not successful and he was confined to his bed with frequent, violent attacks of pain. His wife was disabled by Parkinson's disease and had been partly paralyzed for 15 years.[37]

Perhaps the most preventable are the suicides related to *depression*. Albert Camus, French novelist and essayist, saw suicide as submission and stated, "there is only one truly serious problem and that

---

[35] Wylie, F.M.: Attitudes toward aging and the aged among black Americans: some historical perspectives, Aging and Human Development **2**:66-70, 1971.

[36] From Cohen, J.: Forms of suicide and their significance, Triangle **6**:280-286, 1964.

[37] Ibid.

is suicide.''[38] Suicide in these cases is a passive, perhaps desperate, giving up. Depressive reactions are very widespread and important in old age. They include not only psychotic depression or the special depression associated with lucid moments of the cerebral arteriosclerotic patient, but also those of an everyday nature resulting from loss, grief, and despair. Depressions frequently follow physical illnesses, including viral illnesses, and are not uncommon in Parkinson's disease. Varying degrees of depression may be observed in connection with lowered self-esteem because of reduced social and personal valuation and status. Retirement may be a factor. Finally, guilt over one's actions in either the past or the present can lead to depression. Organic brain syndromes are a serious and complicating factor in late-life depressions.

Older people use all the usual methods of killing themselves: drugs, guns, hanging, and jumping off high places. In the United States firearms and explosives are at the top of the list. Suicide may also be accomplished ''subintentionally,'' by the slower means of not eating, not taking medicines, drinking too much, delaying treatment, and taking risks physically. This long-term process of suicidal erosion is of course not part of suicide statistics, since suicide is seen as a single act. Most laws regarding commitment require specific evidence of danger to oneself or to others (rightfully protecting the civil liberties of people). Therefore such long, drawn-out self-destructive behavior often presents a touchy legal problem: does one try to intervene or not?

■ A 72-year-old woman insisted on living by herself and not with her daughter and the latter's family. She did not want to be a burden. Nonetheless, she had diabetes and congestive heart failure. By living alone she reduced the ''threat'' of effective prompt care in any emergency. Moreover, she lived in a cheap inner-city boarding house. It was unsanitary, the heat was not always adequate, and she had to walk up three flights of stairs.

It seems clear to us, in the above situation, that the woman's right to make her own choice is para-

mount, regardless of concern for her health. Indeed, it may be far more beneficial for her to have such choices than to be in a ''safe'' environment. The decision to take away choice must always be made very conservatively, seeking out every possible alternative. However, the concept of ''danger to oneself or others'' needs to be rethought with the long-term suicide in mind.

Mental health personnel should take suicide threats of older persons seriously. Persons attempting suicide are more likely to fail if below age 35 and to succeed if over 50. It is most rare for an attempt by anyone over 65 to fail. Men are more successful than women. (For suicidal clues, see Chapter 9.) Reducing the frequency of depression and providing for its effective treatment when present are the major ways of reducing suicide in old age. One must be especially alert with people whose depressions seem to have lifted. They may be gathering enough energy to commit the suicide they had contemplated earlier. When there is evidence of suicidal preoccupations, one must schedule extra time and additional sessions. It is important to openly discuss the subject rather than, ostrichlike, hope it will go away. Rescue fantasies—that the therapist will always be on call or will rush to save them—must be dealt with and clarified. Grueling as it may seem, a ''psychological autopsy'' following a committed suicide is mandatory to try to understand what happened and whether anything could have been done. The Weisman-Kastenbaum procedure is useful.[39] Outreach services are imperative to reach depressed people who may have withdrawn and become isolated. Old age must offer the older person something to live for. Bartko et al.[40] reported that the degree of organization (activities, friendships, family relationships, interests, usefulness) in the daily life of older men was a good predictor of survival in originally healthy

---

[38] Camus, A.: The myth of Sisyphus, New York, 1959, Vintage Books.

[39] Weisman, A.D., and Kastenbaum, R.: The psychological autopsy (monograph), New York, 1968, Community Mental Health Journal, Inc.

[40] Bartko, J., Patterson, R., and Butler, R.N.: Biomedical and behavioral predictors of survival among normal aged men: a multivariate analysis. In Palmore, E., and Jeffers, F.C., editors: Prediction of life span, Lexington, Mass., 1971, Heath Lexington Books.

subjects. Jung was correct when he said that human beings cannot stand a meaningless life. Suicide is evidence of that.

Physical effects of "giving up" psychologically

Suicide is not the only consequence of giving up. A team of researchers headed by George Engel (Schmale and Engel)[41] at the University of Rochester Medical Center explored the relationship between psychological attitudes and the onset of physical disease. The found that between 70% and 80% of patients had felt like "giving up" at the time their illness developed. The study suggests that if a person responds to his life with hopelessness, depression, and submission, he may trigger a biological change that encourages the development of an already present disease potential. Their work included patients with infections, cancer, cardiovascular diseases, rheumatoid arthritis, diabetes, and diseases of the nervous system. Predictions of physical illness were able to be made on the basis of psychiatric interviews. Engel emphasized that it was not the magnitude of an event but the way in which a person reacted to it that determined whether one "gave up." Again, the treatment of despair and depression must be emphasized.

1968 DIAGNOSTIC NOMENCLATURE (DSM-II) OF THE AMERICAN PSYCHIATRIC ASSOCIATION (SELECTED SECTIONS)[42]

II. Organic brain syndromes (OBS)

A. Psychoses
Senile and presenile dementia
290.0   Senile dementia
290.1   Presenile dementia

Alcoholic psychosis
291.0   Delirium tremens
291.1   Korsakov's psychosis
291.2   Other alcoholic hallucinosis
291.3   Alcohol paranoid state
291.4   Acute alcohol intoxication
291.5   Alcoholic deterioration
291.6   Pathological intoxication
291.9   Other alcoholic psychosis
Psychosis associated with intracranial infection
292.0   General paralysis
292.1   Syphilis of central nervous system
292.2   Epidemic encephalitis
292.3   Other and unspecified encephalitis
292.9   Other intracranial infection
Psychosis associated with other cerebral condition
293.0   Cerebral arteriosclerosis
293.1   Other cerebrovascular disturbance
293.2   Epilepsy
293.3   Intracranial neoplasm
293.4   Degenerative disease of the CNS
293.5   Brain trauma
293.9   Other cerebral condition
Psychosis associated with other physical condition
294.0   Endocrine disorder
294.1   Metabolic and nutritional disorder
294.2   Systemic infection
294.3   Drug or poison intoxication (other than alcohol)
B. Nonpsychotic OBS
309.0   Intracranial infection
309.13 Alcohol (simple drunkenness)
309.14 Other drug, poison, or systemic intoxication
309.2   Brain trauma
309.3   Circulatory disturbance
309.4   Epilepsy

---

[41] Schmale, A.H., Jr., and Engel, G.L.: The giving up–given up complex illustrated on film, Archives of General Psychiatry **17**:135-145, 1967.

[42] From Committee on Nomenclature and Statistics of the American Psychiatric Association: Diagnostic and statistical manual of mental disorders, ed. 2 (DSM-II), Washington, D.C., 1968, American Psychiatric Association. In the World Health Organization's *International Classification of Diseases* (ICD), 28 basic three-digit numbers have been assigned for mental disorders (numbers 290 through 319). The standard international guide to classifying and coding diseases and other medical conditions is the ICD, published by the World Health Organization and its forerunners in roughly decennial revisions since the issuance in 1900 of the first *International Classification of Causes of Death*. The ninth revision of the *International Classification of Diseases* (ICD-9) was adopted worldwide on Jan. 1, 1979.

309.5 Disturbance of metabolism, growth, or nutrition
309.6 Senile or presenile brain disease
309.7 Intracranial neoplasm
309.8 Degenerative disease of the CNS
309.9 Other physical condition

III. Psychoses not attributed to physical conditions listed previously

Schizophrenia
295.0 Simple
295.1 Hebephrenic
295.2 Catatonic
295.23 Catatonic type, excited
295.24 Catatonic type, withdrawn
295.3 Paranoid
295.4 Acute schizophrenic episode
295.5 Latent
295.6 Residual
295.7 Schizo-affective
295.73 Schizo-affective, excited
295.74 Schizo-affective, depressed
295.9 Chronic undifferentiated
295.99 Other schizophrenia

Major affective disorders
296.0 Involutional melancholia
296.1 Manic-depressive illness, manic
296.2 Manic-depressive illness, depressed
296.3 Manic-depressive illness, circular
296.33 Manic-depressive, circular, manic
296.34 Manic-depressive, circular, depressed
296.8 Other major affective disorder

Paranoid states
297.0 Paranoia
297.1 Involutional paraphrenia
297.9 Other paranoid state

Other psychoses
298.0 Psychotic depressive reaction

IV. Neuroses

300.0 Anxiety
300.1 Hysterical
300.13 Hysterical, conversion type
300.14 Hysterical, dissociative type
300.2 Phobic
300.3 Obsessive compulsive
300.4 Depressive
300.5 Neurasthenic

300.6 Depersonalization
300.7 Hypochondriacal
300.8 Other neurosis

V. Personality disorders and certain other nonpsychotic mental disorders

Personality disorders
301.0 Paranoid
301.1 Cyclothymic
301.2 Schizoid
301.3 Explosive
301.4 Obsessive compulsive
301.5 Hysterical
301.6 Asthenic
301.7 Antisocial
301.81 Passive-aggressive
301.82 Inadequate
301.89 Other specified types

Sexual deviation
302.1 Fetishism
302.2 Pedophilia
302.3 Transvestitism
302.4 Exhibitionism
302.5 Voyeurism
302.6 Sadism
302.7 Masochism
302.8 Other sexual deviation

Alcoholism
303.0 Episodic excessive drinking
303.1 Habitual excessive drinking
303.2 Alcohol addiction
303.9 Other alcoholism

Drug dependence
304.0 Opium, opium alkaloids, and their derivatives
304.1 Synthetic analgesics with morphinelike effects
304.2 Barbiturates
304.3 Other hypnotics and sedatives or "tranquilizers"
304.4 Cocaine
304.5 Cannabis sativa (hashish, marihuana)
304.6 Other psychostimulants
304.7 Hallucinogens
304.8 Other drug dependence

VI. Psychophysiological disorders

305.0 Skin
305.1 Musculoskeletal

305.2 Respiratory
305.3 Cardiovascular
305.4 Hemic and lymphatic
305.5 Gastrointestinal
305.6 Genitourinary
305.7 Endocrine
305.8 Organ of special sense
305.9 Other type

VII. Special symptoms

306.2 Tic
306.3 Other psychomotor disorder
306.4 Disorders of sleep
306.9 Other special symptom

VIII. Transient situational disturbances

307.3 Adjustment reaction of adult life
307.4 Adjustment reaction of late life

X. Conditions without psychiatric disorder and nonspecific conditions

Social maladjustment without manifest psychiatric disorder

316.0 Marital maladjustment
316.1 Social maladjustment
316.2 Occupational maladjustment
316.3 Dyssocial behavior
316.9 Other social maladjustment

Nonspecific conditions

317 Nonspecific conditions

No mental disorder

318 No mental disorder

XI. Nondiagnostic terms for administrative use

319.0 Diagnosis deferred
310.1 Boarder
310.2 Experiment only
319.9 Other

Fifth-digit qualifying phrases

Section II   .x1 Acute
                    .x2 Chronic
Section III   .x6 Not psychotic
                        now
Sections IV through .x6 Mild
    IX   .x7 Moderate
All disorders   .x5 In remission

1980 DIAGNOSTIC NOMENCLATURE (DSM-III) OF THE AMERICAN PSYCHIATRIC ASSOCIATION[43]

Organic mental disorders

[**Section 1.** *Organic mental disorders whose etiology or pathophysiological process is listed below (taken from the mental disorders section of ICD-9-CM).*]

Dementias arising in the senium and presenium
Primary degenerative dementia, senile onset
  290.30 With delirium
  290.20 With delusions
  290.21 With depression
  290.00 Uncomplicated
  Code in fifth digit:
  1 = with delirium, 2 = with delusions, 3 = with depression, 0 = uncomplicated.
  290.1x Primary degenerative dementia, presenile onset, _____
  290.4x Multi-infarct dementia, _____
Substance-induced
Alcohol
  303.00 Intoxication
  291.40 Idiosyncratic intoxication
  291.80 Withdrawal
  291.00 Withdrawal delirium
  291.30 Hallucinosis
  291.10 Amnestic disorder
  Code severity of dementia in fifth digit: 1 = mild, 2 = moderate, 3 = severe, 0 = unspecified.
  291.2x Dementia associated with alcoholism, _____
Barbiturate or similarly acting sedative or hypnotic
  305.40 Intoxication (327.00)
  292.00 Withdrawal (327.01)
  292.00 Withdrawal delirium (327.02)
  292.83 Amnestic disorder (327.04)
Opioid
  305.50 Intoxication (327.10)
  292.00 Withdrawal (327.11)
Cocaine
  305.60 Intoxication (327.20)
Amphetamine or similarly acting sympathomimetic
  305.70 Intoxication (327.30)
  292.81 Delirium (327.32)

---

[43] From Committee on Nomenclature and Statistics of the American Psychiatric Association: Diagnostic and statistical manual of mental disorders (DSM-III), Washington, D.C., 1980, American Psychiatric Association.

292.11 Delusional disorder (327.35)
292.00 Withdrawal (327.31)
Phencyclidine (PCP) or similarly acting arylcyclohexyl-amine
305.90 Intoxication (327.40)
292.81 Delirium (327.42)
292.90 Mixed organic mental disorder (327.49)
Hallucinogen
305.30 Hallucinosis (327.56)
292.11 Delusional disorder (327.55)
292.84 Affective disorder (327.57)
Cannabis
305.20 Intoxication (327.60)
292.11 Delusional disorder (327.65)
Tobacco
292.00 Withdrawal (327.71)
Caffeine
305.90 Intoxication (327.80)
Other or unspecified substance
305.90 Intoxication (327.90)
292.00 Withdrawal (327.91)
292.81 Delirium (327.92)
292.82 Dementia (327.93)
292.83 Amnestic disorder (327.94)
292.11 Delusional disorder (327.95)
292.12 Hallucinosis (327.96)
292.84 Affective disorder (327.97)
292.89 Personality disorder (327.98)
292.90 Atypical or mixed organic mental disorder (327.99)

[**Section 2.** *Organic brain syndromes whose etiology or pathophysiological process is either noted as an additional diagnosis from outside the mental disorders section of ICD-9-CM or is unknown.*]

293.00 Delirium
294.10 Dementia
294.00 Amnestic syndrome
293.81 Organic delusional syndrome
293.82 Organic hallucinosis
293.83 Organic affective syndrome
310.10 Organic personality syndrome
294.80 Atypical or mixed organic brain syndrome

Substance use disorders

Code in fifth digit: 1 = continuous, 2 = episodic, 3 = in remission, 0 = unspecified.
305.0x Alcohol abuse, _____
303.9x Alcohol dependence (Alcoholism), _____

305.4x Barbiturate or similarly acting sedative or hypnotic abuse, _____
304.1x Barbiturate or similarly acting sedative or hypnotic dependence, _____
305.5x Opioid abuse, _____
304.0x Opioid dependence, _____
305.6x Cocaine abuse, _____
305.7x Amphetamine or similarly acting sympathomimetic abuse, _____
304.4x Amphetamine or similarly acting sympathomimetic dependence, _____
305.9x Phencyclidine (PCP) or similarly acting arylcyclohexylamine abuse, _____ (328.4x)
305.3x Hallucinogen abuse, _____
305.2x Cannabis abuse, _____
304.3x Cannabis dependence, _____
305.1x Tobacco dependence, _____
305.9x Other, mixed or unspecified substance abuse, _____
304.6x Other specified substance dependence, _____
304.9x Unspecified substance dependence, _____
304.7x Dependence on combination of opioid and other nonalcoholic substance, _____
304.8x Dependence on combination of substances, excluding opioids and alcohol, _____

Schizophrenic disorders

Code in fifth digit: 1 = subchronic, 2 = chronic, 3 = subchronic with acute exacerbation, 4 = chronic with acute exacerbation, 5 = in remission, 0 = unspecified.
Schizophrenia
295.1x Disorganized, _____
295.2x Catatonic, _____
295.3x Paranoid, _____
295.9x Undifferentiated, _____
295.6x Residual, _____

Paranoid disorders

297.10 Paranoia
297.30 Shared paranoid disorder
298.30 Acute paranoid disorder
297.90 Atypical paranoid disorder

Psychotic disorders not elsewhere classified

295.40 Schizophreniform disorder
298.80 Brief reactive psychosis
295.70 Schizoaffective disorder
298.90 Atypical psychosis

Neurotic disorders

These are included in Affective, Anxiety, Somatoform, Dissociative, and Psychosexual Disorders. In order to facilitate the identification of the categories that in DSM-II were grouped together in the class of Neuroses, the DSM-II terms are included separately in parentheses after the corresponding categories. These DSM-II terms are included in ICD-9-CM and therefore are acceptable as alternatives to the recommended DSM-III terms that precede them.

Affective disorders

Major affective disorders

Code major depressive episode in fifth digit: 6 = in remission, 4 = with psychotic features (the unofficial non-ICD-9-CM fifth digit 7 may be used instead to indicate that the psychotic features are mood-incongruent), 3 = with melancholia, 2 = without melancholia, 0 = unspecified.

Code manic episode in fifth digit: 6 = in remission, 4 = with psychotic features (the unofficial non-ICD-9-CM fifth digit 7 may be used instead to indicate that the psychotic features are mood-incongruent), 2 = without psychotic features, 0 = unspecified.

Bipolar disorder
296.6x Mixed, _____
296.4x Manic, _____
296.5x Depressed, _____
Major depression
296.2x Single episode, _____
296.3x Recurrent, _____

Other specific affective disorders
301.13 Cyclothymic disorder
300.40 Dysthymic disorder (or Depressive neurosis)
Atypical affective disorders
296.70 Atypical bipolar disorder
296.82 Atypical depression

Anxiety disorders

Phobic disorders (or Phobic neuroses)
300.21 Agoraphobia with panic attacks
300.22 Agoraphobia without panic attacks
300.23 Social phobia
300.29 Simple phobia
Anxiety states (or Anxiety neuroses)
300.01 Panic disorder
300.02 Generalized anxiety disorder
300.30 Obsessive compulsive disorder (or Obsessive compulsive neurosis)

Post-traumatic stress disorder
308.30 Acute
309.81 Chronic or delayed
300.00 Atypical anxiety disorder

Somatoform disorders
300.81 Somatization disorder
300.11 Conversion disorder (or Hysterical neurosis, conversion type)
307.80 Psychogenic pain disorder
300.70 Hypochondriasis (or Hypochondriacal neurosis)
300.70 Atypical somatoform disorder (300.71)

Dissociative disorders or hysterical neuroses, dissociative type)
300.12 Psychogenic amnesia
300.13 Psychogenic fugue
300.14 Multiple personality
300.60 Depersonalization disorder (or Depersonalization neurosis)
300.15 Atypical dissociative disorder

Psychosexual disorders

Gender identity disorders
Indicate sexual history in the fifth digit of Transsexualism code: 1 = asexual, 2 = homosexual, 3 = heterosexual, 0 = unspecified.
302.5x Transsexualism, _____
302.60 Gender identity disorder of childhood
302.85 Atypical gender identity disorder
Paraphilias
302.81 Fetishism
302.30 Transvestism
302.10 Zoophilia
302.20 Pedophilia
302.40 Exhibitionism
302.82 Voyeurism
302.83 Sexual masochism
302.84 Sexual sadism
302.90 Atypical paraphilia
Psychosexual dysfunctions
302.71 Inhibited sexual desire
302.72 Inhibited sexual excitement
302.73 Inhibited female orgasm
302.74 Inhibited male orgasm
302.75 Premature ejaculation
302.76 Functional dyspareunia
306.51 Functional vaginismus
302.70 Atypical psychosexual dysfunction

Other psychosexual disorders
302.00 Ego-dystonic homosexuality
302.89 Psychosexual disorder not elsewhere classified

Factitious disorders

300.16 Factitious disorder with psychological symptoms
301.51 Chronic factitious disorder with physical symptoms
300.19 Atypical factitious disorder with physical symptoms

Disorders of impulse control not elsewhere classified

312.31 Pathological gambling
312.32 Kleptomania
312.33 Pyromania
312.34 Intermittent explosive disorder
312.35 Isolated explosive disorder
312.39 Atypical impulse control disorder

Adjustment disorder

309.00 With depressed mood
309.24 With anxious mood
309.28 With mixed emotional features
309.30 With disturbance of conduct
309.40 With mixed disturbance of emotions and conduct
309.23 With work (or academic) inhibition
309.83 With withdrawal
309.90 With atypical features

Psychological factors affecting physical condition

Specify physical condition on Axis III.
316.00 Psychological factors affecting physical condition

Personality disorders
Note: These are coded on Axis II.

301.00 Paranoid
301.20 Schizoid
301.22 Schizotypal
301.50 Histrionic
301.81 Narcissistic
301.70 Antisocial
301.83 Borderline

301.82 Avoidant
301.60 Dependent
301.40 Compulsive
301.84 Passive-aggressive
301.89 Atypical, mixed or other personality disorder

V codes for conditions not attributable to a mental disorder that are a focus of attention or treatment

V65.20 Malingering
V62.89 Borderline intellectual functioning (V62.88)
V71.01 Adult antisocial behavior
V71.02 Childhood or adolescent antisocial behavior
V62.30 Academic problem
V62.20 Occupational problem
V62.82 Uncomplicated bereavement
V15.81 Noncompliance with medical treatment
V62.89 Phase of life problem or other life circumstance problem
V61.10 Marital problem
V61.20 Parent-child problem
V61.80 Other specified family circumstances
V62.81 Other interpersonal problem

Additional codes

300.90 Unspecified mental disorder (nonpsychotic)
V71.09 No diagnosis or condition on Axis I
799.90 Diagnosis or condition deferred on Axis I

V71.09 No diagnosis on Axis II
799.90 Diagnosis deferred on Axis II

REFERENCES

Allen, E.B.: Functional psychoses in the aging simulating organic syndromes, Geriatrics **2:**269-279, 1947.
Birren, J.E., Butler, R.N., Greenhouse, S.W., Sokoloff, L., and Yarrow, M.R., editors: Human aging: a biological and behavioral study, Pub. No. (PHS) 986, Washington, D.C., 1963, U.S. Government Printing Office (reprinted as Pub. No. [HSM] 71-9051, 1971, 1974).
Busse, E.W., Barnes, R.H., Silverman, A.J., Thaler, M., and Frost, L.L.: Studies of the processes of aging, X. The strengths and weaknesses of psychic functioning in the aged, American Journal of Psychiatry **111:**896-901, 1955.
Busse, E.W., and Pfeiffer, E., editors: Mental illness in later life, Washington, D.C., 1973, American Psychiatric Association.
Cannon, W.B.: Voodoo death, American Anthropologist **44:** 169-181, 1942.
Choron, J.: Death and Western thought, New York, 1963, Collier Books.
Committee on Nomenclature and Statistics of the American Psychiatric Association: Diagnostic and statistical manual of mental disorders, ed. 2 (DSM-II), Washington, D.C., 1968, American Psychiatric Association.

Committee on Nomenclature and Statistics of the American Psychiatric Association: Diagnostic and statistical manual of mental disorders, ed. 3 (DSM-III), Washington, D.C., 1980, American Psychiatric Association.

Cumming, E., and Henry, W.E.: Growing old: the process of disengagement, New York, 1961, Basic Books, Inc., Publishers.

Durkheim, E.: Suicide (originally 1897), London, 1952, Routledge & Kegan Paul, Ltd.

Faris, R.E.L., and Dunham, H.W.: Mental disorders in urban areas, Chicago, 1939, The University of Chicago Press.

Feifel, H., editor: The meaning of death, New York, 1961, McGraw-Hill Book Co., Inc.

Fish, F.: Senile schizophrenia, Journal of Mental Science **106:** 938-946, 1960.

Freud, S.: Mourning and melancholia, In Standard edition of the psychological works of Sigmund Freud, vol. 14, London, 1957, Hogarth Press.

Goldfarb, A.I.: Psychiatric disorders of the aged: symptomatology, diagnosis and treatment, Journal of the American Geriatrics Society **8:**698-707, 1960.

Goldfarb, A.I.: Prevalence of psychiatric disorders in metropolitan old age and nursing homes, Journal of the American Geriatrics Society **10:**77-84, 1962.

Havighurst, R.J., Neugarten, B.L., and Tobin, S.S.: Disengagement, personality and life satisfaction in the later years. In Hansen, P.F., editor: Age with a future: proceedings of the Sixth International Congress of Gerontology, Copenhagen, 1963, Copenhagen Munksgaard, 1964.

Hollingshead, A.B., and Redlich, F.C.: Social class and mental illness: a community study, New York, 1958, John Wiley & Sons, Inc.

Inglis, J., Colwell, C., and Post, F.: Evaluation of the predictive power of a test known to differentiate between elderly functional and organic patients, Journal of Mental Science **101:**281-289, 1955.

Kaplan, O.J.: Mental disorders in later life, ed. 2, Stanford, Calif., 1956, Stanford University Press.

Kaplan, O.J., editor: Psychopathology of aging, New York, 1979, Academic Press, Inc.

Kral, V.A.: Psychiatric observations under severe chronic stress, American Journal of Psychiatry **108:**185-192, 1951.

Kramer, M., Taube, C., and Starr, S.: Patterns of use of psychiatric facilities by the aged: current status, trends and implications. In Simon, A., and Epstein, L.J., editors: Aging in modern society, Psychiatric Research Report No. 23, Washington, D.C., 1968, American Psychiatric Association.

Lindemann, E.: Symptomatology and management of acute grief. American Journal of Psychiatry **101:**141-148, 1944.

Lowenthal, M.F.: Lives in distress: the paths of the elderly to the psychiatric ward, New York, 1964, Basic Books, Inc., Publisher.

Lowenthal, M.F.: Social isolation and mental illness in old age, American Sociological Review **29**(1):54-70, 1964.

Marris, P.: Widows and their families, London, 1958, Routledge & Kegan Paul, Ltd.

Menninger, K.A.: Man against himself, New York, 1938, Harcourt Brace, & World.

Mental health problems of aging and the aged, sixth report of the Expert Committee on Mental Health, WHO Technical Report Series No. 171, Geneva, 1959, World Health Organization.

New York State Department of Mental Hygiene Mental Health Research Unit: A mental health survey of older people, Utica, 1960, New York State Hospital Press.

Parkes, C.M., Benjamin, B., and Fitzgerald, A.: Broken heart: a statistical study of increased mortality among widows, British Medical Journal **1:**740-743, 1969.

Patterson, R.D., Freeman, L.C., and Butler, R.N.: Psychiatric aspects of adaptation, survival and death. In Granick, S., and Patterson, R.D., editors: Human aging, II, Publ No. (HSM) 71-9037, Washington, D.C., 1971, U.S. Government Printing Office.

Perlin, S., and Butler, R.N.: Psychiatric aspects of adaptation to the aging experience. In Birren, J.E., Butler, R.N., Greenhouse, S.W., Sokoloff, L., and Yarrow, M.R., editors: Human aging: a biological and behavioral study, Pub. No. (PHS) 986, Washington, D.C., 1963, U.S. Government Printing Office (reprinted as Pub. No. [HSM] 71-9051, 1971, 1974).

Post, F.: The significance of affective symptoms in old age: a follow-up study of one hundred patients, London, 1962, Oxford University Press, Inc.

Report of the Task Panel on Mental Health of the Elderly, submitted to the President's Commission on Mental Health, Feb. 15, 1978.

Roth, M.: The natural history of mental disorders in old age, Journal of Mental Science **101:**281-301, 1955.

Sainsbury, P.: Suicide in later life, Gerontologica Clinica **4:** 161-170, 1962.

Shanas, E.: The health of older people: a social survey, Cambridge, Mass., 1962, Harvard University Press.

Sheldon, J.H.: The social medicine of old age: report of an inquiry in Wolverhampton, London, 1948, Oxford University Press.

Shneidman, E.S., and Farberow, N.L., editors: Clues to suicide, New York, 1957, McGraw-Hill Book Co., Inc.

Shreber, D.P.: Memoirs of my nervous illness, London, 1955, Dawson.

Stenback, A.: On involutional and middle age depression, Helsinki, Finland, XIII. Nordiska Psykiaterkongressen, 1962.

Stern, K., Williams, G.M., and Prados, M.: Grief reactions in later life, American Journal of Psychiatry **108:**289-294, 1951.

Verwoerdt, A.: Clinical geropsychiatry, Baltimore, 1976, The Williams & Wilkins Co.

Vispo, R.H.: Pre-morbid personality in the functional psychoses of the senium. A comparison of ex-patients with healthy controls, The Journal of Mental Science **108:**790-800, 1962.

5

Organic brain disorders

It is predicted that the organic brain disorders, long neglected by American medicine and by society at large, will become a focus of greater and greater interest and even excitement. Lipowski[1] neatly summarizes the forces that are building up to this change:

1. The growing numbers and proportion of older people
2. Advances in the neurosciences that are pointing toward unraveling the mysteries of organic brain disease
3. A growing focus in medicine on both chronic diseases and critical care medicine (intensive care units, emergency medicine, etc.), bringing to greater attention the organic brain disorders occurring in these circumstances
4. Improvements in the classification of organic brain disorders, as exemplified in the new *1980 Diagnostic and Statistical Manual of Mental Disorders* of the American Psychiatric Association (It is hoped that this will improve teaching and stimulate research.)

PROBLEMS IN NAMING DISORDERS (NOMENCLATURE)

Before the twentieth century, the organic brain disorders of late life were grouped together in a category known as organic senile dementia. But at the turn of the century, with an increasing number of older people, neuropathologists examining the brain at autopsy began separating arteriosclerotic conditions from senile dementia and both of these from neurosyphilis. Kraepelin, in emphasizing description and symptomatology while ignoring the person's inner life, described five signs of an organic brain disorder. He failed to note the affective reactions to brain diseases as well as the reversible brain disorder.

Senile dementia, now separated from arteriosclerotic processes, became divided by symptoms in the older textbooks, as follows: (1) simple dementia, (2) delirium, (3) paranoid states, (4) depressed and agitated types, and (5) presbyophrenic types; but these subdivisions did not differentiate between the mental conditions themselves and the affective reactions to and in connection with such mental changes. In England, work was done on hospital admission, following up patients when discharged until the time of their death. It was realized that everything could not be explained on an organic basis, and Roth, one of England's foremost clinical investigators, devised a more sophisticated classification by dividing all the disorders of old age into (1) affective psychoses, (2) senile psychoses, (3) arteriosclerotic psychoses, (4) delirious states, and (5) late paraphrenia.[2]

---

[1] Lipowski, Z.J.: A new look at organic brain syndromes, American Journal of Psychiatry **137**(6):674-678, 1980.

[2] Paraphrenia is a diagnosis used by some investigators to apply to paranoid-hallucinative disturbances in late life. Others deny the existence of the late-life schizophrenia implied in this description.

The American Psychiatric Association's *Diagnostic and Statistical Manual of Mental Disorders* (DSM) and its revisions further complicated the picture.[3] DSM-I (1952) presented the acute and chronic brain disorders, with qualifying psychotic, neurotic, and behavioral reactions; DSM-II (1968) reversed the emphasis by describing psychotic and nonpsychotic disorders, with a single introductory remark distinguishing acute from chronic conditions. DSM-III (1980) does not divide the "organic mental disorders" into psychotic/nonpsychotic or acute/chronic forms. Instead, the new classification contains seven descriptive organic brain syndromes[4] and uses the concepts of acuteness and chronicity to refer to mode of onset and duration of a disorder rather than reversibility or irreversibility of the disorder.

Until DSM-III, no clinician specializing in the field of aging had ever served on the Committee on Nomenclature and Statistics of the American Psychiatric Association—which perhaps accounts for such early age-prejudicial and invalid statements as the following parts of the 1952 definition of senile dementia: "Even mild cases will manifest some evidence of organic brain syndrome: *self-centeredness,* difficulty in assimilating new experiences, and *childish emotionality*"[5] (italics added).

The student and practitioner need to refer to the DSM-III for hospital diagnoses, insurance forms, etc. but should evaluate the definitions and classifications carefully since they may not always clearly reflect reality for the older person and will eventually need further refinement. Diagnostic criteria are still being field-tested. (We have included pertinent sections of the DSM-II and DSM-III classifications in Chapter 4.)

In clarifying one last major confusion, it can be observed that senile dementia and senile psychosis have been used interchangeably in some texts. In the past, however, senile dementia meant that the classic five basic signs of the chronic brain syndrome were more or less present; senile psychosis was used when obvious psychotic behavior was also manifested. This may be particularly important to know in reading old patient charts.

DESCRIPTION

The general characteristics of organic mental disorders found in older persons, as outlined in DSM-III, are described here.

1. The term "organic brain syndrome" now refers to a constellation of psychological or behavioral signs and symptoms (for example, delirium or dementia) without references to etiology. "Or-

---

[3] We will include here a few words on the evolution of the DSMs since the changes in the three editions have been confusing to many. The American Psychiatric Association adopted an official classification of mental disorders for the United States in 1952, called the *Diagnostic and Statistical Manual of Mental Disorders* (DSM-I, 1952). The primary concern for this classification was to facilitate communication. The DSM-I represented a series of compromises with a conglomeration of different conceptual approaches to the area of psychopathology. Psychiatry next became concerned with differences in nomenclature across national boundaries. The second edition of the DSM (DSM-II, 1968) was formed in conjunction with the World Health Organization, and the result was intended to form the basis for international communication. Because the two editions of the DSM were designed primarily for communication purposes, their scientific quality left much to be desired. Studies concluded that the reliability of these systems was mediocre. In DSM-III (1980) the emphasis has been put on enhancing the scientific value of the new classification, studying it through field trials at approximately 125 different institutions in the United States. Cate-

gories within the DSM-III are accompanied by detailed descriptions with explicit diagnostic rules.

Although the American Psychological Association's DSM-III liaison committee has given partial, qualified endorsement to DSM-III, a task force within the association concerned itself with creating a new classification designed to compete with the DSM-III. This classification emphasizes abnormal behaviors and their correlates, as contrasted with the categorical disease approach of the DSMs. Such a classification could provide a useful description of behaviors and their environmental contexts with the potential of being testable and responsive to contemporary scientific knowledge about psychopathology.

[4] The organic brain syndromes are (1) delirium, (2) dementia, (3) amnestic syndrome, (4) organic hallucinosis, (5) organic personality syndrome, (6) organic delusional syndrome, (7) organic affective syndrome.

[5] From Committee on Nomenclature and Statistics of the American Psychiatric Association: Diagnostic and statistical manual of mental disorders, ed. 1 (DSM-I), Washington, D.C., 1952, American Psychiatric Association, p. 24.

DEFINITIONS OF THE FIVE MENTAL SIGNS IN ORGANIC BRAIN SYNDROMES

1. **Impairment of memory.** There are three components to check: initial registration of the stimuli in the mind, retention of the memory that was registered, and ability to recall the memory voluntarily.
2. **Impairment of intellect.** This involves comprehension, calculation, general fund of information, and ability to learn.
3. **Impairment of judgment.** Comprehension and ability to weigh options and formulate decisions and actions must be checked.
4. **Impairment of orientation.** Orientation for time, place, and person depend on the capacities for attention, perception, and memory. Time is the first sphere to be impaired, place is next, and the identities of others and of oneself are the last sphere to be affected.
5. **Lability and shallowness of affect.** Excessive emotional responses, blunting of feeling and response, and shallowness and inappropriate affect are demonstrated.

---

ganic mental disorder'' means a particular organic brain syndrome in which the cause is known or presumed (for example, multiinfarct dementia). Thus ''organic brain syndrome'' is a more general term while ''organic mental disorder'' is more specific.

2. The classic distinctive features of an organic brain syndrome are (a) disturbance and impairment of memory, (b) impairment of intellectual function or comprehension, (c) impairment of judgment, (d) impairment of orientation, and (e) shallow or labile affect (see box above). These five mental signs may not all be seen at the same time or to the same degree, but they represent the core elements of organic brain disorder, particularly in full-blown and advanced states. The signs range in severity from barely perceptible changes to a profound loss of functioning and may be reversible or irreversible, with gradual or precipitous decline of mental abilities. Table 5-1 delineates the early warning (prodromal) characteristics of organic brain syndromes. These are extremely important to watch for since they represent the subtle beginnings of potentially devastating conditions.

3. The organic cause of an organic mental disorder may be a primary disease of the brain, a systemic illness secondarily affecting the brain, a chemical agent such as drugs or alcohol that dis-

turbs the brain transiently or permanently, or the withdrawal of a substance on which the person has become physiologically dependent.

For diagnostic purposes DSM-III emphasizes that a diagnosis of organic mental disorder should be based whenever possible on evidence from the history, the physical examination, or the laboratory tests of a specific organic factor judged to be etiologically related to the disturbance. This is to avoid trying to distinguish an organic from a functional disorder simply on psychopathology alone. There are probably both underdiagnosis and overdiagnosis of organic brain disorders. For example, Duckworth and Ross found that organic brain disorders were diagnosed with more than 50% greater frequency in New York than in either Toronto or London.[6] Diagnostic accuracy should improve in the future as knowledge and technical tools improve.

4. Organic brain syndromes have an extremely variable course depending on the underlying disorder. In the past, ''acuteness'' of onset was generally seen as synonymous with ''reversibility,'' while a ''chronic'' disorder was synonymous with

---

[6] Duckworth, G.S., and Ross, H.: Diagnostic differences in psychogeriatric patients in New York, Toronto, and London, England, Canadian Medical Association Journal **112:**847-851, 1975.

Table 5-1. Prodromal characteristics of organic brain syndrome

Early characteristics	Potential signs and symptoms*
Cognitive	
"Intellectual" decline	Perseveration
Reduced tempo of stream of thought	Increasingly impaired comprehension
Impoverishment of ideas	
Concreteness: impaired abstraction	Increasing memory loss (recent and remote)
Decline of recent memory	Confabulation
Registration, retention, recall, organization†	
Difficulty in maintaining attention and set	Perseveration, irrelevance
Behavioral and affective	
Reduced attentiveness	Progressive withdrawal and self-isolation
Reduced responsiveness	Apathy
Decreased interpersonal interaction	Pseudo-depression vs. depression
Less direct, immediate affective expression	
Liability to "disintegration" during stress	"Inappropriate" affect
Later characteristics	
Emotional lability	Emotional incontinence
Impaired orientation	Confusion
Impaired judgment	

Modified from Perlin, S., and Butler, R.N.: Psychiatric aspects of adaptation to the aging experience. In Birren, J.E., Butler, R.N., Greenhouse, S.W., Sokoloff, L., and Yarrow, M.R., editors: Human aging: a biological and behavioral study, Pub. No. (PHS) 986, Washington, D.C., 1963, U.S. Government Printing Office (reprinted as Pub. No. [HSM] 71-9051, 1971, 1974).
*A one-to-one relationship between presenting characteristic and potential symptom is not implied. Other symptoms may include irritability, apathy, suspiciousness, and slovenliness.
†Impaired organization refers to the inability to remember (and utilize) items in a time-related sequence.

"irreversibility." However, such pairing of concepts has not been demonstrated to be clinically accurate. Thus acuteness is now used simply to indicate a sudden onset, while chronicity refers to disorders lasting months or years. Yet both may be reversible or irreversible, depending on the disorder that is causing them. Often a program of treatment is the only way to discover what is reversible and what is not, especially when two or more disorders are existing together.

5. The outcome of organic mental disorders can be summarized as follows: Disorders like metabolic disturbances, ingestion of toxic substances, and systemic illnesses are more likely to be temporary and may allow full recovery if properly treated. Any disorder causing structural damage in the brain itself is likely to cause permanent impairment. But even when damage is permanent, many of the emotional and physical symptoms can

be treated, resulting in support and actual improvement of functioning.

6. The two most common organic brain syndromes found in older people are delirium and dementia. Delirium is roughly equivalent to the earlier DSM-I concept of acute brain syndrome and dementia to chronic brain syndrome. Both syndromes imply relatively global cognitive impairment. Delirium is most often seen in the very young or the old (after age 60), while dementia is predominately seen in the old or, less commonly, in those approaching old age.

These syndromes overlap and may represent different phases of widespread brain pathology. Delirium is currently viewed as an acute brain failure resulting from widespread derangement of cerebral metabolism and neurotransmission disturbance. Dementia is viewed as a result of pathologic changes in cerebral neurons or their death.

7. The two most common forms of dementia in later life are primary degenerative dementia with senile onset (atrophy of the brain) and multiinfarct dementia (damage to the brain associated with vascular disease). These two disorders account for approximately 80% of the dementia of later life.

8. An accompanying feature of all the previously mentioned disorders is a psychological or behavioral change in the older person. It is often difficult to determine whether this is caused by direct damage to the brain or by the person's emotional reaction to cognitive and other psychological changes caused by the brain disorder. A course of treatment, both physical and psychological, often helps to clarify the diagnosis, although diagnostic fine-tuning in this area may be impossible with our present state of knowledge.

Delirium (previously known as ''acute'' or ''reversible'' brain syndrome)

Senile confusional states and senile delirium are other names for delirium in the medical literature.[7] Delirium usually develops over a short period of time, from hours to days. However, the concept of ''acuteness'' as it applies to brain syndromes should be clarified here since it has been the traditional term used in this context. Acute carries with it the notion of rapid onset, dramatic symptoms, and short duration—none of which is reliably present in the delirium of older people. Delirium may evolve slowly, especially if it results from systemic illness or metabolic imbalance. The term ''reversible'' is a more useful description; reversibility of the clinical course, even if not the cause of the brain pathology, remains the one consistent characteristic, especially if the diagnosis and treatment are applied promptly and accurately.

Delirium in its more subtle forms remains a frequently undiagnosed illness, more so in the United States than in some other countries, for example, England. The concept of delirium characterized as a reversible brain syndrome first began appearing in the literature in the 1930s, and in one study of a large municipal hospital, 13% of the patients were found to have reversible brain syndromes while 33% exhibited mixed reversible and irreversible disorders.[7a]

Symptoms

A sign of delirium is a fluctuating level of awareness, which may vary from mild confusion all the way to stupor or active delirium. Hallucinations may be present, particularly of visual rather than auditory type. The person typically is disoriented, mistaking one person for another, and other intellectual functions can also be impaired. Speech may be incoherent and thinking is disordered. Remote as well as recent memory is lost. Behaviorally, restlessness, a dazed expression, or aggressiveness may show themselves, and the person can appear frightened either by the disorientation or as a result of the vivid visual hallucinations. Delusions of persecution may be present. A predominant feature is disturbance of the sleep-waking cycle. Anxiety and lack of cooperativeness are other symptoms. Disturbances tend to fluctuate unpredictably in the course of a day and are often most severe at night.

It is important to note that there are no consistent or characteristic neuropathological findings in delirium, except for the presence of abnormal movements like various forms of tremors. Autonomic signs (tachycardia, sweating, flushed face, dilated pupils, and elevated blood pressure) are common.

Causes

Obtaining a detailed history from an observer (family, friend, acquaintance) is important, since the patient is unlikely to be able to supply it. Onset of the illness should be explored, with an account

[7] See the early paper of Engel, G.L., and Romano, J.: Delirium: a syndrome of cerebral insufficiency, Journal of Chronic Disease **9:**260-277, 1959.

[7a] Simon, A., and Cahan, R.: The acute brain syndrome in geriatric patients. In Mendel, W.M., and Epstein, L.J., editors: Acute psychotic reaction, psychiatric research reports of the American Psychiatric Association, Washington, D.C., 1963, American Psychiatric Association.

of preexistent disorders, and exposure to toxic substances should be carefully checked. Myriad possible causes for delirium exist, and we discuss the most prevalent later in this chapter (p. 105). (See Chapter 9 for a staged approach to the diagnosis of these conditions and a comprehensive tabulation of causes.)

Course of illness and treatment

Delirium has a relatively brief duration, usually less than a week. One consequence of failure to identify and treat delirium is death from the underlying and undiagnosed cause; another is that the disorder may shift to a more stable organic brain syndrome and the older person then becomes a chronic patient, often in a long-term institutional care facility or nursing home. Active hospital care and in most cases return to the community are the appropriate course of treatment. Currently even with proper diagnosis and treatment, a high immediate death rate during delirium is common (an estimated 40% die, either from exhaustion or from accompanying physical illness); but of those who survive the immediate crisis, a fast recovery and discharge from the hospital are also common. The person who survives the crisis has a good chance of returning to the community. It appears that much delirium can result in complete recovery, although little follow-up work has been done on older recovered patients to determine whether their health is maintained. Other delirium is revealed to be only partially reversible, with an underlying chronic disorder.

Psychiatric disorders can be a first signal pointing toward a developing delirium accompanied by dehydration and electrolyte disturbances. Psychiatrically oriented medical facilities should be available to deal with the pathophysiological crisis that brings the person to the attention of others. All medical personnel should be aware of and prepared to handle delirium since it is a true medico-psychiatric emergency. Treatment must be intensive but can often be short-term, with malnutrition usually causing the longest hospital stay.

Dementia (previously known as "chronic" or "irreversible" brain syndrome)
General observations

Dementia is a phenomenon that many lay people and all too many medical personnel refer to by the inaccurate and emotion-laden term "senility." Many times, for lack of a thorough evaluation, the usually more reversible diagnosis of delirium is also subsumed under this category and the entire conglomeration termed untreatable. As mentioned earlier it was only about 40 years ago that reversible and chronic disorders began to receive differential diagnosis and treatment. It is now becoming clear that one must look for reversibility in *all* disorders, even in those like dementia, which have been considered irreversible. A prime example is the dementia accompanying hypothyroidism. Some chronic conditions that have lasted months or even a year or more may be partly or completely reversible. But even when this is not the case, a careful plan of treatment should be initiated to make the patient as comfortable and functional as possible.

In some older persons with dementia, the brain impairments may represent the only behavior disturbance observed, with the rest of the personality and behavior remaining unchanged. These cases are uncomplicated in the sense that the person attempts to make suitable adjustments to disorders and has insight into what has happened to his or her intellectual abilities, especially in early stages.

■ Mrs. J, a hearty, good-natured woman of 83, compensated for her waning memory in a variety of ways. She made lists of things to remember, she tied letters to be mailed to the doorknob so she would see them when she went out, she attached her wallet and keys onto her belt or slip strap. She asked friends to call and remind her of appointments and she made deliberate efforts to read and talk about the daily newspapers "to keep my brain active."

Such a person can function fairly adequately with little assistance. Even when impairment has progressed to a more severe stage, the person can live at home if proper supports are given. Some persons also realize when they can no longer remain at home, and they seek institutional care on their own.

■ Sam B, a 79-year-old farmer, appeared sad, anxious, and perplexed. He was garrulous, agitated, and occasionally irritable and contentious. He showed flight of ideas and was distractable, with difficulties in maintaining attention and set. Affect was usually appropriate and of sufficient depth, yet he had marked shifts of mood.

He was diagnosed as having dementia, moderate and of 7 years' duration. His second diagnosis was personality trait disturbance, passive-aggressive personality, passive-dependent type, chronic and severe. His lifelong pattern was one of indecisiveness, dependency, and helplessness.

He had definite cognitive losses resulting in severe impairment. These were defects in remote memory, with unreliable judgment and somewhat shaky orientation. Performance on the mental status examination was patchy. His appearance was slovenly. Mr. B lacked insight into his cognitive losses and denied both these losses and his aging state.

In spite of the severity of his losses and his dependent personality, Mr. B made a decision completely on his own to seek admission to an old age home. He decided he would prefer to do this rather than live with a nephew. Mr. B predicted a good home adjustment for himself and did in fact adjust well.

When there are accompanying emotional symptoms, the situation, of course, becomes more complex. Associated behavioral reactions fall into several categories: first are the reactions caused by the deficit itself, as in senile dementia; second are emotional reactions and adaptations to the deficits; and third are reactions termed "release phenomena." The latter appear as latent personality traits and tendencies as a result of brain damage. Nearly every known morbid psychic phenomenon may be seen in organic brain syndromes, especially in the early stages of the syndrome. It is now generally agreed that not only the organic disorder but also the individual's basic personality, his inherited or constitutional traits, and the environmental situation affect the kind and severity of

symptoms that appear. People react to threats to their intellectual capacities in highly individualized ways, and this is most true in the beginning phases of decline. A conspicuous feature is often the presence of a successful social facade in which everything looks normal until one begins to examine responses more carefully, as in the case of the woman discussed below.

■ In a group of friends she enters into the conversation by taking an anecdotal role, discussing the older material that is well embedded in her memory. Only after one listens for a time does it become clear that she is circumstantial, slightly irrelevant, and telling the same stories over and over again to the same friends.

A leveling effect takes place as impairment increases, and in the final stages—"end-stage dementia"—the effect is one of "look alike" or sameness in response as vital basic capacities drop away. People may become completely mute or inattentive. There is also less immediate individuality of reaction when damage is sudden and massive (as with cerebrovascular accidents) rather than gradual.

Some clinicians believe that a pronounced emotional reaction is a hopeful sign, indicating that brain damage is minimal enough to allow the person energy and resources to elaborate on an emotional response. Goldfarb and others[7b] have observed that the presence of disorder or affect or thought content is indicative of a more favorable outlook for improvement, since the emotional reaction may be treatable. One must caution here that the emotional reaction itself can be intractable, particularly if it is associated with long-term personality problems. Actual treatment is the only reliable way to judge the reversibility of symptoms. We also wish to emphasize that advanced dementia is not necessarily the fixed condition it first appears to be and may respond to treatment. Orientation, for example, may be improved by providing direct instruction and supplying orientation aids such as lights, signs, colors, and sounds as

---

[7b]Goldfarb, A.I., personal communication, 1972.

well as clocks and calendars. Chronicity is often used as an excuse for not doing anything when there may be many treatment techniques that could comfort, support, and even greatly increase the functioning of brain-damaged individuals.

Memory changes are one of the most obvious and noticeable symptoms of dementia, since memory so intimately affects interpersonal relationships with family and friends. Everyone has seen the older person whose memory for past events is clear although he or she is unable to remember who came to visit today or what happened yesterday. It is a common notion that recent memory becomes destroyed in some manner by a deteriorative process in the brain, with memories from the past remaining intact longer. This conjures up a picture of a cranial filing system for memory storage, which protects its contents proportionate to the time elapsed since filing. Studies of the brain have not confirmed any such occurrence, nor are there reliable tests for remote memory that enable us to judge how accurate past reminiscences are. A more relevant explanation for recent memory loss is the postulation that brain damage interferes with registration of incoming stimuli and affects the ability for retention and recall. In this event, an experience that ordinarily would become a memory registers either inaccurately or not at all.

■ I feel very often that Henry is simply not receiving new knowledge, that he does not retain the facts and experiences he does receive, that he is not registering visual experience. . . . On a recent trip he tried to follow the instructions of tour guides ("on your left you see . . .") but would look straight ahead or turn to the left long after the scene had passed.

An added factor in memory loss is the possibility of emotional influence on recall capacities. Older people may need to deny, to disremember, or to distort that which is overwhelming or too painful to face; depression and preoccupation with problems may not be noticed yet can interfere with learning and memory.

■ Judge G has been experiencing slow, progressive, organic changes but is only numbly aware of them. He cannot face up to the degree and the implications of what is happening to him. He seems to live in a state of constant fear, inadequate to even small demands on him, forgetting everything, missing trains, and becoming confused about schedules or well-rehearsed plans. I am never sure whether the confirmation of his fears that he will do everything badly is a true mental disability or a self-fulfilling prophecy.

Disorientation is a more easily and accurately tested symptom. Disorientation about time (the day, the hour, the year) is the first major confusion to occur as a result of dementia. Loss of sense of place (where am I, what is this place, what country am I in) is likely to follow and, last, the person loses the ability to recognize other people and eventually cannot remember who he or she is. One sees this in individuals who do not recognize themselves in the mirror, do not know their own names or the names of loved ones, etc.

Neurological deficits such as the following may be found, especially in multiinfarct dementia:

acalculia Loss of a previously possessed facility with arithmetic calculation.

agnosia Inability to recognize objects presented by way of one or more sensory modalities that cannot be explained by a defect in elementary sensation or a reduced level of consciousness or alertness.

agraphia Loss of a previously possessed facility for writing.

anosognosia The apparent unawareness of or failure to recognize one's own functional defect, for example, hemiplegia, hemianopia.

aphasia Loss of a previously possessed facility of language comprehension or production that cannot be explained by sensory or motor defects or diffuse cerebral dysfunction.

    anomic or amnestic aphasia Loss of the ability to name objects.

    Broca's aphasia Loss of the ability to produce spoken and (usually) written language with comprehension retained.

    Wernicke's aphasia Loss of the ability to comprehend language, coupled with the production of inappropriate language.

apraxia Loss of a previously possessed ability to perform skilled motor acts that cannot be explained by weakness, abnormal muscle tone, or elementary incoordination.

> **constructional apraxia** An acquired difficulty in drawing two-dimensional objects or forms or in producing or copying three-dimensional arrangements of forms or shapes.

confabulation Fabrication of stories in response to questions about situations or events that are not recalled.

dysarthria Difficulty in speech production as a result of incoordination of speech apparatus.

perseveration Tendency to emit the same verbal or motor response again and again to varied stimuli.[8]

In older people there are two predominate types of dementia: primary degenerative dementia with senile onset (in DSM-II it is known as "senile dementia" under an added heading labeled "psychosis"; other former terms are "senile brain disease," "senile psychosis," and "progressive idiopathic dementia") and multiinfarct dementia (called "psychosis associated with cerebral arteriosclerosis" in DSM-II). For purposes of brevity we will refer to primary degenerative dementia with senile onset as "senile dementia." See Table 5-2 for an example of one study of the incidence of various types of dementia.

Senile dementia and multiinfarct dementia may look a good deal alike and thus, as mentioned earlier in the chapter, were not differentiated from each other until recently.

■ An 80-year-old, male, state hospital patient was diagnosed as having an organic brain syndrome, but differentiation between senile dementia and multiinfarct dementia was not possible. The patient was wizened, physically deteriorated, weak, and somewhat sloven in appearance. His sense of balance and direction was impaired, and his verbal productivity was increased although not to the point of garrulousness. He was distractable (as by noises in the hall or by room fixtures), occasionally irrelevant, and at times perseverative and had a delayed reaction time.

---

[8] Modified from A psychiatric glossary, ed. 5, Washington, D.C., 1980, American Psychiatric Association.

Table 5-2. Causes of dementia in 140 hospital autopsies

Cause	Occurrence (%)
Alzheimer's disease	48
Mixed Alzheimer's disease and arteriosclerosis	12
Arteriosclerosis	20
Other (pernicious anemia, hypothyroidism, tumor)	12
No explanation	8

From Tomlinson, B.E., personal communication, 1976.

It was not possible to obtain a history because of his confusion. But, confused as he was, he was able to maintain emotional contact with the nurse on the ward. He was disoriented with respect to time, place, and person and was unable to give his own name.

Some of his responses were seen as defensive (he denied his hospitalization and his age). He confabulated, weaving memory and fantasy into answers to questions that he either could not or would not answer in a more direct manner. He complained about his memory. There was some question as to his being at times aphasic rather than uncomprehending.

He was confused over once-familiar procedures, such as lighting cigarettes. On several occasions he would have placed the lighted end of a cigarette in his mouth had the interviewer not intervened.

In short, he had severe impairment in intellectual functioning, memory, judgment, and orientation; yet he retained occasional glimmers of insight and appropriate emotional response.

Pathological examination provides the most useful and reliable data on differences between the two, since clinical examination may be less precise and even contradictory. The two disorders have been thought to occur simultaneously in about 20% of the cases.[9]

As Rothschild (1956) pointed out, early psychi-

---

[9] Some investigators suggest an even higher association between the two disorders. See Müller, C., and Ciompi, L., editors: Senile dementia, Berne, Switzerland, 1968, Hans Huber.

atry attempted to link the cause of mental disorders with demonstrable cerebral changes. Because of the observable brain damage found in senile dementia and multiinfarct dementia, it was widely believed that such damage was the only cause of mental symptoms. However, later research in the 1940s and 1950s found generally poor correlation between the degree of deterioration and neuropathological changes as it became evident that many inconsistencies existed between the extent of brain damage and the severity of mental symptoms, Grünthal[9a] and Rothschild, in the past, have noted the discrepancies. Persons who had little change neuropathologically sometimes showed serious mental and psychiatric change, while others with profound brain damage had only mild psychiatric disorders. Even normal older individuals can have brain changes that appear as marked as those in individuals with clinically obvious senile dementia or multiinfarct dementia. Thus the anatomical brain changes are only part of the factors determining the psychiatric symptoms; one must consider the individual's own constitutional char-

acteristics, personality, heredity, and environmental stress. Thus we repeat and reemphasize that the organic disorders, like so many other disorders in late life, must be viewed socially and psychologically as well as medically—in diagnosis, prognosis, and treatment—particularly in early stages before the damage is too global and leveling. The DSM-III multiaxial evaluation is a positive move in this direction.

Studies of the 1960s and 1970s have shown that despite discrepancies, there are significant correlations between scores for dementia and counts of senile plaques.[10] Roth et al. believe the critical plaque count is 14 per microscopic field (in postmortem examination tissue); in other words, dementia is likely to be present above a count of 14.[11]

[9a] Grünthal, E.: Klinisch-anatomisch vergleichende untersuchungen über den Greisenblödsinn, Zeitschrift für de gesamte Neurologie und Psychiatrie **111:**763, 1927.

[10] Corsellis, J.A.N.: Mental illness and the aging brain, London, 1962, Oxford University Press. See also Roth, M., Tomlinson, B.E., and Blessed, G.: Correlations between scores for dementia and counts of "senile" plaques in cerebral gray matter of elderly patients, Nature **209:**109-110, 1966.

[11] Roth, M., Tomlinson, B.E., and Blessed, G.: Correlations between scores for dementia and counts of "senile" plaques in cerebral gray matter of elderly patients, Nature **209:**109-110, 1966.

POSSIBLE CONNECTIONS BETWEEN AGING AND THE DEVELOPMENT OF ALZHEIMER'S DISEASE

1. The core of each neuritic plaque is composed of amyloid, an abnormal protein not usually found in the brain. Amyloid formation has been linked to "free radicals," a highly reactive class of molecule fragments (with unpaired electrons) that combine readily with other pieces of molecules. One theory of aging is that it is a result of damage of free radicals. Alzheimer's disease may be connected with this process.
2. The neurofibrillary tangles and neuritic plaques seen in Alzheimer's disease occur in the course of "normal" aging to some extent, independent of disease.
3. If slow viruses turn out to be a factor in Alzheimer's disease they are themselves age-related or time-related. In short, they require time to develop.
4. There are age-related changes in the immune system that may bear on the development of autoantibodies, which may have an etiological relationship to Alzheimer's disease.
5. A slow accumulation of aluminum with the passage of time or aging may be a factor in Alzheimer's disease.
6. In the familial form of Alzheimer's disease (there are two forms—the familial and sporadic) there is a genetic penetrance that is age-related.

*Primary degenerative dementia with
senile onset (also known as senile dementia
of the Alzheimer type[12])*

Senile dementia (the abbreviation for the above phrases) refers to a usually chronic progressive decline in mental functioning. This is associated with changes in the brain, primarily the dissolution of brain cells themselves. The disorder occurs much more frequently in women than in men, probably because of their longer life expectancy, with age of onset from 60 to 90 years (the average is 75 years). However, sex linkage itself may be a factor. Surveys indicate that although men have a shorter life-span than women, they are, when they do survive, generally healthier—both physically and mentally. Significant memory impairment is more frequently found in older women than in older men of the same age. Estimates made on the basis of community surveys in the United Kingdom report about 4.1% of the population over 65 years have senile dementia, and 10% to 11% have some degree of dementia.[13] The disorder may look similar to involutional melancholia, Korsakoff's syndrome (pp. 134-135), and many other men-tal disturbances caused by such conditions as malnutrition, heart disease, and toxemia.

Brain pathology. The brain cells themselves atrophy and degenerate, independent of vascular change, most strikingly in the cerebral cortex. Senile plaques, neurofibrillary tangles,[14] and gran-ulovacuolar degeneration of cells in the hippocampal cortex occur in brains of normal older people as well as of demented individuals but differ in amount and distribution in the two groups.[15]

Other parts of the body's soft tissue may also atrophy but not as severely as the brain, which actually loses weight. Single nervous cells are destroyed in a widespread manner, without breaking down the structure of nervous tissue as a whole. Additionally, about 50% of patients also show changes caused by vascular disease with moderate atherosclerosis, but these changes usually are of minor importance.

Clinical symptoms. The older person may pass slowly from normal old age to senile dementia with no abrupt changes (unless accompanied by arteriosclerotic disease).[16] Friends and relatives gradually notice small differences in physical, mental, and emotional functioning.

■ He has called our house, where we have lived for nearly 5 years, an "unhappy" one, comparing it unfavorably to the small, crowded house we had lived in previously where things had been all right. He thus

---

[12] The alternative name "senile dementia of the Alzheimer type" derives from the fact that most 65-year-old and above (senium) patients with clinically defined senile dementia have the same pathological changes in their brain (confirmed through autopsy) as do patients younger than 65 (presenium) who have what is called Alzheimer's disease. (See pp. 107-108 for discussion of Alzheimer's disease.) It is not known whether these are both the same disease regardless of age of onset or whether they are two or more separate diseases that look similar but have different causes. Until further research is done, it has been recommended during the course of a symposium on Alzheimer's disease that the dementia be called Alzheimer's disease before age 65 and senile dementia of the Alzheimer type after 65. See Katzman, R., Terry, R.D., and Bick, K.L., editors: Alzheimer's disease: senile dementia and related disorders, New York, 1978, Raven Press.

[13] Prevalence has been estimated conservatively at ages 65 to 74 as 0.5% in men and 1% in women; corresponding figures for men and women age 75 and over are 4.4% and 9.3% respectively (Kay, D.W.K.: Epidemiological aspects of organic brain disease in the aged. In Gaitz, C.M., editor: Aging and the brain, New York, 1972, Plenum Publishing Corp., pp. 15-27).

[14] The cellular and subcellular elements of these plaques and tangles have only begun to be understood through the use of the electron microscope. In 1963 Terry and Kidd independently reported on the structure of the neurofibrillary tangles in Alzheimer's disease. See also Terry, R.D., and Wisniewski, H.: The ultrastructure of the neurofibrillary tangle and the senile plaque. In Wolstenholme, G.E.W., and O'Connor, M., editors: Alzheimer's disease and related conditions, London, 1970, J. & A. Churchill, Ltd. Terry and Wisniewski concluded that each twisted fiber is made up of paired helical filaments (PHF).

[15] Ball, M.J.: Topographic distribution of neurofibrillary tangles and granulovacuolar degeneration in hippocampal cortex of aging and demented, Acta Neuropathollogica (Berlin) **42:** 73-80, 1978.

[16] For a highly personal account written by the grandsons of an older man, see Jury, M., and Jury, D.: Gramp, New York, 1976, Grossman Publishers, Inc.

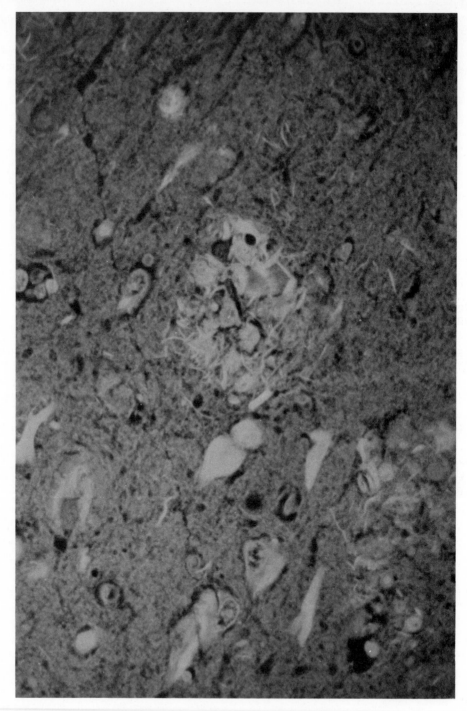

Senile plaque—sign of senile dementia.

Photo micrography courtesy Dr. Robert Terry, Department of Pathology,
Albert Einstein College of Medicine, New York.

comes close to realizing how long the present development has really gone on. I would say that I have been conscious of changes in him for perhaps 6 years. But only in the last 2 years could I have put my finger on definite differences, and the last year has unquestionably been worse of the 2.

Previously personality traits may become exaggerated.

■ A patient's husband writes, "In areas where she has always deferred to me for either judgment or action, she is abdicating more and more, hardly participating even passively. This does not represent so severe a departure from the past pattern: I have always been the more practical and commonsensical of the two—but it now means that she depends on me wholly instead of heavily."

Early features of senile dementia are errors in judgment, decline in personal care and habits, impairment of capacity for abstract thought, and lack of interest and apathy. Loosening of inhibitions can be an early sign. A host of emotional reactions are possible with depression, anxiety, and irritability being the most frequent, particularly in early stages. Depression is usually superficial rather than profound and is based on anxiety and loss. As the deterioration increases, mental symptoms proliferate and the traditional five signs of organic dysfunction become more evident (see description of organic brain syndromes, pp. 90-93). Hallucinations can be present, especially at night. Poor orientation as to time, place, and person as well as confused comprehension (for example, registering a single impression but not the whole picture), rambling incoherent speech, and fabrication may be seen. Sleeplessness and restlessness are common, and the person may wander away from home. Paranoid tendencies may be exacerbated or appear for the first time, and one occasionally sees manic or hypomanic states. There is frequently loss of sphincter control, often with urinary incontinence, even fecal incontinence.

Review of traditional types of "senile psychosis." We wish to review briefly the traditional but now outmoded classification of "senile psychosis," since literature in the field of aging contains many references to it that might otherwise be confusing to the reader. Five types of "senile psychosis" were described as follows.

1. *Simple deterioration.* A progressive memory loss occurs, with loss of contact and initiative, combined with irritability and eventual mild stupor.

2. *Depressed and agitated type.* The usual senile changes are accompanied by restlessness, self-centeredness, depression, and hypochondriasis.

3. *Delirium and confused type.* A generally reversible process with acute onset, this represents a reaction to physical and/or social stress rather than a strictly senile process. However, chronic confusional states are sometimes seen.

4. *Presbyophrenic type.* Literally meaning "old brain," the term "presbyophrenic" refers to psychosis that occurs more often in women than in men. It is marked by confabulation and retention defect and is often thought of as a presenile disorder rather than a senile psychotic classification. The presbyophrenic patient seems alert on the surface, with normal-appearing social manners and level of awareness. But in discussion or interview it soon becomes clear that there is much damage behind the normal facade, particularly in orientation and memory. The retention deficit is covered up by confabulation, in which the person fills in gaps in memory by fabricating and by accepting facts offered to him as his own ideas. The person sincerely accepts the fabrication as real and has no understanding of his memory impairment. Such a person may be jovial and good-natured, restless in an aimless fashion, talkative, and rambling. The picture is similar to that of Korsakoff's syndrome.

5. *Paranoid type.* Memory loss and other evidence of decreased mental functioning may be slight in early stages.[17] A delusional system is

---

[17] There are state hospital data comparing preservation of intellectual abilities among the subtypes of schizophrenia. The paranoid subtype appears to be relatively protected against deterioration, as compared to other types. It has been surmised that this is a result of the continued intellectual stimulation required to build paranoid defenses (Albert, H.S., Bigelow, N.J.T., and Bryan, L.L.: Cerebral arteriosclerosis in the paranoid state, The Psychiatric Quarterly **21**:305-313, 1947).

formed, often accompanied by hallucinations. An earlier, lifelong tendency toward suspiciousness and projection is a factor in the development of the paranoid type. The delusions are most often persecutory, grandiose, or erotic—with emphasis on money, personal harm, and wish fulfillment. At first the personality may be quite intact, but intellectual impairment gradually develops.

These five types are really all variants of the same process and reflect personal, social, and other reactions and differences. For example, paranoid and depressed states are simply emotional reactions to underlying brain disorders. The classification is of limited practical application, since persons may present one or more types at once or may move from one to another in the course of illness.

Causes. Little is known about the causes of senile dementia, but there are very promising research leads. Spectacular advances in neuroscience (new methodological approaches and technical tools, especially new knowledge of cerebral neurotransmitters and new techniques to measure regional cerebral metabolism) and increased research attention specifically given to senile dementia may lead to answers. Already, promising evidence exists of a deficiency in the central cholinergic systems in senile dementia.[18] The enzymes that synthesize and degrade acetylcholine—choline acetyltransferase (CAT) and perhaps acetylcholinesterase (AChE)—are decreased.

There is as yet no agreement on what the difference between normal and pathological aging is or what the aspects of pathological aging are. Changes similar to those seen in senile dementia occur to a lesser degree in normal old age. Some have argued that senile dementia is a quantitative increase in normal involutional change, while others believe that it is qualitatively different. Dorken,[19] the NIMH aging study, and other researchers have provided work that supports the latter view, as does our own clinical experience. But there is consensus that senile dementia is a disease highly associated with but not inevitable to aging. Some theorize that senile dementia is an autoimmune disease.[20] There is also the aluminum hypothesis[21] (next to oxygen and silicon, aluminum is the third most ubiquitous element in the universe). Additionally, a slow virus etiology has been proposed. Others implicate genetics as a causative factor. (See the box on p. 103.) The morbidity risks for senile dementia among relatives of senile dementia patients are about 4.3 times the corresponding risks for the general population.[22] There also appears to be a strong environmental and personality factor, more so than in multiinfarct dementia. In fact in a few instances, what is seen as senile dementia may be a massive defense against the reality of old age and death.[23] Stress itself may play a role in reinforcing or accelerating senile dementia.[24]

Course of illness and treatment. Senile dementia is eventually fatal, with a fairly steady and progressive course. It is one of the main causes of death in old age. Persons may live 10 years or

---

[18] Davies, P.: Studies on the neurochemistry of central cholinergic systems in Alzheimer's disease. In Katzman, R., Terry, R.D., and Bick, K.L., editors: Alzheimer's disease: senile dementia and related disorders, New York, 1978, Raven Press, pp. 453-460.

[19] Dorken, H.: Normal senescent decline and senile dementia: their differentiation by psychological tests, Medical Services Journal **14:**18-23, 1958.

[20] Nandy, K.: Brain-reactive antibodies in aging and senile dementia. In Katzman, R., Terry, R.D., and Bick, K.L., editors: Alzheimer's disease: senile dementia and related disorders, New York, 1978, Raven Press, pp. 503-512.

[21] Crapper, D.R., Krishnan, S.S., and Dalton, A.J.: Brain aluminum distribution in Alzheimer's disease and experimental neurofibrillary degeneration, Science **180:**511-513, 1973. See also Arieff, A.I., Cooper, J.D., Armstrong, D., and Lazarowitz, V.C.: Dementia, renal failure, and brain aluminum, Annals of Internal Medicine **90:**741, 1979.

[22] Larsson, T., Sjogren, T., and Jacobson, G.: Senile dementia, a clinical, sociomedical and genetic study, Acta Psychiatrica and Neurologica Scandinavia **39**(supp. 167):1-259, 1963. It has also been suggested that there is a predisposing autosomal dominant gene with age-related penetrance that may be as high as 40% by age 70.

[23] Gillespie, W.H.: Some regressive phenomena in old age, British Journal of Medical Psychology **56:**303-309, 1962.

[24] Kral, V.A.: Stress and mental disorders in the senium, Medical Services Journal (Canada) **18:**363-370, 1962.

**PROMISING "LEADS" FOR THE CAUSATION OF
PRIMARY DEGENERATIVE DEMENTIA OF THE ALZHEIMER TYPE**

1. Cholinergic system deficiency: reduced enzyme activity
2. Genetic theories
   a. Familial form
   b. Epidemiological relation to Down's syndrome (trisomy 21) and hematological malignancies
3. Increased aluminum/parathyroid disease
4. Autoimmune disease/antibrain antibodies
5. Slow and latent viruses

---

more after onset of symptoms, but average survival is 5 years. (Antibiotics and modern care have prolonged the "natural" survival rate of such diseases.) Emotional reactions may respond to treatment. However, eventually, in many cases, the personality dies or fades away before the death of the body. Physical functioning can improve with proper support even though the physical loss itself is irreparable. Many persons would be able to remain in their own homes throughout most of the course of illness if adequate services and assistance were available.

Multiinfarct dementia (previously known as "psychosis with cerebral arteriosclerosis")

Multiinfarct dementia is a chronic disorder that often shows an uneven and erratic downward progression, as compared to the more steady decline seen in senile dementia. The disorder is associated with damage to the cerebral blood vessels through arteriosclerosis (a term that includes both *arteriosclerosis* —a hardening of the vessel wall—and *atherosclerosis* —a narrowing and closing of the vessel itself).[25] The blood flow to the brain is inter-

Table 5-3. Mean values of cerebral oxygen metabolic rate ($CMRO_2$) in various groupings of subjects

Groupings	Number	$CMRO_2$
Normal young	15	3.5
Normal healthy aged	28	3.3
Aged with chronic brain syndrome without psychosis	2	2.7
Aged with chronic brain syndrome with arteriosclerosis with psychosis	10	2.7

Based on data from Butler, R.N., Dastur, D.K., and Perlin, S.: Relationships of senile manifestations and chronic brain syndromes to cerebral circulation and metabolism, Journal of Psychiatric Research **3:**229-238, 1965.

fered with and, as a result, insufficient oxygen and nutrients reach the brain. Hypertension and/or diabetes are frequently present. Table 5-3 compares the cerebral oxygen circulation[26] in various age groups and diagnostic categories.

Multiinfarct dementia is found in middle and later life because it is a progressive disease that may remain asymptomatic until that point. Age of onset is between 50 and 70 years, with an average age of 66 years. It is much less common than senile dementia and appears more common in men than in women.

---

[25] The presence of retinal arteriosclerosis does not establish the presence of cerebral arteriosclerosis, nor does its absence assure the absence of arteriosclerosis in the brain. (See Alpers, B.J., Forster, F.M., and Herbut, P.A.: Retinal cerebral and systemic arteriosclerosis, a histopathologic study, Archives of Neurology and Psychiatry **60:**440-456, 1948.) Similarly, evidence of peripheral arteriosclerosis is not diagnostic of cerebral changes. Arteriosclerosis is not a generalized condition: not all organs and tissues of the body are uniformly affected.

[26] Using the technique of Kety and Schmidt (Kety, S.S.: Human cerebral blood flow and oxygen consumption as related to aging, Journal of Chronic Diseases **3:**478-486, 1956).

Brain pathology. The brain typically shows areas of softening with complete deterioration of cerebral tissue over a circumscribed, limited area. The damaged area may be anemic or hemorrhagic resulting from the inadequate blood supply caused by blocked vessels.[27]

Clinical symptoms. Early symptoms are dizziness, headaches, decreased physical and mental vigor, and vague physical complaints. Onset can be gradual or sudden, with over 50% of cases occurring acutely in the form of a sudden attack of confusion. Cases with slower onset can look much like senile dementia. There is usually a gradual intellectual loss, and *impairment of memory tends to be spotty* rather than complete. A person may be unable to remember one minute and regain total capacity the next. There may be a certain degree of insight and judgment, again in a spotty sense. The course is up and down rather than progressively downhill. (Note the ''lucid interval'' in forensic psychiatry; see Chapter 9.) The person may hallucinate and become delirious, indicating the insufficiency of cerebral circulation. Focal neurological abnormalities are often present along with dysarthria (speech disturbance) and an abnormal gait with short steps. The limbs may be spastic, the reflexes brisk.

Paranoid reactions are often misdiagnosed as multiinfarct dementia. One of us (R.N.B.) went into a state hospital to gain volunteers for research and requested the hospital to indicate definitive cases of multiinfarct dementia. In 30% of the cases referred, patients showed clear instances of paranoid reaction with minimal or no evidence of brain damage. An example was the following.

■ Diagnosis for this 74-year-old female hospital patient had been probable organic brain syndrome, specifically multiinfarct dementia. However, her faculties were quite clear except for mild memory impairment and impaired judgment as a consequence of her delusional system (not a cognitive defect). She did not show the classic signs of a person with an organic brain syndrome. There was no disorientation, no substantial decline in intellectual functions, nor a lability of affect.

The woman had a hearing impairment and language difficulty (she was born in Europe), which made interviewing difficult and undoubtedly contributed to her poor performance on vocabulary tests. During the mental status examination she had good retention, logical memory, and minimal difficulty in abstracting. She adapted well to the interview, was not depressed, and was likable and affable.

Her predominant symptoms were those of paranoia. Her delusional system concerned her admission to the hospital, and she implicated her daughter-in-law and other family members as conspirators in an elaborate plot to ''put her away.'' (Her general sense of being abandoned by her family was built into a complicated delusional process, which nevertheless had some roots in reality.)

The misdiagnosis of such cases is too often the result of careless examination and unclear diagnostic thinking.

Causes. The causes of arteriosclerosis are still unclear, although many explanations have been offered. Lipid dysfunction, heredity, diet (especially cholesterol), smoking, environmental pollution, lack of exercise, and other elements have been held contributory. Some claim that a head injury may accelerate cerebral arteriosclerosis, but we have not seen examples of this.

Fisher[28] stated that cerebrovascular dementia ''is a matter of strokes, large and small,'' over a period of time rather than a single stroke. (Pearce and Miller[29] observed that it is rare for a patient with a stroke in a single hemisphere of the brain to have significant residual global intellectual deficit.) Roth[30] reported a relationship between the demen-

---

[27] See Hachinski, V.C., Lassen, N.A., and Marshall, J.: Multiinfarct dementia: a cause of mental deterioration in the elderly, Lancet **2**:207-210, 1974.

[28] Fisher, C.M.: Dementia in cerebral vascular disease. In Toole, J.F., Siekert, R.G., and Wisnant, J.P., editors: Cerebral vascular diseases, sixth Princeton conference, New York, 1968, Grune and Stratton, Inc., p. 232.

[29] Pearce, J., and Miller, E.: Clinical aspects of dementia, London, 1973, Baillière Tindall, p. 30.

[30] Roth, M.: Classification and aetiology of mental disorders of old age: some recent developments. In Kay, D.W.K., and Walk, A., editors: Recent developments in psychogeriatrics, Ashford, England, 1971, Headley Brothers, Ltd., p. 1.

tia score during life and the volume of infarcted (destroyed) cerebral tissue found at autopsy. The severity of the dementia seems to be related to repeated infarcts of the brain rather than to the extent of cerebral arteriosclerosis.

Course of illness and treatment. There is great diversity from person to person and even with the same person at different times. A cerebrovascular accident causing confusion or clouding of the mental state can lead quickly to a fatal outcome or may produce an organic condition lasting as long as 10 to 15 years. The average survival of those admitted to a mental hospital has been estimated in the past to be 3 to 4 years.

The hospitalized cardiac patient or the patient with a general vascular disease may also develop multiinfarct dementia. A goodly number die, but those who survive may experience subsidence of the problem, with varying amounts of intellectual impairment. Good remissions may be possible in a number of cases, when intellectual capacity is retained. Early treatment of hypertension and vascular disease may prevent further progression. However, if new attacks follow, each does additional damage. Often the person's physical condition is worse than that seen in senile dementia because of the neurological or cardiac problem; many are bedridden, at least during acute stages. Death, when it occurs, is usually from cerebrovascular accidents, arteriosclerotic heart disease, or pneumonia.

In treatment there is a greater need for special medical care because of the critical physical involvement in multiinfarct dementia.[31] If and when remission occurs, the person can often benefit from psychotherapy, physical therapy, recreation, and all the usual therapeutic supports and services. Physical capacities are often a greater problem than intellectual capacities, although intellectual damage can be profound after massive or repeated cardiac attacks or strokes.

Reversible causes of mental impairment resulting in delirium, dementia, or both

Because reversibility may be possible in both dementia and delirium, we have organized a list of some of the most prevalent reversible causes of these two mental impairments. (See Chapter 9 for a more comprehensive list of reversible disorders leading to delirium and dementia or both.)

Heart diseases

Congestive heart failure refers to decompensation resulting from the heart's declining capacity to pump blood. Thus oxygen, sugar, and necessary nutrients are undersupplied to the brain; a conservatively estimated 13% of acute myocardial infarctions come to medical attention primarily as confusional states.

Malnutrition and anemia

A large proportion of the older population of the United States is undernourished, although this is vehemently denied by some medical and lay people. Older people develop reversible brain syndromes associated with avitaminosis, pellagra,[32] and metabolic disorders. Malnourishment in older persons has both social and economic associations. Poverty forces many to go hungry, while social isolation and depression from living alone can result in persons' simply not eating regularly or well. Older people may have problems in getting to stores for shopping, especially when physical infirmities are present. Appetites may decline as a result of depression, anxiety, or illness, and the loss of teeth can interfere with eating solid foods. Therefore, even middle-class and upper-class older persons may be surprisingly malnourished.

---

[31] In an occasional case, surgical treatment (endarterectomy or angioplasty) is indicated in instances of occlusive disease of the extracranial cerebrovascular supply, particularly in early and incomplete obstructions.

[32] Pellagra is a disease characterized by mental, neurological, cutaneous, mucous membrane, and gastrointestinal symptoms. It is caused by a severe deficiency of niacin (nicotinic acid) or its amide (niacinamide) along with their amino acid precursor, tryptophan. As late as 1945, H.A. Meyersburg reported cases of brain syndrome from pellagra in older people in his work (See Meyersburg, H.A.: Senile psychosis and pellagra: a report of two cases, New England Journal of Medicine **233:**173-176, 1945).

Infection

Infection may not provoke the same level of effective bodily protection as in the young (fever, increase in blood white cell count, etc.). With infection comes fatigue and sometimes dehydration, which leave the individual vulnerable to mental confusion.

Cerebrovascular accidents

A temporary lack of blood supply to the brain (transient ischemic attack [TIA]) can result in an undersupply of oxygen (hypoxia), followed by aphasia (the loss of the ability to speak), interference with vision, and paralysis. A common event among older persons is a stroke; the person becomes unconscious and, on regaining consciousness (if he or she survives), may pass through an acute state of confusion before a restoration of mental normality. If strokes are massive or repeated, chronic disorders eventually result.

Variations are described by Alvarez—the so-called little strokes—which probably occur much more frequently than realized. These produce transient confusion, nausea and vomiting, dizziness, and numbness of the extremities but not full-scale paralysis and aphasia.[33]

Drugs and other toxic substances

With increasing use of drugs of all kinds in the medical and psychiatric management of older people, drug reactions are a significant cause of reversible disorders. Suicide attempts through use of drugs or toxic materials are another factor. Barbiturates, tranquilizers, bromides, thiocyanates, gases, and hormones are not unmixed blessings: for example, both reversible and irreversible organic brain disorders can occur with use of the cortisone series; tranquilizers may cause damage if prescribed too long; steroids can affect mood, with manic or depressive manifestations. Older people who are undernourished or who have markedly reduced kidney function or arteriosclerosis may show

---

[33] One must always beware not to misread aphasia as intellectual deterioration. Aphasia may be transitory, partial (called dysphasia), and responsive to treatment.

greater negative response to even small amounts of drugs. The pathologic brain conditions resulting from medications ordered by doctors are termed "iatrogenic" disorders, meaning they have resulted paradoxically from medical treatment itself and not from any usual physical dysfunction. Diuretics (such as the thiazides) may lead to dehydration and mental confusion. Levodopa (anti-parkinsonian) and indomethacin (antiarthritic) may cause psychotic behavior.

Older people may also have exaggerated drug reactions that do not reach acute confusional proportions; examples are agitation from barbiturates or depression from tranquilizers. Such reactions can increase if the person is not clear about the side effects of various drugs and adds his or her own fears to the clinical picture. Thus tranquilized persons may become extremely depressed if they fear loss of physical powers and are not aware that this is transitory. Doctors and medical personnel owe each person an exact description of what to expect from drugs, so unnecessary emotional complications can be avoided.

Head trauma

For people over age 65, 72% of all deaths from falls and 30% of all pedestrian fatalities are a result of head trauma. Older people are more subject than younger ones to brain injuries in any type of accident, even minor ones. Nonfatal head injuries may leave the older person severely disabled (for example, by the subdural hematomas that occur after falls resulting from weakness, lack of coordination, or alcoholism). Tumor growths (neoplasms) and brain surgery are other traumas that can impair brain functioning.

A trauma can result in delirium followed by an irreversible disorder; for example, a head injury may lead to concussion and/or coma, traumatic delirium, and then Korsakoff's syndrome with confabulation and fabrication.

Alcohol

Alcoholism is more common in old age than is generally recognized. Alcohol, as a central nervous system depressant, impairs intellectual functioning. Intoxication at any age results in a reversible brain syndrome.

Other causes

Diabetic acidosis, liver failure, dehydration, uremia, emphysema, hypothyroidism (myxedema), brain tumors, general surgery, blindfolding during eye surgery, drastic environmental changes, and bereavements are some of the other common causes of reversible brain syndromes. Another cause is hypercalcemia caused by metastatic carcinoma of lung or breast, primary hyperparathyroidism,[34] multiple myeloma, or Paget's disease. Nonketotic hyperosmolarity syndrome, in which hyperglycemia and confusion occur without any ketosis, is not an uncommon cause of reversible brain syndrome.

Older persons show much the same reactions as younger people to exhaustion, vitamin deficiencies, and general disease—but they are likely to be more vulnerable. In a study of admissions at San Francisco General Hospital, Simon (1963) referred to the social and environmental aspects of reversible brain syndrome. Persons with reversible brain syndrome tended to be removed from family ties, were more often men than women, and in many instances were alcoholic. In a number of cases the reversible syndrome was followed by or occurred simultaneously with an irreversible disorder because of permanent damage done to the brain, as in cerebral embolism, arterial hypertension, cardiorenal disease, cardiac decompensation, or circulatory disturbances. In these situations, some improvement was at times possible, but residual disorders remained. In persons with mixed reversible brain syndrome and irreversible brain syndrome, the environmental influence did not appear to be so prominent; physical deterioration, most often cardiovascular disease, was more evident.

PRESENILE DEMENTIA

Presenile dementia[35] includes a group of cortical brain diseases that clinically look like the senile dementia seen in older people; however, they occur earlier, in the 40- and 50-year age groups. Intellectual deterioration and personality disintegration are two predominant features, just as they are in senile dementia. A successful social facade may be maintained in the early states. These presenile conditions are unforgettable and tragic when seen clinically, for they so globally affect the lives of the middle-aged people who are the victims. Alzheimer's and Pick's diseases are the two common forms. While many regard Alzheimer's disease to be simply an early form of senile dementia,[36] all agree that Pick's disease is an independent entity.

With the present knowledge of these diseases, it is of little practical benefit to the patient to diagnostically differentiate among the various forms of presenile dementia. Once it is clear that a chronic process rather than a reversible one is taking place, the clinical pictures of the presenile disorders are practically similar. But brain pathologies after death reveal rather distinct differences and thus may be useful for research and further knowledge into the aging process and the origins of organic disorders.

Alzheimer's disease

In 1907, Alois Alzheimer described a "peculiar disease" involving a 51-year-old woman. It began with declining memory and disorientation coupled over time with signs of depression, delusions of persecution, jealousy, and an apraxia (a problem with skilled motor activity). The brain appeared atrophic. Bielschowsky's method of silver impreg-

---

[34] Aurbach, G.D., Mallette, L.E., Patten, B.M., Heath, D.A., Doppman, J.L., and Bilezikian, J.P.: Hyperparathyroidism: recent studies, Annals of Internal Medicine **79**:566-581, 1973.

[35] See Slaby, A.E., and Wyatt, R.J.: Dementia in the presenium, Springfield, Ill., 1976, Charles C Thomas, Publisher.

[36] Shelanski, M.L.: The aging brain: Alzheimer's disease and senile dementia. In Ostfeld, A.M., and Gibson, D.C., editors: Epidemiology of aging, Washington, D.C., 1975, U.S. Department of Health, Education and Welfare, pp. 113-127.

nation of autopsy material revealed the presence of tangles or clumps of cortical neurofibrils.[37]

Alzheimer's disease became the name applied to the most frequently seen type of presenile dementia, although comprehensive data on incidence are not available. The clinical appearance is one of rapid mental deterioration, beginning with marked mental deficits as well as tendencies toward agitation. It proceeds toward more severe symptoms such as incoherence, aphasia, agnosia, apraxia, gait disturbances, and convulsive seizures. Later the person becomes rigid and may be unable to stand or walk; eventually utter helplessness prevails, with incontinence and marasmus. The average age of onset is 58, the earliest usually 49, and an individual seldom lives longer than 4 or 5 years after illness begins. Remissions can occasionally occur. Treatment is limited to attention to symptoms and patient comfort.[38]

In its early stages Alzheimer's disease can be mistaken for a behavioral disorder and also may be complicated by emotional reactions to the organic changes. One may see depression, denial, and anxiety as the person has not yet lost capacity for insight and attempts to deal with phenomena that begin to subtly manifest themselves. There is yet little known about the cause of the disease (see the box on p. 103); however, it is suspected that three elements play a part: the process of aging, constitu-tional and genetic factors (there is an occasional familial incidence of the disease), and pathogenic factors in the environment—perhaps toxins or infection.

Pathologically the brain as a whole shows atrophy, generally of a more severe nature than is found in senile brain disease. This may result from the greater vigor of pathological processes in a younger person or may simply be a reflection of the fact that younger persons tend to live longer and the pathology has more time to progress.

Pick's disease

Pick's disease is clinically very similar to Alzheimer's and differentiation, as we have already stated, may be impossible until autopsy reveals the distinctive pathologic brain condition. There is usually an earlier onset (in the fourth decade), although it may occur also after age 65. General behavior is most often a lack of initiative rather than the overactivity of the Alzheimer patient. Symptomatology includes early selective impairment of mental functioning with the memory reasonably intact except for new material. Focal signs begin to appear at a later stage (aphasia, aphrasia, apraxia, etc.), and eventually the person sinks into a vegetative existence before death. The cause is unknown, but genetic factors appear relevant. The prognosis is always fatal, with survival from 2 to 15 years. The course of illness is steadily progressive, and treatment of symptoms is all that can presently be done.

Pathologically the brain shows a clear-cut and circumscribed rather than global atrophy, concentrating on the anterior portions of the frontal and temporal lobes of the brain.

Binswanger's disease (subcortical arteriosclerotic encephalopathy)

Binswanger's disease is a slowly progressing dementia and subcortical demyelination, apparently resulting from arteriosclerosis of small arteries supplying the white matter. It occurs in persons between the ages of 50 and 65, and evidence of focal cerebral disease is always present. Diagnosis is impossible until autopsy.

---

[37] For original papers see Alzheimer, A.: Ueber eigenartige Krankheitsfälle des spatern Alters, Z. Ges. Neurol. Psychiat. **4:**356-385, 1911; Alzheimer, A.: Ueber eine eigenartige Erkrankung der Hirnrinde, Allg. Z. Psychiat. **64:**146-148, 1907; Alzheimer, A.: Ueber eine eigenartige Erkrankung der Hirnrinde, Zentralbl. Nervenheilk. Psychiat. **30:**177-179, 1907; and Alzheimer, A.: Ueber einen eigenartigen schweren Erkrankungsprozess der Hirnrinde, Neurol. Zentralbl. **25:** 1134, 1906.

[38] The Alzheimer's Disease Center at the Albert Einstein College of Medicine (1300 Morris Park Avenue, Bronx, New York 10461) and the National Institute on Aging created a booklet for the use of the public and families and friends of Alzheimer's disease patients: Q and A: Alzheimer's disease, NIH Pub. No. 79-1646, 1979. There is now an Alzheimer's Disease and Related Disorders Association, 32 Broadway, New York, New York 10004.

Normal pressure hydrocephalus

Normal pressure hydrocephalus is an uncommon but treatable dementia. First described by Hakim and Adams, it is marked by three major symptoms—dementia, gait difficulty or apraxia, and incontinence of urine.[39] It is associated with gradual enlargement of ventricles while cerebrospinal fluid pressure remains normal. The cause is thought to be an obstruction to the absorption of spinal fluid, and the syndrome may follow a subarachnoid hemorrhage, meningitis, or previous head trauma. There is no evidence of cortical atrophy or of air over the surface of the brain when tested by a computer-assisted tomography of the head. Treatment consists of shunting the cerebrospinal fluid from the ventricular space to the peritoneal space, the atrium of the heart, or the pleural cavity.[40]

Creutzfeldt-Jakob disease (CJD)

Creutzfeldt-Jakob disease, a rare progressive neurological and dementing disorder (also called spongiform encephalopathy), begins in the fourth or fifth decade of life. Death may occur within 9 to 12 months. Myoclonus, seizures, motor findings, and gross EEG abnormalities develop. CJD has been successfully transmitted from a patient to a chimpanzee by Nobel Prize winner D.C. Gajdusek and C.J. Gibbs,[41] scientists at the National Institute of Neurological and Communicative Disorders and Stroke (1968), suggesting that CJD is caused by a slow virus. One transmissible viral dementia might suggest others.

[39] Hakim, S., and Adams, R.D.: The special clinical problem of symptomatic hydrocephalus with normal cerebrospinal fluid pressure: observations on cerebrospinal fluid hydrodynamics, Journal of the Neurological Sciences **2:**307-327, 1965.

[40] Adams, R.D., Fisher, C.M., Hakim, S., Ojemann, R.G., and Sweet, W.H.: Symptomatic occult hydrocephalus with "normal" cerebrospinal fluid pressure; a treatable syndrome, New England Journal of Medicine **273:**117-126, 1965.

[41] Gajdusek's original work was on kuru, a disease observed in New Guinea in the South Pacific. See Gibbs, C.J., Jr., and Gajdusek, D.C.: Biology of kuru and Creutzfeldt-Jakob disease. In Zeman, W., and Lennette, E.H., editors: Slow virus disease, Baltimore, 1973, The Williams & Wilkins Co., pp. 39-48; and Gibbs, C.J., Jr., et al.: Creutzfeldt-Jakob disease (subacute spongiform encephalopathy): transmission to the chimpanzee, Science **161:**388-389, 1968.

Huntington's disease (HD)

Huntington's disease is a hereditary disease (an autosomal [non-sex-linked] dominant trait) that usually begins in middle age but can occur in children and octogenarians. It progresses inexorably to death some 10 to 20 years following inception. Early clumsiness becomes the incessant, uncontrollable, twisting, choreiform movements associated with progressive dementia. Each child of an affected family has a 50% chance of developing HD, but there is no diagnostic test. Therefore, it is not possible to tell if an individual will become diseased until his or her thirties or forties. Efforts are underway to determine if there are characteristic deficiencies in neurotransmitters, for example, GABA (gamma-aminobutyric acid).

The parkinsonism-dementia complex of Guam (PD)

The parkinsonism-dementia of Guam, particularly common among the Chamorro population of this and other Mariana Islands (parts of the United States), strikes primarily in the later–middle age population.[42] Amyotrophic lateral sclerosis is also notably present. (Some believe they may be variants of the same disease process.) On pathological examination, the brain is unusually small, and the bilateral atrophy is most striking in the frontal and temporal lobes. Pigmentation is lost in the portions of the brain called the substantia nigra and locus ceruleus (not true in Alzheimer's disease). The face may be so expressionless that the term "reptilian stare" has been used. There are neurofibrillary changes in the neurons of both the cerebral cortex and the brainstem, similar to those found in dementia of the Alzheimer type. However, senile plaques are not present. PD occurs in males two or three times more frequently than in females and accounts for some 7% of deaths among adult Chamorros. The onset is generally in the late fifties, with death occurring in an average of 4½ years. PD is seen as commonly among stateside Chamor-

[42] Hirano, A., Kurland, L.T., Krooth, R.S., and Lassell, S.: Parkinsonism-dementia complex on Guam, II. Pathological features, Brain **84:**662-679, 1961.

ros (for example, those in San Diego and San Francisco) suggesting that environmental factors are unimportant.

OTHER MANIFESTATIONS OF ORGANIC DISORDERS
Pseudobulbar palsy

Pseudobulbar palsy is marked by poor control of emotions (laughing and crying), which is organically based. The labile emotionality must be differentiated from psychological behavior of a hysterical nature. Dysarthria (deficient articulation of speech) and dysphasia (disturbance in motor production of speech) are common. There is almost always a history of strokes affecting each side of the body. In contrast to progressive bulbar palsy, there is no atrophy or fibrillations of the tongue. The emotional instability is both inappropriate and uncontrollable and can occur in a less marked manner after even minor strokes.

Tremors

Tremors are involuntary movements occurring in one or more parts of the body and produced by alternate contractions of opposing muscle groups. They are symptoms rather than clinical entities in themselves.

In diagnosing a tremor, one should note the rate, the rhythm, the distribution, and the effect of movement or rest. A rapid tremor is one that oscillates 8 to 10 times per second; a slow tremor is one oscillating 3 to 5 times per second. Tremors may be fine or coarse. Intention tremors appear during or are accentuated by a volitional movement of the affected part. Rest tremors are present when the involved part is at rest, but they diminish or disappear with active movements.

Tremors associated with organic diseases of the central nervous system

Parkinsonism. Parkinsonism evidences a coarse, alternating tremor of about 4 to 8 movements per second, which is usually present during rest and tends to diminish or disappear on movement and during sleep. It is most commonly pres-

ent in fingers, forearm, eyelids, and tongue. Rigidity, masklike facies, and slowness of movement are also noted.

General paresis (dementia paralytica). A fine, rapid tremor involving the face (especially periorally [around the mouth]), tongue, and hands is an early symptom of general paresis, a syphilitic disease. It is probably caused by damage to the frontal lobe and its connections with the brainstem and cerebellum. It may be increased by voluntary movements.

Asterixis. Asterixis involves a peculiar "flapping" tremor of the hyperextended hands. It is frequently present in cases of mental impairment associated with metabolic derangements (for example, hepatic encephalopathy) but absent in Alzheimer's disease, multiinfarct dementia, and depression.

Cerebral arteriosclerosis. The tremor in cerebral arteriosclerosis may either be of the intention type or resemble that of parkinsonism, depending on the part of the central nervous system involved. The tremors associated with "senility" probably fall into this group.

Intoxication. Tremor is a prominent symptom of intoxication. Opiate addicts show a fine tremor of the facial muscles and fingers. The most common toxic state in which tremor is seen is alcoholism. In this condition there is a rapid, coarse tremor involving fingers, tongue, limbs, and head.

Tremors associated with functional disease

The tremors appearing in functional disorders may simulate those of organic, central nervous system disease. A psychiatric evaluation helps in making a diagnosis. Tremor is a fairly common symptom in both chronic and acute anxiety states. It may be seen in anxious depressions and in hysteria.

Benign essential tremor

Benign essential tremor principally affects hands, head, and voice and is often called a *familial tremor* since it runs in families. In older persons it is known as *senile tremor* (there is no rigidity or poverty of movement).

General paresis (general paralysis of the insane or dementia paralytica)

General paresis is a form of central nervous system syphilis and is characterized by ideas of grandeur, often of gigantic proportion. With recurrent episodes of venereal disease in the general population, we can expect to see much more of this disorder in the future. Many contemporary older persons received forms of therapy that were not as effective as penicillin (which began to be available only in 1941). Some were treated with arsenicals, whereas others with paresis were treated by the fever therapy of Wagner von Jauregg. Thus syphilis must always be given diagnostic consideration in older people. The effectiveness of intensive penicillin treatment (15 to 25 million units is one course) is limited by the amount of brain damage.

Anosognosia

Anosognosia is an interesting symptom that may be viewed as a defensive denial of severe organic change. The person "does not know *and* he does not know that he does not know the nature of his condition."

■ A 64-year-old black engineer had a residual paralysis of his right side (hemiparesis). He refused to admit that he could not move either extremity. When confronted by his doctor on this point, he would lift his right arm or leg with his left arm and say, "See, I can move them."

Anosognosia was described in a blind person in 1896 (Anton's syndrome) and by Bakinski in 1914 as he discussed patients with left hemiplegia who denied their paralysis. Denial may occur in both brain-damaged and non-brain-damaged persons and in response to many disabilities. It serves as a means of escaping pain and reality, as an excuse to refuse help, as a way to minimize depression, and as a technique to try to carry on while moving slowly toward acceptance of the disability. It affords time to absorb the shock of the situation. Denial may become untenable as the illness progresses or as the person is challenged by others to see what is really there. Alcoholism and drug abuse are both easily subject to denial, as is mental illness. Family members or friends may initiate or participate in the denial.

Mental retardation

It was estimated in 1970 that older persons constituted only 2.4% of the retarded population because of early deaths in this group. With better care, survival is expected to improve in the future. Much of the "deterioration" and early death of retarded persons has resulted from poor institutional care and no rehabilitation. Further, as DiGiovanni points out, "institutionalization tended to cut off communication between retarded individuals and their extended families."[43]

CONCLUSION

Even the so-called organic disorders in late life are multicausal—with social and personal as well as organic roots. We emphasized in this chapter the possibilities of treatment of the organic brain syndromes. In Chapter 9 we detail methods of making important diagnostic distinctions, and in Part Two we deal more extensively with treatment.

[43] DiGiovanni, L.: The elderly retarded: a little-known group, The Gerontologist **18**:262-266, 1978. In our own clinical work we also see older people who struggle to care for a mentally retarded child who is also aging, while they carry the added fear of what will happen to that child when they die.

REFERENCES

Alpers, B.J., Forster, F.M., and Herbut, P.A.: Retinal, cerebral and systemic arteriosclerosis, a histopathologic study, Archives of Neurology and Psychiatry **60**:440-456, 1948.

Bergmann, K.: The epidemiology of senile dementia, British Journal of Psychiatry **9**:100-109, 1975.

Butler, R.N.: Aging: research leads and needs. Recent studies of senile dementia of the Alzheimer's type suggest new approaches to treatment of aged persons, Forum on Medicine **2**:716-721, 723-725, 1979.

Butler, R.N., Dastur, D.K., and Perlin, S.: Relationships of senile manifestations and chronic brain syndromes to cerebral circulation and metabolism, Journal of Psychiatric Research **3**:229-238, 1965.

Committee on Nomenclature and Statistics of the American Psychiatric Association: Diagnostic and statistical manual of mental disorders, ed. 1 (DMS-I), Washington, D.C., 1952, American Psychiatric Association.

Committee on Nomenclature and Statistics of the American Psychiatric Association: Diagnostic and statistical manual of mental disorders, ed. 2 (DSM-II), Washington, D.C., 1968, American Psychiatric Association.

Committee on Nomenclature and Statistics of the American Psychiatric Association: Diagnostic and statistical manual of mental disorders, ed. 3 (DSM-III), Washington, D.C., 1980, American Psychiatric Association.

Cosin, L.Z., Post, F., Westropp, C., and Williams, M.: Persistent senile confusion: study of 50 consecutive cases, International Journal of Social Psychiatry **3:**195-202, 1957.

Davies, P.: Studies on the neurochemistry of central cholinergic systems in Alzheimer's Disease. In Katzman, R., Terry, R.D., and Bick, K.L., editors: Alzheimer's disease: senile dementia and related disorders, New York, 1978, Raven Press, pp. 453-460.

Dunea, G., Mahurkar, S.D., Mamdani, B., and Smith, E.C.: Role of aluminum in dialysis dementia, Annals of Internal Medicine **88:**502-504, 1978.

Gaitz, C.M., editor: Aging and the brain: advances in behavioral biology, vol. 3, New York, 1972, Plenum Publishing Corp.

Goldfarb, A.I.: Prevalence of psychiatric disorders in metropolitan old age and nursing homes, Journal of the American Geriatrics Society **10:**77-84, 1962.

Granacher, R.P.: The Capgras syndrome in old age (letter), American Journal of Psychiatry **135**(6):758-759, 1978.

Gruenberg, E.M.: The epidemiology of senile dementia. In Schoenberg, B.S., editor: Advances in neurology, New York, 1978, Raven Press.

Kallman, F.J.: Genetic differences in aging: comparative and longitudinal observations on a senescent twin population. In Hoch, P.H., and Zubin, J., editors: Psychopathology of aging, New York, 1961, Grune and Stratton, Inc.

Katzman, R.: The prevalence and malignancy of Alzheimer's disease: a major killer, Archives of Neurology **33:**217-218, 1976.

Katzman, R., Terry, R.D., and Bick, K.L., editors: Alzheimer's disease: senile dementia and related disorders, New York, 1978, Raven Press.

Kay, D.W., and Roth, M.: Environmental and hereditary factors in the schizophrenias of old age (''late paraphrenia'') and their bearing on the general problem of causation of schizophrenia, Journal of Mental Science **107:**649-686, 1961.

Libow, L.S.: Pseudo-senility: acute and reversible organic brain syndromes, Journal of the American Geriatrics Society **21:** 112-120, 1973.

National Institute on Aging: Senility reconsidered: treatment possibilities in mental impairment of the elderly, Journal of the American Medical Association **244**(3):259-263, 1980.

Post, F.: The clinical psychiatry of late life, London, 1965, Pergamon Press Ltd.

Roth, M.: The natural history of mental disorders in old age, Journal of Mental Science **101:**281-301, 1955.

Rothschild, D.: Senile psychoses and psychoses with cerebral arteriosclerosis. In Kaplan, O.J., editor: Mental disorders in late life, Stanford, Calif., 1956, Stanford University Press.

Simon, A., and Cahan, R.: The acute brain syndrome in geriatric patients. In Mendel, W.M., and Epstein, L.J., editors: Acute psychotic reaction, psychiatric research reports of the American Psychiatric Association, Washington, D.C., 1963, American Psychiatric Association.

Sjögren, H.: Neuropsychiatric studies in presenile and senile diseases, based on material of 1,000 cases, Acta Psychiatrica Scandinavica **106**(supp.):9-36, 1956.

Tomlinson, B.E., Blessed, G., and Roth, M.: Observations on the brain of demented old people, Journal of the Neurological Sciences **11:**203-242, 1970.

Weinstein, E.A., and Kahn, R.C.: Denial of illness: symbolic and physiological aspects, Springfield, Ill., 1955, Charles C Thomas, Publisher.

Wells, C.E., editor: Dementia, ed. 2, Philadelphia, 1977, F.A. Davis Co.

Wolanin, M.O., and Phillips, L.R.: Confusion: prevention and care, St. Louis, 1981, The C.V. Mosby Co.

6

Special concerns

racism, sexism, retirement, crime, alcoholism, deafness, blindness, and sexuality

How does racism affect the lives of older people? Should older women join the women's liberation movement? Do alcoholics live long enough to become old? Are there "geriatric criminals"? Do older people like to make love? Can they? We consider in this chapter some of the important human issues that are part of old age. Misunderstandings abound in the folklore created around aging.

RACISM AS IT AFFECTS MENTAL HEALTH CARE

Older people are a multiracial and multicultural group. Many are immigrants from other countries. More than 2 million are persons of minority-group background—blacks, Latinos, American Indians, Chinese, Japanese, Koreans, Pilipinos, Vietnamese.[1] A nation as diverse as the United States needs transcultural studies of the older persons within its own borders. Different cultural and racial groups have different conceptions of the life cycle; each has been treated somewhat differently by the majority culture. Research on older black

persons has become more active in recent years and attention has been focused on them through the National Center on Black Aging, formed in 1970.[2] But the same is less true for other minority groups. The U.S. Senate Special Committee on Aging under the leadership of Senator Frank Church established special advisory groups for blacks, Cubans, and American Indians and also published a report from delegates of the 1971 White House Conference on Aging, which deals with older blacks, Asian-Americans, American Indians, and Latinos.[3] The concerns of the minority aged received special emphasis at the 1981 White House Conference on Aging.

There are two major and distinctly separate issues regarding minority-group older people. First are the unique cultural elements found in each minority group, which have bearing on the lives of its older members; second are the effects imposed on the older persons as a result of living in a majority culture. We would like to touch on both of these issues, but it is clear that most available research centers around vital statistics, social and economic

---

[1] There are other ethnic groups that have been or are still subject to prejudice—Poles, Jews, Italians, Greeks, and Arabs, among others. With rising ethnic consciousness, it has become difficult to define minorities for purposes of the U.S. census.

[2] Dr. Delores Davis, Executive Director, National Center on Black Aging, 1424 K St., N.W., Washington, D.C. 20005.

[3] Report to the Delegates from the Conference Sections and Special Concerns Sessions, 1971 White House Conference on Aging, Washington, D.C., 1971, U.S. Government Printing Office.

113

conditions, and the effects of racism rather than the cultural life of individual groups. In Chapter 1 we present some of the facts and figures of minority old age in America. This chapter deals with the direct effects of racial and ethnic prejudice on the mental health care of older people. We look forward to the time when more will be done to recognize the varied and distinctive life-styles inherent in each culture. One would hope such variety could be preserved, protected, and used as a primary consideration in physical and mental health treatment. A richer diagnostic and treatment picture would result.

Black older persons

Black psychiatrists at the annual meeting of the American Psychiatric Association, May 1970, called racism the number 1 mental health problem in America. This was echoed by the black caucuses of the American Orthopsychiatric Association and the National Association of Social Workers. The National Urban League in 1964 published a significant study called "Double Jeopardy," which described the dual discrimination of ageism and racism experienced by the black aged.[4] Black people who face racial prejudice all their lives are met with the added burdens of age prejudice when they grow old. Dr. Jacqueline Jackson, who has contributed much to the understanding of the black aged, has added a third "ism"—sexism—to the jeopardies confronting older black women, for they are in even worse circumstances than black men, despite myths to the contrary.

Two of the most obvious effects of discrimination have been the overrepresentation of black older people on Supplemental Security Income and their shorter life expectancies. Whites often have Social Security and private pensions, while many jobs open to blacks were never or only recently covered by Social Security. And since black older

Multiple jeopardy: age, blackness, poverty, widowhood, womanhood.

Courtesy Zebra Associates, Inc., Advertising, New York. Photographer, Hugh Bell.

people die at a younger age, especially black men, they may never become eligible for retirement benefits even if they have accumulated them.

Outpatient mental health care

Racial prejudice and discrimination affect both the quality and the amount of mental health care available to black older persons. A Washington, D.C., psychiatrist describes a problem that has been crucial in many community mental health centers:

The majority of CMHC [Community Mental Health Center] staff have at best only a superficial understanding of the culture, life experiences, and needs of their clients. It is a widely acknowledged fact that most psychiatric professionals, products of white middle-class America, are unable to bridge the cultural chasm be-

---

[4]Double jeopardy, the older Negro in America today, New York, 1964, National Urban League.

tween themselves and poverty stricken black people in the context of mental health work. Diagnosis and treatment are based on traditional psychiatric concepts of mental health and mental disorder. These in turn hinge on white middle-class norms and values. It is clear that traditional psychiatry cannot be applied to the situation of black people. Effective mental health workers must be able not only to identify with the culture of their clients, but also to distinguish between the effects of societal pathology and individual psychopathology.[5]

In describing the experiences of his staff in the black community, Dr. William A. Reid states: "Clinically we are finding depression and reactions of anxiety, shame, and guilt. Some few show classical neuroses and psychoses." He emphasizes that too many mental health workers arbitrarily assign individual responsibility for misfortune rather than considering social factors. Successful treatment must challenge society's assumptions and not deny the reality of blackness. Psychoanalyst Franz Fanon[6] in 1967 wrote that any study of the psychology of a black person must include (1) a psychoanalytic interpretation of the life experience of the black man [and woman] and (2) a psychoanalytic interpretation of the Negro myth. Grier and Cobbs[7] make similar points. A body of theory and treatment techniques designed especially for the black population has begun to emerge.

The amount of outpatient care offered to the black aged is small. Hospital emergency rooms give minimal attention to psychiatric problems, particularly if the patient is old and poor. Voluntary nonprofit hospitals tend to refuse admission at the gate, a practice that now segregates by income (or class) rather than strictly race, with almost the same effect. Older people of all races make up only 4% to 5% of community mental health clientele, so one can see that only a small fraction of the total are black. Day hospitals and day-care center accommodations are equally rare. These services receive little priority in municipal and county hospital budgets, and private sponsorship is difficult to obtain.

Home care

It is a commonly held view that the black community does not readily seek admission of its older people for institutional care. Some explain this as indicative of a greater tolerance for abnormal behavior and a view of mental illness as a weakness or stigma. Others, such as Carter,[8] believe that it may represent a basic distrust of institutions because of previous life experiences. It is also apparent that there simply are not many institutional facilities other than state hospitals available for the older black person.[9]

Home care services are scarce, and families have been forced to provide care by themselves. Some studies suggest that the older person is more respected and considered less of a burden than in white families. True or not, this is no defensible reason for failing to provide supportive services in black homes.

Institutional care

It appears that staying out of institutions is not as serious a problem for older blacks as is getting into them when they are needed.

Nursing homes and homes for the aged. These homes remain largely segregated even though segregation is usually not openly stated as a policy. Less than 3% of residents are black. Whites rarely apply for admission to black homes, and white homes frequently claim they have not received any "qualified" black applicants. Carter refers to the

[5] Dr. William A. Reid, personal correspondence, 1972.

[6] Fanon, F.: Black skin, white masks, New York, 1967, Grove Press, Inc.

[7] Grier, W.H., and Cobbs, P.M.: Black rage, New York, 1968, Basic Books, Inc., Publishers.

[8] Carter, J.H.: Psychiatry, racism and aging, paper presented at the Research Conference on Minority Group Aged in the South, Durham, N.C., Oct. 12, 1971.

[9] Jackson, H.C.: Alternatives to institutional care for older Americans: practice and planning: "Planning for the specially disadvantaged," presentation for the Conference on Alternatives to Institutional Care, Duke University, June 3, 1972.

difficulty of finding homes for black men, who appear to be even more discriminated against than black women. Black-owned facilities having difficulty in meeting health, fire, and building standards may be closed rather than given assistance and encouragement.[10] Many nonprofit, church-sponsored homes avoid integration by restricting admissions to their own parishioners, already a self-selected group in terms of race and social class.

Mental hospitals. When a black older person requires institutional care, state hospitals are the only facilities routinely available. The integration of mental institutions has occurred relatively recently in most cases. St. Elizabeths Hospital in Washington, D.C., one of the well-known hospitals in the nation, was segregated until 1955; the hospitals in North Carolina were segregated until 1966. Segregated black hospitals were underfinanced and consequently in worse condition than the already inadequate white hospitals. With integration and the sharing of facilities, blacks fared somewhat better than before in terms of physical accommodations, but it is doubtful that their medical or psychiatric treatment improved, since custodial care rather than active treatment is still customary. White aides and attendants are frequently unknowledgeable and insensitive to the cultural aspects of black life. They may not wish to provide personal services like giving baths, carrying out bed pans, and giving enemas. Open neglect frequently occurs. White doctors and other professionals may share in the same insensitivity, lack of knowledge, and, at times, directly racist attitudes. Black aides and attendants who accept the "servant" role tend to be overly solicitous of older white patients, infantilizing them, while others may be passive-aggressive, ignoring patient needs. Direct hostility toward white and black patients alike is not uncommon from "caregivers" of both races. Thus aggression, passive and active, flows between white and black staff members to white and black patients.

Lifelong attitudes and conditioning often persist in old age, even after mental impairment occurs. An aged white woman with strong racial prejudices managed in spite of brain damage and incoherence to consistently call black staff members, including her psychiatrist, "niggers." Sometimes older black patients are seen waiting on white patients by performing personal services, while the whites give orders. There may be rebellion in older blacks; in one case an elderly black man spent his last years giving verbal vent to his murderous feelings toward whites, which had been stored up for a lifetime. Older blacks may share the belief that black professionals are inferior. It is not unusual in an integrated institution for them to confuse a white social worker as their doctor and relegate the black doctor to an attendant status, for as Pinderhughes[11] has observed, we all have shared a "pro-white, anti-black group-related paranoia."

Community-resident black older persons

Because of joint poverty, the aged of both races tend to inhabit the inner city. It is a dangerous area for both groups, particularly since they are vulnerable to robberies, muggings, and fraud. The shared sense of danger can bring them together against the young. Both groups in Washington, D.C.'s Project Assist program expressed a fear of the young men who menaced them, and both willingly accepted help from black and white staff. On the other hand, older whites may attempt to compensate for their own fears and loss of social status by expressing outspoken hatred of the black community, including older blacks.

Research is beginning to explore some of the specific psychological and cultural implications of black old age. There are differences between rural and urban dwellers, Northerners and Southerners,

---

[10] Position statement on Sarah Allen Nursing Home in West Philadelphia by the Board of Directors, Stephen Smith Geriatric Center, 1972.

[11] Pinderhughes, C.A.: The universal resolution of ambivalence by paranoia with an example in black and white, American Journal of Psychotherapy **24:**597-610, 1970.

upper- and middle-income citizens versus those with lower income, as well as the various age groups and professions. For example, very old blacks, according to Dr. Ira Reid, prefer the name "colored," while younger people are most comfortable with "Negro" and the very youngest demand "black." The "black revolution" has not escaped the aged. They may admire the young and support them, or they may be confused, isolated, and labeled by the young as "Uncle Toms." The concept of retirement may be meaningless for poor blacks who cannot afford to stop work. Thus "retirement crisis" does not apply to people who are in a "survival crisis." The black church has proved to be a stabilizing force, providing older persons with social participation, prestige, and power in the internal life created by parishioners.

"Hispanic" or Latino older persons

Racial discrimination has had many of the same social and economic effects on all racial minorities. For example, the Mexican-American population is heavily weighted with the young because of high fertility, low life expectancy, and the return of some older persons to Mexico.[12] There are great cultural differences from region to region in the United States and such diversity makes it impossible to generalize about any given situation in aging or about relationships with family and community. The notion of close family support is challenged because many older persons have become isolated physically and emotionally by the mobility and poverty of their children. Older persons in the Southwest have experienced strong anti-Mexican discrimination, particularly in the 1920s and 1930s

[12] For data on Mexican-Americans see Reich, J.M., Stegman, M.A., and Stegman, N.W.: Relocating the dispossessed elderly: a study of Mexican-Americans, Philadelphia, 1966, University of Pennsylvania, Institute for Environmental Studies; Steglich, W.G., Cartwright, W.J., and Crouch, B.: Survey of needs and resources among aged Mexican-Americans, Lubbock, 1968, Texas Technological College; and Eribes, R.A., and Bradley-Rawls, M.: The underutilization of nursing home facilities by Mexican-American elderly in the Southwest, the Gerontologist **18:**363-371, 1978.

when mass deportations occurred. Inability to speak English is a common handicap. As with blacks, many Latinos, especially those from Mexico, never live to retirement age. Other Latino groups like the Cubans are longer-lived.

American Indian older persons[13]

An estimated 800,000 Indians live in the 50 states, speak some 300 languages, and have diverse customs and traditions. The sole source of income for many of the older people is welfare, with only the minimum level of Social Security

[13] See The Indian elder: a forgotten American, final report on the First National Indian Conference on Aging, Phoenix, Ariz., June 1976; and The continuum of life: health concerns of the Indian elderly, final report on the Second National Indian Conference on Aging, Billings, Mont., Aug. 1978. Both of these can be ordered from the National Indian Council on Aging, P.O. Box 2088, Albuquerque, N.M. 87103.

The first American: old age and poverty.

Courtesy H. Armstrong Roberts, Inc., Philadelphia.

at age 72. The federal government through the Bureau of Indian Affairs did not set up retirement programs so that the older persons could participate in company retirement plans, insurance plans, private investments, and in many cases Social Security. State public assistance programs have pressured older Indians to sell their allotted reservation land, even though the federal government has claimed it supports the Indians' desire to retain their tribal property. Because of jurisdictional questions, some states have refused to license nursing homes on reservations; therefore federal funds, which must be given only to state-licensed homes, are not authorized. Indian spokesmen have stated that federal funds should be released to them directly, administered as part of the Indian Health Service. We discuss the older Indians' plight in Chapter 1. They have been forced to give up much, receiving very little in return, and the damage done to their lives can only be described as incalculable.

Asian-American and Pacific Island– American older persons

Cultural barriers, language problems, and discrimination have added to the old-age burdens of yet another group, Asian-Americans and Pacific Island–Americans. Spokesmen point to a pervasive myth that has excluded these older persons from services:

This emasculating myth that discriminates against Asian-American elderly is that Asian-American aged do not have any problems, that Asian-Americans are able to take care of their own and that Asian-American aged do not need nor desire aid in any form. Such assertions which are generally accepted as valid by society are false. . . . it is impossible for Asian-Americans to look only to their families for help.[14]

[14] From Asian-American elderly, Report to the Delegates from the Special Concerns Sessions, 1971, White House Conference on Aging, Washington, D.C., 1971, U.S. Government Printing Office, p. 61. See also Fujii, S.: Older Asian Americans: victims of multiple jeopardy, Civil Rights Digest **9**: 25, 1976.

There are five basic groups—Chinese, Pilipinos, Japanese, Koreans, and Samoans—as well as Indonesians, Guaminians, Thai, Vietnamese, and others, all with their own languages and cultures; yet they are often lumped together as Orientals.[15] Most older persons are immigrants, and many are literate in their native language although they may not speak English. There is need for a diverse number of services that cannot be met solely by families.

Basic differences exist among the older persons of each cultural group, which reflect not only their inherent uniqueness but also the patterns of racial discrimination they have faced in this country.

When many now-elderly Chinese were brought to the United States in the late nineteenth century as "coolies" (from the Chinese *ku li,* meaning "bitter labor"), whites had already become frenzied by the imagined threat of inundation from Chinese "hordes." Therefore Chinese men were prohibited through the Chinese Exclusion Act of 1882 from bringing their wives and children with them, and they were forbidden to intermarry in America.[16] Others chose to come alone as young men, hoping to make money quickly and then return to live in China. War and the subsequent Communist takeover prohibited their return. "This produced the sex ratio which has plagued Chinese communities ever since. In most areas with large

[15] From Kalish, R.A., and Yuen, S.: Americans of East Asian ancestry; aging and the aged, The Gerontologist **11**:41, 1971.

[16] From 1848 to 1882 over 100,000 Chinese men, as compared to 9,000 Chinese women, had immigrated, mostly to California and the Rocky Mountain states, where they mined gold (they made up 25% of California's gold miners), worked on the railroad (helping to complete the first transcontinental railroad by 1869), and were employed in forestry. The Chinese Exclusion Act of 1882, which also disenfranchised Chinese immigrants and barred them from certain jobs, had as its most long-lasting effect the barring of wives and children from joining their men—by 1943 when the law was repealed, the ratio of males to females in New York's Chinatown was an incredible 17:1 (historical data from Tanzer, A.: The American experience of Chinatown's elderly, unpublished paper, 1980).

Chinese-American populations there are groups of single males who have been derailed, as it were, from the normal cycle of life.''[17] It is considered a great misfortune for a Chinese man to fail to produce sons who will care for him in old age and in afterlife. But racism and political change have caused the breakdown of these traditions. Many older men live isolated lives, addicted to opium and uncompensated for their years of hard labor. Mental illness is extreme: suicide rates among Chinese pioneer generations (*idai*) in the United States far exceed those of Anglos and comparable Chinese populations in Hong Kong and Singapore.

Perhaps for similar reasons the Pilipino population has an unusually large proportion of men in psychiatric hospitals. Some Pilipinos came to the United States as farm laborers; others came because they were awarded U.S. citizenship as veterans of the U.S. armed forces after World War II. Most have no families here and have lost contact with their relatives in the Philippines. The most recent wave of immigration came in the early 1970s because of political problems in the Philippines, doubling the size (now about 300,000) of the Pilipino population in California alone. Many of these later immigrants arrived in families.

Another group, the ''young old'' Chinese, is beginning to appear as a result of the liberalization of immigration laws in 1965, which permitted the reunion of long-separated families, including parents and other older relatives of American citizens. This group appears to have a larger proportion of older women than men. Added to these are the increasing numbers of persons who were born in the United States and are now growing older, again a higher proportion of whom are women.[18] Many of these older Chinese-Americans prefer to live in ethnic communities rather than with their children in outlying areas.

Economic circumstances are at least as important as cultural tradition in determining attitudes toward older persons in the Asian-American communities, as in all communities. Osako describes the effects of socioeconomic class among the Japanese:

Confucianism, the dominant official ideology of feudal and Meiji Japan, preached that the child must respect parents in any circumstance and support them, at any cost, in their old age . . . for the child owes to his parents his birth, nurturing, and family property. Samurai families accepted the norm and strove to observe it. However, the reality of Japanese peasant households [representing the majority of Japanese] significantly deviated from this norm. . . . the traditional Japanese family stresses its corporateness. The family as a corporate entity owns and manages property to insure the survival of its members and to perpetuate the family occupation. Consequently, the individual's role in the corporate activity is a more important basis of his status than his biological attributes, such as age, sex, and blood tie. . . . In the peasant household, all the members worked because farming was intensive and daily survival was problematic. As the old members' contribution declined, their influences and status also diminished. They customarily gave up privileges and authority to the younger generation at a customary retirement age or as their capacity declined. Thus, the actual filial relationship among peasants departed considerably from the Confucian norms.[19]

The widespread belief that respect for older persons is culturally stronger in Asian societies needs to be reevaluated from the viewpoint of economic and social class. Tradition of course has a powerful effect on shaping an individuals' attitudes, but economic and social circumstances affect tradition by either supporting or undermining it.

Early Japanese immigration policies in the United States were not so devastating and dehu-

---

[17] From Kalish, R.A., and Yuen, S.: Americans of East Asian ancestry; aging and the aged, The Gerontologist **11**:41, 1971.

[18] Kalish, R.A., Lurie, E., Wexler, R., and Zawadski, R.T.: On Lok Senior Health Services: evaluation of a success, HEW final report, AOA Research and Demonstration Project No. 93P-75204/9, 1975.

[19] Osako, M.M.: Aging and family among Japanese-Americans: the role of ethnic tradition in the adjustment to old age, The Gerontologist **19**(5):448-455, 1979. Reprinted by permission of *The Gerontologist*.

manizing as those of other Asians. Women and children were allowed to accompany men, and this has had a profound effect on the lives of present-day older persons. Family structure is much more stable and supportive. Japanese older people were able to weather the World War II internment in relocation centers with the loss of jobs and their roles in American society primarily because their children could carry on for them. Many of the children have become highly educated and successful while retaining patterns of loyalty to parents.[20]

What can be done to improve mental health care for minority-group older persons?

1. Income maintenance is a prime requirement for improving health care for older members of minority groups. Social Security age-eligibility rules should reflect the life expectancies of minority groups. For example, a rural, migrant Mexican-American should be eligible for benefits at an earlier age. Private and government pension plans should be portable from job to job. A system of income maintenance that is not related to earnings and is available to all on an equal basis would do much to provide a base of support. Supplemental Security Income, tied to a "means test" and costly in administration, should be replaced by a minimum guaranteed annual income.

2. Minority professionals and older persons themselves should be in key decision-making and advisory positions in any actions affecting older persons.

3. Mental health staffs should reflect the racial composition they serve. Training in the mental health field should be widely available for minority-group members.

4. At present, treatment cannot be handled by minority personnel alone, since there are so few of them. Nonminority personnel should have special training[21] and supervisory monitoring by minority-group professionals if they work with minority clientele.[22]

5. Research from the minority perspective should be funded and encouraged. Problems pertinent to minority aged (for example, hypertension among blacks) need emphasis.

6. More alternative methods of care must be made available—home care services, nursing homes and homes for the aged, psychiatric hospitalization outside of state hospitals, day care, and day hospitals. Techniques of individual and group psychotherapy relevant to minority needs should be developed. Meals-on-Wheels could supply ethnic foods, and food stamps should be usable in ethnic groceries. Recreation and leisure therapy should be aimed at cultural interests. Information systems, service workers, legal assistance, and psychiatric therapy should all be provided on a bilingual basis for older persons who do not speak English.

The On Lok Senior Health Service program in San Francisco began in 1973 as a rather rare example of the provision of ethnic-related services. On Lok is a day treatment center for the frail older persons in San Francisco's Chinatown/North Beach area and serves those who would otherwise be placed in nursing homes or intermediate care facilities. Participants are primarily of Chinese,

---

[20] The Issei (Japanese who were born and raised in Japan before immigrating to the United States) were discriminated against before World War II and placed in internment camps during the war (Bosworth, A.R.: American's concentration camps, New York, 1967, W.W. Norton & Co.; and Kitagawa, D.: Issei and Nisei: the internment years, New York, 1967, Seabury Press, Inc.). Despite adversities the Issei encouraged and supported the education of their children, the Nisei, one third of whom now have professional and technical occupations (Kitano, H.L.: Japanese Americans: the evolution of a subculture, Englewood Cliffs, N.J., 1969, Prentice-Hall, Inc.). For an informative bibliography on older Japanese see Montero, D.: The elderly Japanese American: aging among the first generation immigrants, Genetic Psychology Monographs **101:**116-119, 1980.

[21] The Center on Aging of San Diego State University, San Diego, Calif., holds an Institute on Minority Aging each year (349 Cedar St., San Diego, Calif. 92101).

[22] The "curanderos," traditional healers of Mexico and Latin America, are examples of folk healers that might be encouraged to collaborate with "Anglos" in reaching older persons effectively.

Pilipino, and Italian background and usually do not speak English. Participants receive medical evaluation, health services, occupational, physical, and reality therapy, nutritional services, recreation, transportation, home care services, and brief nursing home care and hospital placement when needed. Staff members at On Lok must be able to speak at least one of the three languages represented by participants, in addition to English. Programs are geared to the ethnic cultures; for example, Chinese as well as American food is served.[23]

SEXISM AND THE PROBLEMS OF OLDER WOMEN

In the United States 14.6 million women were 65 years of age and older in 1979. This constitutes 6% of the total population, 12% of all women, and 57% of the older population. Sexism and ageism are the twin prejudices directed against them. They have experienced sex discrimination all their lives, but age discrimination begins only after they have lost their youth and accelerates as they age. The end result is a greater rate of poverty and social unacceptability than for men, combined ironically with a longer life-span. The cultural denigration of the older woman is taught at an early age through fairy tales that depict old hags, evil crones, scary old witches, and nasty biddies of all kinds. Mother-in-law stories abound. Doctors and medical students call older female patients "crocks." Unmarried aunts are scorned as "old maids." Even grandma becomes a family nuisance as she outlives grandpa and experiences and expresses the emotional and physical facts of aging. Thus the message comes across that a woman is valuable for bearing and rearing children and perhaps to nurse her husband in his dotage and often through his terminal illness, but after that it is

clearly useless and even burdensome to have her around. The mistreatment of older women is a national shame that has yet to be fully challenged even by older women themselves.

Low visibility of the older woman

One of the traditions of the American social system is to keep its "undesirables" out of sight. For years we pretended to know little about the poor or the blacks until they were "discovered" with great alarm. The same can be said for older women. The elderly condition in general is rarely seen as newsworthy unless something extraordinary occurs. Older women must be truly exceptional to be noticed—Helena Rubenstein at 92 running a business empire, Grandma Moses painting primitive art, Martha Graham still dancing at 76, or Helen Hayes performing on the stage at 70. To be less than remarkable is to be invisible.

Profile of the older woman

What is the life of an *average* older woman like? In many cases it means being widowed and living alone, on a low or poverty-level income, perhaps in substandard housing, with minimal medical care and little chance of employment to supplement resources.

Income

A small proportion of older women are well off financially, and some few have inherited enormous wealth. At the other end of the spectrum are those women who have been poor all their lives and who can expect even greater poverty in old age. But in between these two groups is a multitude of women who have lived comfortably throughout their lives and first experience poverty after they are old: the newly poor. Poverty is not reserved for women alone, since older men, too, are often in dire financial condition. Yet whenever poverty is found, it is generally more profound and of greater consequence for women. In 1976 the average monthly Social Security benefits were $218. Retirement benefits for women workers in general averaged 76% of the amount for men. For-

---

[23]Kalish, R.A., Lurie, E., Wexler, R., and Zawadski, R.T.: On Lok Senior Health Services: evaluation of a success, HEW final report, AOA Research and Demonstration Project No. 93P-75204/9, 1975; and Lurie, E., Kalish, R., Wexler, R., and Ansak, M.L.: On Lok Senior Day Health Center: a case study, The Gerontologist **16**(1):39-46, 1976.

An older woman speaks up.

Photo by Patricia and William Oriol.

tunately by 1980 this disparity had evened out, with the average monthly Social Security benefits of $330 for both men and women.

According to the official poverty index, about three fourths of all of the older poor are women alone, most of them widows. Of women over age 72, 42% live in poverty. Only 9% of women over 65 receive private pensions, as compared to 25% of men.

Even women with sufficient income have problems because many of them do not know how to handle money for their own benefit. It is here, particularly, that societal patterns of passivity and assent to masculine financial management show themselves. Women are encouraged to turn their money over to men to manage—to bank representatives, guardians, lawyers, male children—

and those women who do take care of their own finances are often untrained and ill-prepared to make sound decisions. An early study of business and professional women found that they were good savers but suffered badly from inflation because of the way they invested.[24] These were women who were well above average in income, job level, education, and years of experience; but they knew little about investments or how to increase capital. Money management was for them a passive activity in which they preferred the false security of savings, cash, and annuities over a sounder investment program that required an un-

[24] Erb, C.: Do women invest wisely? A study of savings for retirement. Summary of research, Washington, D.C., 1970, Business and Professional Women's Foundation.

derstanding of economics and finance. Courses in finance designed especially for women are fortunately beginning to help educate older women. Their younger counterparts are finding increasing opportunities to learn money management in the same way that men do.

Employment

Over 1 million or 8% of older women are employed, often out of necessity. Many never worked outside their homes until their children left home and they are employed in dead-end and unskilled jobs. Others were employed all their lives but usually earned much less than men of comparable talent and initiative. All of this results in lower Social Security and private retirement benefits and, combined with a longer life-span for women, produces lower income that must be stretched over a greater number of years.

Employers are reluctant to hire older women because of stereotyped attitudes that they are not adaptable to today's jobs and technology; older women are seen as cantankerous, sexually unattractive, overly emotional, and unreliable because of health problems. Yet studies indicate that they make exceptionally good employees, with lower turnover, higher productivity, and less absenteeism than men or younger women. At one point in 1969 the Department of Health, Education and Welfare itself closed the door on women who were over 35 years of age as potential appointees for high-level jobs in the department.

Social Security discriminates against older women in a number of ways. We have mentioned that women earn less and therefore receive less in benefits. Many jobs held by women have only recently been covered under Social Security—agriculture, hotel and restaurant work, hospital jobs, and domestic work (the latter is still frequently uncovered). Much work done by women, primarily work as housewives and mothers, has earned them nothing. Until 1973 a widow received only 82.5% of her husband's benefits even though she had worked all her life as a full-time employee in her home. A divorced woman whose former husband died before 1979 must have been married to him 20 years in order to get Social Security survivor benefits. If a man died after 1979 his divorced wife (if she is at least 60 years old) must have been married 10 years to collect benefits. If a man and woman are married, they may get less Social Security than if they were not married. Thus some older couples live together without marrying in order to obtain the benefits they both may have earned. The Social Security "means test," which limits the amount of income that can be earned, is especially hard on women, since they live longer and use up their resources; many are reduced to doing bootleg work to hide their income from the government because they need to survive. Finally, Social Security is a regressive tax with a base rate of $29,700 as of 1981; therefore women pay proportionately more than men because of their lower incomes.

Marriage

The average American woman can anticipate about 10 years of widowhood. Of the 13.9 million older women, more than 6 million are widows and an additional 1.2 million are divorced or single. (Approximately 7% of all women never marry.) Thus 65% of older women are on their own, an interesting fact when one remembers that they, more than any younger group, were raised from childhood to consider themselves dependent on men.

Why so many widows? Women outlive men their own age and also tend to marry men who are an average of about 2.5 years older than themselves. The difference in life expectancy seems to be a rather recent and poorly understood occurrence. In 1920 men could expect to live 53.6 years and women a year longer, but by 1978 a 7.8-year spread was evident, with a life expectancy of 69.3 for men and 77.1 for women.

Older men have a tremendous advantage over older women when it comes to marriage. Because they tend to marry younger women who will outlive them, they are much less likely to be widowed. More than that, they can count on a fairly

Hugh Downs, host of television show *Over Easy*, discusses widowhood with actress Maureen O'Sullivan and Helen Coston, an Arizona housewife.

Courtesy *Over Easy*, Public Broadcasting System.

healthy spouse to nurse them as they age. Should the wife die prematurely, they have plentiful options for remarriage. At age 65 when men number 10 million, the 14.6 million women already outnumber them by over 4 million and the odds improve as men grow older. In remarrying, men can bypass their own age group altogether and marry women from 65 all the way down to girls in their twenties or teens. One can readily see what is happening to older women in all of this; their chances for remarriage are small, and only 21,000 in 1979 found a second husband. It is socially frowned on for an older woman to date or marry a man much younger than herself, a blatant form of discrimination when men are freely allowed this option.

Motherhood

Mary Grace Kovar brings attention to the childlessness of many contemporary older women. The cohort (generation) of women born between 1905 and 1909, now around 70 years old, is a "famous low-fertility cohort," since these women produced fewer children than any recorded group of American women before or since. At the height of its childbearing years, this group was confronted with the worst economic depression in American history, with 25%—one of every four—workers unemployed. Many couples felt they could not support a large or even moderately sized family. About 20% of the women had no children, another 22% had only one, and another 20% two. The long-term result is that about 25% currently have no living children. (Nearly 30% of black women in this age group are childless.) They are, however, likely to have brothers and sisters (and therefore nieces and nephews), because their own mothers had large families. Thus there may be extended family support for some of the childless.

Interestingly, the 1925 to 1930 cohort women, now around age 50, were the high-fertility post–World War II cohort, and so while many will face divorce or become widowed because of the male-female differential life expectancy, they will have children. Only about 10% never had a child and the "ideal" was four children.

Living arrangements

Currently, 34% of older women live alone, 18% live with husbands, 39% with relatives, 4% with nonrelatives, and only 5% in institutions. Many women have never lived alone until old age. It is estimated that up to 60% live in substandard housing.

Health

Older women cannot count on the medical profession. Few doctors are interested in them. Their physical and emotional discomforts are often characterized as "postmenopausal syndromes" until they have lived too long for this to be an even faintly reasonable diagnosis. After that, they are assigned the category of "senility." Doctors complain about being harassed by their older female patients, and it is true that many are lonely and seeking attention. Yet more than 85% have some kind of chronic health problem, and both depression and hypochondriasis commonly accompany the physical ailments.

Research efforts

The National Institute on Aging and the National Institute of Mental Health held a major workshop/conference, The Older Woman: Continuities and Discontinuities, in 1978,[25] focusing on the woman over 70. The key demographic issues included emphasis on cultural, racial, and socioeconomic variables as they influence health and disease. A principal goal of the workshop was to promote research activity—including surveys, life history approaches, network analysis,[26] and cross-cultural methods—on the understanding of mental health and disorder as well as the family and social systems of older women. The continuities and discontinuities in the lives of women were stressed. As "kin-keepers," women's emotional relationships with parents, siblings, offspring, and friends are seen as major sources of continuity throughout their lives, as is responsibility for housework. On the other hand, intermittent labor force participation produces pronounced discontinuities in the lives of many women.

Emotional results of prejudices against older women

The phenomenon of "self-hatred" is found in most groups of people who are the victims of discrimination. If enough people tell you something negative about yourself for a long enough time, you end up believing it. Thus older women typically discredit themselves in both obvious and subtle ways. A successful film star of 72 admits that men are favored as actors over women in old age. Yet she insists she has no use for women's liberation: "No, no, no. I want a man to know more. . . . Physically I want him stronger, mentally I want him stronger." A representative of the Department of Labor's Women's Bureau said many older women have a "Uriah Heep" attitude about employment, feeling they must appear obsequious and obedient because they feel they have little of value to offer an employer.

There are women who profit from and exploit the insecurities of their contemporaries. Helena Rubenstein, one of the world's wealthiest self-made women, is a fascinating example of a female

---

[25] Summary available from National Institutes of Health, National Institute on Aging, Bethesda, Md. 20014.

[26] An analysis of the interpersonal connections between people, involving their affiliation and contacts with kin, friends, neighbors, acquaintances, and the community at large.

who maintained her own power and influence until age 92 while making millions off the cravings of women to stave off inevitable aging.

A pervasive theme in the efforts of older women to find a meaningful life is the preference for male company and the downgrading of female companionship. Many cannot see themselves as fulfilled unless they have a husband or at least some male to whom they can relate, and this becomes more frustrating as the male population thins out. Some women compensate with an overbearing idolization of a son or grandson. Others make sad, futile efforts to appear young and thus recapture the lost rights of their youth and early adulthood. The top-heavy ratio of women to men encourages an already culturally established pattern of competition with fellow females for the few remaining men. The mother-in-law syndrome is another way women may express their disdain toward their own sex (their daughters-in-law), as well as the envy an older woman can feel toward a younger woman. The harsh experiences of women during the aging process make it understandable that they may see the young as rivals not only for the attention of males but also for the very economic resources necessary for their survival in old age.

Some older women turn to religion, in a passionate excessive manner that is less a spiritual search than a way of filling the void of their former family. If a man is not available, then perhaps a masculine god-figure may give some sense of comfort and meaningfulness. Religion can be truly beneficial, but it can also serve as a cover-up for terribly lonely women who have no relevant human beings in their lives.

The "club and charity" set is a further example of the attempt to find meaning. Here, again, such activities can be highly beneficial both to the donor and to the receiver of charity. Yet it is quickly evident in many cases that the real purpose is to fill empty time—rather than getting to the task of relieving the suffering of others. There are, of course, remarkable exceptions but many older women congregate together in dilettante fashion instead of using their considerable abilities in more constructive and creative attempts to alleviate social miseries.

What's good about being an older woman?

We have detailed some of the difficulties of older women. But there is more. Many older women have learned much about the double whammy of sex and age discriminations and have a great deal to teach the young. Their experiences give us guidelines for combating prejudice and supporting older women in their efforts to find a satisfying life.

Older women today have unexplored potential in terms of personal expression. In addition to their increasingly good records of health and longevity, they do not have to struggle with the conflicts between mothering and careers, which, even with day care, often trouble younger women. They are in the interesting position of being the only adult females who are truly free of the demands of child responsibility and, in many cases, marital responsibility. The idea of dependency on a male is deeply ingrained in white and in many minority cultures, but older women could conceivably challenge this tired stereotype. For example, many women who were forced into marriage by cultural and family pressures might have been happier single, as career or professional women. Educational programs should be designed especially for them to explore late-life careers. Other older women are homosexuals who have been hiding as "heteros" for a lifetime and might be willing to "come out" if the climate were favorable.[27] Numbers of others could have satisfied heterosexual companionship and maternal needs without marriage or children and still can. They could also adopt the sexual option now reserved for men. We might, for instance, be surprised at the number of secret liaisons between young males and older females,

---

[27] A rare description of a 75-year-old woman's attitudes toward her own lesbianism and that of others is found in Klaich, D.: Woman + woman: attitudes toward lesbianism, New York, 1974, Simon & Schuster, chap. 10.

A 91-year-old winner of a state senior talent contest after giving a
dramatic reading on women's rights.

Photo by Patricia and William Oriol.

which could surface if they became socially acceptable.

Older women by example could give younger women confidence to resist the mania to remain young, with the knowledge that a rich life can await them as they age. Young women and even the middle-aged are floundering for viable female models to follow. A considerable number of older women have forged unique positions for themselves in terms of identity, personal achievement, and even financial and political power, but they need to be located and made visible.

Politically the older woman is in an advantageous position and it is likely to improve. With a voting strength of almost 14 million, 90% of whom are registered voters and most of whom vote regularly, they represent a major and fast-growing constituency that already could elect their own congresspersons in those states where they reside in high proportions. They have the available time and energy to lobby, campaign, and promote candidates, since 90% are retired from active employment. There is reason to suppose that women as candidates for the presidency and as appointees to the Supreme Court may come from this age group, since older people often fill these positions.

In spite of widespread poverty for many women, there are tremendous sums of money in the hands of widows and female heirs. Women might take on their own financial management instead of entrusting it to male husband-surrogates. Women of wealth could exert much greater influence in economic, social, and other spheres if they used the resources they already have. They could provide backing for the women's movement and specifically for their own age-group problems.

Advocacy groups specifically for older women are beginning to form. The Older Women's League was begun in 1978 by Tish Sommers and Laurie Shields and became a national organization in 1980.[28] The National Action Forum for Older Women also began in 1978, under the leadership of Jane Procino and Nancy King.[29] The Women's Studies Program at George Washington University, directed by Charlotte Conable, formed a coalition with the Congressional Women's Caucus in 1980 to draft and promote legislation to benefit older women.[30]

Many older women have lived out their last years in the way thus characterized by Edna St. Vincent Millay: "Life must go on—I forget just why." But there is a sturdy and hopefully growing group of older women who are undaunted and look to life with continued enthusiasm. An 83-year-old former suffragist who recently became excited by the women's movement states, "I don't want to leave the world without being a part of this."

RETIREMENT

Because fewer than 10 population-based studies have dealt with the vital issue of the effects of retirement on mortality and health, most of what we know about retirement is information gathered from small studies of specific groups of people or from our own personal experience with retired persons. In the population-based studies, mandatory retirement at age 65 has *not* been shown to be im-

mediately or chronically related to increased illness or death. But at least three studies suggest a temporary increase in morbidity (illness) and mortality 3 to 5 years after retirement, predominately among blue-collar workers.

Recent changes in the law have ended mandatory retirement in the public sector. In most cases, it has been moved up to age 70 in the private sector, with the exception of certain business executives. This was largely the result of efforts by Congressman Claude Pepper (D-Fla.).

Everyone "reacts" to retirement, but not everyone goes through a "retirement crisis." Retirement does not mean the same thing for everybody. Some view it as the end of their worthwhile life and think that anything beyond is downhill. This is particularly true of men who tend to identify strongly with their jobs. Some are "workaholics" who are addicted to continuous laborings. Other people see retirement as a relief from hard work, a chance to rest, a period of passive enjoyment and relaxation. Still others believe that it marks the completing of their commitment to society and the beginning of their active commitment to themselves and all the things they have been waiting and wanting to do. It is not unusual to see second and even third careers occurring in late life, creative ventures begun, whole new personalities emerging as people discover and rediscover themselves. Max Lerner once said that retirement should enable people to move into work they love to pursue, after leaving work that has pursued them. The emotional quality of retirement depends on the individual personality, income, health, social circumstances, and sense of worth.

Work has long been recognized as a useful defense that occupies minds and bodies and keeps feelings in control. This brings to mind the individuals who become sick, anxious, or upset on Sundays, holidays, or vacations and feel fine once they are back at work. In retirement, these symptoms can become everyday occurrences unless work substitutes and a satisfactory new life-style are found; otherwise perfectly healthy men and women may develop headaches, depression, gas-

[28] Older Women's League, 3800 Harrison St., Oakland, Calif. 94611.

[29] National Action Forum for Older Women, 2000 P St., N.W., Suite 508, Washington, D.C. 20036.

[30] Women's Studies—George Washington University, 2025 I St., N.W., Washington, D.C. 20052.

Congressman Claude Pepper, political leader responsible for successful
Congressional legislation regarding mandatory retirement.

Courtesy Congressman Claude Pepper's Congressional Office.

trointestinal symptoms, and a pattern of oversleeping. These disorders can begin even in anticipation of retirement. Irritability, loss of interest, lack of energy, increased alcoholic intake, and reduced efficiency are all familiar and common reactions. Many people have work dreams in which they dream of being back on the job. In many cases these feelings are transitional as the retired person adjusts to a new life and new associations. Consideration must be given to the tremendous changes that take place over a relatively brief period of time, including the absence of structured work and one's role as a producer of work, the removal from working colleagues, the absence of travel to and from work, the change in daily scheduling, and the reduction in income—usually to about one half of its former level.

Retirement comes in three phases: The actual day itself is perhaps a day of celebration or commemoration. Then comes the longer period of working through feelings and adjusting to a new life. Finally people arrive at a state in which they think of themselves as "retired." At this point the adjustment has been made and people become identified with a new life condition.

The phenomena of both overpreparation and underpreparation for retirement can be observed. The overly prepared are those who anxiously begin to plan ahead in early middle age, with elaborate attentions to the details of their future life. Such overachievers are usually indicating that they are unhappy or insecure in their present life and are trying desperately for something better in the future. On the other extreme are those who do not even conceive of, let alone prepare for, retirement and who are sadly surprised when it catches them unaware. The most successful retirees are those who take reasonable precautions for their old age but enjoy living in the present rather than expecting some future "golden age."

Many women have dual roles as homemakers and career working women, which may be an unfair burden in earlier years but can serve them well as they retire from employment. Keeping a home always provides a familiar pattern of life to fall back on. The majority of men have no such diverse identity (which may also be true of some unmarried women). In Chapter 3 we describe the need for male as well as female liberation to allow men a sense of themselves apart from their work. The present overidentification with work may be a factor in the high rate of suicide in older white men.

We wish to reemphasize that not everyone dreads retirement. Many people never identify personally with their jobs but use them only to survive financially. Countless numbers are only too delighted to get rid of work that has been backbreaking, boring, dead-end, demeaning, or demanding. And there are numerous older people who truly look forward to and enjoy the freedom and possibilities of a new way of life.

CRIME[31]

Older people commit very little crime. There are a few "geriatric criminals." In one study of 722 persons over 60 arrested for minor causes by the San Francisco police, 82.3% were charged only with drunkenness.[32] Yet older persons are the frequent victims of crime, especially robbery and, in the case of older women, rape (see the National Institute on Mental Health's report on rape and the older woman[33]). Experience can do little to protect the older person today, particularly the urban dweller in the inner city and other low-income areas.

Traditionally the older person in the community had a role in that he had lived longer, he therefore had more experience, he was wiser. . . . he knew where the tigers were in the jungle.

NATHAN W. SHOCK

---

[31] See House Select Committee on Aging, Research into crimes against the elderly, parts I and II (hearings), Jan. 31 and Feb. 1, 1978, Pub. No. (Comm.) 95-122, Washington, D.C., 1978, U.S. Government Printing Office.

[32] Epstein, L.J., Mills, C., and Simon, A.: Antisocial behavior of the elderly, Comprehensive Psychiatry **11:**36-42, 1970.

[33] National Institute of Mental Health, National Center for the Prevention and Control of Rape: Rape and the older woman: a guide to prevention and protection, Pub. No. (DHEW) Adm 78-534, Washington, D.C., 1979, U.S. Government Printing Office.

Crime in cities is widespread, as is the fear of crime. According to some figures the actual incidence of crime against persons over age 65 is not higher than other age groups. However, the quality of the data (for example, reporting of crimes) must be questioned since many older persons are afraid to report crime for fear of retaliation by the criminal. Moreover, older people live in fear—especially in cities—and often stay indoors to an unnatural degree, thereby protecting themselves from crime by virtual self-imprisonment in their own homes.

The *District of Columbia Report to the 1971 White House Conference on Aging,* subtitled "Metropolitan Police Contact with the Elderly,"[34] is among the few documents of even relatively recent date that show the degree to which crimes are committed against older persons. In Project Assist, Brostoff pointed to "a large group of old people (over 60) . . . a depressed underclass . . . who are particularly vulnerable to crime, easy victims of street robbery, unable to move out of high-crime

[34] In June 1970, the Office of Services to the Aged, Human Resources Administration, D.C. Government, awarded a contract to the Washington School of Psychiatry to study the relationship between older people and the metropolitan police department. The purposes of the research contract were as follows:
1. To determine the extent to which older persons are victims of crime in the District of Columbia
2. To discover what social or health problems result from such victimization and how they are dealt with
3. To ascertain under what circumstances older persons come to the attention of the police when no crime has been committed, but aid of police is sought because other community resources are unknown or not available
4. To explore methods and techniques for quick and appropriate referral for service by police in disposing of problems of older persons encountered as victims of crime or as persons needing or seeking help

Project Director Phyllis Brostoff, MSW, conducted the study, called Project Assist, and compiled the above-mentioned document for the White House Conference. (For additional information see Brostoff, P., Brown, R., and Butler, R.N.: The public interest: report no. 6: beating up on the elderly: police, social work, crime, Aging and Human Development **3**:319-322, 1972.)

neighborhoods . . . and likely to have no other community resource to turn to other than the police if trouble occurs. . . ." Police reports often do not indicate the ages of victims. However, the incidence of crime that is recorded against older persons suggests that crimes occur primarily where large numbers of older people are concentrated. Public housing complexes are a prime target, since almost 20% of people in such housing are 65 years of age or older. Bus and subway stops, basement laundry rooms in apartment buildings, dark halls, back doors, elevators, and shortcuts (paths, passageways hidden from view) can all be dangerous places for older people. Mailboxes in unguarded apartment vestibules are the province of thieves who know when Social Security and welfare checks arrive. Food stamps are a frequently stolen item. The disabilities of old age—deafness, slowness, blindness, spotty memory—make older people more vulnerable.

In Washington, D.C., about 90% of crimes against older persons were robberies and 8% were assaults. Most robberies take place on the streets rather than at home. The methods used are purse-snatching, frightening, and strong-arming. The amount of money stolen is often under $5, and little is ever recovered. Stolen checks and food stamps are recoverable, but the delay can mean having no food or rent money when it is needed. Many of the poor aged have no phone on which to notify police of crime. Crimes committed by relatives or landlords against older people rarely are prosecuted because they get lost in the law enforcement system. Butler has described the "battered old person syndrome" (known in England as "gran-slamming") in which battering and abuse take place within the home or family circle, perpetrated by relatives or acquaintances.[35] Columnist Russell Baker's article "On Beating Grandmother" in *The New York Times* (Nov. 16, 1976) also summarizes the issues. Steinmetz additionally has

[35] Butler, R.N.: Why survive? Being old in America, New York, 1975, Harper & Row, Publishers, Inc.

done research on violence in the family, including its younger and older members.[36]

Older persons seek police help with social problems as well as those caused by crime; for example, 15% of telephone calls to the police during Project Assist were about crimes, while 40% came from people asking for help and information (how to get an ambulance, heat in an apartment, etc.). Thus the police are excellent sources for the location and referral of isolated older people. They are contacts for people with chronic brain syndromes who wander from home, older alcoholics, and acute brain syndrome victims who are in difficulty on the street or at home.[37]

Naturally the main responsibility of the police is law enforcement and their focus is on prevention of crime and apprehension of criminals. Many object to providing social services and want a "magic number" they can call for referral of social problems. Social agencies could work more closely with the police than they now do. Multiservice senior centers would be an ideal resource for the variety of problems older people bring to the police.

Protection of older people from crime should be improved.[38] Escort services could be arranged by volunteer groups; dead bolt locks should be provided for the older person's residence. The federal government now arranges to send checks directly to banks free of charge for those persons who would prefer this, thus reducing the theft of checks. Special low-cost checking account service might encourage people not to carry cash but to establish credit and to pay by check whenever possible. It has been said that if it were generally known that older people no longer dealt in cash, the incentive for criminal attack would be markedly reduced. Vertical policing throughout all the floors in high-rise buildings should be done by police on the beat or by volunteers. Police could perform security audits of buildings to spot crime hazards. Tenants themselves could guard mailrooms at the beginning of each month to protect against check thefts. The older woman might carry an old empty purse or the older man a wallet with a few dollars as decoys to give up under attack.

A safe environment (versus one of fear and genuine danger) is crucial to the mental health of older people. No one can live under threat of harm without physical and emotional repercussions. Older persons need protection also when they get into trouble (forgetfulness, getting lost, home accidents, isolation, and self-neglect) because of their own disabilities. And finally, they need protection against the fraud (for example, medical quackery) or deceit that preys on their vulnerabilities. (See the excellent selected bibliography, *Criminal Justice and the Elderly,* organized by topic, including impact of crime on older persons, consumer fraud, and victim assistance and restitution.[39])

---

[36] Steinmetz, S.K.: Violence in the family, testimony prepared for the Senate Sub-Committee on Child and Human Development, March 1978. See also Block, M.R., and Sinnott, J.D., editors: The battered elder syndrome: an exploratory study, College Park, 1979, University of Maryland, Center on Aging; and Lau, E.E., and Kostberg, J.: Abuse of the elderly by informal care providers: practice and research issues, paper presented at 31st Annual Meeting of the Gerontological Society, Dallas, Nov. 20, 1978.

[37] Matthews, R., and Rowland, L.: How to recognize and handle abnormal people—a manual for the police officer, New York, 1960, The National Association for Mental Health, Inc., chaps. 6 and 10.

[38] See Elderly are crime targets, SOS, Senior Opportunities and Services Technical Assistance Bulletin 2(4):1-3, 1972. Also a useful booklet entitled "Your Retirement Safety Guide" has been prepared by the American Association of Retired Persons, 1225 Connecticut Ave., N.W., Washington, D.C.

[39] Boston, G., Nitzberg, R., and Kravitz, M., (compilers), U.S. Department of Justice, Law Enforcement Assistance Administration, National Institute of Law Enforcement and Criminal Justice, Jan. 1979. For free copies write to the National Criminal Justice Reference Service (NCJRS), Department F, Box 6000, Rockville, Md. 20850.

ALCOHOLISM[40]

Alcoholics live to old age in greater numbers than ever. In addition, some older people become alcoholics only after becoming old.[41] Studies indicate that the overall incidence of alcoholism in older people is lower than among younger people, but is it more often a hidden condition in later life because most older problem drinkers are retired. In addition, certain groups of older people are highly prone to alcoholism. Elderly widowers have the highest rate of alcoholism of all age groups.

Alcoholism is a condition resulting from excessive ingestion of or idiosyncratic reaction to alcohol. A *problem drinker* is one who drinks enough to cause problems for him- or herself and society.[42] *Acute* alcoholism is a state of acute intoxication with temporary and reversible mental and bodily effects. *Dipsomania* refers to periodic or "spree" drinking. *Chronic* alcoholism is the fact and consequence of habitual use.

The National Council on Alcoholism, formed in 1971, issued a set of criteria to diagnose the "disease" of alcoholism.[43] Major criteria include the following:

1. Drinking a fifth of whiskey a day, or its equivalent in wine or beer, for a 180-pound person[44]

DIAGNOSTIC CLUES FOR THE CLINICAL PRESENTATION OF ALCOHOLISM IN OLD AGE

1. Insomnia
2. Impotence
3. Problem with control of gout
4. Rapid onset of confusional state
5. Uncontrollable hypertension
6. Unexplained falls

---

2. Alcoholic "blackouts"
3. Withdrawal syndrome—gross tremor, hallucinosis, convulsions, or delirium tremens (DTs)
4. Blood alcohol level above 150 mg/100 ml without seeming intoxicated
5. Continued drinking despite medical advice or family or job problems clearly caused by drinking

Minor criteria include such signs as gulping drinks, frequent car accidents, surreptitious drinking, repeated "going on the wagon," and drinking to relieve anger, fatigue, or depression.

Thus major criteria are symptoms that represent conclusive evidence of physiological or psycho-

---

[40] The National Council on Alcoholism (NCOA) estimates that There are about 9 million alcoholics in the United States. The Langley Porter studies under Simon and Lowenthal provide information on alcoholism in older people. The NCOA (1424 16th St., N.W., Suite 401, Washington, D.C. 20036) established a blue ribbon commission on alcoholism and the aged in 1980, chaired by Wilbur Mills.

[41] For further information on alcoholism in old age see Mishara, B.L., and Kastenbaum, R.K.: Alcohol and old age, New York, 1980, Grune & Stratton, Inc.; Mayfield, D.G.: Alcohol problems in the aging patient. In Fann, W.E., and Maddox, G.L., editors: Drug issues in geropsychiatry, Baltimore, 1974, The Williams & Wilkins Co., pp. 35-40; Riccitelli, M.C.: Alcoholism in the aged—modern concepts, Journal of the American Geriatrics Society **15**:142-147, 1967; Rosin, A.J., and Glatt, M.M.: Alcohol excess in the elderly, Quarterly Journal of Studies on Alcohol **32**:53-59, 1974; and Zimberg, S.: The elderly alcoholic, The Gerontologist **14**:221-224, 1974.

[42] As defined by the U.S. Department of Health and Human Services' National Institute on Alcohol Abuse and Alcoholism (NIAAA).

[43] During the 1950s the World Health Organization and the American Medical Association declared alcoholism a disease. This, of course, raised the issue of whether personal responsibility (self-control) plays a role in addiction. For example, drug addiction is still treated as a crime rather than as a public health problem similar to alcoholism. There is great question as to the conceptual validity and the therapeutic wisdom of regarding alcoholism solely as a disease. A balance must be struck between that which the individual can control and that which is beyond his or her control.

[44] Beers and wines have a relatively higher concentration of various kinds of solids, which accounts for slower absorption. The alcohol in whiskey, brandy, vodka, and gin is absorbed more rapidly.

logical dependence, while minor ones are symptoms usually associated with, but not specific to, alcoholism.[45] (For diagnostic clues for the clinical presentation of alcoholism in old age, see the box on p. 133.)

Alcoholism is the third leading health problem in the United States, after heart disease and cancer.[46] Most deaths directly caused by alcoholism are a result of cirrhosis of the liver. A substantial portion of highway and home accidents are the result of drinking. It is estimated that alcoholism shortens life expectancy by 10 to 12 years. It may cause heart disease of several kinds and can damage the brain. It may lead to chronic impotence in men by damaging the central nervous system and upsetting hormonal balance. (Transient impotence from excessive drinking may also occur but is reversible.) Alcoholism also contributes to falls and other serious accidents as well as fires. (On the other hand, there is evidence that drinking in moderation may be healthful—for example, in helping prevent heart disease by converting low-density lipoproteins to high-density lipoproteins.[47])

There are numerous opinions as to what causes alcoholism. Some believe it is genetically determined; others see it as a learned adaptation to psychological stresses. It may be secondary to depression, for example, or it may be an inability to tolerate frustration. Still others view alcoholism as a reflection of social conditions such as poverty or an outgrowth of the encouragement of drinking by various cultures.

Alcohol is a central nervous system depressant. It is not, as many believe, a stimulant except as it indirectly inhibits cortical control (higher intellectual functions are associated with the cerebral cortex) and thereby releases emotional reactions. With inhibition and impairment of intellectual functions comes failure in judgment, which adds to impairments that may already exist as a result of cerebral arteriosclerosis and senile brain disease. Alcohol can affect muscular coordination and bodily equilibrium, causing falls and accidents in old age.

Studies at the National Institute on Aging have shown that alcohol more severely impairs old subjects (55 to 80 years) than young (20 to 54 years) on a number of important behavioral measures, including reaction time and delayed recognition (memory). Aging does not significantly influence alcohol metabolism but does impair physiological tolerance to alcohol. The older subjects not only were more severely impaired immediately after drinking but also recovered significantly more slowly.

Chronic alcoholism usually involves poor nutrition primarily caused by vitamin and protein deficiencies and liver dysfunction. In addition to a general deterioration of the personality, one may see delirium tremens[48] followed by Korsakoff's

---

[45] See National Council on Alcoholism, Criteria Committee: Criteria for the diagnosis of alcoholism, American Journal of Psychiatry **129**:127-135, 1972; and Chafetz, M.E., Seixas, F.A., Kaim, S.C., and Cloud, L.A.: Alcoholism criteria: an important step, American Journal of Psychiatry **129**:214-216, 1972.

[46] Federal agencies concerned with alcoholism (and drug abuse): (1) Alcohol, Drug Abuse, and Mental Health Administration (ADA-MHA): A government agency within the U.S. Department of Health and Human Services responsible for administering federal grant programs to advance and support research, training, and service programs in the areas of alcoholism, drug abuse, and mental health; (2) National Institute of Alcohol Abuse and Alcoholism: An institute within ADA-MHA responsible for programs dealing with alcohol abuse and alcoholism; and (3) National Institute on Drug Abuse; An institute within ADA-MHA responsible for programs dealing with narcotic and drug abuse.

[47] See the National Heart, Lung and Blood Institute–supported Honolulu Heart Study.

[48] An acute and sometimes fatal brain disorder (in 10% to 15% of untreated patients) caused by withdrawal or relative withdrawal from alcohol, usually developing in 24 to 96 hours. A hisotry of excessive and unusually prolonged intake is present, and the symptoms of the syndrome include fever, tremors, ataxia, and sometimes convulsions, frightening illusions, delusions, and hallucinations. The condition is often accompanied by nutritional deficiencies. It is a medical emergency.

psychosis. Confabulations or fabrications of memory and inability to retain new information (retention defect) are the latter's most striking symptoms. Short-term memory loss (amnesia) and disorientation are present.

Wernicke's encephalopathy may also occur with chronic alcoholism. It is characterized by mental changes such as delirium, apathy, and/or Korsakoff's syndrome, ataxia, and eye signs (for example, motor palsies and nystagmus). Thiamine deficiency is the major cause, and prompt intravenous administration may be life saving.

The alcoholic amnestic syndrome (a loss of memory for events occurring during a drinking session, probably caused by bilateral damage to the hippocampal and limbic systems of the brain) has led some to postulate an ''alcoholic dementia''—with mental and personal deterioration. However, the latter clear up on cessation of drinking and the provision of care. Only the amnestic syndrome remains. Sir Martin Roth has written that the evidence for a dementia associated with alcoholic damage of the central nervous system is not very convincing.

Alcoholism in old age is of two types in terms of duration: lifelong and late-life. The former used to result in death of middle-aged persons, but because of antibiotics, better nutritional care, and hospital management, many alcoholics now live to grow old. In addition, some older people first turn to alcohol in old age because of grief, depression, loneliness, boredom, or pain. A grief-stricken widow who drinks is an example of this. Another pattern in alcoholism is a lifelong habit of drinking that becomes even more pronounced as life stresses increase.

■ Mr. D, the black gardener and handyman in a white, wealthy neighborhood, was only 65 years old, but he looked much older. His eyes were tired and sometimes vacant. He worked at hard, backbreaking tasks, and each family in the neighborhood expected him to do the bulk of the work on their property. There were no paid vacations, no sick leave, and no retirement pension beyond the Social Security based on payments that were subtracted from his already meager paychecks. He had become arthritic, with painful, swollen joints. But his employers did not relax their expectations of him as he aged and grew more feeble. In fact, one employer called all the others when the worker became eligible for Social Security and said, ''We must be sure Billy doesn't take advantage of Social Security and earn more than he is supposed to.'' Mr. D had drunk steadily for years, on weekends, but now began coming to work drunk. His employers wondered, ''What has come over Billy?''

One sees a high proportion of alcoholism among older patients, mostly men, in Veterans Hospitals and Domiciliaries. It has been suggested that war experiences and exposure to the cultural drinking patterns of the armed services play a causative role, not to mention the special cut-price liquor ''package'' stores run by the military in the United States and around the world.

One also sees many older men and women among the homeless derelicts who sleep on sidewalks, doorsteps, park benches, subway trains, and train stations.[49] The stereotype of the ''Bowery bum'' applies to about 5% of alcoholics in the United States. The Salvation Army and other religious groups provide free care, food, and lodging. Dorothy Day's exemplary work in her bowery mission concentrated on the homeless alcoholic.

Alcoholism in nursing homes and homes for the aging is another problem. Family members may bring alcohol to the patient directly or in a disguised bottle. (Old Listerine bottles are favorites for this use.) In some homes patients are able to bribe staff members to get them drinks. Alcoholics Anonymous has become involved in several homes with good results.

Treatment of chronic alcoholism usually consists of detoxification or ''drying out,'' supple-

---

[49] For the moving account of an older man's life as an alcoholic see Straus, R.: Escape from custody: a study of alcoholism and institutional dependency as reflected in the life record of a homeless man, New York, 1974, Harper & Row, Publishers, Inc.

mented by vitamins, meals, fluids, rest, and medical care. There can be many associated physical
problems. A full physical examination should be
done, checking for such conditions as diabetes,
pancreatitis, tuberculosis, peripheral neuropathy,
and subdural hematomas. Many alcoholics who
are poor or isolated from their families come to
medical attention through police. The middle- or
upper-income alcoholic is often hospitalized under
a disguised diagnosis, for example, malnutrition or
gastritis, in order to avoid the stigma of alcoholism.[50]

Disulfiram (Antabuse) is a drug used to maintain
sobriety while a person undergoes supportive or
psychotherapeutic treatment. If taken as prescribed on a regular basis, it produces highly unpleasant symptoms whenever a person drinks, including pounding of the heart, nausea, vomiting,
and shortness of breath (the result of acetaldehyde
production). Side effects in the usual dose range of
0.25 gm daily include fatigue, reduced libido, and
reduced potency. Toxic psychoses can occur at
higher doses. In a patient over 60 it is of utmost
importance to evaluate his or her cardiovascular
status, since myocardial and coronary diseases are
definite contraindications. Diabetes mellitus, cerebral damage, kidney disease, hypothyroidism, and
hepatic cirrhosis or insufficiency all require extreme caution because of possible accidental reactions. Disulfiram may also affect the metabolism
of other drugs.

Mild tranquilizers (for example, chlordiazepoxide [Librium], diazepam [Valium]) are used in the
management of some patients as they withdraw
from alcohol. However, they must be prescribed
carefully, since alcohol and these drugs may potentiate each other (synergism). Heavy tranquilizers and sedatives mixed with alcohol can be life
threatening. Dependency on drugs is also a danger,
and many doctors believe that drugs should only be
given to inpatients.

Alcoholics Anonymous (AA)[51] has an impressive record of helping alcoholics achieve sobriety.
This organization of about 700,000 members
worldwide consists of recovered alcoholics who
collectively assist alcoholics through personal and
group support. AA also has a program for spouses
and other relatives of alcoholics (Al Anon) and one
for teenagers whose parents drink (Alateen). Because of the magnitude of drinking problems
among older people, we would like to see an
AA program set up especially for them—perhaps
called Alaelder. Their adult children and their
grandchildren should also be involved where possible, since families tend to be more negative and
unsupportive to the older person who drinks heavily.

Nursing homes and other institutions could develop treatment programs.[52] Group therapy (alone
or with supportive psychotherapy and family counseling), is another useful approach. Recreation
therapy and pastoral counseling may be helpful.
Labor-management programs to treat problem
drinking among employees have been successful
because of the powerful added incentive of avoiding the loss of one's job. In general, however,
alcoholism is extremely difficult to control. Determination and patience on the part of both the
alcoholic and doctor or therapist are crucial. It may
be necessary to start over again and again; the
treatment of alcoholism is often long term or lifelong. Family and other social supports are immensely important.

HEARING IMPAIRMENT[53]

Hearing is so crucial to mental health in old age
that we wish to give it special emphasis. Hearing

---

[50] The American Hospital Association claims that 25% to 30%
of all adult medicosurgical patients in metropolitan hospitals,
regardless of diagnosis, have been found to be suffering from
alcoholism.

[51] Most towns and cities have an AA listing in the telephone
book. If not, information may be obtained by writing to General Service Office, Box 459, Grand Central Station, New
York, N.Y. 10017. There are no dues or fees for membership.

[52] For example, the Queen Nursing Home and Treatment Center
in Minneapolis, Minn., treats only older alcoholic persons.

[53] Schow, R.L., et al.: Communication disorders of the aged. A
guide for health professionals, Baltimore, 1978, University
Park Press, p. 1.

loss is more common than visual loss, although both increase with age. Hearing impairments rise gradually with age and then increase sharply over the age of 60.[54] About 19% of individuals age 45 to 54 have some problem in hearing; as compared to 75% in the 70- to 79-year-old age group. The National Health Examination Survey of 1961-1962 studied pure tone audiometric measurements at six different frequencies in persons 18 to 79 years of age. Nearly 30% of persons age 65 to 74 and almost half of those age 75 to 79 showed hearing loss for speech alone, as compared to 10% in the general population. In the older age group 450,000 people were profoundly deaf and totally isolated from any sound. In the National Health and Nutrition Examination Survey (HANES I) of 1971, 23% of those 65 to 74 years of age and 40% of those age 75 and above reported that they had hearing impairments that were somewhat handicapping. These surveys provide general estimates of the prevalence of hearing loss but do not characterize the loss by type or cause.

HANES I, conducted in 1971 and 1972, included audiometric testing that is now being analyzed. More recent epidemiological surveys also have explored hearing. A currently unpublished report on the 1977 Health Interview Survey indicates that 29.3% of persons age 65 and over reported hearing impairments. Hearing loss is more common among older men than older women; perhaps one of the explanations is their greater rate of exposure to noise in the workplace.[55] However, for reasons still unknown, *severe* hearing loss is more common among older women than among older men. Depression and paranoid ideation are the most common severe emotional consequences of hearing loss.

When a person becomes deaf through disease . . . not knowing what his fellow men are saying he becomes doubtful of auditory memories and images; he misinterprets auditory sense impressions which have been distorted by disease, and incorporates tinnitus caused by such disease into his world of inner phantasy. He projects his inner feelings of inferiority caused by his deafness onto his environment and develops ideas of reference. Systematization soon follows, with active delusions of persecution. If the personality is sufficiently unstable a psychotic illness results.[56]

In Chapter 3 we discuss the relationship between hearing loss and depression. Hearing defects create irritation in others because they interfere so markedly with communication. The loud, badly articulated speech of the hard-of-hearing person and the need to shout and speak slowly make simple conversations frustrating. The hard-of-hearing may find themselves isolated in a crowd or at a large dinner party because the background noise exacerbates the hearing problem. Persons with hearing problems appear to be constantly afraid of embarrassment that might follow from missing or misunderstanding a comment in the conversation. It is not yet well understood why people are embarrassed by disability, but with the hearing impaired it clearly must have something to do with the tendency of others to be impatient and insensitive to a person with such a deficit. The hard-of-hearing are often mistakenly thought to be retarded or mentally ill. The dramatic story of Ludwig Van Beethoven notwithstanding, the hearing impaired receive much less empathy than the visually impaired and are more subject to depression, demoralization, and psychotic symptomatology.

[54] Leske, M.C.: Prevalence estimates of communicative disorders in the U.S., report prepared for the National Institute of Neurological and Communicative Disorders and Stroke, 1978.

[55] Kovar, M.G.: Elderly people: the population 65 years and over. In Department of Health, Education and Welfare, National Center for Health Statistics: Health, United States 1976-1977, Pub. No. (HRA) 77-1232, Washington, D.C., 1977, U.S. Government Printing Office.

[56] From Houston, F., and Royse, A.B.: Relationship between deafness and psychotic illness. The Journal of Mental Science **100**:990-993, 1954. See also Cooper, A.F., et al.: Hearing loss in paranoid and affective psychoses of the elderly, Lancet **2**:851-854, 1974.

The phenomenon of increased reaction time associated with decreased auditory acuity in the presence of depression needs investigation,[57] as well as the association of mild hearing losses in the aged with diminished performance on verbal tests of intellectual ability.[58]

In the late years one is likely to observe nerve as well as conduction deafness.[59] Another source of hearing impairment involves the cochlea, a spiral tube of the inner ear, which resembles a small shell. The cochlea contains about 20,000 hair cells at birth, which gradually die off and cannot be replaced. Loss of these ganglion cells is called ''presbycusis'' and is believed to be associated with the aging of the body and/or brain. The central nervous system also is very important in hearing loss because it is the analyzing mechanism for sounds. Older people may be able to hear sounds but not understand them. Immigrants who have learned a second language appear to have special difficulty in this respect with their second language as they age. It is important not to overlook impacted wax (cerumen) in the ear as a cause of reduced hearing, although wax secretion probably diminishes with age.

Diseases like Meniere's syndrome may be char-

FACTORS TO CONSIDER IN DIAGNOSING HEARING LOSS
1. Excess noise exposure on the job during recreation, or in an individual's living situations
2. Middle ear infections
3. Circulatory diseases
4. Medications

---

acterized by hearing loss and are often treatable. Infections, diabetes,[60] cancer, chronic cardiovascular disease,[61] and many other conditions can also cause ear problems; thus referral to the ear-nose-and-throat specialist is always indicated. Special measures may be necessary to differentiate hearing loss from cognitive impairment in older persons who are severely disabled by conditions such as stroke.

Medicines can have a cumulative effect leading to hearing loss. Extensive use of aspirin, antibiotics such as the aminoglycosides, certain common diuretics, antitumor agents, and other medications have a known ototoxicity (literally meaning ''ear poisoning''), as well as drugs whose effects on hearing remain unknown. Many of the 38% of the older population who have arthritis undoubtedly consume large enough quantities of aspirin to affect their hearing. The increases in hypertension and heart failure with age signify a heightened probability of diuretic use and thus the danger of hearing loss. The possible effects on hearing must be part of the consideration when prescribing any drugs in large quantities and/or over a long term.

The hearing impairment occurring during aging is noted first in the higher sound frequencies and begins to be observed after age 50. This does not

---

[57] Birren, J.E., Butler, R.N., Greenhouse, S.W., Sokoloff, L., and Yarrow, M.R.: Interdisciplinary relationships: interrelations of physiological, psychological, and psychiatric findings in healthy elderly men. In Birren, J.E., Butler, R.N., Greenhouse, S.W., Sokoloff, L., and Yarrow, M.R.: Human aging: a biological and behavioral study, Pub. No. (PHS) 986, Washington, D.C., 1963, U.S. Government Printing Office (reprinted as Pub. No. [HSM] 71-9051, 1971, 1974).

[58] Granick, S., Kleban, M.H., and Weiss, A.D.: Relationships between hearing loss and cognition in normally hearing aged persons, Journal of Gerontology 31:434-440, 1978.

[59] Conduction deafness is caused by middle or external ear pathologic conditions (sound waves are blocked before they reach the inner ear), whereas nerve deafness results from interruption of the auditory nerve pathway. Nerve deafness is much more serious since it implies damage to the nerve that carries impulses to the brain or damage to the brain itself (see Ruben, R.: Aging and hearing. In Rossman, I.: Clinical geriatrics, Philadelphia, 1971, J.B. Lippincott Co., chap. 14).

[60] Taylor, I.D., and Irvin, J.: Some audiological aspects of diabetes mellitus, Journal of Laryngology and Otology 92:99-113, 1978.

[61] Rubinstein, M., et al.: Chronic cardiovascular pathology and hearing loss in the aged, Gerontology 23:4-9, 1977.

in itself interfere with normal speech, but the person may miss the song of birds, a distant telephone ring, or the ticking of a watch. A person with no hearing defect can hear a whispered message at 20 feet in a reasonably quiet room. When a whisper cannot be heard at 3 feet, the person already has a moderate hearing loss and probably has difficulty with ordinary conversation. This is especially true if the speaker talks rapidly or there is background noise. If a conversational voice cannot be heard 1 foot away, the person has severe hearing loss. Obviously the loss is profound if the person cannot hear a loud shout with the mouth to the ear. For older people there are often some problems involving consonants like *p* as in pay, *s* as in sam, *th* in then, *t* as in to, *k* as in could, *h* as in house, *sh* as in shoe, or *ch* as in church. They simply may not hear any of these sounds or may hear only some of them.

Noise pollution is increasingly a factor in hearing loss. The decibel level of one's environment can become great enough to permanently damage the tiny hairs in the inner ear. (The decibel, named after Alexander Graham Bell, is the smallest difference in loudness the human ear can detect.) For example, violinists tend to develop slight deafness in their left ear. Many experts predict hearing loss for young people who listen to loud rock music with high decibel levels. The increasing noise of city life portends hearing problems for the population in general. Studies of the Mabaans of Sudan, a tribe so isolated that they do not even use drums, show very clearly how lack of noise protects hearing, for they live with a background noise of 40 decibels and experience very little hearing dam-

age. Hospitals themselves have a high decibel level in spite of their "Quiet, please" signs. Following are examples of noises and their decibal levels.

Normal breathing	10 decibels
Leaves rustling in the breeze	20 decibels
Whisper	30 decibels
Quiet restaurant	50 decibels
Normal speech	60 decibels
Busy traffic	70 decibels
Niagara Falls	90 decibels
Subway	100 decibels
Pneumatic riveter	130 decibels
Jet takeoff (discomfort)	140 decibels

Of the estimated 14.5 million persons of all ages in the United States with hearing impairments, more than 10 million have not received medical attention to determine what steps can be taken to improve their hearing. This holds true for the estimated 5.5 million persons over 65 with hearing defects. Careful diagnosis is critical to restoring as much function as is recoverable. The results of careful diagnosis and treatment can be favorable even in a large population of institutionalized patients.[62] Institutions themselves should be places where verbal communication is both necessary and rewarding to patients.[63]

VISUAL IMPAIRMENT

The four most common causes of visual impairment in people over 65 years are macular degeneration, cataracts (lens opacities), glaucoma,[64] and diabetic retinopathy.[65] These account for 20%, 17%, 13%, and 12%, respectively, of all blind-

[62] Smith, C.R., and Fay, T.H.: A program of auditory rehabilitation for aged persons in a chronic disease hospital, ASHA; Journal of the American Speech and Hearing Association **19:** 417-420, 1977.
[63] Alpiner, J.G.: Rehabilitation of the geriatric client. In Alpiner, J.G., editor: Handbook of adult rehabilitative audiology, Baltimore, 1978, Williams & Wilkins Co.
[64] Glaucoma patients should avoid emotional upsets and beware of tricyclic antidepressants, since both may increase intraocular pressure.

[65] *Macular degeneration* affects a vital part of the retina and leads to loss of central vision, leaving peripheral vision intact. *Glaucoma* involves increased tension within and hardening of the eyeball as a result of increased fluid. There are two basic types: acute congestive (narrow-angle) and chronic (wide-angle). The latter is the most common form of the disease. *Diabetic retinopathy* is a deterioration of the retina caused by chronic diabetes.

ness in people over 65.[66] Nearly half of the legally blind[67] population is 65 years of age or older. In 1971, 9.6 million persons in the United States had visual impairments. Much of this loss is avoidable either through prevention or treatment of the disability. Glaucoma screening tests, for example, are an age-specific preventive health care measure recommended for persons over 40 years of age. It should be noted that only 35% of the adult population received glaucoma screening tests in a recent 2-year period of study.

Nonmedical members of mental health teams should learn the common physical symptoms of eye problems, to avoid putting a psychiatric label on a physical process and to increase empathy and understanding. For instance, if a person reports colored halos around lights, this could be one of the classic prodromal symptoms of glaucoma and not an illusion caused by psychological processes. Such knowledge can result in quicker and more accurate diagnosis and treatment.

Nearly all older people wear glasses because of presbyopia (a form of farsightedness occurring after middle age, caused by diminished elasticity of the crystalline lens). But other than this, about 80% of older people have reasonably good sight until age 90 and beyond. In many cases at least one eye functions well, even though the other may lose vision. There may be an increased slowness in visually adapting to darkness; proper lighting is especially important, including night lights. Psychologically older persons fear going blind and tend to overestimate the possibilities of this. But actual vision impairment can be devastating, in terms of both psychological isolation and physical immobilization. With many people vision loss is gradual, and they are able slowly to compensate

and adjust. A sudden loss of vision or a loss occurring when the person is feeble and unable to muster resources is usually the most difficult.

SEXUALITY IN OLD AGE
Societal attitudes toward sexuality in old age

Many people, young and old, are astonished at the idea of human beings making love in their seventies, eighties, and even beyond.[68] It is assumed that (1) older people do not have sexual desires, (2) they could not make love even if they *did* want to, (3) they are too fragile physically and it might hurt them, (4) they are physically unattractive and therefore sexually undesirable, and (5) anyway, the whole notion is shameful and decidedly perverse. There may also be anxieties on the part of young people related to oedipal connections with parents (we all know that, God forbid, *our* parents were not interested in sex). Yet, in work with older people it is clear that sex is a major concern in late life. Fear about loss of sexual prowess is a common preoccupation for the older man and can reach devastating proportions. Older women will often describe sexual desires, but many regard such feelings as undignified, if not depraved. Some older persons can freely accept their interest in sex, but their children and grandchildren may disapprove and make them feel guilty.

Older persons become the butt of jokes. Older men are frequently ridiculed as impotent or as "dirty old men." (A California bumper sticker protesting this idea read "I'm not a dirty old man. I'm a sexy senior citizen.") Older women fare even worse in the public eye. They are the neuters of our culture, who have mysteriously metamorphosed from desirable sexy young things to mature and sexually "interesting" women; finally, at about age 50, they steadily decline into sexual oblivion, according to popular opinion.

Homes for the aged, nursing homes, and mental

---

[66] Moorhead, H.B., et al.: Causes of blindness in 4,965 persons whom it stated were added to their MRA registers in 1966. In Proceedings of 1960 Conference of Model Reporting Area for Blindness, Washington, D.C., 1969, U.S. Public Health Service.

[67] In legal blindness, central visual acuity does not exceed 20/200 in either eye with corrective lenses, or the visual field is less than an angle of 20 degrees.

[68] Butler, R.N., and Lewis, M.I.: Sex after sixty. A guide for men and women for their later years, New York, 1976, Harper & Row, Publishers, Inc. (paperback title: Love and sex after sixty [1977]).

institutions all add to the impression that older persons are sexless.[69] There are no provisions for privacy; in fact, there seems to be an agreement that the aged must be prevented from having *any* sexual contacts. They are often rigidly segregated, men from women, with no visiting in each other's rooms. Conjugal visits with spouses are seldom provided for. Even husbands and wives living in the same institution may not be allowed to live or sleep together. Nursing staffs become anxious and upset when older persons, understandably, resort to masturbation. The problem is often no less difficult for older people who live with their children or in other people's homes.

Curiously enough, even the Social Security system has been a barrier to remarriage, and consequently sex, because widows who remarried were forced to give up their former husbands' Social Security benefits. A reporter for the *Miami News* in 1965 described the practice known as "Social Security sin" wherein thousands of older people were living together in common-law arrangements to preserve their pensions. The problem was partially alleviated when Congress passed legislation allowing a widow to retain her previous pension or choose her new husband's benefits, whichever sum was greater.

The fear of death is another factor affecting sexuality. There are many symbolic associations between sexual activity and death—as in the French word for orgasm, "petit mort" or little death. Fears of the occurrence of heart attacks or strokes during the course of sex may lead couples to acquire twin beds, separate bedrooms, and a habit of abstinence that may or may not be justified medically. Currents of anxiety, depression, and hostility can accompany these fears as sexuality is inhibited.

Female longevity creates another baffling situation. Since 7% of women never marry, many others are widowed relatively early, and still others have husbands who are older than they and perhaps sickly, there are many women without partners. What alternatives do they have? Women as a group do not yet have the cultural prerogatives of men to socialize with younger members of the opposite sex. There are not enough older men available. Extramarital affairs are difficult for many to reconcile religously or morally. Masturbation, although increasing in old age, is still considered shameful or harmful. Thus women legitimately complain that society has not provided suitable sexual expression or even information that is relevant to sexual needs in late life. Someone half-seriously, half-facetiously suggested that polygamy legalized after age 60 might be a sensible solution to the undersupply of men. Older women reacted sharply. One said, "I am lonesome, but not that lonesome!" Better solutions might be the equalizing of the life-span through research, the equalizing of sex roles to give women the same opportunities as men, the encouragement of dating and marriage with younger men, and the development of more lenient attitudes toward the homosexuality that already exists.[70]

Homosexuality as a life-style has both advantages and disadvantages in the later years. The stereotype of the aging homeosexual is that of a lonely, bitter, isolated person. The reality, according to the few studies in this area, is much more complex and includes close, satisfying relation-

---

[69] Three empirical studies concern sexuality among older institutionalized persons: Wasow, M., and Loeb, M.: Sexuality in nursing homes. In Solnick, R.L., editor: Sexuality and aging, Los Angeles, 1978, The University of Southern California Press; Kaas, M.J.: Sexual expression of the elderly in nursing homes, The Gerontologist **18**(4), 1978; and Blackwell, D.L., and Hunt, S.S.: Sexuality and aging: staff attitudes toward sexual expression among aged nursing home residents, paper presented at the 31st Annual Scientific Meeting of the Gerontological Society, Dallas, Nov. 17, 1978. Another such study, Sexuality and Aging Research Project Within Nursing Home Settings, is being conducted by the Senior Citizen's Provincial Council, 1914 Hamilton St., Regina, Saskatchewan SN6 (Harry J. Mullens, Executive Director).

[70] Homosexuality per se was eliminated as a mental disorder by the American Psychiatric Association in DSM-II (1973). Thus homosexuality itself is no longer seen as psychopathological; only when it is "ego-dystonic" (the individual does not accept being a homosexual), causing distress or disability, is it deemed a mental disorder.

ships that have lasted as long as 40 years or more.[71] Kimmel's study of 14 aging gay men, ages 55 to 81, found older gays were used to taking care of themselves, with fewer role disruptions than older men with wives and families. On the negative side, gay men experienced both age and sexual-choice discrimination, and the combination contributed to a tendency among older gay couples to withdraw from society. Bereavement, disablement, problems of inheritance and other legal issues, and ageism within the gay community itself can obviously all become problems for older gays. A program called Senior Action in a Gay Environment (SAGE) is being developed by the gay community in New York to offer free social services to older gay men and women.

Research findings

The data that have been accumulating on the sexuality of older persons have generally supported the view that sexual capacity has been underestimated except where illness or lack of sexual partner is a factor. Kinsey can be considered the pioneer in modern-day studies of sexuality in older people. The aged constituted only a small part of his sample, but his findings were useful in beginning to demolish the notion of termination of sexuality in late life. It was found that most men at age 60 were sexually capable and that there was

little evidence of sexual decline in women until late in life.

Masters and Johnson's contributions have been exceedingly useful, since they include direct clinical observations of sexual performance as well as interviews. The Duke longitudinal studies examined 250 people between ages 60 and 94 every 3 years. Interestingly, these studies found that about 15% of older persons actually *increased* their patterns of sexual activity and interest as they aged.

Physical characteristics of sex in old age
Older men

Changes that occur with aging are often misinterpreted as evidence that older men are becoming impotent. "From a psychosexual point of view, the male over age 50 has to contend with one of the great fallacies of our culture. Every man in this age group is arbitrarily identified by both public and professional alike as sexually impaired."[72]

For a variety of causes associated with chronological aging there are age-related sexual changes. The older man ordinarily takes longer to obtain an erection, but as Masters and Johnson point out, "One of the advantages of the aging process with specific reference to sexual functioning is that, generally speaking, control of ejaculatory demand in the 50-75 year age group is far better than in the 20-40 year age group."[73] Translated, this means the older man can remain erect and make love longer before coming to orgasm. There is also the advantage of lovemaking experience gained throughout a lifetime.

Older men experience a reduction in the volume of seminal fluid, which explains the decrease in the pressure to ejaculate. Orgasm begins to be experienced in a shorter one-stage period, as compared to two stages in earlier life, but it remains

---

[71] The work in this area includes the following: Kelly, J.: Brothers and brothers: the gay man's adaptation to aging (Ph.D. dissertation), Ann Arbor, Mich., 1974, University Microfilms; Kelly, J.: The aging male homosexual; myth and reality, The Gerontologist **17**:328-332, 1977; McDevitt, R.J.: The older homosexual, Medical Aspects of Human Sexuality **2**:191-192, 1974; Minnigerode, F.A.: Age-status labeling in homosexual men; Journal of Homosexuality **1**: 273-276, 1976; Minnigerode, F.A., and Adelman, M.R.: Elderly homosexual women and men: report on a pilot study, The Family Coordinator **27**:451-456, 1978; Laner, M.R.: Growing older male: heterosexual and homosexual, The Gerontologist **18**:496-501, 1978; Kimmel, D.C.: Life-history interviews of aging gay men, International Journal of Aging and Human Development **10**:239-248, 1979-80; and Kimmel, D.C.: Adult development and aging: a gay perspective, Journal of Social Issues **34**:113-130, 1978.

[72] From Masters, W.H., and Johnson, V.E.: Human sexual inadequacy, London, 1970, J. & A. Churchill, Ltd., pp. 316 and 318.
[73] Ibid.

pleasurable. There is, after age 50, a physiologically extended refractory period, meaning that the capacity for erection following ejaculation cannot be regained as quickly as in younger men. It may be 12 to 24 hours before sex is again possible. Couples who are aware of this may want to delay ejaculation in order to make love as long as they wish. No panic is called for when the male's penis becomes flaccid more promptly on ejaculation. This is natural and not a sign of impairment.

A vital point to remember is that the older man does not lose his facility for erection as he ages unless physical or emotional illness interferes. Psychiatrist Charles Fisher of the Mount Sinai Hospital Sleep Laboratory found that most of his 21 subjects, all men over 60, had penile erections with their sexual dreaming, including one who was 96. Most men over 60 are satisfied with one or two ejaculations a week but can enjoy sex and satisfy a partner more frequently than that because erections are possible whenever stimulated. A consistent pattern of sexual expression helps to maintain sexuality.

Older men are usually able to continue some form of active sex life until their seventies, eighties, and perhaps beyond. If they lose interest or become impotent, there can be a number of factors involved: boredom, fatigue, overeating, excessive drinking, medical and psychiatric disabilities (impotence can be one of the first signs of depression), and fear of failure. The last is common and often based on misinformation about what is normative in old age. Among physical causes of impotence are arteriosclerotic, cardiorespiratory, endocrine, genitourinary, hematological, neurological, and infectious disorders. Frequently perineal prostatectomy and occasionally suprapubic and urethral prostatectomy can be factors. Drugs are also responsible. Chlordiazepoxide (Librium), imipramine (Tofranil), phenothiazines (especially thioridazine, known as Mellaril), methyldopa (used in parkinsonism), and alcohol have all been reported as inducing impotence. For women also, any tranquilizing drug can act as a depressant for sexual feelings.

Older women

Biologically the older woman experiences little impairment as she ages. If she is in reasonably good health, she can expect to continue sex activities until late in life, assuming she has maintained a frame of mind that encourages this and has a sexual partner with whom to enjoy it. Menopause, also called "change of life" or "climacterium," occurs with the cessation of menstruation, usually between the ages of 45 and 50. Certain myths have surrounded menopause, including a fear of insanity, the ending of sexual desire and attractiveness, and the myths of inevitable depression, adverse physical symptoms, and defeminization. These have been disputed by Helene Deutsch, Therese Benedek, Bernice Neugarten, and others who have written about the female climacterium. It is generally concluded that most women experience minimal physical problems; but because of cultural expectations and varying amounts of misunderstanding, there can be adverse psychological reactions. These are, however, not inevitable.

The physiological situation of older women during and after menopause requires review. They commonly suffer from the effects of gradual steroid insufficiency, which causes a thinning of the vaginal walls. Cracking, bleeding, and pain (dyspareunia) can result during sexual intercourse. There may be vaginal burning and itching ("senile vaginitis"[74]). The urethra and bladder become more subject to irritation as they are less cushioned by the atrophied vaginal walls, and there can be burning or frequency of urination for several days after sex. The loss of sex steroids also reduces the length and diameter of the vagina and may shrink the major labia. However, sex-steroid replacement therapy can substantially reduce many of these menopausal symptoms. The nautral estrogen complex (conjugated estrogens, USP) has been in use for more than 30 years. It is inexpensive and can be helpful against osteoporosis (chronic backache, compression fractures, and "dowager's hump"),

---

[74] We believe this term is demeaning and prefer "estrogen-deficient vaginitis."

estrogen-deficient vaginitis, pruritus, and other aggravating symptoms. Recent reports, however, suggest an increase of cancer of the lining (endometrium) of the uterus with use of estrogens. The doctor and patient must carefully evaluate the risk against the benefit.[75]

Vaginal secretions that lubricate the vagina may decrease with age. But this does not seem to occur in women who were sexually stimulated on a regular basis once or twice a week from youth on. As with men, a consistent pattern of sexual activity is beneficial to women in maintaining their sexual capacities. Muscle tone affecting the "grip" of the vagina on the penis during intercourse can be improved through special exercises (Kegel) designed for this purpose.[76]

Sex and chronic physical conditions

The realization that people with chronic illnesses have sexual interests may be unexpected and even unwelcomed. It complicates the medical picture for doctors. The well spouse may not know how to respond. Yet patients may live for years with the help of medical treatment and want as normal a life as possible, including sex. Most current studies of sex concentrate on healthy populations rather than including people with disabling conditions. Sexual activity may be both therapeutic and preventive medicine. There is some evidence, for example, that sexual activity helps arthritis, probably because of adrenal gland production of cortisone. The sexual act is itself a form of physical activity, helping people stay in good physical

condition. It helps to reduce tensions, which are both physical and psychological.

Cerebrovascular accidents and coronary attacks cause concern because patients and doctors may not discuss if and when sex can be safely resumed. The oxygen cost in sexual intercourse is equivalent to that in climbing a flight of stairs or walking briskly. The heart rate ranges from 90 to 150 beats a minute, with an average of 120 beats—about the level for light to moderate physical effort. There is not yet a conclusive mass of data regarding sudden death during sex, but it probably occurs much less often than patients fear and somewhat more than the reported incidence (because of reluctance to report accurately). A conservative estimate is that 1% of sudden coronary deaths occur during intercourse. Potency may be affected psychologically because heart disease is not only frightening but also tends to undermine confidence in physical capacities. For some people the anxiety caused by restricting sex may be greater than the actual physical risk from participating in it.

Diabetes mellitus is common in old age and causes impotence two to five times as often as in the general population, although sex interest and desire may persist. Impotence from poorly controlled diabetes usually disappears when control is established. But the adequately controlled diabetic man who develops impotence usually has a more permanent problem. The effects of diabetes on the sexuality of women are unknown.

Pelvic surgery must be carefully planned to avoid unnecessary sexual impairment. Of men who have had prostatectomies, 70% remain potent. Three types of prostatectomy are listed.

1. *Transurethral resection (TUR)*. A thin Bakelite or plastic sheath is inserted in the penis, a tungsten wire is maneuvered through the tube, and the gland is removed. The tissue may grow back; therefore TUR is indicated for men in their seventies or if other severe disease is present.

2. *Perineal*. An incision is made between the scrotum and anus, removing most of the prostate.

3. *Suprapubic*. The incision is made through the abdomen.

---

[75] The dosage for menopausal and postmenopausal estrogen deficiency, including atrophic vaginitis and pruritus vulvae, has generally been 1.25 to 3.75 mg daily, 3 weeks on and 1 week off. The dosage level and the duration of treatment is now being reevaluated in light of the 1975 findings of a possible link to uterine cancer in some women. Estrogens in a vaginal cream can also be used. The general use of testosterone replacement therapy in men is presently not justified on the basis of reliable knowledge.

[76] Butler, R.N., and Lewis, M.I.: Sex after sixty. A guide for men and women for their later years, New York, 1971, Harper & Row, Publishers, Inc., pp. 36 and 71 (paperback title: Love and sex after sixty [1977]).

After a prostatectomy the semen is deposited in the bladder rather than ejaculated. Potency is rarely affected with the TUR and suprapubic approaches, and some men even have increased potency. Impotence may occur for psychological reasons. Nonpsychological, physical impotence is most often associated with the perineal approach.

There is no evidence that hysterectomy, with or without oophorectomy, produces any change in sexual desire or performance in women. If change does occur, it is usually psychological. The fear of sexual impairment, fear of loss of sexual desire, and fear of becoming unattractive to men are most commonly seen. People tend to become upset about any subtractive surgery, especially if it is a major subtraction like hysterectomy. Mastectomies, ileostomies, and colostomies are other common surgical procedures that can lead to sexual concern and possible problems.

Peyronie's disease can interfere with sexual performance in men unless it responds to treatment or regresses spontaneously. The symptoms are an upward bowing of the penis, with a shift angled to the right or left. Hard tumors in the corpora cavernosa cause the symptoms, but the cause of these tumors is unknown. Intercourse may be difficult and painful or completely impossible. A variety of treatments may be used and the disease itself may regress in about 4 years.[77] This disease has been thought to be rare, but judging from our own clinical experience, we suspect it is more common than is believed.

Mental health treatment considerations

Sex, self-esteem, and self-image are closely related. A task of the mental health specialist is to help older people deal with their personal feelings, fears, and possible misunderstandings about sex in old age as well as to recognize and support the special developmental qualities of sex and intimacy that can occur in the later years. One of these special qualities we call "the second language of sex"—a growing capacity, seen in many emotionally healthy older persons, to develop intimacy and communication in a love relationship to new levels.[78] If sexual activity and potency decline while interest remains high, the therapist and patient must consider whether improvement is possible or some divergent activities can be substituted. Marital counseling, individual and group psychotherapy, and family counseling may be indicated and can be quite successful.[79]

Masters and Johnson, in treating older people in their clinic, report a higher incidence of referrals of men with sexual dysfunction than women, probably because of the need for erective capacity in male sexuality. They report a higher failure rate with their older patients, which they attribute to the length of time the problem has existed and not the ages of the patients. Nonetheless, there was a more than 50% success rate even when the problem may have existed 25 years or longer. They state, "The fact that innumerable men and women have not been sexually effective before reaching their late fifties or early sixties is no reason to condemn them to continuing sexual dysfunction as they live out the rest of their life-span. The disinclination of the medical and behavioral professions to treat the aging population for sexual dysfunction has been a major disservice perpetrated by those professions upon the general problem."[80]

Sex education for older people is important. Normal age changes need to be understood so that neither men nor women mistake such changes for loss of sexuality. Techniques of sexual intercourse

---

[77] McDonald, D.F.: Peyronie's disease, Medical Aspects of Human Sexuality **6**:64-70, 1972.

[78] Butler, R.N., and Lewis, M.I.: Sex after sixty. A guide for men and women in their later years, New York, 1971, Harper & Row, Publishers, Inc., pp. 136-145 (paperback title: Love and sex after sixty [1977]).

[79] A bachelor participating in the NIMH Human Aging Studies undertook intensive psychotherapy 4 times a week at age 65 and married for the first time. As another example, the English sexologist Havelock Ellis overcame lifelong impotence in his old age with the help of a loving and responsive woman (Calder-Marshall, A.: The sage of sex, a life of Havelock Ellis, New York 1959, G.P. Putnam's Sons.)

[80] From Masters, W.H., and Johnson, V.E.: Human sexual inadequacy, London, 1970, J. & A. Churchill, Ltd., p. 344.

especially pertinent to old age should be clarified. (For example, sex in the morning may be preferable for those older persons who fatigue easily.) The importance of masturbation when sexual partners are unavailable should be emphasized for those who do not find its practice personally upsetting. Masturbation helps preserve potency in men and the sexual functioning in women, releases tensions, stimulates sexual appetite, and contributes to general well-being. It must be remembered that many older people were brought up to believe that masturbation is harmful physically and mentally. Such cultural and historic viewpoints cannot be lightly dismissed, but people may be responsive to new information.

Another cultural element is seen in the reluctance of some older women to go to a doctor for help with gynecological problems. Women with even advanced carcinoma of the vulva may delay asking for medical care. Some older women tolerate general prolapse of the uterus for long periods of time, and it is not unusual to find infection and edema from such untreated conditions. Women may need encouragement in accepting examinations on a regular basis.

Regular physical examinations, proper medical treatment, and adequate diet and exercise all help to preserve sexual capacities. As Masters and Johnson have so encouragingly reported, the two major requirements for enjoyable sexual activity until later in life are reasonably good health and an interested and interesting partner.

REFERENCES

Bernstein, M.C.: Forecast of women's retirement income: cloudy and colder; 25 percent chance of poverty, Industrial Gerontology 1(2):1-13, 1974.

Block, M.R., and Sinnott, J.D., editors: The battered elder syndrome: an exploratory study, College Park, Md, 1979, University of Maryland, Center on Aging.

Brog, S.K., and Hersch, C.: A successful model for community support of low-income minority group aged, Aging and Human Development 3:243-252, 1976.

Burgess, E.W., editor: Aging in western societies, Chicago, 1960, University of Chicago Press.

Butler, R.N., and Gastel, B.: Hearing and age: research challenges and the National Institute on Aging, Annals of Otology, Rhinology and Laryngology 88(5):676-682, 1979.

Butler, R.N., and Lewis, M.I. Sex after sixty. A guide for men and women for their later years, New York, 1976, Harper & Row, Publishers, Inc. (paperback title: Love and sex after sixty [1977]).

Clark, M., and Anderson, B.G.: Culture and aging. An anthropological study of older Americans, Springfield, Ill., 1967, Charles C Thomas, Publisher.

Comfort, A.: Sexual consequences of disability, Philadelphia, 1978, George F. Stickley Co.

Dancy, J., Jr.: The black elderly: a manual for practitioners, Ann Arbor, 1977, University of Michigan, Institute of Gerontology.

Dlin, B.M.: Sex after ileostomy or colostomy, Medical Aspects of Human Sexuality 6:32-43, 1972.

Double jeopardy, the older Negro in America today, New York, 1964, National Urban League.

Elderly are crime targets, SOS, Senior Opportunities and Services Technical Assistance Bulletin 2(4):1-3, 1972.

Fanon, F.: Black skin, white masks, New York, 1967, Grove Press, Inc.

Ferenczi, S.: Sunday neurosis (1919). In Rickman, J., editor: Theory and technique of psychoanalysis, New York, 1952, Basic Books, Inc., Publishers.

Finkel, A.L., Moyers, T.G., Tobenkin, M.I., and Karg, S.J.: Sexual potency in aging males, Journal of American Medical Association 170:1391-1393, 1959.

Fisch, L.: Special senses: the aging auditory system. In Brocklehurst, J.C., editor: Textbook of geriatric medicine and gerontology, Edinburgh, 1973, Churchill Livingstone.

Gaitz, C.M., Characteristics of elderly patients with alcoholism, Archives of General Psychiatry 24:372-378, 1971.

Gaitz, C.M., and Scott, J.: Mental health of Mexican Americans: do ethnic factors make a difference? Geriatrics 29:103-110, 1974.

Gochros, H.L.: The sexually oppressed, Social Work 17:16-24, 1972.

Golden, H.M.: Black ageism, Social Policy 7:40-42, 1976.

Hellerstein, H.K., and Friedman, E.H.: Sexual activity and the postcoronary patient, Archives of Internal Medicine 125:987, 1970.

House Select Committee on Aging: Research into crimes against the elderly, parts I and II (hearings), Jan. 31 and Feb. 1, 1978, Pub. No. (Comm.) 95-122, Washington, D.C., 1978, U.S. Government Printing Office.

Houston, F., and Royse, A.B.: Relationship between deafness and psychotic illness. The Journal of Mental Science, 100:990-993, 1954.

Jackson, J.J.: The blacklands of gerontology, Aging and Human Development 2:156-172, 1971.

Jackson, J.J.: The plight of older black women in the United States, Black Scholar 7:47-85, 1976.

Kalish, R.A., and Yuen, S.: Americans of East Asian ancestry: aging and the aged, The Gerontologist **11**:36-47, 1971.

Kastenbaum, R.J., editor: Special issue—black aging, Aging and Human Development **2**:155-231, 1971.

Kent, D.P.: The elderly in minority groups: variant patterns of aging, The Gerontologist **11**:26-29, 1971.

Kinsey, A.C., Pomeroy, W.B., and Martin, C.R.: Sexual behavior in the human male, Philadelphia, 1948, W.B. Saunders Co.

Kinsey, A.C., Pomeroy, W.B., Martin, C.R., and Gebhard, P.H.: Sexual behavior in the human female, Philadelphia, 1953, W.B. Saunders Co.

Lau, E.F., and Kosberg, J.: Abuse of the elderly by informal care providers: practice and research issues, paper presented at 31st Annual Meeting of the Gerontological Society, Dallas, Nov. 20, 1978.

Lewis, M.I.: Sex and aging. In Goldstein, K.K., Salisbury, P.A., and Davison, W.P.: Aging: research and perspectives: a briefing for the press, New York, 1979, Columbia Journalism Monograph No. 3.

Lewis, M.I., and Butler, R.N.: Why is women's lib ignoring old women? Aging and Human Development **3**:233-231, 1972.

Maldano, H.D.: The Chicago aged, Social Work **20**(3):213-216, 1975.

Masters, W.H., and Johnson, V.E.: Human sexual response, Boston, 1966, Little, Brown & Co.

Masters, W.H., and Johnson, V.E.: Human sexual inadequacy, London, 1970, J. & A. Churchill, Ltd.

Misharo, B., and Kastenbaum, R.: Alcohol and old age, New York, 1980, Grune & Stratton, Inc.

Moore, J.W.: Mexican-Americans, The Gerontologist **11**:30-35, 1971.

Neugarten, B.L., and Kraines, R.J.: "Menopausal symptoms" in women of various ages, Psychosomatic Medicine **27**:266-273, 1965.

Newman, G., and Nichols, C.B.: Sexual activities and attitudes in older persons, Journal of the American Medical Association **173**:33-35, 1960.

Pfeiffer, E.: Geriatric sex behavior, Medical Aspects of Human Sexuality **3**:19-29, 1969.

Ruben, R.: Aging and hearing. In Rossman, I.: Clinical geriatrics, Philadelphia, 1971, J.B. Lippincott Co.

Rubin, I.: Sexual life after sixty, New York, 1965, Basic Books, Inc., Publishers.

Schneider, E.L.: The aging reproductive system, New York, 1978, Raven Press.

Schuckit, M.A., and Pastor, P.A., Jr.: The elderly as a unique population: alcoholism, Alcoholism: Clinical and Experimental Research **2**(1):31-38, 1978.

Shanas, E., and Sussman, M.B.: Family, bureaucracy and the elderly, Durham, N.C., 1977, Duke University Press.

Stanford, E.P.: The elderly black, San Diego, 1978, The Campanile Press.

Streib, G.F., and Schneider, C.J.: Retirement in American society, New York, 1971, Cornell University Press.

Taylor, B.J., and Peach, W.N.: Social and economic characteristics of elderly Indians in Phoenix, Arizona, Journal of Economics and Business **26**:151-155, 1974.

U.S. Senate Committee on Aging: Proceedings of the ninetieth and ninety-first Congress, availability and usefulness of federal programs and services to elderly Mexican Americans, parts 1-4, Washington, D.C., 1969, U.S. Government Printing Office.

U.S. Senate Committee on Labor and Public Welfare: The education of American Indians, Washington, D.C., 1969, U.S. Government Printing Office.

U.S. Senate Special Committee on Aging: A working paper, Advisory Council on the Elderly American Indian, Washington, D.C., 1971, U.S. Government Printing Office.

U.S. Senate Special Committee on Aging: The multiple hazards of age and race: the situation of aged blacks in the United States, working paper prepared by Inabel B. Lindsay, DSW, Consultant, Washington, D.C., Sept. 1971, U.S. Government Printing Office.

White House Conference on Aging, 1971: A report to the delegates from the Conference Sections and Special Concerns Sessions, Nov. 28-Dec. 2, 1971, Washington, D.C., 1971, U.S. Government Printing Office.

Wylie, F.M.: Attitudes toward aging among black Americans: some historical perspectives, Aging and Human Development **2**:66-70, 1971.

Older people and their families

The 1980 White House Conference on Families addressed some of the problems confronted by older people and their families. Significantly, one of the conference's five top recommendations was a change in tax policies to encourage the care of older people at home. Perhaps such recommendations will translate into appropriate public policy decisions, for example, family payments for home care.

American older persons have been pictured as isolated and rejected by their families. Adages such as "one mother can raise 10 children but 10 children cannot care for one old mother" are solemnly cited as typical of the attitudes of American children toward their aging parents. The urban, industrialized society, which thus far, indeed, has placed little value on the virtues of old age, has been singled out as the annihilator of the extended family and its network of mutual assistance. But is there evidence to support this generally accepted view of American family life? Can a culture so institutionalize its prejudice against older people that ties of affection and loyalty between parent and child are discarded? The tenacity of kinship bonds throughout history—in spite of wars, conquest, slavery, immigration, political ideology, and cultural change—would lead one to doubt easy assumptions concerning demise of the parent-child relationships. From the standpoint of mental health it is questionable whether young human beings can ever function or grow in a rea-

sonably healthy manner without emotional and interactive bonds with adults who care about them. This drive for emotional sustenance is not likely to dry up as people reach adulthood. Survival in a productivity-minded society may in fact make kinship support *more* necessary and meaningful as human beings are buffeted by constant challenges and reexaminations of their worth in the outside world.

FAMILY LIFE CYCLE[1]

Four fifths of all older people have living children. (Half of these have only one or two and half have three or more children.) A family may span three to five living generations, complete with a past reaching farther back than one can trace and a future stretching beyond the lives of any present family members. Each person experiences his own individual life cycle from birth to death while at the same time participating as an integral part of a family with a collective life cycle of its own. It is rare to find an older person who truly

---

[1] Models of the developmental processes of families are as important as models of individual personality development. Sociology, anthropology, psychiatry, and social work all have valuable experience in this area, which they do not often share with each other. Margaret Mead has said, "We've never adequately differentiated between a household, a biological nuclear family and whatever else people think the family really is. . . . We have no way of dealing with people who are members of a biological family but who aren't living within the nuclear family."

148

has no "family," even if it means only distant relatives. The closeness of kin in terms of blood relationships and the numbers of kin give no clear indication of the amount of meaningful contacts. But they do indicate the kin potential, implying usually an emotional tie, whether positive or negative. A person cannot easily "divorce" his blood relatives, since his or her own identity is intricately bound up with those to whom he is related. (For example, adopted children seem to inevitably yearn at some point in their lives for knowledge of their kin and may actively search for them even though their lives may be otherwise satisfactory.) A feeling of kin relatedness is probably an essential element in orienting oneself in time and space as a significant human being.

The number of people who are considered "family" by an older person may change markedly throughout a lifetime. Some older people have grown up with brothers and sisters but never married and therefore have no "immediate" family of children and grandchildren. Others may have expanded from a small childhood family unit to produce a large number of sons, daughters, grandchildren, and great-grandchildren with their assorted in-laws. Some older people relate closely to distant kin, and others even adopt as kin people to whom they are not related at all. One should never be deceived by statements from older people claiming they have broken off contact with a family member (for example, not speaking to a brother or sister for 30 years). Such relationships usually have as much emotional content as more directly active ones—or even more—as demonstrated by the concerted effort to avoid contact.

The development and changing use of birth control has greatly altered the "traditional" kin family. As we discuss in Chapter 6, people over 70 are likely to have larger numbers of brothers and sisters (and nephews and nieces)[2] and smaller numbers of children than the middle generation (over 50), which has fewer siblings and more offspring because of the post–World War II baby boom. The baby boom children themselves, ages 23 to 34 in 1980, will be somewhat like their grandparents, with more siblings and fewer children of their own than their parents.

People who are now 25 years of age or younger are the first generation to truly feel the birth control–produced "kin-squeeze": many have few or no brothers and sisters and most will have no more than one and at the most two children. Yet this generation is likely to have parents, grandparents, and even great-grandparents in their immediate family. The kin family is shrinking increasingly within each generation, but on the other hand, it is stretching out for the first time in human history over four and even five generations. It is fascinating to speculate on the consequences of large numbers of people from multiple generations interacting with one another. For one thing it means that the greater part of one's life will be spent relating to other family members as fellow adults.

The concept of the family itself is changing—the great "classical family of western nostalgia," as Stanford University sociologist William J. Goode calls it, does not exist and probably never existed to any great degree. The so-called extended family of early America often consisted of conglomerations of nuclear family members, unmarried siblings of the nuclear couple, lodgers, hired hands, slaves, indentured servants, apprentices, and a relatively small number of older kin who managed to survive the infections, ailments, and accidents that made life so generally short and brutal. Whether older people fared any better in these households than they do today is still a matter of debate, as is the romantic urban view that the early American rural existence was a gentler

---

[2] A 1975 national survey found 8 out of 10 old people had living siblings (75-year-olds came from families with an average of five children). Those who were unmarried had closer bonds with their siblings and many lived in the same house. See Shanas, E.: Social myth as hypothesis: the care of the family relations of old people, The Gerontologist **19**(1):3-9, 1979. Also see U.S. Bureau of the Census: Marital status and living arrangements, March 1978, Series P-20, No. 338, Washington, D.C., 1979, U.S. Government Printing Office.

Table 7-1. Present American families*—1979

Father—sole wage earner Mother—fulltime homemaker One or more children at home	17% (7% have the classic two children)
Father—wage earner Mother—wage earner One or more children at home	28%
Married couples No children, or none at home	32.4%
Single mothers One or more children at home	6.6%
Single fathers One or more children at home	0.7%
Unrelated persons living together	3.1%
Single parent, relatives and children	5.3%
One person living alone (one- third of whom are women over 65)	22%

*There is some overlapping of categories.
From Betty Friedan's article in *The New York Times,* March 23, 1980. © 1980 by the New York Times Company. Reprinted with permission.

way of life for older folks. Table 7-1 details the contemporary family of America. Imagine the families of late life of the next decades!

Families will come in increasingly multiple forms—single-parent family, two-paycheck couples, and intergenerational communes (see the box below). A rising new pattern is a return of an adult child to the nest after a personal setback or to conserve financial resources. Even now only 7% of American families meet the traditional concept of husband-breadwinner, housewife, and two dependent children. Some of the likely consequences will be more effective child-care and day-care programs for older persons who cannot be left alone and more opportunities for families to work at home, with spouses sharing in the care of the children and infirm older parents.

A whole new possibility of kin networks for the old is hoving into view with rising divorce rates. While one third of all marriages now end in divorce, three fourths of all divorced women and five sixths of divorced men remarry, bringing a whole clan of step-relatives along to add to their partner's kin network. Two or more divorces bring even more kin potential. Even though the popular image of step-families is usually something similar

---

DEFINITIONS OF FAMILIES AND OTHER FAMILYLIKE ARRANGEMENTS

General definition of family Those who consider themselves economically and emotionally related to each other by blood (consanguinity) or by marriage (conjugality).

Nuclear family A married pair (conjugal) with dependent children and an independent household, bound to outside kin by voluntary ties of affection or duty.

Extended family All of those related to one another by blood or marriage.

Modified and extended family Separate households for all but very old or sick, with a complex, viable, supportive pattern of family relationships with kin. The nuclear family is part of the extended kin family. The latter is a highly integrated network of social relations and mutual assistance—vertical over generations and bilateral to other kin.

Household A number of persons who share a residence, exchange services, and give emotional support to each other.

Social network Those individuals with whom one interacts during the course of one's daily life.

Support system A group of individuals who join together to give support and assistance to each other, sometimes for a specific purpose.

to the feud between the Hatfields and the McCoys, with each side of the family staking out its emotional territory, the reality is that many amicable and lifelong alliances form among family members who become related through first, second, or more marriages even though the marriages themselves may or may not succeed.

DO AMERICAN FAMILIES "ABANDON" THEIR OLDER MEMBERS?
Research evidence

Urbanization and industrialization have led to theories about changes and/or breakdown in family structure.[3] The nuclear family consisting of mother, father, and several children has been postulated as the most functional family unit in a society that requires mobility, compactness, and emotional self-sufficiency to be built in and carried along. Older people and other extended-family members are seen as not fitting into this streamlined picture, so the nuclear family supposedly has closed its ranks and its heart, determined to go it alone. Older parents and grandparents have been pictured as left to shift for themselves. This may *sound* plausible, but it has not happened and is not likely to. The emerging pattern of family life is one of separate households for all but the very old or sick, while at the same time maintaining a complex pattern of family relationships that are viable and supportive. Sussman calls this the "modified and extended" family system in which the nuclear family is not isolated but is part of "an extended kin-family system, highly integrated within a network of social relationships and mutual assistance that operates along bilateral kin lines and vertically over several generations."[4]

Litwak earlier defined the modified extended family in relation to what he calls the "classical extended" and nuclear types:

[It] differs from the "classical extended" family in that it does not demand geographical propinquity, occupational involvement, or nepotism, nor does it have an hierarchical authority structure. On the other hand, it differs from the isolated nuclear family structure in that it does provide significant continuing aid to the nuclear family.[5]

Aid to older persons takes the form of economic help, living arrangements with families when this is imperative, and affection and companionship. Brothers, sisters, children, grandchildren, aunts, uncles—even nephews, nieces, and cousins—may be involved in the flow of mutual aid.[6] When families do not offer help to their older members, a whole range of personal, social, and economic forces are usually at work rather than a simple attitude of neglect and abandonment.

Many studies have verified the continuing existence of strong family ties in the United States and elsewhere. A World Health Organization report states:

Wherever careful studies have been carried out in the industrialized countries, the lasting devotion of children for their parents has been amply demonstrated. The great majority of old people are in regular contact with their children, relatives, or friends. . . . Where distance permits, the generations continue to shoulder their traditional obligations, of the elders toward their children, and the children to the aged.[7]

Townsend, in England, found that the families of institutionalized aged showed ". . . much more

---

[3] Parsons, T., and Bales, R.: Family, socialization and interaction process, New York, 1955, Free Press of Glencoe, Inc.

[4] From Sussman, M.B.: Relationships of adult children with their parents in the United States. In Shanas, E., and Streib, G.F., editors: Social structure and the family: generational relationships, Englewood Cliffs, N.J., 1965, Prentice-Hall, Inc.

[5] From Litwak, E.: Extended kin relations in industrial democratic societies. Occupational mobility and extended family cohesion, American Sociological Review **25**:9-21, 1960. See also Litwak, E.: Geographic mobility and extended family cohesion, American Sociological Review **25**:385-394, 1960.

[6] For a moving account of one family's care of an older member, see Jury, M., and Jury, D.: Gramp, New York, 1976, Grossman Publishers, Inc.

[7] From World Health Organization: Mental health problems of the aging and the aged, Technical Report Series No. 171, Geneva, 1959, The Organization.

evidence of genuine affection and loyalty than the reverse. . . .''[8]

Approximately 2 out of every 10 older people in the United States live alone. Most of these are single, widowed, or divorced, and a large proportion are women. Many have children but prefer to live apart from them. Naturally a greater proportion of the very old (over 80) live with family members because of declining capacities. Unmarried people may live with siblings and friends. Studies indicate that the majority of older people choose independent living quarters with a spouse or alone as long as this is possible and then expect to move in with family members when their health or financial situation deteriorates.

In spite of the desire for separate households on the part of both parents and children, Shanas has observed:

> While the proportion of old people who live with their children has decreased over the last 20 years, the proportion living close to children has increased substantially. In 1975, the proportion of old people living in the same household with one of their children was 18 percent. Thirty-four percent of all persons over 65 with children, however, live apart from children, but within 10 minutes distance from at least one of them. As a result, in 1975, half of all people with children (52 percent) lived either in the same household with a child, or next door, down the street or a few blocks away. Old people who live alone are commonly considered a particularly vulnerable group among the elderly. Yet, among those old people who have children and who live alone, half are within 10 minutes distance of a child.[9]

Shanas believes that the ''myth of alienation'' has been created and perpetrated by two groups: *professional workers* in the field of aging, who

tend to see those older persons who do not have normal family supports, and *childless old people,* who constitute one fifth of all older people and are likely to believe that the aged are neglected by their children. In our experience also, gross negligence of parents by children has been exaggerated, but there is of course no doubt of its existence. Subtle and open disparagement and cruelties are not uncommon and require attention, even though they may not be the norm.[10]

Three-generational household

Twelve percent of older married persons and 17% of unmarried older persons (single, widowed, and divorced) live in households that include one or more of their children. Such arrangements generally occur when the older person has become too infirm or impoverished to live alone. Since most people move in with their relatives at an advanced age, the average length of their stay is not a long one because of the death of the older person or serious illness requiring hospital or nursing care. In most instances the pattern is one of an older mother moving in with her daughter and family. The manner in which these two women relate is often the key to success or failure of the living arrangement. Most families manage the problems quite well, perhaps realizing that precedents are being set for the next generation of children and parents. Genuine affection combined with a sense of ethical responsibility motivates many children to voluntarily assist their elderly parents.

''Filial'' economic responsibility

Filial responsibility[11] includes more than just law and custom, since it refers also to the personal attitudes of responsibility toward parents: the ethical and emotional responses of children to their

---

[8] From Townsend, P.: The effects of family structure on the likelihood of admission to an institution in old age: the application of a general theory. In Shanas, E., and Streib, G., editors: Social structure and the family, Englewood Cliffs, N.J., 1965, Prentice-Hall, Inc., pp. 163-188.

[9] Shanas, E.: Older people and their families: the new pioneers, Journal of Marriage and the Family **42**(1):12, 1980. This three-decade-old study focuses on those 4 out of 5 noninstitutionalized older persons with living children.

[10] See p. 131 for ''battered old person syndrome.'' Such ''parent abuse'' is almost impossible to document unless the older person cooperates in providing evidence.

[11] Schorr, A.L.: Filial responsibility in the modern American family, U.S. Department of Health, Education and Welfare, Social Security Administration, Washington, D.C., 1960, U.S. Government Printing Office.

mothers and fathers. But we discuss here the legal and social requirements and expectations. Children were held accountable for the care of their parents under medieval church law and it was not until the Elizabethan Poor Law that the concept of community assistance was introduced. However, families were expected to do everything they could before receiving outside help. During the early part of the twentieth century, filial responsibility versus governmental aid began to be tested to a greater degree. There were greater numbers of older people, sometimes two generations of them in one family, and the preindustrial, agricultural society was disappearing. In its place came industrialization, separating wages from the ownership of the means of production. Older people no longer had the power of ownership of land, tools, and animals or the sustenance of the agricultural community; therefore they became more vulnerable economically as they aged. Their children were forced to take on more responsibility for them or look to the government for assistance. Social Security, beginning in 1935 in the United States, provided basic economic maintenance for increasing numbers of older people. Instead of individual families paying for their own older members, Social Security is based on a concept of intergenerational support whereby the entire middle-aged generation in the labor force supports the older generation.[12]

There is much talk about the "graying society" (or "aging society"), as if it were tragic that more and more people are living out their lives. A major concern is that the old will use up a disproportionate amount of the nation's resources. Of course the economics of aging are important and the subject of intergenerational transfer is an issue for econometricians and public policymakers as well as the public to study; moreover, decisions must be made to ensure that the costs of caring for the old are appropriate, that programs are managed

efficiently, and that equity is served through use of sound economic and social principles. But it is necessary to avoid selective focus on the intergenerational transfer of funds that underlies Social Security. A much broader understanding of the intergenerational transfer of *all* funds and assets is called for.[13]

In 1975, 7 out of every 10 older persons age 65 and older in a nationwide probability survey of the noninstitutionalized reported helping their children and grandchildren with services, money, or gifts. Five out of 10 reported helping their great-grandchildren. At the same time 7 out of 10 older people also reported receiving similar help from their children.[14] (Interestingly, a growing task for the middle-aged is to help older parents with the bureaucratic red tape surrounding the varied benefits to which they are entitled.)

Although governmental agencies are necessarily and increasingly providing financial support and services for older persons, some policies still reflect the earlier traditions of total filial or family responsibility. The "responsible relative" clause in many welfare programs is the most obvious example. Families usually turn to welfare for help with older persons only when they are already in desperate straits. But certain localities still insist that close relatives must exhaust their own resources before their aged can receive assistance. Such requirements force a lower standard of living not only on the older people but also on their families. Savings may be completely used up, endangering the family's future. Families may have to deny other family members' needs in order to finance the older person's care. The spouses of older persons may lose the accumulated resources of a lifetime and have to also accept welfare themselves to survive. (We have seen this happen

---

[12] Kreps, J.M.: The economics of intergenerational relationships. In Shanas, E., and Streib, G.F., editors: Social structure and the family: generational relationships, Englewood Cliffs, N.J., 1965, Prentice-Hall, Inc.

[13] See The economics of aging, a National Journal Issue Book, Washington, D.C., 1978. In the National Journal Book, pp. 65-70. Note the critique, "The Economics of Aging: We Are Asking the Wrong Questions," by one of the co-authors (R.N.B.).

[14] Shanas, E.: The family as a social support system in old age, The Gerontologist **19**(2):169-174, 1979.

with applications for welfare assistance with nursing home placements and we see the painful pauperization required to gain Medicaid coverage in nursing homes.) Middle-aged persons may have as many as four parents and eight grandparents who are living; thus they simply cannot afford to be financially "responsible" relatives to all. The government and welfare agencies must remove the financial burdens from families so that they can attend to the many other emotional and personal needs of older people.

In Denmark, for example, older persons are completely independent financially from their children because of the comprehensive welfare structure; yet they maintain a high degree of interaction and mutuality with their families in every other respect. Old people are not dependent on the politics of potentially emotion-laden family largess for necessary services. Instead, the interaction with family members is voluntary, based on mutual interest in seeing one another.

Are older people "dumped" into institutions?

This is another of the myths that confuse the realities of life in old age. There are, of course, some families who do unload their responsibilities to older family members despite ensuing guilt. In addition, isolated, familyless older people may be placed in an institution when they become ill or feeble, simply because there is no other place for them to go. But most people who have families move in with their relatives when they can no longer live independently. Older people shudder at the thought of institutions, as do their children. Institutions are reserved as the last recourse after everything else has been tried, and families will often go through unbelievable hardship before giving in to placement. The following is a letter we received from a son seeking help for his mother:

My 84-year-old mother lives with me in my four-room apartment. Her senility has become worse and she is totally confused, unable to sit still, care for herself, or even remain continent. Three years ago I had to quit my

job in order to stay home with her, as she used to wander the streets and get lost. I lived on my savings; I am unmarried. I am 52 years old, still unemployed and have passed up two good jobs. Three weeks ago I placed her in an expensive, beautiful, nursing home but she became more confused, totally dependent, and overmedicated. She lost 7 pounds and her bowels became impacted. In desperation I took her back home. I am at my wit's end. What should I do? I love the poor woman. But I cannot enjoy life at all. What is the best thing for her? And me?

Families such as this one may be forced to accept permanent institutional care simply because there are no other alternatives available. And in this particular case, an enormous amount of money was expended, for very poor care, during a brief trial placement. Families should have a whole range of services to assist them in keeping the older person at home, including economic aid. (See Chapter 10 on home care.) One of the fears of public policymakers is that liberalization of Medicare home care benefits might lead to withdrawal of support of older persons by families already providing support. Thus there would be a "raid on the federal treasury." However experiences of other nations that offer such assistance do not confirm this fear.[15]

When institutional care is absolutely necessary, it should be reliable, therapeutic, and reasonably priced. Families could organize with each other in a variety of ways to protect their older family members, for example, to improve nursing home conditions (see p. 341) and to support research

---

[15] See Department of Health, Education and Welfare, National Center for Health Statistics: Home care for persons 55 and over, U.S., July 1966–June 1968, Vital and Health Statistics, Series 10, No. 73, Pub. No. (HSM) 72-1-620, 1972. According to this study, families provide 80% of home health care to older persons. Of intact families studied, 70% were willing to provide intensive personal care without outside help to extremely disabled persons returning home from the hospital the first time. But after the second hospitalization, only 38% of the same relatives felt they could continue to give intensive care without outside assistance. They were wary of the prospect once they had previous experience with it.

against Alzheimer's disease. Over a dozen family groups have emerged in the United States and Canada to stimulate better services and new dollars for research for the personally devastating and socially costly Alzheimer's disease, one of the diseases of old age that can begin in middle age and often leads to institutionalization (see Chapter 5).

MULTIPLE GENERATIONS

Longer lives have increased the likelihood of families with three, four, or even five generations. Increased survivorship is a result of a dramatic reduction in the number of women dying in childbirth, children dying of childhood disease, infants dying in utero or at birth, and older people dying of infections as their bodies lose some of their former resiliency. Modern medicine and improved public health measures can be thanked for these life-giving contributions. Shanas reports that almost one half of all persons 65 and over with living children are members of four generation families. A sizable number of persons over 65 years of age have one or two living parents. About 1 out of 10 older people has a child over 65. Likewise, aging parents may have their aging children living with them, rather than vice versa. We have seen parents in their eighties who were caring for aging and ailing children in their sixties. Townsend[16] calls attention to the existence in Western nations of increasing numbers of older persons with great-grandchildren.

Reliable nationwide figures for the number of older people with living children and grandchildren (and those older persons with living parents) are not available. These questions have not been included in any known U.S. census survey or other large representative sampling.[17] Such important data are necessary to evaluate the amount of potential family support an older person has available

to him or her. However in 1975 in a national survey,[18] nearly three fourths of those studied who were 80 and above were great-grandparents, as were one fourth of those 65 to 66. These figures may increase through continuing improvement in life expectancy and through an increasing fertility rate. Some of the public pressures in the 1980s that are involved in projections for a rise in the fertility rate are listed below:

1. General business/marketing community
2. Selected business/marketing community
   a. Baby food
   b. Toy industry
   c. Maternity clothes
   d. Baby equipment
3. Education industry
4. Roman Catholic Church
5. People fearing to be without children in their old age
6. Parents who want grandchildren

The implications of these new phenomena in human societies have yet to be understood.

GRANDPARENTS

Of the four fifths of persons over 65 with living children, 94% are grandparents and 46% are great-grandparents. The following reveals how the chances of being a grandparent have increased dramatically over the last 50 years:

Studies show that in 1920 only four out of five children at the age of 10 were apt to have one living grandparent whereas 50 years later 19 out of 20 were apt to. In 1920 the chance of a 10-year-old child having at least two grandparents alive was two in five. In 1970 it was three in four. The chance of a 10-year-old having at least three living grandparents has risen from one in ten to three in eight. The chance of having all four has gone from one in 90 to one in 14. (These figures pertain to white children.)[19]

[16] Townsend, P.: The emergence of the four-generation family in industrial society. In Neugarten, B.L., editor: Middle age and aging: a reader in social psychology, Chicago, 1968, University of Chicago Press.

[17] According to Paul Glick, Senior Demographer, U.S. Bureau of the Census, Population Division, 1980.

[18] Shanas, E.: A national survey of the aged, final report to the Administration on Aging, Washington, D.C., 1978, U.S. Department of Health, Education and Welfare.

[19] From Metropolitan Life Statistical Bulletin **52**:8-10, 1972.

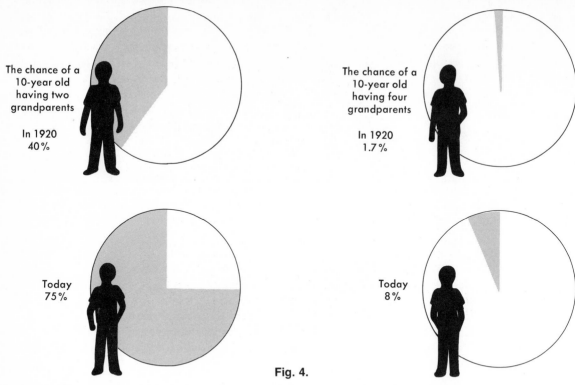

The chance of a 10-year old having two grandparents

In 1920
40%

Today
75%

The chance of a 10-year old having four grandparents

In 1920
1.7%

Today
8%

Fig. 4.

National Institute on Aging. In Metropolitan Life Statistical Bull. **53**:8-10, 1972.

Grandparenthood, like many of the other aspects of late life, has received only meager research attention, primarily in the form of small pilot studies, which may or may not be generalizable to grandparents as a whole. But they do add intriguing pieces of clarifying information about a function so familiar to us.

Early psychoanalytic interpretations of grandparenthood were rather grim and villainous, reflecting patriarchal values. Ferenczi[20] pictured the grandfather as either an imposing, authoritarian old man who frightened and challenged his grandchild or a helpless, feeble person who invited the grandchild's disparagement because he was weak and near death. Ferenczi conceded that boy children may learn about death for the first time

through contacts with grandfathers, but he viewed this essentially in an oedipal context as an opportunity to learn a new way of getting rid of father.

Grandmothers likewise received stern treatment from scholars and practitioners (for example, Abraham, 1955). An overly zealous social worker defending children from the evils of grandmothers wrote an article in 1942 titled "Grandma Made Johnny Delinquent," in which the author argued that grandparents "interfering with the raising of a child" should be removed from the home. La-Barre, Jessner, and Ussery (1960) wrote in the same vein in their paper, "The Significance of Grandmothers in the Psychopathology of Children."[21] Actually, evidence shows that few grand-

[20] Ferenczi, S.: The grandfather complex. In Rickman, J., editor: Theory and technique of psychoanalysis, New York, 1926, Basic Books, Inc., Publishers.

[21] Presented at 1958 annual meeting, University of North Carolina School of Medicine, Chapel Hill.

Grandparenthood.

Photo by Myrna Lewis.

parents (less than 10%) function as surrogate parents, and many of these have been lifesavers rather than evildoers in the lives of grandchildren.

In a more positive mood, Benedek has identified the grandparent role as one available universally to most older people:

Grandparenthood is a new lease on life because grandparents—grandmothers more intensely than grandfathers—relive the memories of the early phase of their own parenthood in observing the growth and development of their grandchildren. Grandparenthood is, however, parenthood one step removed. Relieved from the immediate stresses of motherhood and the responsibilities of fatherhood, grandparents appear to enjoy their grandchildren more than they enjoyed their own children. Their instinctual wish to survive being gratified, they project the hope of the fulfillment of their narcissistic self-image to their grandchildren. Since they do not have the responsibility for raising the child toward

that unconscious goal, their love is not as burdened by doubts and anxieties as it was when their own children were young.[22]

Neugarten and Weinstein (1964) have differentiated types of grandparents in their study of 70 middle-class, older couples: the formal grandparent, the fun seeker, the surrogate parent, the reservoir of family wisdom, and the distant figure who arrives only on holidays and family occasions. They found the fun seeker and the distant figure most common of the types. It was noted that not all older people wanted the grandparent role, although some expressed satisfaction with it. Some felt exploited by their children (as babysitters, etc.); others expressed negative attitudes

---

[22] From Benedek, T.: Parenthood during the life cycle. In Anthony, E.J., editor: Parenthood, Boston, 1970, Little, Brown & Co., p. 201.

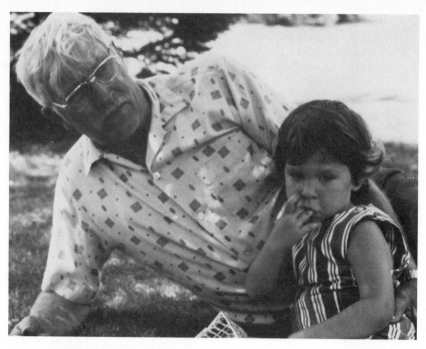

Grandparenthood.

Photo by Myrna Lewis.

toward their own children through their grandchildren. Some joined forces with the young in secret struggles against the middle generation. Biological continuity, emotional self-fulfillment, vicarious accomplishment, teaching, and helping in various ways were some of the meaningful roles in grandparentage.

Kahana and Kahana (1970) have studied grandparenthood from the grandchild's perspective (white, middle-class sample). The feelings of grandchildren depend on the amount of contact, grandparents' behavior toward them, parents' relationships with grandparents, and the child's perceptions of older people in general and grandparents in particular. Children's responses to grandparents change as the youngsters develop; very young children react to gifts, favors, and open affection, whereas slightly older ones prefer sharing activities and having mutual fun.

Grandparenthood now occurs in middle age as well as old age and great-grandparents are not uncommon. The possible roles a grandparent can play are becoming more open to individual interpretation. When grandparents have power and responsibility (as in the role of surrogate parents), they are likely to be more formal and perhaps authoritarian. But when removed from responsibility, they tend to be indulgent, enjoying the grandchildren but not feeling burdened. Some volunteer to be surrogate grandparents to other people's children, as in the Foster Grandparent Program (a component of Action). Youthful grandparents may avoid any element of the traditional grandparent role, preferring to be called by their first names and functioning as friends. The image of the white-haired, elderly grandpa and grandma may eventually have to be reserved for great-grandparents.

An older couple's wedding and fiftieth wedding anniversary pictures.

Courtesy Emil and Irene Eickhoff.

OLDER MARITAL COUPLES

The ''postparental'' period (after the children have grown up and gone) of life for older couples has been extended because of greater longevity, generally earlier marriage, and fewer children. In 1890 the last child married an average of 2 years *after* the death of one of the parents; in 1950 the last child married 13 to 14 years *before* the death of one parent.[23] Most parents have completed childrearing by their late forties and early fifties, leaving them an average of 13 years alone together, or one third of their entire married life.

Care during illness, household management, and emotional gratification are three expectations found in older marriages. The older couple married for many years will find they have a different marriage in old age than they had in middle or early life. Each of them has been changing and experiencing life individually as well as together.

They may have grown more different or more alike. Conflicts between them can intensify or dissipate as they age, with more tolerance or, on the other hand, more rigidity in their expectations of each other. Some have maintained that there is some degree of deterioration in up to one third of older marital relationships.[24] It is difficult to assess an adult in his or her total environment because the circumstances are much more complicated than those of a child. Many more people, life experiences, accidental happenings, stresses, losses, and accomplishments are involved, and prediction of

---

[23] Glick, P.C.: American families, New York, 1957, John Wiley & Sons, Inc.

[24] Yarrow, M.R., Blank, P., Quinn, O.W., Youmans, E.G., and Stein, J.: Social psychological characteristics of old age. In Birren, J.E., Butler, R.N., Greenhouse, S.W., Sokoloff, L., and Yarrow, M.R., editors: Human aging: a biological and behavioral study, Pub. No. (PHS) 986, Washington, D.C., 1963, U.S. Government Printing Office (reprinted as Pub. No. [HSM] 71-9051, 1971, 1974). See also Pineo, P.C.: Disenchantment in the later years of marriages. In Neugarten, B.L., editor: Middle age and aging, Chicago, 1968, University of Chicago Press, pp. 258-262.

eventual individual outcome is precarious. It requires an innocent and hopeful faith to promise in marital vows to love and honor someone "until death do us part," for in 20, 30, or 40 years the partner one married may have become quite a different human being. Men who married "sweet young things" may not accept the fact that women age just as they themselves do. Women who doted on their roles as wives and mothers may rebel at the thought of being nursemaid to an ailing and aging husband. Of course there are people who expect and accept change with dignity and constructive response, having reached maturity with relatively few personality handicaps that would impede adaptability. Environmental influences, physical and mental health, and the historical period of time in which one is living are other variables affecting marriages over a long span of time.

Most older marriages are broken by death rather than divorce. Divorce can be more easily risked in youth or middle age when resources and options are greater. Children and grandchildren serve as a strong bond between marital partners. Couples who reach old age have usually adapted to each other in a way that each finds supportive or at least more acceptable than the unknown.[25] And when so many other losses are occurring naturally, marriage may be one of the more familiar and comfortable patterns remaining. Older people can become intensely dependent on each other for intimacy, personal services, and mutual support; a major psychological blow then occurs when one partner dies. As we have said before, factors of the immediate environment are *very* closely related to the older person's behavior and attitudes, with significant persons being the most important of

these factors. Thus, in general, divorce occurs before old age, if it is to occur at all, and older people perceive threats to themselves emanating from outside the marital relationship as more significant than those from within. Marriage becomes a more valued human relationship by the very fact of powerful outside forces and eventual death.

Older marriages, although less likely to dissolve, do have problems that carry over from the past or develop as a result of current stress.

■ Mr. and Mrs. H had been married 40 years. They had arrived at serious disagreements and mistrust early in the marriage but had stayed together because of the children. They reached a state of truce in which there was as little contact between them as possible. Mr. H obtained employment that required him to travel about 80% of the time. For 30 years he devoted his energy and interest to his work and to impermanent, extramarital relationships. After retirement at 65, he returned to their loveless home. He became depressed and thought often of death. Finally he developed numerous hypochondriacal symptoms, which occupied his time and energy in much the same manner as had his former job. He and Mrs. H continue to live together, each obviously unwilling to leave the other.

A common difficulty in older marriages is the disequilibrium caused by the physical or emotional illness of either spouse. Major chronic changes occurring with senile brain disease, for example, can drastically alter the marital relationship. One partner may become the caretaker or nursemaid for the other, often with little help from elsewhere. Illnesses can drain the physical, emotional, and financial capacities of the caretaker spouse. Anger and depression may occur, and it is not unusual to find the formerly well spouse develop physical or psychiatric symptoms of his or her own.

Patterns of dominance may shift in old age, with the female assuming a more active and responsible role than formerly. Many of today's older persons were brought up in a male-dominant, female-subordinate culture. But with shorter life expectancies for men and their practice of marrying women younger than themselves, they are usually older than their mates and consequently less capable

---

[25] It is noteworthy that in the NIMH study of healthy older men, there were many criticisms and complaints about wives, yet only one man reported even considering separation from his spouse, and none believed that either his marriage or his choice of a spouse was a mistake. Whether this is a tribute to the success of these marriages or an indication that such an indictment of a large segment of their lives was too painful to face is an interesting question. Generally, however, these men appeared to "tell it like it was," or at least close to like it was, about their marriages.

Late-life marriage.

Photo by David S. Strickler.

physically. As early as 1960 Gold, in studying age and sex patterns of familial dominance in 24 preliterate societies, found a shift to female dominance in later life in 14 of these. She states, "Although old women did not gain the upper hand in all societies studied, aging in no instance led to the husband's gaining in authority."[26] She suggests that husbands may be willing to accept female domination as the price of security as they age. Women, having been deprived of equal cultural status all their lives, may even enjoy the opportunity to exert their influence as men become more dependent and infirm with age. Unfortunately their taste of greater status is frequently mitigated by the need to provide nursing services to their husbands. When that is accomplished and their husbands die, they are left to nurse themselves through old age or accept help from someone else. The ascendance to dominance may be short-lived and unrewarding. Mutuality and equality (for example, in sex roles and age of marriage) throughout life would be a more sensible pattern and carry over to a more consistently mutual relationship in old age.

There seems to be some interdependence between the life-spans of husband and wife; studies have shown an association between the length of life of husband and wife (for example, the early study of Ciocco, 1941). It has been suggested that this is a result of selection (healthy people may select other healthy people as partners, while frailer men and women may not marry) or to the marital environment itself, which supposedly encourages a moderate, temperate life. Suicide rates are lower for married men and higher for divorced. In old age the mutual aid and support in a marriage can become a crucial factor in the health of each partner, just as depression and loss of support after the death of a spouse can contribute to the deterioration of the surviving partner's health. For many people the maintenance of closeness with another is the center of existence up to the very end of life.

Remarriage, after death or divorce of a spouse, does occur with some frequency. There are May-December marriages in which an older man marries a much younger woman; but marriages between people of approximately the same age are more usual. Children from an earlier marriage may or may not bless the new union. Their negative attitudes may be voiced strongly, particularly if they believe a parent is being taken advantage of, is acting foolishly, or is endangering their inheritance; on the other hand, children may actively encourage parents to find new lives for themselves through remarriage. McKain[27] found that the success of late-life marriage was related to the following factors: the children encouraged marriage, the couple knew each other at least 11 years before marriage, there was sufficient income, the couple pooled financial resources, and both were reasonably satisfied with their lives.

IN-LAWS

Sooner or later almost everyone becomes an in-law. Each person who marries receives an average of six members of the spouse's family as in-laws. In the public mind, "in-law" means "trouble," especially if it happens to be a mother-in-law closely involved with her son's or daughter's life. Although no one knows for sure, our guess is that the mother-in-law "problem" stems from the cultural encouragement of competition among women from the time they are small girls. Added to this are the stresses facing the older woman because of her longer life-span and low social status. Overinvolvement with children is another possible factor. But the entire problem is very likely exaggerated, since numbers of people manage to get along reasonably well with in-laws, including

---

[26]From Gold, S.: Cross-cultural comparisons of role change with aging, Student Journal of Human Development, Spring 1960, p. 11a.

[27]McKain, W.C.: Retirement marriage, Storrs, 1969, University of Connecticut, p. 168.

mothers-in-law. In-laws can be supportive as well as trouble-making. Personality factors are probably more critical than the social roles as in-laws in establishing relationships.

OLDER "ISOLATES"

Isolation as we are defining it here refers to individuals who have minimal or no contact with other human beings. Some people become isolated in old age because of life circumstances and would choose to live differently if they could. Others isolate themselves by choice, often following a lifelong pattern of existence as "loners." Townsend distinguishes between isolates and "desolates": "Those who are secluded from family and society, as objectively assessed on the basis of defined criteria, are the isolates. Those who have been recently deprived by death, illness or migration of someone they love—such as a husband or wife or child—are the desolates. A major conclusion of the present analysis is that though the two are connected, the underlying reason for loneliness in old age is desolation rather than isolation."[28] The emotional meaning of isolation depends on whether it is a habitual life-style or whether it has come about or been exacerbated by emotional loss.

Shanas (1963)[29] makes much the same point when she comments that isolation is not synonymous with loneliness, neither is it a direct causative factor in mental illness. Some older people have lived alone so long they have lost the notion of what loneliness means. Shanas found that the loneliest and most isolated people appear to be those widowed persons who have no children and live alone. On the other hand, isolation and loneliness of people are not necessarily relieved by closeness of children or frequent contact with them. In this case, isolation is a state of mind rather than actual social alienation.

Attempting to explain the fact that a greater number of single or widowed people over 65 are admitted to mental hospitals, as compared to married people, Shanas believes the blame cannot be placed on social isolation. Instead, she postulates that serious illnesses can devastate the person who is alone because there is no one to care for him or her; thus continuation in the community becomes impossible, whereas this would not be the case for someone with family or friends. Lowenthal (1968) in tracing the connection between social isolation and mental illness in old age states:

Lifelong extreme isolation (or alienation) is not necessarily conducive to the development of the kinds of mental disorder that bring persons to the psychiatric ward in their old age; lifelong marginal social adjustment may be conducive to the development of such disorder; late-developing isolation is apparently linked with mental disorder but it is of no greater significance among those with psychogenic disorders than among those with organic disorders, and may be more of a consequence than a cause of mental illness in the elderly; finally, physical illness may be the critical antecedent to both the isolation and the mental illness.[30]

The choice to be a loner must be respected. As we have seen, people who isolate themselves are not all frail, dependent, lonely persons. We must be able to differentiate this group from those older people who truly want and need assistance in making changes in their lives. Above all, both loners and those isolated unwillingly by circumstance should have the needed help they require in order to maintain the kind of life most satisfactory to them.

---

[28] From Townsend, P.: The emergence of the four-generation family in industrial society. In Neugarten, B.L., editor: Middle age and aging: a reader in social psychology, Chicago, 1968, University of Chicago Press.

[29] Shanas, E.: The older person at home—a potential isolate or participant. Reprinted from National Institute of Mental Health. In Research utilization in aging, an exploration, proceedings of a conference sponsored by Community Research and Services Branch, April 30–May 3, 1963, Washington, D.C., 1964, U.S. Government Printing Office.

[30] From Lowenthal, M.F.: Social isolation and mental illness in old age. In Neugarten, B.L., editor: Middle age and aging: a reader in social psychology, Chicago, 1968, University of Chicago Press, p. 234.

INHERITANCE AND THE FAMILY

The issue of who gets the inheritance, if there is any, is a sensitive one for many families, and the manner in which this is handled is a good indicator of family problem solving. Some older people make their wills early and in secret. Others fully inform each child. For many people, making a will is such a painful process that it is put off and they die intestate (without a will). Children who are used to sharing with each other and who have resolved their major conflicts with parents may be able to settle an estate amicably with no will. But for others this is precisely the time for angry, hurt, and disappointed feelings to come to the fore, and a royal battle ensues.

The making of a will can be therapeutic for several reasons. The older person, by his or her own action, takes the potential for conflict out of the hands of the children. The estate will be handled according to the parent's own wishes. The disposing of the burden of possessions through a will can free older people and simplify their lives; many give things away even before they die. The will tells a great deal about the relations of the legator to his or her legatees (children, charitable interests, etc.). The nature of wills varies according to the stage of life of the testator. For example, if one has young children, trusts may be set up. Selection of executors and trustees is important: the executor is appointed to execute the will; the trustees are persons or agents, such as a bank, holding legal title to property in order to administer it for a beneficiary.

In some states a person may make an oral or nuncupative will; in others a holographic will—one written in the testator's own handwriting and unwitnessed—is acceptable. Older people may need to know that there are two main classes of property: real and personal. The former refers to such immovable objects as land, houses, and trees. The latter includes all other kinds of property (called legacy). If no will has been made, the property descends to lawful heirs, as legally prescribed, or to the state. Property passes into the hands of the executor who sells it and divides the proceeds among the next of kin. If a will has been made and the person dies, the will must be probated, or proved to be authentic. The executor brings the will before the court (probate or surrogate's court), and any possible heir is given the opportunity to object to the probate of the will.[31]

It is likely that the future will bring changes in laws of inheritance, since many question the right of ownership in fee simple—that is, absolute ownership—in a complex society providing many goods and services funded through public revenues.

The use of *prenuptial agreements* is a time-honored method, in most states, of allaying the fears of children when their parents remarry in old age. Such agreements also protect older people themselves by keeping their resources intact and unavailable to anyone but designated persons. Wealthy people are inclined to use prenuptial agreements even in earlier marriages to protect family estates. With people now living longer, with more late-life marriages, and with more inherited wealth, prenuptial agreements are increasingly common. Legal consultation is necessary. The agreement customarily describes what will *not* be available to the opposite spouse. Trusts can be alternatives to prenuptial agreements.

FAMILY INVOLVEMENT IN MENTAL HEALTH CARE OF OLDER PERSONS
Family therapy

Empirical evidence has made it clear that most older people are *not* alienated from their families; therefore one must go further and assume that any problems, crises, and changes affecting an older person also affect his or her family. The newly forming field of family therapy, begun about 20 years ago, has recognized that the problems of older people have impact on the entire kinship network. Even the youngest family members will be

---

[31] For a useful resource on wills, see Porter, S.: Sylvia Porter's money book, New York, 1980, Doubleday & Co., Inc.

reacting emotionally to the events in the lives of grandmother and grandfather. It is through these experiences that they learn firsthand about late life, and many of their attitudes toward older persons and their own eventual aging will be modeled after the situations and attitudes in the family circle. Family therapy involving everyone from young to old can be a way of helping to understand what is happening to the older person, clarify feelings, review and deal with old conflicts (which may be surprisingly undiluted by the passage of time), and mobilize everyone in the care and concern for the older member. (See Chapter 12 for discussion of family counseling.)

"Filial maturity"

Blenkner[32] has used the term "filial maturity" to describe a middle-aged developmental stage beyond the usual freudian framework. (The latter encompasses development from birth through early adulthood, with little theoretical consideration given to middle and late life.) Adults in their forties and fifties experience a "filial crisis" when it becomes evident that their parents are aging and the offspring will be called on to provide the support and comfort that older parents need. This may contrast with childhood visions of parents as powerful and nurturing individuals who assist and support their offspring, rather than vice versa. In view of the vicissitudes of early parent-child relationships, there is often unfinished developmental work to be done in freeing middle-aged adults from hostile, ambivalent, or immature parental ties that impede a healthy relationship. Maturity for the middle-aged child "involves being *depended on* and therefore being dependable insofar as his parent is concerned," with full recognition of the parent as an individual with his or her own rights, needs, limitations, and life history. "It is often necessary to assist the child to complete his unfinished emancipation from the parent *in order that he may then be more free to help his parent*."[32a] Neurotic guilt toward parents must be differentiated from the real guilt of failure to assume filial responsibility.

Blenkner reminds us that much psychiatric and social work literature treats the interactions between older people and their children in a negative, patronizing fashion. The term "role-reversal" has become a favored concept because it fits so comfortably with the negative stereotypes depicting the aged as dependent or regressed; the child supposedly becomes the parent to his or her own parents as they slip from self-sufficient adulthood to a state of childish dependency. Surely a more derogatory interpretation of the realities of old age could not be imagined, especially when adult dependency in this society is consistently equated with laxness and moral decline. Certain other societies have managed a very different view.

An Igbo elder [Eastern Nigeria] is no more productive than his American counterpart, but can demand care in his old age as his publicly acknowledged right, without any sense of guilt, ego damage, or loss of face. Whoever fails in giving such care is culpable and subject to scorn and ridicule, and runs the risk of being cut off from the ancestors.[33]

Thus the older Igbo has the powerful authority of the ancestor world to back his claim to respect and care, while the older American must rely on the good will of his or her children and/or society. Some of the more practical matters of helping

---

[32] For an excellent summary on family relationships in old age see Blenkner, M.: Social work and family relationships in later life with some thoughts on filial maturity. In Shanas, E., and Streib, G.F., editors: Social structure and the family: generational relations, Englewood Cliffs, N.J., 1965, Prentice-Hall, Inc., pp. 46-59.

[32a] Blenkner, M.: Social work and family relationships in later life with some thoughts on filial maturity. In Shanas, E., and Streib, G.F., editors: Social structure and the family: generational relations, Englewood Cliffs, N.J., 1965, Prentice-Hall, Inc., p. 50.

[33] From Wylie, F.M.: Attitudes toward aging and the aged among black Americans: some historical perspectives, Aging and Human Development **2:**68, 1971.

older family members can be easily learned.[34] Indeed, several rehabilitation centers and hospitals now teach families how to perform required therapies and other services. For example, at Montefiore Home in Cleveland, Ohio, the social service department has expanded its contact with the family to include classes for adult children in order to provide knowledge about aging and the illnesses frequently occurring in old age, means of coping, and an opportunity for sharing concerns with others.[35] Visiting nurses and home health specialists perform a teaching function within the family (see Chapter 10). Many more older people could be treated at home if their problems were detected early and prompt psychiatric, social, medical, and economic resources were made available. Families could then be free to provide the blend of affection and personal services so essential to mental health in old age.

---

[34] Recent books for the families of older persons are: Bumagin, V.E., and Hirn, K.F.: Aging is a family affair, New York, 1979, Thomas Y. Crowell Co., Inc.; Otten, J., and Shelly, F.D.: When your parents grow old, New York, 1976, Funk and Wagnalls Book Publishing; and Silverstone, B., and Hyman, H.K.: You and your aging parent, New York, 1976, Pantheon Books, Inc.

[35] Dorrucci, F.: Classes for adult children of the aged, Social Work **19:**732-733, 1974.

REFERENCES

Abraham, K.: Some remarks on the role of grandparents in the psychology of neuroses. In Abraham, H., editor: Selected papers: clinical papers and essays in psychoanalysis, vol. 2, New York, 1955, Basic Books, Inc., Publishers.

Brody, E.M.: Aging is a family affair, Public Welfare **25:**129-141, 1967.

Brody, E.M., and Spark, G.M.: Institutionalization of the aged: a family crisis, Family Process **5:**76-90, 1966.

Ciocco, A.: On the interdependence of the length of life of husband and wife, Human Biology **13:**505-525, 1941.

Duval, E.M.: In-laws in your life, Pastoral Psychology **52:**39-47, 1954.

Farrar, M.S.: Mother-daughter conflicts extended into later life, Social Casework **36:**202-208, 1955.

Glick, P.C.: Updating the life cycle of the family, Journal of Marriage and the Family **39:**5-13, 1977.

Harevan, T.K.: The last stage: historical adulthood and old age, Daedalus **105:**13-28, 1976.

Harevan, T.K.: Family time and historical time, Daedalus **106:** 57-70, 1977.

Harevan, T.K., editor: Transitions: the family and the life course in historical perspectives, New York, 1979, Academic Press.

Hill, R.B.: Strengths of black families, New York, 1972, Emerson Books, Inc.

Hill, R.B., Foote, N., Aldous, J., Carlson, R., and MacDonald, R.: Family development in three generations, Cambridge, Mass., 1970, Schenkman Publishing Co., Inc.

Jacobs, S.C.: Grief: a mediating process between a loss and illness, Journal of Comprehensive Psychiatry **20:**165-176, 1979.

Jacobs, S.C., and Ostfeld, A.M.: The effects of illness and death of one family member on other family members: a review with some recommendations for research and medical practice, prepared for the National Institute on Aging, Departments of Psychiatry and Epidemiology and Public Health, New Haven, Conn., 1978, Yale University School of Medicine.

Jury, M., and Jury, D.: Gramp, New York, 1976, Grossman Publishers, Inc.

Kahana, B., and Kahana, E.: Grandparenthood from the perspective of the developing grandchild, Developmental Psychology **3:**98-105, 1970.

Kahana, E., and Kahana, B.: Theoretical and research perspectives on grandparenthood, Aging and Human Development **2:**261-268, 1971.

Lowenthal, M.F., and Haven, C.: Interaction and adaptation: intimacy as a critical variable. In Neugarten, B.L., editor: Middle age and aging: a reader in social psychology, Chicago, 1968, University of Chicago Press.

Munnichs, J.: Linkages of old people with their families and bureaucracy in a welfare state, the Netherlands. In Shanas, E., and Sussman, M.B., editors: Family, bureaucracy and the elderly, Durham, N.C., 1977, Duke University Press.

Neugarten, B.L.: Continuities and discontinuities of psychological issues into adult life, Human Development **12:**121-130, 1969.

Neugarten, B.L., and Weinstein, K.K.: The changing American grandparent, Journal of Marriage and the Family **26:** 199-205, 1964.

Parsons, T., and Bales, R.: Family, socialization and interaction process, New York, 1955, Free Press of Glencoe, Inc.

Rosenmayr, L.: The family—a source of hope for the elderly? In Shanas, E., and Sussman, M.B., editors: Family, bureaucracy and the elderly, Durham, N.C., 1977, Duke University Press.

Rosenmayr, L., and Kockeis, E.: Propositions for a sociological theory of ageing and the family, International Social Science Journal **15**(3):410-426, 1963.

Ryder, N.B.: The cohort as a concept in the study of social change, American Sociological Review **30:**843-861, 1965.

Shanas, E.: The health of older people: a social survey, Cambridge, Mass., 1962, Harvard University Press.

Shanas, E.: The unmarried old person in the United States: living arrangements and care in illness, myth and fact, paper prepared for the International Social Science Research Seminar in Gerontology, Markaryd, Sweden, August 1963.

Shanas, E., and Streib, G.F.: Social structure of the family: generational relations, Englewood Cliffs, N.J., 1965, Prentice-Hall, Inc.

Shanas, E., and Sussman, M.B., editors: Family, bureaucracy and the elderly, Druham, N.C., 1977, Duke University Press.

Sussman, M.B., and Burchinal, L.: Kin family network: unheralded structure in current conceptualization of family functions. In Neugarten, B.L., editor: Middle age and aging: a reader in social psychology, Chicago, 1968, University of Chicago Press.

Townsend, P.: The family life of old people, London, 1957, Routledge and Kegan Paul, Ltd.

Treas, J.: Aging and the family. In Woodruff, D., and Birren, J.E., editors: Aging: scientific perspectives and social issues, New York, 1975, D. Van Nostrand Co.

Troll, L.K.: The family of later life: a decade review, Journal of Marriage and the Family **33:**263-290, 1971.

Uhlenberg, P.: Cohort variations in family life cycle experiences in U.S. females, Journal of Marriage and the Family **36:**284-292, 1974.

U.S. Senate Special Committee on Aging: Sumary of developments and data, a pre–White House Conference on Aging report, Nov. 1971.

TWO

EVALUATION, TREATMENT, AND
PREVENTION

8

General treatment principles

We are writing the treatment section of this book on two levels: one describing what we consider to be appropriate and ideal mental health care of older people and the other dealing with contemporary realities, far from ideal. Our aim is to keep in sight the direction for improvements, while also advising mental health personnel, older people themselves, and anyone involved in their welfare on how to make the best of what is now available.

NEW ATTITUDES TOWARD MENTAL HEALTH TREATMENT OF OLDER PERSONS

There has been a steady growth in theory and practice in the psychiatric treatment of older persons, which emphasizes the importance of active as well as restorative and rehabilitative possibilities. Most important, the potentiality of reversibility has been demonstrated, both in the functional disorders and in some of the organic disorders, particularly delirium.[1] Prevention, comprehensive evaluations, and genuine therapeutic efforts have begun to be accepted as worthwhile activities on behalf of older persons.

Changes in psychiatric perspectives

Psychiatry, at the turn of the century, had a detached view of abnormal behavior—observing and cataloging exterior behavior. Later, dominated by freudian thinking, it moved to the interior and the inner life of humans—probing subjective experience and internalized modes of adaptation. Since World War II, psychiatry has moved out somewhat (but only *somewhat*) into the community—examining the influences of institutions and environmental conditions on human behavior, inner experience, and adaptations. This is reflected in the American Psychiatric Association's 1980 *Diagnostic and Statistical Manual,* which requires consideration of social stresses as part of a psychiatric diagnosis. Recently some attention has turned to the inherent changes of the individual as he or she progresses through the life cycle. Thus in about 80 years, psychiatry has looked at people's outward behavior, their inner life, their environment, and finally their passage through their finite existence—the life cycle. This includes a new interest in the psychology of old age.[2] There are also exciting recent developments occurring in the neuro-

---

[1] Private mental hospitals demonstrate the correlation between financial capacity and reversibility. In studies done in private institutions, Dr. Robert Gibson and Dr. J.M. Myers stressed the reversibility of the psychiatric conditions of old age. From 54% to 75% of patients over 65 were able to be discharged to their own homes in 2 months. Thus if one can afford private care, the chances are greater for reversibility. See Gibson, R.W.: Medicare and the psychiatric patient, Psychiatric Opinion **7:**17-22, 1970.

[2] Berezin, Busse, Eisdorfer, Gaitz, Gitelson, Goldfarb, Greenleigh, Grotjahn, Linden, Pfeiffer, Rothschild, Simon, Thompson, and Weinberg are among the few American psychiatrists whose work has stimulated research into the psychopathology and psychodynamics of aging as well as contributed to the development of treatment approaches.

sciences that are ultimately likely to make great contributions to understanding human behavior and to the treatment of mental disorders. An example is the catecholamine hypothesis of the origins of affective disorders like depression (see p. 71).

However, psychiatry as a practicing specialty has not kept pace with the theoretical aspects of the discipline. It is the private psychotherapy and analytic practice that remains psychiatry's chief preoccupation, with little active participation in the broader field of community psychiatry. The financial opportunities in private practice have militated against the application of new understanding in the area of human behavior.[3] Other disciplines have become more involved than ever in mental health work. Nurses, social workers, psychologists, pastoral counselors, paraprofessionals, and members of still-forming specialties are doing much of the work traditionally thought of as "psychiatry" in the past.

Life cycle theory—what is it?

A science, or perhaps more humbly, a perspective and body of knowledge of the life cycle, is barely born. Social, biological, medical, and other changes have led to longer life and increased visibility of the stages of the life cycle. Improved sanitation and medical care have prolonged life in both the formerly dangerous years of infancy and the often frail years of late life. The middle years of life stand as a fulcrum and largely support the two ends of the life cycle—childhood and old age. This is true for individuals, when parents are responsible both for their children and for their own parents; it is true also in society, where middle-aged people hold the power, make the decisions, and produce the goods. We do not yet know to what extent normative, modal features of the life cycle account for the varying patterns of change and adaptation we see. A few investigators like Matilda White Riley are engaged in endeavoring to disentangle the features of the successive phases of the life cycle from the contributions of such influences as social change, medical disease, and historical variation.[4] Butler (1968) has used the term "average expectable life cycle" as a counterpart to Heinz Hartman's concept "average expectable environment"[4a] to bring focus to the notion that there are average, normative experiences against which to measure individual patterns. If, for example, we see correlations of conservative behavior with age, are these a result of the conditions of youth carried forward in time, or are they intrinsic to aging? If we observe preoccupation with bowel function in aged persons, is it a result of the popular lore of the turn of the century or a consequence of the inherent character of old age? Are the declines in memory associated with aging to be interpreted as a consequence of brain disease, educational obsolescence, social anomie, depression, and/or the mysterious, inevitable, irreversible process called aging?

There is not yet a sufficiently sensitive methodology to weigh the relative significance of the many elements that are involved in the production of changes in people and adaptation to those changes. We believe the life cycle itself—the changes inherent in the rhythm of a life from birth to death—makes profound contribution to the variability. The study of human development has tended in the past to stop with adolescence. Recently social scientists have begun to study the psychology of mid-life. Persons involved in fact gathering and theoretical formulations now need to build up a head of steam and plunge through middle to old age instead of losing interest after surveying the "achievement" of adulthood. Contemporary personality and developmental theories need enlargement and expansion to provide a full account of human nature. Naturally such an effort

---

[3] England takes a straightforward approach to the issue of economic incentive by offering "capitation payments" (special payments for each older person receiving treatment) in order to encourage work with persons who ordinarily are not treated.

[4] Riley, M.W.: Aging from birth to death and social change, paper prepared for a session on New Frontiers in Science, American Association for the Advancement of Science, San Francisco, 1980.

[4a] Hartman, H.: Ego psychology and the problem of adaptation, New York, 1958, International Universities Press.

would give further direction to the treatment of older people.

In clinical work and reflections Butler speaks of the development of an *individual inner sense of the life cycle,* which is neither the same as the average expectable life cycle nor the same as a personal sense of identity, although it is related to both. It is a subjective feel for the life cycle as a whole; its rhythm, its variability, and the relation of this to the individual's sense of self. This inner sense seems to be a necessary personal achievement in order for individuals to orient themselves wherever they happen to be in the life cycle. It becomes particularly important as people age and begin to comprehend their own eventual end.

In adolescents, the middle-aged, and older persons, such a personal sense of the cycle of human life is a necessary adaptive mechanism. To understand the kinds of changes to be expected and face the reality and inevitability of these changes, including death itself, is important to individual security. It gives people the opportunity to prepare themselves, to plan and order their lives in more meaningful ways, and (perhaps more important), to be assured that they are not alone in their experiences. All former and future generations and all of their fellow living human beings share many of the same basic realities. The understanding of this is part of what humans long for when they speak of searching for the meaning of life through religion or a personal philosophy of life. An inner sense of the life cycle—often unspoken—produces a profound awareness of change and evolution—birth, maturation, obsolescence, and death—and therefore a profound but nonmorbid realization of the precious and limited quantity of life. For older people it is not the same as "feeling old"; it is instead a deep understanding of what it means to be human.

One sees all kinds of people struggling for greater sensibility about life but, for various reasons, not being able to face what is there. There are adolescents who can comprehend the notion of suicide (perhaps because the person kills himself and thus has control over his death) but cannot imagine death in old age or even that they themselves will grow old. Middle-aged persons often develop anxiety symptoms about aging and try to turn the clock back to youth by dressing and acting young. Even in their old age one sees Peter Pans—those who have never grown up to face their age and the fact of death.

In our own work we have seen what an inner sense of the life cycle can mean in old age. It can portend adaptation to inevitable changes in the best manner possible; or its absence can guarantee maladaptation, wherein the older person reacts with terror, dependency, and prolonged grief to personal change. The following case examples are illustrative.

■ A still handsome, warm, and magnetic 78-year-old former politician, who had received many public awards, called for a psychiatric consultation, his voice full of despair. He had always been healthy and unusually vigorous until the previous summer, at which time he developed glaucoma. Shortly thereafter he began to notice weakness of his left arm. By means of a myelogram, electromyelographic studies, and other tests, it was determined that the patient had anterior horn cell disease.

He had been an unusually healthy man all his life, extremely vigorous, very proud of his sexual prowess and attractiveness. He had been married three times and had had many private affairs.

However, until his recent problems, he had never taken seriously the fact that he could become old. Moreover, his much younger brother was suffering from severe chronic brain disorder and was residing in a nursing home; this fact began to preoccupy him.

Our patient remained somewhat busy in public life but had recently given up his last private love affair. During a warm and somewhat grief-stricken lunch together, the two quoted Ecclesiastes to each other: "Everything in its season. . . ."

Yet he never prepared for old age. He never thought about old age when he was younger; in fact he gave it little thought until his glaucoma. On the rare occasions when he did, he would say to himself, "Why shouldn't I live to be 100?" Whenever he rarely thought about death, he wished for, and he thought that he would have, a quick sudden death, He had turned aside suggestions that he write his memoirs.

Now he felt helpless. His sense of omnipotence was under sudden seige and near collapse. He became extremely hypochondriacal. He not only went to physicans from a whole range of specialties but sought out possible quacks.

In summary, he had not experienced aging or the diseases associated with aging gradually. All was precipitous, with no stepwise intimations of mortality!

Although he had five children, he was not in any sense strongly involved with them, which suggests that he had not grown or fulfilled the life-cycle task of parenthood.

He became very much dependent on the therapist. Although the psychotherapist was obviously doing nothing "material," he believed the therapist was the only physician who was "doing anything" for him—in spite of the fact that the others had offered drugs and had conducted a variety of tests. Emphasis in psychotherapy was on consideration of the unfolding of the life cycle and on renunciation and restitution; that is, on grieving and accepting things as they were and finding other avenues for personal pleasure and development—particularly those pertinent to later life such as teaching, counseling, and leaving "traces." It was necessary to reduce the number of sessions to help him resolve his sudden (but not unexpected) dependency. He improved, but any lenghty separations from the therapist created setbacks.

■ In 1965 an 87-year-old former schoolteacher sustained a stroke from which she recovered except for a residual right hemiplegia. There was no aphasia. She had always been an extremely independent person, and she was quite agitated and depressed over what happened to her. Unlike the first patient, however, she did not respond with helplessness. She was a very courageous fighter, pulling herself up and down stairs for dinner each day. This was still true 5 years later at age 92. The therapist was seeing her at that time, although the agitated depression had gone. They seemed unable to give each other up. They would meet approximately once monthly, usually on Saturday afternoon, at which time at her insistence they would have a fine sherry or Madeira together. There were occasions when she would put herself to bed and seem to be failing. However, nothing would be amiss on physical examination, and it became clear that these episodes were related to the thought on her part that maybe she was just about to die. In view of her advanced age, this was not such an irrational idea! Then, after several days in bed, she would awaken to the realization that she was neither dead nor dying and would be back up functioning again.

At other times the therapist would simply tell her she was alright, whereupon she would agree and resume life. These episodes were characterized psychologically by great preoccupation with leaving things and with what the recipients would do with the objects of her legacy. It was very important to her that she not be falsely reassured about death but that respectful attention be given to her ideas about dying, death, burial, and the objects of her legacy—religious items, pictures of her parents, old favorite books, etc. Unlike the first patient, she had always had a sound sense of the evolving process of life, the life cycle. But her advancing age—or diseases—narrowed the opportunities in which she could express her personality. Thus she had to rely more and more on verbal or bodily expression of needs (rather than action). She had responsiveness in abundance from her daughter as well as from her therapist. She continued to do quite well.

Rites of passage

Rites of passage are the cultural observances of biological and social changes. Christenings, confirmations or bar mitzvahs, marriages, and burials are the most obvious, but there are countless others, all adding structure and meaning to lives. They lend predictability and help to ease the individual's movement from one stage to the next. Such rites help us to "know the score"; offer social supports from time of birth and early development; confirm our religious, sexual, occupational, and social identity; consecrate marriages as well as provide for their dissolution; and offer models for dealing with happiness and fulfillment as well as with failure, grief, loss, and eventual death. However, rites of passage, as with all other cultural institutions, are often out of tune with human needs as history unfolds. It is necessary to understand the nature of the particular life cycle in order to judge the validity of the rites of passage associated with it. Rites of passage undergo constant revision—and when the revision is delayed, complicated, incomplete, or aborted, humans flounder and suffer from the lack of a meaningful structure. An example in the present is the problem in handling grief that has resulted from increasing secularization and the loss of religious supports. Older people, and especially their children, often do not know what to do with grief. Should they cry, maintain a stoic front, deny it, become angry, or what? For many there is no longer a structured and supportive mourning period. Some mourners pretend the loss never happened; others wait silently, hoping grief will go away. Yet we know theoretically what "grief work" is and what could be done to help find the best possible psychological resolution to loss. It remains for such knowledge to become part of popular psychology. People who no longer belong to an institutionalized religion must learn to do for themselves some of the work they formerly left up to the church or synagogue.

Other parts of the life cycle are changing as a result of alterations in biology and changes in the life-span. Changes occur so quickly that people may be left bewildered. The bewilderment is greatest in those for whom the change is greatest. Small children born today have never experienced anything but accelerating change, and it has been suggested that change itself is an accepted way of life for them. But for the present generation of older people who remember a more slowly moving past, the contrast with the present can be horrifying, disconcerting, and disorienting, particularly if the older person feels or is in some way personally victimized by change.

New rites of passage are needed to support new developments. Recent and still-growing controls of the events of the life cycle bear comment. Flexibility of classic rites is needed to cope with birth control, liberalized abortion, genetic manipulation, sex prediction before birth—all of which could (and already do) allow considerable control over the occurrence and timing of birth and quality of children. The arrival of menstruation for girls has moved ahead thirty-six months in the last hundred years. The rite of marriage (which first became a sacrament in the ninth century AD, when people seldom lived longer than 40 years) is being influenced by trial marriages, the ability to control births, and the notion of divorce by consent.

The event of death is subject to greater control. Organ transplants, new thoughts about criteria for death (as a result of medical discoveries), interest in passive and active euthanasia—all produce legal, ethical, and medical considerations that will become part of the evolving rites surrounding death.

One feature of present life—retirement—has almost no formal rites of passage and no precedent historically. The institution of retirement is barely 80 years old and is a consequence of the lengthening of the life-span for vast numbers of people. In the next 25 years, 65 million people will have retired, and in the year 2000, about 33 million of these will still be alive. Similar demographic changes are occurring in other countries, some of which are responding more positively than we. Our present lack of structured and meaningful rites for retirement has led to anomic nonparticipation of many people in American life.

Biological control can create social innovation and vice versa. Thus people can become freer of the previously fixed, unalterable biological states that have long controlled the culturally defined rites of passage. What such freedom means for the future is hard to fathom. We do know that present generations of older people need to have a secure place for themselves in a society that makes sense to them. Good mental health is not possible in chaos and meaninglessness.

OBSTACLES TO TREATMENT IN OLD AGE
Ageism and countertransference

We have described the many negative attitudes toward older people under the general term "ageism"—the prejudices and stereotypes that are applied to older people sheerly on the basis of their age.[5] (Another term, "gerontophobia," refers to a more rare "unreasonable fear and/or constant hatred of older people whereas ageism is a much

---

[5] Butler, R.N.: The effects of medical and health progress on the social and economic aspects of the life cycle, Industrial Gerontology **1:**1-9, 1969.

more comprehensive and useful concept.'')[6] Ageism, like racism and sexism, is a way of pigeon-holing people and not allowing them to be individuals with unique ways of living their lives.[7] Prejudice toward older people begins already in childhood[8] and is an attempt by younger generations to shield themselves from the fact of their own eventual aging and death and to avoid having to deal with the social and economic problems of increasing numbers of older people. It provides a rationalization for pushing older people out of the job market without spending much thought on what will happen to them when they are no longer allowed to work. (The new retirement law, which drops mandatory retirement in the public sector and raises the retirement age in the private sector to 70, is a powerful counterforce to this trend.) Ageism is the sacrifice of older people for the sake of ''productivity'' and the youth image that the working world feels compelled to project. A terrible awakening comes when these younger people themselves grow old and suddenly find that they are the victims of attitudes they once held against others.

In mental health field, ageism has become professionalized—often, to the point where it is not recognized. Gibson[8a] noted in 1970 that psychiatrists were pessimistic about the treatability of older persons.[9] In reviewing the records of 138 patients over 65 who were admitted to a private hospital during a 3-year period, it was found that the prognosis was considered poor in 80% of the patients; yet 60% were discharged as improved to their homes within 90 days. Gallagher et al.[10] also found age correlating with therapeutic pessimism. Of patients between 15 and 29 years of age, 66.7% received psychotherapy; of patients who were 30 to 39, 38.5% did; and of those 40 to 65, only 15.4% did.

A study of 179 psychiatrists, published in 1980, corroborates what we know from earlier studies:

1. These psychiatrists regarded older patients as less ideal to work with than younger patients with identical symptoms.
2. The prognosis for older persons was considered poorer than for the young, even though the data (admittedly limited) on the prognosis of older persons do not support this conclusion.
3. Psychiatrists were much less likely to use psychotherapy, especially with older depressed women, then they did with younger persons. Instead they gave drugs, with the implication that psychotherapy would not be worthwhile.[11]

Other mental health professionals are no less pessimistic. Countertransference in the classic sense occurs when mental health personnel find themselves perceiving and reacting to older persons is ways that are inappropriate and reminiscent of previous patterns of relating to parents, siblings, and other key childhood figures. Love and protectiveness may vie with hate and revenge. Ageism takes this a step further. Staff members not only have to deal with leftover feelings from their personal pasts, which may interfere with their perceptions of an older person; they must also be aware of a multitude of negative cultural attitudes toward

[6] Palmore, E.: Gerontophobia versus ageism, The Gerontologist **12:**213, 1972.

[7] Palmore, E.R., and Manton, K.: Ageism compared to racism and sexism, Journal of Gerontology **28:**363-369, 1973.

[8] Ansello, E.F.: Ageism and picture books, Interracial Books for Children Bulletin **7:**4-10, 1976; and Age and ageism in children's first literature, Educational Gerontology **2:**255-274, 1977.

[8a] Gibson, R.W.: Medicare and the psychiatric patient, Psychiatric Opinion **7:**17-22, 1970.

[9] One study found that older psychiatrists see a higher proportion of older patients, advocate more comprehensive treatment, and find older patients more interesting and gratifying. See Garetz, F.K.: The psychiatrist's involvement with aged patients, American Journal of Psychiatry **132:**63-65, 1975.

[10] Gallagher, E.B., Sharaf, M.R., and Levinson, D.J.: The influence of patient and therapist in determining the use of psychotherapy in a hospital setting, Psychiatry **28:**297-310, 1965.

[11] Ford, C.V., and Sbordone, R.J.: Attitudes of psychiatrists toward elderly patients, American Journal of Psychiatry **137:**571-575, 1980.

older persons, which pervade social institutions as well as individual psyches.

The Group for the Advancement of Psychiatry report, "The Aged and Community Mental Health," in 1971 listed some of the major reasons for negative staff attitudes toward treating older persons.[12]

1. The aged stimulate the therapist's fears about his own old age.
2. They arouse the therapist's conflicts about his relationship with parental figures.
3. The therapist believes he has nothing useful to offer older people because he believes they cannot change their behavior or that their problems are all due to untreatable organic brain diseases.
4. The therapist believes that his psychodynamic skills will be wasted if he works with the aged, since they are near death and not really deserving of attention (similar to the triage system of the military, in which the sickest receive the least attention because they are least likely to recover).
5. The patient might die while in treatment, which could challenge the therapist's sense of importance.
6. The therapist's colleagues may be contemptuous of his efforts on behalf of aged patients. (One often hears the remark that gerontologists or geriatric specialists have a morbid preoccupation with death; their interest in older persons is therefore "sick" or suspect.)

Another factor in ageism is what appears to be a human propensity for hostility toward the handicapped. There is often an unconscious overidentification with older people, especially those who are physically handicapped: they are thought of as "defective," "crippled," "powerless," or "castrated." Excessive sentimentality, sympathy, avoidance, or hostility may result. It is estimated that some 300 million people in the world have highly visible deformities. These cause emotional problems—in part because of the attitudes of society. In primitive cultures such "cripples" (and, we might add, old people) were often put to death. This "final solution" is not so obvious in present societies, but attitudes remain surprisingly similar. In a study done by two German psychologists on attitudes of normal school-age children and adults toward the handicapped, most (63%) thought the victims should be institutionalized (in short, keep out of sight). Many believed "they probably would rather be dead." The younger the children, the less pity they felt and the more aversion. The same thing has been found for differences in skin color. Fear is the basis for the hostility, and ignorance prolongs it. The fear is that this might happen to me, so I must either run away or fight it actively.

Some people have described the treatment they have received as handicapped patients. An American writer, Eric Hodgins, in his book *Episode: Report on the Accident Inside My Skull*[13] tells of his own doctor, an old friend of many years, who talked to others about him in the hospital room after his stroke as though Hodgins were no longer an aware human being.

Another man, younger and partially blind, has described the confusions he created in a state service for the blind because he had been accepted into a well-known university's Ph.D. program and was applying to the state for educational assistance. The counselors, with their bachelor's and master's degrees, did not know how to react to a blind person who was obviously not acting "handicapped." They finally resolved their dismay by allotting the money to the man for 3 successive years of doctoral training without any personal staff contact with him, an apparent collusion aimed at avoiding a confrontation with their own preconceptions.

---

[12] Group for the Advancement of Psychiatry, Committee on Aging: The aged and community mental health: a guide to program development, vol. 8, series no. 81, New York, Nov. 1971.

[13] Hodgins, E.: Episode: report on the accident inside my skull, New York, 1964, Atheneum Press. This superb account should be required reading for all who work with patients of any age.

Publications in the field of mental health contain evidence of ageism. One respected and relatively recent edition of a well-known clinical psychiatric textbook states:

A dislike of change, a reduction in ambition and activity, a tendency to become constricted and self-centered in interests, an increased difficulty in comprehension, an increase in time and effort in adapting to new circumstances, a lessened sympathy for new ideas and views and a tendency to reminiscence and repetition are scarcely signs of senile dementia, yet they pass imperceptibly into mental destitution and personality regression. Many elderly people have little capacity to express warm and spontaneous feelings toward others. . . .

The patient resents what he considers as interference by younger persons and may complain that he is being neglected. Some show a hostile but anxious and fearful dependence. Natural affections become blunted and may turn to hatred. A certain tendency to isolation occurs.[14]

There are half-truths in this statement in the case of persons with senile dementia. But more obvious is the pessimistic, patronizing view of old age, tempered only slightly by hints that some of the changes might be psychological reactions to loss and stress. The student reading such material is confirmed in his or her negative attitudes.

Reactions of older persons against treatment

Force, deceit, or any other measure taken by mental health personnel ''for the older person's own good,'' when it is against the wishes of the older person, cannot be justified morally or legally, except in those cases in which the person is a clear and present danger to the life of himself or others. Older people may resist mental health intervention in their lives for many reasons: desire for independence, fear of change, suspiciousness based on past experiences, realistic appraisal of the inadequacies of most ''helping'' programs for older persons, clumsy, insensitive, or patronizing intervention techniques on the part of mental

[14] From Noyes, A., and Kolb, L.: Modern clinical psychiatry, ed. 8, Philadelphia, 1973, W.B. Saunders Co., p. 289.

health staff, etc. Many times older people will tenaciously hold on to what little they have rather than risk the unknown. They may prefer to live in their own homes despite crime, dilapidation, and isolation. They may resist medical examinations, surgery, and medications. Some have been known to keep guns to use on themselves or others if someone comes to take them to a nursing home—a fate feared by many as worse than death. Pride and desire for self-reliance, as well as depression and mental confusion, must be considered as factors in resistance.

One approaches the resistance of older persons just as one would the resistances of any age group—by gradual development of trust, provision of information, and a commitment to self-determination and civil rights. Members of the clergy can often be helpful in talking through problems and decisions, as can family members, neighbors, and friends. The older person must be closely involved in any decision making about him- or herself. Action, rather than just verbalization by mental health staff, can bring satisfying results. An example is the case of an older New York woman with mild intellectual impairment who refused to move out of her condemned apartment. No amount of talking could convince her. Finally a staff member offered to physically help her move and stay with her the first night. The old woman accepted. Her fears had met with response.

Another problem affecting treatment is the low self-esteem of some older people, who have incorporated the negative cultural view of themselves. This reaction of the victims of discrimination has been called ''self-hatred'' and takes the form of depression, with passive giving up or active self-denigration. They look at themselves as so many younger people see them and thus do not like what they see. Open discussions about ageism can help such people reexamine their self-views, particularly if at the same time they begin to experience new acceptance on the part of people around them. Age-integrated group therapy is especially useful in this regard.

Lack of knowledge

We simply do not know much specifically about old age, especially about healthy old age. Most clinical experience and studies have been of the sick and institutionalized aged. Generally, older persons are not admitted to research and training centers. And most experience has been limited to brief periods of contact—to short-term evaluation rather than to treatment.[15]

One major consequence of this limitation is the loss of the more enduring, intensive relationship of treatment personnel and patients, which can be an important source of data about the older person as well as a check on one's evaluation of him or her. Indeed referral for psychiatric (mental health) treatment is not only relatively uncommon in the community, but when it does occur, it is usually late in the course of illness, again affecting the accumulation of basic knowledge for evaluation as well as militating against the likelihood of therapeutic success.

Financial and bureaucratic impediments

Mental health care is expensive, especially when private psychiatrists, other psychotherapists, private-duty nurses, and private hospitalization are involved. Such care is far beyond the budget of most older people. Public care is occasionally adequate and at times exemplary, but usually it is a far cry from satisfactory. Older people are one of the last priorities on budgets and the last in line on waiting lists. Medicare has not proved to be the godsend hoped for. Nonetheless, pending adoption of a comprehensive medical insurance plan for all Americans, the major method of obtaining care for older persons will continue to be the Medicare sys-

tem. Medicare now covers only 38% of the average older person's health expenses (down from 42% in the previous edition of this book). The deductibles (that which the patients pays) are just that—deductions from the care of the aged. Older people often just do not purchase the excluded items (including dentures, eyeglasses, outpatient drugs, physical examinations) because they cannot afford to. Ironically, the out-of-pocket cost of medical care has actually risen for older people since the introduction of Medicare because of increases in physician's fees, hospital costs, and the general inflationary spiral. There is also no proof that the deductible features of Medicare deter unnecessary use of health services. Instead, the exclusions may actually increase the government's bill by discouraging preventive and early rehabilitative care.

It is necessary to be well informed on the financial aspects of psychiatric care for older persons in order to avoid professional overoptimism and pie-in-the-sky planning. We can speak of ideal community mental health programs and about the facts that more is known than is applied and that our society has not yet made a major commitment to the care of the aged. But we cannot maintain an artificial distinction between care and basic political/financial obstacles. The body politic is not to be underestimated. Mental health personnel must acknowledge and deal as creatively as possible with the socioeconomic framework under which research, care, and treatment occur.

Medical coverage for psychiatric disorders is unrealistically limited and was inserted in the Medicare legislation as a kind of afterthought. There is a 190-day lifetime limit on treatment in mental hospitals; and the patient must pay 50% of outpatient services from a physician. There is an annual limit of $250 on outpatient care. Social workers, psychologists, and other mental health personnel are not appropriately covered on an outpatient basis. The system obviously affords inadequate coverage—and, contrary to sound psychiatric practice, it promotes hospitalization rather than

---

[15] In 1963 Butler and Sulliman found that 40% of all contact between privately practicing psychiatrists and older people in the greater metropolitan Washington community was for consultation only (Butler, R.N., and Sulliman, L.G.: Psychiatric contact with the community-resident, emotionally disturbed elderly, Journal of Nervous and Mental Diseases **137:**180-186, 1963). Little has changed in the ensuing years.

care in the community.[16] Some older people have themselves checked into a hospital just to get a physical examination (basing it on some physical complaint) because this will not be paid for on an outpatient basis.

Nursing homes unfortunately have gotten into the business of providing "care" for psychiatric patients; yet they are not in any sense of the word psychiatric institutions. The conditions for eligibility for extended care under the Medicare program are both inadequate and inadequately applied. As a result, thousands of older patients, including those with psychiatric problems, are receiving no more than routine custodial care. Many nursing home facilities are substandard (the frequent occurrence of fires in nursing homes is one example). Too often a nursing home can be defined as a place with few nurses and few of the characteristics of home. Social and restorative services hardly exist, and activity programs usually receive more advertising than implementation. It is very rare for psychiatric or social work services to ever play a part in the nursing home program.[17] Approximately 95% of commercial nursing homes and about 70% of voluntary homes do *not* provide a social work staff.[18] In addition, a good deal of nursing home care is not even financed through Medicare[19]; rather it is funded by Medicaid and public assistance, ensuring even more deplorable conditions and lack of standards.

Bureaucratic impediments present many obstacles. There is much confusion among services for older persons. There is a lack of centralized information and referral services. Property and insurance liens prevent some older people from seeking help, since they do not want to sign over all their earthly possessions in return for assistance. The "responsible relative" clause in some jurisdictions, which requires relatives to assume financial responsibility for parents, siblings, and other relatives, denies assistance to older persons and forces hardships on families.

The stress and frustration older people go through to collect Medicare and private health insurance must be experienced to be believed. We present a case that is not atypical in our work with older people.

■ We attempted to assist one of our clients who was having trouble collecting payments for psychotherapy. Medicare was sending payments in different amounts for the same service and the same fee, and Mrs. K wanted to know why. In addition, her supplementary major medical insurance with Blue Cross—Blue Shield was refusing to pay for psychiatric services even though the insurance agent handling the policy assured us the woman was covered.

In a 5-month period we made multiple calls to Medicare (Mrs. K had already talked to no avail to eight different people there during the previous 6 months), asking for an explanation and a list of allowable charges. We were told that a computer was faulty, and an audit was being done. Five months later Mrs. K received a notice that she had been overpaid $60 and that she must

---

[16] Social Security Administration, Office of Research and Statistics: Financing mental health care under Medicare and Medicaid, Research Report No. 37, Washington, D.C., 1971, U.S. Government Printing Office.

[17] A 1971 study of 214 proprietary nursing homes in Chicago revealed that only two had fulltime social work staff, 21 had a parttime social worker, and 180 had no social workers at all. The 1971 Social Security Amendments rescinded the requirement for social services to be provided for Medicare-reimbursed extended care, thus reducing the beginning expansion of social services in at least Medicare-certified nursing homes. In a 1974 survey of 114 Ohio nonprofit institutions for the aged, it was learned from the 106 respondents that 58% had no social work staff. Of the 45 having social work staff,

the staff was fulltime in only 25. See Kosberg, J.I., and Tobin, S.S.: Variability in nursing homes, The Gerontologist **12**:214-219, 1972; and Hefferin, E.A.: Rehabilitation in nursing home situations: a survey of the literature, Journal of the American Geriatrics Society **16**:293-313, 1968.

[18] For a discussion of the role of the social service consultant in nursing homes see Dickstein, H.W.: The social service consultant, Nursing Home **23**(4), 1974; and A guide for social services in nursing homes and related facilities, Pub. No. (HEW) 1878, Washington, D.C., 1969, U.S. Government Printing Office.

[19] In 1975 only 3.2% of nursing home care was financed through Medicare.

pay it back. There was still no explanation or list of allowable charges. Mrs. K refused to believe anything any longer and decided to ignore the $60, feeling sure another mistake had been made.

During the same 5 months we were told twice by Blue Cross–Blue Shield that Mrs. K was eligible for psychiatric services and three times that she was not. We were twice asked to resubmit *everything* (previous material had been lost, couldn't be transferred from one part of BC-BS to another, etc.). After 5 months of work on our part, Mrs. K still had not been paid. Like the carrot on a stick, there was a constant promise of payment—"in a month or 6 weeks."

We checked with Mrs. K 10 months after our first contact. She had finally been paid by BC-BS. She had never paid Medicare the $60 and was never billed for it. She continued to get different payments from them for the same service and said, "but I don't question it anymore—as long as I get something back." Medicare never sent a list of allowable charges, and BC-BS said they could not furnish her with a list of covered services or allowable charges for people who also had Medicare, because "each case is considered separately." We and she remain to this day in the dark about exactly what is happening, but at least some payments are coming through.

When an older person with anxiety, anger, and frustration about public and private health insurance programs comes to the attention of mental health personnel, there are some things to remember before simply deciding that the person is "acting dependent" or that he or she "can't cope."

1. It is difficult to reach the proper insurance or government official by phone. (About half of our clients' and our own calls regularly never reached their target.)
2. Phone calls are often not returned; neither are messages received. Materials that are promised may not be sent.
3. Conflicting information is given.
4. Many health insurance employees do not know their own office procedures or the specifics of the programs they serve.
5. Clients are shifted from one person to another person to another and tend to give up before they reach the "right" person.
6. Records seem, routinely, to get lost. Then the client must start all over again.
7. There may be no explanation about payments or inconsistent payments, especially in Medicare.
8. When a mix-up occurs, clients often hear an insurance representative say, "It's out of my hands" (in the computer, another office, etc.); there seems to be no way then to retrieve it promptly.
9. Even though insurance or government personnel may be pleasant and interested, they give the impression of being "helpless" in straightening out problems efficiently. Thus the older person feels guilty about complaining or causing a fuss.

As we mentioned in Chapter 7, one of the new, major, time-consuming functions emerging for middle-aged offspring is to help their older parents deal with and untangle bureaucratic red tape in order to collect the benefits to which they are entitled. To assist them, and older persons in general, federal agencies should work toward:

1. Centralizing or unifying offices in each locality to which older people must go for assistance under various federal and state programs.
2. Developing a common application form for various programs.
3. Arriving at uniform definitions.
4. Unifying and simplifying procedures for determining eligibility and recertification of eligibility under various programs.
5. Unifying hearing and appellate procedures for various benefit programs.

STAFF CONSIDERATIONS
What kind of people work with older persons?

It has been suggested that few mental health personnel actively choose to work with older people and that most of them fall into the work by chance.

Professionals tend to deny having an original, personal attraction to the field, preferring to say they have responded to a "need" in society or to an intellectual curiosity about aging. Directors of institutions for older people will state that most of their employees developed interests and satisfactions after beginning their work. We suggest that these may be subtle denials, concealing a reluctance to admit an interest in old age—a reluctance fostered by the societal devaluation of the aged and by the often heard professional opinion that an interest in aging represents a morbid preoccupation with decline and death. Naturally chance plays a part in determining one's career opportunities. But conscious or unconscious personal factors are as important in choosing and remaining in the field of aging as they are in any other human decisions. We offer the following as a number of possible emotional motivations for working professionally with older people.

1. Particularly warm relationships in childhood with grandparents, who then leave their grandchildren a legacy of natural sympathy and an interest in older people

2. Early dependence on grandparents (for example, the "grandmother's children" who were not reared by their own parents) or on older persons (Parents may have been already older than average when they had children; or there may have been a young mother and a much older father.)

3. Death or painful illness of an important older person when a child is young and extremely impressionable. (In studies of physicians, for example, it has been found that a significant number experienced an early death of a loved person. Medicine then became a way of gaining power over death and the helpless feelings of childhood.)

4. Unconscious counterphobic attempt to conquer one's own personal fear of aging and death

5. Conscious attempt to "prepare" for one's own old age, especially if the models of parents or grandparents are unacceptable (A 58-year-old social worker interested in working professionally in the field of the aging joined one of our age-integrated therapy groups to prepare, as she said, for old age. She was terrified at seeing herself become more and more like her mother, whom she viewed as a bitter, disillusioned old woman. She felt helpless in the grip of the model her mother presented her.)

6. Personal sense of inferiority that causes one to identify with older people, who are culturally defined as inferior

7. Guilt and subsequent reaction formation for feelings of fear and revulsion toward the aged

8. Admiration for and identification with someone working in the field of aging

The importance of determining one's personal motivation is obvious. A mental health specialist must know from where he or she is starting, emotionally, in order to more effectively help others.

PROFESSIONAL DISCRIMINATION AGAINST THE POOR AND THE OLD

We have touched on professional discrimination a number of times but want to keep emphasizing it from different angles because we believe it is so crucial. Enforcement of the Age Discrimination Act of 1975[20] would significantly reduce, if not eliminate, discrimination against older persons in the delivery of mental health services. Psychiatrists must reconsider medical education, psychiatric residency programs, and subsequent postgraduate medical and psychiatric training. We cannot move blissfully along in our efforts toward meeting the psychiatric problems of older persons without recognizing the need for far-reaching changes in education and emphasis.

---

[20] The hearings conducted by Dr. Arthur S. Flemming, Chairman of the Civil Rights Commission, were of great importance in passing this bill.

Private psychiatrists see patients who are mostly from a small upper segment of the socioeconomic and intellectual population. For instance, an earlier study of private psychiatrists in Boston revealed the following:

About one-quarter of all Bostonians who are private patients are young women in their twenties and early thirties who live within an area of less than 100 blocks. Most are college educated.[21]

Another study, done by the American Psychoanalytic Association, showed that of the private patients seen by its members, 98% were white and 78% were educated at the college level or above.[22] Other studies by Hollingshead and Redlich,[23] Schaffer and Myers,[24] and Brill and Storrow[25] have confirmed these findings. They were summarized by Schofield,[26] who called the selection of private psychiatric patients the YAVIS syndrome—young, attractive, verbal, intelligent, and successful.

In large and small ways this attitude has improved very little.[27] Doctors in nursing homes frequently tell older patients and their families, "Don't call me directly, I'll deal with your problem through the nurse." It is extraordinary that the premium prices paid for care do not guarantee personal contact with the physician. Occasionally foreign-born doctors present another problem. Approximately 20% of newly licensed physicians in the United States are foreign-trained. Many of them work in public hospitals and clinics because of the medical discrimination against them in private facilities. Thus the poor and older persons are especially likely to be treated by foreign-born physicians and psychiatrists, who have language and cultural differences from their clientele. In addition, the aged and the poor are still the training material in the emergency rooms and the wards. Professor Alonzo Yerby once said that the poor have had to barter bodies and dignity in return for medical treatment. This was to have ended with Medicare, but it has not.

Although the 1980 Mendenhall psychotherapy study reports that the average psychiatrist spends only 5.3% total patient time on patients over 65,[28] over 1,500 psychiatrists now identify themselves as having a primary interest in older patients (the extent of their knowledge or ability to work with older persons is unknown). More than 400 of these have joined the American Association for Geriatric Psychiatry in its first year (1978) of existence. In 1979 the American Psychiatric Association showed a commitment to aging by establishing a Council on Aging. In general, clinical interest is slowly rising, but research is scanty and the clinical psychology of old age is a patchwork of theories and improvisations.

There are major labor needs in the present and the future for both psychiatry and primary care medicine.[29] There is beginning movement toward high-quality geriatric medicine. The Beeson Report of the Institute of Medicine, *Aging and Medical Education,* was an important catalyst along with the National Institute on Aging's Geriatric Medicine Academic Awards, open to departments

[21] From Ryan, W., editor: Distress in the city, Cleveland, 1969, Case Western Reserve University Press, pp. 16-17.

[22] Hamburg, D.A., et al.: Report of ad hoc committee on central fact gathering data of the American Psychoanalytic Association, Journal of the American Psychoanalytic Association **15**:841-861, 1967.

[23] Hollingshead, A.B., and Redlich, F.C.: Social class and mental illness, New York, 1958, John Wiley & Sons, Inc.

[24] Schaffer, L., and Myers, J.: Psychotherapy and social stratification, Psychiatry **17**:83-89, 1954.

[25] Brill, N.W., and Storrow, H.A.: Social class and psychiatric treatment, Archives of General Psychiatry **3**:340-344, 1960.

[26] Schofield, W.: Psychotherapy: the purchase of friendship, Englewood Cliffs, N.J., 1964, Prentice-Hall, Inc.

[27] Kucharski, L.T., White, R.M., Jr., and Schratz, M.: Age bias, referral for psychological assistance and the private physician, Journal of Gerontology **34**:423-428, 1979.

[28] University of Southern California, Division of Research in Medical Education: Psychiatry practice study report, Los Angeles, Calif., 1978.

[29] Kane, R., Solomon, D., Beck, J., Keelor, F., and Kane, R.: The future need for geriatric manpower in the United States, New England Journal of Medicine **302**:1327-1332, 1980.

of internal medicine, family medicine, and psychiatry.[30] There is also now an American Geriatric Psychiatry Association, begun in 1978 and organized by Sanford Finkel.

The American Psychological Association's task force on training and aging submitted a report in December 1976, including a paper on graduate education prepared by Martha Storandt.[31] Two hundred thirty-eight departments of psychology offering Ph.D.s and listed in the American Psychological Association's publication *Graduate Study in Psychology for 1976-1977* were queried. One hundred ninety responded. Sixteen of the departments, or about 7%, had programs in gerontological psychology. Another 11, or about 5%, were planning or developing such programs. Another 17% indicated at least one course offering in the psychology of aging but no program. Eight percent indicated one or more faculty members interest in aging but no course offering. Thus, apparently over 60% of the departments have no faculty, courses, or programs related to aging. Further, another study by Division 20 of the American Psychological Association showed only 9% of the psychology departments reporting undergraduate courses in aging.

Nurses have, of course, always taken care of older people, and those in the nursing field have been showing increasing interest in such care.[32] Nurses[33] are usually the first medical contact older

people have (61% of RNs work in acute care hospitals and 8% in nursing homes; the rest are in clinics, private doctors' offices, and public health programs, with a few in private practice). Therefore their training, skills, and sensitivity are crucial in creating positive and effective health care for the old. Because of their pioneering work as a profession in the field of aging, we have compiled a historical summary of their activity (see the box on p. 185). In the 1970s nurses began moving away from primary emphasis on a medical model to a "nursing model," emphasizing health and prevention of illness as well as care during illness (rising out of the tradition of the public health nurse). At the same time they began to move away from their previous focus on institutionalized older persons to care in other settings, such as home care. Leadership in teaching nurses to work with other professions in a multidisciplinary approach to the problems of old age became a focus of the nursing profession.

Unfortunately, the broadening role of nurses — for example, as nurse practitioners—combined with poor pay, low status, and often difficult working conditions (largely because it has been a "female" profession) have led to an estimated shortage of 220,000 nurses[34]—a shortage in the first line of defense for medical care for the old. Furthermore, cutbacks in federal funds for nursing research in the 1980s, if upheld, will hamper the dis-

---

[30] For valuable assessments of these areas see National Academy of Sciences, Institute of Medicine: Aging and medical education, Washington, D.C., 1978; National Institute of Health, National Institute on Aging: Recent developments in clinical and research geriatric medicine: the NIA role, Bethesda, Md., April 1979; and U.S. Senate Special Committee on Aging: Medicine and aging: an assessment of opportunities and neglect, 94th Congress, 2nd Session, Oct. 13, 1976.

[31] Storandt has compiled a list of universities that offer graduate training in the psychology of aging (Storandt, M.: Graduate education in the psychology of adult development and aging. Results of a survey conducted by the Education Committee of Division 20 [Adult Development and Aging], Washington, D.C., June 1976, American Psychological Association.)

[32] For example, see Irene M. Burnside's excellent book: Nursing and the aged, New York, 1976, McGraw-Hill Book Co. Nurses who have taken leadership with regard to aging are Faye G. Abdullah, Doris Alford, Myrtle I. Brown, Sister Erika Bunke, Irene M. Burnside, Sally Busch, Barbara Davis, Priscilla Ebersole, May Futrel, Laurie M. Gunter, Barbara W. Hansen, Jacqueline Heppler, Lois Knowles, Helen Monea, Dorothy Moses, Maxine Patrick, Valencia Prock, Sister Marilyn Schwab, Doris Schwartz, Eldonna Shields, Edith Stilwell, Virginia Stone, and Mary O. Wolanin.

[33] There were an estimated 1,400,000 RNs in 1980, and 70% of these (990,000) were in active practice.

[34] Of the 1.4 million registered nurses in the United States in 1980, 25% have left the field. Hospitals alone have vacancies for nearly 100,000 nurses.

THE PIONEERING INVOLVEMENT OF THE NURSING PROFESSION IN WORK WITH OLDER PERSONS*

1943-1948—Two articles appeared in *American Journal of Nursing,* giving geriatric nursing direction and value and viewing geriatric nursing as a potential specialty.

1950—First nursing textbook for care of the elderly published (Newton, K.: Geriatric nursing, St. Louis, 1950, The C.V. Mosby Co.).

1950 on—Nursing literature about nursing and the aged proliferated.

1955—American Nurses' Foundation established to promote nursing research, much of which has been concerned with care of the aged.

1958—American Nursing Association (ANA) became first health profession to support health insurance for elderly (culminated in Medicare in 1965).

1959—ANA testified before U.S. Senate Subcommittee on Aging about low standards of care in nursing homes and also recommended expansion of home care programs.

1960—ANA adopted statement on standards for nursing care in nursing homes.

1961—ANA formed conference group for geriatric nurses, which met for first time in 1962 (70 nurses).

1966—Conference group became one of five clinical divisions in the ANA.

1966—A professional publication, *Geriatric Nursing,* appeared (discontinued in 1968).

1970—ANA published its standards of geriatric nursing practice. These were revised in 1976 (see Standards: gerontological nursing practice, 1976, American Nurses' Association, 2420 Pershing Rd., Kansas City, Mo. 64108). These were designed for all areas of nursing practice, not just for "gerontological nurses."

1972—ANA committee formed to develop program to certify nurses to work with the aging. First group of nurses (74) was certified in 1974. In 1980 there were over 280 such nurses. (Nurses must be RNs. Training is 9 months to 1 year, offered by at least nine nursing programs around the United States.)

1973—National project of continuing education on geriatric nursing started.

1974—Geriatric nurse practitioner programs were being developed.†

1974 on—Department of Health, Education and Welfare made grants to nursing schools to develop curricula on aging. By 1976, 9% of nursing schools had required courses in gerontological nursing.

1974 on—Nursing textbooks on aging began to appear.

1975—Membership in ANA gerontological (formerly geriatric) group rose to 30,000.

1975—ANA published *Nursing and Long-Term Care: Toward Quality Care for the Aging,* report from the American Nurses' Association, Committee on Skilled Nursing Care, prepared for the Subcommittee on Long-Term Care of the U.S. Senate Committee on Aging.

1975—*Journal of Gerontological Nursing* appeared.

1975—Nurses' Training Act gave special emphasis to work with older persons.

1980—Four doctoral nursing programs had either an individualized program or a major in gerontological nursing. Twenty-three universities had master's degree nursing programs with specialization in geriatric/gerontological nursing.‡ About 100 baccaulaureate nursing programs included specific focus on geriatrics.

*Adapted from Reif, S.D., and Hoffman, T.: Have nurses made a difference: a historical perspective, paper presented at a conference for gerontological nurses entitled "Nurses Make a Difference," St. Paul, Minn., Oct. 6, 1977; Brimmer, P.F.: Past, present and future in gerontological nursing research, Journal of Gerontological Nursing 5(6):27-31, 1979; and Martinson, I.M.: Gerontological nursing, presentation to the National Institute on Aging, Bethesda, Md., Oct. 1980.

†Guidelines for the preparation of geriatric nurse practitioners and Guidelines for short term continuing education programs preparing the geriatric nurse practitioner, 1974, American Nurses' Association, 2420 Pershing Rd., Kansas City, Mo. 64108.

‡See Brower, T.H.: A study of graduate programs in gerontological nursing, Journal of Gerontological Nursing 3(6):40-46, 1977, for a more complete account of graduate programs.

covery of new techniques for caring for older persons on the most practical levels of care.

Nurses can be certified in geriatric nursing. Certification recognizes the registered nurse who practices in a health care setting or performs health care functions where the primary responsibility is the care of the aged, where actions are focused on a particular patient, and where there is personal responsibility and accountability to the patient for the outcome of such actions. Only those who are in the clinical practice of nursing qualify. Consultants, researchers, administrators, and educators are eligible to seek certification if they are also in clinical practice and can meet the criteria as specified.[35]

There are now a number of nursing schools that offer gerontological courses at the undergraduate and graduate levels. Duke University was the first to offer a master's degree in gerontological nursing (under the direction of Dr. Virginia Stone). Several schools have geriatric nurse practitioner programs.[36] But lack of interest and resistance against work with older persons remains.

Despite the leadership of social workers in the field of aging,[37] their numbers remain a handful—rather like the situation in psychiatry. Social work is unique in the opportunity for one-to-one contacts with older people in the community and in institutions. This happens in the daily course of the many different functions social workers serve in the United States. Yet, in spite of this frequent contact, social work has not adequately recognized work with older people as a special clinical focus. Social work schools have inadequate curricula and students are not yet attracted in any significant numbers to the idea of working with older people. Professional social work services in the long-term care of the old, whether in institutions or in the community, are already meager; for example, in 1972 an amendment to the Social Security Act (P.L. 92-603) removed staff requirements for social workers with master's degrees from nursing homes. Current cost containment efforts nationwide will reduce services even further. Only a few of the 82 accredited schools of social work offer courses in gerontology. A review of 618 doctoral dissertations between 1920 and 1968 revealed that only 14 dealt with subjects related to aging.[38] The Council on Social Work Education has encouraged schools to include study of the middle and later years in the entire curriculum. Certain social agencies began some years ago placing greater emphasis on work with older persons; for example, the Family Service Association of America did a 4-year study, 1961 to 1965, with Ford Foundation support, to upgrade the content of their casework with older people and their families in the 40 Family Service agencies in the United States and Canada.[39]

The National Association of Social Workers (NASW) in 1974 to 1975 conducted an 18-month Project Provide, funded by the Department of Health, Education and Welfare, to assist in training social workers and social service designees

---

[35] Candidates who achieve a passing score on the examination must submit additional documentation on their practice, reference vouchers, and evidence of continuing education. Case studies, clinical research, or a pilot project complete the requirements. Information on certification can be obtained from the Coordinator of Certification, American Nurses' Association, 2420 Pershing Rd., Kansas City, Mo. 64108.

[36] See Standards of geriatric nursing practice (Appendix A) and Guidelines for short term continuing education programs preparing the geriatric nurse practitioner (Appendix B). In Burnside, I.M.: Nursing and the aged, New York, 1976, McGraw-Hill Book Co.

[37] Among them are Walter M. Beattie, Jr., Marie L. Blank, Margaret Blenkner, Elaine M. Brody, Helen Turner Burr, James J. Burr, Rose Dobrof, Rebecca Eckstein, Monseignor Charles Fahey, Bernice Harper, Theodore Isenstadt, Hobart C. Jackson, Wilma Klein, Ruth Knee, Virginia Lehmann, Inabel Lindsay, Helen Lokshin, Louis Lowe, Jean M. Maxwell, Robert Morris, Helen Padula, William Posner, Ollie A. Randall, Herbert Shore, Barbara Silverstone, Barbara Soloman, Cleo Tavani, Sheldon S. Tobin, Edna Wasser, Ruth Webber, and Ellen Winston.

[38] Baldi, J.J.: Doctorates in social work, 1920-1968, Journal of Education for Social Work **7:**11-22, 1971.

[39] Wasser, E.: Creative approaches in casework with the aging, New York, 1966, Family Service Association of America. Unfortunately the book that resulted from this study in 1966 was still the only one on casework with the aging offered by FSA in its 1980 book catalogue.

involved in long-term care facilities. Approximately 2,700 people in 31 states participated in the workshops, and in 1979 a position paper on long-term care was published.[40] The NASW policy statement on aging was adopted in 1977[41] and a committee on aging formed. The NASW Committee on Aging is promoting the development of local committees on aging. By 1980 about half of the 55 chapters of NASW had viable committees on aging and/or long-term care.

Another development is the appearance of the *Journal of Gerontological Social Work,* edited by Rose Dobrof.

A valuable expanding resource of capable counselors is found in many areas. Within the American Personnel and Guidance Association (APGA)[42]—with 41,000 members—are various counselors: mental health, school, employment, etc. Counselors work in a variety of settings, including community mental health centers, as professionals and paraprofessionals. Standards-setting, state licensure, and third-party reimbursement are current issues confronting counselors. The APGA has a 2-year cooperative agreement with the Administration on Aging to support the National Project on Counseling Older People. Through this project, various service providers who work with older persons—social service aides to administrators and attorneys—will be provided continuing education in basic gerontological counseling skills. Under the direction of Mary L. Ganikos, APGA has produced two guides for counseling older persons.[43] Two additional gerontological counseling manuals are presently underway.

Discrimination that prevents utilization of skills

Physicians will be more and more obliged to reconsider their own roles vis-a-vis those of other mental health personnel. There are not enough physicians available or willing to do the mental health work that is being demanded. The American Psychiatric Association supports the requirement of health insurance carriers that psychotherapy be carried out only by physicians or be supervised by them. Thus social workers and psychologists in private practice must be supervised by psychiatrists—an open form of discrimination when there are no empirical data to suggest that this produces more effective work. In fact, there is increasing evidence that the successfulness of psychotherapy is based more on the personality factors of the therapist than on the kind or length of his or her training or the acquiring of a medical degree. Recently, by imposing more stringent restrictions, a number of insurance companies have made it difficult or impossible for nonphysicians to practice. Patients are required to choose higher priced care from physicians.

Because of the realities under which the poor, the black, the Spanish-speaking, and the aged exist, social workers, paraprofessionals, community workers, and others are in many respects better and more appropriately ''trained'' to offer therapy and others services than are psychiatrists. This is not said to let psychiatrists off the hook with the poor; it is intended to point to the additional knowledge and skills that physicians have yet to learn.

---

[40] NASW Committee on Aging: Long-term care for the elderly, chronically ill and disabled: a position paper, National Association of Social Workers, 1425 H St., N.W., Suite 600, Washington, D.C. 20005.

[41] See Aging: an NASW policy, as adopted by the 1977 Delegate Assembly of National Association of Social Workers (85,000 members).

[42] American Personnel and Guidance Association, 2 Skyline Pl., Suite 400, 5203 Leesburg Pike, Falls Church, Va. 22041. (Note especially the division called the American Mental Health Counselors Association.)

[43] Ganikos, M.L., editor: Counseling the aged: a training syllabus for educators, Falls Church, Va., 1979, American Personnel and Guidance Association; and its companion piece, Ganikos, M., Grady, K., Olson, J., Blake, R., Fitzgerald, P., and Lawrence, P., compilers: A handbook for conducting workshops on the counseling needs of the elderly, Falls Church, Va., 1980, American Personnel and Guidance Association.

Paraprofessionals

Paraprofessionals are also known as "new professionals," "nonprofessionals," "lay therapists," "community workers," "community aides," "indigenous workers," and even, condescendingly, "subprofessionals." The abundance of names points to the newness of the concept and the disagreement about roles. We prefer the term "paraprofessional" because its Greek roots mean "along side of" professionals, implying a working together rather than working under other staff members. Paraprofessionals should and will play increasingly more important roles in evaluation and treatment of older persons. A National Institute of Mental Health study of more than 10,000 mental health paraprofessionals reported in 1969 as follows:

Non-professionals are utilized not simply because professional manpower is unavailable but rather to provide new services in innovative ways. Non-professionals are providing such therapeutic functions as individual counseling, activity group therapy, milieu therapy; they are doing case finding; they are playing screening roles of a nonclerical nature; they are helping people adjust to community life; they are providing special skills such as tutoring; they are promoting client self-help through involving clients in helping others having similar problems.[44]

Paraprofessionals have certain skills and knowledge often lacking in their colleagues, built from their own personal experiences. One must caution against overromanticizing the capacities of paraprofessionals; if they can effectively help other people, their skills are real enough and need no embroidery. But there are, of course, those who are ineffective, just as in every profession, and this too should be honestly acknowledged. Training and supervision are crucial to growth and utilization of inherent skills. Reasonable and uniform

standards of performance ensure better treatment capabilities.

A "power" issue occurs in most settings where paraprofessionals begin to function effectively and autonomously. Professionals may become threatened, may feel pushed out and insecure, or insulted and angry. It is difficult to share power and status, let alone to give some of it over completely to a new group. Power must be discussed openly, but it *must* be shared.

We have alluded before to the dangers of developing a two-class system of care, with paraprofessionals caring for the poor and psychiatrists caring for the rich. Obviously this is unhealthy, undesirable, and unfair. All the professions need to work together to utilize each other's assets and provide optimal care.

In the future, various new careers may evolve—one example, a "personal care worker" who would be trained to absorb a variety of functions now distributed among members of many occupations, from home health aide to homemaker to occupational therapy assistant. This would avoid the jurisdictional disputes that now arise, as shown by the homemaker who will not or cannot change a cancer dressing, the home health aide who will not clean the kitchen, etc.

The changing mental health team concept

The community mental health team is likely to become more comprehensive, either by its members' taking on more functions, or by its absorption of more occupations (for example, family physicians, physical and occupational therapists, homemakers, visiting nurses, and home health aides, in addition to the more traditional participation of psychiatrists, social workers, psychologists, nurses, and nursing assistants). The leadership of teams is becoming diversified—some centers now are headed by nurses, social workers, and psychologists rather than psychiatrists.[45] Perhaps

---

[44] From Sobey, F.: Non-professional personnel in mental health programs, a summary report based on a study of projects supported by the National Institute under contract number PH-43 66-967, National Clearinghouse for Mental Health Information Pub. No. 5028, Nov. 1969.

[45] The *Federal Register* (June 7, 1969) states, "The direction of a center may be carried out by a properly qualified worker of any one of the mental health professionals."

one third of all centers are directed by nonphysicians.

The following list shows some characteristics of older persons, per 150,000 population of an average community mental health center catchment area (the area designated to be served by a particular center).

15,000 over 65 years of age
  14,250 in community (95%)
  750 in institutions, nursing homes, state hospitals (5%)
4,500 over 75 years of age
1,100 black people
3,750 below "official" poverty line
3,000 living alone
130 women to 100 men

STAFF TRAINING

General therapeutic principles should be applicable in all settings—private offices, community mental health centers, hospital wards, service agencies—where older people are seen in a mental health context. Intrapsychic phenomena, mechanisms of defense, developmental theory, the structure of grief, and the dynamics of dependency are some of the key areas of knowledge. Everyone, including the paraprofessionals, should have a working knowledge of this material. Even difficult concepts can be presented in inservice training in a clear, simplified, but accurate manner if the person presenting such material takes the time and thoughtfulness to do so.[46]

Mental health personnel working as a team can reach each other from their collective backgrounds. Anyone with special training or skills should, ideally, share such knowledge openly rather than retaining it as "secret" prerogatives. Psychiatrists, psychologists, and nurses have particular bodies of information to teach others, but they need to learn much more about social, economic, and cultural considerations and thus will have to be students as well. Social workers can use increased skills and knowledge in understanding and recognizing medical symptoms and in sharpening diagnostic skills. Paraprofessionals are usually weak on formal knowledge of psychopathology and psychodynamics but may be exceedingly sensitive about environmental conditions and cultural factors. A successfully working team will eventually end up sharing a mutual body of knowledge, with the end product being qualitatively more useful than the sum of its parts. Individual disciplines can maintain their individual skills while at the same time gaining from and adding to a larger whole. The result can be a rich blend of similarities and differences stimulating and teaching each other. The danger, of course, lies in the competition and power struggles that seem to arise naturally under such circumstances. These reactions should be anticipated and a plan of action agreed on before they occur. There is no reason why human beings who have chosen a career of helping others should not be able to help themselves in working peacefully and constructively with their colleagues. Much is theoretically known about group behavior. It remains for us to apply it in our hopefully humane dealings with each other as mental health practitioners.

In working specifically with the aged, it is safe to assume that all staff members will have some attitudes toward older people that are unclear, untrue, and even prejudicial. Major tasks in staff training are to clear up uncertainty and misinformation and to make personnel aware of negative countertransference and ageist feelings. Sometimes this can be accomplished by simply providing accurate information. At other times it may require sensitivity training of a sort that brings a staff member's feelings to his awareness and invites and stimulates him to reexamine them. Supervisory sessions, both group and individual, are useful. It is wise to see many kinds of older people in many different settings and circumstances. It is

---

[46] For general interviewing principles presented simply and clearly we recommend Garrett, A.: Interviewing—its principles and methods (ed. 2 revised by E.P. Zuki and M. Mangold), New York, 1972, Family Service Association of America. Also see Redlich, F., and Freedman, D.: The theory and practice of psychiatry, New York, 1966, Basic Books, Inc., Publishers, chap. 7.

also desirable to work with persons from all age groups and not overspecialize—a life cycle view is helpful.

Inservice training, planning, and problem-solving programs are ways of wrestling with staff conflicts and antagonisms when they arise, providing a forum for resolving countertransference, setting policy and programs, and planning formal and informal learning experiences. Outside teachers and consultants can be used to avoid inbreedings of ideas and outlook. Staff members generally rebel at the thought of extensive outside reading, which should be kept at a minimum and be carefully selected for its clarity and direct usefulness.[47]

Research should be built into any ongoing program. Any unusual observations of the older person or his or her family, responses to drugs, or other pertinent information should be recorded in a special observation book kept available for that purpose, as well as in the person's individual records. Such a practice can result in serendipitous findings that would otherwise be lost and may add to an accumulating body of general knowledge about older people. The material could be available for such uses as staff discussion or written research. Another form of research is a routine, periodic reevaluation of the program or service itself. Both of these research methods can be uncomplicated, do-it-yourself ways of learning more and of revitalizing services. Cooperative and more sophisticated research can be arranged from time to time among various similar institutions or services in an area. Grants can be obtained for applied research studying delivery systems. The National Institute of Mental Health in Rockville, Maryland, can be contacted for ideas and support.

TREATMENT POINTS TO REMEMBER
What's in a name?

What we call someone often defines how we will treat him or, at least, how we view him.

---

[47] See references at end of each chapter as well as lists of films and fiction in Appendixes.

What should an older person be called? Some of the names one hears are aged, elderly, senior citizen, retiree, gramps, granny, old biddy, old fogy, old gal, or just plain old. If the older person comes for mental health care, is he or she a patient? a client? a "health consumer"? In our experience, people prefer the simplest and most dignified title. "Older person" can be used for anyone from a 60-year-old to one of 90 or more years. "Elderly" is accepted in advanced old age—the seventies and eighties. "Aged" to some has implications of decrepitude and is not as favored. We have used the terms "older person" most frequently and "elderly" less often and have referred to the older person as "patient" only when it was confusing not to do so. "Patient" implies a limited role in relationship to a doctor or therapist, and we are interested in presenting the older person as a whole. Viewing someone as a patient encourages his self-evaluation as dependent and inferior.

In contacts with particular older persons it is important to respectfully address them as Mr. or Mrs. unless they specifically ask to be called by their first names. Young students, interns, and trainees are especially tempted to use first names brashly, either through habit or as an attempt to overcome feelings of intimidation. Older people may find this insulting. Black and other minority elderly may be even more sensitive and angered or depressed at being called by their first names. The presumptuous use of first names or nicknames implies a careless, thoughtless, even contemptuous attitude toward the feelings of older people, who grew up at a time when this was a demeaning and disrespectful gesture. In the case of black people, they have too long been known only as "James" while the white person was "Mr. Jones."

There is also the habit, especially rampant in medical schools, of medical students and interns referring to older patients as "gomers," "turkeys," "dirtballs," "trolls," and the apparent all-time favorite "crocks." Students are too often socialized into being impatient and bored with the old, as well as resentful and fatalistic about the physical and mental deterioration found in many of the older people they see.

Who decides?

Treatment is a collaboration among older people, their families, and mental health personnel. Decisions should be mutually agreed on unless physical or mental incapacity prevents this. Some treatment personnel are beginning to use contracts between the patients and themselves, stating specific goals of treatment, as well as the cost and length of sessions, measures for renegotiation after a stipulated period, and provisions for cancellation.

Need for full attention to physical complaints

It is very important emotionally for the older person to feel that medically everything possible is being done, even when there is really little that can be done. To exhaust the limits of the possible is very reassuring. The arthritic pain, the hypertensive flare-up, the constipation, nerves, irritable colon syndrome, unsightly varicose veins, stress incontinence, estrogen-deficient vaginitis, urinary tract infections, dry and itchy skin, gout, parkinsonism, osteoporosis, cold extremities, painful calves, fatigue, edema, irregular pulse, headaches, dizziness, shortness of breath, and confusion are all common complaints that must be treated with seriousness and competence. Sometimes side effects of the treatments must be treated. For instance, magnesium-aluminum hydroxide helps alleviate gastric distress associated with prolonged salicylate therapy for arthritis.

It is extraordinarily painful for a human being to be sold short, to be considered unreachable, beyond help, having received the ''maximum benefits'' of physical therapy and other treatment. Imagine the sense of numbing despair. It is equally true, of course, that doing for the sake of doing can be a pointless charade. What is necessary is a continuing collaboration with objective assessment, including the person's morale. Treatment should never be discontinued in a vacuum without explanation and some acceptance from the patient. To do so is to risk depression and despair.

Because Medicare does not cover physical workups, mental health personnel should become alert to signs of physical illness. For example, early signs of peripheral vascular disease (arteriosclerosis obliterans) such as mild calf pain, loss of hair on toes, slow or unusual toenail growth, cold sensitivity, and shiny skin may be presented as part of an older person's complaint. Early diagnosis obviously means early treatment.

Older people often have a dilemma with regard to their family doctor. Usually one's doctor is older than oneself. As one gets older that is often disadvantageous. It would be ageist to recommend against the older, experienced doctor; but the potential reality of retirement, disability, or death of such a physician must not be overlooked. In some cases this can be overcome by building a parallel relationship with a younger colleague of the doctor. Group practice is another solution.

Psychoanalytic theory as it applies to older people

Psychoanalytic theory provides a valuable means of viewing old age. The ego, the id, the superego, and the ego ideal are useful constructs. In the presence of brain damage, impulses may overrun inhibitions; that is, the id may overpower the superego and the ego, executive functions having been damaged. Incomplete fulfillment of one's ego ideal occupies an important part of the content of the life review in both the brain-damaged and the unaffected. In the person not brain-damaged, considerations pertinent to ego psychology indicate the continuing capacity of the older ego to grow and the superego to become more flexible. The notion of the weakening of the id or libido (vitality) with age is reminiscent of Aristotle's observation contained in the *Rhetoric* that older persons love and hate less strongly. We do not yet know enough about outer influences on ego structure or even the id to be certain how intrinsic any observed weakening of the id or ego may be.

The full range of transference possibilities can be seen in older persons as with any age group. One may see role reversal, with the older person taking the role of parent to the therapist. Coercive, dominating, or patronizing behavior may occur. In older people who manifest helplessness, the therapist may be imbued with magical powers.

How to estimate treatability

When in doubt, treat and see if improvement occurs. This is, of course, an obvious role with respect to brain disorders like delirium but should also be applied elsewhere. Improvements can occur in people who are considered hopeless. Overt behavior is too often taken as innate rather than adaptive. On the other hand, patients with apparently positive treatment possibilities may not respond well at all because of hidden, underlying processes. Treatment should be used to both rule in and rule out a diagnosis and should not be separated from evaluation.

Emotional self-treatment

Much mental health treatment is done by older people on their own. One should be alert for this and encourage it. We include an example of Christmas greeting oratory, which hints at self-treatment in progress. A description of catastrophe is followed by the implication of recovery in a vacation resort. The life review search for names in the cemetery shows a self-conscious sense of how this must appear to others. Finally the last stanza proclaims another year of life over, with a sense of stoic realism and a certain air of self-congratulation.

> "Again this year the Christmas spree
> Was held at our house, but no tree.
> The old folks failed to get up steam
> To decorate a tree, 'twould seem.

• • •

> "Then finally _____'s luck ran out.
> She'd stretched it far without a doubt.
> She's fallen many times before
> But this time hit the ''ice box'' door.
> The door won out—broke a rib.
> It hurt a lot, and that's no fib.

> "Last fall we took another trip.
> We went by car, not plane or ship.
> New England and New York our goal,
> Back roads, slow speed, we paid no toll.

> "_____ prowled a cemetery there
> He came away with notes for fair.
> His family tree is growing big,
> But there's a lot more dope to dig
> Before the job is really done.
> It's queer what some folks think is fun.

• • •

> "Now Year's end's drawing near again,
> Just like it always does, but then
> Each time it does we're one year older,
> And ev'ry winter seems some colder
> We're both alive and fairly well.
> How we hold up, just time will tell."

Use of nonverbal communication

Because of the greater likelihood of physical impairments, nonverbal communication can facilitate treatment and in some cases become a dominant part of the relationship. Persons who are hard of hearing need to be able to see the lips of the person talking to them in order to "read" them. (We all do this to some degree, and it is not hard to learn to read lips.) It may be necessary to speak very close to the ear, and it is important to learn if one ear is a "good ear," better than the other. Eye contact also is useful in relating; one can learn to "read" the eyes of a stroke victim or of someone with throat problems or certain forms of aphasia. Older people seem to be very alert and responsive to the tone and inflection of an interviewer's voice—able to judge rather accurately the personality behind the voice. Touch and tactile communication become extremely important. There is often a desire to be literally "in touch" with the person speaking. People who are very sick may respond more to holding their hands than to talking. Shared tears of happiness or sadness on the part of both mental health personnel and older people are common and can be therapeutic. When the older person is physically unable to talk, interviews can be carried out via intuition: the therapist surmises what is on the older person's mind and verbalizes it for him; then the person signals in some way, a smile, nod, frown, if he is being understood. Affection from an older person should be accepted graciously and warmly—and returned—when appropriate. A kiss on the cheek or pat on the hand for the therapist may become part of the ritual of therapy.

Patience is needed for those struggling to speak. We never shall forget the 75-year-old woman who had had a stroke and was attempting to express her emotional feelings about her suffering. She struggled mightily for a number of minutes, but the words just would not come. Finally everything fell momentarily into place and she shouted "Shit" to the heavens, with a triumphant voice and a gleam in her eye—summing up her feelings succinctly. We and she alike considered it a therapeutic victory.

"Listening" as a form of therapy

Listening is an important ingredient in therapy with older persons.[48] Some older people have a great need to talk, and their talking should not be dismissed as boring or garrulousness. Reminiscence has meaning for the life review that occurs in nearly all people. Feelings of guilt that result from such reminiscing should not be treated as irrational, to be patched up by patronizing reassurance. Guilt is as real in old age as in any other age and must be dealt with therapeutically.

---

[48] One might imagine the creation of a National Listeners Corps whose members would function in nursing and old age homes, mental hospitals, etc. We would predict consequent reductions in need for nursing services, drug use, etc. Older people themselves and high school students would be appropriate listeners.

Race and culture—language differences

In Chapter 6 and elsewhere we emphasize the importance of racial, cultural, and ethnic backgrounds in diagnosis and treatment. We wish to add here the problems of language differences, whether these be regional dialect, slang, or accent differences or use of a totally different language—such as Chinese, German, or Spanish. (For example, between 1959 and 1971, some 600,000 Cubans fled their native land to the United States. By 1971, 40,000 were over 65 and 150,000 were between 45 and 64. Nearly half the exiles settled in Florida. In 1980 a new wave of Cubans arrived, but the proportion of older people in this immigration is not yet known.) Members of minority groups should be employed in every level of mental health care. Bilingual interpreters having skill in slang or dialect interpretation, as well as actual dual language ability, should be used to train staff, provide direct interpretation, and help older members of minority groups obtain needed services. In addition, hospitals and services that hire foreign personnel, including doctors, have a responsibility to adequately train them in English or provide interpreters. Older persons should not have to bear the burden of treatment personnel's language handicaps.

Myth of termination of treatment

Older persons need the opportunity for continuing support and easy reavailability of services, even when a particular problem has been resolved. Traditional psychiatric and social work thought stresses working through to termination of mental health care, and there is a considerable literature on countertransference and the problem of termination of treatment. With older people it may be necessary to continue the treatment and care, varying it according to changing conditions until a quite different termination—death.

Three directions to move in treatment

Older people need a *restitution capacity,* the ability to compensate for and recover from deeply felt losses. They also need the opportunity for *growth and renewal,* which represent the opposite of obsolescence or stagnation. This can be defined as the effective striving toward discovery and utilization of innate potential. It can mean a rediscovery or even a first discovery of the self. Jung has written of individuation as one of the tasks of late life. Consequent to a successful psychotherapeutic process (or occurring naturally in a private life review) one may see either the emergence of a qualitatively different personality or identity or a renewal.

I for one have never touched bottom in self, nor even struck against the surface, the outlines, the boundaries of the self. On the contrary, I feel the self as an energy only which expands and contracts.

BERNARD BERENSON AT 83

And, finally, they require *perspective,* the ability to see themselves and their lives as wholes rather than fixating on any particular aspect. This is the ability to perceive one's place in the world, free from distortion, and extends to both the outer world and the inner world. It is the sense of "putting one's house in order." Inherent in perspective is a time framework that includes both past and future orientation and that is longitudinal rather than merely situational. The end result is to make acceptable "sense" out of one's life.

We discuss other treatment directions in later chapters: what to do when that which is "possible" becomes limited for older persons; the psychotherapy surrounding death, loss, and their emotional trappings; and advocacy—including the therapist as advocate.

RIGHT TO TREATMENT

The right to treatment is more than a moral obligation—it is now a legal right and requirement. Mental health personnel have too long had the unjustified luxury of "deciding" whether to offer services or treatment of or being able to weigh the wisdom of expending resources on older persons. (See Chapter 11.) Mental health care is the promotion of human well-being and the alleviation of suffering—from birth to death. If we are serious about this, it must be a right rather than a privilege.

REFERENCES

Aries, P.: Centuries of childhood: a social history of family life, translated by R. Baldick, New York, 1962, Alfred A. Knopf, Inc.

Bazelon, D.: Lake vs. Cameron. In Allen, R.C., Ferster, E., and Rubin, J.G., editors: Readings in law and psychiatry, Baltimore, 1975, Johns Hopkins University Press.

Birnbaum, M.: Some comments on the right to treatment, Archives of General Psychiatry **13:**33-45, 1965.

Burnside, I.M.: Nursing and the aged, New York, 1976, McGraw Hill Book Co.

Busse, E.W.: Therapeutic implications of basic research with the aged, Strecker Monograph Series No. 4, Philadelphia, 1967, The Institute of Pennsylvania Hospital.

Butler, R.N.: Research and clinical observations on the psychological reactions to physical changes with age. In Proceedings of the Conference on Psychological Reactions to Physical Changes with Age, Rochester, Minn., 1966, Mayo Clinic.

Butler, R.N.: Toward a psychiatry of the life cycle: implications of socio-psychological studies of the aging process for policy and practice of psychotherapy. In Simon, A., and Epstein, L.J., editors: Aging and modern society—psychosocial and medical aspects, Washington, D.C., 1968, American Psychiatric Association.

Feldstein, D.: Do we need professions in our society? Professionalism vs. consumerism, Social Work **16:**5-12, Oct. 1971.

Finkel, S.I.: Geriatric psychiatry training for the general psychiatric resident, American Journal of Psychiatry **135:**101-103, 1978.

Ford, C.V., and Sbordone, R.J.: Attitudes of the psychiatrists toward elderly patients, American Journal of Psychiatry **137**(5):571-575, 1980.

Frankl, V.: Man's search for meaning (original, 1959), New York, 1963, Washington Square Press, Inc.

Garrett, A.: Interviewing—its principles and methods (ed. 2 revised by E.P. Zuki and M. Mangold), New York, 1972, Family Service Association of America.

Goldfarb, A.I.: Psychotherapy of aged persons, I. The orientation of staff in a home for the aged, Mental Hygiene **37:**76-83, 1953.

Group for the Advancement of Psychiatry, Committee on Aging: The aged and community mental health: a guide to program development, vol. 8, series no. 81, Nov. 1971.

Henry, W.E., Sims, J.H., and Spray, S.L.: The fifth profession, San Francisco, 1971, Jossey-Bass, Inc., Publishers.

Hollingshead, A.B., and Redlich, F.C.: Social class and mental illness, New York, 1958, John Wiley & Sons, Inc.

Lowy, L.: Social work with the aging: the challenge and promise of the later years, New York, 1979, Harper & Row, Publishers, Inc.

Lutz, C., and Guitz, C.M.: Psychiatrists' attitudes toward the aged and aging, The Gerontologist **12:**163-167, 1972.

Perlin, S., and Butler, R.N.: Physiological-psychological-psychiatric interrelationships. In Birren, J.E., Butler, R.N., Greenhouse, S.W., Sokoloff, L., and Yarrow, M.R., editors: Human aging: a biological and behavioral study, Pub. No. (PHS) 986, Washington, D.C., 1963, U.S. Government Printing Office (reprinted as Pub. No. [HSM] 71-9051, 1971, 1974).

9

Diagnostic evaluation

how to do a workup

PURPOSE OF EVALUATION

The mental health evaluation in its simplest sense is a method of looking at the problems of older people, arriving at decisions that are as accurate as possible as to what is wrong, and concluding what can be done to try to alleviate or eliminate these problems. The older person and the evaluator together try to discover whether the problems are originating from inside (long-term personality factors or personal reactions to situations) or from outside (environmental or social causes); whether there are physical components; and whether the problems represent a new, first-time experience, an old experience with new implications, or something new superimposed on already existing difficulties. A gathering together and assessment of the many factors that affect the emotional life of an older person is the process by which such evaluation is carried out. Evaluators use historical data from the person's past; current medical, psychiatric, and social examinations; and their own personal interactions with the individual to get a many-sided and, one hopes, a coherent picture of what is happening.

On the basis of the evaluation, decisions must be made as to reasonable, reachable treatment goals: Can the problem at hand be reversed or merely ameliorated? Should treatment be aimed at total recovery, partial restitution, maintaining the status quo, or—of equal importance—supporting the person during some inevitable decline? Is environmental change indicated, would direct medical treatment be useful, or does the individual need psychotherapy? These are some of the possibilities. It is, of course, necessary to know what resources are available for treatment purposes: the older person's own emotional and physical capabilities, the assets in his or her family and social structure, and the kind of services and support available in the community.

An aggravating, ever-present factor in working with and planning for older people is the difficulty in obtaining needed services. For example, it is increasingly evident that older people make good use of individual psychotherapy; yet it is seldom offered, even when they can afford to pay. In some cases such services are not available for any age group, and older persons are excluded along with everyone else. However, in many instances, a service may be offered to the general public but older people find themselves put at the bottom of the waiting list or totally denied access to what is theoretically available. This is an example of institutionalized ageism—discrimination on the basis of age. All too many mental health personnel, because of training and background, assume that certain services are not applicable for older people and thereby deny treatment possibilities. We hope that Part Two of this book will help to overcome the pessimism that has prevailed regarding rehabilitation and treatment in the later years and especially in very old age.

CONDITIONS FOR A GOOD EVALUATION
Rapport

It is an old mental health principle that the first contact for evaluation is also the first therapeutic treatment hour; the two cannot be separated. Unfortunately, for many older people it may be the first and last time they will have a structured opportunity to talk about their problems and feelings. As discussed more fully in Chapter 8, the older person needs to sense certain things in order to feel comfortable about revealing him- or herself. The individual must perceive that (1) the interviewer is not repulsed or frightened by the physical or mental changes in old age but can accept these changes as a matter of fact and can see through them to the person inside, (2) the interviewer knows what he or she is talking about when dealing with old age (the psychological aspect of being old), (3) the interviewer understands the social problems of old age, having a broad and accurate knowledge of conditions as they exist for the majority of older persons, and (4) the interviewer has the professional skills and empathy that will inspire older people to trust him or her with their confidence, in the expectation that help will follow.

Confidentiality and privileged communication

Confidentiality is a critical element in gaining an accurate history and in establishing and maintaining rapport. "Privilege" is the legal right of the person to privacy of communication. With the advent of the team concept, using paraprofessionals and peer review, the legal situation has not yet been clarified. In most states a patient can sue the physician who does not preserve privileged communication, but what about the nurse, the social worker, the nursing assistant, and others? The increase in insurance forms and computer use complicates the picture. Until clarification, it is essential that practitioners recognize the seriousness of protecting the patient's/client's privacy. For instance, a designing relative may be trying to get an older person's house and attempt to gain significant information from mental health personnel. It is well known that the privacy of the poor who are served in community mental health centers, public clinics, and the like is less protected than that of the privately paying person. Legal suits may curb such practices.

Setting

All persons should be interviewed wherever possible in dignified, private surroundings—not on the run, in public hallways and open clinic areas.

Time

The older person should be given more time when there is evidence of intellectual retardation (slowing), whether this be caused by depression or organic changes. Interviews and examinations should be unhurried and relaxed. Instructions of any kind should be written out after they have been given verbally. When organicity, severe depression, or paranoid reactions are suspected, there must be several sessions, preferably at different times of day, to take into account variation in general and cerebral circulation. Early-morning confusion—before the older person has shaken off sleep—can be mistaken as chronic, fixed disorientation. There is also a "sundown syndrome"—the increased disorientation and agitation at night resulting from loss of visual orientation when daylight is gone or electric lights are turned off. If this is organically based, it has been called "senile nocturnal agitation."

Clarity of purpose

It is beneficial to clarify with older persons the reason for seeing a mental health evaluator and what they can expect during and as a result of the evaluation. It is usually wise to make certain persons understand the setting in which they are being seen (for example, a clinic or a counseling agency), unless this is totally obvious. Older persons also have the right to know who is interviewing or examining them (a psychiatrist, a mental health specialist, a visiting nurse, etc.).

The hard-of-hearing

When hearing loss is a problem, interviews should take place in settings with minimal background noise. The interviewer should feel free to ask directly about the hearing loss (this will be seen by most older people as a sign of sensitivity and concern). If one ear is better than the other, the interviewer should sit near and speak into that ear. The voice volume should be constant and distinct, with no trailing off at the end of a sentence. The expression on the patient's face should be noted to be certain that he or she is hearing and understanding. Many older people read lips to augment their hearing; it is difficult for them if the interviewer's face is not turned toward them or his or her mouth is covered. Beards and mustaches can be a problem.

Persons with stroke

Just as with the hard-of-hearing, the interviewer should sit on the "good" side of the stroke patient, since there may be damage to hearing and vision on the other side. When the patient has difficult speaking (aphasia), the interviewer should allow him or her to struggle to speak. The word should be supplied only when absolutely necessary. The person should be reassured that the interviewer wants him or her to try to talk. If words won't come, the person can try to write on a large pad or a blackboard. When asking questions, the interviewer should phrase them so the patient can respond yes or no or shake his or her head. Above all, it should *not* be assumed that the patient's intelligence has been affected. Stroke victims frequently complain that people routinely treat them as though they are intellectually impaired.

Recognizing the Goldstein catastrophic reaction[1]

The Goldstein catastrophic reaction describes the tendency of brain-damaged persons to become flooded with anxiety and irritability when confronted with a task they cannot handle. Weinberg's "exclusion of stimuli" may have a similar basis.[1a] Any examination may provoke this reaction and thus complicate or delay findings. The careful, skilled interviewer can alleviate unnecessary stress by being sensitive to the reaction of the person. (It is also, of course, important to note the presence of this reaction in diagnosing brain damage.)

When talking to brain-damaged older people, an interviewer should be sure to get their attention, speak slowly with good light on the interviewer's face, and use short, meaningful sentences with appropriate gestures. If the answer seems to be inappropriate, the interviewer may try phrasing the question in several different ways. For example, "Did you take your pill?" might be varied by saying, "What medicine have you taken today?" The purpose of all of this (and the interviewer can develop other techniques through trial and error) is to try to tap into the remaining intellectual capacity of the older person through any device that works with that individual. Only careful observation will tell if one is succeeding.

HOW COMPREHENSIVE SHOULD AN EVALUATION BE?

We recognize the range of opinion regarding the length, style, and content of an evaluation and the methods by which it should be conducted. A number of variations can be justified on the basis of the treatment method and setting under consideration as well as the individual's specific request for help. For example, an older person wanting only brief assistance in dealing with feelings about retirement may not require the same workup as the person needing evaluation for placement in a nursing home. But in general we believe that a comprehensive evaluation has much to recommend it. There is an astounding lack of uniformity in what

[1]Goldstein, K.: Aftereffects of brain injuries in war and their evaluation and treatment, New York, 1942, Grune & Stratton, Inc., pp. 71-73, 77-78, 93.

[1a]Weinberg, J.: Personal and social adjustment. In Anderson, J.E., editor: Psychological aspects of aging, Washington, D.C., 1956, American Psychological Association.

happens when an older person meets with mental health practitioners or institutional facilities. Even routine information may not be gathered. An individual may or may not get treatment, which may or may not be based on a solid evaluation and recommendation. Busy agencies and personnel with limited resources plead that their hands are tied. Yet even the shoddiest medical facility or the busiest family doctor would not be able to deal quite as cursorily with patients if they presented physical (rather than emotional) complaints—as least some minimal workup would be done. Nonprivate mental health specialists have operated, often out of necessity and sometimes out of laxness, in a piecemeal, second-rate manner and then have had to take the blame for their "failures." Fortunately the 1980 *Diagnostic and Statistical Manual* of the American Psychiatric Association (APA) is a useful and thorough guide in arriving at a psychiatric diagnosis. But training sessions may be necessary to learn how to use it because of its complexity.

Court suits are now being instituted claiming the "right to treatment" for persons requiring care, particularly in the case of the poor. It is hoped that this will result in more meaningful standards of mental health treatment. The older person not only has a right to expect treatment (as opposed to custodial care or no care) but also to expect that it be based on a thorough evaluation.

The following categories of treatment encompass the major services to older persons in terms of evaluation

Emergency-crisis intervention
Evaluation for brief service
Evaluation for extended service
Evaluation for referral elsewhere (for example, a mental health evaluation for referral to a psychiatric hospital or nursing home)
Evaluation for legal purposes (psychiatric commitment, guardianship, etc.)

In all these categories a complete evaluation is indicated for optimal and often timesaving intervention. An emergency, of course, requires atten-

tion to the immediate crisis, but with older people a crisis often points to underlying problems and requires extended periods of recovery. Thus an evaluation can be begun as soon as the emergency subsides. The evaluation should ideally fulfill a *preventive, screening* function as well as a diagnostic one. As with all ages, the problem first presented by older persons is often not their major or only difficulty. They may be reluctant to reveal intimate matters or be fearful of appearing demanding and complaining. They sometimes may deny actual problems or are totally unaware of their presence. When older people do not receive competent mental health care, the twin culprits are usually lack of finances for private care and prejudice against them in both public and private circles because of their age.

WHAT CONSTITUTES A "DIAGNOSIS"?

A diagnosis is not simply a matter of psychiatric nomenclature that an evaluator, by the process of elimination, plucks out of the APA's *Diagnostic and Statistical Manual*. One must know the strength of persons psychologically (for example, their defenses and personality assets); their physical capabilities; and the familial, social, and cultural climate and structure of their lives. The direct and immediate environmental influence on people's lives is finally receiving its due share of importance along with the more traditional emphasis on early developmental and constitutional factors of personality. It is vital also to recognize the vast implications of prejudice in its institutional and personal forms as they affect the lives of black, Asian-American, American Indian, Latino, and other minority and ethnic elderly (Chapters 1 and 6). The serious mental disorders and the emotional reactions seen in old age are multicausal.

A problem may not only have many causes; it may itself be multiple, that is, a combination of many problems. Simon and Cahan have rightly stated that "the doctrine of the single diagnosis, as it occurs in many psychiatric institutions, has probably interfered with a more complete understanding of the individual geriatric patient.''[2] A serious case in point is a diagnosis of senile, multi-infarct, or other dementia while omitting an additional diagnosis of superimposed delirium. Another serious and frequent oversight is the failure to recognize the emotional component or overlay to physical illness of the body or brain. An evaluator must search for possible combinations of problems where some may be less obvious than others but no less damaging.

Diagnosis is best viewed as a continuing, dynamic assessment, particularly in the case of older persons. Old age, indeed life at any age, is more similar to a motion picture than a still photograph; it is constantly changing. Because of this ongoing, altering process, evaluation, too, must be continuous, with treatment intervention varied accordingly.

A BASIC EVALUATION

The concept of "multiple evaluations" describes the way in which an older person's problems can best be diagnosed. A basic evaluation should include a core collection of material: basic personal information, a psychiatric assessment, a medical assessment, a sociocultural assessment with the older person and, if possible, his relatives, and an on-the-spot evaluation of the home environment where indicated. In addition, any number of special evaluations may be deemed valuable in arriving at a clear understanding of the older person (for example, special medical tests, nutritional evaluation). The following outlines list the elements of such an appraisal as well as some of the special consultants who can be used. It is important that members of consultative specialities be willing to see older people as well as being readily available to people of all incomes. The evaluator may have to act on the older person's behalf in persuading reluctant consultants to participate,

particularly if they are being used for the first time. The professional bias against older persons remains an interference to collaboration and must be confronted whenever possible.

Comprehensive basic examination of the older person

Basic background information: personal, family, economic, social
Psychiatric assessment
   Personal and family history
   Psychiatric examination, including Mental Status Evaluation (or, if time is limited, the Mental Status Questionnaire or other "screening test")
   Psychiatric Symptoms Checklist
Medical assessment
   Medical history, including reports from family doctor
   Physical examination, including neurological, rectal, and pelvic examinations
   Computerized axial (or transaxial) tomography (CAT or CT scanner)
   Electroencephalogram (brain wave test)
   Skull films
   Electrocardiogram
   Chest radiograph (x-ray film)
   Laboratory tests
      Complete blood count
      Hematocrit
      Urinalysis (albumin, glucose, and ketone levels and microscopic examination) and culture
      Fasting blood sugar
      Blood urea nitrogen
      Electrolytes
         Serum sodium
         Potassium
         Chloride
         Carbon dioxide
         Calcium
         Phosphorus
         Magnesium
      Thyroid tests
         Protein-bound iodine (PBI)
         Triiodothyronine (T_3) resin uptake
         Serum thyroxine (T_4)
         Bilirubin
         Vitamin B_{12} and folic acid
      Serum cholesterol
      Triglycerides
      Serology
      Erythrocyte sedimentation rate

---

[2] From Simon, A., and Cahan, R.: The acute brain syndrome in geriatric patients. In Mendel, W.M., and Epstein, L.J., editors: Acute psychotic reaction, Washington, D.C., 1963, Psychiatric Research Report No. 16, p. 10.

Stool for occult blood
Hearing test: audiometry
Visual examination
  Refraction
  Glaucoma check
  Retinal examination
  Visual fields examination (peripherals, centrals)
Dental examination
Sociocultural assessment
  Intimates: family and friends
  Financial status/work
  Housing/transportation
  Social status and participation
On-the-spot home evaluation (where indicated)

Special evaluations

Studies for blood levels of toxins or therapeutic drugs
Psychological tests
  Bender Visual-Motor Gestalt Test
  Wechsler Adult Intelligence Scale (WAIS)
  Wechsler Memory Scale
  Kent E-G-Y Test
  Raven Progressive Matrices
Tests of the central nervous system
  Lumbar puncture (for pressure, cells, protein, serology)
  Brain scan
  Ventriculography
  Pneumoencephalography
  Angiography
  Echoencephalography
  Isotope cisternography*
Medical tests
  Liver functions
  Serum and red cell folate
Other specialties to consider
  Internal medicine
  Neurology
  Ophthalmology
  Otorhinolaryngology (ENT)
  Physiatry/rehabilitation
  Dermatology
  Radiology
  Podiatry
  Physical therapy

---

*The technique of intrathecally administered, radioiodinated human serum albumin (RISA) for cisternography has been well described.

Occupational therapy
Pharmacology
Homemakers–home health aides
Visiting nurses
Recreation
Education
Employment opportunities
Home economics
Nutrition/dietetics
Transportation
Legal services
Shopping services
Meals-on-Wheels
Visitation services
Telephone reassurance service

Basic background information

The question of how to collect background information or "histories" for use in mental health evaluations has always been a controversial and confused one. This is largely because mental health as we define it today encompasses every aspect of a person's life, and the task of collecting and assimilating so much information boggles the mind. Add to this the need to take a longitudinal life cycle view, as in the evaluations of older people, and the problem grows. In an era of specialization, medical doctors have tended to limit themselves to the body and its ills, traditional psychiatrists to "inner" problems (although this is becoming less and less true—the trend is toward a psychosocial approach), social service workers to "outer" difficulties, and members of the clergy to spiritual life—but mental health personnel, who can be from any of these professions and more, must familiarize themselves with the whole picture in order to prescribe and carry out sound treatment.

Collection of basic background information should be done in a manner that ensures comprehensiveness without being rigid. The goal is a high-quality evaluation, whether it takes place in a private hospital, a public clinic, a doctor's office, or a nursing home. The following elements are important considerations in planning data or "history" collection.

1. The method of obtaining the data desired must be flexible in terms of how it is collected and who can collect it. Some psychiatric facilities may provide only one interview for this purpose while others may offer a more leisurely accumulation of the data during actual course of treatment. Anyone from a psychiatrist to a paraprofessional may do initial interviewing. At times, the older person's relatives or even the older person himself may be the most appropriate person to collect the data, independent of outside assistance.

Maddox and Douglas found good agreement between self-assessment and physician assessment of health status; when inconsistent, the tendency was for patients to overestimate health.[3] Another issue is the underreporting of illness such as Sir Ferguson Anderson observed in reporting of symptoms by older people. He has intensively observed 3,000 people over 55 in a working-class section of Glasgow, Scotland. Under the United Kingdom's National Health System, care is free—yet many did not report symptoms of obvious disease. Anderson's explanations are:

a. Old people accept society's message that sickness and disability are inevitable with age.
b. Incapacity and death may not be so much frightening as welcomed.
c. Mental impairment obscures detection and reporting.

Certain material—name, addresses, reason for needing help, etc.—naturally must be available shortly after the first contact; but other background material should be collected in a way that is compatible with the needs and personality of the older person, the realistic working conditions faced by mental health staffs, and the setting in which service is being given. We stress, however, that the end result should be a broad and thorough review of the person's history and current life situation.

2. With the patient's permission, data should be in a transferable form, able to be passed from one staff member to another and from one treatment setting to another. This is particularly true with older people because numerous personnel may participate in their care, and the elderly frequently move from one setting or agency to another as their conditions change. Sharing information is timesaving and protects patients from repeating themselves—the confidentiality being maintained by sharing appropriately.

3. Data collection ideally serves an organizing function for experienced evaluators (by organizing their manner of thinking about a person) and a teaching function for less experienced personnel (by guiding them in what to look for and what to consider important). The problem-oriented medical record (POMR) is becoming widely used in medicine[4] and to a lesser degree in psychiatry.[5] This is a method of creating a more useful record by compiling a data base, list of problems, plans for each problem, and progress notes on each problem. In contrast to this is the traditional source-organized record in which information from each source of input (doctor, nurse, x-ray report, laboratory test, referring source, consultant, and others) is put in a separate place in the patient's chart, making integration of problems more difficult.

4. Taking data on the life history is organizing for the patient. Using the opportunity to review one's life—to take an inventory and to evaluate the meaning(s) of one's life—should be encouraged. The sense of approaching death is believed to be related to the life review. Reactions to one's death—equanimity, fear, or denial—should be appraised. The life history becomes both diagnostic and therapeutic. We consider the concept of the life review in several contexts in this book (Chapters 3 and 12).

5. Research potential should be built into any data collection system. There are still tremendous

[3] Maddox, G.L., and Douglas, E.B.: Self-assessment of health: a longitudinal study of elderly subjects, Journal of Health and Social Behavior **4**:37-93, 1973.

[4] Weed, L.L.: Medical records that guide and teach, New England Journal of Medicine **278**:593-600, 652-657, 1968.
[5] Ryback, R.S.: The problem oriented record in psychiatry and mental health care, New York, 1974, Grune & Stratton, Inc.

gaps in our knowledge about old age, and direct treatment contact is, of course, a rich source of information.

As a result of our own work experiences in various hospitals, welfare departments, community mental health clinics, nursing homes, research, and private practice, we have devised a method of collecting data, which combines for us an adaptable format with a thorough content. (See the Personal Mental Health Data Form for Older Persons below.) It can be compiled either piecemeal or all at once, and at any time during contact with a patient. For example, when seeing a person in crisis, one must deal with the immediate situation and may not be able to obtain much background data until the crisis subsides. When we know we will be seeing the person over a period of time, we generally fill out the form ourselves in an unhurried manner as the data accumulate. However, in a period of crisis or shortage of time, a relative may complete the form, either at home or in the office. (Material of course is not as rich as when the patient is directly involved.) In other cases it is appropriate and even highly therapeutic for the patient to fill out the form alone. Patients report that it is a life review process that is organizing to them in evaluating themselves and planning for their future. We would generally not recommend this for patients having obvious severe organic brain disorders, poor eyesight, or severe hand tremors or for those who would become frustrated without help. It can, on the other hand, be extremely useful for the hard-of-hearing patients (with whom interviewing is difficult) and for those who pride themselves on their independence. We also use the form this way for patients who are entering group therapy and may be seen in only one, individual, pre-group session.[6]

Text continued on p. 224.

---

[6] Another means of assessment is the Older Americans Resources and Services (OARS) methodology, produced under the direction of Dr. Eric Pfeiffer at Duke University. OARS' objectives are to develop models for mental health care, social services, and multidimensional techniques for evaluating the functional status of older people. The program serves persons over age 50 in Durham County. See Pfeiffer, E., editor: Multidimensional functional assessment: the OARS methodology, Center for the Study of Aging and Human Development, Durham, N.C., 1975, Duke University Press. Also see the discussion on the Patient Appraisal and Care Evaluation (PACE) instrument in Chapter 11.

PERSONAL MENTAL HEALTH DATA FORM FOR OLDER PERSONS

Note to patients   **Confidential**

This Personal Data Form is an inventory, an overview of your past and present situation. For our purposes, it provides basic background data. For you, it is a way to begin reviewing your life, finding themes, in terms of both strengths and difficulties.

The material is confidential and will be treated with care. We do not share this material with **anyone** outside our office, unless specifically given permission by you. Thus candor and comprehensiveness, which add to the value, are encouraged. Some of the questions will be irrelevant, in which case simply leave blanks. If more writing space is needed, add an extra sheet.

You may be asked to write to other psychotherapists, doctors, and hospitals who have knowledge of you, giving them permission to send us extended summaries of their contacts with you. If you wish, we will furnish you with a copy of this form for your own use or for use with other health personnel such as your internist.

Thank you very much,

(signed by chief administrator)

INFORMATION FOR OUR USE IN YOUR INSURANCE FORMS

TO BE COMPLETED BY PATIENT   Date: _____

Patient's name: _____

Social Security no.: _____ Medicare no.: _____

Medicaid no.: _____ Supplemental Security Income (SSI): _____

Date first seen at our office: _____

Approximate date symptoms appeared: _____

Health coverage *(indicate by a check mark)*

☐ None

☐ Blue Cross–Blue Shield: ☐ High option   ☐ Low option

☐ Aetna

☐ Group Health Association

☐ Champus

☐ Medicare: ☐ Part A   ☐ Part B

☐ Medicaid

☐ Veterans Administration

☐ Other *(name):* _____

TO BE COMPLETED BY THERAPIST

Psychiatric diagnosis (NOTE TO PATIENTS: *We shall discuss any diagnosis with you before submitting it to your insurance company.*)

_____

Nature of treatment *(indicate date treatment began)*

Consultation alone (diagnosis and evaluation): _____

Individual psychotherapy: _____

Group psychotherapy: _____

Couples (conjoint) therapy: _____

Family therapy: _____

Drug therapy: _____

Referral for ECT: _____

Referral for hospitalization: _____

Other (specify): _____

PERSONAL DATA FORM (LIFE REVIEW FORM)

I. BASIC BACKGROUND INFORMATION   Date: _____

A. Patient's full name: _____

Nickname(s): _____ _____ Preferred first name: _____

Age: _____ Complete birth date: _____

Birthplace: _____

Present addresses: Residence: _____

(Street)

_____

(City)   (State)   (Zip)

Work: _____

(Place of employment)

_____

(Street)

_____

(City)   (State)   (Zip)

Telephone numbers: Residence: _____ Work: _____

NOTE: *If you do not wish to be called at work except for emergencies, check here* ☐.

If you cannot be called at work at all, check here ☐.

REFERRAL SOURCE

Patient referred by: _____

IN CASE OF MEDICAL EMERGENCY: *Current doctor(s)*

Name: _____

Address: _____

Phone: _____ Specialty: _____

IN CASE OF EMERGENCY: *Nearest relatives and/or friends*

Name: _____

Address: _____ Phone: _____

Name: _____

Address: _____ Phone: _____

If you live alone, please give the name and phone number of a nearby neighbor or friend.

Name: _____ Phone: _____

B. Religion

Of family of origin: _____

Present religious affiliation, if any: _____

Are you active religiously? _____

Any religious conflict? _____

Continued.

PERSONAL DATA FORM—cont'd

I. BASIC BACKGROUND INFORMATION—cont'd

C. Ethnic, racial, or cultural background: _____

    Year of immigration to U.S.: _____

    From where: _____

D. Family status

    Present marital status: ☐ Single ☐ Separated ☐ Widowed ☐ Married ☐ Divorced ☐ Living with someone

    Marriage or living partner *(circle which)*, most current:

        Full name of spouse or living partner: _____

        Age difference: _____ (years older than you)

                    _____ (years younger than you)

        Religion of spouse or living partner: _____

        Place of birth of spouse or living partner: _____

        Your courtship duration: _____

        Date of marriage or when you began living together (month, day, year): _____

        Closest anniversary attained: _____

        Date of separation: _____

        Date of divorce or widowhood (month, day, year): _____

    Marriage or living partner *(circle which)*, previous:

        Full name of spouse or living partner: _____

        Age difference: _____ (years older than you)

                    _____ (years younger than you)

        Religion of spouse or living partner: _____

        Place of birth of spouse or living partner: _____

        Your courtship duration: _____

        Date of marriage or when you began living together (month, day, year): _____

        Closest anniversary attained: _____

        Date of separation: _____

        Date of divorce or widowhood (month, day, year): _____

    Other marriages or partnerships *(describe):* _____

PERSONAL DATA FORM—cont'd

Children:	Name	Sex	Age	City and state of residence	If deceased, date and cause of death
1.					
2.					
3.					
4.					

(Add an extra page for children if needed; include miscarriages, stillbirths, etc.)

Your age when last child left home: _____

What are your feelings about being a parent? _____

_____

Grandchildren:	Name	Sex	Age	City and state of residence	If deceased, date and cause of death
1.					
2.					
3.					
4.					

(Add an extra page for grandchildren if needed.)

Your age at birth of first grandchild: _____

What are your feelings about being a grandparent? _____

_____

Great-grandchildren:	Name	Sex	Age	City and state of residence	If deceased, date and cause of death
1.					
2.					
3.					
4.					

(Add an extra page for great-grandchildren if needed.)

Your age at birth of first great-grandchild: _____

What are your feelings about being a great-grandparent? _____

_____

Members of current household (include everyone who lives with you):

	Name	Sex	Age	Relationship to you
1.				
2.				
3.				

Continued.

PERSONAL DATA FORM—cont'd

I. BASIC BACKGROUND INFORMATION—cont'd

E. Family history

Parents

Father's full name: _____

    Occupation: _____

    Year of birth: _____ Birthplace: _____

    If dead: Year of death: _____ Age at death: _____

        Cause of death: _____

        Your age at his death: _____

    Educational level attained: _____

    Brief description of his personality: _____

    _____

    _____

Mother's full name: _____

    Occupation: _____

    Year of birth: _____ Birthplace: _____

    If dead: Year of death: _____ Age at death: _____

        Cause of death: _____

        Your age at her death: _____

    Educational level attained: _____

    Brief description of her personality: _____

    _____

    _____

With whom did you live up to age 21? _____

Were you raised in a rural, small town, urban, or suburban setting? *(describe)* _____

_____

During childhood, who lived in your home other than immediate family? *(include relatives, nurses, maids, boarders, etc.)* _____

Did anyone other than your parents help care for you? *(describe)* _____

_____

PERSONAL DATA FORM—cont'd

Siblings:	**Name**	**Age**	**City and state of residence**	**If deceased, date and cause of death**
1.				
2.				
3.				
4.				

(Add an extra page for siblings if needed.)

Grandparents (amount and quality of contact with them)

Paternal: _____

Maternal: _____

Your socioeconomic conditions during childhood: ☐ Poor ☐ Average ☐ Wealthy

F. Education (your years of schooling): _____

Description of schools:	**Name of school**	**Year of graduation**	**Degree**
Grammar school:			
High school:			
Trade, technical, or vocational school:			
College:			
Graduate or professional school:			
Later courses; other education:			

Self-rating, as a student *(check):* ☐ Above average ☐ Average ☐ Below average

Any honors, awards, scholarships: _____

Who was the first person in your immediate or extended family to have a college education? _____

_____

Would you like to obtain further education? *(describe)* _____

_____

G. Work

Your occupation or profession: _____

G.S. level (if applicable): _____

Your second occupation or profession *(describe):* _____

_____

Last three jobs and the durations of employment:

1. _____

2. _____

3. _____

Continued.

PERSONAL DATA FORM—cont'd

I. BASIC BACKGROUND INFORMATION—cont'd

Average number of hours a day that you work: _____

Occupation of spouse: _____

What are your major work interests? _____

Were you in military service? _____ Which branch? _____

Did you experience age, sex, racial, ethnic, or other discrimination at work? *(describe)* _____

_____

How physically active was your work? _____

_____

Postretirement

Did you work after retirement? _____

If so, describe employment: _____

How many hours per week? _____

Employed or self-employed? _____

Did you experience any form of discrimination at work? *(describe)* _____

_____

Are you currently employed? _____ If not, would you like to be? _____

H. Retirement

Your age at retirement: _____

Date of retirement: _____

Was it voluntary? _____ Welcomed? _____

Was it compulsory through company or union? _____

Was it forced because of illness? _____

Did you have preretirement preparation (seminars, etc.)? _____

_____

Did you have postretirement counseling? _____

I. Economic status *(check source[s] of income, not amount[s])*

☐ Employment   ☐ Private pension plan

☐ Social Security   ☐ Public assistance

☐ Veterans benefits   ☐ Insurance payments

☐ Disability benefits   ☐ Annuities

☐ Teachers' Insurance and Annuity Association   ☐ Savings

☐ College Retirement Equities Fund   ☐ Investments

☐ Railroad Retirement   ☐ Assistance from family

☐ Other: _____

Do you pay or receive alimony? _____

PERSONAL DATA FORM—cont'd

Do you pay child support? _____

Your annual family income:

    ☐ $60,000 or more ☐ $30,000-$60,000 ☐ $15,000-$30,000 ☐ $10,000-$15,000

    ☐ $5,000-$10,000 ☐ $3,000-$5,000 ☐ Less than $3,000

Do you have serious financial problems? *(describe)* _____

_____

Has there been a recent income drop? _____

If so, what is the reason? _____

Have you given over power of attorney? _____ To whom? _____

Have you established a guardianship? _____

Have you established a conservatorship? _____

J. **Residence** *(check)*

  ☐ House ☐ Condominium ☐ Apartment (☐ Owned ☐ Rented)

  ☐ Hotel

  ☐ Rooming house

  ☐ Boarding house

  ☐ Nursing home

  ☐ Home for aged

  ☐ Mental hospital

  ☐ Chronic disease hospital

  ☐ Personal care home

  ☐ Foster care

  ☐ Public housing

  ☐ Mobile home, trailer

  ☐ "202"

  ☐ No regular residence

  ☐ Other *(describe):* _____

Total monthly cost of housing: _____

Any problems with living situation *(describe):* _____

_____

How many flights up? _____ Is there an elevator? _____

Any problems in neighborhood *(describe):* _____

_____

If you are temporarily not in your own home, is someone caring for your

    ☐ Possessions? ☐ Plants? ☐ Pets?

Have you moved since retirement? _____ From where? _____

Continued.

PERSONAL DATA FORM—cont'd

I. BASIC BACKGROUND INFORMATION—cont'd

K. Transportation and mobility

Do you drive a car? _____ Do you own one? _____ Do you have access to one? _____

How do you usually get around? _____

Is public transportation available? _____ Do you use it? _____

Any physical disabilities that affect your mobility (describe): _____

_____

Do you feel safe going out during the day? _____

Do you feel safe going out during the night? _____

Do you have a telephone? _____

L. Interests and pleasures (describe)

Avocations or hobbies: _____

Sports: _____

Commercial recreation (movies, nightclubs, etc.): _____

_____

Music: _____

Languages: _____

Travel (places and years): _____

_____

Vacation habits (what do you do and how often?): _____

_____

Gardening: _____

Collect anything: _____

Pet(s): _____

Use of community centers, senior centers, etc.: _____

What is the *most* characteristic thing you do to relax and unwind? _____

_____

How many hours a day do you watch T.V.? _____

How many hours a day do you engage in your other interests and pleasures (excluding T.V.)?

_____

Are you satisfied with the balance between work and play in your life? _____

_____

PERSONAL DATA FORM—cont'd

M. Active community involvements *(describe)*

Memberships-organizations, clubs, etc.: _____

Retiree or "senior citizens" groups: _____

Political activity: _____

Veterans organization: _____

Voluntary work: _____

Church work: _____

N. Friendship patterns

Do you have someone to depend on in an emergency? _____

If so, who? _____

Are you lonely? _____

Is there someone you can talk to whenever you feel like it? _____

If so, who? _____

Who are the three closest living persons in your life?

	Name	**How are they important?**
1.	_____	_____
2.	_____	_____
3.	_____	_____

Describe contacts (list names, frequency of contact, and nature of contact; is the relationship a good one for you?)

1. Children: _____

2. Grandchildren: _____

3. Great-grandchildren: _____

4. Siblings: _____

5. Other relations: _____

6. Friends: _____

7. Neighbors: _____

(Add an extra page for these descriptions if needed.)

Continued.

PERSONAL DATA FORM—cont'd

I. BASIC BACKGROUND INFORMATION—cont'd

O. Prejudice (directed against you?) *(describe)*

Age: _____

Sex (male or female): _____

Race: _____

Ethnic origin: _____

Religion: _____

II. MEDICAL INFORMATION

List significant doctors or medical specialists you see now or saw in the recent past:

	Name	Address	Phone	Problem
1.				
2.				
3.				

Date of your last medical checkup: _____

How do you rate your general medical health? *(check)*   ☐ Excellent   ☐ Good   ☐ Fair   ☐ Poor

History (any health problems)

When born: _____

When growing up: _____

List any illnesses that seem to run in family: _____

_____

Heart disease: _____ Cancer: _____ Senile dementia: _____

Were you subject to any medically dangerous work hazards such as chemical exposure, polluted air? _____

Asbestos dust: _____ Cotton dust: _____ Coal dust: _____

Blood type: _____

Have you ever had the following? *(list dates)*

1. Accidents, injuries, and falls

Concussion or other head injury: _____

Fracture: _____

Hip injury: _____

Other: _____

Any operation as a result: _____

PERSONAL DATA FORM—cont'd

2. Operations:

Date	Type of operation	Name of hospital	City

3. Circulatory disorders

Heart disease: _____

    History of rheumatic fever: _____

High blood pressure: _____

Transient ischemic attack (TIA): _____

Stroke: _____ Any residual: _____

Leg cramps: _____

Cholesterol levels: _____

    HDL (high-density lipoprotein): _____

    LDL (low-density lipoprotein): _____

Triglycerides: _____

4. Angina: _____

5. Heart attack: _____

6. Arthritis: _____

Rheumatoid arthritis: _____

Osteoarthritis: _____

Gout: _____

7. Lung conditions (bronchitis, emphysema, tuberculosis): _____

8. Diabetes: _____

9. Cancer: _____

10. Thyroid problems (hyper- or hypo-): _____

11. Anemia: _____

12. Gastrointestinal problems: _____

Diverticulitis: _____

Constipation: _____

Diarrhea: _____

13. Bladder problems: _____

Decline in continence: _____

Nocturia (need for night time urination): _____

Continued.

PERSONAL DATA FORM—cont'd

II. MEDICAL INFORMATION—cont'd

14. Kidney problems: _____

15. Prostate problems: _____

16. "Change of life" or menopausal problems: _____

17. Allergies (hay fever, drugs, etc.): _____

18. Foot problems: _____

19. Other symptoms

    Nervousness, tension: _____

    Frequent, severe headaches: _____

    Other pain: _____

    Difficulty in breathing (dyspnea): _____

    Dizziness: _____

    Fainting spells: _____

    Fever: _____

    Ringing or buzzing in ears: _____

    Bleeding: _____

20. Psychosomatic disorders

    Asthma: _____

    Peptic ulcer: _____

    Essential hypertension: _____

    Ulcerative colitis: _____

    Ileitis: _____

    Other: _____

21. Osteoporosis: _____

22. Epilepsy or seizures: _____

23. Parkinsonism: _____

    Flu from the epidemic of 1918-1919: _____

24. Venereal diseases: _____

25. Other: _____

Do you have anything that you consider to be a significant handicap? *(describe)* _____

_____

Do you have any chronic health problems? *(describe)* _____

_____

PERSONAL DATA FORM—cont'd

Do you have any of the following physical limitations?

  ☐ Hearing loss

   Do you wear a hearing aid? _____

   Do you have any problems with your hearing aid? _____

  ☐ Vision loss

   Do you wear glasses? _____

   Cataracts: _____

   Glaucoma: _____

  ☐ Memory loss

Do you wear dentures?   ☐ Partial   ☐ Complete

Do you have any problems with your dentures? _____

Do you have a need for any other medical equipment or prosthetic devices? _____

Are you receiving any of the following therapies?

  ☐ Physical   ☐ Occupational   ☐ Speech   ☐ Inhalation   ☐ Recreational

  ☐ Other (specify): _____

Daily living habits

  Do you consider any of the following to be a serious personal problem?

   ☐ Overeating   ☐ Overdrinking   ☐ Smoking   ☐ Underactivity

  Alcohol consumption

   How many cocktails, highballs, etc. a day? _____

   How many glasses of beer a day? _____

   How many glasses of wine a day? _____

   Do you drink in the morning? _____

   How much before dinner? _____

   How much before bed? _____

  Water consumption: _____ (glasses a day)

  Caffeine consumption a day: Coffee _____ Tea _____ Cola _____

  Carbonated drink consumption a day: _____

  Do you smoke cigarettes, cigars, or a pipe? _____

   How much do you smoke a day? _____

   How long have you smoked? _____

   Do you chew tobacco? _____

Continued.

PERSONAL DATA FORM—cont'd

II. MEDICAL INFORMATION—cont'd

Are you on a special diet? *(describe)* _____

_____

    ☐ Diabetic   ☐ Low-salt   ☐ Low-fat   ☐ Low-cholesterol

Is diet medically prescribed or self-prescribed? _____

How many meals a day do you eat? _____

Are you a vegetarian? _____

Do you take vitamins? _____ What kind? _____

    ☐ Vitamin B   ☐ Vitamin C   ☐ Vitamin D

Do you drink milk? _____

   How many glasses a day? _____

   Lactose intolerance? _____

Do you take calcium? _____

Do you take iron? _____

Current weight: _____ Has there been recent loss or gain? _____

What has been your maximum and minimum weight? Maximum: _____ Minimum: _____

Current height: _____ Any shrinkage in your original height? _____

Exercise

   Do you exercise regularly? _____

   What kind of exercise? _____

   How often each week? _____ How long each time? _____

Sleep

   Any difficulty falling asleep? _____

   Any difficulty staying asleep (sleep fragmentation)? _____

   Early awakening? _____

   Do you take naps? _____

   Average number hours of sleep a day: _____

   Have your sleeping patterns changed recently? _____

   Any sleep reversal with wakefulness at night and sleepiness in day? _____

   Do you take sleeping pills? _____ What kind? _____

   Do you snore? _____

PERSONAL DATA FORM—cont'd

Describe recurrent dreams (e.g., examination dreams, flight, falling, or chase dreams): _____

_____

_____

_____

Is there any dream that seems highly significant to you? _____

_____

Drug usage *(dates drugs recently were or are now taken as well as schedule and amount of dosage)*

Prescription drugs

Sedatives: _____

Tranquilizers: _____

Antidepressants: _____

Lithium: _____

Stimulants: _____

Diuretics: _____

Digitalis: _____

Reserpine: _____

Antihypertensives other than reserpine: _____

Hormones: _____

Premarin (estrogens): _____

Thyroid replacements: _____

Nitroglycerin: _____

Over-the-counter drugs

Laxatives: _____

Aspirin: _____

Others: _____

Sexual activity and concerns

Do you experience a desire for sexual activity? _____

Has there been a recent change in your sexual desire? *(describe)* _____

Do you currently have sexual outlets? *(describe)* _____

How frequently? _____

Continued.

PERSONAL DATA FORM—cont'd

II. MEDICAL INFORMATION—cont'd

Are there any problems—emotional, physical, social—as far as you are concerned regarding sex? *(describe)* _____

_____

    Males: Any problems with potency? _____

    Females: Any vaginal pain or irritation? _____

        Any uterine prolapse? _____

        Do you do special (Kegel) exercises? _____

How important is sexual activity in your life?

    □ Very important   □ Moderately important   □ Unimportant

III. PSYCHIATRIC INFORMATION

A. General

What brought you here (complaints, concerns, symptoms)? _____

_____

_____

_____

How long have you had the above problems? _____

Have you recently felt

    □ Depressed   □ Anxious   □ Lonely   □ Guilty   □ Angry   □ Resentful

    □ Fearful *(describe specific fears):* _____

Have you had recent losses of any kind (health, loved ones, job, etc.)? _____

_____

Previous psychiatric contact

    Name(s) of therapist(s): _____

    Discipline (psychiatrist, psychologist, social worker, nurse, other): _____

_____

    City where therapy was received: _____

    When: _____

    Describe general form of treatment (individual or group therapy, family therapy, couples therapy, parent and child therapy, sex counseling, other): _____

_____

_____

PERSONAL DATA FORM—cont'd

Have you had a specialized form of therapy or experience such as Gestalt, encounter, EST, biofeedback, behavior modification, hypnosis, primal therapy, psychodrama, reevaluation counseling, feminist consciousness-raising, or other *(identify)*? _____

_____

_____

How long were you in treatment? _____

Were drugs given? _____ Which ones? _____

Did you receive electroshock treatments? _____

Were you hospitalized? _____

Outcome of treatment in your opinion: _____

_____

_____

Have you belonged to any self-help organizations such as Weight Watchers, Alcoholics Anonymous, Recovery, Inc., Parents without Partners, or others? _____

_____

_____

When? _____

What was the outcome? _____

Has your spouse or partner had psychiatric problems? _____

Is there anyone in your current or previous family with psychiatric problems? _____

_____

Have you ever taken psychological tests? _____

Which ones? _____

Done by whom? _____

For what purpose? _____

Briefly, what is your own theory as to why you are currently having difficulties? _____

_____

_____

What "first-aid" techniques or home remedies have you found that make you feel or function better (e.g., "keeping busy," going to sleep, prayer, shopping, talking, sports)? _____

_____

_____

How long does improvement last? _____

_____

Continued.

PERSONAL DATA FORM—cont'd

III. PSYCHIATRIC INFORMATION—cont'd

Therapy goals

What are the goals you wish to achieve in treatment? _____

_____

_____

_____

If married, do you feel your spouse would benefit from the following? *(check)*

☐ Individual psychotherapy ☐ Group psychotherapy ☐ Brief consultation around your problem ☐ Couples therapy ☐ Family therapy

B. Your attitudes toward aging and death

First experience with death *(describe):* _____

_____

Losses of loved ones (include relatives, friends; describe person and date)

When you were a child (up to 10 years of age): _____

_____

From 10 to 21 years: _____

From 21 to 60 years: _____

After age 60: _____

What are your feelings about old age? _____

What are your feelings about death? _____

Do you worry much about illness? _____

Do you worry much about your own death? _____

Do you worry much about death of others? _____

Describe any arrangements you have already made concerning your death (funeral arrangements, a "living will," donation of your body for science and medicine, donation of various organs for transplant, etc.): _____

_____

_____

Are you a member of a memorial society? _____

Have you made a will? _____

Are there any further arrangements you still wish to make? _____

Describe the old age of your parents: _____

_____

_____

PERSONAL DATA FORM—cont'd

Describe the old age of your grandparents: _____

_____

_____

Have you modeled your own later life after that of anyone else? _____

_____

If so, who? _____

C. Self-view *(use extra space as needed)*

Describe yourself (appearance, personality, personal assets, and liabilities): _____

_____

_____

_____

_____

_____

How do you feel about your present status in life? _____

_____

Do you feel you have much control over your own life? _____

Do you feel you have much influence on others? _____

_____

Have you been an independent person in the past? _____

Are you now an independent person? _____

Do you live alone? _____

Have you lived alone in the past and for how long? _____

What are your feelings about living alone? _____

Describe persons or things that have most influenced your life (friends, family, teachers, books, etc.):

_____

_____

_____

Do you tend to reminisce? _____

    What is the most frequent subject matter? _____

What are your earliest memories? _____

Who loved you most as a child? _____

Who disliked you most? _____

Continued.

PERSONAL DATA FORM—cont'd

III. PSYCHIATRIC INFORMATION—cont'd

Who hurt you most? _____

Who disappointed you most? _____

Have you composed a diary? _____

   kept a photograph album? _____

   written an autobiography? _____

   saved letters, mementoes, souvenirs? _____

What are the two or three most traumatic events (and your approximate age at the time) in your life

that specifically stand out in your memory (e.g., accidents, deaths, fires, moves, divorces, personal

failures of any kind, illnesses, etc.)? _____

_____

_____

_____

What are the two or three happiest and most satisfying events that specifically stand out in your

memory (and your approximate age at the time)? _____

_____

_____

_____

CONCLUSION

What have been your reactions to this review of your life? _____

_____

_____

_____

A completed personal data form is like a baseline electrocardiogram: it indicates the person's present situation and provides a standard against which to measure changes in the future. It is often not accurate to think in terms of eventual "discharge from treatment" for older people in the same way as for the young. Since many will need various kinds of service the rest of their lives, it will save time to collect adequate information right from the start. Mental health personnel need to review their own thinking and attitudes about the quality of evaluation given to older people. A sloppy, haphazard approach cannot be rationalized as time-saving nor as humane care.

Psychiatric assessment

The traditional psychiatric interview derives from the medical model; it can be an unimaginative, tedious, rigid procedure of limited usefulness in mental health care unless attention is given also to psychodynamics[7] and socioeconomics. A completed personal data form such as we have described can provide background and direction for the psychiatric interview. But we also urge caution in the opposite direction. In the interest of dealing with the crises of the moment, or at any time concerning oneself only with the immediate environmental context, the value of the psychiatric view can be overlooked completely. A psychiatric diagnosis, perhaps more for older people than any other age group, is immensely important. One must be ever alert to the possible presence of reversible delirium and functional disorders, both of which can be treated if properly diagnosed. A psychiatric look at the everyday crises of living, too, can be valuable. Much that is swept under the rug as "senility," or even viewed as reaction to environmental stress, may have a psychiatric component that rightly deserves clarification and treatment.

In conducting a psychiatric examination, it is obviously not wise to be bound to a cookbook routine. Rather, one must continue to build on one's skill in observation, perception, and intuition (for hypothesis making), while at the same time taking a comprehensive approach. The degree of comprehensiveness—the width and depth—of the study will vary according to time pressures, purposes, motivation, and (sadly) the patient's economic status and ability to pay.

We will not discuss the general techniques of psychiatric examination, since these are well described elsewhere.[8] Instead, those components of the examination that are found to be especially pertinent to older people will be stressed. The appearance and general behavior of the person can offer significant clues: Does she walk like an "old" person, or does her walk belie her age? Does he dye his hair and pretend to be youthful? Is there a peculiar gait (for instance, the distinctive

parkinsonian "march," the marche à petits pas with its characteristic short shuffling steps, the patient leaning forward so that the gait is propulsive, the arms not swinging)? Does she look blank-faced (indicating organicity? depression?)? An ironed-out, masklike facies may point to parkinsonism. Is he slow moving in speech and action, distractable, flighty, incoherent, or irrelevant? Does she speak sotto voce, quietly, while looking about suspiciously (possible paranoid feature)? Is the appearance one of premature age and debilitation (there may be a basic physical process or illness underlying the psychiatric symptomatology)? One must also be aware of behavior that might be inappropriate for younger people but is "normal" in old age—a good example is the fact that an older person may arrive an hour or more early for an interview. This should not instantly be given the label "obsessive-compulsive." Older people often are highly time-conscious and want to compensate for any unavoidable delays along the way that may be hard for them to cope with; thus they tend to overcompensate by starting very early.

At the beginning of an interview, it must be made clear to the older person what the purpose of the interview is. Many people still see attention from psychiatrists and other psychiatric staff as indications that they are "crazy," and they need reassurance that the examination is taking place to help to discover what is causing discomfort, pain, or anguish for them—that it is a way to get to know them better. Some need to be told this directly, others will assume it from the general manner of the examiner, and still others arrive already convinced. One generally starts off the examination by asking the person what brought him or her for treatment—what is the chief problem or complaint. The history of the problem in the person's own words is next. Family and chronological life histories follow. Careful questioning is necessary to discover how the older person feels about his family: does he see himself as a burden, is he angry at them, do they indicate annoyance with him? At every step, care must be taken to watch the non-verbal communications and revelations of the unconscious. One should try to record important

---

[7] The systematized knowledge of theory of human behavior and its motivation, the study of which depends largely on the functional significance of emotion. Psychodynamics stresses the role of unconscious motivation.

[8] For example, see Lewis, N.D.C.: Outline for psychiatric examinations, ed. 3, New York, 1943, New York State Department of Mental Hygiene.

aspects of the person's description in his or her own exact words, not only for any latter medicolegal reasons but also for later reflection on psychodynamics.

A psychiatric checklist as the one opposite is a useful device for ascertaining symptoms on admission and for comparison with follow-up impressions.

The examiner must also be especially alert for "new" and "peculiar" behavior—keeping in mind the immediacy of the life situation as well as the life history. Immediate precipitants are crucial in old age when change, loss, and deprivation are so powerful in their effects.

Certain symptoms in old age practically guarantee medical and/or psychiatric problems. Persons with organic brain disorders and severe depressions may survive—even well—in the community, and then suddenly a change in their lot makes the pathologic condition visible. Wandering at night, evident confusion, and incontinence are examples of problems that are usually organic in nature—all of which can, however, be functional. Wandering, for instance, may have as its psychogenic root the need to escape. Incontinence may be an expression of anger.

The alert facade or appearance and normal-looking social habits can be deceptive, masking the presence of severe brain damage. Korsakoff's syndrome, presbyophrenia, and the presenile dementias are conditions in which an observer can be misled by first impressions.

■ Two sisters were admitted to the National Institute of Neurological Diseases and Blindness in 1960 for studies of familial essential hypercholesterolemia and general research studies. One was 57, the other 55. They were anxious, depressed, fearful, restless, and perplexed. Verbal productivity was somewhat increased. There was slurring of speech as well as delay in responses and little spontaneity of thinking. They had difficulty finding words; they were distractable. There was perseveration of ideas, but in these patients, not of words.

They appeared outwardly intact. Their personal habits and conduct were fine. The successful social facade, however, fell away drastically when tested in the mental status examination. They knew all the "right things" to say. They just didn't know such simple facts as what day it was.

Intellectual deficiency, memory loss, acalculia, inability to abstract proverbs, and impaired judgment were present. Both began to show signs of illness in their early fifties. Their courses were insidious and progressive. There was a family history of Alzheimer's disease, one of the presenile dementias. Four of five siblings showed signs. Brain biopsies confirmed our studies, which showed reduced cerebral blood flow and oxygen consumption.

Concentration, memory retention and immediate recall, mental grasp and comprehension, counting and calculation, and judgment must be appraised with delicacy. Although there have been advances in recent years in psychiatric techniques for rating or measuring the psychological functioning, mental status, and symptoms of older persons, much work remains to be done. The clarification and differentiation of age-relevant behavior from lifelong behavior (as well as disease-determined, culture-deprived, and other behavior) are unsettled problems. There have been efforts toward the development of quantified forms for mental status examination, covering areas such as memory, orientation, and judgment, but none has been generally accepted for standard use. The Mental Status

---

MENTAL STATUS QUESTIONNAIRE— "SPECIAL TEN"

1. Where are we now?
2. Where is this place (located)?
3. What is today's date—day of month?
4. What month is it?
5. What year is it?
6. How old are you?
7. What is your birthday?
8. What year were you born?
9. Who is President of the United States?
10. Who was President before him?

Modified from Kahn, R.L., Goldfarb, A.I., and Pollack, M.: The evaluation of geriatric patients following treatment. In Hoch, P.H., and Zubin, J., editors: Evaluation of psychiatric treatment, New York, 1964, Grune & Stratton, Inc.

PSYCHIATRIC SYMPTOMS CHECKLIST

	At time of admission	At time of follow-up
1. Conversion symptoms		
2. Hypochondriacal ideas		
3. Somatic delusions		
4. Suspiciousness		
5. Persecutory trend		
6. Idea of unreality		
7. Depersonalization		
8. Nihilistic ideas		
9. Depressive trend		
10. Suicidal attempts		
11. Elation		
12. Grandiose ideas		
13. Hallucinatory experiences:		
a. Auditory		
b. Visual		
c. Tactile		
d. Gustatory		
e. Olfactory		
14. Illusions		
15. Misinterpretations		
16. Obsessions (including death)		
17. Compulsions		
18. Phobias		
19. Anxiety; fear (including death)		
20. Nightmares; dreams		
21. Sexual adaptation		
22. Psychosomatic symptoms		
23. Psychogenic exacerbation of somatic pathology		

From Perlin, S., and Butler, R.N.: Psychiatric aspects of adaptation to the aging process. In Birren, J.E., Butler, R.N., Greenhouse, S.W., Sokoloff, L., and Yarrow, M.R., editors: Human aging: a biological and behavioral study, Pub. No. (PHS) 986, Washington, D.C., 1963, U.S. Government Printing Office (reprinted as Pub. No. [HSM] 71-9051, 1971, 1974).

Table 9-1. Rating of mental functional impairment by mental status questionnaire

No. of errors	Presumed mental status
0-2	Chronic brain syndrome absent or mild
3-8	Chronic brain syndrome moderate
9-10	Chronic brain syndrome severe
Nontestable	Chronic brain syndrome severe*

Modified from Kahn, R.L., Goldfarb, A.I., and Pollack, M.: The evaluation of geriatric patients following treatment. In Hoch, P.H., and Zubin, J., editors: Evaluation of psychiatric treatment, New York, 1964, Grune & Stratton, Inc.
*In the noncooperative person without deafness or insuperable language barriers.

Questionnaire of Kahn et al. (included here) is probably the most widely used, but it is no substitute for a full mental status examination. The Mental Status Questionnaire is correctly used when a quick mental appraisal is required for screening and cursory diagnostic purposes. A rough estimate of impairment of mental functioning is given in Table 9-1. The Kahn-Goldfarb screen was developed chiefly for institutionalized patients. Pfeiffer[9] developed the Short Portable Mental Status Questionnaire to cover both community and institutional populations. Also valuable are the Folstein-Folstein-McHugh "Mini-mental State" (see p. 229-230) and Libow's Mental Status Text.[10] We prefer the more comprehensive Mental Status Evaluation (pp. 231-232), derived from the National Institute of Mental Health's human aging studies, comparing state hospital and healthy community populations.

Mental status examinations are not really adequate. For example, orientation is not necessarily a sensitive indicator of mental dysfunction.[11] Visual and auditory deficits (as with aphasia) may lead to misdiagnosis. The truth is that a powerful, precise range of well-validated neuropsychological tests do not yet exist. Central nervous system functioning is too delicate and comprehensive to be left to "simple tests" except as crude screening devices.

A note should be made here with respect to two special features in evaluation, which are of interest to us: observation of handwriting and interviewing in front of a mirror. Parkinsonian patients typically write in small script (micrographia); thus attention to handwriting can be diagnostic. Mirror interviewing also has diagnostic value in revealing a patient's self-image. It is not a routine procedure but can be quite helpful for in-depth evaluations. A fuller description will follow later.

We wish to point out also that psychiatrists are by no means the only people qualified to do "psychiatric" evaluations. In community mental health centers, psychiatric hospitals, and elsewhere, a team of persons from many disciplines may arrive at a joint evaluation. In addition, well-trained paraprofessionals can learn to assess the psychiatric condition of patients. With inadequate psychiatric coverage in most public and many private facilities, such skills can and should be learned by others.[12] Responsible supervision and competent training can ensure quality care, regardless of the primary discipline.

Medical assessment

A thorough physical examination is mandatory, in addition to a medical history (we use the medical section of a patient's complete personal data form to provide some beginning background infor-

Text continued on p. 233.

---

[9] Pfeiffer, E.: A Short Portable Mental Status Questionnaire for the assessment of organic brain deficit in elderly patients, Journal of the American Geriatrics Society 23:433-441, 1975.

[10] Libow, L.S.: Senile dementia and "pseudosenility": clinical investigation by appropriate laboratory tests and new mental status evaluation technique. In Eisdorfer, C., and Friedel, R., editors: Cognitive and emotional disturbances in the elderly: clinical issues, Seattle, 1977, Medical Yearbook Publishers, pp. 78-81.

[11] Jacobs, J.W., Bernhard, M.R., Delgardo, A., and Strain, J.J.: Screening for organic mental syndrome in the medically ill, Annals of Internal Medicine 86:40-46, 1977.

[12] There is a danger, mentioned previously but worth repeating, that must be avoided, wherein psychiatrists will care for the well-to-do and paraprofessionals care for the poor.

"MINI-MENTAL STATE"

Maximum score	Score	

Orientation

5 (_____) What is the (year) (season) (date) (day) (month)?

5 (_____) Where are we (state) (county) (town) (hospital) (floor)?

Registration

3 (_____) Name 3 objects: 1 second to say each. Then ask the patient all 3 after you have said them. Give 1 point for each correct answer. Then repeat them until he learns all 3. Count trials and record.

☐ Trials

Attention and calculation

5 (_____) Serial 7's. 1 point for each correct. Stop after 5 answers. Alternatively spell "world" backwards.

Recall

3 (_____) Ask for the 3 objects repeated above. Give 1 point for each correct.

Language

9 (_____) Name a pencil, and watch (2 points).

Repeat the following "No ifs, ands or buts." (1 point)

Follow a 3-stage command:

"Take a paper in your right hand, fold it in half, and put it on the floor." (3 points)

Read and obey the following:

Close your eyes (1 point)

Write a sentence (1 point)

Copy design (1 point)

_____ TOTAL SCORE

Assess level of consciousness along a continuum

Alert	Drowsy	Stupor	Coma

INSTRUCTIONS FOR ADMINISTRATION OF "MINI-MENTAL STATE" EXAMINATION

Orientation
1. Ask for the date. Then ask specifically for parts omitted, e.g., "Can you also tell me what season it is?" One point for each correct.
2. Ask in turn "Can you tell me the name of this hospital?" (town, county, etc.) One point for each correct.

Registration
Ask the patient if you may test his memory. Then say the names of 3 unrelated objects, clearly and slowly, about 1 second for each. After you have said all 3, ask him to repeat them. This first repetition determines his score (0-3) but keep saying them until he can repeat all 3, up to 6 trials. If he does not eventually learn all 3, recall cannot be meaningfully tested.

Attention and calculation
Ask the patient to begin with 100 and count backwards by 7. Stop after 5 subtractions (93, 86, 79, 72, 65). Score the total number of correct answers.

If the patient cannot or will not perform this task, ask him to spell the word "world" backwards. The score is the number of letters in correct order, e.g., dlrow = 5, dlorw = 3.

Recall
Ask the patient if he can recall the 3 words you previously asked him to remember. Score 0-3.

Language
Naming: Show the patient a wrist watch and ask him what it is. Repeat for pencil. Score 0-2.

Repetition: Ask the patient to repeat the sentence after you. Allow only one trial. Score 0 or 1.

3-stage command: Give the patient a piece of plain blank paper and repeat the command. Score 1 point for each part correctly executed.

Reading: On a blank piece of paper print the sentence "Close your eyes," in letters large enough for the patient to see clearly. Ask him to read it and do what it says. Score 1 point only if he actually closes his eyes.

Writing: Give the patient a blank piece of paper and ask him to write a sentence for you. Do not dictate a sentence, it is to be written spontaneously. It must contain a subject and verb and be sensible. Correct grammar and punctuation are not necessary.

Copying: On a clean piece of paper, draw intersecting pentagons, each side about 1 inch, and ask him to copy it exactly as it is. All 10 angles must be present and 2 must intersect to score 1 point. Tremor and rotation are ignored.

Estimate the patient's level of sensorium along a continuum, from alert on the left to coma on the right.

MENTAL STATUS EVALUATION

1. Retention

Say to the patient: "I am going to tell you an address which I want you to remember.
I will ask for it at a later time."

This is the address: Apartment C Arbor Estates   Alternate: Room 7 Carrier Hotel

Then say, "Repeat that for me now." This is essential to be certain the address has been registered in the memory. Then continue with the examination, 2. Remote memory (time interval: 5 minutes).

Then, "Do you remember the address I gave you a few minutes ago?"

RAW SCORE: (−1, 0, 1, 2, 3, or 4).   _____

2. Remote memory

Write out subject's response. Score 1 point for each correct answer.)   **Score**

1. Where were you born?

   _____

2. Where did you go to school?

   _____   _____

3. Highest grade completed?

   _____   _____

4. How old were you when you finished school?

   _____   _____

5. How old were you when you began work?

   _____   _____

6. Name of first employer?

   _____   _____

7. Address of first employer?

   _____   _____

8. Mother's maiden name?

   _____   _____

9. Who was President of the United States when you began your first job (in this country when foreign born)?

   _____   _____

REMOTE MEMORY SCORE: Sum of correct answers*   _____

3. Orientation

(Rate 1, 2, or 3 for A, B, and C.)   **Score**

A. Time: _____   _____

   What is the date today?

   What year (month, day) is it? What season is it?

   1. No awareness of correct time (e.g., does not know month, season, or year).

   2. Disturbed orientation, but some degree of awareness (e.g., knows season or year, etc.).

   3. Knows exact time (month, approximate day, year, and season).

From Perlin, S., and Butler, R.N.: Psychiatric aspects of adaptation to the aging process. In Birren, J.E., Butler, R.N., Greenhouse, S.W., Sokoloff, L., and Yarrow, M.R., editors: Human aging: a biological and behavioral study, Pub. No. (PHS) 986, Washington, D.C., 1963, U.S. Government Printing Office (reprinted as Pub. No. [HSM] 71-9051, 1971, 1974).
*Authentication of the correctness of answers should be based, where possible, on information obtained from family members, records, etc.

Continued.

MENTAL STATUS EVALUATION—cont'd

3. Orientation—cont'd

B. Place: _____   _____

What is the name of this place?

Where is it?

1. No awareness of location.

2. Disturbed orientation, but can give an approximation that is reasonably accurate.

3. Knows exact location.

C. Person: _____   _____

What is my job? (Other members of the staff?)

1. No knowledge of above.

2. Some knowledge of above.

3. Knows exactly who and what they are.

ORIENTATION SCORE: Sum of A, B, and C   _____

4. Recent memory
(Check when you are certain he is correct; otherwise write in subject's response. Leave blank if incorrect. One point for each correct response.)

1. Where do you live? _____   _____

2. How long have you lived there? _____   _____

3. How long have you been here? _____   _____

4. Where were you a week ago? _____   _____

5. How many meals have you had today? _____   _____

6. What did you have for breakfast?* _____   _____

_____   _____

7. What is my name? _____   _____

8. When did you see me for the first time? _____   _____

9. Have you been in this room before? _____   _____

_____   _____

RECENT MEMORY SCORE: Sum of correct answers

5. Reading *(logical memory)*†
"I am going to read you a story. Listen carefully." Then, "Now tell me what I read. Begin at the beginning and tell me everything that you can remember . . . and what else?"

(21 possible memories. Check every memory. Leave spaces beside wrongly remembered or omitted facts blank. When in doubt write out response. One point for each memory.)

LOGICAL MEMORY SCORE: Sum of memories   _____

*The evaluator should check beforehand where possible to uncover confabulation, that is, some patients with organic problems cover up their memory loss.
†From Terman, L.M., and Merrill, M.A.: Measuring intelligence, Boston, 1937, Houghton-Mifflin Co., pp. 255-256.

mation)[13] and recent reports from the patient's family doctor or other involved physicians. The latter reports are often obtained verbally by phone but should be summarized in written form in the patient's record. It must be known what drugs are being taken, for what condition, for how long, and what, if any, have been the side effects, especially adverse reactions. A routine physical examination includes the laboratory tests listed in the outline on p. 200, supplemented by any further tests suggested by the patient's symptomatology.

Electroencephalography (brain wave test) is the process or method of making a graphic record of the electrical activity of the brain. Healthy aged persons have essentially the same records as younger people with the exception of the observation of Busse and Silverman of left temporal foci, the meaning of which remains unclear. (Obrist has not found these to be associated with intellectual impairments.[14]) Thus evidences of diffuse or focal changes are significant indications of organic brain disorders. The degree of EEG slowing is related to the severity of intellectual impairment; the slower and more abundant the waves are, the greater the deterioration. Similar relationships have been reported by Mundy-Castle et al.[15] and by Weiner and Schuster,[16] who also rated the severity of dementia.

Computerized axial tomography (CAT)[17] is a technique introduced in 1973 for assaying brain pathology. It is based on two principles: (1) tomography, that is, radiological serial sectioning, and (2) computerization, that is, the rapid integration of thousands of pictures via computer. A narrow beam of x-rays passes through the head rapidly in a series of thin "slices," hitting radiation detectors that feed signals into a high-speed computer. At each of tens of thousands of points in the plane of the scan, the computer calculates the absorption coefficient of the intervening tissues, blood, and bone—that is, the difference between the x-rays originally emitted and those received on the crystal detectors. The technique is 100 times more sensitive than the conventional x-ray examination. The computer also produces an oscilloscopic picture the physician can view on what resembles a television screen or can record as a photograph. The technique is noninvasive (unlike the injection of radioactive isotopes for x-ray purposes) and uses no more radiation than is required for a traditional x-ray film of the skull. X-ray films are only two-dimensional and thus flat, as compared to the multidimensionality of CAT. This technique is able to replace the higher risk and unpleasantness of pneumoencephalography, in which air is injected into the central nervous system. It also essentially replaces angiography, isotope scanning, and some exploratory surgery.

Work in progress strongly suggests that CAT is a major medical breakthrough. As its capacity for resolution (refined differentiation) of central ner-

---

[13] The Cornell Medical Index is a well-standardized questionnaire (195 questions on symptoms, complaints, and health habits) that is also helpful, since it provides a general picture of symptoms and medical history from the patient's point of view. It can be administered by a nurse or an assistant or self-administered by the patient before the actual medical examination (Brodman, K., Erdmann, A.J., and Wolff, H.G.: Cornell Medical Index Health Questionnaire Manual [revised edition], New York, 1956, Cornell Medical College, p. 15).

[14] Obrist pioneered the three-compartment analysis that separates the cerebral blood flow (CBF) values into flow in the gray matter, the white matter, and the extracerebral tissue. The CBF technique may have differential diagnostic value in separating various types of dementia. Hachinski and others, in 1975, showed mean hemispheric flow reduction in patients believed demented for vascular reasons (multiinfarct dementia) but not in patients with primary neuronal degenerative dementia, for example, of the Alzheimer type.

[15] Mundy-Castle, A.C., Hurst, L.A., Beerstecher, D.M., and Prinsloo, T.: The electroencephalogram in the senile psychoses, Electroencephalography and Clinical Neurophysiology **6:**245-252, 1954.

[16] Weiner, H., and Schuster, D.B.: The electroencephalogram in dementia: some preliminary observations and correlations, Electroencephalography and Clinical Neurophysiology **8:** 479-488, 1956.

[17] Readers may be more familiar with the commerical name, EMI scanner, derived from Electric and Musical Instruments, an English company that devised the instrument in England in 1971 and introduced it into the United States in 1973. Physicist A.M. Cormack and electronics engineer G.N. Hounsfield (with EMI, Ltd.), pioneers in the development of the CAT scanner, received the 1979 Nobel Prize in medicine for their work.

vous system tissue is enhanced, its value will be increased. One drawback is that although CAT may be able to differentiate between, for example, a hemorrhage or a blood clot, it cannot, of course, diagnose cerebral circulatory insufficiency. CAT scanning can reliably detect subdural and epidural hematomas, tumors, intracerebral hemorrhage, brain abscess, subdural empyema, hydrocephalus, and nonhemorrhagic stroke. The CAT scan is able to tell a physician whether a patient's stroke resulted from a blood clot or a cerebral hemorrhage (the symptoms look the same but the treatment is different). In addition to focal lesions, the CAT scan delivers information about ventricular size and width of cortical sulci. However, these measures are *not* diagnostic of clinical dementia! In other words, the CAT scan can rule in or out certain treatable causes but can not give a definitive diagnosis of senile dementia/Alzheimer's disease.

CAT will become a routine diagnostic procedure. Its cost is covered by Medicare, and it may reduce expenses of long-term hospitalization and chronic care of older persons through improved diagnosis and treatment.[18]

Tests measuring the cerebral blood flow and oxygen consumption by the brain would be invaluable diagnostically, but the present methods, including the original nitrous oxide method of Kety and Schmidt (1948), are too dangerous for routine clinical use, requiring the skills of highly trained medical personnel. It is hoped that a simple and safe test will be developed so that it can be part of the basic examination. There has been promising work using xenon 133.

Outstanding neurophysiologists such as Sokoloff and Lassen have addressed the task of relating regional cerebral blood flow, oxygen utilization, and biochemical functions with cognition, memory, consciousness, and sensory and motor functions in health or disease throughout life, including old age. Sokoloff and his colleagues did the first unique major study on mean total cerebral blood flow and metabolism in normal men in relation to

aging and on changes induced by vascular disease and dementia in aged men. They found that these did not change with age but changes were seen in cerebral vascular disease.[19] Sokoloff discovered the use of a glucose analogue,[20] which is transported into the brain like glucose, for animal studies. For human studies, he uses deoxyglucose[21] and application of positron emission tomography (PETT), a unique, noninvasive technique.

PETT is an exciting new experimental procedure that records chemical changes in the brain. The deoxyglucose, which has been made radioactive, is injected into a patient and is absorbed by the brain cells. These isotopes soon emit positively charged particles called positrons, which collide with negatively charged electrons normally present in the cells. Each collision produces high-energy particles called photons, whose speed and path are recorded by PETT. A computer processes the information in color on a screen, showing biochemical activity in the living brain. Thus, with computerized tomography one can see structure (anatomy and pathology), but with positron emission transverse tomography one can study function and metabolism. At present, it would appear to be much more important for research (for example, probing for biochemical abnormalities in senile dementia/Alzheimer's disease) than for any diagnostic or treatment purposes.[22] (*Note:* PETT is not yet available for clinical diagnostic purposes; it is only being used experimentally.)

In preliminary studies researchers have found altered glucose metabolism in schizophrenia and

---

[18] Fox, J.H., Topel, J.L., and Hackman, M.S.: Dementia in the elderly: a search for treatable illnesses, Journal of Gerontology **30:**557-564, 1975.

[19] Dastur, D.K., et al.: Effects of aging on cerebral circulation and metabolism in man. In Birren, J.E., Butler, R.N., Greenhouse, S.W., Sokoloff, L., and Yarrow, M.R., editors: Human aging: a biological and behavioral study, Pub. No. (PHS) 986, Washington, D.C., 1971, U.S. Government Printing Office (reprinted as Pub. No. [HSM] 71-9051, 1971, 1974).

[20] 14c-2-deoxy-D-glucose, called 2DG.

[21] 18F 2-deoxy-D-glucose.

[22] The PETT technique does require a cyclotron in order to produce the isotopes, which have short lives. It also requires a large back-up scientific team, including a radiochemist to isolate and purify isotopes and an organic chemist who can label the substances to be studied.

manic-depressive psychosis, a finding that may become useful in differential diagnosis of the two. PETT may become useful also in the treatment of epilepsy by helping surgeons locate and destroy seizure-inducing cells.

Hearing tests, a visual examination with a check of eyeglasses, and a dental examination are obviously important for older people. Nutrition and sleeping habits must be noted. Because of widespread poverty among older persons, combined with the physical incapacity of some to care for themselves, many suffer from malnutrition in subtle or gross forms.[23] Malnutrition and dehydration therefore are among the major medical problems to recognize. Dehydration without malnutrition is also common. The evaluator should also be familiar with changes in touch, pain sensitivity, and other functions that tend to occur over time.[24]

The medical evaluation should be comprehensive, multiphasic, continued at regular intervals, and when feasible, computerized. It is hoped there will soon be a baseline body of quality data available through automated technology and telemetry (to send information quickly, long distance) to aid in diagnosis. Heart disease, diabetes, glaucoma, emphysema, and cancer are particular foci. Indeed, after age 45 there should be regular medical checkups for the healthy and more frequent ones for the ill. Unfortunately, Medicare does not cover routine checkups, making it difficult for older persons to take advantage of the early detection and prevention possible through regular physical examinations.

Another difficulty for older people is lack of knowledge about health, medicine, and their own bodies. For obvious reasons they know less than later generations will know. Physicians have not been the major source of health education that they could be for older people. Often they are reluctant to impart information—saying it takes too much time, there is no good purpose to it, etc.—while older persons remain unenlightened as to what is being done to them. Many, for example, are given medication without knowing what it is for or what the side effects may be. Numerous other examples could be given of medical care administered in a manner that produces needless anxiety and emotional anguish.

Besides the usual diagnostic benefits, medical evaluation has two particularly important functions for the older patient. First, the examination is essential for the detection and early treatment of reversible delirium. These syndromes must be diagnosed early or they can become complicated, losing their reversibility. Second, the medical examination helps to "rule in" the functional disorders by clarifying those situations in which no physical basis can be found. Thus an evaluator is clued into the possibility of a functional disorder (depression, paranoid states, etc.) and is more inclined to explore psychogenic processes.

Socioeconomic assessment

The immediate social environment has substantial influence on the older person's psychological behavior and attitudes, and this has been investigated in studies at NIMH and elsewhere. "As the environment showed qualities of deprivation or displacement of the person (in loss of intimate persons, loss of income, in cultural displacement), the attitudes and behaviors of the aged showed more deteriorative qualities. Losses of significant persons were especially associated with deteriorative functioning,"[25] and further, "findings of this study lead to the suspicion that psychological reactions to the loss of friends and other environmental supports may amplify if not initiate changes in the

---

[23]One should not overlook the possibility of pellagra in the workup. The complete syndrome of this vitamin deficiency disease may not be present. One can look for redness of the mouth and tongue (more obvious in acute cases), skin changes, and—of special interest to mental health personnel —evidence of intellectual changes in a chronic brain disorder.

[24]Kenshalo, D.W.: Age change in touch, vibration, temperature, kinesthesis, and pain sensitivity. In Birren, J.E., and Schaie, K.W., editors: Handbook of the physiology of aging, New York, 1977, Van Nostrand Reinhold Co.

[25]From Birren, J.E., Butler, R.N., Greenhouse, S.W., Sokoloff, L., and Yarrow, M.R., editors: Human aging: a biological and behavioral study, Pub. No. (PHS) 986, Washington, D.C., 1963, U.S. Government Printing Office, p. 314 (reprinted as Pub. No. [HSM]71-9051, 1971, 1974).

older nervous system and thereby the rest of the organism."[26]

Having intimate friends in whom one can confide is very important. It must be recognized, however, that social isolation per se is not always causative of emotional and mental reactions in old age. Persons who have lived isolated lives throughout the years—"loners"—are not necessarily more liable to the occurrence of late-life psychopathology. It is those persons who become isolated relatively late in life, through no choice of their own, who have the most difficulties.

A socioeconomic evaluation should include general background information concerning details of family structure, housing, work or retirement, friendship patterns, economic circumstances, social roles, activities, and interests. (See example of personal mental health data form, pp. 203-224.) Interviews with the older person and members of his or her family can provide valuable insight into the contribution of social factors to the patient's problem and into potential assets that can aid and support treatment. An assessment should include the amount and quality of love and affection that exist between the family and the older person. The evaluation of the family itself is crucial, since the genesis, precipitation, and maintenance of disorders may derive from a family context. The older person may be expressing what is really a family-wide pathology in which he or she is the scapegoat or the victim of ancient angers. Sometimes the "problem" of the older person is the means by which a son or daughter seeks treatment when unable to ask for it directly. A skilled evaluator may be able to detect this phenomenon and help the younger family members to obtain treatment themselves. In other situations the older person may exploit the family; an example is the domineering parent who becomes even more tyrannical in old age by playing on guilt feelings of children toward the aging and decline of a parent. A prideful overemphasis on independence and a manipulation of others through passivity are other patterns

---

[26]Ibid., p. 316.

of behavior in older persons that can cause family conflict. Older people must not routinely be judged helpless or fragile. Indeed, a fair number of them wield substantial influence over family and friends.

In working with the total family, it is imperative to share evaluation findings as openly as possible with all members, guided by judgment as to the effects of such sharing on the older person. Family therapy involving the older person may be indicated—couples' therapy with the patient and spouse can be beneficial even in marriages that have been difficult for years and/or have deteriorated. At times, the family approach is used as a rationale to exclude the older patient (usually the result of countertransference problems on the part of treatment personnel).

There is no point seeing the patient—you know his memory is gone. He feels rejected—I find it more useful to see the son and daughter-in-law.

One must recognize the vast implications of race as well as racism in the lives of older blacks, Asian-Americans, American Indians, Latinos, and older members of other groups. A knowledge of cultural patterns and traditions and the discriminatory practices and prejudices experienced in a lifetime are fundamental parts of a thorough evaluation. This applies also to ethnic origins, since so many older persons are immigrants. However, a note of caution is warranted here: at times, race or ethnic origin may be used to rationalize another form of prejudice. For example, the older black person can be denied psychiatric care because his or her problems are viewed as social or racial, while intrapsychic problems remain unnoticed. People in every culture develop internalized emotional difficulties that are not necessarily directly attributable to the social condition and that require treatment.

Treatment should ideally be planned to coincide with those cultural elements that are familiar and valued by the older person. An elderly black man in a nursing home might prefer "soul food," whereas a Norwegian immigrant could long for "lutefisk." Patient comfort, satisfaction, and dignity are important in a positive treatment program.

Not least among the steps in an adequate evaluation is determining the patient's health care coverage and economic circumstances. Pending the introduction of a truly comprehensive national health insurance, it is usually necessary to appraise the patient's "ability to pay" for treatment, although this notion of personal financial responsibility is generally obsolete, given the realities of escalating costs and, for older persons, the denial of adequate income programs and job opportunities. Third-party medical payments include Medicare, Medicaid (see box), and sometimes insurance supplementary to Medicare. A routine check should be made to determine whether the older person is a member of one of the national organizations for older people that sell such supplementary insurance. The National Council of Senior Citizens and the American Association of Retired Persons offer policies, as do the so-called nonprofit Blue Cross–Blue Shield plans and the commercial insurance carriers. One must be on the lookout for fly-by-night, fraudulent Medicare supplements that have been sold to older people. A check of the additional income resources listed on a personal mental health data form (pp. 203-224), and information about average living expenses will

---

HEALTH INSURANCE FOR THE AGED—HOSPITAL INSURANCE
(Popular name: Medicare—Part A)

This program provides hospital insurance protection for covered services to any person 65 or over who is entitled to Social Security or Railroad Retirement benefits. A dependent spouse 65 or over is also entitled to Medicare, based on the worker's record. The covered protection in each benefit period includes hospital inpatient care, posthospital extended care, and home health visits by nurses or other health workers from a participating home health agency. It does not include doctors' services.

Under Social Security, workers, their employers, and self-employed people pay a contribution based on earnings during their working years. At age 65, the portion of their contribution that has gone into a special Hospital Insurance Trust Fund guarantees that workers will have help in paying hospital bills.

HEALTH INSURANCE FOR THE AGED—SUPPLEMENTARY MEDICAL INSURANCE
(Popular name: Medicare—Part B)

Social Security's medical insurance program helps pay for doctor bills, outpatient hospital services, medical supplies and services, home health services, outpatient physical therapy, and other health care services.

Medical insurance is not financed through payroll deductions and is not based on earnings or period of work. As a voluntary supplemental extension of Medicare's hospital insurance protection, it helps pay for many of the costs of illness not covered by hospital insurance.

MEDICAL ASSISTANCE PROGRAM
(Popular name: Medicaid Title XIX)

This program provides grants to states to administer medical assistance programs that benefit (1) the needy—all Supplemental Security Income recipients and public assistance families with dependent children—and those who would qualify for that assistance under federal regulations, (2) at a state's option, the medically needy—people in the four groups mentioned above who have enough income or resources for daily needs but not for medical expenses, and (3) all children under 21 whose parents cannot afford medical care.

State plans must include at least five basic services for the needy, and a similar or less extensive program for the medically needy. Family planning services may be included in both.

complete the economic assessment. Older people, like others, may be sensitive to questions about economics, fearing that they will be billed unjustly for treatment or simply resenting an intrusion into their privacy. Some are ashamed to admit their meager incomes and out of pride may refuse to accept financial benefits to which they are entitled. Every effort should be made to help them exploit all possible outside resources in order to protect their own incomes during treatment. (The task of mental health personnel is made more difficult by the lack of systematic training in the ever-changing and complicated system of benefits available through Medicare and Medicaid.)

Medicare coverage may be expanded and will probably be incorporated within a national health insurance plan. In the meantime, actual coverage is limited (38% of the health bill of older persons in 1978). There are many exclusions—outpatient drugs, eye glasses, dentures, blood transfusions, routine physical examinations—all of particular importance to older people. No third-party payment covers the medical problem of malnutrition resulting from inadequate income or difficulty in obtaining food. Referral for Supplemental Security Income (SSI), food stamps, and Meals-on-Wheels programs are among some available resources.

On-the-spot home evaluation

To see how older people of all socioeconomic classes live is a first-rate diagnostic tool. Extreme privation is not unusual.

■ The old man lived in an unpainted, roach-infested, windowless closet, sleeping on a urine-smelling mattress that could not be fully extended because of the small size of the closet.

With 95% of older persons residing in the community, a home evaluation is a logical way to get a sense of the day-to-day existence of the patient. One looks for pets (companionship), calendar (to what month is it turned?), clock (is it running and set properly?), odors (gas leaks, spoiled food, signs of incontinence), food supply (is the person

eating regularly and adequately?), mementoes (what does the person consider important?), family pictures, temperature of house (potential accidental hypothermia resulting from a cold home), and medication cabinet and night stand (to see what and how prescription and nonprescription drugs are being taken). The safety and security of the home, the ability of the person to get around the house, and the presence of others can be assayed. (It is not uncommon to find an older person caring for someone who may be even sicker than he or she.) A realistic evaluation of the fear of crime and financial and physical limitations to transportation can be made.

Such outreach services as home visiting are still insufficient in the United States. Some cities (for example, Baltimore) have health aides who work for the city health department's bureau of special home services. These workers collect data about older persons in their homes and are a useful adjunct to the mental health specialist. The physician, the psychiatrist, the psychologist, the social worker, the nurse, and the paraprofessional all should make use of home visiting to keep in touch with the realities of life of older persons from various backgrounds—urban, suburban, or rural. Measures of activities of daily living (ADL) in various settings are valuable.[27]

PSYCHOLOGICAL TESTS

Although we do not necessarily believe that psychological tests must be done in every case, they can be most useful when indicated. When there is uncertainty about the differential diagnosis of organic brain damage versus depression, such tests can be invaluable; but one should not forget that the patient with an organic problem can still be depressed. A patient with chronic organic brain disorder generally produces lower test scores than one with acute brain disorder; however, at the height of the acute reversible crisis (for example, delirium), the patient is likely to be untestable.

[27] Katz, S., Downs, T.D., Cash, H., and Grotz, R.C.: Progress and development of the index of ADL, The Gerontologist **10:**20-30, 1970.

The Bender Visual-Motor Gestalt[28] is the most useful measure of organic change. The person is presented with a series of cards, one at a time, with a simple geometric figure on each. The patient's task is to copy each figure on a sheet of paper. The first card shows a circle flanked by a diamond, with one corner of the diamond touching the circle. The second card shows a series of dots in a straight line. The person must be able to retain his or her spatial orientation. The patient having organic difficulty may rotate the figures, misplace them, or perseverate (for example, be unable to stop making the series of dots).

The Wechsler Adult Intelligence Scale[29] is a standardized test of intelligence, for which national figures are available. The Wechsler Memory Scale[30] may also help in the differentiation. Moreover, there are standardized figures for older people, taking education into account to some extent. However, a cultural bias is present against foreign immigrees, blacks, and other racial minorities. The WAIS can be given in abbreviated form by asking the odd-numbered items—1, 3, 5, and so forth—of Information, Comprehension, Calculations, Similarities, Vocabulary. The verbal subtest—Similarities—is an excellent measure of the ability to abstract; patients with organic disorders will tend to be concrete on this test. The Raven Progressive Matrices, utilizing geometric figures, is presumably culture-free, but there is some question of this.

Another popular test is the Kent E-G-Y,[31] a 10-item, quick-screening test for intelligence. Some people, such as Goldfarb, find M. Bender's

Double Simultaneous Tactual Stimulation (Face-Hand) Test[32] of value in the important differential diagnosis between organicity and depression. The Face-Hand Test (see the box below) is also of value in attempting to determine the degree of brain damage. The failure to properly report touch on the back of the hands is a valid and reliable suggestion of brain damage of senile brain disease. The errors made are failure to report the touch at all (extinction), displacement of the hand touch to another part of the person's body, and exomesthesia (the touch somewhere ''out there'' or ''over there''). The number of errors is recorded for the test done with the eyes closed and then for the test repeated with the eyes open.

The Life Satisfaction Measure of Neugarten et al.[33] isolates five components of an individual's positive life satisfaction: (1) taking pleasure from the round of activities that constitutes his everyday life, (2) regarding his life as meaningful and accepting resolutely that which life has been, (3) feeling he has succeeded in achieving his major

[28] Bender, L.: A visual-motor Gestalt test and its clinical use. Research Monograph No. 3, New York, 1938, American Orthopsychiatric Association.

[29] Wechsler, D.: WAIS manual: Wechsler Adult Intelligence Scale, New York, 1955, The Psychological Corporation.

[30] Wechsler, D.: A standardized memory scale for clinical use, Journal of Psychology **19:**87, 1945.

[31] Kent, G.H.: Kent E-G-Y test: series of emergency scales, manual, New York, 1946, The Psychological Corporation. See Delp, H.A.: Correlations between the Kent E-G-Y and the Wechsler batteries, Journal of Clinical Psychology **9:** 73-75, 1953.

[32] Bender, M.B., Fink, M., and Green, M.: Patterns in perception in simultaneous tests of the face and hand, Archives of Neurology and Psychiatry **66:**355-362, 1951.

[33] Neugarten, B.L., Havighurst, R.J., and Tobin, S.S.: The measurement of life satisfaction, Journal of Gerontology **16:**134-143, 1961.

ORDER OF STIMULATION USED IN FACE-HAND TEST

1. Right cheek—left hand
2. Left cheek—right hand
3. Right cheek—right hand
4. Left cheek—left hand
5. Right cheek—left cheek
6. Right hand—left hand
7. Right cheek—left hand
8. Left cheek—right hand
9. Right cheek—right hand
10. Left cheek—left hand

Modified from Bender, M.B., Fink, M., and Green, M.: Patterns in perception in simultaneous tests of the face and hand, Archives of Neurology and Psychiatry **66:**355-362, 1951.

goals, (4) holding a positive image of self, and (5) maintaining happy and optimistic attitudes and moods.

Lawton's Morale Scale[34] was specially designed to assess morale of the aged. This scale determines self-perceptions of mood, adjustment, and well-being.

Projective tests elicit spontaneous and personal responses to a vague stimuli, thus giving valuable psychological insight into the person being tested. The Rorschach Inkblot Test[35] is a series of 10 cards, each containing a different inkblot to which the patient associates whatever thoughts may occur to him or her. This provides information on the formal organization of the personality and some of its unconscious features. The Thematic Apperception Test (TAT) stimuli are more suggestive but still unspecific. The test consists of 20 pictures to each of which the patient associates a story. The Sentence Completion Test is a group of unfinished sentences that the patient is asked to complete with the first thought that comes to mind.

The Minnesota Multiphasic Personality Inventory (MMPI) assesses personality structure and diagnostic classification through a paper and pencil inventory. Of the nine dimensions of the personality that are measured, the aged do not appear to deviate from other age groups except in the D scale, which measures depression.

Graham and Kendall's Memory for Designs Test[36] has also been found useful for assessment of older people.

A self-rating test for depression, developed by Zung[37] and containing 20 multiple-choice questions, has been criticized by Blumenthal as not suitably geared to older people. She states that "depressive" complaints are "not depressive in nature but are referrable to other symptoms"—for example, constipation can present some of the same symptoms as depression.[38]

Eisdorfer has reported that heightened arousal, as measured by multiple concurrent indices of nervous system and endocrine activity as well as by subjective reports, improves learning performance in older people.[38a] We need much more new knowledge regarding problem solving, learning, and memory, such as that accruing from the NIA Baltimore Longitudinal Study of Aging.[29]

Special services for persons with memory loss are few and far between; one such is a Memory Disorder Clinic at the New England Medical Center Hospital that offers diagnostic and comprehensive care for patients with all kinds of memory loss, including that resulting from Alzheimer's disease.

DIAGNOSTIC USE OF MIRROR AND SELF-DRAWINGS

Any technique that is useful in eliciting rich, spontaneous information and response from older people can become part of one's diagnostic repertoire. Such techniques may be discovered by accident. Clinical experiences by the author (R.N.B.) of observing certain older people communicating with their mirror images led to investigation of self- and body concepts through the experimental use of the mirror and self-drawings. These techniques were introduced as cues for a collaborative

[34]Lawton, P.: The Philadelphia Geriatric Center morale scale: a revision, Journal of Gerontology **30**:85-89, 1975.

[35]Ames, L.B., Metraux, R.W., Rodell, J.L., and Walker, R.N.: Rorschach responses in old age, New York, 1974, Brunner/Mazel, Inc.

[36]Graham, F.K., and Kendall, B.S.: Memory for Designs Test: revised general manual. Perceptual and motor skills **7**(supp. 2), 1970 (monograph).

[37]Zung, W.W.K.: A self-rating depression scale, Archives of General Psychiatry **12**:63-70, 1965; and Zung, W.W.K.: Depression in the normal aged, Psychosomatics **8**:287-292, 1967.

[38]Blumenthal, M.: Measuring depressive symptomatology in a general population, Archives of General Psychiatry **32**: 971-978, 1975.

[38a]Eisdorfer, C.: Intelligence and cognition in the aged. In Busse, E., and Pfeiffer, E., editors: Behavior and adaptation in late life, ed. 2, Boston, 1977, Little, Brown & Co.

[39]Arenberg, D.: A longitudinal study of problem solving in adults, Journal of Gerontology **29**:650-658, 1974; and Arenberg, D.: Differences and changes with age in the Benton Visual Retention Test, Journal of Gerontology **33**:534-540, 1978.

self-exploration *with* the older person as an active participant—how does he view himself now, how did he in the past, and what does he see in his future?

Mirror

To help illustrate the psychological significance of one's mirror image, let us quote from a Tolstoi short story, *The Death of Ivan Ilych* (1886).

And Ivan Ilych began to wash. With pauses for rest, he washed his hands and then his face, cleaned his teeth, brushed his hair, and looked in the glass. He was terrified by what he saw, especially the limp way in which his hair clung to his pallid forehead. While his shirt was being changed he knew that he would be still more frightened at the sight of his body, so he avoided looking at it.

Asking an older person to look into a mirror and tell about what he sees is an exceptionally excellent way of acquiring data about body images and

Diagnostic use of the mirror.

From Butler, R.N.: Geriatrics **18**:220-232, 1963.

reactions to changes with age. The mirror is a powerful trigger or cue to thoughts and observations about oneself and one's changes. One often obtains much richer data in less time than by ways of elaborate verbal questioning about physical, personality, and other changes. The range of reactions may be accounted for by (1) reality factors in appearance, (2) personality factors, whether lifelong or in reaction to old age, and (3) organic factors. (See following outline.)

1. Reality factors in appearance
   a. Skin-wrinkling; pigmentation; flabbiness; leathering
   b. Bodily movements—slowing
      Physical impairments
         Arthritis
         Palsies—tremors
   c. Facial changes—palsies; wrinkling
   d. Hair—balding; graying
   e. Eyes—opacities of the lens
   f. Teeth—absence; discoloration
   g. Cartilage growth—ears; nose
   h. Chest—increased diameter; breathing rate
   i. Abdomen—protuberance
   j. Weight—loss; shrunken
2. Personality factors
   a. Lifelong
      Focal emphasis on (cathexis of) parts vs. whole—for example, nose; profile vs. frontal view; sexual organ
      Character—narcissism, self-hate, etc.
      Identity—crisis
      Mood—depression, hypomania, etc.
   b. Old age
      Fear—shudder—tension—aging and death
      Denial of aging changes
3. Organic factors
   a. Perceptual factors
      Vision affected (can be defensive; cf. exclusion of stimuli—Weinberg)
   b. Organic factors
      Organic brain damage: ''Not me''
      Disorientation for person

As is known, cartilage continues to grow in old age, so the ears and nose may consequently become more prominent, but these changes are not mentioned as often as wrinkling, sagging around the eyes, hair loss, and general appearance of "oldness." On the other hand, most healthy older people find it difficult to see themselves as having essentially changed. Of course, much turns on the term "essentially." It appears that they are in effect recognizable to themselves, and in their own minds they have not drastically altered in their character and nature in the course of time; their identity has remained solid. A sudden and rapid deterioration and change of appearance can cause an identity crisis or reaction, even in otherwise healthy people. Adjustment and acceptance are much easier when physical change comes slowly. A clue to shaky identify or difficulty in adapting to changes can be seen in people who reject their mirror image.

■ A middle-aged woman who expressed a profound fear of aging could not accept her mirror image as herself. She regarded the image as something foreign and experienced her "real" self as being on the inside of her body, feeling and reacting, while people responded to her "foreign" outside image in a way that was unacceptable to her.

Personality factors before the mirror can be strikingly obvious. People exhibiting defensive preoccupation with themselves (narcissism) are pleased and attracted by their image, whereas those who are ashamed and guilty shun the mirror, reject their images, become anxious. A focal emphasis on or cathexis of a particular body part (for example, the nose) is observed and provides diagnostic clues. Usually a part rather than the whole is seen by the older person. Other common reactions are fear, shudders, suddenly occurring thoughts about aging and approaching death, or, conversely, a denial of aging changes and denial of fear of death.

Organic factors can affect the mirror reactions. Persons with organic brain damage may insist the image is "not me" or illustrate vividly a "disorientation for person" by not recognizing the person in the mirror. Perceptual impairments of vision can be actual or defensive in nature, the latter re-

calling Weinberg's concept of exclusion of stimuli, in which the person blocks out images that are too painful.

Self-drawings

Some classic examples of the emotion-laden quality of self-drawings are the variety of self-portraits done by well-known artists (many using their mirror image). A 1972 museum exhibit displayed such portraits with expressions ranging from pleased and serene to displeased and tortured. Goya made his self-portrait defiantly ugly and troubled, not bothering to idealize himself or impress his audience. Cezanne dressed himself in overalls and a lumpy, battered hat, beneath which he seemed to be shy and retiring. The self-portrait of Dürer was exquisitely and lovingly drawn.

Self-drawings by patients are revealing, whether done in front of the mirror or by themselves. The technique is to focus the person directly on himself. Self-drawings of older persons with and without the mirror often suggest a self-view of dissolution, sometimes bizarre; they do not appear, as some have said, similar to the drawing of children. The illustrations on pp. 243-244 show examples of self-drawings of normal older men.

Barring severe hand tremors or profound visual problems that would affect expression, drawing provides other clues to the feelings of older people. Things to look for in drawings are the size of the image and placement of figures on the page, amount and kind of detail, underemphasis or overemphasis of a body part, omissions, facial expressions, activity or inactivity of the figure, and the general emotional quality of the picture.

"Draw your insides"

"Draw your insides" is an interesting device because of the preoccupation of so many older people with their bodily ailments and changes. One can get clues about the emotional impact of such changes by observing the older person's response in this kind of drawing. Shown on p. 245 is the figure provided for the male subject. A female figure should be provided for women.

SUBJECT 16

In front of mirror ▶

Subject 16. *This 76-year-old retired merchant's counterphobic activity helped him to ward off depressive symptoms. Although emphasizing his physical well-being, his self-drawing suggests incompleteness. Character trait disorder.* Subject 20. *This 78-year-old retired clerk has recurrent nightmares related to death. He describes himself as a "silent worrier." No psychiatric diagnosis.*

SUBJECT 20

In front of mirror ▶

● Placement of original drawings on paper

SUBJECT 19

In front of mirror ▶

◀ Draw a person

Subject 19. *This 75-year-old physically healthy man did not have diagnosable psychopathology. He first drew a female figure in the "draw-a-person" test; his second draw-a-person figure is essentially the same as his self-drawings.*

Continued.

Self-drawings of normal older men.

From Butler, R.N.: Geriatrics **18:**220-232, 1963.

Subject 27. *This 71-year-old professional man was diagnosed obsessional-compulsive reaction. His narcissism was demonstrated in his pleasure before the mirror. Subject 12. This 75-year-old man with obvious artistic talent drew an actual likeness of himself in the mirror. No psychiatric diagnosis was made.*

SUBJECT 27

In front of mirror ▶

SUBJECT 12

In front of mirror ▶

SUBJECT 39

◀ In front of mirror

SUBJECT 35

◀ In front of mirror

Subject 35. *This 79-year-old retired businessman appeared happy, youthful, and alert. He had no psychiatric diagnosis, yet his self-drawings were surprising. A suprapubic prostatectomy had been performed for an obstruction twenty-three years before, after which he was sexually inactive. Subject 39. At 73 years of age, this man returned to work after retirement, which he found to be a "drudgery." His self-drawing became more orderly in front of the mirror.*

Self-drawings of normal older men—cont'd.

From Butler, R.N.: Geriatrics **18**:220-232, 1963.

Figure given to patient when he is asked to draw his insides.

Items most commonly drawn are intestines, heart, lungs, and stomach. Placement and size of these organs in the drawing can given indications of their meaning emotionally. In experimental tests, 20% of inner body parts were drawn as protruding out from the body or as completely outside, suggesting possible mental confusion and organicity.

Since comparative data for other age groups or various diagnostic entities are not available, no concise inferences can be drawn from findings; indeed, anatomical knowledge may be limited in the older population, which did not receive as much educational emphasis on biology, health, etc. as more recent generations have. But the draw-your-insides procedure, along with mirror reactions and self-drawing, produces rich emotional data without unduly threatening the older person. In the same way, reviews of family photo albums and scrapbooks can provide stimulation and diagnostic clues, while often giving immense pleasure to the older person in the process.

COMMUNITY ASPECTS OF AN EVALUATION

The older person's community should be included in the evaluative process, both to determine what the community has to offer and to engage community services in ongoing evaluations of patients. A homemaker working in a patient's home may be able to furnish a picture of the person's day-to-day life. Visiting nurses, working in Meals-on-Wheels programs, occupational therapists, and others can offer their particular viewpoints.

STUDIES OF COMMUNITY-RESIDENT "HEALTHY" OLDER PERSONS
Quests for a psychological baseline against which to measure "illness"

Busse's group and the NIMH group are among those which have evaluated community older persons. In the NIMH studies, begun in 1955, physical and emotional health was a criterion in selection for study. Part of the purpose in such work was to obtain, for evaluating older people, a baseline consisting of a composite of the statistical norm (the average) and the healthy (the ideal). A longitudinal view of the life cycle has begun to receive attention. Senescence as a developmental stage or process in the course of the life cycle has a psychology of its own, which thus far has only been crudely delineated.

Evaluation of the effects of lifelong personality

The list given here indicates the contribution of some aspects of lifelong personality to the psychological nature of older people.

1. Adaptive qualities
   a. Candor, ease of relationships, independence, affirmation, positive self-concept, sense of usefulness
   b. Defense mechanisms: insight, denial, use of activity
2. Maladaptive qualities
   a. Paranoid isolation
3. Maladaptive in early life—adaptive in late life
   a. Obsessive-compulsive features
   b. Schizoid mechanisms
   c. Dependent personality

Both adaptive and maladaptive features are brought by the person into old age. We must caution observers, however, that only through a careful knowledge of life history can differentiation be made between those qualities possessed by the individual throughout his or her life and those which first came into being in old age through a reorganization of personality. The Swedish film "Wild Strawberries" reflects the potential of an older man, set in his ways, to make rather basic changes in his personality late in life.

Lifelong personality traits that have been found useful in old age are a sense of self-esteem, candor, ability to relate easily with others, independence and self-motivation, and a sense of usefulness. Measures of the "ego strength" (the ego's function as the moderating and reality-testing component of the personality) enable judgments to be made regarding the capacity to cope and adjust. Some defense mechanisms (by which the ego copes) are more useful than others. Naturally, insight is a valuable aid in alleviating anxiety and guilt by realistically appraising the changed circumstances of life and body. Denial can be beneficial if it does not interfere with needed medical or emotional care and if it facilitates relationships and activities. Older people who use appropriate activity, ranging from the creative to merely "keeping busy" in order to counteract fear or depression, also have a defense that is an asset. Less adaptive are the counterphobic defenses, wherein some older people undertake excessive and dangerous activities in order to prove their continued prowess, youthfulness, and fearlessness.

In judging the adaptations of older persons, it is vital to remember that they commonly deal with more stresses (in actual number, frequency, and profundity) than any other age group. Thus evaluation of restitutive attempts must be viewed with this in mind. Sometimes maintenance of the status quo may be all that is possible; indeed, this may be a triumph under the circumstances. A pride in present accomplishments, no matter how small, is appropriate.

Paranoid personality features have a particular maladaptiveness in old age, since so much happens to reinforce the notion that the problems are all "out there." In addition, hearing and other sensory losses increase the inability to deal with threatening forces and compound the isolation of the person with paranoid tendencies. A defensive use of perceptual loss, such as "hearing what one wants to hear," may be present. Tendencies to use age, disease, or impairment as a defense (by acting more helpless than is warranted) are common problems. Personality characteristics of rigidity, despair, depression, and the whole range of psychopathological reactions can further hamper adaptation to old age.

As we state in Chapter 4, certain psychopathology can become increasingly adaptive as people age. Obsessional maneuvers fill the emptiness of retirement; schizoid detachment apparently insulates against loss; dependency can result in a welcoming of greater care and help from others.

Diagnostic attention to the inner experience of old age

Aside from the complex of reality factors and the influences of the individual personality, there are inner reactions to old age, which seem to be part of the developmental work of late life. One of these inner processes, the life review, appears to be of universal occurrence. (See Chapters 3 and 12.) It takes place through reminiscence accompanied by feelings of nostalgia, regret, and pleasure. Complications that can occur are extreme emotional pain, despair, guilt, obsessive rumination, panic, and suicide. A resolution or working through of the life review may bring atonement,

Table 9-2. The social readjustment rating scale

Life event	Mean value
1. Death of spouse	100
2. Divorce	73
3. Marital separation	65
4. Jail term	63
5. Death of close family member	63
6. Personal injury or illness	53
7. Marriage	50
8. Fired at work	47
9. Marital reconciliation	45
10. Retirement	45
11. Change in health of family member	44
12. Pregnancy	40
13. Sex difficulties	39
14. Gain of new family member	39
15. Business readjustment	39
16. Change in financial state	38
17. Death of close friend	37
18. Change to different line of work	36
19. Change in number of arguments with spouse	35
20. Mortgage over $10,000	31
21. Foreclosure of mortgage or loan	30
22. Change in responsibilities at work	29
23. Son or daughter leaving home	29
24. Trouble with in-laws	29
25. Outstanding personal achievement	28
26. Wife begin or stop work	26
27. Begin or end school	26
28. Change in living conditions	25
29. Revision of personal habits	24
30. Trouble with boss	23
31. Change in work hours or conditions	20
32. Change in residence	20
33. Change in schools	20
34. Change in recreation	19
35. Change in church activities	19
36. Change in social activities	18
37. Mortgage or loan less than $10,000	17
38. Change in sleeping habits	16
39. Change in number of family get-togethers	15
40. Change in eating habits	15
41. Vacation	13
42. Christmas	12
43. Minor violations of the law	11

From Holmes, T.H., and Rahe, R.H.: The social readjustment rating scale, Journal of Psychosomatic Research **11**:213, 1967. Used by permission of Pergamon Press, Inc. See the article for complete wording of items.

serenity, constructive reorganization, and creativity.

The Holmes rate scale provides a constructive approach to evaluating the impact of various life events affected, of course, by the character of the person (Table 9-2).

PROBLEMS COMMONLY MISDIAGNOSED OR OVERLOOKED

Some conditions that require special diagnostic care are listed. These conditions, commonly overlooked, are recoverable and treatable. Look for the following.

1. Delirium
   a. Alone
   b. Superimposed on dementia
2. Depressive reactions simulating organic brain disorders
3. Paranoid states without organic brain disease
   a. Generalized
   b. Circumscribed
   c. Chronic paranoid state with superimposed, reversible crises
4. Subdural hematomas
5. Drug reactions

The list below contains key diagnostic concepts.

1. Insight and depression may be present in early phase of multiple infarct.
2. Depression may mask itself as organic confusion.
3. Reversible brain syndromes are often misdiagnosed as irreversible brain syndrome.
4. Reversible and irreversible brain syndromes may coexist.
5. Depression and brain syndromes may coexist.
6. Retinal arteriosclerosis is *not* diagnostic of cerebral arteriosclerosis.
7. Suicide is frequent in older men.
8. Paradoxical excitatory drug reactions to barbiturate sedatives may occur.
9. Tranquilizer-induced (''iatrogenic'') brain syndromes occur.
10. Tranquilizer-induced depressions are not uncommon.

Senility reconsidered

We bring special attention to the treatment possibilities for mental impairment of older persons and recommend the reader study "Senility Reconsidered," the result of a search for consensus by a wide range of authorities concerning the diagnostic and treatment approaches to the potentially reversible deliria and dementia of old age.[40]

The most common causes of reversible impaired intellectual functions are therapeutic drug intoxication, depression, and metabolic or infectious disorders. An enormous number of drugs have

[40] See NIA Task Force: Senility reconsidered: treatment possibilities for mental impairment in the elderly, Journal of the American Medical Association **244**:259-263, 1980. This is one of consensus efforts conducted by the National Institutes of Health (in this instance by the National Institute on Aging). The consensus task force was composed of R.W. Besdine, J.A. Brody, R.N. Butler, L.E. Duncan, L. Jarvik, and L.S. Libow.

Table 9-3. Reversible causes of mental impairment

	Dementia	Delirium	Either or both
Therapeutic drug intoxication			Yes
Depression	Yes		
Metabolic			
a. Azotemia or renal failure (dehydration, diuretics, obstruction, hypokalemia)			Yes
b. Hyponatremia (diuretics, excess antidiuretic hormone, salt wasting, intravenous fluids)			Yes
c. Hypernatremia (dehydration, intravenous saline)		Yes	
d. Volume depletion (diuretics, bleeding, inadequate fluids)			Yes
e. Acid-base disturbance		Yes	
f. Hypoglycemia (insulin, oral hypoglycemics, starvation)			Yes
g. Hyperglycemia (diabetic ketoacidosis, or hyperosmolar coma)		Yes	
h. Hepatic failure			Yes
i. Hypothyroidism			Yes
j. Hyperthyroidism (especially apathetic)			Yes
k. Hypercalcemia			Yes
l. Cushing's syndrome	Yes		
m. Hypopituitarism			Yes
Infection, fever, or both			
a. Viral			Yes
b. Bacterial			
Pneumonia, Pyelonephritis, Cholecystitis, Diverticulitis		Yes	
Tuberculosis			Yes
Endocarditis			Yes
Cardiovascular			
a. Acute myocardial infarct		Yes	
b. Congestive heart failure			Yes
c. Arrhythmia			Yes
d. Vascular occlusion			Yes
e. Pulmonary embolus		Yes	

From NIA Task Force: Senility reconsidered; treatment possibilities for mental impairment in the elderly, Journal of the American Medical Association **244**(3):261-262, 1980.

Table 9-3. Reversible causes of mental impairment—cont'd

	Dementia	Delirium	Either or both
Brain disorders			
a. Vascular insufficiency			
Transient ischemia		Yes	
Stroke			Yes
b. Trauma			Yes
Subdural hematoma		Yes	
Concussion/contusion		Yes	
Intracerebral hemorrhage		Yes	
Epidural hematoma			
c. Infection			
Acute meningitis (pyogenic, viral)		Yes	
Chronic meningitis (tuberculous, fungal)			Yes
Neurosyphilis			Yes
Subdural empyema			Yes
Brain abscess			Yes
d. Tumors			
Metastatic to brain			Yes
Primary in brain			Yes
e. Normal pressure hydrocephalus	Yes		
Pain			Yes
a. Fecal impaction			
b. Urinary retention		Yes	
c. Fracture		Yes	
d. Surgical abdomen		Yes	
Sensory deprivation states such as blindness or deafness			Yes
Hospitalization			
a. Anesthesia or surgery			Yes
b. Environmental change and isolation			Yes
Alcohol toxic reactions			
a. Lifelong alcoholism	Yes		
b. Alcoholism new in old age			Yes
c. Decreased tolerance with age producing increasing intoxication			Yes
d. Acute hallucinosis		Yes	
e. Delirium tremens		Yes	
Anemia			Yes
Tumor—systemic effects of nonmetastatic malignant neoplasm			Yes
Chronic lung disease with hypoxia or hypercapnia			Yes
Deficiencies of nutrients such as vitamin B_{12}, folic acid, or niacin	Yes		
Accidental hypothermia		Yes	
Chemical intoxications			
a. Heavy metals such as arsenic, lead, or mercury			Yes
b. Consciousness-altering agents			Yes
c. Carbon monoxide			Yes

been implicated—diuretics, psychopharmacological agents, sedatives, digitalis, oral antidiabetic agents, analgesics, and antiinflammatory agents. Table 9-3 is a comprehensive portrayal—useful as a checklist of reversible causes of mental impairment.

Depression versus organicity

It is imperative to diagnose depressions that may be masked as organic states. Observe the content of thought and capitalize on the sense of interpersonal responsiveness. The depressed are prone to express a sense of worthlessness. The patient with an organic disorder is likely to be perceived as presenting a "biological" rather than an "emotional" problem. Depressive episodes are self-limited; organic states are not. Identify the specific events or stimuli that precipitated the feelings of depression. Many depressive episodes are realistic responses to loss. Some are influenced by the unconscious or the past history, but because they cannot be readily explained by the present, they are referred to as "exogenous" rather than "reactive." There is a relief of symptoms when actual loss or threat is relieved, compensated for, or replaced; but this is not so with organic disorders. Depression may look similar to the organic disorders, but careful evaluation can differentiate the two. (See Chapter 5.) Here psychological tests, the Goldstein catastrophic reaction, EEG, and other components of the comprehensive examination are most helpful. It must not be forgotten, however, that depression and organic brain disorder can coexist. In depressions one may also see a paranoid trend.

The following letter from the relative of an older woman to a therapist is an example of the kind of evidence often presented.

In order to help you [the therapist] with your evaluation of her problems, I [her relative] thought it best to let you know what I have observed in her behavior, attitude, appearance, and general demeanor the last 6 months. She puts clothes on backwards, inside out, sometimes leaving nightclothes underneath street clothes, and shoes on the wrong feet. She has lost interest in books, television, letter writing. When in my home she follows me constantly. When she can't find me, she goes all over house and garden looking for me and calling my name. She is extremely restless no matter what the situation—she cannot wait for anything, which is one reason we were an hour early for your appointment. When she is in her own apartment and not having dinner in the communal dining room, she is on the phone dialing me every 10 minutes for hours on end. If my husband and I are out, she then dials my friends until our return. She has a habit of making loud "sighs" in my presence and says aloud, "I don't know what I'm going to do." At this time she has made no effort to make new friends at the residential home for older people where she now lives although outwardly she is an extremely friendly and gregarious person.

The diagnosis was that of organic brain disorder with a concurrent depression.

Paranoid states without organic brain disorder

Look for ideas of ruin and for delusions of noxious fumes, delusions of marital infidelity, and the like. Note isolated evidences of projection as well as comprehensive delusional systems. Be aware of cases of folie à deux.[40a] Check for hearing loss, which is associated with suspiciousness and paranoid states.

Subdural hematomas

Falls and fractures are common in old age. Persons over 65 account for 72% of all fatal falls and 30% of all pedestrian fatalities. Subdural hematomas are collections of blood between the dura mater (the hard outer membrane over the brain) and the skull. They may be clinically silent. Again, a careful history may elicit a story of head injury (although the person may not remember falling, because of memory loss), concussion, perhaps coma, delirium, or a syndrome (Korsakoff's) marked by fabrication and confabulation. Papilledema (swollen optic nerve head) and possibly

---

[40a] As described earlier, folie à deux is a form of psychosis in which symptoms, especially paranoid delusions, are shared by two people—most often mother and daughter, two sisters, or husband and wife.

headaches are more common in younger persons. Mental symptoms such as somnolence (sleepiness), confusion, memory loss, and hemiparesis (paralysis on one side) are more common in older persons. The hematomas of older persons are thicker than those in younger persons. This may be because of the decreasing weight of the brain that occurs with age, thereby increasing the space between the brain and skull and making room for the hematoma to expand without increasing intracranial pressure. Subdural hematomas, as well as brain tumors, hypertension, and extracerebral vascular occlusion or narrowing, can often be successfully treated—provided they are discovered.

Drug reactions

The prevalent wide use of drugs, from tranquilizers to antidepressants, has produced a number of negative drug reactions. Although they are useful when properly prescribed and controlled, drugs are also overused and misused. A striking illustration is the use of chemical straightjackets (heavy doses of quieting drugs) to handle patients in nursing homes. Drugs may make a differential diagnosis between functional and organic disorders exceedingly difficult, and discontinuation of the medications during an evaluation period may be required.

SUICIDE INDICATIONS

Suicide in old age is discussed in Chapter 4. We wish to list here (not necessarily in order of frequency or importance) some of the major diagnostic clues for suicide in old age.

Depression (with no anger outlet)
Withdrawal
Bereavement (especially within first year after loss)
Isolation: widowed; single
Expectation of death from some cause
Less organization and complexity of behavior
Induced helplessness
Institutionalization
Physical illness
Alcoholism
Desire and rational decision to protect survivors from financial disaster

Philosophical decision: no more pleasure or purpose
Meaninglessness of life
Decreased self-regard
Organic mental deterioration
Changes in sleep patterns: nightmares
Male
NOTE: A threat to commit suicide is relatively uncommon in this age group. Older people tend to simply kill themselves.

One must be alert for statements from people about killing themselves and be aware of any previous suicide attempts. Self-destruction can be abrupt or drawn out over long periods of time (not eating, not taking one's medicines, alcoholism, delay in seeking treatment, excessive risk taking). Older people account for one fourth of all reported suicides. Therefore a mental health evaluation should give serious consideration to behavior that might indicate self-destructive tendencies.

LEGAL EXAMINATION

Medical doctors, especially psychiatrists, may be called on to evaluate an older person's need for involuntary commitment to an institution or to ascertain aspects of competency (contractual or testamentary capacity). Human beings have a fundamental right to make their own decisions, enter into contracts, vote, make a will, and refuse medical or psychiatric treatment. Each of these decisions represents one's control over one's own life, with the understanding that the consequences may be unfortunate as well as fortunate, folly as well as wisdom. Limitations of such rights or freedom ideally come about only when illnesses invalidate the capacity to make choices or, in the case of legal commitment, when the older person is a danger to him- or herself or to others, physically, or is in clear and present need of immediate care or treatment. Older people also need protection when they are vulnerable to exploitation by others.

In examining an older person for forensic (legal) purposes, the examiner should spell out in detail that fact. The person needs to know that he or she can be represented by an attorney and that statements to the examiner will *not* be protected either by privilege (the legal concept) or by confidentiality (the relationship). The examination should be thorough, and we again suggest use of the personal mental health data form on pp. 203-224.

What is the test of incompetency? "Understanding" is the crucial criterion: the person must have sufficient mental capacity to *understand* the nature and effect of the *particular* transaction in question. The psychiatric diagnosis is not considered, in courts of law, to be as important as judgment.[41]

Contractual capacity (the ability to make contracts) is related to the degree of judgment required—selling a major business is a complex situation that may require a greater degree of judgment than selling a car. One problem sometimes emerging in contractual cases is that in which an older person's judgment may, indeed, be adversely affected by mental or physical disorders, but this fact is unknown to the other party in the contract.

■ A 69-year-old woman was profoundly depressed but outwardly cheerful. She sold her $75,000 home for $55,000. It was a bona fide sale, so there was no later recourse.

The concept of the "lucid interval" is a vague and difficult one, implying the capacity to exercise sound judgment at one time and not another. The multicausal aspects of the emotional and mental disorders of old age indicate the possibility of such intervals. For example, a person with cerebral vascular insufficiency may do well until severe emotional stress (for example, death of a spouse) compromises the equilibrium; after a period of time he or she may again stabilize and be considered "lucid." An evaluator must be extremely thorough in examining the older person for such a possibility.

Testamentary capacity (the ability to make a will) requires that the testator (person who makes the will) be "of sound mind and memory," knowing the condition of his estate, his obligations,

and the import of the provisions of the will. The psychiatric examiner must consider whether the older person is unduly suggestible or under "undue influence" from others. Severe depression and paranoid states, as well as organic brain disorders, may affect the capacity to write a will; however, diagnosis of psychosis, adjudication of guardianship, or commitment per se does not invalidate a will. "Extreme age, mental sluggishness, and defective memory do not render a testator incapable of making a will if he is able to recall to mind his property and the natural objects of his bounty." Alcoholism, addictions, and unusual beliefs (for example, spiritualism) do not by themselves invalidate wills. When there is any doubt of testamentary capacity or when a contesting of the will is anticipated, it is wise of the testator to arrange for a comprehensive medical and psychiatric evaluation while he or she is alive, with a careful and complete report filed until death. By so doing further grief and turmoil can be prevented for the family.

■ An 87-year-old man married his nurse and rewrote his will. Other members of the family challenged his mental soundness and pushed for a postmortem examination of his brain, resulting in bitterness and anguish for everyone concerned.

Guardianship, the appointment of a committee for a person or his estate, should be solely for his benefit and protection. The test is whether the person can or cannot protect himself or arrange his own affairs.[42] Emotional disability, as well as intellectual impairment, is important. (Guilt or feelings of worthlessness may lead a person to give everything away.) Injudicious management and improvidence are difficult to evaluate and are not precisely correlated with intellectual debility. Laws are unclear on many points, and there is a

---

[41]Commitment to a mental hospital is *not* the equivalent of incompetency.

[42]An older person can turn over responsibilities to others without being declared incompetent by (1) appointing a "representative payee" who handles all income and pays bills, (2) authorizing a power of attorney to handle financial affairs (a broader function than a representative payee), or (3) setting up a trust fund.

quality of all-or-none, whereas a continuum or scale of impairment would be more appropriate. Certain disabilities are not considered at all by the law—visual and auditory impairments, loss of speech, and others. Poor people are disadvantaged because of the legal costs of conservatorships[43]; since few states provide for public guardianship (the poor man's conservatorship), estates are easily eroded. The poorly educated and the uninformed are not protected, and the Roman injunction "caveat emptor" (let the buyer beware) holds sway to a greater degree in old age than ever before.

Involuntary commitment is examined more thoroughly in Chapter 11, but we wish to discuss here the question of court cases for mental patients and older people in general. In what passes for kindness, it is often argued that court appearances are too disturbing for the older patient. Even when a hospitalized person decides to call for a jury trial, the hospital psychiatrist may back away and discharge the patient first. We believe there are serious faults with these attitudes. They conceal from the public, from the person involved, and from the psychiatrist and mental health personnel the realities of legal processes and of property and personal rights. Patients often learn from the painful court proceedings; it becomes clear what the situation really is, and the process can have therapeutic effects. Our traditional overestimation of the fragility of patients and, indeed, our paternalism and infantilization can deny people their rights and the opportunity for self-expression.

Court appearances may also assist mental health personnel in sharpening up their diagnostic thinking. A few embarrassing moments under cross-examination in a court of law can be a humbling experience and worth hours of postgraduate training or review. Psychiatrists and other staff who complain of wasting time in court might be well

advised to keep eyes and ears open, taking the occasion to learn something more of the human condition as it unfolds in a courtroom.

The adversary system does have its cruelties, and one might argue for dispassionate commissions wherein commitment, competency, and contractual and testamentary capacities are evaluated. We would support the use of independent commissions comprised of physicians, mental health personnel, and lawyers but subject to administrative and judicial reviews. Hearings must include patients, well represented by counsel. The amount of time provided must be adequate, not just a token. (In Washington, D.C., it was found that the mental health commission operative at St. Elizabeths Hospital often made judgments within minutes.) We also believe, along with others, that the various capacities under consideration (contractual, testamentary, etc.) should be considered separately and in their special contexts, rather than under a global concept called "competence."

REFERENCES

Birren, J.E.: A factorial analysis of the Wechsler-Bellevue Scale to an elderly population, Journal of Consulting Psychology **16:**399, 1952.

Busse, E.W.: Treatment of the non-hospitalized, emotionally disturbed, elderly person, Geriatrics **11:**173-179, 1956.

Busse, E.W., editor: Cerebral manifestations of episodic cardiac dysarrhythmias, Amsterdam, 1979, Excerpta Medica.

Busse, E.W., and Blazer, D.G., editors: Handbook of geriatric psychiatry, New York, 1980, Van Nostrand Reinhold Co.

Butler, R.N.: The facade of chronological age, American Journal of Psychiatry **119:**721-728, 1963.

Butler, R.N.: The life review: an interpretation of reminiscence in the aged, Psychiatry **26:**65-76, 1963.

Butler, R.N., and Perlin, S.: Physiological-psychological-psychiatric interdisciplinary findings. In Birren, J.E., Butler, R.N., Greenhouse, S.W., Sokoloff, L., and Yarrow, M.R.: Human aging: a biological and behavioral study, Pub. No. (PHS) 986, Washington, D.C., 1963, U.S. Government Printing Office (reprinted as Pub. No. [HSM] 71-9051, 1971, 1974).

Costa, P.T., Jr., and McCrae, R.R.: Objective personality assessment. In Storandt, M., Siegler, I.C., and Elias, M.F., editors: The clinical psychology of aging, New York, 1978, Plenum Publishing Corp.

Ehrentheil, O.F.: Differential diagnosis of organic dementias

---

[43]See discussion of role of social service as conservator and New York State's Conservatorship Law of 1973 in Schoenfeld, B., and Tuzil, T.J.: Conservatorship: a move towards more personalized protective service, Journal of Gerontology and Social Work **1:**225-234, 1979.

and affective disorders in aged patients, Geriatrics **12:**426, 1957.

Eisdorfer, C., and Lawton, M.P., editors: The psychology of adult development and aging, Washington, D.C., 1973, American Psychological Association.

Fox, J.L.: Methods map brain function chemically, Chemical Engineer News **56:**20-22, 1978.

Goldstein, K., and Scheerer, M.: Abstract and concrete behavior, Psychological Monograph **53**(2):239, 1941.

Holmes, T.H., and Rahe, R.H.: The social readjustment rating scale, Journal of Psychomatic Research **11:**213-218, 1967.

Jacobs, J.W., Bernhard, M.R., and Delgado, A.: Screening for organic mental syndromes in the medically ill, Annals of Internal Medicine **86:**40-46, 1977.

Kahn, R.L., and Miller, N.E.: Assessment of altered brain function in the aging. In Sporandt, M., Elias, M.F., and Siegler, I.C., editors: The clinical psychology of aging, New York, 1978, Plenum Publishing Corp.

Kety, S.S., and Schmidt, C.F.: The nitrous oxide method for the quantitative determination of cerebral blood flow in men: theory, procedure, and normal values, Journal of Clinical Investigation **27:**476-483, 1948.

Klisz, D.: Neuropsychological evaluation in older persons. In Storandt, M., Elias, M.F., and Siegler, I.C., editors: The clinical psychology of aging, New York, 1978, Plenum Publishing Corp.

Lawton, M.P.: The functional assessment of elderly people, Journal of the American Geriatrics Society **19:**465-481, 1971.

Libow, L.S., and Sherman, F.: The core of geriatric medicine: a guide for students and practitioners, St. Louis, 1980, The C.V. Mosby Co.

Norris, V., and Post, F.: Treatment of elderly psychiatric patients: use of diagnostic classification, British Medical Journal **1:**675-679, 1954.

Perlin, S., and Butler, R.N.: Psychiatric aspects of adaptation to the aging experience. In Birren, J.E., Butler, R.N., Greenhouse, S.W., Sokoloff, L., and Yarrow, M.R., editors: Human aging: a biological and behavioral study, Pub. No. (PHS) 986, Washington, D.C., 1963, U.S. Government Printing Office (reprinted as Pub. No. [HSM] 71-9051, 1971, 1974).

Rahe, R.H., McKean, J.D., and Arthur, R.J.: A longitudinal study of life-change and illness patterns, Journal of Psychosomatic Research **10:**355-366, 1966.

Rossman, I., editor: Clinical geriatrics, ed. 2, Philadelphia, 1979, J.B. Lippincott Co.

Roth, M.: Natural history of mental disorder in old age, Journal of Mental Science **101:**281-301, 1955.

Rypins, R.F., and Clark, M.C.: A screening project for the geriatric mentally ill, California Medicine **109:**273-278, 1968.

Schaie, K.W.: Developmental processes and aging. In Eisdorfer, C., and Lawton, M.P., editors: The psychology of adult development and aging, Washington, D.C., 1973, American Psychological Association.

Schaie, K.W., and Schaie, J.P.: Clinical assessment and aging. In Birren, J.E., and Schaie, K.W., editors: Handbook of the psychology of aging, New York, 1977, Van Nostrand Reinhold Co.

Simon, A., and Cahan, R.B.: The acute brain syndrome in geriatric patients. In Mendel, W.M., and Epstein, L.J., editors: Acute psychotic reaction, Psychiatric Research Report No. 16, Washington, D.C., 1963.

Wells, C.E., and Buchanan, D.C.: The clinical use of psychological testing in evaluation in dementia. In Wells, C.E., editor: Dementia, ed. 2, Philadelphia, 1977, F.A. Davis Co.

Werner, M.M., Perlin, S., Butler, R.N., and Pollin, W.: Self-perceived changes in community-resident aged: "aging image" and adaptation, Archives of General Psychiatry **4:**501-508, 1961.

10

How to keep people at home

Do older people who are ill really prefer staying home if they can get the help they need? Would the rest of us? Knowing what we all know about hospitals and other institutions—the high-priced, impersonal, medically oriented concepts of care and the grim reputations of most institutions for older persons—it seems clear that some alternatives would be eagerly and even desperately welcomed. Institutions seldom feel like home to people who were raised from infancy in family units, and little is done to make them feel homey. Still worse, little is done to make them therapeutic or even livable. A tour of many state hospital geriatric wards, nursing homes, and other treatment and custodial settings designed "especially" for older persons is often enough to frighten otherwise brave people and turn steady stomachs. The concept of "long-term care" is used when older people need care of any sort for chronic impairments. Many people use the term "long-term care" only in connection with institutionalization; but in fact it also covers care in the older person's home or any other location. For a succinct definition:

Long-term health care refers to any professional or personal services required on a recurring or continuing basis by an individual because of chronic physical or mental impairment. It may be provided in a variety of settings including the client's own home.[1]

We talk here about acute and long-term care in the home. In the next chapter we concentrate on acute and long-term care in institutions.

HOW IMPORTANT IS "HOME"?

Home is extraordinarily significant to many older persons. It is part of their identity, a place where things are familiar and relatively unchanging, and a place to maintain a sense of autonomy and control. Some insist on remaining at home "at all costs" to their emotional and physical health and personal security. Such tenaciousness can be laid to a desire for freedom and independence; a fear of loss of contact with familiar and loved people, places, and things; a fear of dying, because of the reputation of hospitals and nursing homes as "houses of death" from which there is no return; and a trepidation about change and the unknown, which frightens people of all ages. In this nation of homeowners where 67% of older people own their homes, the idea of a personal house is deeply ingrained; communal living is viewed as a loss of personal liberty and dignity. The notion of home can refer primarily to the four walls surrounding one, to the neighborhood in which one is located, or to the possessions that make one feel at home. Home may mean certain other individuals living with one or it may mean neighbors, pets, and

[1]U.S. Department of Health, Education and Welfare, Public Health Service, Office of Health Policy, Research and Statistics National Center for Health Statistics: Long term health care: minimum date set, preliminary report of the Technical Consultant Panel on Long Term Health Care Data Set, U.S. National Committee on Vital and Health Statistics, Sept. 8, 1978.

255

plants. It can either be a place where one has lived a good part of one's life or a new place, as when older people move into a retirement community or leave the farm for a home in town. Thus home is whatever the "concept of home" means to each person.

Home can be a euphemism. In our eagerness to recognize the importance of a feeling of home, we must not overlook those older people who dislike their living conditions, who have never felt "at home" where they are, and who are eager to move somewhere else—even to an institution. They may live in a dilapidated rooming house, having a bare room with a lone light bulb suspended from the ceiling, in a boarding house with skimpy meals, in a cheap "retirement hotel" where the bath is shared with drug addicts, alcoholics, or street drifters. Some older people are themselves drifters with no regular residence, no fixed address. They sleep on park benches or in subways, bus and train stations, bowery missions, doorways.

Home may be fine physically but miserable emotionally because of family circumstances. The in-law problem is classic when an older person moves in with a son or daughter. Everyone may end up bitterly unhappy.

■ One 69-year-old woman was living with her son and daughter-in-law. The mother and daughter-in-law had never gotten along and couldn't tolerate talking to each other. The mother was discouraged from participating in housework. She therefore would remain in her pajamas all day, watching television. When her son was due home, she would dress, put on her makeup, and become warm and friendly. She and her daughter-in-law vied for his attentions. The mother complained that she was not invited to help the family and was considered a burden. The daughter-in-law stated that the mother expected total care. The son, caught in the middle between the two women in his life, finally asked his mother to leave.

Many situations with an older parent in the home fortunately work out much more satisfactorily. But one must avoid falling prey to one's own slogans, such as "keep people in their own homes" when this may be totally inappropriate and even cruel. The other battle cry of reformers, "return institutional patients to the community," needs to be looked at with the same careful skepticism. What kind of community? What kind of home will be involved? Successful adjustment and adaptation is no more ensured in the community than anywhere else. Each new generation of reformers and each new change in political administration tend to grab that easy problem-solving device known to bureaucrats as "reorganizing"—to give the impression of progress (change names and titles, shift personnel, start new programs, abandon old ones, move patients around: into institutions, back to communities, into nursing and foster homes, or back to institutions with new names). Actual provision of care is rarely improved by all this shuffling. Each decision concerning home care versus institutional care must be based on the older person's needs, but both alternatives should be as attractive and as therapeutic as it is possible to make them. In general, we believe that home care offers the best treatment location except when people are physically dangerous or require inpatient medical treatment. But it is beneficial only when the home is an adequate place to begin with or can be made adequate by selected interventions.

ADVANTAGES OF HOME CARE

One of the obvious advantages of home care is that most older people prefer it. Care at home offers better morale and security as long as proper services are given to provide comfort, support, and direct treatment of physical and emotional ills. Relatives and service personnel such as homemakers and home health aides can often give more individualized care than nursing staffs in institutions. Families tend to become intimately involved in treatment. Familiar surroundings are reassuring, and the older person does not have to be separated from family members, friends, possessions, and pets. Earlier intervention is possible, since it is not necessary to wait until hospitalization to begin treatment. Hospital beds can be saved for those who are more critically ill. Older people who are very ill or who are not ambulatory are not forced to leave home and travel to get treatment. Physicians, nurses, social workers, and members of all other disciplines involved can become more familiar with community resources and use them more fully as well as point up the need for services not presently available. Older people and their families can receive not only medical and psychiatric care but also social and economic help. And, finally, the older person and the people in his or her life receive a different view of illness and treatment. Instead of being whisked off to the hospital or an institution, people remain where their care can be observed and participated in. It becomes evident that mental or physical illness can be lived with. Life does not have to stop or become totally disrupted, and rehabilitation and recovery may be seen occurring even in the very old and sick. It is clear that removal from home for treatment or long-term care is perceived by many older people as a "punishment" for getting sick. They fear the isolation, the loneliness, and the separation from familiar patterns and people, not to mention the boredom. The thought of "dying alone" becomes a frightening preoccupation. Older people should not have to "serve time" in an institution just because they become ill, unless such care is an absolute necessity or their own personal preference.

It should also be mentioned that home care is a potential consumer market, which could create many new jobs and a whole new service industry. It could open up the mental health professions to an influx of new personnel and new ideas. Some day home services (and nursing homes themselves) may be operated as social or public utilities, well regulated and run in the public interest. New professions may well evolve, having a broader base of skills than is now seen.

USE OF THE HOME FOR SCREENING AND EVALUATION

Keeping older people at home can begin as early as when a request or referral for mental health services is received. Part or all of the evaluation can be done at home, except for technical (usually medical) examinations that require a specific set-

ting. Even when most of an evaluation must be carried out elsewhere, it is important that a direct evaluation of the person's home situation be made. In addition to telling much that is useful about people's lives, such evaluations make it possible to bring services to those older persons who cannot or will not leave their homes to come to a clinic, a hospital, or an agency.

Referral requests for mental health care come from older people themselves, their families, agencies, the police, and other sources, as shown in the following list.

Self-referral
Family
Friends and neighbors
Members of the clergy
Doctors—often internists
Visiting nurse service
Welfare department
Community agencies
Police

The more isolated the older person, the more likely it is that his or her difficulties will remain unnoticed until an emergency occurs and the police are called. Health inspectors, shopkeepers, and service workers such as meter readers, mail carriers, and hotel and apartment clerks may be the link that connects the isolated older person with the police after something obviously begins to go wrong.

After an evaluation of the specific nature of the person's problem has been completed (Chapter 9), a mutually agreeable decision must be made among family members, the older person, and mental health personnel as to the nature and location of treatment to be given. Does mental health care include such diverse services as provision of adequate income, homemakers, or even podiatry (foot treatment)? Our view is that a comprehensive, broad concept of care includes whatever has to be done. We are interested in preserving and rebuilding any aspects of the older person's life that contribute to his or her physical and emotional well-being. Rather than offering the rather narrow specialty skills most of us learned during professional and vocational training, we advocate learning the additional skills necessary to meet the variety of needs older people present. This is both good mental health treatment and good preventive care, as well as sound education for mental health personnel.

SOME FACTORS TO CONSIDER REGARDING HOME CARE

The decision to provide treatment in the home is influenced by what the older person needs and/or wants, the family situation, and the services and choices of care available in a community. In terms of the individual, one must know if he or she is physically and mentally capable of self-care, either alone or with assistance.[2] The list below gives the most important of the skills needed for living at home, particularly if one is alone part or all of the time.

Orientation to time, place, person
Cooking and feeding oneself
Bathing
Dressing
Grooming
Toileting
Continence
Transferring from bed to chair
Standing and walking
Climbing stairs
Fire and accident security
Shopping
Money management
Ability to follow instructions (for example, medication)
Ability to seek assistance when needed
Social participation

Other considerations are adequate transportation, socializing opportunities, quick availability of emergency medical care, financial circumstances, and the neighborhood crime conditions. Can the rent or mortgage be paid—and the utilities, repair costs, and property taxes? Does the older person have the inner resources to manage on his or her own? Are there interests and activities? Personal relationships? Sexual outlets? Religious and spiritual supports?

One must also consider those people whom the older person will be living with or relying on heavily. Does home include other family members, roomers, or companions? Is it possible to be at home in someone else's home, perhaps with sons or daughters? Can sharing and communal living work in the average family? Or would the older person be more content in a communal arrangement with elderly persons or mixed with other age groups? Relatives or friends with whom an older person lives may not be willing or able to care for the person at home any longer. Sometimes there are no comfortable or easy solutions as the needs of the elders clash with those of younger family members. In most situations families will make every sacrifice to keep an older person and may need help in reconsidering whether this is the wisest course of action. In other cases they need support and opportunity for respite if they do decide on home care. It should be known that in the United States 80% of home health care for older people is performed by families, primarily by the middle-aged daughters of older men and women. As these women become increasingly employed outside the home, less free care will be available and more supplemental care will be needed.[3]

What happens when the "women in the middle" (ages 40 to 55) go to work? Brody[4] sees a shift toward the "young-old" women, ages 55 to 74, who become responsible for the care of the old-old—those over 75. The young-old themselves are increasingly in the paid workforce, and many will have to earn enough to buy "parent care" when the older people of the family are no longer autonomous. Brody sees the danger of women over age 50 becoming a new high-risk group be-

---

[2] For one approach, see Lawton, M.P., and Brody, E.M.: Assessment of older people: self-maintaining and instrumental activities of daily living, The Gerontologist **9:**179-186, 1969.

[3] Brody, E.M.: Economic and environmental issues relating to aging, with some thoughts about women in the middle. In Aging: research and perspectives, Monograph No. 3, New York, 1979, Columbia University, Graduate School of Journalism, pp. 37-45.

[4] Ibid.

cause of their many roles: wife and possibly caregiver to a husband when he is ill, out-of-home worker, parent of young adults, grandparent, and caregiver to own or husband's parents (the great-grandparents).

The 1980 HEW Task Force on Implementation of the Report to the President from the President's Commission on Mental Health recognized that

> Women, in particular, already provide a great deal of the unpaid, day-to-day care of the dependent young, old, and sick. It is important for federal, state, and local governments to continue to develop formal support systems to supplement these already existing informal supports. With half of the women in America in the work force, women cannot be expected to provide volunteer support for all of those in need. It is important that women not be stereotyped into the role of caregivers, and, as informal support systems are developed, it will be important for men to be active participants in the system.

The essential consideration in opting for home care is the kind of services one can expect to be available to the older person. Often these will ultimately determine whether it is possible for the person to stay at home. In this chapter we go further than in any other in describing care that should and may exist but probably does not. Coverage under Medicare and the insurance programs for older people encourage hospitalization rather than outpatient care. The very poor may be able to get some home services through welfare, but self-supporting people tend not to be able to afford them. Free care or care based on the ability to pay is sporadically available through charitable agencies and United Fund organizations. The federal government, through Medicare, has weakly sponsored provisions for home health aides, cutting back funds in the 1970s.

HOME CARE—WHAT *REALLY* EXISTS AND WHAT *IDEALLY* SHOULD EXIST

Any truly serious national effort to keep people in their own homes requires provision for direct home delivery of health services. The middle class as well as the poor suffer from the unavailability

of such care. Home care should be available to the chronically ill, to those recuperating from hospitalization, to those who may be acutely ill but can be treated outside a hospital, and finally to all those older people who simply need some help here and there to fills in the gaps left by various losses or declining functions. We will describe the services we believe are essential if home care is to be a comprehensive approach to the treatment and prevention of mental illness. Evaluations, treatment plans, and coordination of care by some responsible person or group are, of course, essential. It is usually not difficult to figure out who the responsible coordinating person should be because there are precious few agencies and individuals, professional or otherwise, who work directly in the community, despite much rhetoric to the contrary. In the past the family doctor took care of physical problems (using the house call, long since placed on the endangered list of extinct medical practices) and members of the clergy attended to spiritual and/or emotional matters, buttressed by neighbors and nearby family members.[5] However, doctors and the clergy began spending more time in their offices, and crime, especially in urban areas, frightened away many of those who might have preferred direct community work. Now only two major groups routinely make house calls: public health nurses and social workers. Much to their credit, members of these professions—usually women—continue working unarmed and often alone in high crime areas where the poor and many urban older persons reside. Some medical doctors, psychiatrists, and related professionals are becoming reinterested and involved in community work, particularly through community mental health centers and outreach programs. Paraprofessionals of all kinds are beginning to do mental health work. But the faithful standbys are still the nurses and social workers, and they are likely to be the cen-

---

[5] As can be seen, home care is not a radical new idea but a return to some of the sound principles of the past, strengthened by newer medical and psychiatric understanding and techniques.

tral coordinating figures in any plans for provision of home care.

The outline here summarizes the range of services that should be part of the repertoire of home care.

Mental health intake, screening, and evaluation
Mental health care
Physician's services
Nursing services
Homemaker–home health aides
Physical therpay
Occupational therapy
Speech therapy
Inhalation therapy
Dental care
Nutrition service (Meals-on-Wheels, group dining, food distribution programs)
Health education
Laundry service
Social services
   Information and referral
   Financial support
   Legal services
   Personal needs (transportation, telephone reassurance, grooming, shopping, companions, friendly visitors, pets)
   Family "respite" services
   Night sitters (for short-term illnesses)
   Home safety
   Chore services (handyman) or home maintenance repairs
   Recreation (community center, senior center)
   Employment and volunteer work (VISTA, Senior Aides, SCORE, Peace Corps, Foster Grandparent, Green Thumb, etc.)
   Education (home library service, academic courses)
Religious support (clerical or pastoral counseling, "practical" ecumenism)
Police assistance
Outpatient care in clinics, community mental health center, day hospitals, day-care centers
Multipurpose senior centers
Protective services
Screening before hospital admission

We repeat that many communities will not have all or even most of these resources. Some can be created at little or no cost by volunteer groups; others can be lobbied for in state legislatures. Pressure can be put on professional groups and voluntary agencies to make their services available or create new services. Below are listed six sources of financial support for home health care services.

1. Medicare.
2. Medicaid.
3. Social Services: Under Title XX (SSA), matching payments to states are provided.
4. Older Americans Act: Under Title III (OAA), payments are made to states for distribution to local Area Agency on Aging (AAA).
5. Veterans Administration: The VA provides aid and assistance grants to families caring for disabled veterans for purchase of home health service. The VA also furnishes these services directly, usually through a VA hospital.
6. Internal Revenue Service: The IRS provides for an exemption under the income tax law for families purchasing home health care for a dependent parent.

Section 222 of the Social Security Amendments of 1972 provides authority for research, experiments, and demonstration projects related to health care reimbursement and financing policy in a number of areas, including day care, intermediate care, and homemaker services. Using Section 222, a variety of alternatives to institutionalization are being studied, such as (1) Homemaker and Day Care Demonstration Experiments and (2) Triage—Coordinated Delivery of Services to the Elderly. The Triage project provided for a single-entry system involving the assessment of the older client's needs and the coordination and development of services to older persons in a seven-town region of central Connecticut. The main purpose of the experiment was to find out whether the availability of a full spectrum of coordinated health and health-related services for impaired older persons would result in better health and lower costs than under the existing health care system.

In planning a program of home care, one must be clear about the objectives, whether rehabilitation, maintenance of the status quo, or support through decline and eventual death. Older people themselves should voice their opinions about the kind of mental health care they want in old age.

Change is the most constant factor in the treatment of older persons. Treatment must be constantly evaluated for its appropriateness and be altered whenever circumstances change in the direction of either improved functioning or greater illness. It can be as harmful to overtreat someone who is trying to get better as to undertreat. Dependency and loss of functioning can result if people of any age are overprotected and coddled when they do not need it.

The passage of the 1980 Mental Health Systems Act was aimed at correcting the many inadequacies found in the Community Mental Health Center (CMHC) Program (begun in 1963) by the 1979 President's Commission on Mental Illness. The Act, if adequately funded each year by Congress, contains the following features.

1. More community care will be provided for those who have been underserved by the current CMHC programs—namely the old, the young and adolescent, the chronically mentally ill, and certain racial and ethnic minorities. Projects can be specifically targeted for these groups.

2. All federal funding for community care must go through the states, which will act as service coordinators and program evaluators. There will be no direct federal funding to local communities as in the 1963 CMHC Act. The purpose is to return authority to the states and avoid a two-tiered federal-state system of authorization and review.

3. However, none of the money authorized can go to state hospitals. All of it must go to community-based care; thus states are being required to commit themselves to community care of chronic-care patients if they want federal funds.

HOME DELIVERY OF SERVICES
Mental health services

All the services mentioned in this chapter are considered by us as part of mental health care. In addition, the specific services of psychiatrists, so-cial workers, and all other members of mental health teams should be routinely available in people's homes. The two major types of psychiatric outreach care are emergency care (usually for persons making suicide threats and attempts or for those wandering in the streets as a result of brain damage or functional psychosis) and ongoing therapy for those who find it difficult to leave home. Evaluations for mental health services as well as screening for institutional admissions can be done in homes.[6] Screening should of course emphasize keeping people out of institutions, when appropriate, by use of home care. Mental health services are discussed more fully in Chapter 12. With outreach services one sees many people who would never appear at clinics and would only be seen in hospitals as a result of an emergency.

Physicians' services

Physicians should be on call for emergency home visits on a 24-hour basis and for ongoing medical evaluation and management of patients. Contact may vary from brief intensive care to weekly or monthly medical supervision and treatment. Laboratory services can also be provided. Specimens—blood, urine, feces, etc.—can be obtained from the person at home and analyzed in the laboratory. Electrocardiograms and other selected studies can be made in the home.

There are two major problems standing in the way of home medical care: doctors' reluctance to make house calls and a lack of financial resources that might make it possible to tempt them from their offices. Government figures document the decline in house calls. In 1957-1958 doctors made about 45.7 million calls; in 1966-1967 only 27.3 million were made, although the population had risen. By 1972 less than half the doctors in the country still made house calls, and most of these

---

[6] Arne Querido's famous Amsterdam psychiatric emergency service sent teams to the homes of persons in crises. The San Francisco Geriatrics Screening Project and the Baltimore City Health Department Geriatric Evaluation Service are illustrative of the better screening programs in the United States that stress home visits.

practiced in rural areas. In most cases doctors believe they can treat a patient better in an office or in a hospital emergency room and that the house calls take too much time. "It is rare that a house call is justified" is a common viewpoint.

Profit-making house call organizations have been established but so far only in a few large cities. The oldest is Health Delivery Systems, Inc., of New York City. Next is the Bridge Medical Associates of New York. Los Angeles has Health Systems, Inc. Some local medical societies offer emergency services. Residents in teaching hospitals, older semiretired doctors, newly licensed doctors, and moonlighting military and government doctors make up the bulk of the staff of these organizations. Armed guards are sometimes available to accompany doctors into "hazardous" neighborhoods. Radio equipment vans are used by the Los Angeles organization. The patient's own doctor receives a report from the house call doctors. Medicare will cover 80% of what is determined to be the customary and prevailing fee for a particular area.

Doctors who make house calls catch emergency situations such as heart attacks and appendicitis in early stages as well as providing relief from relatively minor but extremely painful ailments such as ear infections. They can determine if hospitalization is called for or if other services are needed. And they provide an enormous sense of security to the older person who may be worried about health or unable to leave home for care of aggravating but noncritical illnesses.

■ Mrs. H, a black woman of 85 years, lives in a public housing project with her daughter's family. She is confined to her second-floor room because of arthritis and a disabled hip. She seldom sees a doctor because her son-in-law has a heart condition that prohibits him from carrying her down the stairs. In addition, her daughter must take off a day's work to transport her in the family car. Mrs. H does not want to put an extra burden on them, so she seldom mentions her aches and pains. She wept with disbelief and happiness at the sight of the physician from the neighborhood community mental health service who came to see her in her room.

Doctors are poorly distributed geographically. Some areas—the urban poor and the rural—typically have few doctors and other health personnel. In Washington, D.C., 90% of doctors are located west of Rock Creek Park, which essentially divides white (west) from black Washington, where some 60% of the black population live.

The National Health Service Corps is the unit in the U.S. Public Health Service charged with carrying out the emergency Health Personnel Act of 1970 (Public Law 91-623). This Act authorizes the assignment of commissioned officers and civil service personnel of the Service to areas in the United States where health services are inadequate because of critical shortages of health personnel. This program is not meant to solve the problem of the overall shortage of physicians and other health personnel in the nation but is aimed at alleviating some of the more acute problems stemming from the maldistribution of U.S. health workers.

The United States has 1 physician for every 650 people, compared to 580 in Italy and 400 in the U.S.S.R. The 1970 report of the Carnegie Commission on Higher Education prescribed a shortened program for medical schools and residency programs. Women and minority group members, who now make up only 7% of doctors, should be vigorously encouraged. One state, California, has passed a law permitting physicians' assistants to work under doctors' supervision, doing much of the medical work. Highly trained medical corpsmen discharged from the military services have a knowledge of emergency medicine that is often far superior to the experience of doctors in civilian life. There are training programs for assistant physicians who are known as paramedics, clinical associates, and health practitioners. Nurses also are taking over certain functions of the physician and are called "nurse practitioners."

Specialization by doctors is another problem for older people. Older people frequently look in vain for a "family doctor." Although there has been insufficient congressional emphasis on geriatrics, in the 1970s congressional legislation aimed at encouraging doctors to enter family practice. Geriatric medicine has not been recognized as a specialty in the United States, although 40% of internists' patients are older people with whom they spend 60% of their time. In spite of the fact that older people are medically underserved, a 1980 report by the Graduate Medical Education National Advisory Committee (GMENAC) failed to consider the impact on physicians of the growing number of older people. Others have recognized that physicians in nearly all specialties need special training in geriatric medicine, in addition to their regular training; this would open up a whole new area of expertise as well as a new clientele.[7]

Nursing services

The services included under home nursing care are those of *registered nurses* (RNs), whose two specialties pertinent to older persons are public health nursing and psychiatric nursing; *licensed practical nurses* (LPNs); and *home health aides*. The last two groups are supervised by registered nurses.

We shall attempt to clarify the work of each of these groups as they care for older persons. *Public health nursing* refers to RNs and sometimes to LPNs who work for tax-supported city or county health departments. They visit families in their homes, provide direct nursing care, give health guidance, participate in communicable disease control programs, and staff public health clinics. They may give emergency care as well as care for acute and chronic illness. They can instruct people in the use of community health and social resources and make authorized investigations of convalescent homes, nursing homes, and other institutions. Referrals usually come from public health clinics or city and county hospitals as well as other public agencies. There is a heavy concentration of poor and inner-city people as clientele. Services are free of charge to those eligible.

Another group of nurses works with the *Visiting Nurse Association* (VNA),[8] a voluntary organization supported by local United Givers' funds, endowments, gifts, patients' fees, and contracts with health and welfare departments, the American Cancer Society, the Multiple Sclerosis Association, the local Heart Association, the Veterans Administration, Medicare, and others. These nurses provide approximately the same services as public health nurses[9] but tend to have smaller caseloads and can devote more time to individual patients. Public health nurses may each have several hundred patients as well as responsibilities in clinics and schools. Both groups wear similar blue uniforms, and community familiarity with these uniforms gives them protection as they work in high crime neighborhoods. Visiting nurses do more direct home nursing, while public health nurses carry an added responsibility for preventive and community work. Referrals to visiting nurses come from private doctors and private hospitals, in the form of patient and family self-referrals, and from overloaded public health nurses. Visiting nurses care for both poor and middle-class patients. Older people are required to pay a fee adjustable to their income or may be eligible for free service through one of the organizations contracting with VNA and the third-party payments of Medicare and Medicaid.

LPNs work under the supervision of RNs and perform many of the same nursing skills. *Home health aides* also provide simple nursing care, to be discussed later. For those who can afford very expensive services, a number of agencies supply *private duty RNs, LPNs,* and *nurses aides* for up to 24-hour total nursing care.

Home nursing service enables older people to leave hospitals sooner, as well as keeping them at home longer before institutionalization. Some of the common ailments for which persons are treated

[7] Kane, R., Solomon, D., Beck, J., Keeler, E., and Kane, R.: The future need for geriatric manpower in the United States, New England Journal of Medicine **302**(24):1327-1332, 1980.

[8] Other services provided by the VNA include homemaker–home health aides, physical and speech therapies, medical social work, and psychiatrically trained nurses.

[9] In some communities visiting nurses and public health nurses have merged their staffs and functions, while in others they work separately.

are strokes, cerebrovascular accidents, arthritis, cancer, hip fractures, paraplegia, and minimal to moderate chronic brain syndromes. Teaching is another nursing function; an example is the self-administration of insulin for diabetes. Family members can be taught to do a variety of tasks, including physical therapy. Problems with incontinence, bedsores, personal care of teeth and mouth, bed baths, skin care, grooming, and feeding are tasks of the nursing personnel. They are also trained to look at the patient's family from a life cycle perspective: If there are children, are they immunized? Is the mother receiving prenatal care? What can be done about the father's chest pains? All this is in addition to the original reason for the visit, which was to serve the older patient.

There has not been an increase in nursing personnel to meet the growing numbers of older people in the community. Federal and state funding programs have not recognized the need for care other than for short-term intervention linked to acute illness. Relatively few professional nurses and LPNs are employed in home health agencies. Many agencies are now cutting back on nursing staff because of restrictive Medicare regulations, curtailment of Medicaid benefits, and reduced voluntary support.

Homemaker–home health aide services[10]

The term "homemaker–home health aide" refers to one and the same person, although in some parts of the nation these functions are distributed among several persons, for example, a housekeeper and a nurses aid. "Homemaker" describes the full range of homemaking activities available to people with either short-term or long-term physical and emotional illness or disability. "Home health aide" is a title found in Medicare regulations and involves a somewhat narrower definition of care, somewhat like a nurs-

ing assistant or nurses aide in a hospital who complements RNs and LPNs by performing simple medical procedures as well as "personal care." Home health aides may take the patient's vital signs, apply simple dressings, and give massages, baths, grooming assistance, and physical therapy. Anything directly connected with an individual's care is part of their work: light cooking, cleaning the patient's room, and washing clothes for the patient. Strictly speaking, they are not allowed to provide the broader, family-wide care of the home, which is the realm of the homemaker. Training and supervision emphasize both aspects of the homemaker–home health aide: the performance of household tasks and the nursing care that is medically prescribed.

Homemaker–home health aides are always employed by an agency, organization, or administrative unit that selects, trains, and supervises them. They can be obtained through the recommendations of physicians, nurses, social workers, and health institutions as well as on a self-referred basis. Services may be free (for those eligible for welfare assistance) or paid for by third-party payments. In some cases fees are charged according to ability to pay or on a straight fee basis. The Upjohn Homemakers, Inc. is an example of a private pharmaceutical company's offering a wide range of home care services, from nurses to homemakers and live-in companions, in 50 metropolitan areas.

Many communities across the nation are without homemaker–home health aide services, according to the National Council for Homemaker–Home Health Aide Services.[11] There were an estimated 60,000 homemaker–home health aides available in 1975,[12] as compared to an estimated need for 300,000.[13] The latter figure is based on Western European experience—for example,

---

[10] Home health aide services are covered by Medicare, whereas homemaker services are not. As of June 1975, Part A of Medicare allowed 100 free home health visits during 1 year after discharge from a hospital or a participating skilled nursing facility. Part B allows an additional 100 visits per year, but the patient pays the first $60.

[11] National Council for Homemaker–Home Health Aide Services, 67 Irving Pl., New York, N.Y. 10003. One can obtain a "Directory of Homemaker Services" from the Superintendent of Documents, U.S. Government Printing Office, Washington, D.C. 20402.

[12] According to the U.S. Labor Department's *Occupational Outlook Quarterly* in 1975.

[13] Reference omitted in proof.

Holland, Scandinavia, and Great Britain—of 1 homemaker per 1,000 people under 65 years of age and 1 homemaker per 100 persons age 65 and older. England, with a population of nearly 50 million (one fourth of the United States population), has 60,000 persons serving as home helpers. Sweden, with a population of 8 million, has 35,000 homemakers (called "samaritans").

Homemaker–home health aide services in the United States began more than 50 years ago (by 1958 there were still only 1,700 homemakers in the United States); they were first founded voluntarily. Later they were included on a limited basis in public welfare programs, but financing for the most part still comes chiefly from voluntary sources such as United Community Funds. Federal funds are usually small and available only for pilot programs to establish services or innovative features in an ongoing program.[14] Medicare and Medicaid provide limited coverage, and federal matching funds have helped finance services in a few areas under public welfare auspices. The National Council for Homemaker–Home Health Aide Services sets national standards for aides and is supported by 109 agency members, 150 agency associates, and 36 organizations, plus scores of foundations, corporations, and volunteers.

Quality homemaker–home health aide services that meet national professional standards will not be purchased cheaply, yet the cost is a small fraction of the expense of supporting an infirm or disabled person in a public or private institution. This is illustrated by the estimate of the Department of Health, Education and Welfare that shortening each hospital stay by a single day would reduce the present astronomical cost of hospital care in the United States by over $1 billion a year. The average cost for homemaker–home health aide services across the country is $6.00 per hour. This includes administrative costs, cost of training the aide, and the aide's time for service. (Cost per

hour varies depending on whether the aides are unionized or not.)[15]

The 1971 White House Conference on Aging delegates urged provision of broadened services in the home and other alternatives to nursing home care, as a public service, without out-of-pocket payments required under Medicare. The National Council of Senior Citizens has long urged homemaker and home health services as an alternative to nursing home care. A resolution adopted by the 1971 National Council convention reads as follows:

A nationwide program of comprehensive long term care is urgently needed and should be developed without further delay. The deficiencies of long term care, so evident in existing health services, are becoming more and more acute.

Programs of long term care, sought by delegates to the National Council's tenth annual convention, should recognize the potentials of such innovations as day care hospitals and neighborhood health services so as to obviate the need for expensive nursing home care and provide a more pleasant environment for those requiring long term care.

Physical, occupational, and speech therapies

Physical, occupational, and speech therapies, especially physical and speech, are partly reimbursable under Medicare, but severe restrictions limit their use. Thus patients may receive a great deal of rehabilitative work in hospitals following bone and joint diseases and strokes, but the investment is lost because home care follow-up is not given.[16]

---

[14] For example, the Office of Economic Opportunity funded a pilot training program for "family health workers," recruiting trainees with a minimum fifth-grade education from welfare rolls.

[15] The General Accounting Office recently published two reports: *Home Health Care Services: Tighter Fiscal Controls Needed* (Dec. 30, 1977), assessing the cost-effectiveness of home care, and *Home Health: The Need for a National Policy to Better Provide for the Elderly*, (Dec. 30, 1977). For a copy of these reports write to the U.S. General Accounting Office, DHISF, P.O. Box 6015, Gaithersburg, Md. 20760.

[16] The Curative Work Shop in Milwaukee is an example of an outstanding rehabilitation agency. This comprehensive community outpatient center offers among its components an adult rehabilitation program and a home services program. It is a voluntary agency, begun more than 50 years ago, and is certified under Medicare and Medicaid.

The physical therapist should be responsible for any equipment and appliances necessary for rehabilitation, in addition to the actual provision of therapy. Physical exercise on a daily basis should be introduced, following an appropriate medical evaluation, if the older person does not exercise regularly. Two kinds of exercise are usually indicated: one to keep the body and its muscles and joints limber and the other to increase the endurance and capacity of the cardiovascular system.[17]

Massage is one of the oldest forms of healing art and is beneficial in later life. It may be used to relax muscle tension, improve circulation, reduce edema and induration, and stretch adhesions from surgery. It is not a means of weight reduction. It has psychological value in providing "touching" from one person to another. It can be taught to spouses and other family members of the older person.[18]

Occupational therapy (O.T.) is often stereotyped as "arts and crafts" or is considered "infantilizing" or "paternalistic." This is unfortunate. Properly prescribed O.T. is of great value in maintaining or restoring one's self-mastery.

Occupational therapy is concerned with a person's ability and capacity to perform tasks of daily living which enable him to be productive and maintain a satisfying life. Through the use of activities, selected according to the individual's developmental level and health needs, the occupational therapist evaluates the areas related to psychological and social functioning, motor and sensory integrative functioning, cognitive and performance abilities. Occupational therapists seek to teach, restore, and maintain the occupational performance skills, behaviors, and attitudes crucial to independent and healthy functioning. Home and daily family role demands, work and play needs, and social or community factors which impede or contribute to health form the primary perspective of occupational therapy practice.[19]

At its best, O.T. is geared toward helping the individual improve his functioning in any way possible, as defined by the person, his family, and the therapist. This can be done through any form of therapeutic activity that encourages self-expression and use of those resources available to the individual. For example, one occupational therapist uses the "life review" concept in her O.T. group program to encourage older people to examine their lives in a constructive way.[20]

Dental services

"Visiting dentists" are available in some areas and should be provided for all older people who find it difficult to leave their homes. Dentistry is not covered by Medicare, even though it is a critical element of nutrition and general health.

Nutrition services

Food stamps, governmental supplemental food programs, Meals-on-Wheels, group dining, and homemaker–home health aides who shop for and prepare food are some of the means of combating the hunger and malnutrition found in many older people. The best medical prescription for countless older persons would be a prescription for food rather than drugs. Reversible (and ultimately irreversible) brain syndromes can result from malnutrition. It is imperative to examine for evidences of malnutrition and hypovitaminosis even in the affluent, whose eating habits may be poor. Low-income older persons must scrimp on food. Psy-

---

[17] *The Fitness Challenge in the Later Years,* prepared jointly by the Administration on Aging and the President's Council on Physical Fitness and Sports, Pub. No. (OHD/AOA) 73-20802, May 1968 (reprinted Nov. 1973). Available from the U.S. Department of Health, Education and Welfare, Office of Human Development, Administration on Aging, Washington, D.C. 20201.

[18] Downing, G., and Rush, A.K.: The massage book, New York, 1972, Random House, Inc.

[19] Janet B. Sheridan of the Occupational Therapy Association, Rockville, Md., personal communication, 1978. See also American Occupational Therapy Association: Occupational therapy: its definition and functions, American Journal of Occupational Therapy **26:**204-205, 1972.

[20] Kiernat, J.M.: The use of life review activity with confused nursing home residents, American Journal of Occupational Therapy **33:**306-310, 1979. For a general overview of occupational therapy, see Lewis, S.C.: The mature years: a geriatric occupational therapy text, Thorofare, N.J., 1979, Charles B. Slack, Inc.

chological conditions—loneliness, depression, apathy, confusion—can induce malnutrition, which in turn furthers these symptoms. Physical disabilities can keep people from shopping and cooking.

Congress passed legislation in 1972 for a national program for one nutritiously planned hot meal a day, 5 days a week, to people over 60 years of age. The meals are served in the form of group dining in schools, churches, synagogues, and community centers and are also delivered to people's homes. The federal government provides 90% matching money, with state and local governments or private nonprofit organizations providing the remaining 10%. Although the measure emphasized that the projects be located in low-income areas, having a low income is not a requirement and there is no eligibility test. Anyone over 60 can eat the meals. This is particularly important, in our opinion, because "means tests" or special low-income programs for the poor lead to angry public feelings toward the poor and humiliation for the recipients of such programs. By 1980 some 600,000 people participated daily in the nutrition program for older persons (Title III of the Older Americans Act).

The Department of Agriculture has a Commodities Distribution or Donable Foods Program that dates back to the Depression. For example, the District of Columbia distributes this food through the D.C. Department of Public Health under the title "Supplemental Foods Program," but people over 65 are not eligible. (Only children and pregnant women or new mothers are eligible.) The food in the program consists of evaporated milk, canned meats, scrambled egg mix, canned juices and vegetables, farina, and other staples.

The Food Stamp Act was passed by Congress in 1964 to provide immediate food for needy families. The program is part of the Department of Agriculture. Low-income people purchase stamps at less than face value and redeem them for food in standard food stores. Of the 19 million registered in 1976, about 15% were 65 and older. Food stamps can also be used for Meals-on-Wheels but not for group dining.

In some areas nutritionists are available to consult with patients and families about food needs and food preparation.

Social services

Social services are services that are not strictly medical or psychiatric but instead represent economic and social supports. In the past, social service has been synonymous with social work, but this is no longer true. Many other professions have become involved: members of the clergy, police officers, nurses, government officials, volunteers, paraprofessionals, and physicians who are actively working in the community. In home care, however, it is still most often the social worker who works together with nursing personnel to coordinate a program designed for an individual. Many homemaker—home health aide services are administered and/or supervised by professional social workers. However, only 20% of certified home health agencies offer social services.

Information and referral

How does the older person find out about services? Some cities have information and referral services especially for the elderly. If not, local or state commissions or advisory committees on aging may be helpful. Social services, human resources, or welfare departments (the names vary in municipalities and states) usually have information numbers to call. The same is true of local health and welfare councils and local mental health associations. The 1,160 Social Security district and branch offices can provide information. Family Service agencies are another resource. There are over 200 of these in the United States.[21]

Some of the agencies and institutions furnishing direct service to older people are welfare offices, voluntary agencies (the Hearing Aid Society, Societies for the Blind, etc.), public health departments, including community mental health centers, hospitals (both medical and psychiatric), visiting nurse services, nursing homes, employ-

---

[21] For information contact the Family Service Association of America, 44 E. 23rd St., New York, N.Y. 10010.

ment offices, departments of vocational rehabilitation, religious organizations, and the police.

Financial support

Regardless of potential benefits of home care, one must be realistic about whether a person can survive financially. All sources for financial support must be explored for the older person at home, including free or low-cost services and any pensions or financial assistance for which he or she might be eligible. It is not unusual to find older people who do not know they are eligible for Medicare, Medicaid, Supplemental Security Income, Veterans benefits, and even Social Security and income tax benefits. Federal tax laws allow a double exemption for people over 65 years of age and two double exemptions for a married couple. For the blind, still another exemption is allowable. It is hoped that in the future there will be money available for families to keep older people at home —direct payments, monies for construction of home additions or renovations, and other expenses.

For homeowners it is important to understand the upkeep and property tax situation. Many older homeowners face financial crises and may be forced to sell their homes. Older renters experienced substantial rent rises, partly necessitated by property tax increases. Energy costs spiraled to such an extent that many older persons were forced to cut back on heat, air conditioning, light, and other energy expenses. One effect was an increase in accidental hypothermia—lowering of body temperature to such an extent that coma and even death can result. Older people are particularly susceptible to temperature changes because their bodies no longer regulate their temperature as well as in the past.[22]

For the very poor, welfare is usually the last resort. Supplemental Security Income is not enough for decent subsistence but at least promotes a slower rate of starvation than would occur without it. Money for food must often be sacrificed for medical care and medical supplies as well as other crucial living expenses. Clothing is not a part of many welfare budgets; neither are household articles and furniture.

Personal needs (companions, pets, telephones, shopping, transportation, grooming, etc.)

Older persons may need live-in or parttime companions, help with shopping and transportation,[23] instructions or direct help with grooming (home visits from beauticians and barbers do wonders for mental health), and appliances and aides to support or compensate for various disabilities (special handles near toilet and tub, wheelchairs, wide doorframes, etc.).

A telephone can mean a longer life. The National Innovations Center of London, England, reported in 1972 that people without a phone had significantly higher mortality. In increasing numbers of urban, suburban, and rural areas, telephone reassurance services have been established under the auspices of private and public agencies. Volunteers often work the phones and check to see if older people living alone are all right.[24] Special

---

[22] Besdine, R.W.: Accidental hypothermia: the body's energy crisis, Geriatrics **34**:51-59, 1979; Butler, R.N.: Energy and aging: the impact of rising energy costs on older Americans; testimony before the U.S. Senate Special Committee on Aging, Apr. 5, 1977; and U.S. Department of Health, Education and Welfare, National Institute on Aging: A winter hazard for the old: accidental hypothermia, Pub. No. (NIH) 78-1646, 1978.

[23] An interdisciplinary workshop conducted by the Administration on Aging and the Departments of Transportation and Housing and Urban Development has provided a multifaceted depiction of the interrelationships of transportation and aging (Cantilli, E.J., and Shmelzer, J.L., editors: Transportation and aging: selected issues, Washington, D.C., 1970, U.S. Government Printing Office). An especially valuable description of older people's medical and physiological characteristics was included (Libow, L.S.: Older people's medical and physiological characteristics: some implications for transportation. In Transportation and aging: selected issues, Washington, D.C., 1970, U.S. Government Printing Office, pp. 14-18).

[24] Guidelines for a telephone reassurance service, Superintendent of Documents, Washington, D.C., 1972, U.S. Government Printing Office. (Booklet gives a description of the service along with instructions on how to initiate such a service.)

telephones are available for the hard-of-hearing.

Given the state of loneliness and isolation affecting significant numbers of older people, pets can be directly supportive of mental well-being. Dogs and cats are the most favored pets, in that order. For the older person a dog has the added advantage of providing some protection. Size, the need for exercise, and economy are three key points in selection. A large dog requires a daily walk and eats a great deal. On the other hand, a small dog like a poodle can be expensive to maintain because of necessary grooming every 6 weeks to avoid skin problems, sore feet, and eye problems. Poodles and certain other dogs have the advantage of not shedding, helpful to allergic persons and to housekeeping. One can acquire a dog from the Humane Society or an animal shelter free or at a modest cost, depending on locale. A female dog is usually more tractable. Big dogs may bark less than little dogs, and the bark of a little dog may fend off an intruder. In England one can get house insurance at lower premiums if one owns a dog, and in the United States a dog is tax deductible if obtained *after* a robbery. Older people may enjoy participating in dog shows.

Cats are easier to train than dogs and cost less to maintain. Birds bring pleasure to many older people. Canaries, finches, and parakeets are especially popular. Perhaps the easiest, least expensive, and least time-consuming pets to care for are fish. Plants are ''pets'' to many older people.

Family ''respite'' services

Although home care may be the treatment of choice for most older persons, it can place such a strain on other family members in the household that care is undermined and the family's own mental health compromised. Any program of care must therefore consider regular social supports to the families themselves.

''Respite'' services (more available in England than here) are a great relief to families and can make it possible for the generations to live together under even stressful circumstances. Such respite includes sending someone to care for the older person at home so the family can take holidays, weekends, and vacations by themselves. At times of particular stress or when the older person needs more attention, it should be possible to admit the individual briefly to an institution to give the family a chance to rest and recover. This also helps to acquaint the older person with institutional life and reduces the symbolic and real associations of institutions as places of no return. Day and night sitters should be available when the family wants to go out or when the older person requires inordinate attention at night, exhausting family members. Home appliances and aids—wheelchairs, special handles and bars to assist walking, or anything else that alleviates undue dependency or physical stress on the family—can make care easier. The availability of psychiatric, medical, and social assistance on an emergency or routine basis can provide significant relief to a family.

Home safety

Accidents both in and out of the home are an area of legitimate concern. Among people 65 and older, accidents are the third leading cause of death, claiming about 30,000 victims yearly and disabling 800,000 more.[25] Although older people make up only 11% of the population, 26% of all accidental deaths and 17% of all accidental injuries happen to people over 65. Accidents that do not result in death can have permanent physical and emotional repercussions and may end the older person's independence of movement. A fall may so seriously undermine self-confidence that mobility is curtailed.

Falls lead as the cause of accidental injuries and deaths. See Table 10-1 for the dramatic upsurge of falls for those over 75. To get an idea of the impact of falls leading to hospitalization and nursing home admissions, consider the following:

1. People over 60 make up almost one fourth of all hospital admissions for fall injuries.

---

[25] A useful booklet called *Handle Yourself With Care* has been prepared by the Administration on Aging and the National Safety Council. It is for sale by Superintendent of Documents, U.S. Government Printing Office, Washington, D.C. 20402.

Table 10-1. 1977 death rate from falls

Age category	Deaths per 100,000 persons
All ages	6
65-74	14
Over 75	87

Data from U.S. Department of Health and Human Services, 1980.

2. Even more significantly, the previously mentioned one fourth of admissions for fall injuries is responsible for over 80% of all hospital stays for falls. Older people require longer periods to recover than younger people.
3. Hip fractures alone are responsible for the admission of 8% of all nursing home residents.
4. Another 4% of nursing home admissions are the result of bone fractures other than hip fractures.
5. The median length of stay in a nursing home for a hip fracture is 85 days. One third of hip fracture patients stay 6 months or more. About one fourth never leave until their death.

Most falls occur in the home. Losses in muscle strength and coordination (often resulting from failure to actively maintain physical conditioning), sense of balance, and speed of reaction are factors. Reduced blood flow and oxygen to the brain can result in dizziness and faintness. Older people should beware of sharp moves of the head because of changes in the balancing mechanism of the inner ear. Some people suffer ''drop attacks''—sudden and unexpected falls without loss of consciousness but with loss of muscle power of body and legs. Drugs, especially sedatives and tranquilizers, may confuse and slow response. For example, phenothiazine medications may cause falls following a drop in blood pressure on standing up (postural hypotension).

The home should be made as safe as possible. Staircases are especially dangerous at the top and bottom steps. Steps should be highly visible and have good illumination, nonskid treads, and handrails. Slippery floor coverings should be eliminated. Linoleum, small mats, and sliding rugs are offenders. Nonskid floor waxes, wall-to-wall carpets or rubber-backed rugs, and tacking are wise. Corrugated shoe soles help. Nonskid mats and grab rails should be used in bathtubs and near toilets and beds. One must also be alert to the disorientation that can follow a move to a new residence.

■ A 73-year-old carpenter moved to Florida after living in his home for 36 years. He was accustomed to turning to the left from his bedroom door to enter the bathroom. Suffering from nocturia, he had to get up several times a night. In his new home a stairway was to the left. Several nights after moving, he fell down the stairs and fractured his hip.

Burns, cuts, and poisonings are other hazards. Especially dangerous practices like smoking in bed should be stopped. Room heaters and heating pads must be carefully controlled. Fires can occur when one is cooking while wearing long sleeves or bed clothes. Medicine bottles must be read with caution; it is recommended that they be read *twice* before medicine is taken and *once* afterward.

Loss of one's driver's license can be a blow to self-esteem as well as mobility. But losses of visual and auditory acuity, slower reflexes, poor night vision, and arthritic limitations on neck movements can affect the ability to drive a car. Only 14% of older people have licenses to drive, partly because of disabilities but largely because many of the current elderly have never learned to drive. Interestingly, studies show that older drivers have lower accident rates than younger drivers.

Friendly visiting and outside contact

The world must be brought inside to the bedridden and the homebound. There are friendly visitors programs provided by many voluntary organizations, including the Salvation Army and other religious groups, through which visits are made to isolated individuals. Studies indicate that such visiting has a positive effect on the mental health of those who must stay in bed or in their homes.[26] Frequent contacts with family, friends, and neighbors help keep emotions responsive and minds interested. Television, radio, phonographs, and newspapers can be rich sources of enjoyment. Older people have been known to sacrifice food to pay for television repairs because it is so important to them. Some people leave their television on all day ("like a friend in the house") or sleep with it on at night. Large screens are a visual help, and volume can be adjusted for hearing difficulties. Television and radio offer recreation, education, and religious services. One man described watching television as rather like sitting on the park bench and watching the world go by, a continuous nonstop show. Another spoke of the sense of having world events at his fingertips; he had two sets, one on top of the other, which he watched simultaneously. People call or write to broadcasting stations, avidly follow their favorite newscasters and masters of ceremonies, and participate in audience talk shows.

Recreation, education, and employment

Since 1969, the most broadly accepted definition of therapeutic recreation describes it as "a process that utilizes recreation services for purposive intervention in some physical, emotional, and/or social behavior to bring about a desired change in that behavior and to promote the growth and development of the individual." Recreation specialists use recreation as a medium to assist disabled people to change certain physical, emotional, or social characteristics so they may live their leisure life-styles as well and as independently as possible.[27] Treatment settings include acute care hospitals, physical rehabilitation centers, prisons, skilled care facilities, mental health centers, and the community.

For those who can leave their homes, senior centers and community centers may offer a variety of possibilities. There are increasing numbers of senior centers[28] and also a National Institute of Senior Centers (a program of the National Council on the Aging).[29] Their primary aim is no longer simply recreation; they now provide a range of social and health services. About 1,000 have some kind of health education in addition to direct medical services, which includes professional clinics, screening programs, immunizations, or physical examinations. They may have activities a few hours each week or may be open all day 5 days a week. Shows, parties, music,[30] beauty salons, handicrafts, candle-making, cooking, flower-arranging, trips, discussion groups (also group therapy), games, television, walks, group shopping trips, and special programs for the blind are some of the activities in a well-functioning center. Some offer vacations.[31]

Continuing their education is an interest expressed by many older people. Some communi-

---

[26] Milligan, M.A., and Bennett, R.: Assessment of mental health and social problems during multiple friendly visits: the development and evaluation of a friendly visiting program for the isolated elderly, International Journal of Aging and Human Development **8**:43-65, 1977-1978; and Wright, H., Bennett, R., Simon, R., and Weinberg, G.: Evaluation study of the exploratory visit: an innovative outreach activity of the ILGWU's Friendly Visiting Program, International Journal of Aging and Human Development, **8**:67-82, 1977-1978.

[27] To be eligible for registration as a therapeutic recreation specialist it is necessary to meet the requirements set by the National Therapeutic Recreation Association, a branch of the National Recreation and Park Association, 1601 N. Kent St., Arlington, Va. 22209.

[28] Almost 5,000 senior centers are operated in the United States, sponsored by churches, synagogues, clubs, and non-

profit corporations. Financial support derives from private donations and from local, state, and federal governments.

[29] For information, see Directory of senior centers and clubs: a national resource, National Institute of Senior Centers, National Council on the Aging, Inc., 1818 L St., N.W., Washington, D.C. 20036.

[30] Books and articles are beginning to appear emphasizing the recreational preferences and treatment possibilities of certain recreation for older persons. See Gibbons, A.C.: Popular music preferences of elderly people, Journal of Music Therapy **14**:180-189, 1977; and Palmer, M.D.: Music therapy in a comprehensive program of treatment and rehabilitation for the geriatric resident, Journal of Music Therapy **14**:190-197, 1977.

[31] See Vacations for the Aging and Senior Centers Association (VASCA), 225 Park Ave., S., New York, N.Y. 10003.

Contestant in a statewide senior talent show.

Photo by Patricia and William Oriol.

ties offer home library service. Inexpensive or free correspondence courses should be offered by high schools and colleges, and older people could be encouraged to enroll in regular academic classes if scholarships and low fees were possible. Elementary and junior and senoir high schools located in communities where older people live could remain open after the regular class day and provide recreation, education, and food service. Colleges could work up curricula especially designed for older people; already some are doing this. In the summer of 1975, five New Hampshire colleges, in a small pilot project, opened their campuses to "hostelers" of retirement age. The result was the Elderhostel program,[32] now found on a number of campuses, where older people can take a wide va-

riety of courses, live in dormitories on campus, and generally enjoy student life at reasonable costs during the off-seasons of vacation time and summers. In 1979 more than 20,000 Elderhostelers studied at over 300 colleges and universities in the United States and Canada. In 1981 the first foreign programs were offered—16 in Great Britain and four in Scandinavia—arranged in connection with "partner" organizations abroad. There are a sequence of three 1-week programs at three different campuses. Fairhaven College, a semiautonomous campus of Western Washington State College, is perhaps the ultimate example of year-around intergenerational learning.[33] The 500-member student body ranges in age from 2 to 82.

About one third of the 3,000 colleges and uni-

---

[32] Elderhostel, National Office, 55 Chapel St., Newton, Mne. 02160, or 100 Boylston St., Suite 200, Boston, Mass. 02116.

[33] The Bridge Project, Fairhaven College, Bellingham, Wash. 98225.

versities in the United States (a 10% increase since 1970) are now offering some kind of continuing education aimed at those over 25. The returning adult is welcomed at a time when college enrollments of younger students are slipping. Many of the returnees are middle-aged women re-entering the job market. But increasingly, when it becomes clear how eager older people are to have just such an opportunity, schools will also attempt to enroll older people to fill the empty slots. The American Association of State Colleges and Universities sees universities developing into "three-tiered" institutions, serving the traditional student, the middle-aged student, and retirees.

In their book, *You Are Never Too Old to Learn*,[34] Cross and Florio report on a survey taken by the Academy for Educational Development. Program directors at several hundred colleges and universities with large numbers of older students were asked what were the most popular subjects with these students. The nine most popular subjects were history, psychology, health, foreign languages, literature, painting, creative writing, religion, and needlework. Philosophy, preretirement planning, and physical fitness were tied for tenth place.[35]

Employment and volunteer work allow older persons to supplement their incomes and involve them in absorbing activities that benefit them and the community. In Bethesda, Maryland, the Over-60 Counseling and Employment Service of the Montgomery County Federation of Women's Clubs, Inc. developed a program that provides job opportunities for older men and women—acting as companions for other older persons, caring for children, doing yard work and carpentry, etc. There have been other scattered programs to train unskilled older persons as family aides. In 1966 an experimental project in New Jersey, known as Operation BOLD (Blot Out Long-term Dependency), financed under Title V of the Economic Opportunity Act of 1964, taught homemaking skills and home care of the sick to aides. Volunteers in Service to America (VISTA), Senior Aides, Service Corps of Retired Executives (SCORE), the Peace Corps, Foster Grandparent programs, Green Thumb, Mature-Temps, Retired Senior Volunteer Program (RSVP)[36] and other employment and volunteer activities are designed especially to accommodate older persons.

Those with handicaps must be given every opportunity to take an active part in such activities. Section 504 of the 1973 Rehabilitation Act states:

No otherwise qualified handicapped individual in the United States . . . shall, solely by reason of his handicap, be excluded from the participation in, be denied the benefits of, or be subjected to discrimination under any program or activity receiving Federal financial assistance.

The purpose of the Act is to ensure that federally funded programs and activities are accessible to handicapped persons. The objectives are to ensure equal opportunity, equal access, and equally effective services and treatment for handicapped individuals.

Religious support

Members of the clergy of all faiths are involved in the care of older people. Some concentrate only on spiritual aspects, while increasing numbers of others become directly involved in social services, counseling, and other secular activities. Many older people are deeply religious, and members of the clergy can become an integral part in planning and providing for their care. The clergy has tra-

---

[34] Cross, W., and Florio, C.: You are never too old to learn, New York, 1978, Academy for Educational Development.

[35] For further information on education programs for older persons, see Tuition Study, Institute of Lifetime Learning, 1909 K St., N.W., Washington, D.C. 20049; National University Extension Association, Suite 360, 1 Dupont Circle, N.W., Washington, D.C. 20036; and Institute of Retired Professionals, The New School, 66 W. 12th St., New York, N.Y. 10011. For a free directory of accredited schools that offer home-study courses, write to the National Home Study Council, 1601 18th St., N.W., Washington, D.C. 20009.

[36] RSVP evolved out of the project SERVE. See Sainer, J.S., and Zander, M.L.: SERVE: older volunteers in community service: a new role and a new resource, New York, 1971, Community Service Society.

ditionally formed one of the few professional disciplines whose members are specifically trained to care for dying people. Home visiting with the sick and infirm is also common practice, and members of the clergy therefore are an important source of referral for medical and psychiatric problems.

Religious groups have for centuries given special attention to older people. Some of the better, as well as the worst, examples of homes for the aged and old age–oriented community activities can be found under their auspices. But the need to maintain doctrinal differences has led to fragmentation of services. Each denomination builds its own little island of concern, isolated from everything else. A "practical ecumenism" could allow churches and synagogues to protect their identities yet pool their resources in a planned effort to help older persons.[37] For example, buying necessary supplies together for old age homes could sharply cut costs. Pooling skilled personnel would increase the range of services each home could give. Cooperative planning of vital community programs such as Meals-on-Wheels[38] and friendly visitors could reach many more people, with the churches of all denominations acting as neighborhood bases for all older persons, regardless of denomination. A national church program including all denominations could register all eligible older people for health programs, coordinate food programs, provide friendly visitors and telephone reassurance, set up information and referral services nationally, help coordinate home care programs, and much more. Members of the clergy could receive special training for work with older persons. Religious groups should use their power and influence for improvement of older people's economic and social conditions.

---

[37] Butler, R.N.: Toward practical ecumenism, Bulletin of the American Protestant Hospital Association **34:**6-12, 1970. See also Hospital Progress, Journal of the Catholic Hospital Association, July 1970.

[38] The coordination of 11 separately sponsored church and community programs serving over 1,300 older recipients is described by McLaughlin, C.B.: Meals on Wheels reach Baltimore's elderly, Food and Nutrition **3:**204, 1973.

New housing arrangements

When it becomes difficult or undesirable for an older person to live separately in his or her own home, there are beginning to be alternatives to the nursing home or other institutions.

Congregate housing

Martin Janis established two "Golden Age Villages" in Columbus and Toledo, Ohio, during his tenure as director of the Ohio Department of Mental Hygiene and Correction. These continue to be the only two such congregate housing units for older persons in the nation and are seen as model facilities for low-income elderly. They provide personal-care services such as meals, a health clinic, and barber and beauty shops as well as housing.

Shared living concept

The shared living concept is the brainstorm of Mr. and Mrs. Jim Gilles of Winter Park, Florida, who tried it in their own home. The idea centers around a "family" of nonrelated older adults (sometimes with younger adults included) who share a household and divide the expenses of running it. It has grown into a nonprofit, volunteer-staffed, nationwide organization known as Share-A-Home of America, Inc.

Others

A variety of boarding homes, retirement hotels, and other facilities can be found here and there that offer a variety of services and a somewhat protected environment.

OUTPATIENT CARE

Outpatient services (sometimes called "ambulatory care") refer to care given to people who live in the community rather than in institutions. This care is provided by hospital outpatient clinics, neighborhood health centers, family agencies, day hospitals, and day-care centers. Outpatient service may be given in or outside of the home, either bringing the person to the service or taking the service to the person. We have already described home care; therefore this section emphasizes the facilities where people can go for outpatient care rather than having it brought to them.

Hospital emergency rooms are the major 24-hour facilities available for medical and psychiatric emergencies. In addition, hospitals generally offer *outpatient medical clinic care;* some have *outpatient psychiatric clinics* as well. Currently only 2% of patients in outpatient psychiatric clinics are over 60 years of age. Few of the clinics offer the services necessary for older people, especially psychotherapy.

Community mental health centers are another potential but thus far unrealized resource for older persons. In 1961, proposals regarding the establishment of community mental health centers were made and published by the Joint Commission on Mental Illness and Health in *Action for Mental Health.* This first publication was very hopeful and stands in contrast to such later books as *The Community Mental Health Center: an Interim Appraisal,* by the Joint Information Service of the American Psychiatric Association and the National Association for Mental Health.[39]

The Federal Community Mental Health Centers program was enacted by Congress in 1963 and amended in 1965, 1967, and 1975. If nothing else, it has certainly focused attention on the fact that the system of delivery of mental health services is woefully inadequate. The community mental health center is required to offer a minimum of five services, four of which are direct clinical activities: inpatient care, outpatient care, partial hospitalization (such as day care), and around-the-clock emergency service. The fifth required program element is community education and consultation services oriented toward prevention. In addition, Public Law 94-63, the Public Health Service Act of 1975, requires that the community mental health centers provide "a program

of specialized services for the mental health of the elderly, including a full range of diagnostic, treatment, liaison, and follow-up services."[40] Community mental health centers are responsible for specific catchment areas, but certain of the center programs (such as those for children, older persons, and drug addicts) may serve several catchment areas.

Both public and private agencies have participated in the establishment of centers. It should be pointed out that whatever the nature of its sponsorship, the typical community mental health center is supported through a combination of public and private funds. Public monies meet 75% of the total operating costs of typical centers during the first year of operation. Private funds derived from varying combinations of patient payments, third-party payments made in behalf of patients, and voluntary contributions meet the remaining 25%.

By 1979 some 700 centers were operating. On the basis of an average of 155,000 persons to be served per center, about a fourth of the country's population is included in the catchment areas of the funded centers. It is estimated that the nation needs between 1,800 and 2,000 such centers. They might eventually be absorbed within health maintenance organizations.

The community mental health centers have been criticized. The facts are that they have never been adequately funded, housed, and staffed. There are no standards. Inservice training and personnel development have lagged. Racism and stereotypes about "the poor" have been negative influences. As is usual when some ideal hope does not work out to eminent satisfaction, there are those who are ready to do away with these ventures, not realizing (or in fact realizing very well) that the reasons they failed are related to inadequate support and the fact that they have not been validly tested.

The Glasscote study explores the many reasons

[39]Glasscote, P.M., Sussex, J.J., Cumming, E., and Smith, L.R.: The community mental health center: an interim appraisal, Washington, D.C., 1969, The Joint Information Service of the American Psychiatric Association and the National Association for Mental Health.

[40]For a different perspective, see Patterson, R.D.: Services for the aged in community mental health centers, American Journal of Psychiatry **133:**271-273, 1976.

why the community centers have not fulfilled the key purpose of federal funding, which is to appreciably diminish the flow of mentally ill patients of all ages to state hospitals.[41] The Glasscote work also points out the slowness of progress toward meeting the problems of the indigent mentally ill, who make up a large share of the state hospital–bound patients. Many explanations can be given for this slowness, including insufficient and ill-timed appropriations, rigid geographical guidelines, inadequate psychiatric training and experience of operating personnel, and lack of consensus as to the purpose of the center. The work of Hollingshead and Redlich is pertinent to the problems of middle-class mental health professionals attempting to serve the poor of varied ages and races.[42] Older people make up only 4% to 5% of community mental health center clientele.[43]

Day hospitals for patients with psychiatric problems enable persons to come to the hospital for any indicated treatment during the day and return home at night. This provides a degree of care intermediate between outpatient therapy and total institutional care. It is particularly useful for former mental hospital patients and persons with significant organic mental impairment. In this way families obtain substantial support in keeping an older person at home. Nursing and old age homes should offer similar partial care. One of the greatest problems with day hospital programs is the need for transportation, particularly in rural areas. In England, ambulances are used to transport people. Taxis (paid for by Medicaid in some states), volunteers' cars, and staff cars may be used. An ideal day hospital service should offer medical care, individual and group psychotherapy, drug therapy, occupational and physical therapy, entertainment, education, a library, a store, beauty and barber shops, free lunches, baths, some form of patient government, and plenty of opportunities for congenial socializing. Day hospitals can ease the return of former mental hospital patients to community life and monitor the physical condition and reactions to medications of all patients. Relatives, friends, and community volunteers should have free access and play vital roles.

Day-care centers offer day care in a nonhospital setting but provide many of the same social and recreational services.[44] There are presently only a few geriatric day-care centers in the United States. The first recreational day center for the aged, the William Hodson Community, was set up in 1944 as part of New York City's Department of Public Welfare.[45] This center emphasized self-government, poetry, music, dramatics, woodwork, painting, birthday parties, discussion groups, counseling, and an added fillip in the form of country vacations.

Various other groups now offer similar programs, of which the following is an example:

■ Levindale Hebrew Geriatric Center and Hospital in Baltimore, Maryland, provides day care and a community orientation. A bus picks up 20 to 30 mentally or physically handicapped older people daily at their own homes and takes them to Levindale for a schedule of activities, including meals.

MULTIPURPOSE SENIOR CENTERS

Congressman John Brademas (D-Ind.) introduced legislation in December 1971 to authorize construction of multipurpose senior citizen community centers. A revolving fund was to be established to ensure mortgages for such centers. The senior center movement illustrates the continuing debate over the development of comprehensive

[41]Glasscote, P.M., Sussex, J.J., Cumming, E., and Smith, L.R.: The community mental health center: an interim appraisal, Washington, D.C., 1969, The Joint Information Service of the American Psychiatric Association and the National Association for Mental Health.

[42]Hollingshead, A.B., and Redlich, F.C.: Social class and mental illness, New York, 1958, John Wiley & Sons, Inc.

[43]"The area of mental health services represents one of the most glaring examples of discrimination on the basis of age," according to the U.S. Commission on Civil Rights: The age discrimination study, Washington, D.C., 1979, U.S. Government Printing Office, p. 6.

[44]Matlack, D.R.: The case for geriatric day hospitals, The Gerontologist **15:**109-113, 1975.

[45]Kubie, S.H., and Landau, G.: Group work with the aged, New York, 1953, International Universities Press, Inc.

Senior aides at a day-care center.

Photo by Patricia and William Oriol.

versus categorical programs: whether the services needed by older people should be assured within comprehensive programs for people of all ages or be provided in specialized ways. Philosophically, socially, and psychologically, integration of services is the more desirable. Experience demonstrates, however, that older people get lost in the shuffle, and fall through the cracks. Until there is a finely honed change in the cultural sensibility so that older persons do not get lost, it is necessary to press for special, highly visible programs.

Multipurpose senior centers can provide a range of services beyond the walls of their facilities. Social workers and aides (paraprofessionals, who are sometimes called "geriatric aides") and friendly visitors may visit the homes of clients. Residential homes may be organized. Group shopping trips by bus, for check-cashing as well as shopping, may be chaperoned. Little House in Menlo Park, California, has been a pioneer example of a multipurpose senior center since 1949.

PROTECTIVE SERVICES

Protective services is the name for a group of services given to persons who are so mentally deteriorated or disturbed as to be unable to manage their affairs in their own best interest and who have no relatives or friends able and willing to act on their behalf. Social work, legal, medical, psychiatric, nursing, homemaking, and home health aide services may be provided. Small amounts of cash may be available for use in certain situations.

Federal legislation[46] has been enacted that will permit local welfare offices to set up protective service programs, for which the federal government provides 75% of the cost. Adult Protective Services Programs have been developing more rapidly since the passage in 1974 of Title XX of the Social Security Act. Nearly 20 states have organized programs combining service and intervention.

Protective service clients often need assistance because of some mental condition such as paranoid ideas, organic brain syndrome, overwhelming anxiety, or severe personality disorder. Most of these clients are best helped by social workers and nurses who are generalists in the sense that they manage their cases with the support of medical, legal, and psychiatric consultations and can call on homemakers, visiting nurses, and paraprofessionals for help. A typical case illustrates the importance of such services to mental health.

■ A mildly confused older woman developed paranoid ideas about the gas company, which resulted in her not paying her bills for several months. She was threatened with having the gas turned off, which would leave her without heat in midwinter. Had she been without help, her gas probably would have been turned off; after a while police and medical help would have been called for, and her eventual transfer (probably in a very deteriorated condition) to an inpatient psychiatric ward would have been necessary. With protective services, the crisis with the gas company was averted. A casework aide, under the supervision of a social worker, was able to gain the woman's confidence enough to convince her to pay the gas bill. Since she had no money for an immediate payment, protective services made a partial payment of the bill and arranged with the gas company for the woman to pay the rest later. Continuing contact

with the protective service worker enabled the woman to continue living in her own home. A homemaker was also provided for a few hours a week. All these helpers used psychiatric consultants to help them react appropriately to the client's psychiatric condition.

The protective service and the community mental health approaches are closely related in that both provide a variety of services to meet a person's needs while the person remains in his or her home, thus utilizing less-than-total-care institutions whenever it is in the patient's best interest. The patient is seen not just as having a certain illness but in the context of psychological, social, physical, and economic conditions. Also, psychiatric needs may be met without requiring the person to accept the idea that he or she is a "mental patient."

Historically, legal concern for older persons centered on the protection of property holdings against dissipation and exploitation. In recent times there has been more emphasis on protection of the person. In 1962 the Social Security Administration made a grant to the Benjamin Rose Institute of Cleveland, one of the few agencies providing extensive protective services to older people, for a research and demonstration project. Margaret Blenkner,[47] director of this research, has contributed to our understanding the problem of protective services.

It has not been established how many people need protection. The number who have mental impairment is substantial, and this applies in institutions as well as in the community. Early studies showed that about 50% of institutionalized populations had mental impairment.[48] Other studies sug-

---

[46] 1962 Public Welfare Amendment to the Social Security Act. Among pioneering books on protective services is that of Lehmann, V., and Mathiasen, G., editors: Guardianship and protective services for older people, Albany, N.Y., 1963, National Council on Aging Press.

[47] Blenkner, M., Bloom, M., Wasser, E., and Nielsen, M.: Protective services for old people: findings from the Benjamin Rose Institute study, Social Casework **52**:483-522, 1971.

[48] Goldfarb, A.I.: Prevalence of psychiatric disorders in metropolitan old age and nursing homes, Journal American Geriatric Society **10**:78-84, 1962. See also U.S. Department of Health, Education and Welfare, National Center for Health Statistics: Characteristics of residents in institutions for the aged and chronically ill, United States, Apr.-June 1963, Pub. No. (PHS) 100, Series 12, No. 2, Washington, D.C., 1965, U.S. Government Printing Office.

gest that one sixth of the noninstitutionalized population—3 million older people—has some degree of mental impairment. Even if these figures include unrecognized or simulated depression, for practical purposes this describes a vulnerable population. Some of the earliest studies concerning "certifiable" persons in the community[49] estimated 5% in need of protection. Less stringent studies by Blenkner, Goldfarb, Lowenthal, and others have estimated closer to 16%. (These studies are not strictly comparable because of varied criteria.)

Burr cites data indicating that 10% of the adult caseload of public welfare agencies (largely Old Age Assistance) are in need of protective services.[50] However, most welfare departments still do not supply them.

In 1967 the Administration on Aging of the Social and Rehabilitation Service (HEW) began its National Protective Services Project in three rural Colorado counties and Washington, D.C.[51] Referrals for protective services came from county welfare departments, AOA, Social Security offices, housing authorities, health programs, social agencies, counseling, referral, and information services, and probate courts. Some of the referred older people were rootless, isolated "loners," reflecting a multigenerational chain of psychopathologic conditions. Some had chronic brain syndromes, others were severely depressed or neurotic, and a few were mentally retarded. Physical disease was common. Most were poor, with less than grammar school education.

In Blenkner's approach, social casework was the core service and the directive was "do, or get others to do, whatever is necessary to meet the needs of the situation." Rapport, trust, mutual respect are necessary. In our Washington work we found gradualism (nonprecipitous, careful intervention) a guiding concept; we did not accept the idea that it was crucial to think in terms of completing a case, except as nature dictated through death. Needs included, of course, medical, financial, home health aide, homemaker, nursing care, psychiatric, and legal services. Following are some principles crucial to protective services.

1. Entrust client or patient with decision-making power.
2. Establish trust and rapport; before all else, do not violate that trust.
3. Use gradualism—do things nonprecipitously and carefully.
4. Do not kill with kindness.
5. Work with assets.
6. Respect resistance.
7. Do not move people if it can be avoided and if it is against their will.

In Blenkner's intriguing work, upsetting to some, she and her colleagues found that the protected group as compared to the control group had higher rates of institutionalization and death. They attribute this to hopelessness (we would add helplessness) engendered by *things being done* for people. Members of the protected group were institutionalized earlier than they would otherwise have been and "contrary to intent . . . did not . . . prove protective of the older person although it did relieve collaterals and community agents." We believe it essential that studies be designed to confirm or refute the Benjamin Rose studies. In the meantime we favor continuing intervention but take seriously this injunction of Blenkner et al.: "We should . . . question our present prescrip-

[49] New York State Department of Mental Hygiene, Mental Health Research Unit: A mental health survey of older people, 1960, New York State Hospital Press.

[50] Burr, J.J.: Program goals and the specialist's function in public welfare. In Planning welfare services for older people, paper presented at the Training Institute for Public Welfare Specialists on Aging, Cleveland, Ohio, June 13-24, 1965, Washington, D.C., 1966, U.S. Department of Health, Education, and Welfare, pp. 5-12.

[51] One of us (R.N.B.) was the consulting psychiatrist of the Washington project, excellently directed by George Roby, MSW. Dr. Jack Kleh and Mrs. Virginia Lehmann were the medical and legal consultants, respectively. See U.S. Department of Health, Education and Welfare, Social and Rehabilitative Service, Community Services Administration: Report of the National Protective Services Project for Older Adults, Pub. No. (SRS) 72-23008, 1971.

tions and strategies of treatment. Is our dosage too strong, our intervention too overwhelming, our takeover too final?''[52]

PRE-HOSPITAL-ADMISSION SCREENING[53]

In 1965 the Langley Porter Institute and the California State Department of Mental Hygiene established a pilot program to screen older persons on the brink of commitment to state mental hospitals. It was hoped that the project would provide *alternatives* to hospitalization and promote the proper care of older persons outside the institution. Innovations included the following.

1. Screening of persons over 65 years of age when involuntary commitment was under consideration
2. Screening in the patient's home by a team physician, psychiatrist, and social worker
3. Appropriate alternatives, including placement, to provide for total needs of the patient

One California study by Simon and Lowenthal[54] showed that a common cause of commitment was acute brain syndrome, or ''delirium'' as it is now called. This disorder is a temporary but usually reversible mental disturbance, often brought about by malnutrition, uncontrolled diabetes, decompensated heart disease, and other diseases. Since delirium is closely related to physical illness, it could be treated in a general hospital, with continuing care at home or in a protective care facility (nursing home or convalescent home). It would then not be necessary for such persons to be committed for treatment in a mental hospital.

State institutions could effectively conduct screening in the hospitals themselves and then make proper alternative placement if necessary. Baltimore and some other cities have programs similar to that of San Francisco.

MODELS OF MULTIPLE SERVICE PROGRAMS

The Minneapolis Age and Opportunity Center (MAO)[55] is a comprehensive program of health and social services founded in 1969 and directed by Daphne Krause. It is a nonprofit organization owned by senior citizens. The purpose of MAO is to give older people an alternative form of care, with direct services to the partially incapacitated and those who need services on a temporary basis. Krause calls the program ''medi-supportive.'' The goal is independence. Services include daily meal deliveries; homemaker services (including bathing, housework, laundry, and home maintenance); 24-hour transportation for medical services, shopping, and emergencies; legal and employment services; once-a-day telephone reassurance; a ''food closet'' for emergency or supplementary food; dial-a-friend; and assistance in obtaining health and counseling services. Contacts between the old and the young are encouraged. A free clinic was opened in 1973, sponsored by the Abbott-Northwestern Hospital, with Medicare accepted as full payment for fees. This clinic offers preventive medical services, diagnosis and treatment services, emergency service, counseling service on health matters, and inpatient service where needed. The hospital provides health care personnel and equipment, and MAO supplies volunteers and professionals for the wide range of services described earlier. Funding for MAO has been provided by Supplemental Security Income, Model Cities funds, Medicare, county welfare, private donations, and other sources.

[52] For further discussion of the need to provide protection for the civil liberties of clients, see Regan, J.J.: Intervention through adult protective services programs, The Gerontologist **18**:250-254, 1978.

[53] We are indebted here to the review of the San Francisco Geriatric Screening Project contained in Mental health care and the elderly: shortcomings in public policy, report of the U.S. Senate Special Committee on Aging, Washington, D.C., 1971, U.S. Government Printing Office.

[54] Lowenthal, M.F.: Lives in distress, New York, 1964, Basic Books, Inc., Publishers.

[55] Minneapolis Age and Opportunity Center, Inc. (MAO), 1801 Nicollet Ave., Minneapolis, Minn. 55403. See also One city's controversial plan to give seniors a fair shake on health, American Medical News, Sept. 9, 1974.

The Council for the Jewish Elderly (CJE) of Chicago is a social agency with transportation, outreach, and homemaker services, Meals-on-Wheels, storefront area service centers, a senior work center, apartments, and liaisons with two hospitals. Another program with a more distinct ethnic orientation is that of the On Lok Senior Health Center for older Chinese, Pilipinos, and Italians (Chapter 6).

CONCLUSION

The Committee on Aging of the Group for the Advancement of Psychiatry (GAP) took the lead in pointing out the deficiencies in the report, *Action for Mental Health,* of the Joint Commission on Mental Illness and in American mental health care for older persons. It offered constructive proposals for community care and a series of publications on the subject.[56]

Although GAP emphasized service in the community, it called for a range of services and facilities including institutionalization to meet the realities of old age:

Old people need a broad range of treatment settings. They must not be lumped into one category. In-depth evaluation must be done before the treatment process is started. Once an elderly patient is sent down one road it is difficult to divert him to another. . . . It is our position that the psychiatric hospital is an integral and necessary component of the therapeutic continuum for elderly psychiatric patients just as quality nursing home care is ideal for elderly medical patients. . . . We favor the development of comprehensive diagnostic and treatment centers, however, at each point along the sequence of neighborhood health centers, community mental health centers, and hospitals. Irreversibility must never be casually (and stereotypically) assumed.[57]

Mental health workers and the people they serve seek to maintain the older person at home so long as it is wise and appropriate. To effectively do so, our communities must develop the necessary services. When reality dictates, however, both workers and older people must share in the decision to accept institutional care. The difficulty of that decision would be lightened by vast improvements in our nation's facilities.

REFERENCES

Beattie, W.: Aging and the social services. In Binstock, R., and Shanas, E., editors: Handbook of aging and the social sciences, New York, 1976, Van Nostrand Reinhold Co.

Bennett, R.: Social isolation and isolation-reducing programs, Bulletin of the New York Academy of Medicine **49:**1143-1163, 1973.

Brickner, P.W.: Home health care for the aged: how to help older people stay in their own homes and out of institutions, New York, 1978, Appleton-Century-Crofts.

Brickner, P.W., et al.: The homebound aged: a medically unreached group, Annals of Internal Medicine **82:**1-6, 1975.

Chu, F.D., and Trotter, S.: The madness establishment: Ralph Nader's study group report on the National Institute on Mental Health, New York, 1974, Grossman Publishers, Inc.

Group for the Advancement of Psychiatry: Crisis in psychiatric hospitalization, Report No. 72, 1969.

Group for the Advancement of Psychiatry: The aged and community mental health: a guide to program development, Report No. 80, 1971.

Joint Commission on Mental Illness and Health: Action for mental health, final report of the Commission, New York, 1961, Basic Books, Inc., Publishers.

Kubie, L.S.: Need for a new subdiscipline in the medical profession, Archives of Neurology and Psychiatry **78:**283-293, 1957.

Kutner, B., Fanshel, D., Togo, A.M., and Langner, T.S.: Five hundred over sixty: a community survey on aging, New York, 1957, Russell Sage Foundation.

MacMillan, D.: Mental health services for the aged, a British approach, Canada's Mental Health, June 1967, pp. 1-17.

Markson, E., Kwoh, A., Cumming, J., and Cumming, E.: Alternatives to hospitalization for psychiatrically ill geriatric patients. In Psychiatry and the elderly (special section), American Journal of Psychiatry **127:**1055-1062, 1971.

Moses, D.V., and Lake, C.S.: Geriatrics in the baccalaureate nursing curriculum, Nursing outlook **16:**41-43, 1968.

Padula, H.: Developing day care for older people: a technical assistance monograph prepared for the Office of Economic Opportunity, National Council on the Aging, Washington, D.C., Sept. 1972.

Project SHARE: Issues in deinstitutionalization, Washington, D.C., 1978, U.S. Government Printing Office.

Regan, J.J.: Intervention through adult protective services programs, The Gerontologist **18:**250-254, 1978.

---

[56] Group for the Advancement of Psychiatry, Publications Office, 419 Park Ave., S., New York, N.Y. 10016.

[57] Group for the Advancement of Psychiatry: Toward a public policy on health care of the elderly, Report No. 79, 1970, pp. 663-664.

Rodstein, M.: Accidents among the aged: incidence, causes and prevention, Journal of Chronic Diseases **17:**515-526, 1964.

Rusk, H.A.: Principles involved in teaching the activities of daily living. In Rusk, H.A.: Rehabilitation medicine, ed. 4, St. Louis, 1971, The C.V. Mosby Co.

Schechter, I.: 1980 chartbook of federal programs in aging, Washington Care Reports, 1980.

Streib, G., and Streib, R.: Communes and the aging: utopian dream and gerontological reality, American Behavioral Scientist **19:**176-189, 1975.

Townsend, P.: The family life of old people: an inquiry in East London, Glencoe, Ill., 1957, Free Press.

Townsend, P.: The last refuge, London, 1962, Routledge and Kegan Paul Ltd.

U.S. Senate Special Committee on Aging: Alternatives to nursing home care: a proposal, prepared by staff specialists at the Levinson Gerontological Policy Institute, Brandeis University, Waltham, Mass. (Dr. Robert Morris, Director), Washington, D.C., 1971, U.S. Government Printing Office.

U.S. Senate Special Committee on Aging: Mental health care and the elderly: shortcomings in public policy, Washington, D.C., 1971, U.S. Government Printing Office.

U.S. Senate Special Committee on Aging: Home health services in the United States, Washington, D.C., 1972, U.S. Government Printing Office.

U.S. Senate Special Committee on Aging: A working paper: adult day facilities for treatment, health care, and related services, Washington, D.C., 1976, U.S. Government Printing Office.

11

Proper institutional care

Nursing home costs in the United States have doubled from 1976 ($10 billion) to 1980 ($21 billion). It is projected that nursing home costs will be in excess of $75 billion by 1990. Spending per capita for the nation's 1.3 million nursing home residents is $17,000 per year, up from $8,250 in 1955. It is little wonder that the U.S. government is becoming increasingly concerned with what is presently called the long-term care issue. The appropriate location for an infirmed or disabled older person and the need for cost-effective quality care will dominate government policy decisions.

We discuss institutional care of all sorts in this chapter, but as with government fiscal preoccupations, our discussion is dominated by the huge issue of nursing home care. Our definition of institutional care includes any care (medical, nursing, psychiatric, or social) given to older people *not* residing in their own homes or the homes of family and friends. Although efforts should be directed toward helping the mentally and/or physically ill

older person remain independent and in his or her own home, there are many situations in which it is simply not possible or advisable to do so. Active outpatient treatment may fail and short- or long-term institutional care is required.[1] Present means of financing care, the inadequacy of facilities and services, and deficiencies in number and training of personnel are among the obstacles to the provision of the spectrum of services and facilities needed to dovetail with the wide range of psychiatric, nursing, medical, and social states of older people. Once again, as in other chapters, we describe what is presently available, balancing this against what would be ideal. Emergency shelter, acute and chronic hospitalization (both medical and psychiatric) nursing homes, homes for the aged, and residential (for example, foster care) homes are the basic forms of institutional care utilized by the older population. We examine what each of these has to offer, both in kind and in quality of service.

---

[1] The Group for the Advancement of Psychiatry took early issue with the premise that "the only good psychiatry is treatment in the community." Its 1969 report entitled "Crisis in Psychiatric Hospitalization" was a "protest against a current band wagon movement" that is exemplified by such slogans as "Keep patients out of psychiatric hospitals" and "Use the psychiatric ward of a general hospital instead of a mental hospital." GAP stressed "the vital role of the psychiatric hospital in a continuum of comprehensive psychiatric treatment." It based its criticism of the movement away from the psychiatric hospital on both theoretical and clinical considerations. As a clinical result of uncritical acceptance, these slogans lead to diagnostic and treatment errors, it contended. Readmission rates increase. A large number of semifunctioning individuals are immobilized through misuse of medications.

DECISION TO INSTITUTIONALIZE AN OLDER PERSON

The unfavorable reputation of American institutions for the elderly combines with the natural reluctance of older people to leave their homes and communities; and the result is active or passive (and often justifiable) resistance to admission. An older woman came to our attention because she kept an arsenal of guns at home to use on herself or others if someone came to take her to a nursing home or mental hospital. Increased morbidity, disorientation, and mortality have been associated with the movement of people to institutions, since the aged are particularly vulnerable to the stress of sudden change. Thus the decision to institutionalize must be made conservatively and with care to fully prepare and cushion the individual against the inevitable shock.[2]

When is institutionalization indicated?

The need for medical care in an institution is fairly apparent and based on a physician's recommendation. However, it has not been possible to construct strict criteria for voluntary admission and involuntary commitment to state and private psychiatric hospitals; and the criteria for nursing homes and homes for the aged are even more nebulous and indefinite.

Lowenthal has identified five factors that influence the decision to place older, mentally ill persons in a hospital—some of which are relevant also for other chronic care facilities.

1. Disturbances in thinking and feeling, such as delusions or depressions
2. Physical illness
3. Potentially harmful behavior such as confusion or unmanageability
4. Harmful behavior such as actual violence to others or refusing necessary medical care

5. Environmental factors such as the unavailability or incapacity of a responsible other person to care for the patient[3]

It is immediately clear that adequate social supports such as home care services could prevent the institutionalization of a portion of the older persons described here. Medical hospitalization would be more appropriate for others, and a differentiation should be made between long-term and short-term or intermittent needs for care. The following outline[4] illustrates an effort to build criteria for mental hospitalization of older persons.

I. Clearly appropriate for admission
 A. Those with functional psychoses and without significant physical illness or disability, for whom outpatient treatment is not feasible
  EXAMPLES
  1. Patients receiving psychiatric treatment in the community who require brief periods of protection from the consequences of their behavior during episodes of acute disturbance or depression (for example, suicide, homicide, spending sprees, refusal to eat)
  2. Chronically mentally ill patients who need protection and management, as well as treatment, during prolonged periods of disruptive or disorganized behavior and require regular and frequent attendance of a physician
 B. Alcoholics without significant physical illness or disability who, following detoxification, need a period of inpatient treatment for their alcoholism
 C. Those with severe organic brain disorders whose usual behavior, intractable to medication, is too disturbing to be managed at home or in another facility

---

[2] To provide an understanding of the impact of institutional care on people, Erving Goffman's powerful essay, "On the Characteristics of Total Institutions" (1957), should be required reading, along with Stanton and Schwartz's classic study, "The Mental Hospital" (1956).

[3] Lowenthal, M.F.: Lives in distress, New York, 1964, Basic Books, Inc., Publishers.

[4] This outline (somewhat paraphrased) illustrates the effort of one state (Maryland) to establish guidelines (developed when Helen Padula was Coordinator, Services to the Aged, Maryland). Maryland was influenced by a preceding New York State effort. We emphasize that this is merely a guideline and should not be used in a rigid, immutable manner.

EXAMPLES

The physically agressive patient, the fire set-
ter, the eloper, or the person otherwise dangerous to himself or others when physically
able to carry out his potentially destructive behavior

II. Clearly inappropriate for admission

A. Those with delirium, symptomatic of a grave
physical illness, requiring urgent admission to a
general hospital

B. Those who are moribund or comatose

C. Those with major medical problems and minor
mental symptoms

EXAMPLES

Patients who become mildly confused or disturbed as a result of or in conjunction with
recent head injury, cardiovascular disease,
diabetes, metabolic disturbance, terminal
malignancy, etc. (Psychiatric consultation
might be utilized, if required, rather than mental hospital admission.)

D. Those with inconsequential lapses of memory
and mild disorientation as a result of organic
brain disorders, who are more effectively treated
or managed in their own homes or, if necessary,
in a foster home, a home for the aged, etc. (A
state mental hospital has little to offer and, in
view of the large wards in most state mental hospitals, may aggravate the patient's confusion.)

E. Those who need only adequate living accommodations, with economic or other social support services

As a footnote to the preceding discussion, it is
important to remember that self-destructive or
suicidal behavior in older persons may be a slow
process associated with prolonged and intense
grief, loneliness, and progressive organic disease
and may manifest itself in malnutrition, failure to
take medicine, and other forms of deteriorating
self-care.

Advisability of voluntary admission

Wherever possible, the older person—like a person of any age—should participate fully in all
decisions regarding him- or herself, including
those of institutionalization. The family, of course,
should also be closely involved. Making the decision to admit a person to a nursing home, a home
for the aged, or a hospital can be extremely difficult, since all these facilities are so disliked and
feared by both older persons and their families.

Almost all older people view the move to a home for
the aged or to a nursing home with fear and hostility. . . . All old people—without exception—believe that
the move to an institution is the prelude to death. . . .
[The old person] sees the move to an institution as a
decisive change in living arrangements, the last change
he will experience before he dies. . . . Finally, no matter
what the extenuating circumstances, the older person
who has children interprets the move to an institution as
rejection by his children.[5]

Considerable change should be made regarding
the concept of care, preparation of older people
and their families, and longevity of residents in
such a facility. Many people could be admitted
much later if they were given more support at
home. In addition, there should always be an expectation and actual possibility of discharge and
return home after response to treatment and
changes in the person's condition and circumstances.

Involuntary commitment to state and private psychiatric facilities

Admission to any institution should ideally be
voluntary, but there are some circumstances that
may require commitment against a person's
wishes. Extreme civil libertarians urge that legal
involuntary commitment to mental hospitals be
done away with (but, strangely, have not com-
mented on the de facto assignment of older people into nursing homes and related facilities—with
few of the protections afforded in connection with
admission to mental hospitals). Others insist that
people who are a danger to themselves or to others
need the protection of commitment procedure.
Such procedures are not uniform from state to
state, but in general the legal justification for action is (1) imminent physical danger to self, (2) im-

---

[5] From Shanas, E.: The health of older people: a social survey,
Cambridge, Mass., 1962, Harvard University Press.

minent physical danger to others, or (3) a clear and present need of immediate care or treatment.

Doctors are the only practitioners who are allowed to perform commitment proceedings. Since a large percentage of the U.S. population has no access to a psychiatrist, the family physician is, by default, pressed into service in times of psychiatric emergency. Many doctors fear signing commitment papers because of possible malpractice suits. Following are some of the safeguards to remember when commitment is under consideration—for the protection of both the older person and his or her doctor.

1. Know and observe laws regarding involuntary commitment. Get to know the local judge or clerk of court available for assistance and advice. Examine the patient within the legal time limit before signing papers.
2. Avoid shortcuts in examination (see discussion of the legal examination in Chapter 9). Watch for sedatives by giving the person time to recover. If the person is comatose, decide if this is medically or psychiatrically caused. If psychiatric, double check again at a later time.
3. Remember that taking the word of relatives is always risky.
4. Avoid personal conflict of interest.
5. Avoid use of force (for example, injections, electroshock treatment).
6. Avoid illegal transportation. Most states rule that only a police officer can transport someone against his or her will.[6]
7. Avoid institutions that are unfamiliar. Get to know all local facilities.
8. Avoid acting alone when consultation is available.

The informal, nonprotesting admission or emergency admission procedure is helpful when the person is too confused to comprehend what is happening.

DIFFERENT KINDS OF SHORT- AND LONG-TERM INSTITUTIONAL CARE
Emergency care

Many older people remain in their homes until an acute psychiatric and/or medical crisis occurs, necessitating emergency care. Emergency rooms of hospitals have become the primary mode of providing initial care; this means, of course, that the patient must transport him- or herself, must be transported to the hospital independently, or must obtain the services of an ambulance. Fire departments, police, and rescue squads (often voluntary) may provide ambulance services, depending on the particular community, with fire departments the most commonly involved. As we mentioned earlier, psychiatric emergencies are regulated differently from locale to locale, and in a number of communities only the police can legally transport such a patient.

Ambulance service staffs can range from untrained volunteers to paramedics with modern, mobile intensive care units (MICU) that transmit physiological data from the field to the hospital through telemetry. In some countries, such as France, Ireland, the Soviet Union, and even in some parts of the United States, physicians have staffed mobile coronary care units. However, personnel training[7] and financing of emergency care are problems; for example, Medicare does not cover ambulance services.

Although emergency care in the United States has been generally poor, "emergentology" is now a medical specialty and undergoing reform. Improvements will reduce disabilities in all ages, and there is no doubt, according to various studies, that many more lives could be saved. Unfortunately, even in emergency rooms age prejudice exists; both private and public hospitals respond less favorably to older than to young persons.[8]

---

[6] In some jurisdictions (for example, the District of Columbia) where liability insurance is lacking or inadequate, the police themselves fear legal action.

[7] The traditional American Red Cross training is not adequate. A pamphlet on the training of ambulance personnel may be obtained from the National Academy of Sciences, 2101 Constitution Ave., N.W., Washington, D.C. 20418.

[8] Sudnow, D.: Passing on: the social organization of dying, Englewood Cliffs, N.J., 1967, Prentice-Hall, Inc.

Emergency shelter

One of the saddest problems is that of passing the buck by shunting the older person from one place to another. "Decisions" are made by avoidance, by taking minimal responsibility, and by failing to consult with the patient, his or her family, and (often) the family doctor. Voluntary hospitals are renowned for their ethically dubious practice of dropping the "Medicare patient" on the doorsteps of the municipal hospital.

Emergency shelter admission is mandatory and should be made available in any and all hospitals— to allow, at the very least, for a period of decision making. This is as true for the so-called social admissions (the person may have no place to sleep, etc.) as it is for medical and psychiatric episodes, especially the reversible brain syndromes (delirium), which require emergency action. Not only is the brief admission useful to effect a proper work-up, but also during that time therapy can begin and changes may be seen that may alter the original diagnostic impression and individual treatment program. The idea of hospitalization for several days in a unit attached to the emergency room of the hospital, for crisis intervention in all age groups, would be a step forward in evolving comprehensive social, medical, nursing, and psychiatric care in our general hospitals. Physicians, police, judges, and other community agents as well as families are frequently at a loss to know where to take an older person for comprehensive diagnosis. Complete diagnostic evaluations and a therapeutic trial should precede any admission to long-term mental hospitals or nursing home facilities. This requires a team approach with medical, nursing, mental health, and social evaluations.

Acute hospitalization

The term "acute hospitalization" usually applies to hospital stays lasting from a few days to 3 months, during which diagnosis and treatment take place simultaneously.[9] Transient confusional states (reversible brain syndromes) and functional disorders can respond to acute care, sometimes with dramatically positive results.

Psychiatric units in profit-making or in voluntary general hospitals usually provide short-term psychiatric care independent of age; in other words, when an older person is able to pay, he or she is more likely to receive the same degree of care as that given to younger people. If it is believed (either correctly or mistakenly) that the person is suffering from dementia, he or she will at least receive decent care until transfer elsewhere is arranged. Private mental hospitals also do effective work in the acute hospitalization of older persons. In addition, the inservice units of community mental health centers (usually public hospitals), as well as municipal, county, and state hospitals, provide this service with varying degrees of quality. Preadmission screening units, whether in the community or in general or state mental hospitals (Chapter 10), should be alert to the disorders that can respond to acute hospitalization.[10]

In Pennsylvania under Mental Health Act No. 143, persons who are labeled "senile" are specifically excluded from mental health treatment. Section 102 of the Act reads as follows:

It is the policy of the Commonwealth of Pennsylvania to seek to assure the availability of adequate treatment to persons who are mentally ill, and it is the purpose of this Act to establish procedures whereby this policy can be effected. Treatment on a voluntary basis shall be preferred to involuntary treatment; and in every case, the least restrictions consistent with adequate treatment shall be employed. Persons who are mentally retarded, senile, alcoholic, or drug dependent shall receive

---

[9] The work of Cosin in England, with patients moving in and out of the hospital depending on their condition at given times, is illustrative of good care.

[10] Some states (for example, New York and Pennsylvania) exclude older people who are regarded as "simply senile" (those with organic brain disorders who are neither psychotic nor severely depressed) from psychiatric admission and/or payment for psychiatric treatment. A study of 53 such people excluded by the New York State mental hospital system found that these patients are usually severely ill and often need psychiatric hospitalization before their placement in the community. See Feldshuh, B., Sillen, J., Parker, B., and Frasch, W.: The nonpsychotic organic brain syndrome, American Journal of Psychiatry **130**:1026-1029, 1973.

mental health treatment only if they are also diagnosed as mentally ill, but these conditions of themselves shall not be deemed to constitute mental illness.

Monica D. Blumenthal[11] has written,

The effect of this act has been to exclude persons suffering from chronic organic brain syndromes who are elderly from receiving care in the state mental hospitals. This creates a major difficulty in the management of those patients who require 24-hour-a-day supervision because they have great day-night confusion, they are wanderers, they are hostile and their care generally creates a great drain on the family. We have under our care a number of such patients whom we have not been able to manage successfully on an outpatient basis who live in families who are being driven to the limits of their endurance by the care required by their elderly person. Many families find it difficult to manage patients who disturb their sleep over long periods of time and we are not able to change this pattern in all our clients, although we are able to effect changes in some.

In families where the patient with organic brain syndrome is particularly disruptive, the care-takers who are often also elderly tend to develop a depressive reaction which in some instances has led to suicidal ideation and serious clinical depression requiring hospitalization.

The Mental Health Centers also interpret the law to mean that they are not responsible for providing care to patients with chronic brain syndromes.

During acute hospitalization it is important to maintain orientation—through unrestricted visiting hours, personal belongings and the like, and family liaison. Home pressures, unattended pets and plants belonging to older persons, and mail (especially Social Security, pension, and Supplemental Security Income checks) may need attention from hospital social aides or community agencies.

Chronic hospitalization

Organic brain damage is the major psychiatric reason for permanent hospitalization. Persons with chronic physical conditions (for example, stroke victims) may be admitted to chronic disease and geriatric hospitals, even though many such persons have accompanying or previously existing mental problems.

In 1976 approximately 49,100 persons over 65 were residents of state and county mental hospitals, with an additional 1,800 in private mental hospitals and 5,800 in Veterans Administration hospitals. Approximately two thirds of these persons were first admitted at age 65 or older, and the remaining one third was hospitalized at a younger age. Females outnumber males 2 to 1 in private mental hospitals, whereas in state and county hospitals the sex ratio is about 100 females to 97 males. In contrast, the VA hospital population is almost exclusively male.

Private mental hospitals, both voluntary non-profit and profit-making, offer care that is of adequate to high quality, at high prices, and thus they are beyond the resources of all but a few older people. The Veterans Administration provides services to a predominately male population that includes Spanish-American and World War I and II veterans.[12] There are 172 VA hospitals throughout the country as well as regional offices, 16 domiciles, 88 nursing homes, and 228 outpatient clinics. Of these, 33 are predominately psychiatric, although the others often provide psychiatric services. Most of these hospitals were built in the 1920s. Relatively little psychotherapy and few social services are offered. Drugs and custodial care are the norm. VA hospitals are neither better nor worse than state mental hospitals, and there is a great need for increasing resources.

The Veterans Administration states that it "has the most comprehensive program for continued treatment and follow-up of the aging patient to be found anywhere in the free world."[13] By law, the

---

[12] The average age of the World War I veterans was 83 in 1979, while the 13.5 million World War II veterans had an average age of 60.

[13] Dr. Paul A.C. Haber, Assistant Chief Medical Director for Professional Services. The VA has conducted a Normative Aging Study at the VA outpatient clinic in Boston since 1963, beginning with 2,135 men. See *Aging and Human Development,* (special issue), 1972. There are now eight Geriatric Research, Education, and Clinical Centers (GRECC). The Bedford (Mass.) VA Hospital, the location of one GRECC, is undertaking a study of senile dementia.

---

[11] Blumenthal, M.D., Geriatric Psychiatric Program Director, University of Pittsburgh, personal communication, 1980.

VA must provide medical care for 25 million veterans whose average age in 1972 was 45. In the same year, 1972, there were 2 million over 65, but by 1992 there will be 7 million, as World War II veterans grow older. Approximately 2 out of every 3 males over age 65 in the United States will be veterans, comprising about one fourth of the total male population. By the turn of the century, veterans age 65 and older will comprise more than 60% of all males age 65 and older. Thus, most of the nation's older men will be eligible for various veterans' benefits.[14]

State and county medical hospitals have been the center of long-standing controversy, and we have come full circle in our attempts to provide proper mental health care. When the American social reformer Dorothea Lynde Dix (1802-1887) began her efforts, there were practically no hospitals for the mentally ill. The first American asylum for mental patients was established in Williamsburg, Virginia, in 1773, and it was the only such "state hospital" of its kind for 50 years. Toward the midnineteenth century, the belief grew that the mentally and emotionally ill could be helped and that the state owed them help. Miss Dix pressed the idea of hospital care. A state-by-state system of hospitals was established, which now has come increasingly under criticism because of the quality of care and the basic concepts of treatment that it represents. With cries of "bring the patient back to the community," we seem panicked into an unfortunate and precipitous course of dismantling the hospital system without establishing valid alternatives.

It can be argued that there is no reason for chronic hospitalization, since nursing homes and other facilities could provide the appropriate care. (See the overview presented in Chapter 4.) Many older people are in mental institutions not because they need to be, but simply because there is no other facility for them. But paralleling the studies purporting to show that older people need not be

in mental hospitals are reports that older persons need not be in nursing homes. Older people seem never to belong anywhere!

Yet there is a grain of truth in all these points of view. These people frequently are misplaced; many could remain at home with supportive services. For those who do require permanent residential treatment for medical and/or psychiatric reasons, there is only a narrow range of choices available, which may not fit their particular situations. Neither present-day nursing homes nor mental hospitals can escape justly deserved criticism. The financing arrangements, often politically inspired, that support the growing nursing home industry have led to numbers of older persons with chronic organic brain disorders being given custodial care in nursing homes rather than mental hospitals. The nursing home (especially the intermediate care facility) becomes a de facto location for mental patients, with few of the attributes of a mental hospital.

Many nursing homes are unsafe in terms of fire protection and patient supervision. They may provide poor nursing and medical care, little or no psychiatric care, and minimal rehabilitation and recreation. Living in a nursing home is too often like being confined to a motel (in fact a number of homes seem designed for quick renovation into motels should the present clientele prove unprofitable). State mental hospitals, on the other hand, generally have a mixed age range of people, more grounds than typical nursing home facilities, a larger number of staff, more activities and social programs, theaters, churches, gymnasiums, job opportunities (including sheltered workshops), gardening, and stores. There is an atmosphere of greater hustle and bustle, more like that of a community. Safety and fire security regulations are usually more strictly enforced. If the massive mental hospitals could be refurbished or be physically moved out of their usual geographical location (too far from the community); if the "back wards" were abolished and all custodial care replaced with active treatment programs; and if admissions, periods of residence, and discharges became more fluid and flexible procedures aimed at integration

---

[14] Veterans 65 and over are considered by law to be "permanently and totally disabled" and thus eligible for pensions if their incomes are below an amount set by law.

with family and community life, then the concept of the mental hospital might become accepted by older people, their families, and professionals. As it is now, the mental hospital symbolizes being "old and crazy," whereas the nursing home means that one is "old, incapacitated, and about to die." Neither represents a positive approach to mental health care.

The 1980 Mental Health Systems Act (see Chapter 10) is one effort to help overcome some of the negative consequences of deinstitutionalization of mental patients and enable more of such persons to live in the community. Title I, for example, focuses on increasing state involvement in developing a comprehensive network of community support services for those with chronic mental illness.

Meanwhile, the American Federation of State, County, and Municipal Employees (AFSCME) launched a massive public relations and lobbying campaign in 1978-1980 to reverse the national trend of "deinstitutionalizing" chronic mental patients. The AFSCME, whose 1 million members makes it the nation's largest public employee union, is concerned with protecting the jobs of its many members who work in the large state hospitals. Rather than closing down or cutting back hospital care, the AFSCME advocates expanding the national mental health care program, including improved institutions for those who need constant care, publicly operated community-based facilities, and psychiatric care that is accessible and affordable for low- and middle-income people, as well as the affluent.

Foster care

"Foster care" originated as foster parent programs for children; efforts to encourage families to take in older people who are unrelated to them have never been very successful, presumably because older people are not so "attractive" as children. Foster care has become a euphemism for foster family care and really describes, in many areas, an underfinanced, unregulated, unprofessional series of "homes" operated for profit. Since some

states have sought to reduce state mental hospital rolls, many older people—usually long-term and predominately schizophrenic patients—have been transferred, often indiscriminately, into foster care, intermediate care, and other so-called nursing homes, as well as boarding homes of various types.[15] Finding locations for community residential facilities is difficult because of state and local zoning legislation and regulations. Often such facilities are forced into high-density, commercial, transient, and low-income areas.[16]

The passive, supine nontroublemakers are most likely to be chosen for these dubious exchanges, since foster care and personal care homes will take only tractable persons who have minimal nursing

---

[15] Butler, Goldfarb, Weinberg, and others protested indiscriminate transfers to unacceptable settings (Trends in long-term care, hearings before the U.S. Senate Special Committee on Aging, Subcommittee on Long-term Care, Dec. 17, 1970). The vulnerability of the aged to death or illness as a result of transfer ("transfer mortality") is a serious cause for concern (Butler, R.N.: Immediate and long-range dangers to transfer of elderly patients from state hospitals to community facilities [guest editorial]; The Gerontologist 10:259-260, 1970; see also Aldrich, C.K., and Mendkoff, E.: Relocation of the aged and disabled: a mortality study, Journal of the American Geriatrics Society 11:185-194, 1963; and Killian, E.C.: Effect of geriatric transfers on mortality rates, Social Work 15:19-26, 1970; there are numerous papers showing the same mortal and morbid effects). Lieberman's studies have shown that a year or more of preparation may be necessary to increase survival during the first 6 months in an institution, even when the institution is adequate (Lieberman, M.A.: Psychological effects of institutionalization, Journal of Gerontology 23:343-353, 1968).

Of course, movement of patients is not necessarily an evil in itself. Some facilities are so terrible that transfer is humane. *Where* the person is being moved is important. For instance, in Pennsylvania in 1967, a program was developed at the South Mountain Geriatric Center. Patients were moved out of the state mental hospitals and into this facility designed exclusively for the use of older people. Favorable results have been reported (Cohen, E.S., and Kraft, A.C.: The restorative potential of elderly long-term residents of mental hospitals; paper presented at Twentieth Annual Meeting of the Gerontological Society, St. Petersburg, Fla., Nov. 9, 1967).

[16] Oriol, W.E.: Housing the elderly deinstitutionalized mental hospital patient in the community, Washington, D.C., 1980, International Center for Social Gerontology, Inc.

needs. The average payment through Supplemental Security Income to such "homes" is hardly enough to provide decent food and the basic amenities, let alone medical, nursing, psychiatric, and social care. Safety and fire inspections are notoriously negligent.

> The chief D.C. fire marshall yesterday ordered the immediate inspection of all foster care homes used by St. Elizabeths Hospital after two patients died early yesterday in a fire at one such home in Southeast Washington.
>
> THE WASHINGTON POST
> *December 15, 1971*

Boarding homes are equally at fault in terms of safety hazards. In the winter and spring of 1979, 45 patients died in boarding house fires in Missouri, Pennsylvania, and the District of Columbia. Boarding homes and foster care homes are often not covered by safety codes because they fall into a "residential" rather than an "institutional" category.

Nursing homes

More than a million older people live in nursing homes in the United States, and these homes have received considerable adverse attention from legislators, the press, and the general public. We wish to emphasize that there are a number of fine commercial nursing homes (often called "proprietary" homes) that give good care to older persons, and we would hope to encourage and support their efforts. However, a significantly larger number of homes are correctly described as human dumping grounds and even as "halfway houses somewhere between society and the cemetery."[17] We focus here on the deficiencies of nursing home care—not to moralize but to present the reader with a picture of what remains to be accomplished in upgrading patient care.[18] We also provide a brief

---

[17] Former Congressman and now Senator David Pryor (D-Ark.), 1970.

[18] A special debt is owed former Senator Frank Moss (D-Utah), ably assisted by staff director, Frank Frantz, of the U.S. Senate Subcommittee on Long-term Care, for its pioneer hearings on nursing homes in the pre-Medicare period.

description of some of the reasons why nursing home care has evolved into its present form.

Categories of nursing homes

Commerical nursing homes are, of course, available to people who can afford to pay for their own care. However, because costs of care have risen so precipitously,[19] a number of financing mechanisms have been created to assist the majority of people who could not otherwise afford care. There continue to be many problems; for example, middle-income people may have too much income to be eligible for assistance but not enough to pay for care by themselves.

The various categories of nursing homes, which are directly defined by their federal and state financing, do not always clarify the actual kind and amount of service offered. Therefore one must check on the *actual* service rendered (for example, how *much* nursing care) in a particular home, regardless of category.

There are two major types of long-term care institutions for the aged that the federal government subsidizes through Medicare and Medicaid (Title 18 and 19, respectively, of the Social Security Act). These are known as skilled nursing facilities (SNF) and intermediate care facilities (ICF). These categories are often referred to as "levels of care." Entire sets of standards and reimbursement systems are based on these levels of care. *Skilled nursing care* refers to those services that must be performed under the supervision of professional or registered nurses. *Intermediate care* is "more than room and board, but less than skilled nursing." These terms are very unclear to the public as well as to health professions, Congress, and the press. There is a tendency to use the term "nursing home" to cover everything here described. The degree of confusion involved in applying the definitions of skilled nursing and intermediate care can be observed in noting the percentages of patients classified into the two levels in different states. In New York State, approximately 80% of

---

[19] Some nursing home fees range well beyong $1,000 a month.

patients are in "skilled nursing," while in New Mexico and Iowa only 15% are classified in this category. Because reimbursement for skilled nursing care is higher than for intermediate care, some states have simply transformed (often without much change) ICFs into questionable SNFs. Another problem is the tendency of some nursing home operators to collude with doctors to have most people designated as SNF clients.

Originally SNF's were divided into two categories, extended care facilities (Medicare) and skilled nursing care facilities (Medicaid). The 1972 Social Security Amendments created a single definition and set of standards for ECFs and SNFs; thus the new category "skilled nursing facility" was introduced.

An ICF may approximate what the public has in mind when it refers to a "nursing home." (Some communities as large as San Francisco do not have ICFs, apparently because the reimbursement rates for the ICF level of care do not encourage their development.) Personal care, simple medical care, and intermittent nursing care are the services under the jurisdiction of ICFs.

Number of nursing home beds available

Nearly 20,000 care facilities were certified in 1980 by federal and/or state agencies to receive

Table 11-1. Number and financing of nursing home beds, 1980

Type of facility	Number of beds	Financing
Intermediate care facilities	905,000	Medicaid only beds
Skilled nursing facilities	433,715	Both Medicaid and Medicare beds
	144,000	Medicaid only beds
	27,000	Medicare only beds
TOTAL	1,509,715	

Data from Department of Health and Human Resources, Health Care Finance Administration, 1980. There may be an additional 700,000 beds in other facilities for long-term care—mainly residentail beds in domicilary or personal care homes that are not federally certified.

financing for providing nursing home care. The number of beds available is shown in Table 11-1. Assuming a 10% bed vacancy rate and the fact that some patients are young or disabled persons, it was estimated that in 1977, 1,126,000 older people were nursing home patients.[20] (The 1980 Census will provide a more current count of nursing home patients.) The major associations of nursing homes and homes for the aging, including figures on the number of beds each organization represents, are listed at the end of this chapter.

Financing of nursing homes

In discussing nursing home care, it is important to clarify a few points about the commercial nursing home industry. The United States is one of the few countries in the world where care of sick older persons has become "big business," run primarily for commercial gain. The number of nursing homes has proliferated since 1965.

The nursing home industry consists of some 23,000 homes[21] with 1.5 million beds. About 90% of the homes are profit making, some owned by large chains with publicly sold stock. Others have nonprofit sponsors such as churches and community organizations. A total of $21 billion was spent on nursing home care in fiscal 1980. These 23,000 homes are more than twice the number that existed around 1960. This growth began partly in response to the increasing demand for beds as the aging population increased and was accelerated by the passage of Medicare and Medicaid. Guaranteed payments to nursing homes convinced investors that it was a no-lose proposition. By 1969, Wall Street considered nursing homes a glamour industry. Investments came from real estate developers, insurance men, used cars businessmen, and others outside the health field. Physicians, despite obvious conflict of interests, invest in and own nursing homes.

Government officials estimate about one half of the United States' 1.5 million nursing home beds are controlled by profit-making corporate chains

---

[20] According to U.S. Public Health Service data.

[21] There are differing counts of the numbers of nursing homes.

that operate five or more homes each. The top 20 chains run one third of the industry and are buying out more and more of the smaller owners. The major reasons for this phenomenon are the following.

1. With inflation and a squeeze in health care dollars, chains can outdo small owners by buying in volume, centralizing accounting, and sharing specialists' services. As one executive said, "We can McDonaldize."
2. Chains can buy the sophisticated management necessary to streamline compliance with federal, state, and local standards that often overlap. Small operators are swamped by the paperwork. The chains hire specialists to handle it.
3. Many large firms look at nursing homes as a real estate investment.
4. Corporations can write off a failing or foundering nursing home as a tax loss.
5. There is money to be made. For example, nursing homes took about 53 to 54 cents of every Medicaid dollar in 1980.

It should be also mentioned that the same thing is happening with psychiatric hospitals. According to a study by the National Institute of Mental Health, the number of chain-owned psychiatric hospitals rose 66% from 1968 to 1975. Chains now own more than 57% of the nation's 180 private psychiatric hospitals.

In 1970 and 1971 many nursing homes withdrew from the Medicare program that had so encouraged their growth. Some did so because they had not met standards (and a number of them could not afford to do so even if they had wished to), whereas others were frustrated and impatient with the bureaucratic confusion, laborious and contradictory rules and regulations from the federal government, retroactive denial of claims, and other administrative difficulties. It must also be noted that these institutions have had to adapt to rapidly changing federal law—the Kerr-Mills program, Vendor Medical Programs, and Medicare. On the other hand, cases have been documented in which the nursing homes overbilled, billed for services never delivered, billed after a patient's death, and double-billed to different governmental programs

for the same patient. The government has also charged that services were overutilized, thus costing more than originally anticipated.

Conditions in nursing homes

There are, as we have said, some excellent homes in which emphasis is on meeting patients' needs in every way possible within financial limits. But the remainder of homes run the gamut from filthy and unsafe to clean but cheerless and depressing. The worst of the homes are firetraps, with unhealthy living conditions and neglect of patient care. Other homes are stylized, motel-like, antiseptically clean horrors—patients sit in numb silence with dejected faces or pace endlessly down hallways. There may be little commotion or communication except for the one-way mumble of television. Nutrition is often inadequate. Poor food-handling standards have resulted in food poisoning such as in the July 1970 *Salmonella* epidemic in a nursing home in Baltimore, Maryland, where 107 patients became ill and 25 died. Personal abuse of patients by the staff can occur because the older people are ill, vulnerable, and unable to defend themselves, and the staff may be untrained, unmotivated, and improperly supervised. Many nursing home administrators themselves have had no specific training directly related to their work, although this is changing, happily. There is a shortage of physician services, skilled nursing care, dental care, social services, and psychiatric care. Patients often are overmedicated and deprived of any responsibility or decision making on their own behalf.[22]

Nursing home standards

Individual nursing homes are subject to state and/or federal standards, depending on their financing, but the federal government gives enforcement functions to the states. Yet even those states that have receivership laws, civil financial penalties, and the authority to withhold placements in

---

[22] For a view of the depersonalization that can occur, see Barron, E.: When you're old, money is honey, Social Work **20:** 230-232, 1975.

inadequate facilities have not been altogether effective in providing quality care or in preventing facilities from violating regulations. Homes that do not meet standards are often allowed to remain "temporarily" open, with the explanation given that patients would have no other place to go. Basic fire and safety standards may go unheeded, and nursing home disasters are inevitable under the circumstances.

As the result of a 1972 directive by President Nixon, the Department of Health, Education and Welfare established a new office to oversee all HEW programs relating to nursing homes. The Office of Nursing Home Affairs (ONHA) was responsible for coordinating efforts by different agencies in the Department to upgrade standards nationwide for the benefit of the more than a million Americans living in nursing homes. Establishment of ONHA with a director meant that for the first time, a single official was responsible for pulling together different HEW nursing home efforts into a single coordinated program.

In 1975 ONHA was given lead responsibility for home health services as well as nursing home services. In 1976 the organizational title of ONHA was changed to the Office of Long Term Care (OLTC) to better reflect the idea that care may need to be long term, whether in or out of institutions.

The list below gives President Nixon's 8-point nursing home program,[23] announced in 1971.

1. Training state nursing home inspectors
2. Completion of federal support of state inspections under Medicaid
3. Consolidation of enforcement activities
4. Strengthening federal enforcement
5. Short-term training for professional and paraprofessional nursing home personnel
6. Assistance for state investigative units
7. Comprehensive review of long-term care
8. Cracking down on substandard nursing homes

---

[23] From the President's message on aging to Congress, March 23, 1972.

Despite this high-sounding rhetoric, in 1974 the U.S. Senate Special Committee on Aging reported major deficiencies in fire safety and sanitation alone in 50% of American nursing homes. Public Law 94-182, signed in December 1975, mandated the use of the 1973 edition of the Life Safety Code in all long-term care facilities.[24] The Life Safety Code has been the most successfully enforced of the nursing home standards, since the technical requirements are clearly stated, nursing home owners are fearful of facing legal charges if patients die or are injured, and judges usually move quickly to enforce standards if a risk of fire is uncovered.

A nursing home may voluntarily apply for accreditation by the Joint Commission on Accreditation of Hospitals (JCAH) on the recommendation of the Accreditation Council for Long Term Care Facilities (ACLTCF). A certificate of accreditation from the JCAH means that certain basic standards have been met. The standards are developed by health professionals and relate to all aspects of a facility's operation, including organization and administration; fire safety and construction; nursing, dietetic, and pharmaceutical services; medical/health records; and social, environmental, and other essential services. There are also standards requiring a facility to evaluate continuously the

---

[24] The Life Safety Code of the National Fire Protection Association (NFPA) does not require sprinklers in buildings that are fire resistant for 2 hours or in buildings of one story that are protected and noncombustible for 1 hour. One-hour "protected combustible" residences (that is, frame construction buildings) must have sprinklers throughout. In all buildings, however, sprinklers are required in hazardous areas—kitchens, storage areas, and trash rooms. Sprinkler systems are life-savers. The NFPA has *never* received a report of a multiple-death fire in a hospital, a nursing home, or a home for the aged that had sprinklers throughout. NFPA recorded that in the 28-year period from 1951-1978, 73 multiple-death (three or more fatalities) fires occurred in facilities that were without sprinklers, causing a total of 682 deaths.

For further information on safety in long-term care institutions see Life Safety Code, National Fire Protection Association, 470 Atlantic Ave., Boston, Mass. 02210; and Long-term care safety standards, Joint Committee on Accreditation of Hospitals, 875 N. Michigan Ave., Chicago, Ill. 60611.

quality of the care and the services it provides.[25] Two specific categories of long-term care facilities are included under the standards: (1) "a long-term health facility"—which must have inpatient care; an organized medical staff, a medical staff equivalent, or a medical director; and continuous nursing service under professional nurse direction, and (2) a "resident care facility"—which must provide a safe, hygenic, living arrangement for residents who do not need or do not desire the more intensive care provided by a long-term health care facility.

Dissatisfaction has been expressed about the usual certification process for long-term care facilities. Although regulations are established for the proper conduct of such facilities for reimbursement purposes, most reimbursements rely on the determination of whether a facility is *capable* of providing the needed service, not on whether it has delivered such a service. There has been no systematic way to identify whether the patient is receiving the service or making the progress that he or she should. In other words, survey and certification

only evaluate paper compliance, not the quality of care rendered.

The Patient Appraisal Care Planning and Evaluation (PACE)[26] is an evaluation approach that can be used to determine the care a patient needs and the effects of that care after it is provided. It is built on a health care model rather than a medical (sickness) model. By using the PACE instrument, the appraiser (provider of care in a nursing home, usually a nurse) observes and records data about patient characteristics and functional capacity, plans for an individual's goals, and determines if those goals have been met.

Patient Care Management System (PCMS), developed by the Department of Health and Human Services, incorporates concepts of the PACE instrument. It is a formal assessment of each patient's needs, a plan to meet those specific needs, and a care outcome evaluation. It provides a way to periodically assess medical, nursing, nutritional, and psychosocial conditions as well as the discharge potential of each patient.

In another attempt to assess and standardize care, the Long Term Care Minimum Data Set of the National Center on Health Statistics was designed to standardize information in medical records. It requires the inclusion of four major areas in medical records: demographic-health status, service, administrative, and procedural areas. This data set can be tied into the PACE instrument both to improve the assessment of care and to assist re-

---

[25] These standards are published by the JCAH in the *Accreditation Manual for Long Term Care Facilities*. A not-for-profit, nongovernmental organization, the JCAH is sponsored by four major hospital and medical groups: The American College of Physicians, the American College of Surgeons, the American Hospital Association, and the American Medical Association. Its accreditation programs receive technical and professional advice from an advisory group made up of the following members:

    American Association of Homes for the Aging
    American College of Nursing Home Administrators
    American College of Physicians
    American Congress of Rehabilitative Medicine
    American Health Care Association
    American Medical Association
    American Nurses Association
    American Podiatry Association
    American Psychiatric Association
    Center for Study of Aging and Human Development
    National Association of Social Workers, Inc.
    National Council of Health Care Services
    National Association of State Mental Health Program Directors
There are no public or consumer members.

---

[26] Conceived, after studying about 50 quality-of-care evaluation instruments, by Clare Ryder (M.D., M.P.H.). Faye Abdellah, assistant surgeon general and chief nurse officer, Department of Health, Education and Welfare, Public Health Service, directed the initial efforts leading to the development of PACE during her term as director of the HEW office of Long Term Care. See Abdellah, F.G., Foerst, H.V., and Chow, R.K.: PACE: an approach to improving the care of the elderly, American Journal of Nursing **79**(6):1109-1110, 1979.

Other references on patient assessment are Densen, P.M., and Jones, E.W.: The patient classification for long-term care developed by four research groups in the U.S., Medical Care **14**:137-144, 1976; and Jones, E.W., McNitt, B.J., and Densen, P.M.: Patient assessment and its use in long-term care facilities, American Health Association Journal **1**:74-80, 1975.

searchers by providing standardized data. Sidney Katz's index of the activities of daily living (ADL)[27] is compatible with the work done by the National Center on Health Statistics in its 1977 National Health Interview Survey and the National Nursing Home Survey.

The Multidimensional Functional Assessment Questionnaire developed by the Older American Resources and Services Program (OARS) at the Duke University Center for the Study of Aging and Human Development is a method for testing impaired adults and in particular older people. It is designed to provide information on the level of functioning in five areas—physical health, mental health, social resources, economic resources, and self-care capacity—as well as the need for services.

Patient characteristics

The average age of nursing home residents is 80 years; 70% are women and 90% are white. Some 85% to 90% of persons who enter nursing homes do not leave them alive. The average length of stay is 1.6 years, with one third of the residents dying within the first year and another third between the first and third years. The final third live 3 or more years (see Table 11-2). Breaking down these figures somewhat further, the average stay in a skilled nursing facility is 25 days and in an intermediate care facility 2½ years.

As with all of the institutions for older persons, "large numbers of the disabled are forced into nursing homes . . . at a very high charge to the public treasury simply because public programs could not give attention to alternative ways of meeting their needs outside of institutions."[28] See

Table 11-2. Length of stay of nursing home residents, 1977

Distribution of length of stay	Percentage of residents
Less than 3 months	13
3-6 months	10
6-12 months	14
1-3 years	32
3-plus years	31

Median length of stay: 582 days or 1.6 years

Data from U.S. Public Health Service, National Center of Health Statistics, Washington, D.C., 1977.

Table 11-3 and Fig. 5 for descriptions of the physical illnesses and diseases found among nursing home patients. A 1971 study by Brandeis University's Levinson Gerontological Policy Institute of nursing home inhabitants in Massachusetts showed that of 100 persons, 37 needed fulltime skilled nursing care, 26 needed minimally supervised "living," 23 could get along at home with periodic home visits by nurses, and 14 needed nothing.

The numbers of people in nursing homes who suffer from psychiatric disorders have been variously estimated; Goldfarb, for example, in 1962, found that 87% of patients showed significant evidence of chronic brain syndrome. As we have emphasized previously, persons with chronic physical disorders generally have psychiatric symptom manifestations. Added to these patients are the numbers of people now being transfered from mental institutions.[29] Despite the need, it is rare for psychiatric care to be available. Nursing homes tend to select persons with kinds of psychiatric symptoms that cause the least problems. Suicidal, boisterous, or hostile persons are likely to be rejected, along with those who wander off, smoke in

[27] Katz, S., Downs, T.D., Cash, H., and Grotz, R.C.: Progress and development of the index of ADL, The Gerontologist **10**:20-30, 1970.

[28] U.S. Senate Special Committee on Aging: Alternatives to nursing home care: a proposal, prepared by Levinson Gerontological Policy Institute (Robert Morris, Director), Brandeis University, Waltham, Mass., Oct. 1971, Washington, D.C., 1971, U.S. Government Printing Office.

[29] Kramer, M., Taube, D., and Starr, S.: Patterns of use of psychiatric facilities by the aged: current status, trends, and implications, proceedings of the American Psychiatric Association Regional Research Conference on Aging, "Aging in Modern Society," 1967.

Table 11-3. Number and percentage of nursing home residents, by selected health statuses, United States, 1977

Health status	Residents	
	Number	Percentage
TOTAL	1,303,100	100.0
PRIMARY DIAGNOSIS AT LAST EXAMINATION		
Diseases of the circulatory system		
TOTAL	516,800	39.7
Congestive heart failure	52,800	4.1
Arteriosclerosis	264,400	20.3
Hypertension	47,700	3.7
Stroke	103,500	7.9
Heart attack, ischemic heart disease	22,500	1.7
Other	25,800	2.0
Mental disorders and senility without psychosis		
TOTAL	266,100	20.4
Senile psychosis	21,200	1.6
Other psychosis	57,400	4.4
Chronic brain syndrome	96,400	7.4
Senility without psychosis	26,600	2.0
Mental retardation	42,400	3.3
Alcoholism	6,800	.5
Other mental disorders	15,300	1.2
Other diagnoses		
TOTAL	429,700	33.0
Diseases of the musculoskeletal system and connective tissues		
Arthritis and rheumatism	56,200	4.3
Diseases of the nervous system and sense organs		
Blindness	5,100	.4
Multiple sclerosis	7,300	.6
Epilepsy	6,800	.5
Parkinson's disease	23,300	1.8
Accidents, poisonings, and violence		
Hip fracture	29,300	2.2
Other bone fracture	10,600	.8
Endocrine, nutritional, and metabolic diseases		
Diabetes	71,700	5.5
Neoplasms		
Cancer	28,900	2.2
Diseases of the respiratory system		
Emphysema	8,000	.6
Pneumonia		
Other respiratory diseases	18,500	1.4
Diseases of the digestive system		
Ulcers	8,600	.7
Diseases of the blood and blood-forming organs		
Anemia	7,300	.6
Diagnosis unknown		
TOTAL	90,500	6.9

Data from U.S. Public Health Service; National Center for Health Statistics, 1977.

Fig. 5. *Includes neoplasms, respiratory, digestive, genito-urinary, eye, ear, and others. Surveyed: 283,300 residents of 6,591 skilled nursing facilities.

U.S. Department of Health, Education and Welfare, Office of Nursing Home Affairs: Long-term care facility improvement study. Introductory Report, Stock No. 017-001-00397-2, July 1975.

bed, or are addicted to drugs or alcohol. The tractable, depressed, withdrawn persons are more acceptable, as well as those with incontinence and definite nursing needs.

The ongoing nursing home debate

The latest round in the continuing national debate over nursing homes is worth noting. Some insist that too many people are in nursing homes. Vladeck's controversial book, *Unloving Care: The Nursing Home Tragedy*,[30] advocates phasing out the worst one third of the nation's 17,000 nursing homes and using the approximately $5 billion saved by this move to supplement the $1 billion currently spent on special housing and home-based services for older people. Vladeck divides the current nursing home population into three categories.

1. The 100,000 to 200,000 people who are fatally ill or recuperating from acute illnesses who would be better off in a hospital extended care facility where they could get the medical attention they need. The majority of these persons die soon after admission to a nursing home (the average stay is 6 months). Vladeck suggests they could use the estimated 100,000 beds now empty in hospitals.
2. The half million patients with physical disabilities who are in nursing homes because they have no one at home to care for them. Although chronically ill, these patients could live, with support, outside the nursing home in, for example, congregate housing where housekeeping services, meals, medical services, etc would be available.
3. The more than one half million persons who need round-the-clock custodial care. Vladeck believes that nursing homes are necessary for this group, but only they should be institutionalized.

On the other hand, Dunlop[31] and others question

whether a significantly reduced rate of institutionalization in nursing homes is feasible. Those older persons with family members who are available to care for them are generally very severely impaired by the time they enter a nursing home. This is because family members tend to help the older person remain at home as long and sometimes much longer than is reasonable. Housekeeping, personal care, and errands are common forms of assistance given by families. When chronic and extensive nursing care becomes necessary, most families turn to nursing homes. How many could be encouraged to care for sicker relatives than they now do, even with nursing and medical support? The question becomes more complicated when we remember what is happening to the family and to American women. More and more middle-aged women, the traditional caregivers to the old, are going to work outside the home. The size of the family itself is thinning out because of a lowered birth rate. And the increased life expectancy is bringing more four and five generation families, with a host of older people for the middle-aged and younger family members to be responsible for. Increased home care might bring more rather than less burden to these family members by enabling more of the aged to remain home in a chronically ill condition.

Although generally healthier as a group than patients with families, those nursing home patients with no family on whom to rely would frequently have to have some form of protected living (like congregate housing) as an alternative to a nursing home. This becomes an enormously expensive proposition requiring a whole new set of structures or the remodeling of older structures. Although this might be desirable for older persons, it would not necessarily reduce the cost of long-term care and could conceivably increase it. Furthermore, unless a whole new approach were taken, these new "quasiinstitutions" might prove to be little improvement over the present intermediate care facilities where most such older people now live.

All in all, many persons knowledgeable in the field of nursing homes in the United States believe

[30] Vladeck, B.C.: Unloving care: the nursing home tragedy, New York, 1980, The Twentieth Century Fund.
[31] Dunlop, B.B.: Expanded home-based care for the impaired elderly: solution or pipe dream? American Journal of Public Health **70**(5):514-519, 1980.

that, at most, 10% of nursing home patients could live on their own in the community with home health or other supports. But this has to be balanced with the thought that perhaps that same number of persons are now existing in the community under unacceptable circumstances and really should be in institutions. Sophisticated epidemiological studies are needed to determine the facts.

Selecting a nursing home[32]

Mental health personnel should be thoroughly familiar with any nursing homes to which they refer older people and their families. Initially one should know whether the home is state-licensed, whether it is certified to participate in government financial assistance programs, whether the administrator is state-licensed, and whether the home provides such services as physical therapy, social work, and specially prescribed diets. Visits to the nursing home in question are useful in order to talk to staff, observe the home and its operations, and view the patients firsthand. Families can contact local agencies (usually public health departments, voluntary and family agencies) and physicians who may be able to give an idea of the quality of individual homes. Local health and welfare councils, welfare departments, and mental health associations may provide help in selection. (A provision of the 1972 Social Security Act gives consumers the right to ask at any Social Security or welfare office for the records of deficiencies found in government inspections of all Medicare- and Medicaid-funded nursing homes. The full reports can be obtained on written request from regional Social Security or welfare offices at a minimal cost.) Proper placement must, of course, be based on a comprehensive evaluation of the older person's condition and needs.

Homes for the aging

Homes for the aging are voluntary, nonprofit institutions, usually sectarian (religious) but also under the auspices of benevolent and fraternal associations, trusts, or municipalities. Increasingly, homes for the aging have nursing home components.

They are not at this time totally satisfactory community resources because many of them have not yet achieved full social responsibility. Religious, fraternal, and trust homes tend to be very selective in their admissions, and persons without some wealth and a sustaining family are more likely to be rejected. The homes ordinarily exclude the overtly mentally ill, the severely mentally impaired, and the acutely or notably physically ill. When illnesses develop after admission, transfer to municipal, county, and state facilities is probable because most homes for the aging have insufficient services and personnel to provide the necessary care. Members of minority groups are generally excluded through overt or covert means; less than 3% of residents are black. (Failure to comply with Title VI of the Civil Rights Act has left some homes out of Medicare.) Waiting periods for admission are long—several months to several years. Persons on waiting lists are not usually provided with outreach services, although these services are developing in some areas.

Since homes for the aging do depend on voluntary contributions, it is understandable how difficult it has been for them to offer a range of services on a multilevel basis in accordance with the changing medical and psychiatric statuses of older people. There is growing public support for diversion of public taxpayers' money from the commercial nursing home industry to nonprofit homes.[33] Table 11-4 describes the associations involved in long-term care.

There are beginning to be major progressive

---

[32] See Nassau, J.B.: Choosing a nursing home, New York, 1975, Funk & Wagnalls Publishing Co., Inc. An excellent guide, *How to Choose a Nursing Home,* is available from the Institute of Gerontology, University of Michigan, 543 Church St., Ann Arbor, Mich. 48104. The American Nursing Home Association will provide single copies free of charge of another brochure, *Thinking About a Nursing Home?* if the request is accompanied by a self-addressed, stamped, return envelope.

[33] The National Council on the Aging support such a diversion.

Table 11-4. Percentages and kinds of institutional homes

Homes	Percentage
Commercial nursing homes	79
Voluntary nonprofit homes for aging: nursing homes and "campus" complexes (religious, benevolent, fraternal, and trust)	14
Governmental homes (federal, state, county, and municipal)	7

changes as homes for the aging move away from the limited historic connotations of "old age homes." A few have evolved into *campuses* where a wide spectrum of services and facilities is created to give progressive, graduated care. It has long been realized that older individuals do not fall neatly into institutional categories. Living "independently" in apartments can be possible if medical services and ready access to hospital facilities are provided. And many can live in a home for the aging or a nursing home rather than a state hospital if such facilities offer therapeutic programs and can draw on personnel usually found in a hospital. How can all these services be offered? The Philadelphia Geriatric Center has included all the combinations suggested above in one city block: a hospital, the Home for the Jewish Aged (which was the parent institution), two residential apartment buildings, a research institute, and several small-unit, intermediate boarding facilities. A day-care center for older persons exists in another part of the city.

Other homes for the aging have moved beyond their physical structure into the community. Social services, Meals-on-Wheels, and day-care centers are developing in some areas. "Drop-in" centers with recreational service, arts, and crafts may occasionally be found, along with sheltered workshops.

An outstanding long-term care facility is the Jewish Home and Hospital for the Aged in New York, founded in 1870. It is the largest nonprofit institution for the care of the aged in New York City, with many programs in teaching (The Fred-

eric D. Zeman Center for Instruction) and research. Over 1,600 individuals are cared for through an integrated group of facilities. The aged in the community are served by a day-care center and geriatric outreach program. At its two main centers are intermediate care (health-related) facilities and skilled nursing facilities, and 500 beds accredited as a Chronic Disease Hospital.[34] A middle-income housing project has 320 residents.

Particularly outstanding is the Jewish Institute for Geriatric Care, New Hyde Park, New York, where Leslie S. Libow has done his pioneering work both in geriatric medical education and in developing the body of knowledge of geriatric medicine.

Some homes do accept the so-called senile patient. The Menorah Home and Hospital for the Aged in Brooklyn, New York, a 526-bed institution with 300 senile residents and 500 outpatients, has pioneered in the provision of psychiatric and mental health services for older persons. In 1957 Menorah founded a Geriatric Guidance Clinic and also established the first day center in a home for the aged (with a membership of 250 older people living in the community).

Other exemplary institutions, some of which approximate the campus-type of environment, are the Carmelite Homes (the Mary Manning Walsh Home[35] of New York City and St. Joseph's Manor of Trumbull, Connecticut), the Isabella Home Geriatric Center in New York City, the Avery Convalescent Center in Hartford, Connecticut, the Philadelphia Geriatric Center, Golden Acres (the Jewish Home for the Aged) of Dallas, Texas, the Samarkand of Santa Barbara, California, Lincoln Lutheran of Racine, Wisconsin, Loretto Geriatric

---

[34] Many facilities for older persons do not conduct regular autopsies, thus losing valuable opportunities to discover diagnostic errors and to advance research in aging. The Jewish Home and Hospital, to its credit, has an autopsy rate well over 50%.

[35] Bernadette de Lourdes, Mother: Where somebody cares: the Mary Manning Walsh Home and its program for complete care of the aging, a descriptive account of modern concepts in action, New York, 1959, G.P. Putman's Sons.

Center of Syracuse, New York, Asbury Methodist Village of Gaithersburg, Maryland, the Hebrew Rehabilitation Center for the Aged of Boston, and the Wesley Homes of Atlanta, Georgia.[36]

A number of the American Association of Homes for the Aging's member homes are involved in housing, health-related shelter, and community programs such as day care, home health, and nutrition. Of every 10 AAHA homes, 9 provide some form of "homes without walls" services, for example, outpatient services (3,000 homes for the aging and nursing homes are providing outpatient services, 2,000 with nonprofit support).

FINANCING INSTITUTIONAL CARE

Personal and economic costs of mental diseases are staggering. For example, a private nursing home can cost $1,200 a month, and some families pay another $1,000 a month to obtain a 24-hour private duty nurse in the nursing home. Private mental hospitals may cost $2,000 monthly. Figures on the cost of a Medicaid bed in a skilled nursing care facility for June 1977–July 1978 are as follows.

New York	$16,275
California	$16,713
Iowa	$16,133

A tragic way of cutting costs would be to place older mental patients outside the mainstream of psychiatric care. Therefore a truly appropriate national health plan must cover long-term and terminal care for the psychiatrically and physically impaired patient. Two thirds of our nation's health bill is for chronic illness (two thirds of $118.7 billion in 1975, with the total amount rising rapidly since then). Yet most health insurance plans have tried to sidestep the issue or leave it to the states. Individuals and their families can rarely meet the high costs.

Historically, the care and treatment of the mentally ill have been left to the individual states. The first federal assistance was offered to the states in the National Mental Health Act of 1946. Part of the Medicaid legislation with significance for mental health was sponsored by Senator Russell Long in 1965. It permits federal financial assistance for persons in the group age 65 and over who are patients in institutions for mental diseases. It is a companion piece to the Title XVIII (Medicare) legislation, which provides specifically for those older persons with acute brain disorders and other mental illnesses who can be expected to respond to relatively brief but intensive treatment in mental hospitals.[37] The Long Amendment also makes provisions for the very many aged who are suffering from chronic disorders, either organic or functional, and who need long-term continued care in state mental health facilities. In expressing the intent of the Amendment, the Senate Committee on Finance stated that it

wishes to insure that the additional Federal funds to be made available to the States under the provisions of the bill will assist the overall improvement of mental health services in the State. State and local funds now being used for institutional care of the aged will be released as a result of the bill, but there is great need for increased professional services in hospitals and for development of alternate methods of care outside the hospitals. To accomplish this, States may have to reallocate their expenditures for mental health to promote new methods of treatment and care. The committee bill provides that the States will receive additional Federal funds only to the extent that a showing is made to the satisfaction of the Secretary that total expenditures of the States or its political subdivisions from their own funds for mental health services are increased.[38]

---

[36] Also see Adelman, N.E., compiler: Directory of life care communities, Kennett Square, Pa., 1978, Kendall Grasslands.

[37] Theoretically, the Medicaid legislation is supposed to cover the medically indigent of all ages, not all of whom are on welfare.

[38] From U.S. Senate Committee on Finance: Social Security Amendments of 1965: report to accompany H.R. 6675, June 30, 1965, Washington, D.C., 1965, U.S. Government Printing Office, p. 149.

However, millions of dollars in Medicaid payments have not resulted in better programs or higher medical standards. In most states, monies designated by law for the improvement of the care of older mental patients in state hospitals go into the state general revenue fund and are seldom seen by the hospitals.

The loophole in the legislation that allows this misuse of funds is the "maintenance of state effort" clause, which, for example, required a state to maintain a budget for mental health programs that would "exceed" what was spent in an earlier (defined) period. Two major problems exist in respect to the clause (Section 1903b). First, it is a matter of legal interpretation as to whether the "extent that" the state must exceed the previous budget *includes* the federal payments. Second, for all practical purposes, even if the stricter interpretation is accepted, the various commissioners for mental health would ask for budgetary increases anyway, merely to combat rising costs. Thus there is no guarantee that programs involving patient care will be improved, but rather that the federal government will be paying the increased overhead. The money, in other words, is not earmarked in any significant way, and the intention of Congress that matching funds be spent in developing and implementing a comprehensive mental health program cannot be enforced under the current statute. A tightening up of the ambiguous language is necessary. Federal funds should be paid only when the state shows evidence of expenditures in personnel, equipment, and program development that improve mental health services.

About two thirds of all 244 state hospitals have been certified for the Medicare program. Certification came either from the Joint Commission on Accreditation of Hospitals or from the Social Security Administration. Certified hospitals must maintain comprehensive clinical records and must have sufficient staff to carry out "active" and "intensive" psychiatric treatment. The point of these special rules is to avoid custodial care. The Medicare regulations are spelled out in the Social Security Administration booklet "Health Insurance for the Aged: Conditions of Participation for Hospitals."

FAMILY REACTION TO INSTITUTIONALIZATION

Families often need help in dealing with their feelings about an older family member's going to an institution. In one touching example, we worked with one very conscientious 70-year-old man who was taking care of his 92-year-old mother and his 67-year-old wife, both of whom had severe dementia. He refused institutionalization for either of them and was devoting all of his waking hours to the very difficult task of managing their care by himself in his home. Nursing and social service departments in institutions are especially important in maintaining liaison with relatives. Many family members are extremely ambivalent, both because of the negative reputation of institutional care and because of their own feelings of failing or abandoning the person. Some experience a sense of relief about which they later feel guilty. Families who care (as opposed to those who reject the older person—a much less common category) often experience a grief reaction on admission as though the person had already died. This "death" may be more traumatic than the actual death of the older person later on. In some cases family members may actually stop visiting the person because of inability to tolerate their own grief and ambivalence. We believe that there should be a built-in expectation and real possibility of visits home so that families are not subtly encouraged to cut themselves off emotionally. Families need to be advised that some of the very supportive things they can do for an older person are to visit frequently, take the person on outings and weekend visits home if possible, become involved with the institution by getting to know the staff and administrative personnel, and provide the extra amenities and attention that only a family can give.

The actual day of admission of an older person is often handled insensitively, the person simply being "deposited" without any transition or preparation. This shock approach can result in increased illness and even death; certainly it is questionable psychologically. We advise flexibility and individualization; some persons indeed respond best to a firm, quick (but humane) admission, while many others need to take their time, to absorb things slowly with a good deal of support. The inauguration of day programs, preliminary admissions for weekends or during times when families want to go away on vacation, and provisions for family or friends to sleep in the institution (nearby or even in the same room) when the older person is anxious and frightened could soften the suddenness and harshness of admission. Family and friends could be allowed and encouraged to serve as volunteers in institutional activities, from socializing to performing simple services for residents. Children and grandchildren should be given access to relatives; a little life and noise in most institutions would be a vast improvement. In general, there should be much more fluidity between the institution and the community.

Group and individual therapy with families can be useful in helping to resolve long-term family conflicts and short-term reactions to institutionalization. See Chapter 12 for further discussion of therapy.

OTHER FACTORS IN INSTITUTIONAL CARE
Right to treatment[39]

A second legal concept beyond the question of involuntary admission discussed earlier is the "right to treatment." It is difficult to balance the right to freedom with the right to treatment. A Fed-

---

[39] We are indebted here to the work of Charles Halpern and his brief in the *Wyatt v. Stickney* case in Alabama concerning the right to treatment (Amici's proposed standards for adequate treatment, Jan. 21, 1972).

Kenneth Donaldsen, victor in obtaining release from a mental hospital, testifying on the right to treatment.

Photo by Patricia and William Oriol.

eral District Court for Alabama ruled in 1972 that patients committed involuntarily to a mental hospital through noncriminal procedures have a constitutional right to "adequate and effective treatment." The court further found that the state was failing to provide adequate treatment to the several thousand patients who had been civilly committed to Bryce Hospital in Tuscaloosa. The ruling was made as a result of a class action suit initiated by guardians of patients at Bryce and by certain hospital employees. It was stated that the Constitution requires adequate and effective treatment, because without it the hospital is transformed into a penitentiary where one could be held indefinitely without conviction for any offense. The court ordered a report from the hospital within 90 days that was to include a precise definition of the mission and functions of the hospital and a specific plan to deliver adequate treatment to patients.[40]

U.S. District Court Judge Frank M. Johnson, Jr., established three major aspects of an adequate treatment program: (1) a humane physical and psychological environment, (2) staffing adequate in numbers and training to provide treatment, and (3) an individual treatment plan for each patient.

In reviewing Alabama's mental health and retardation facilities in 1979, 7 years after the *Wyatt v. Stickney* case, Judge Johnson found they still "failed to achieve substantial compliance" with the standards he set down in 1972. He had the institutions placed in receivership and issued two orders aimed at achieving full compliance within 18 months in the class action case, now on its fourth name, *Wyatt v. Ireland*.

The focus has also turned to other states with conditions as deplorable as in Alabama. Litigation for patients' rights has become more sophisticated and complex; for example, how does a hospital give legally required treatment to patients if they refuse treatment and are supported by law in their refusal?

Individual treatment plans

The right to treatment must involve an individual treatment plan for each patient.

The need for an individual treatment plan cannot be over-emphasized. Without such a plan, there can be no evidence that the hospital has singled out the patient for treatment as an individual with his own unique problems.[41]

Preliminary diagnostic formulation and individualized treatment plans should be accomplished within 12 hours of admission to any kind of hospital or institution. Reception units or special psychogeriatric units should be available for brief hospitalizations, perhaps 3 to 5 days up to 3 to 6 weeks, to facilitate proper diagnosis and, in the cases of reversible brain syndromes (like delirium and some dementia) and functional disorders, definitive treatment. The staff should avoid a mental "set" regarding treatability or length of hospitalization. Experience has emphasized that trials at treatment constitute a major part of evaluation; for example, considerable time should be given to make certain that a seemingly fixed and permanent organic brain disorder is not a refractory depression or caused by a reversible underlying physical condition.

Periodic and comprehensive reevaluation is important. Patients who arrive with one condition may develop others during their stay. Changes in psychiatric symptoms are often caused by physical changes that the patient may be unable to report.

Other patient rights and privileges

The many and pervasive aspects of authoritarianism seen in our hospitals and institutions are facets of infantilization and serve the needs of the providers rather than those served. The goal should

---

[40]*Ricky Wyatt et al. v. Dr. Stonewall B. Stickney et al.,* U.S. Court for Middle Dist. of Ala., Northern Div., Action No. 3195-N. The Supreme Court, in handing down its unanimous decision in the landmark case of *Donaldson v. O'Connor* in 1976, avoided the broad issue of "right to treatment" in favor of a more narrow judgment that a state cannot constitutionally confine a nondangerous mentally ill person who is capable of surviving safely on his own.

[41]From Bazelon, Judge D.: Implementing the right to treatment, University of Chicago Law Review, pp. 742 and 746, 1969.

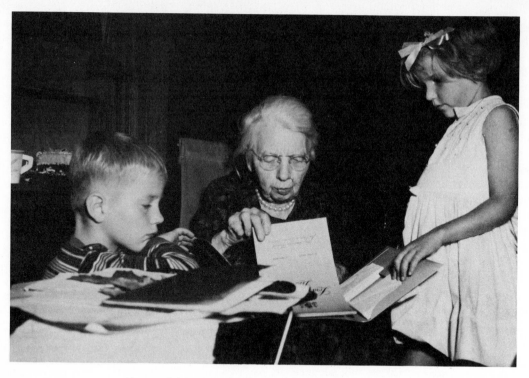

Young visitors: an older person's privilege and right.

Photo by Russell Lewis.

be the fewest restrictive conditions necessary to achieve the purposes of institutionalization. Patients' rights must be preserved in very specific ways. The following list of rights provides good examples.

A hospital patient's bill of rights[42]

1. To considerate and respectful care
2. To obtain from his physician complete current in-information concerning his diagnosis, treatment, and prognosis, in terms he can understand
3. To obtain from his physician information necessary for informed consent before any procedure or treatment is begun; to obtain information on significant alternatives; and to know the name of the person responsible for the treatment
4. To refuse treatment to the extent permitted by law

and to be informed of the medical consequences of refusal
5. To every consideration to his privacy concerning his own medical care; persons not directly involved in his care must have the patient's permission to be present at case discussion, consultation, examination, and treatment
6. To confidentiality of all communications and records pertaining to him
7. To expect that within its capacity a hospital make reasonable response to his request for service and not transfer him to another institution without explanation
8. To obtain information about any relationship of his hospital to other health services that concern his care and about the existence of any professional relationships among individuals who are treating him
9. To be advised if the hospital proposes to engage in human experimentation affecting his care and to refuse to participate in such research

---

[42] Modified from the statement affirmed Nov. 17, 1972, by the Board of Trustees of the American Hospital Association.

10. To reasonable continuity of care, including postdischarge follow-up
11. To examine and receive an explanation of his bill no matter who pays it
12. To know what hospital rules and regulations apply to his conduct as a patient

Patients' rights in skilled nursing facilities[43]

The governing body of the facility establishes written policies regarding the rights and responsibilities of patients and, through the administrator, is responsible for development of, and adherence to, procedures implementing such policies. These policies and procedures are made available to patients, to any guardians, next of kin, sponsoring agency(ies), or representative payee selected pursuant to section 205 (j) of the Social Security Act, and Subpart Q of Part 404 of this chapter, and to the public. The staff of the facility is trained and involved in the implementation of these policies and procedures. These patients' rights, policies and procedures ensure that, at least, each patient admitted to the facility:

1. Is fully informed, as evidenced by the patient's written acknowledgment, prior to or at the time of admission and during stay, of these rights and of all rules and regulations governing patient conduct and responsibilities;
2. Is fully informed, prior to or at the time of admission and during stay, of services available in the facility, and of related charges including any charges for services not covered until titles XVIII or XIX of the Social Security Act, or not covered by the facility's basic per diem rate;
3. Is fully informed, by a physician, of his medical condition unless medically contraindicated (as documented, by a physician, in his medical record), and is afforded the opportunity to participate in the planning of his medical treatment and to refuse to participate in experimental research;
4. Is transferred or discharged only for medical reasons, or for his welfare or that of other patients, or for nonpayment for his stay (except as prohibited by titles XVIII or XIX of the Social Security Act), and is given reasonable advance notice to ensure orderly transfer or discharge, and such actions are documented in his medical record;

---

[43] From Federal Register **39**(193):part II (Oct. 3), 1974.

5. Is encouraged and assisted, throughout his period of stay, to exercise his rights as a patient and as a citizen, and to this end may voice grievances and recommend changes in policies and services to facility staff and/or to outside representatives of his choice, free from restraint, interference, coercion, discrimination, or reprisal;
6. May manage his personal financial affairs, or is given at least a quarterly accounting of financial transactions made on his behalf should the facility accept his written delegation of this responsibility to the facility for any period of time in conformance with State law;
7. Is free from mental and physical abuse, and free from chemical and (except in emergencies) physical restraints except as authorized in writing by a physician for a specified and limited period of time, or when necessary to protect the patient from injury to himself or to others;
8. Is assured confidential treatment of his personal and medical records, and may approve or refuse their release to any individual outside the facility, except, in case of his transfer to another health care institution, or as required by law or third-party payment contract;
9. Is treated with consideration, respect, and full recognition of his dignity and individuality, including privacy in treatment and in care for his personal needs;
10. Is not required to perform services for the facility that are not included for therapeutic purposes in his plan of care;
11. May associate and communicate privately with persons of his choice, and send and receive his personal mail unopened, unless medically contraindicated (as documented by his physician in his medical record);
12. May meet with and participate in activities of social, religious, and community groups at his discretion, unless medically contraindicated (as documented by his physician in his medical record);
13. May retain and use his personal clothing and possessions as space permits, unless to do so would infringe upon rights of other patients, and unless medically contraindicated (as documented by his physician in his medical record); and
14. If married, is assured privacy for visits by his/her spouse; if both are inpatients in the facility, they are permitted to share a room, unless med-

ically contraindicated (as documented by the attending physician in the medical record).

All rights and responsibilities specified in paragraphs 1 through 4 of this section—as they pertain to (a) a patient adjudicated incompetent in accordance with State law, (b) a patient who is found, by his physician, to be medically incapable of understanding these rights, or (c) a patient who exhibits a communication barrier—devolve to such patient's guardian, next of kin, sponsoring agency(ies), or representative payee (except when the facility itself is representative payee) selected pursuant to section 205 (j) of the Social Security Act and Subpart Q of Part 404 of this chapter.

Commitment or voluntary admission to a mental hospital or "assignment" to a nursing home should not per se abrogate the right to manage affairs, to sign contracts, to hold professional, occupational, or vehicle operator's licenses, to marry or obtain a divorce, to register and vote, and to make a will. Direct access to legal counsel is also mandatory.[44] Patients should not be placed incommunicado. Visitation (including small children) and telephone communications should be permitted at all times (a 24-hour basis) except when there are clear indications that such communications and visitations promote disturbances in the patient, which are untherapeutic and harmful at a *particular* time. Any limit on such contact must be periodically reviewed, and renewal or continuation must not be automatic. This should require a physician's decision, and the physician must not have any ownership ties with the facility, in order not to prejudice his or her judgment.

Patients must have the unrestricted right to receive sealed mail except when responsible staff personnel can clearly defend restriction on the basis of an individualized patient plan. Again, periodic review must occur. The physician must bear ultimate responsibility since only the patient's

mental or physical condition could warrant such a restriction on rights and privileges.

Privacy[45] and space to move are other rights. Privacy is obviously qualitative as well as quantitatative, and the availability of at least 4 hours a day alone should be made. There must be a minimum of 100 square feet of floor space in one-patient rooms. No multipatient room should exceed four persons. There must be a minimum of 80 square feet of floor space per patient, with soundproofing, screens or curtains, and at least one toilet, lavatory, shower, or tub for each six persons. Each patient bed should have an electronic signal system to call to the staff for help. A comfortable, attractive day room area (40 square feet per patient) with reading lamps, tables, chairs, and recreational facilities is considered necessary, and a dining room area should include 10 square feet per patient.

Husbands and wives who both are institutionalized should have the option to live together in an institution if they so desire.[46] If problems arise or separation becomes necessary, skilled counseling should be available to them to avoid estrangement and feelings of desertion. When only one partner is institutionalized, arrangements for conjugal visits should be possible.

Food, abundantly and attractively served, is another patient right, unless medically restricted. The diet must, at minimum provide the Recommended Daily Dietary Allowance developed by the National Academy of Science. Opportunities for snack times and raiding an icebox, as well as moderate use of alcohol within medical limits, are psychologically beneficial.

The money available to the older person (from Supplemental Security Income and Social Security checks to private funds) must be safeguarded as there is presently no assurance of this after insti-

---

[44] Ennis, B., and Siegel, L.: The rights of mental patients; the basic ACLU guide to a mental patient's rights, New York, 1973, Richard W. Baron Publishing Co., Inc.

[45] Lawton, M.P., and Bader, J.: Wish for privacy by young and old, Journal of Gerontology **25**:48-54, 1970.

[46] Locker, R.: Elderly couples and the chastification, Social Work **21**(2):149-150, 1976.

tutionalization, particularly if a family is not involved.[47]

Persons should not be stripped of their clothing and made into "patients" with shoddy institutional apparel. Patients have the right to wear their own clothes and have their own possessions with them unless this is legitimately considered dangerous. Personal possessions and clothing help to maintain orientation, self-respect, and identity. Personnel are advised also to avoid calling persons by their first or "pet" names, as this too implies loss of dignity and infantilization. Further, patients should not be on "display" for the amusement of others.

■ On an institutional visit we were introduced by the chief nurse to an 87-year-old woman. The nurse, who, of course, insisted on being referred to as Mrs. L by the patients, said, "Jane, sing your song for the visitors." "Jane," who had formerly been a teacher of some repute, obediently belted out a popular song. Such callous disregard for patient dignity is perhaps not common, but it does occur all too frequently.

All persons should have access to members of the clergy and religious services of their choice.

Community advocates for institutionalized older persons should be given free access to nursing homes, hospitals, and other long-term care facilities. A National Citizens' Coalition for Nursing Home Reform organized for the following purposes.

1. To operate exclusively for charitable and educational purposes
2. To coordinate the efforts and resources of member organizations and individuals to improve the long-term care system and quality of life for nursing home residents
3. To provide resources and information relative to nursing home reform to members and the general public

4. To solicit sources of funding to finance the Coalition's activities
5. To develop and implement nursing home advocacy training programs
6. To study nursing home issues and report and make recommendations to members and the public at large

As of March 1980, the Coalition had 72 membership groups in 24 states (see list in Appendix B).

Physical environment

The environment of hospitals, nursing homes, and other institutions is ripe for change. Clever minds could be put to work to design esthetic and prosthetic environments that would help to compensate for mental and physical losses. Wandering patients who are now often restrained could be encouraged through the use of color coding, the buddy system,[48] and adequate staff to orient themselves. Maximum security atmospheres could be reduced by such devices as attractive wooden fences, gates, and even shrubbery rather than iron bars. (Few geriatric patients break out of institutions! They merely need something to discourage confused wandering.)

Protection from accidents and fires needs to be improved, and all institutions should be subject to the Life Safety Code of the National Fire Protection Association. Air conditioning in summer and control of temperature and humidity in winter are crucial, since older people cannot withstand extreme atmospheric conditions. In unair-conditioned hospitals and nursing homes, excessive numbers of older people die during heat waves.

With the advent of plastic and electronic devices that may be under either direct or remote control, much can be done to make up for deficiencies in ambulation, audition, vision, and general stimulation. Safety devices such as handrails, grab

---

[47] Needed are public guardianships in all our states to provide some measure of legal protection for low-income older persons.

[48] Kosbab, F., and Kosbab, M.F.: A buddy system for hospitalized geriatric patients, Archives of General Psychiatry **7:** 135-139, 1962.

bars, call buttons, and nonslip floors are essential. Calendars, large clocks (set to the *correct* time!), and mirrors are useful orientation devices. The general environment should be reasonably calm but alive with stimuli, lest reactivity become extinguished. Good illumination and colorful decorations are helpful. Beauty parlors, barber shops, and canteens add variety (easy access to cosmeticians, hairdressers, masseuses, and masseurs does wonders for patient morale); music should be available but not, because of the Goldstein catastrophic reaction (Chapter 9), constantly blaring, Muzak fashion. Outdoor activities such as gardening and perhaps even caring for pets in mini-zoos on institutional grounds can be extremely therapeutic.

Physician's care

Only about two fifths of the 23,608 homes for long-term care of older persons and the disabled in the United States had a fulltime or parttime physician on the premises in 1976, according to a Census Bureau survey. Of the institutions surveyed, 84% said they had outside doctors on call to take care of emergencies and other needs of residents.

All institutions should have physicians with central responsibility and commensurate authority to override private doctors of individual patients if necessary. These physicians should plan the general medical program (routine tests, dental care, immunizations), conduct regular rounds, prescribe medications, respond to emergencies, and be available for consultations with families. Physicians must beware that they do not function for the convenience of the institution rather than providing service to patients (for example, prescribing excessive medication may relieve the staff but make "zombies" out of patients). Physicians themselves should be under review by all staff members, regarding their judgments.

Teaching/research nursing homes

The National Institute on Aging is exploring the feasibility of encouraging the establishment of model teaching/research nursing homes at selected academic medical centers[49] to focus on research, education, and service all at once. (Ultimately, of course, it would be ideal if each of the 126 medical schools would have a teaching/research nursing home nearby as part of its program.) They would offer the unique opportunity to study disease processes themselves in older people,[50] as well as the effects of nutrition, drugs, exercise, and social interaction on disease; to investigate better methods of diagnosis and treatment; to analyze the best methods of delivery of services of all kinds to nursing home residents; to train medical, nursing, social work, psychology, and other health professions' students; and to provide continuing education for all mental health professionals involved in the care of the aged.

Nursing care

The role of the registered nurse in administration and in direct care in institutions is absolutely central. A registered nurse's leadership is likely to determine the quality of all aspects of care, including medical care. Supervision and on the job teaching of registered and practical nurses and aides are essential.

Nursing of the older patient requires flexibility, good humor without ridicule, and respect without distancing.[51] Wolanin[52] has described nursing staff

---

[49] The concept of academic (teaching/research) nursing is developed in Butler, R.N.: The impact of Alzheimer's disease on the nation's elderly, testimony before the U.S. Senate Subcommittee on Aging and the Subcommittee on Labor/HEW Appropriation, July 15, 1980; and in Butler, R.N.: The teaching nursing home, J.A.M.A. **245**(14):1435-1437, 1981.

[50] Because many older people are sent to nursing homes rather than general hospitals or mental hospitals, a teaching nursing home would provide the opportunity to study a number of conditions not routinely treated, at least for any great length of time, at hospitals. A major example is senile dementia of the Alzheimer type.

[51] Jaeger, D., and Simmons, L.W.: Humor in nurse-patient relationships. In Jaeger, D.: The aged ill: coping with problems in geriatric care, New York, 1970, Appleton-Century-Crofts.

[52] Wolanin, M.O.: They called the patient repulsive, American Journal of Nursing **64**:173-175, 1964.

reactions to incontinence, difficult self-feeding, obscene language, and other unpleasant behaviors. Basic individualized knowledge of the patient is crucial[53] and in keeping with our stress on comprehensive evaluation. The list below notes problems frequently presented by nursing staffs to medical and psychiatric consultants on the rare occasions when consultants are called in to nursing homes and homes for the aged.

1. Depression
2. Confusion or other symptoms of delirium or dementia
3. Paranoid delusions
4. Noisiness
5. Restlessness or wandering
6. Combativeness
7. Inappropriate dependency on staff
8. Persistent talk of a wish to die
9. Incontinence
10. Families who are unjustifiably critical or demanding of the institution

Bed rest can be dangerous, replicating all the untoward effects of chronic, debilitating illnesses: cardiovascular, respiratory, metabolic, and neuromuscular changes. To illustrate, with decreased respiration can come hypostatic pneumonia, and with immobility a decrease in strength of muscles and weakening of bones (osteoporosis) may occur, with the risk of falls and fractures. People should be ambulated quickly, even after operations.

Bedsores (also called decubiti, trophic ulcers, or pressure sores) can develop quickly, especially in bedridden, debilitated, older persons. Such sores occur at pressure points—the bony areas of elbows, hips, and heels, and the buttocks—and are the result of reduced blood supply caused by the body's weight. Persons who are not turned in bed, who are malnourished or anemic (vitamin C deficiency and low protein intake are most dangerous), or who have been allowed to lie in urine until the skin macerates may develop infections in the sores. These infections are indolent, causing little

or no pain. Care should include ambulation, rotation of the patient.[54] cleanliness and dryness, avoidance of oversedation, and checking of pressure points for early signs of redness. Physiotherapy through overhead trapeze and activity as well as active and passive exercises, including massage, are indicated. Paraplegic patients may need to be placed in frames that turn (Stryker frames). Indwelling catheters may be necessary to control urinary incontinence. Foam rubber, air mattresses and water beds, pillows, and sheepskin sheets are useful. When an ulcer has developed, it should be cleaned (debridement). Trypsin, an enzymatic digestive agent, along with topical antibiotics (for example, neomycin) is appropriate. Oral zinc therapy is controversial.

Incontinence refers to the inability to control bladder and/or bowel. The condition may be permanent as a result of severe injury, central nervous system disease, chronic infections, etc. At other times it is temporary and reversible, related to anxiety, pain, hostility, and inadequate attention. Even persons with organic brain damage may be able to improve control. A careful evaluation and correct assessment as to cause must be made, and a plan for treatment built and kept. Emotional aspects should be dealt with through psychotherapy and staff involvement. The incontinent patient with no permanent physical damage can often be retrained. In urinary incontinence one begins by giving the patient the bedpan or urinal regularly on schedule to develop a habit (for example, every 2 hours or on rising, after eating, and before bedtime). In bowel retraining, proper timing is also of the essence. Good dieting helps. Passive exercises for the bedridden (bending the knees and pressing the thighs against the abdomen) can sometimes stimulate the urge to defecate. Walking and other

---

[53] For selected references in gerontological nursing, see pp. 318-319.

[54] High pressure for a short time is safer than low pressure for longer periods. See Husain, T.: An experimental study of some pressure effects in tissues with reference to the bedsore problems, Journal of Pathology and Bacteriology **66:**57, 1953; and Exton-Smith, A.N., and Sherwin, R.W.: Prevention of pressure sores; significance of bodily movement, Lancet **11:**1124-1126, 1968.

efforts to improve muscle tone help. Adult gauze diapers and underpads should be used and frequently changed until control improves.

Staff morale and dedication are another crucial consideration. Decent care for all patients, rich or poor, depends on the goodwill and skill of all levels of staff; yet much of the time the poor working conditions, low pay, low status, and lack of inservice and outside training for nursing personnel have been ignored. Like many other groups providing human services (police, fire fighters, teachers, government workers), nursing personnel are not allowed to strike, for obvious reasons—the welfare of patients. Yet this moral pressure has amounted to a kind of moral blackmail. Walkouts have occurred in some localities. One would have to suppose that the anger and feelings of exploitation on the part of staff get communicated to patients in active or passive forms.

More than 3 million employees work in hospitals and nursing homes, of which perhaps 12% are unionized. The big three health care unions are the American Federation of State, County, and Municipal Employees (AFSCME), Service Employees International, and the National Union of Hospital and Health Care Employees (formerly Local 1199). All are affiliates of the AFL-CIO. They organize and undertake collective bargaining efforts in hospitals, nursing homes, and other facilities. The American Nurses' Association and the National Federation of Licensed Practical Nurses are not unions, stricly speaking, but they talk and act like unions to some degree. There is also the National Conference of Physicians' Unions. (Important to unionization, too, are the U.S. Senate Committee on Labor and Public Welfare and, of course, the Federal Mediation and Conciliation Service.)

The minimum nursing staff–to–patient ratios in long-term care facilities should be 1 registered nurse per 30 residents per shift. In addition, there should be 1 nursing staff member per 7 residents per day shift; 1 nursing staff member per 12 residents per evening shift; and 1 nursing staff member per 20 residents per night shift. There is a greater need where there are more total care patients.

Perhaps 80% to 90% of care of institutionalized older persons is provided by nursing aides, assistants, and orderlies, yet training for these groups of personnel varies from no training at all to about 160 hours. Only a few states, including Minnesota, Iowa, and Oregon, have specific training programs.

It is estimated that staff turnover is a fantastic 75% per year! Part of the solution to the problem of high turnover is preservice and inservice training and staff development, which should cover learning to relate to patients, giving psychological counseling, and learning to do group therapy. Technical nursing skills, such as dealing with stroke problems and bowel and bladder retraining, need to be constantly reviewed and updated. Much of the ultimate administrative and training responsibility rests on the registered nurse—who is usually overworked and underrewarded.

Since much of the actual care of patients in mental hospitals and nursing homes falls on nursing assistants and aides, adequate pay, continuing education, and opportunities for promotion should be mandatory if good staff morale is to be maintained.[55] In addition, all staff should be included in the planning and carrying out of treatment with patients.[56] See Table 11-5 for the personnel figures for various categories of employees in nursing homes.

Patient restraint

Physical and chemical (by drugs) restraint and seclusions must be avoided except under true emergency conditions. Restraints (called ''poseys'') are not a substitute for personal contact to alleviate the anxiety that often causes the physical agitation. Restraint or seclusion should never

---

[55] See Jackson, H.: Bridging continuing education and mental health in long-term skilled institutional care for the elderly, paper presented at a 1972 conference of the same name.

[56] Shore writes of practical experiences with various kinds of staff meetings in old age homes. See Shore, H.: You can have more effective staff meetings, Professional Nursing Homes, Nov. 1962.

Table 11-5. Personnel data from the 1977 National Nursing Home Survey

	RN	LPN	Nursing aide	Total nursing personnel	Administrative, medical, and therapeutic personnel*
All employees	60,700	82,700	412,800	556,200	68,400
Certification					
SNF only	21,000	19,600	101,300	141,900	17,000
SNF and ICF	25,200	28,800	158,400	212,300	21,500
ICF only	9,700	26,700	115,600	152,000	20,600
Not certified	4,800	7,600	37,600	50,000	9,300

Data from U.S. Public Health Service, National Center for Health Statistics, Washington, D.C., 1977.
*No further breakdown of this category.
SNF, skilled nursing facility; *ICF,* intermediate care facility.
These data are in terms of fulltime equivalent employees (FTE), with each 35 hours work completed the equivalent of 1 FTE.

exceed 2 hours without review and rewriting of the order by a physician. Medications must be under constant monitoring and not be used as chemical straightjackets.

Medical and psychiatric experimentation

The Ten Commandments of Medical Research Involving Human Subjects, as employed by the National Institute of Health, should be in effect. No experimental research on older patients is permissible without express and informed consent, given after consultation with legal counsel. The volunteer should be made fully aware of the risks and benefits of the experiment and his or her right to terminate the experiment at any time. Similarly, any unusual, hazardous, and/or experimental treatment procedures such as new drugs or lobotomy must be introduced only after express and informed consent and consultation on the patient's part with legal counsel. The National Institute on Aging conducted a workshop on human protection in research.[57]

Institutional neurosis

"Institutional neurosis" can occur in hospitals, nursing homes, prisons, or anywhere that persons are removed from society and live in a rigid, isolated community. It can also develop in the person's own home if he or she is isolated. The symptoms are erosion of personality, overdependence, and expressionless face, automatic behavior, and loss of interest in the outside world. Immediate and long-term effects of military or concentration camp imprisonment have been described, much of which applies also to isolated institutions for older persons.[58]

Age, sex, and "clinical state" segregation

Federal regulations issued June 1, 1978, require the right to privacy in nursing homes.[59] Sexual segregation is a very questionable practice. It is cruel to automatically rule out heterosexual (or homosexual) activities with spouses or other consenting adults, including other patients, as long as no clear physical or psychological danger is present. One of us (R.N.B.) participated in studies at Chestnut Lodge in 1958-1959, which did not segregate patients by sex and allowed freedom and

[57] National Institute on Aging: Protection of elderly research subjects, Pub. No. (NIH) 79-180, Washington, D.C., 1978, U.S. Government Printing Office. For a summary paper on the subject see Butler, R.N.: Protection of elderly research subjects, Clinical Research **28:**33-35, 1980.

[58] Segal, H.A.: Initial psychiatric findings of recent repatriated prisoners of war, American Journal of Psychiatry **111:** 358, 1954. See also Kral, V.A.: Psychiatric observations under severe chronic stress, American Journal of Psychiatry **108:**3, 1951.

[59] See Health Standards and Quality Bureau, Office of Standards and Certification, Health Care Financing Administration, Rockville, Md. 20857.

privacy for sexual activities. The results were a more relaxed patient population and a greater respect for patients' adulthood. Older people should not be scolded for masturbation. Masturbation is a normal sexual outlet, and staff members in institutions may need help in overcoming their own anxieties about patients' use of this outlet. Conjugal visits with spouses should be encouraged.

There is question about the wisdom of age-segregation treatment facilities. It is argued that when older persons are placed in age-integrated wards of hospitals they receive less staff attention and may be injured by young, aggressive patients. (Assaults can be minimized if personnel is adequate). On the other hand, restriction to an age-segregated unit can result in monotony and difficulties in recruiting and keeping well-trained, dedicated staff. Some studies have indicated that older persons show greater improvement in age-integrated facilities.

Segregation can also occur based on clinical status. Severely impaired older persons often do better in separate facilities that can offer specialized treatment programs not needed by healthier patients. Research can also more easily take place in these circumstances. But the designation of a floor or a section of an institution as the "senile floor" or "senile wing" can lead to much anxiety in healthier patients ("Will I be transported to the senile wing?" "Does this mean I am losing my mind?") Integration of the severely impaired with the less impaired has some benefits of its own. For example, the healthier patients can benefit from giving help to the more impaired through a "buddy system." But for many patients such integration has a depressing effect. A choice would be ideal, with fluid connections between units to comply with the inclination of patients.

Reality-orientation, remotivation, and rehabilitation programs
Reality orientation[60]

James C. Folsom first organized a "reality-orientation program" in Winter Veterans Administraton Hospital in Topeka, Kansas, in 1958. The bulk of the work was done by the nursing assistants, who spent the most time with the patients. Folsom believes patients are not ready for remotivation until they have gone through the reality orientation classes. The program is ideally suited for patients who have been institutionalized for long periods of time or have moderate to severe organic brain impairment.[61]

■ During the classes, which have four patients each, the instructor presents basic personal and current information over and over to each patient, beginning with the patient's name, where he is, and the date. Only when he has relearned these basic facts is the patient presented with other facts such as his age, home town, and former occupation.

Remotivation

Remotivation has been defined as a "means of reaching the large number of long-term, chronic patients residing in large mental hospitals, who do not seem to want to move toward improvement or discharge."[62] Remotivation must be followed by activities leading toward rehabilitation, such as occupational and recreational therapy, the industrial programs, and finally, vocational and social rehabilitation. It has also been applied to nursing homes. Any effort to stimulate and encourage social participation is undoubtedly therapeutic. Arts and crafts and group activities such as movies or games or singing are important because they offer human contact. All programs must be carefully evaluated to avoid infantilization.

---

[60] Taulbee, L., and Folsom, J.C.: Reality orientation for geriatric patients, Hospital and Community Psychiatry **17:**133-135, 1966. See also Reality orientation: a technique to rehabilitate elderly and brain damaged patients, Hospital and Community Psychiatry Service of the American Psychiatric Association, 1969. Reality orientation must be distinguished from reality therapy, a confrontative psychiatric technique developed by William Glasser.

[61] Sensory training programs, in which the institutionalized geriatric patient is stimulated to use the five senses, exist in a few places. See Downey, G.W.: Sensory training reawakens patients to life, Modern Nursing Home **27:**62, 1971.

[62] Bechenstein, N.I.: Enhancing the gains; remotivation, a first step to restoration, Hospital and Community Psychiatry **7:** 115-116, 1966.

The remotivation technique[63] consists essentially of the following five steps, which the psychiatric aide uses with small groups of 10 to 15 patients.

1. *The climate of acceptance* —establishing a warm friendly relationship in the group.
2. *A bridge to reality* —reading of objective poetry, current events, etc.
3. *Sharing the world* —development of the topic, introduced above, through planned objective questions, use of props, etc.
4. *An appreciation of the work of the world* —designed to stimulate the patients to think about work in relation to themselves
5. *The climate of appreciation* —expression of enjoyment at getting together, etc.

As Robert S. Garber, Chairman, American Psychiatric Association Remotivation Project Advistory Committee wrote,

Each patient has sick roles and healthy roles. The sick ones have come to dominate his life, but the healthy roles are not entirely dead. I as a psychiatrist deal mainly with the sick roles. You as remotivators are in touch with the health roles.[64]

The Veterans Administration Hospital in St. Cloud, Minnesota, began a program in 1972 in which sixth-grade students serve as remotivation therapists for older institutionalized veterans.[65] The students and patients are brought together twice a week for 45-minute periods for 11 weeks at a time. The students are carefully prepared and supervised. Patients are prepared by the staff for separation from the children at the end of the program (although many children keep contact through letters and gifts). Patients demonstrate significant gains in self-awareness and self-esteem during the program but appear to lose some of the gains if continued involvement with therapists is not offered.

Rehabilitation

Mental hospital and nursing home programs could benefit immeasurably from the availability of rehabilitation as a medical specialty (physiatrics), one of the significant developments of twentieth century health care. An important model is the Institute of Rehabilitation Medicine in New York (part of New York University's Medical Center), founded and directed by Dr. Howard Rusk since 1948. The blind, the deaf, the retarded, the hemiplegic, the paraplegic, and those suffering from Parkinson's disease —in short, anyone with losses in their neurosensory and physical functions —can benefit from rehabilitative programs. We review physical, occupational and speech therapies in Chapter 10.

The National Institute on Handicapped Research was given the task by Congress to report on research on the handicapped, including the elderly handicapped, being carried out by government agencies. For example, some of the institutes within the National Institutes of Health are developing various prosthetic and rehabilitative devices that may be useful for older people. This is a field where both the development of new technology and the reengineering of devices originally designed for other purposes (as in the NASA space program) are going on.

Daily exercise should be part of routine physical care in every institution. Each patient should participate, including the bedridden, as long as exercise is geared to physical capacity. Psychological well-being is often improved as an added benefit when exercise is encouraged.[66] Morning exercises

---

[63] Remotivation kits for nursing homes and for mental hospitals, 1968, are available through the American Psychiatric Association, Washington, D.C. A film, *Remotivation—A New Technique for the Psychiatric Aide,* is available on loan from Smith Kline & French Laboratories, Film Center, SK & F Services Department, 1500 Spring Garden St., Philadelphia, Pa. 19101.

[64] From Garber, R.S.: A psychiatrist's view of remotivation, Mental Hospitals **16:**219-221, 1965.

[65] A school-hospital remotivation program (Veterans Administration Hospital, St. Cloud, Minn.), Hospital and Community Psychiatry **25:**661-664, 1974. Information on setting up a similar program can be found in the booklet, *Westwood-Geriatric-Remotivation Program,* Veterans Administration Hospital, St. Cloud, Minn.

[66] Powell, R.R.: Psychological effects of exercise therapy on institutionalized geriatric mental patients, Journal of Gerontology **29:**156-161, 1974.

to music are becoming a regular part of the treatment programs in some nursing homes, old age homes, and other institutions.

The President's Council on Physical Fitness and Sports has co-sponsored a new physical fitness program for older persons in and out of institutions. It consists of a motivational film, *The Good Life,* a leader's discussion guide for group discussion of fitness, and a fitness book for participants entitled *Pep Up Your Life*. The program is designed for senior centers, nursing homes, clubs, and other places where older people are concentrated. Exercises are designed to be done while sitting, standing, or confined to a wheelchair or bed. Individual exercise planning guides in *Pep Up Your Life* help older people keep track of their personal fitness program. The entire packaged program is available without cost as a public service.[67]

Dance therapy expands on the idea of exercise by encouraging emotional and psychological expression. Dance is an expressive medium for self-recognition, communication, release of tension, and socialization.[68]

"Bibliotherapy" is a term used to refer to the healing that lies in the written word. Some institutions are beginning to use circulating libraries as an adjunct to treatment programs rather than simply as a recreational pastime.[69]

A mnemonic procedure, a method of memory therapy known to the ancient Greeks, was used with men and women over 60 years old in two studies of free recall. The learners took a mental trip through their residences, stopping, in order, at 16 places. When they learned a list of words, they retraced the trip, visualizing one of the items in association with each stopping place.[70]

Work therapy and sheltered workshops

"Work therapy" is appropriate only as a truly therapeutic activity and not as compulsory and uncompensated housekeeping and maintenance chores that save the institution money. Patients may volunteer to do work for the institution but should be compensated in accordance with the minimum wage laws of the Fair Labor Standards Act, 29 U.S.C. No. 206, as amended in 1966. Patients who are physically able should, however, make their own beds, dress themselves, and perform other acts ordinarily encompassed under the rubric of self-care.

The handicapped, including the aged, for instance in homes for the aged, may participate in "sheltered workshops."[71]

Sheltered workshop is a work-oriented rehabilitation facility with controlled working environment and individualized vocational goals, which utilizes work experiences and related services for assisting the handicapped person to progress toward normal living and a productive vocational status.[72]

[67] Distributed by the Travelers Film Library. Contact the President's Council on Physical Fitness and Sports, Washington, D.C. Other references on exercise include Barlon, W.: The Alexander technique, New York, 1974, Alfred A. Knopf, Inc.; Feldenkranz, M.: Awareness through movement, New York, 1972, Harper & Row, Publishers, Inc.; deVries, H.: Vigor regained, Englewood Cliffs, N.J., 1974 Prentice-Hall, Inc.; and Spirduso, W.W.: Physical fitness, aging and psychomotor speed: a review, Journal of Gerontology **35:** 850-865, 1980.

[68] Cohen, I., and Segall, J.: Using dance therapy in the extended care facility, Nursing Homes **23:**28-30, 1974; and Caplow-Lindner, E., Harpaz, L., and Sarnberg, S.: Therapeutic dance/movement, expressive activity for older adults; New York, 1979, Human Sciences Press.

[69] Hynes, A.: Bibliotherapy in the circulating library at St. Elizabeths Hospital, Library **25:**144-148, 1975; Crispen, J., editor: Health and rehabilitative library services, vol. 1, Chicago, Oct. 1975, American Library Association.

[70] Robertson-Tchabo, E.A., Hausman, C.P., and Arenberg, D.: A classical mnemonic for older learners: a trip that works! Educational Gerontology **1:**215-226, 1976.

[71] See the handbook Sheltered workshops and homebound programs, ed. 1, 1972. The National Committee on Sheltered Workshops and Homebound Programs (15 W. 16th St., New York), p. 3. See also Shore, H.: The sheltered workshop, Professional Nursing Home, Feb. 1966; and U.S. Department of Health, Education and Welfare, Rehabilitation Services Administration, Social and Rehabilitative Service: Standard for rehabilitation facilities and sheltered workshops, 1969.

[72] Official definition adopted by the National Association of Sheltered Workshops and Homebound Programs, Oct. 1959. (This organization has been renamed the International Association of Rehabilitative Facilities, 5530 Wisconsin Ave., Washington, D.C. 20015.)

This kind of shop gives an opportunity to make a modest amount of money, as well as providing activity and promoting pride. Because industries pay on a piece basis, it is economically feasible for them. Packaging, stuffing, stapling, tag stringing, and various types of simple repetitive assembling are examples of activities.

At the Philadelphia Geriatric Center "the workshop is one of our most successful therapeutic enterprises of all activities in the home; it is the one with the greatest competition for places, and there is always a waiting list and people who wish to put in more than usual possible time per person."[73] The Riverdale Home in New York also conducts a large program.

Patient government

There are many legitimate complaints—about food, lack of entertainment, nursing care—legitimate not only because in too many instances the complaints are valid, but also because of the deep frustration and grief associated with institutionalization and the understandable need to ventilate feelings. Patient government or resident councils, joint patient-staff conferences, and the presence of older people on the boards of trustees of hospitals and homes for the aging should be standard and not just window dressing. Older people living in the community would do well to be their own ombudsmen and check up on the conditions and treatment in institutions.

Volunteers

With careful selection one can assemble a loyal, conscientious group of volunteers who are a valuable adjunct to the quality of an institution. The Red Cross Gray Ladies are an example of a well-trained volunteer group. Most institutions are wary of volunteers—some with good reason, since they do not want their weaknesses exposed to the public.

---

[73] Dr. M. Powell Lawton, Philadelphia Geriatric Center, Philadelphia, Pa., personal communication, 1973.

Research

It is imperative that research be built into institutions. Research should be of two kinds: studies concerned with enhancing the understanding of old age and chronic illness (for example, study of senile dementia) and studies dealing with improvement in services (for example, study of group therapy). Fortunately, nurses are beginning to be trained in research methods. Rarely is research done in either nonprofit or commercial homes. The Philadelphia Geriatric Center is an example of a voluntary institution that has developed a fine research program.

Major associations of nursing homes and homes for the aging

American Association of Homes for the Aging
1050 17th St., N.W., Suite 770, Washington, D.C. 20005.
  Membership—represents nonprofit community-sponsored housing, homes for the aging, and health-related facilities serving older persons. Homes are sponsored by religious, fraternal, labor, civic, and county organizations.
  Size—over 250,000 older persons live in 1,600 AAHA homes.

American Health Care Association
1200 15th St., N.W., Washington, D.C. 20005.
  Membership—a federation of state associations of commercial homes in 49 states (Oklahoma not included). Some 200 nonprofit homes also belong, usually small homes with about 60 beds. This is a nonprofit organization.
  Size—7,500 facilities, with approximately 607,000 beds, belong.

National Council of Health Care Services
1200 15th St., N.W., Washington, D.C. 20005.
  Membership—a voluntary association of proprietary health care companies. Members own and manage nursing homes, hospitals, psychiatric facilities, clinics, home health agencies, and child day-care centers. Members must meet accreditation standards of the Joint Commission on Accreditation of Hospitals. Membership is open to any private company owning and operating three or more medical facilities with a minimum of 300 beds.
  Size—members presently provide 70,000 beds.

NOTE: Some homes, like the Mennonite homes, will not belong to any national organization, nor will they participate in Medicaid or Medicare.

REFERENCES

American Nurses' Association, Division on Gerontological Nursing Practice: The registered nurse consultant to the intermediate care facility, Kansas City, 1978, The Association.

Bozzetti, L.: The aged in Sweden II: a systems approach—the Swedish Model, Psychiatric Annals **7:**63-81, 1977.

Brody, E.M.: Follow-up study of applicants and non-applicants in voluntary homes, The Gerontologist **9:**187-196, 1969.

Brody, E.M.: Long-term care of older people. A practical guide, New York, 1977, Human Sciences Press.

Brody, S.J., Cole, L., Storey, P.B., and Wink, N.J.: The geriatric nurse practitioner: a new medical resource in the skilled nursing home, Journal of Chronic Diseases **29:**537-543, 1976.

Brudno, J.J.: Group programs with adult offspring of newly admitted residents in a geriatric setting, Journal of the American Geriatrics Society **12:**385-394, 1964.

Butler, R.N.: Immediate and long-range dangers to transfer of elderly patients from state hospitals to community facilities (guest editorial), The Gerontologist **10:**259-260, 1970.

Carp, F.: Housing and living environments of older people. In Binstock, R., and Shanas, E., editors: Handbook of aging and the social sciences, New York, 1976, Van Nostrand Reinhold Co.

Cosin, L.Z., Mort, M., Post, F., Westropp, C., and Williams, M.: Experimental treatment of persistent senile confusion, International Journal of Social Psychiatry **4:**24-42, 1958.

Donahue, W.: Action programs to prevent, reduce or improve institutionalization. Mental health care and the elderly: shortcomings in public policy, report by the U.S. Senate Special Committee on Aging, Washington, D.C., 1971, U.S. Government Printing Office.

Droubay, E.H.: Blue is for bathrooms . . . colors guide geriatric patients, Mental Hospitals **15:**386-390, 1964.

Goldfarb, A.I.: Institutional care of the aged. In Busse, E.W., and Pfeiffer, E., editors: Behavior and adaptation in late life, Boston, 1969, Little, Brown & Co.

Halpern, C.: A practicing lawyer views the right to treatment, Georgetown Law Journal **57:**782-817, 1969.

Kahana, E., and Kahana, B.: Therapeutic potential of age integration: effects of age-integrated hospital environments on elderly psychiatric patients, Archives of General Psychiatry **23:**20-29, 1970.

Kane, R., and Kane, R.: Long-term care in six countries: implications for the United States, Washington, D.C., 1976, U.S. Government Printing Office.

Kosbab, F.P., and Kosbab, M.F.: A buddy system for hospitalized geriatric patients, Archives of General Psychiatry **7:**133-139, 1962.

Lawton, M.P., and Brody, E.M.: Assessment of older people: self-maintaining and instrumental activities of daily living, The Gerontologist **9:**179-186, 1969.

Little, V.: Open care for the aged: Swedish model, Social Work **23:**282-287, 1978.

Lowenthal, M.F.: Lives in distress, New York, 1964, Basic Books, Inc., Publishers.

Mendelson, M.A.: Tender loving greed, New York, 1974, Alfred A. Knopf, Inc.

Moss, F., and Halamandaris, V.: Too old, too sick, too bad: nursing homes in America, Germantown, Md, 1977, Aspen Systems Corp.

Nader, R.: Old age: the last segregation, New York,, 1971, Grossman Publishers, Inc.

Randall, O.A.: A 20th century philosophy for homes for the aged, New York, 1949, National Social Welfare Assembly.

Reingold, J.: A master plan approaches its goal, Hospitals **50:**53-57, 1976.

Reinhardt, A.M., and Quinn, M.D.: Current practice in gerontological nursing, vol. I, St. Louis, 1979, The C.V. Mosby Co.

Spirduso, W.W.: Physical fitness, aging and psychomotor speed: a review, Journal of Gerontology **35:**850-865, 1980.

Stilwell, E.M., editor: Readings in gerontological nursing, Thorofare, N.J., 1980, Charles B. Slack, Inc.

Tobin, S.S., and Lieberman, M.A.: Last home for the aged, San Francisco, 1976, Jossey-Bass, Inc., Publishers.

U.S. Public Health Service, National Center for Health Statistics: The National Nursing Home Survey: 1977 summary for the United States, Pub. No. (PHS) 79-1794, Washington, D.C., 1979, U.S. Government Printing Office.

U.S. Senate Special Committee on Aging, Subcommittee on Long-term Care: Nursing home care in the United States: failure in public policy, Washington, D.C., 1974, U.S. Government Printing Office.

Vladeck, B.C.: Unloving care: the nursing home tragedy, New York, 1980, The Twentieth Century Fund.

SELECTED READINGS IN GERONTOLOGICAL NURSING

American Nurses' Association: Standards for geriatric nursing practice, American Journal of Nursing **70**(9):1894-1897, 1970.

American Nurses' Association: Nursing and long-term care: toward quality care for the aging, Kansas City, 1975, The Association.

American Nurses' Association: The registered nurses consultant to the intermediate care facility, Kansas City, 1977, The Association.

Breitung, J.: The geriatric care manual: processes and procedures for nurses, health assistants, and home health aides, New York, 1980, Tiresias Press, Inc.

Brickner, P.W.: Home health care for the aged: how to help older people stay in their own homes and out of institutions, New York, 1978, Appleton-Century-Crofts.

Burnside, I.M., editor: Nursing and the aged, New York, 1976, McGraw-Hill Book Co.

Carnevale, D.L., and Patrick, M.: Nursing management for the elderly, Philadelphia, 1979, J.B. Lippincott Co.

Dufault, K.: Recognition of a classic in gerontological nursing, Journal of Gerontological Nursing **5**(3):56-58, 1979.

Edwards, M.M.: Nursing old people in hospital, Nursing Times **20:**922-923, 1962.

Eliopoulos, C.: Gerontological nursing. New York, 1979, Harper & Row, Publishers, Inc.

Fasano, M.A.: The nurse assistant in long term care, Sacramento, Calif., 1980, Inter Age.

Gunter, L. and Estes, C.: Education for gerontic nursing, New York, 1979, Springer Publishing Co.

Norton, D.: Geriatric nursing—what it is and what it is not, Nursing Times **23:**236-238, 1962.

Norton, D., McLaren, R., and Exton-Smith, A.N.: An investigation of geriatric nursing problems in hospital (originally published in 1962), Edinburgh, 1975, Churchill Livingstone.

Reinhardt, A.M., and Quinn, M.D., editors: Current practice in gerontological nursing, vol. I, St. Louis, 1979, The C.V. Mosby Co.

Schwab, S.M.: Caring for the aged, American Journal of Nursing **73**(12):2049-2053, 1973.

Wells, T.: Toward understanding nursing problems in care of the hospitalized elderly, Nursing Papers: Perspectives in Nursing **9**(1):5-11, 1977.

Wolanin, M.O., and Phillips, L.R.F.: Confusion: prevention and care, St. Louis, 1981, The C.V. Mosby Co.

12

Psychotherapy and environmental therapy

The direct provision of human services during times of dependency and crises for older people would seem to be an unchallengeable and appropriate response, yet psychotherapy continues to be subjected to searching questions of validation. From the scientific perspective, this is as it should be. However, from a historical point of view, we are in a period of considerable national economic austerity, bringing with it national debates over reimbursement by both governmental and private health insurance for psychotherapy. In this chapter we discuss this issue as it affects older persons. We also review the common modalities of *psychotherapy* —individual, group, family— and consider *environmental therapy,* under which we include age awareness and acceptance, federal policies to aid older persons, social roles, location and mobilization of resources, registration drives, self-help and self-care, employment, advocacy, legal and consultative services, and encouragement of political activity on the part of older people.

We consider the roles of the mental health specialists and the team concept in Chapter 8 on therapeutic principles. All forms of environmental therapy and psychotherapy can be provided by the mental health team as a functioning unit (in varied combinations of therapists, older people, family members, or groups) or by individual therapists from all of the disciplines.

INDIVIDUAL PSYCHOTHERAPY

Individual psychotherapy is *least* available to older people and yet should be part of any therapeutic relationship. Older persons need the opportunity to talk and to have a listener. They need the therapist's support in their efforts to "seize the day" and build a "life" during the remaining time available.[1]

There is minimal contact in private practice between therapists and older persons. Public clinics also report low rates of contact of any kind, but especially little in the way of psychotherapeutic work. Psychiatrists, social workers, generally psychologists, members of mental health teams, and other therapists do not see many older people; when they do, the purposes are usually diagnostic and the effort is "disposition."

Old age is the period in life with the greatest number of profound crises, often occurring in multiples and with high frequency. The critical psychological events in this age group are the familiar human emotional reactions to death and grief, diseases and disabilities. Depression and anxiety escalate, defensive behavior is seen, earlier personality components may reappear in exaggerated forms, and newly formed functional states are fre-

---

[1] See *The Shameless Old Lady* (Appendix F), based on a play by Bertolt Brecht in which an elderly widow makes the most of the last 18 months of her life.

quently noted. These conditions require psychotherapeutic efforts, in-depth as well as supportive.

The designation of older people as ''good'' or ''poor'' candidates for psychotherapy should be questioned, especially the implication that a number of people should not be offered treatment because they cannot ''use'' it. We wonder how this judgment can be made before treatment has begun. Some older people who meet all the criteria for ''good'' candidates fail to find therapy helpful, whereas ''poor'' candidates may show unexpected response and results. The test of objectivity is the willingness to give adequate trials to *all* persons without allowing our theories, prejudices, and fears to interfere. Theories, in any case, can be masterful camouflages. For example, Freud was preoccupied with death and pessimistic about old age. His work reflects his avoidance of the issues of late life and his decision to explain the human personality only in terms of the early years. Ironically, we would barely know of him had he died before the age of 40, since his finest work was done in the postmeridian period of his life.

We submit, on the grounds of clinical experience, that older persons, if not brain-damaged, are greatly receptive to psychotherapy and can in no way be considered ''poor candidates.'' They often exhibit a strong drive to resolve problems, to put their lives in order, and to find satisfactions and a ''second chance.'' Their capacity to change has been demonstrated in many instances; the fact that older people spontaneously begin reviewing their lives in a way similar to psychotherapy is indicative of the manner in which this process is part of the natural course of late life. Even the brain-damaged elderly can gain from psychotherapy as Goldfarb, among others has demonstrated.[2]

Any evidence pointing toward older people as untreatable is usually to be found in the minds of therapists rather than in empirical studies. Powerful forces of countertransference and cultural

prejudice are at work, including personal fear and despair over aging and death. Therapeutic pessimism and nihilism are inappropriate, invalid, and inhumane. Older people, like the young, can gain from insight and understanding, from objectivity and empathy. Biology is not destiny in old age any more than in youth. Personal history and culture are of profound importance.

Theoretical considerations

Freud and the vast majority of his followers ruled out psychoanalysis for older persons without ever testing its usefulness. Abraham[3] raised some objections to this general negativism, reporting on five persons he called ''old'' who were in their fifties. He and Jelliffe[4] stated the ''age of the neurosis'' is more important than the age of the patient. Grotjahn[5] reported on analytic work with a 71-year-old client with ''senile brain disease.'' Wayne, Meerlo, Gitelson, Alexander, Atkin, and Kaufman were among those who first described some limited psychotherapeutic efforts with older people.

Goldfarb, Greenleigh, Linden, Weinberg, Butler, and others have devoted substantial amounts of their public and private clinical work to older people. Goldfarb's ''brief therapy''[6] and Linden's

---

[2] For example, see Dodgen, J.C., and Ransom, J.A.: Psychotherapy of a sexagenarian, Diseases of the Nervous System **28:**680-683, 1967.

[3] Abraham, K.: The applicability of psycho-analytic treatment to patients at an advanced age. In Selected papers of psychoanalysis, London, 1949, Hogarth Press.

[4] Jelliffe, S.E.: The old age factor in psychoanalytic therapy, Medical Journal and Record **121:**7-12, 1925.

[5] Grotjahn, M.: Psychoanalytic investigation of a 71 year old man with senile dementia, Psychoanalytic Quarterly **9:**80-97, 1940.

[6] Goldfarb emphasizes the dependent relationships of older patients (comparing them with early parent-child relationships). The physician assumes the role of parent figure pressed on him by the patient. Thus sometimes the therapist will be seen as a scapegoat and sometimes as the omnipotent helper. See Goldfarb, A.I.: Group therapy with the old and aged. In Kaplan, H.I., and Saddock, B.J., editors: Comprehensive group psychotherapy, Baltimore, 1971, Williams & Wilkins Co.; and Goldfarb, A.I.: Psychotherapy of aged persons; IV. One aspect of the therapeutic situation with aged patients, Psychoanalytic Review **42:**100-187, 1955.

work with group therapy became the best known of these efforts in therapy.

Because of the tendency of older people to review their lives, to seek meaning and to deal with death, there is an obvious existential component to any therapeutic work with them. Yet existential therapists have not demonstrated great interest. We have found ideas of Buber[7] (the importance of relationship with others) and Frankl[8] (the possibilities within the confines of the "death camp") to be particularly useful for older people. All forms of psychotherapy—"uncovering" to "supportive" and freudian to jungian to rogerian—can contribute to both a better understanding of the psychology and psychotherapy of old age (for therapy is a major source of knowledge) as well as to direct help for people. Psychoanalytic concepts, Skinner's ideas regarding conditioning and the extinction of dysfunctional patterns of behavior, and Jung's stages of development[9] all apply to the elderly condition. What is obviously needed is an integrated and eclectic utilization of all contemporary personality theories and practices, including the life-cycle perspective of human life. The complexities of late life require complex therapy.

We cannot live the afternoon of life according to the program of life's morning, for what was great in the morning will be little at evening, and what in the morning was true, will at evening have become a lie. I have given psychological treatment to too many people of advancing years, and have looked too often into the secret chambers of their souls, not to be moved by this fundamental truth. . . .

CARL GUSTAV JUNG
Modern Man in Search of a Soul

Common themes in psychotherapy with older persons
New starts and second chances

Older people often express a wish to undo some of the patterns of their life, to unritualize behavior and give some newness to their experiences. These people speak of the monotony or dryness of their experiences, a kind of "salt losing its savor" feeling. This should be met not just with feeble efforts to regain what has been lost but with attempts to build new interests and new possibilities.

Death in disguise

Some older people have resolved their personal feelings about death. Others manage to deny death without serious emotional consequences. But a number of older people need help, first in recognizing the source of their anxieties and fears (death) and then in reaching some degree of accommodation with the inevitable. Therapists must be able to recognize disguised fears of death. For example, one man spoke of "running toward that man and then I saw him and I slowed down to a walk." He was referring to death. In his attempts to revitalize his life, the spectre of death presented him with an omnious impediment that he had to face before therapy could continue in the direction he wanted to go.

Keen awareness of time

There is an obvious concern with time when it is clear that the remaining days are running short. Younger therapists often have great difficulty understanding what it means *not* to think in terms of a future. We must take our cues from older people who have faced this issue squarely; the development of a sense of immediacy, of the here-and-

[7] Buber, M.: The William Alanson White Memorial Lectures, Fourth Series, Psychiatry **20**:95-129, 1957.

[8] Frankl, V.: From death camp to existentialism (1959). In Man's search for meaning, New York, 1963, Washington Square Press, Inc.

[9] It is interesting that two thirds of Jung's practice was made up of middle-aged and older persons, whereas Freud's private practice was composed of younger patients. These differences may help to account for variations in theoretical emphases, with Freud's therapy concentrating on youth and sex while Jung emphasized individuation and creativity.

now, of presentness—all aid in the evolution of a sense of simple enjoyment and tranquility, which we have called elementality.

Grief and restitution

Psychotherapy in old age must deal with grief, with losses of loved ones, and with dysfunctioning of one's own body and its parts. Efforts at restitution are crucial. One of the most important goals in therapy is helping the older person find a secure confidant, either in his family or in his circle of friends and acquaintances.

Guilt and atonement

We have left undone those things which we ought to have done; and we have done those things which we ought not to have done.

The 51st Psalm opens with "Miserere, mei Deus" (Have mercy on me, O God). The cry for mercy, indeed for clemency, in the face of death must be heard. But the therapist does not have it within his or her power to "grant" mercy or bring full alleviation of the distress. One can listen, really listen, bear witness, be able, as it were, to attest to the realities of the life described, and thus help give meaning and validity to that life. Recondiliation may be possible with spouses, siblings, children, and friends.

Reality must be central. If there were simple alignments between our drives, our moral strictures, and the workings of the world, if Freud were dead wrong, we could move merrily along. If aging and disability did not exist; if lives were not filled up with malevolence, acts of violence, and real wrongs done to others and oneself, then we could simply reassure the older people who are sick with guilt. But psychotherapy in old age is a therapy of atonement as well as of restitution. One cannot deny cruel and thoughtless acts, falsely reassuring that all is irrational freudian guilt. Facing genuine guilt as well as the attrition of the person's physical and emotional world is what makes psychotherapy with the aging an intellectually and emotionally powerful experience. The

therapist cannot win out against death, but he or she can win out *for* life, for a sense of the real, for the kind of growth that truly matters, dealing as it does with the evaluation of ways to love—and hate—with the meanings of human conduct, with an appreciation of human nature and the succession of the generations.

Autonomy versus identity

Identity, while an important concept, has been found to be difficult to study in various age groups. In our clinical experience, autonomy should be separated from identity as a concept. The so-called identity crisis of the adolescent is as much a problem of establishing freedom and achieving responsibility and self-sufficiency (autonomy) as it is one of identity ("self-sameness"), if not more so. Erikson deals with only one side of this issue.

The term identity expresses . . . mutual relation in that it connotes both a persistent sameness within oneself (selfsameness) and a persistent sharing of some kind of essential character with others.[10]

In old age most healthy people find themselves essentially the same as they have always been (as in data, for instance, from interviews before the mirror, Chapter 9). With emerging medical (changes in body schema) and psychiatric problems (depression), the sense of self goes through reevaluation, but again more crucial is the problem of autonomy. For example, there is the question, "Can I survive independently without being a burden?" It is true, of course, that if one's identity is closely bound to autonomy, the two merge, as it were, together. The person, for instance, whose identity has been that of a dependent person may find it easier to accept illness and institutionalization than the so-called independent, autonomous person whose identity has been structured accordingly. The latter may suffer more in dependent situations despite a "sound" identity

---

[10]Erikson, E.H.: The problem of ego identity. In Identity and the life cycle, Psychological Issues **1:**101-164, 1959.

by usual standards. Thus it is autonomy that may be more decisive as a determinant of human behavior than identity at all ages, depending on circumstances.

With respect to the life review,[11] identity and autonomy are equally important. But here again we find our experiences at variance with Erikson, for a different reason. We find that older persons often wish to escape their identities and try something new and that the fatalistic acceptance proposed by Erikson in his bipolar view of ego identity versus despair is not universal.

Need for assertion

A sense of helplessness tends to occur especially when one is ill or severely incapacitated in any way. There is seldom adequate opportunity to be assertive in a way that alleviates this feeling. A bedridden person, for example, may finally resort to purposely urinating in bed to express angry feelings. We have known a number of people who have refused to take baths, in what seems to be a direct, angry message to their families or caregivers. Others may become dictatorial to nursing staff or family and friends. Persons caring for the ill or handicapped must assist them in finding ways to assert themselves in a positive manner that brings at least a measure of the self-esteem necessary for human dignity.

Therapeutic issues
Am I a "patient"?

Insight into one's condition—that is, agreement that one has a psychiatric condition—is held by many to be a crucial prognostic indicator. On the other hand, humiliative labeling as a "patient" and all too willing acceptance of the "sick role" are questionable too. We believe it is important that appraisal be flexible and individualized. For some a useful agreement can be made to share in an effort to deal with an "illness," or "emotional problem," while for others it seems more functionally useful to see that the person receives important mental health services without their being identified in that way.

A vigilant search for signs of health

With older people, as with all ages, it is as critical to identify and encourage areas of health as it is to clarify problems. Many beautifully "diagnosed" persons never reach their full potential in treatment because the therapist fails to recognize and utilize their strengths and assets in the therapeutic process.

Significance of certain illusions

The therapist must not in any way be destructive of the processes of illusion and denial needed by older people. One must discuss the fact of death, the facts of loss, and the problems of grief, but this must always be in the context of possibilities, restitution, and resolution. The same principle applies in work with persons of all ages; one must work compassionately and carefully to understand and encourage a realistic lowering of defenses rather than attacking them overtly.

Question of "cures"

Jung wrote,

The serious problems in life are never fully solved. If ever they should appear to be so, it is a sure sign that something has been lost. The meaning and purpose of a problem seems to lie not in its solution but in our working at it incessantly.

The struggle, the need for change, and the opportunity for change—the really profound problems, the deeper intricacies of human existence—

---

[11]The University of Chicago Committee on Human Development has pursued studies of reminiscence. See Gorney, J.E.: Experiencing and age; patterns of reminiscence among the elderly, unpublished Ph.D. dissertation, 1968; Falk, J.M.: The organization of remembered life experience in old age: its relation to subsequent adaptive capacity and to age, unpublished Ph.D. dissertation, 1969; and Havighurst, R.J., and Glasser, R.: An exploratory study of reminiscence, Journal of Gerontology **27**:245-253, 1972.

are genuine problems and subject to alteration up to the point of death.

Value of listening

It is imperative to listen attentively, to bear witness, to heed the telltale echoes of the past, to pick up the flatness of speech where distant feelings have died, to observe outbursts of unresolved issues in lives, and to empathize with the irreconcilable. When the older patient is garrulous, continually reminiscing, importunate, and querulous, the fact is that talk is necessary and listening by another mandatory. (One must also listen to silences.)

The National Retired Teachers Association and the American Association of Retired People (NRTA-AARP) produced a manual in 1980 for reminiscence programs for homebound or institutionalized older persons.[12] "Listeners" are trained to visit the older person and encourage reminiscence for both therapeutic and recreational purposes.

Worth of one therapeutic session

In the best of therapy, each session must involve active work, thinking through, building hypotheses, and persistently searching out ways to assist the person. This is especially true for the older person for whom there may be only one session available (because of impending death, physical weaknesses, or lack of access, financially or transportationwise, to the therapist). When this is the case, much can be done in a short time.

One jungian analyst, Florida Scott-Maxwell, wrote,

A farmer's wife came and told a tragic story where nothing could be done, but her compassion and strength made it possible to continue. As usual with these cases, I asked if she would care to come again; she looked a little surprised, and said, "There is no need, I've told you everything." She had only wanted to confide in someone she respected, in case there was more she could do, and not to be so alone in her hard life. . . . One visit was enough for her.[13]

The brief amount of time must be measured in terms of the quality of the experience rather than the quantity.

Telephone psychotherapy

Because of the financial and physical limitations of older people, the therapist should be very flexible about the use of the telephone in conducting psychotherapy.[14]

■ One 75-year-old man, with a history of heart attacks and continuing angina, would talk by phone when he could not travel. Even then he might have to interrupt his sessions to place a nitroglycerin tablet under his tongue. He never took obvious "advantage" of the situation and attended about 90% of his sessions in person.

Telephone outreach therapy is preferable to denial of the therapy for the homebound older person. It is also an excellent method for giving support and reassurance to an insecure or unstable person who may need something less than a regularly scheduled office appointment. Others (for example, a person with chronic schizophrenia) may need the distancing that a telephone provides, while at the same time achieving some degree of verbal closeness. (Fees for phone calls have been controversial in private psychotherapy but may be justified *when prearranged* because therapists are ordinarily paid on a time basis rather than a fee-for-service basis.)

Volunteers can be used to provide telephone answering services at crisis centers and in telephone reassurance programs.

---

[12] For further training and leadership information, contact the Interreligious Liaison Office, Program Department, NRTA-AARP, 1909 K St., N.W., Washington, D.C. 20049.

[13] Scott-Maxwell, F.: The measure of my days, New York, 1968, Alfred A. Knopf, Inc. [*Note:* Scott-Maxwell was in her eighties and still working as a therapist at the time she wrote her book.]

[14] Unfortunately, about one third of older people do not have telephones, reminding us again of the penury of old age.

Self-confrontation and the use of memory aids

Self-confrontation has been used in research and in clinical practice for various age-groups and diagnostic categories. Still and motion pictures as well as audio and video tape recordings have been employed. Such techniques could be especially valuable, we believe, in work with older people individually and in family therapy. We have used photo albums, the mirror, and the tape recorder; but we (and others) have not yet taken full advantage of the technological possibilities.

The need for self-definition in the life review and the problem of memory argue for the value to the patient of being able to take tape recordings home, for instance, for further listening and reflection. This would also encourage an active participation in the therapeutic process, not a passive, dependent position.

Providing direct instructions, for instance, written or taped, for medication schedules and the statement of general principles and specifics may be useful for the older patient, so long as this is not done with an air of patronization.

Life review therapy

Life review therapy[15] is a more structured and purposive concept than simple reminiscence or recalling the past. It includes the taking of an extensive autobiography from the older person and from other family members as indicated. (Such memoirs can also be preserved by means of tape recordings.) The use of family albums, scrapbooks, and other memorabilia, the searching out of genealogies, and pilgrimages back to places of import all evoke crucial memories, responses, and understanding in patients. A summation of one's life work by some means is useful. For those who have children, a summary of feelings about parenting is important. The goals and consequences of these steps include a reexamination of one's life that results in expiation of guilt, the resolution of intrapsychic conflicts, the reconciliation of family relationships, the transmission of knowledge and values to those who follow, and the renewal of ideals of citizenship and the responsibility for creating a meaningful life.

The life review can also be conducted as part of group activity. Groups of all kinds—nursing home residents, senior center participants,[16] social groups, therapy groups—can use the life review to help older persons reconstruct and reevaluate their lives.[17] The concept of life review has been bolstered by an increasing interest in the United States in finding one's ethnic "roots." Handbooks for composing a personal autobiography are being published to aid nonprofessional writers in exploring and describing their lives.[18] These accounts form a valuable first-person historical source for use by families, sociologists, cultural historians, and others, in addition to providing therapeutic benefits and satisfaction for the older person.

Attempts are rapidly being made to more clearly

---

[15]Lewis, M.I., and Butler, R.N.: Life review therapy: putting memories to work in individual and group psychotherapy, Geriatrics **29**:165-169, 172-173, 1974; and Merriam, S.: The concept and function of the reminiscence: a review of the research, The Gerontologist **20**(5):604-609, 1980.

[16]For an example of reminiscence in a senior center, see the article "Senior Citizens Produce Book of Remembrances," *The Chronicle* (Milford, Del.), June 25, 1980. The article describes a book, *The Times We Remember,* produced by older members of the local senior center.

[17]Dietsche, L.M.: Facilitating the life review through group reminiscence, Journal of Gerontological Nursing **5**:43-46, 1979.

[18]Hendricks, L.: Personal life history. Writing for older adults. A handbook for teaching personal life history classes, Leon County School Board, Tallahassee, Fla, 1979; and Daniel, L.: How to write your own life story: a step by step guide for the non-professional writer, Chicago, 1980, Chicago Review Press.

conceptualize the concepts of reminiscence and life review and test their impact on older persons.[19]

Psychotherapy and public policy

We do not wish to further belabor the lack of Medicare coverage of mental and emotional problems, but we must, for the obvious reason that these facts militate against the provision of the specific treatments we are outlining. For example, the services of social workers and psychologists are ordinarily not covered. In addition, insurance supplementary to Medicare often excludes mental, psychoneurotic, and personality disorders. The U.S. Senate Finance Committee held hearings in 1978 to try to determine how much to pay for psychotherapy under Medicare. It concluded that most of the 700 studies evaluating the worth of psychotherapy were scientifically flawed, and it challenged the mental health professions to provide better evidence. Meanwhile, the question of what to do about Medicare coverage was postponed.

Intensive outpatient psychotherapy (for example, psychoanalysis) is considered a luxury by members of Congress and others. It is usually employed with the upper-income groups, not the poor. Most national health insurance (NHI) plans under consideration provide limited coverage for mental illness. The more generous provide approximately 30 to 90 days for inpatient care and up to 20 outpatient visits a year to private physicians. These provisions tend to be discriminatory with regard to coverage for mental illness as compared to other illnesses.

A 1972 American Psychiatric Association study entitled "Health Insurance and Psychiatric Care: Utilization and Cost"[20] indicated that coverage for mental illness was widespread in existing private insurance plans, that utilization of these benefits was relatively low in comparison with those for all other conditions, and that costs of coverage of mental conditions would undoubtedly be supportable under NHI. For example, charges for hospital inpatient care for mental conditions range from 3% to 6% of charges for inpatient hospital care for all other conditions. Under the high-option Blue Cross–Blue Shield plan for federal employees, total costs of care for mental conditions, both inpatient and outpatient, equaled 6.4% of benefits paid for all other conditions.

Evidence shows that greater availability of psychotherapy on an outpatient basis would reduce chronicity and disability in psychiatric states and reduce the need for general medical care. There are studies (one involving Group Health of Washington, a prepaid group practice) that show a decrease in the use of medical facilities when outpatient psychotherapeutic services are introduced.[21]

Representatives of organizations like the American Psychiatric Association (APA) believe there are enough positive, controlled studies among the 700 studies[22] made thus far to show that psycho-

---

[19] A sample of recent articles includes the following: Coleman, P.G.: Measuring reminiscence characteristics from conversation as adaptive features of old age, International Journal of Aging and Human Development **5**:281-294, 1974; Coleman, P.G.: The role of the past in adaptation to old age, Ph.D. thesis, University of London, 1972; Giambra, L.M.: Daydreaming about the past: time setting of spontaneous thought intrusions, The Gerontologist **17**:35-38, 1977; Haggard, E., Brekstad, A., and Skard, A.G.: On the reliability of the anamnestic interview, Journal of Abnormal and Social Psychology **61**:311-318, 1960; Lewis, C.N.: The adaptive value of reminiscing in old age; Journal of Geriatric Psychiatry **7**:117-121, 1973; Pincus, A.: Reminiscence in aging and its implications for social work practice, Social Casework **15**:47-53, 1970; Weisman, S., and Shusterman, R.: Remembering, reminiscing and life-reviewing in an activity program for the elderly, Concern, Dec.-Jan. 1977; and Zeiger, B.L.: Life review in art therapy with the aged, American Journal of Art Therapy **15**:47-50, 1976.

[20] Reed, L.S., Myers, E.S., and Scheidemandel, P.D.: Health insurance and psychiatric care: utilization and cost, Washington, D.C., 1972, American Psychiatric Association.

[21] Goldberg, I.D., Krautz, G., and Lock, B.Z.: Effect of a short-term outpatient psychiatric therapy benefit on the utilization of medical services in a prepaid group practice medical program, Medical Care **7**:419-428, 1970.

[22] In 1980 the APA had summaries of 12 studies demonstrating the cost-effectiveness of mental health care.

therapy works. But the questions of what specific kind of therapy is best for which condition, how long should treatment last, and which professional is best qualified to do it remain unanswered.[23] The push for inclusion of psychotherapy in public and private insurance plans will require more specific answers.

As a significant move in this direction, the APA appointed a Commission on Psychiatric Therapies in 1977, charged to ''examine critically the somatic, dyadic group/family and social therapies in current use as to technique, duration, results, costs, and other salient characteristics for the purpose of identifying therapeutically effective approaches.''[24] Part of the APA's goal is to develop a manual by 1985 that will recommend specific guidelines for the treatment of all mental disorders. The treatment problems of older persons will be considered for each category of mental disorder, along with recommendations for the most effective therapies, based on a nationwide consensus of clinicians and scientists.

Some personal experiences with older people in psychotherapy

It is quite amazing that the most frequently asked question by professionals and lay persons alike is whether older people can make use of any psychotherapy that goes beyond support and simple guidance. This implies a quite naive assumption that old age brings an inevitable, implacable, and global loss of mental and emotional faculties. The examples in history, philosophy, literature, music, theology, and every other field of human activity ought to be enough to make us stand in awe of the intellectual, spiritual, emotional, and creative capacities of our elders. They have been and are often our most richly endowed leaders,

mentors, and teachers. So let us lay to rest the question of the ability to use psychotherapy and concentrate on the more relevant questions of the kind, the length, and the combinations of therapies that are most useful to the issues of later life.

Although we both have conducted psychotherapy with older persons in a wide assortment of settings and have referred to this work throughout the book, we present here a few brief examples from the recent private practice of one of us (M.I.L.) to give some of the personal flavor and variety of work with older people in a private practice.

■ A married couple in their seventies came for sex counseling. After a number of months of therapy, they wished to work on the sex issue more intensively and contacted Masters and Johnson's clinic. They were accepted as patients, flew to St. Louis, and took the intensive 2-week treatment program (paid for with part of their savings). Medical tests also showed the man to have a physical problem involving vascular difficulties. They are pursuing treatment for this condition as well. Although the final results of all of their efforts are still not in, they remain determined to try whatever possibly can improve their sex life, since both of them had enjoyed it so much in the past.

■ A woman in her early sixties, unmarried, with a dependent, childlike demeanor, wished to become more ''mature'' and less anxious and dependent. During the course of therapy she found a new job where she functioned in a more adult manner, began to move out of her passive habits socially by helping to organize groups for single older persons, and eventually reestablished a former romantic relationship with a man whom she had known for 20 years. She is now involved in working on that relationship with the help of psychotherapy.

■ A male homosexual couple (one man in his late sixties and one in his late fifties) requested help in resolving problems in their relationship. After having lived together 15 years, they eventually decided, during the course of therapy, to live in separate homes and have other intimacies but to continue their close friendship and support of one another. The older man, whose health had been deteriorating, continued to receive aid with his disabilities from the younger one.

---

[23] For a useful discussion of the issues see Parloff, M.: Psychotherapy and research: an anaclitic depression, Psychiatry **43:** 279-293, 1980.

[24] From the working draft proposal from the APA Commission on Psychiatric Therapies to the National Institute of Mental Health on the Development of a Psychiatric Treatment Manual (PTM-1), 1980.

■ A middle-aged brother and sister resolved their differences with one another in helping an aged and mentally and physically infirm mother accept a move to a nursing home. The older woman refused to join them in family therapy but was able to communicate her wishes through her children to the therapist so effectively that a solution was found that was acceptable to her as well as to them.

■ An 80-year-old man was referred by his doctor for depression over his heart problems. However when given the opportunity to talk confidentially, the man revealed the depression centered around his guilt at conducting a long-term affair with a middle-aged woman living in his home while his wife remained unaware of the nature of this relationship. After much soul-searching he concluded that he wished to continue as he was, since his wife, as he put it, was glad to be rid of his requests for sex and affection and seemed totally involved with her many activities. He still phones for an appointment now and then to talk over his concerns about the future of the younger woman when he dies and his own feelings about his death and that of his wife.

■ A retired married couple in their sixties wished to come to a decision about remaining married. Unable to talk civilly with each other even in the therapist's presence, they are each engaged in writing long essays in between therapy sessions about their anger, hopes, disappointments, and memories of the marriage. These are exchanged with each other and form the basis of a beginning analysis of the problems. Meanwhile they are being helped by the therapist to learn the elementary tactics of fair fighting and problem solving.

■ A woman in her middle seventies came, wanting to resolve her lifelong depression and difficulty in relating to people. She felt she was "unable to love." Through careful and often painful intensive psychotherapy aimed at insight, and after several years of treatment, she began to be able to successfully counter her tendency to avoid intimacy by drawing on her understanding of her childhood relationship with a cold, intellectual mother. In her fascination with this process she also became involved in various church groups aimed at enriching emotional responses, and she eventually moved from participant to training as a group leader, teaching others to lead such support groups. She still uses individual psychotherapy to help recognize when she is starting to withdraw and to deal with her disappointment when she does so.

GROUP THERAPY
Group experience for older people

Group therapy is a very valuable procedure that should be widely used in all institutions (nursing homes, hospitals, etc.) and outpatient services. It utilizes psychotherapeutic principles and techniques from individual psychotherapy as well as techniques directly derived from group process.[25]

Group therapy has been more widely used in work with older persons in and out of institutions than is generally realized or reflected in professional and scientific literature. This is partly a function of necessity, an outgrowth of the disinterest of many therapists in individual therapy with older people. It is also selected as more economical than one-to-one therapy. Volunteers as well as administrators, aides, social workers, psychologists, and psychiatrists have been "trained" to varying degrees of competence to conduct group therapy. Nurses probably conduct more group work with older persons than do other professionals[26] because they are already greatly involved in physical care and thus have more direct contact.

Usually sociability and emotional catharsis are the main objectives, but in the institutional setting

---

[25]Following are 10 curative factors in group therapy as listed by I.D. Yalom in his excellent text, The therapy and practice of group psychotherapy, New York, 1970, Basic Books, Inc., Publishers.
1. Imparting of information
2. Instillation of hope
3. Universality
4. Altruism
5. The corrective recapitulation of the primary family group
6. Development of socializing techniques
7. Imitative behavior
8. Interpersonal behavior
9. Group cohesiveness
10. Catharsis

[26]See Blake, D.: Group work with the institutionalized elderly. In Burnside, I.M., editor: Psychosocial nursing care of the aged, New York, 1973, McGraw-Hill Book Co.; Burnside, I.M.: Group work with the aged: selected literature, The Gerontologist **10:**241-246, 1970; and Ebersole, P.: From despair to integrity through reminiscing with the aged. In A.N.A. clinical sessions, New York, 1975, Appleton-Century-Crofts.

the "management" of behavior is a major consideration. The tendency for providers of services to control rather than help resolve the disturbed and upset feelings and actions of their patients needs to be questioned. When group therapy endeavors to understand and not simply "control," it is certainly preferable to chemical restraint through tranquilizer straightjacketing. Group therapy can also be conducted for the staffs of institutions and agencies to help them work through their negative and often unconscious attitudes about older persons. Social agencies, community and day centers, and "golden age" or "senior citizens" groups offer group psychotherapy to community-resident elderly. The utilization rate of golden age or senior citizens centers and clubs is relatively low, and they probably attract the more gregarious older people. The goal of these groups is usually the growth and satisfaction of participating members through positive social experiences. Group workers also develop recreational, cultural, social, and educational group activities in the larger community.

Group therapy has been used with preretirement and retirement problems, but in general, governmental and private preretirement programs fail to deal adequately with psychological and interpersonal aspects of retirement. They tend to stress financial planning and other more tangible matters.

As with group therapy in general, the role of the leader in a group of older persons may be active or passive, from the passive ones who listen to the active ones who question, explain, teach, protect, reassure, and confront. Some prefer to use the term "therapist" rather than "leader," for the latter sets certain expectations. Some consider the central role to be serving as catalyst of emotional interchange while protecting individuals and the group from excessively destructive anger and disruptive anxiety.

Not all groups need leaders.

■ In the city of Washington, one of us (R.N.B.) founded a group for older professionals and executives, with two intents: to provide an activist, advocacy group on behalf of older persons and to provide a setting for mu-

tual mental and emotional interchange. In effect, it became a "leaderless" group. It has never had a professional paid leader and, having begun in 1965, it was still in existence and lively when this volume went to press.

Groups must have momentum and vitality to maintain continuity and reduce absences and dropouts. Selection of members is critical. Heterogeneity (aged-integrated groups) minimizes the sense of isolation of the older person. Indeed, such group members may "forget" the factor of age. Groups of one's age peers have virtues of their own, including a sense of sharing a life stage together. Topics in groups composed largely of older people tend to be illness, death, loneliness, and family conflict; age-integrated groups are more likely to deal with the whole range of the life cycle, enabling older members to review and renew their own experiences and values.

Group therapy should be used with the families of older people. When an older person is admitted to an institution, for example, family members often experience profound conflicts. In one sense, they are already experiencing the death of their older relative and the first grief reaction (the later actual death and subsequent grief reactions may even have less impact). Work with relatives helps ameliorate guilt and grief and builds liaison for visitation, home stays, and discharge when possible.

Group therapy should not be viewed as second rate to individual psychotherapy. Group therapy has it own applicability and is a powerful instrument of itself. Both individual and group therapy may be usefully combined in work with the same person. The person may need the opportunity for reviewing his or her life on an individual basis and for preparing for the impending encounter with death, while at the same time gaining much from the continuing human interchange and the range of emotions — love to hate — that a well-functioning group can provide. Ebersole[27] found that the

---

[27] Ebersole, P.P.: Reminiscing and group psychotherapy with the aging. In Burnside, I.M.: Nursing and the aged, New York, 1976, McGraw-Hill Book Co., chap. 12.

use of group reminiscence was helpful to older persons in working through pain and disappointment from the past. Klein et al.[28] reported that community-resident older persons belonging to groups were eager to learn from and share experiences with each other and their group leaders as soon as they have gotten over initial distrust and suspicion.

Some persons benefit from participating in more than one group. One such man, in his late years, found his "rap sessions" eye-opening because of the differences in the way he was seen by two groups.

Silver[29] introduced group therapy with senile patients in 1950. He found a party atmosphere important—with milk, cookies, and music. Problems with memory and attention were severe in his group. But it was Linden who first described an organized program of group therapy, in 1953.[30] Goldfarb stressed working with new residents of homes to assist with orientation.[31]

"Age-integrated, life-crisis" group therapy[32]

From 1970 to 1975 we conducted and studied four age-integrated life-crisis groups (eight to ten members each) with one contrasting middle-aged group. We experimented with age integration (age range from 15 years to 80 and above), believing that age segregation as practiced in our society leaves very little opportunity for the rich exchange of feelings, experience, and support possible

among generations. "Life crisis" refers to the near-normal to pathological reactions to adolescence, education, married or single life, divorce, parenthood, work and retirement, widowhood, illness, and impending death. Thus such groups are concerned not only with the intrinsic psychiatric disorders but also with preventive and remedial treatment of people as they pass through the usual vicissitudes of the life cycle. Criteria for membership included absence of active psychosis and presence of a life crisis (acute, subacute, or chronic). Reactions to life crises followed traditional diagnostic categories, of course, including depression, anxiety states, hysterical reactions, obsessive-compulsive and passive-aggressive reactions, hypochondriasis, alcoholism, and mild drug use. Groups were balanced for age, sex, and personality dynamics. They met once a week for an hour and a half. We found it useful to have a male and a female cotherapist from different disciplines to provide both a psychodynamic and a sociological orientation for each group, as well as opportunities for transference. Individual membership in a group averaged about 2 years, and new group members were asked to commit themselves to a minimum of 3 months' participation.

The life-cycle crises approach to group therapy need be neither strictly encounter nor strictly psychoanalytic. Rather it can be equally concerned with the interaction among and between group members, as determined by reality and the past histories of each member, and with the individual problems of each member. The goals are the amelioration of suffering, the overcoming of disability, and the opportunity for new experiences of intimacy and self-fulfillment. Expression of both anger and positive feelings should be encouraged—not for a mere defusing of feeling but as a step toward constructive resolution of problems and a positive life experience.

Our patients often continued in individual psychotherapy with the referring doctor. When this was not feasible, individual therapy was encouraged along with group therapy, either with one of the cotherapists or with someone else. However,

[28]Klein, W.H., LeShan, E.J., and Furman, S.S.: Promoting mental health of older people through group methods, New York, 1965, Mental Health Materials Center, Inc.

[29]Silver, A.: Group psychotherapy with senile psychiatric patients, Geriatrics **5**:147-150, 1950.

[30]Linden, M.E.: Group psychotherapy with institutionalized senile women: study in gerontology in human relations, International Journal of Group Psychotherapy **3**:150-151, 1953.

[31]Goldfarb, A.I.: Psychotherapy of aged persons, IV. One aspect of the therapeutic situation with aged patients, Psychoanalytic Review **42**:100-187, 1955

[32]Lewis, M.I., and Butler, R.N.: Life review therapy: putting memories to work in individual and group psychotherapy, Geriatrics **29**:165-169, 172-173, 1974.

Older and younger persons work well together in groups.

Photo by Myrna Lewis.

absence of such therapy did not preclude participation in groups.

Regarding older persons, some of the phenomena we observed included (1) pseudo "senility," (2) a "Peter Pan" syndrome (refusal to grow up), and (3) leadership being preempted by the middle-aged, with neglect or "mascoting" of elderly and young (necessitating therapeutic intervention). Unique contributions of older persons included models for growing older, solutions for loss and grief, creative use of reminiscence, historic empathy, and a sense of the entire life cycle. Possibilities for psychological growth continued to the end of life.

Following are case notes on a 70-year-old woman.

■ Repeated hospital admission for psychiatric depression. Living in retirement village. No genuine financial worries but not rich. Episodes characterized by increasing depression, hopelessness, remorse, insomnia, and anorexia (no appetite). Attributes her illness to worry over daughter, who is subject to manic-depressive disease and hospitalizations.

Gives impression of quiet older lady who moves and talks little, nearly mute. Face looks grief-stricken and full of worry. Hand-wringing. No signs of organic failure. Slow but appropriate answers. Denies suicidal thought but wishes she were dead.

In life-crisis group it comes out that she believes in hereditary and physiological basis of emotional illnesses—and hence blames self for daughter's troubles. Also describes for first time an affair with a married man, conducted at 67 after death of her own husband. She feels unfaithful, disloyal. During the year she has become increasingly bright-eyed and alert, listening with interest to the sexual experiences of younger group members and eliciting their views of her own life.

FAMILY THERAPY

The family, if there is one, should of course be involved in any work with an older person, unless circumstances dictate otherwise. There should also always be clarification as to who constitutes the "patient." Sometimes the older person is "brought in" by a son or daughter, and it is quickly apparent that it is the adult child who needs help. Issues in family therapy include the need for decisions about the older person, feelings of guilt and abandonment, old family conflicts, and the need to provide continuing care and involvement with the older member. The therapist may decide to see the entire family together—not only those living in the household but also those living separately.

In one of the rare articles on psychotherapy with older people by a private practice psychiatrist, Finkel[33] examines family therapy as well as older forms of treatment. He describes the cycle of trouble that can begin in a family when an older person experiences serious losses of some kind. The cycle can take on much of the predictability of a Rube Goldberg contraption once it gets moving. The parent suffers a loss and turns to his or her family for increased support. Frequently, stirred up feelings of sadness, frustration, and anger are present in the parent, awaiting a sympathetic ear. The family initially offers its help generously but soon begins to feel exhausted by the extra demands. Both parent and adult children struggle with their new roles toward each other. Meanwhile the adult children are carrying additional burdens of their own, specific to middle age—seeing children through college and out into the world, coping with beginning bodily changes and ailments, and carrying major responsibility in the working world, the family, and community life. The older person beings to feel he or she is a burden. The adult children feel inadequate and ambivalent about the task of "doing enough" for the older person. Frustrations turn into anger and criticism. The older person may end up feeling rejected, humiliated, and intensely sad. The adult child, seeing this, experiences guilt and remorse. Often there is a brief period of "making up" and reaffirming the old parent-child bond, following by a repeat of the entire cycle. Family therapy can do much to bring understanding and resolution into this cycle.

Older marital couples may also need counseling concerning marital problems, including premarital counseling, confrontations with serious illness and approaching death, and concerns about children and grandchildren.

BEHAVIORAL MODIFICATION AND THERAPY[34]

Lindsley,[35] in 1964, developed a theoretical prospectus for the application of operant conditioning (pioneered by B.F. Skinner) to the older institutionalized person. On the whole, older populations, inpatient or outpatient, have not been studied and treated according to either "behavioral modification" or "behavioral therapy."[36] The former is the practical application of operant conditioning and includes, for example, the use of token economy (reinforcing behavior by reward). Behavioral therapy, pioneered by Wolpe, includes aversion techniques (the use of noxious stimuli). Assertive training may be valuable for older people having difficulty expressing their needs explicitly.

BIOFEEDBACK

Biofeedback refers to techniques that use electronic monitoring devices to teach patients to control selected aspects of their behavior by providing them with continuous information about what they are doing. These techniques have been applied

---

[33]Finkel, S.I.: Experiences of a private-practice psychiatrist working with the elderly in the community, International Journal of Mental Health **8**:147-172, 1980. (Dr. Finkel is convenor of the American Association for Geriatric Psychiatry.)

[34]We are indebted to Dr. Harold Weiner of St. Elizabeths Hospital, Washington, D.C., for his comments on these approaches.

[35]Lindsley, O.R.: Geriatric behavior prosthetics. In Kastenbaum, R., editor: New thoughts on old age, New York, 1964, Springer Publishing, Inc.

[36]For illustrative studies see Hoyer, W.J., Mishara, B.L., and Riekel, R.G.: Problem behaviors as operants: applications with elderly individuals, The Gerontologist **15**:452-456, 1975; Preston, C.E.: Behavior modification: a therapeutic approach to aging and death, Postgraduate Medicine **54**:64-68, 1973; and Lisk, N., Howe, M.W., and Pinkstone, E.M.: Behavioral group work in a home for the aged, Social Work **20**(6):454-463, 1975.

therapeutically to a variety of conditions that afflict older people, including headaches, backaches, and general anxiety. Engel, working at the National Institute on Aging, has successfully applied biofeedback in the reduction of hypertension as well as fecal incontinence with young subjects but not older. Johnson and Garton[37] have been able to retrain muscles through the same techniques.

ENVIRONMENTAL THERAPY

We are using the term "environmental therapy" to encompass the development of age awareness, federal policies to aid older persons, social participation,[38] mobilization of community resources, self-care, self-help, and even registration drives, job placement, direct advocacy, legal and consultative services, and political organization. The courage of many older people in the community is striking, since they must struggle against a system marked by fragmentation and indifference. Self-respect and dignity in old age obviously do not follow from felt and actual powerlessness. Consequently, we regard self-assertion in all the forms just mentioned, including political activism, as supportive of good mental health.

Age awareness and acceptance

We do not mean to be facetious in saying that "old age is beautiful" (it could be but often is not); however, it is important to encourage age awareness and acceptance. Gray hair need not be dyed. Older people should not have to "think" or "act young." For example, prejudice against age has led men and women in business, the professions, politics, and everyday life to seek plastic surgery

to eliminate the stigma of age. Face-lifting operations are frequently undertaken at great expense for dubious reasons, just as people part with money to get rid of "those ugly age spots," otherwise known as "liver spots."

People should neither be compelled nor feel compelled to misrepresent their age for employment or social purposes. A significant number of older people refuse to even identify with people their own age or with the problems that come with age. The well-to-do are especially prone to this, preferring to think of themselves as "different" from the poverty-striken elderly all around them. Yet unless they are extremely wealthy, they too can be devastated financially by just one major illness or period of adversity.

In order to begin to confront the realistic difficulties of late life, older people must first recognize their age, accept it, and even take pride in it. Second, they must recognize themselves in others of their age, empathize with common experiences, and realize "we are all in this thing together" in spite of economic differences, cultural or social backgrounds, or social status. When one is old, there is really no effective way to escape the effects of a culture that denigrates age. The most effective defense is a united challenge that combines practical, direct action with psychological support—both from others and to and from each other.

Federal policies to aid older persons
Age Discrimination Act

Age discrimination in programs receiving federal financial support is prohibited in the Age Discrimination Act of 1975. Yet older people are still often denied access to programs that are not "age-categorical" (that is, programs where age is a specific eligibility criterion). The U.S. Civil Rights Commission, chaired by activist Arthur S. Flemming, issued a report in 1978 showing age discrimination in 10 of the major social programs of the federal government, especially in community mental health programs, legal services, and employment training programs. Claims of age dis-

---

[37] Johnson, H.E., and Garton, W.H.: Muscle reeducation in hemiplegia by use of electromyographic device, Archives of Physical Medicine and Rehabilitation **54:**320-323, 1973.

[38] Cavan's study, now often overlooked, with its sizable sample of 2,988 subjects demonstrated the vast importance of social factors to adjustment. See Cavan, R.S.: Personal adjustment in old age. In Lansing, A.H., editor: Cowdry's problems of aging, ed. 3, Baltimore, 1952, Williams & Wilkins Co.

crimination can be brought before the Federal Mediation and Conciliation Service. However the regulations accompanying the Age Discrimination Act have several serious weaknesses: Although the legislative history confirms that Congress was mainly concerned about discrimination against the elderly, the regulations do not specially emphasize older persons. Second, federal, state, and local laws have been exempted from the impact of the Act.

Older Americans Act

In 1965 Congress passed the Older Americans Act (OAA), creating the Administration on Aging (AOA). With further amendments to the Act, AOA has grown to become the major federal agency in advocacy and services to the aging. Every state has an overall state agency on aging and a number of smaller planning areas, each coordinated by an area agency on aging. The area agencies—which may be either public or private nonprofit agencies—plan continuing services for older persons and coordinate the delivery of services. Generally, they do not deliver services directly, but contract with local providers for homemaker, transportation, nutrition, information and referral, counseling, legal, and other social services.

OAA funds flow from AOA to the state agencies and, in turn, to the area agencies. The money is allocated according to state plans and area plans developed and refined annually, based on the results of public hearings. Each state agency and each area agency must have an advisory council with a membership of at least one half older persons.

One can readily see that an "aging network" has sprung up throughout the United States (see Appendixes). To many workers in the field of aging and to many older people themselves, OAA and AOA have meant major steps forward in spite of problems partly explained by inadequate funding, shortage of trained professionals, and general growing pains. However critics such as Estes and Binstock profoundly question the underlying assumptions of this new establishment. In her book *The Aging Enterprise*,[39] Estes sees a major industry of services for older persons as mainly benefiting the providers and as fostering separatism, stigmatization, and dependency for the aged. She writes, "The needs of the aged are replaced by the needs of the agencies formed to serve the aged, and this transposition turns the solution into the problem." Estes' book has been a constructive contribution toward reexamining public policy related to aging.

Mobilization of community resources

In previous chapters we stress the role of mental health workers in effectively representing the interests of their patients/clients. These persons should also be helped to utilize the system (for example, see discussion of registration drives, next). Social and family agencies could play leading roles in putting pressure on other voluntary agencies as well as institutions of government. For instance, a family agency should insist that community mental health centers (CMHCs) provide outreach care for older patients. In the District of Columbia in 1971, the Jewish Social Service Agency was told that one CMHC did not accept patients over 60. A complaint was lodged through the city's Advisory Committee on Aging, and the exclusion ended.

Community workers can help fabricate networks of care within the community. Community support systems are especially valuable for the older person who has no available family. Friends, neighborhood storekeepers, druggists, and others have all been involved by mental health staff in looking out for the older person. This must be done, of course, with two perspectives in mind: the privacy of the person must not be compromised, and the network must be used for strengthening the status of the person rather than undermining

---

[39]Referring to the collection of programs, organizations, special interest groups, trade associations, and service providers and other professionals serving the aged. See Estes, C.L.: The aging enterprise: a critical examination of policies and services for the aged, San Francisco, 1979, Jossey-Bass, Inc., Publishers.

it through infantilization. An analysis of a person's social supports or "network" is part of a good mental health treatment plan. The availability of support has been found to be more important in adaption to stress than the kind and amount of stress encountered.

Organized sources of information and referral, especially true clearinghouses, should be created in district Social Security offices, voluntary agencies, state commissions on aging, and the like.

In the remainder of this chapter, we focus on specific ways to mobilize the community through efforts made by the mental health worker or made directly by the older person him- or herself.

Registration drives

Registration drives are among important efforts that mental health workers can initiate or support. Cloward and Piven[40] helped generate the idea of registering all eligible recipients for various income and service programs so they could in fact benefit from whatever the programs were offering. George Wiley expanded on this thought with the National Welfare Rights Organization, which later became a nationwide movement of welfare recipients. The operations Medicare Alert and FIND (Friendless, Isolated, Needy, Disabled) were outreach programs for older persons. The first registered older people for Medicare B (for doctors' coverage); the second resulted in the study "The Golden Years: A Tarnished Myth" done by the

National Council on the Aging, demonstrating the enormous needs and poverty of older persons. Workers in specific cities have set up outreach programs designed to get the low-income elderly in touch with the material benefits to which they are entitled under existing state and federal legislation. The work of Benefit Alert in Philadelphia is illustrative. It is important to stress, however, that (to quote Brody et al.) "Prosthetic devices such as Benefit Alert are no substitute for structural changes in program"; these simply make it less easy to ignore older persons, since they are demonstrating their need and eligibility for services and benefits.

Self-help and self-care

The burgeoning self-care, self-help movement in the United States—estimated in 1980 at several hundred thousand individual groups belonging to 400 major groups—promises great, if still not well-defined, potential for older people. "Self-care" refers to actions performed by individuals for their own or their families' health and well-being and the well-being of others; "self-help" is used when groups of people who share a common interest or condition join together to offer one another mutual interchange and support. In essence, the health consumer is taking a more active role in maintaining or improving his or her physical and mental health, sometimes taking over tasks otherwise performed by health care providers and sometimes augmenting such work.

Several social factors have joined to make self-care and self-help popular.

1. A demand for better health care by the consumer movement
2. The rising cost of health care (The cost of medical care rose twice as fast as any other item in the Consumer Price Index between 1950 and 1970). In 1975, 8.3% of the U.S. Gross National Product was spent in health care, as compared to 5.2% in 1960.
3. A maldistribution of professional health care
4. The counter-culture movement of the 1960s urging greater self-reliance for individuals

---

[40] Cloward and Piven argued in 1966 (Cloward, R.A., and Piven, F.F.: The weight of the poor . . . a strategy to end poverty, The Nation **202:**510-517, 1966) that "adding all eligible persons to the welfare rolls would generate a financial crisis of such magnitude that the federal government would be pressured to respond with a plan for a guaranteed annual income." An Advisory Council on Public Welfare the same year suggested, as had others, a "national floor under assistance payments" and federal, rather than state, responsibility for public welfare program studies and financing (Advisory Council on Public Welfare: Having the power we have the duty, report to the Secretary of Health, Education and Welfare, Washington, D.C., 1966, U.S. Government Printing Office). This became one of the historical steps in the development of Supplemental Security Income.

The four steps in self-care are listed below.

1. Self-knowledge (health education)
2. Body monitoring—maintaining healthful habits and detecting health problems in early stages
3. Self-treatment—learning first aid and using a variety of medical tools, like blood pressure cuffs, and simple home treatments[41]
4. Learning when to seek professional help

A few attempts have been made to design self-care programs specifically for older persons. An example is Sehnert's "Activated Patient" program for Medicare recipients in Reston, Virginia.[42] Many self-care concepts are pertinent to old age, from learning to take one's own blood pressure to improvements in diet and exercise.

Self-help groups usually spring up voluntarily around an issue of shared concern. Examples of self-help groups that are especially relevant for older people are Widow Outreach Programs, the Alzheimer's Disease and Related Disorders Association, Emphysema Anonymous, the American Cancer Society, the Arthritis Foundation, Make Today Count (for the terminally ill), the Gray Panthers, Reach to Recovery (for breast cancer patients), Recovery, Inc. (the Association of Nervous and Former Mental Patients), stroke clubs like Opus (Organization of People Undaunted by Stroke, Inc.), the American Diabetes Association, women's consciousness-raising groups, the Parkinson's Disease Foundation, the United Ostomy Association, and the American Heart Association.

The National Institute on Aging has prepared a booklet describing and listing major self-help groups of particular value for the elderly.[43]

A very few self-help groups have been specifically tailored for older persons. One of these is SAGE (Senior Actualization and Growth Exploration),[44] describing itself as a "growth center for people over sixty-five." It was founded in 1974 in California and is now active in 15 states, including groups in convalescent and nursing homes. Groups meet 2 to 3 hours a week. The program combines Eastern philosophy with Western innovations—deep breathing, massage, yoga, biofeedback, counseling, dance, music, and art.

Many self-help groups and self-care concepts have been enthusiastically supported by health care providers.[45] Other providers have been less enthusiastic, fearing encroachment in professional territory, predicting consumers would "go too far" in self-care, or simply doubting the effectiveness of the self-care, self-help movement. Serious studies of the impact of the movement have not yet been done. But the "soft indicators" of client satisfaction show that many find this new health movement satisfying and useful, as judged by their continuing voluntary participation.

---

[41] The following are examples of books in this area: American National Red Cross: Standard first aid and personal safety, Garden City, N.Y., 1973, Doubleday & Co., Inc.; Sehnert, K.W., and Eisenberg, H.: How to be your own doctor (sometimes), New York, 1975, Grosset & Dunlap, Inc. (explains the "Activated Patient" concept); and Vickery, D.M., and Fries, J.F.: Take care of yourself: a consumer guide to medical care, Reading, Mass., 1976, Addison-Wesley Publishing Co., Inc.

[42] Sehnert, K., Awkward, B., and Lesage, D.: The senior citizen as an "activated patient," mimeographed book prepared for the Office of Assistant Secretary for Planning and Education, U.S. Public Health Service, Department of Health, Education and Welfare, March 1976.

[43] A guide to medical self-care and self-help groups for the elderly, Pub. No. (NIH) 80-1687, Washington, D.C., 1979, U.S. Government Printing Office. See also Butler, R.N., Gertman, J.S., Oberlander, D.L., and Schindler, L.: Self-care, self-help and the elderly, International Journal of Aging and Human Development **10**:95-119, 1979.

To find out if an organization is operating in a particular area, the following clearinghouses can be contacted: The National Self-Help Clearinghouse, 33 W. 42nd St., Room 1227, New York, N.Y. 10036, and The Self-Help Institute at Northwestern University Center for Urban Affairs, 2040 Sheridan Rd., Evanston, Ill. 60201.

[44] See Dychtwald, K.: The SAGE project: a new image of aging, Journal of Humanistic Psychology **18**(2):69-74, 1978; and Luce, G.G.: Your second life: vitality and growth in maturity and later years from the experiences of the SAGE program, New York, 1979, Delacourte Press.

[45] Lieberman, M.A., et al.: Self-help groups for coping with crisis: origins, members, processes and impact, San Francisco, 1979, Jossey-Bass, Inc., Publishers.

Employment

If older people are so delighted with retirement, why are older-aged employment services overloaded with applicants?

Some older people need the money because the Social Security or pension checks just will not stretch far enough.[46] Some want to get out of the house to occupy their time. Many want the "meaningfulness" of work. So long as work and money have such profound financial, social, personal, and ethical significance, it is illusory to deny their importance to health, both physical and mental. Some older people are told to do volunteer work—advice that is indeed helpful to some but naive in instances where economic survival is at issue. Arbitrary retirement is often cruel and of questionable constitutionality. Despite the raising of the retirement age to 70 in the private sector, it is anticipated that there will be increasing numbers of legal suits testing the right of any person, regardless of age, to employment.

The National Committee on Careers for Older Americans (chaired by Arthur S. Flemming) wants to reverse public and private policies that have led to premature retirement of able older Americans.[47] The Department of Labor has been urged to provide help to older people through the Comprehensive Employment Training Act (CETA).

Unemployment. Unemployment hangs over the heads of many people who are over 50 years of age. A classic instance of this was seen in 1963 when the Studebaker Corporation announced the end of automotive production in its South Bend, Indiana, facilities. The company plant shutdown affected nearly 10% of the area's total work force of 90,000 people. More than half of those laid off were over 50 years of age. The entire community rallied together with state and federal agencies. The successful Project ABLE (Ability Based on Long Experience) was an experimental action and demonstration program supported through the Department of Labor's Office of Manpower, Automation and Training. It showed that large numbers of unemployed older workers can be returned to productive employment through mobilization of the community, individual counseling, and job development and opportunities. South Bend itself recovered.[48]

Several laws have been enacted to relieve the unemployment difficulties of older workers. There are now "extended benefits" during periods of high unemployment for those whose regular unemployment compensation entitlement has been exhausted. Training, retraining, counseling, and other needed services for middle-aged and older workers are available on a limited basis.

The Senior Opportunities Services (SOS) program of the Office of Economic Opportunity is intended to identify and meet the needs of persons over 60 with projects that serve and/or employ older persons predominately. The various projects include community action programs to provide employment opportunities, home health services, assistance in the Food Stamp plan, and outreach and referral services. As much as possible, these activities are staffed by older citizens, paid or volunteer. OEO's Senior Aides and Senior Community Service Aides are engaged in such activities as homemaker and health assistance, nutrition, institutional care, home repair, child care, and social service administration.

Green Thumb, which involves beautification by planting—for men— and Green Light, which employs aides in libraries, schools, and day-care centers—for women—are federal employment programs for older people. The box opposite lists jobs for older persons that could be developed to meet needs that exist in many communities.

Age discrimination. Age discrimination in employment is directly related to unemployment. The Age Discrimination in Employment Act of 1976[49]

---

[46] Self-employment is often of necessity "bootleg" work: typing, babysitting, housecleaning, handyman services (electrical and carpentry skills), etc., which is *not* reported as income so as to avoid imperiling Social Security pensions.

[47] See National Committee on Careers for Older Americans: Older Americans: an untapped resource, 1979.

[48] United Community Service of St. Joseph County, Inc., Project ABLE (Ability Based on Long Experience), Final Report Contract No. MDS37-64, Older Worker Employment, South Bend, Ind., Dec. 1965.

[49] 29 U.S.C. 621 et seq.

JOB OPTIONS FOR OLDER PEOPLE IN MEETING COMMUNITY NEEDS

Transportation
Station information aides
Bus drivers
Van drivers
Pool arrangers
Improved route sign advisors
Service assistance locators

Cultural activities
Performers and artists
Programmers
Trainers
Sales and promotion workers
Facilities maintenance workers
Fund raising counselors and assistants
Audience development specialists
Arts conservators and technicians
Resource and information assistants

Employment
Job finders
Trainers
Job developers
Career and job counselors

Non-profit activities
Fund raising/membership counselors
Bookkeepers and accountants
Government regulations and compliance counselors
Coordinators of volunteers
Incorporation advisors

Environment
Counselors on pesticide and safety
Extended sanitation and special clean-up workers
Monitors
Materials recycling aides
Environmental impact analysts

Employee relations
Mediation, arbitration, and conciliation specialists (both employee/management and employer/employee relations)

Neighborhood
Guards and monitors
Clean-up aides
Repair workers for substandard housing
Energy conservation advisors and workers
Mediators, conciliators and arbitrators
Fire and safety inspectors
Pest control workers
Translators and communicators

Health
Hospital technicians and aides
Home health care providers and aides
Rehabilitation technicians and aides
Medical equipment operators

Education
Discipline aides
Tutors and resource specialists
Class administration aides
Library workers
Career and other counselors
Special population education programmers and advisors
Fund raisers
Special skill enrichment advisors and aides
Financial aid advisors

Special services to dependent persons
Companions
Nutrition advisors
Form fillers
Eligibility & assistance advisors
Readers & communicators
Recreation advisors and workers
Meal providers and/or feeding helpers
Day care providers
Home health care aides
Rehabilitation technicians & helpers
Representative payees & guardians
Homemakers
Shopping assistance helpers

From National Committee on Careers for Older Americans: Older Americans: an untapped resource, New York, 1979, Academy for Educational Development.

is administered by the Department of Labor, Wage and Hour Administration, in 350 offices throughout the nation (see listings in the telephone directory). The Act prohibits discrimination on the basis of age in hiring, job retention, compensation, and other terms, conditions, and privileges of employment. It originally applied only to those workers between 40 and 65 years of age; however, amendments in 1978 raised the protected age limit for workers in the private sector to 70 years of age and eliminated the upper age limit entirely for most federal employees.

People over 70 in the private sector are totally unprotected by law, although some, through individual and class legal efforts, are attempting to challenge this. Typical ways in which employers avoid hiring the older person are to declare that the person is "overqualified," "unskilled," less needful of a job as compared to the young, and less reliable and flexible. Most of this is false, and the rest could easily be remedied through, for example, training programs that accept the person over 50 years of age.[50]

Job placement. Job placement requires vocational evaluation and counseling as critical first steps. The U.S. Employment Service (USES) has been very disappointing in its feeble efforts to place older workers, but pressure should nonetheless be placed on USES and its various offices. There are Federal Job Information Centers (in various cities), which give advice and information on federal job opportunities. The Women's Bureau in the Department of Labor has taken some interest in the job plight of older women and can offer advice. Various communities offer privately sponsored, nonprofit, over-60 employment and counseling services and agencies. In some there are 40-plus clubs for finding employment after age 40. For the handicapped and elderly, sheltered workshops may be available. (See Chapter 11.) In Ap-

pendix C we have outlined various governmental programs to which older people can apply (some being specifically designed for the low-income elderly).

Advocacy

Advocacy includes use of all means at our disposal, from direct action to moral persuasion, to effectively represent the needs and grievances of older people. The contributions of Saul Alinsky and Ralph Nader should be known to the mental health worker. Class-action cases are essential, for instance, to mandamus (to compel) better treatment in state mental hospitals[51] and other governmental facilities. Legal and protective services,[52] private conservatorships, and public guardianships are essential—not only to protect older people but also to advance their causes such as better housing and administrative and judicial reviews regarding Social Security and Medicare claims. Contemporary grievance mechanisms are being overhauled and improved following court cases.

Nursing home deficiencies must not be covered up by local, state, or federal governments. The Freedom of Information Act should compel the Social Security Administration to reveal the names of specific institutions with their particular deficiencies.

Individual older people have a variety of rights to be protected such as contractual and testamentary rights. Tenant rights have become increasingly important.

The Group for the Advancement of Psychiatry has argued that every community mental health center should have an advocate for the aged, a spokesperson "in negotiations with other agencies or governmental counseling."

There already exist various advocates for older people. Some churches have lay commissions and special ministries to the aging. Cities and states have advisory committees and commissions. Massachusetts created the first cabinet-level De-

---

[50] For the pioneering references see The National Council on the Aging: Utilization of older professional and scientific workers, May 1961; Shock, N.W.: Older people and their potentialities for gainful employment, Journal of Gerontology **2:**92-102, 1947; and McFarland, R.A.: The older worker in industry, Harvard Business Review, Summer 1943, pp. 505-510.

[51] *Wyatt v. Stickney,* Alabama, 1971-1972.

[52] Neighborhood legal services, Legal Aid societies, public defenders, public-interest law firms, and protective services are available for the legal needs of older persons.

partment of Elder Affairs in 1971 to oversee all programs for older persons. The new Department has authority over such functions as Supplemental Security Income, Disability Assistance, and the provision of a program for income maintenance (formerly functions of the Welfare Department); licensing and inspection of nursing homes, rest homes, and similar facilities for the elderly (formerly the responsibility of the Department of Public Health); and construction and administration of housing and transportation services for older persons (previously vested in the Department of Community Affairs).

For advocacy to mean anything there must be *accountability*. Challenging of authority must be handled by "reactions" from the challenged; otherwise the "system" is not working. There has been a crescendo of complaints about the unresponsiveness of the system under which we live. We do not wish to perpetuate any romantic illusions about "working within" the system. We have not been impressed with great progress on behalf of older people in the last decades—nor on behalf of minority or other groups. There was only a 1% change in the distribution of wealth between 1950 and 1970, to take one major indicator, and changes since then have been equally discouraging. To work at all on the problems of the elderly, as with all groups that have suffered or are suffering injustices, one must be willing to be angry and outraged, depressed and despairing, but always ready and spoiling for a struggle. In short, affirmation, anger, and despair in due proportion are appropriate emotions.[53]

---

[53] Joan Colebrook wrote movingly about urban renewal in the South End of Boston (Colebrook, J.: A reporter at large: the renewal, New Yorker, Jan. 1, 1966). She observed: "Social workers were trying to provide some moral support for impoverished and isolated older people who found themselves in the way of the bulldozer." She was writing about older people trying to survive in their run-down neighborhoods with abandoned and substandard housing, garbage-strewn empty lots, dimly lighted streets. They were subjected to mugging and purse-snatching. When urban renewal began, it happened that the possessions of a lifetime were at times thrown into the streets if an older person was in a hospital or for some other reason not able to be home. She also observed some relocation deaths.

The Swedish concept of ombudsman has been proposed for application in the United States. (An ombudsman in Scandinavia is a mediator who protects the rights of individual citizens and works with governmental agencies to ensure fair representation.) We believe older persons themselves should take leadership. They should make unannounced visits to nursing homes. When they do not wish to retire, they should be willing to challenge the pressure to leave their jobs. There are countless ways in which they can counter the myths and prejudices against old age

We have also long urged the formation of a national federation of friends and relatives of nursing home residents rather than depending solely on the establishment of federal, state, and local standards, regulations, and enforcement. The Friends and Relatives of Nursing Home Patients, Inc., a consumer group in Oregon organized principally by Ruth Shepherd in 1972, is an example of a local group whose objective is to have as a member of the organization one family member or friend who is financially or legally responsible for each resident of a nursing home. The development of the National Citizens Coalition for Nursing Home Reform under Elma Griesel is a move toward the monitoring and improvement of nursing homes on a national basis.[54] (See Appendix B for a list of the many organizations belonging to this coalition.)

Legal services

Congress has defined "legal services" in Section 302(4) of the Older American's Act as "legal advice and representation by an attorney (including, to the extent feasible, counseling or other appropriate assistance by a paralegal or law student under the supervision of an attorney) and includes counseling or representation by a non-lawyer where permitted by law, to older individuals with economic or social needs." Amendments to OAA in 1972 specifically included legal services for funding under Title III of the Act through state

---

[54] See Horn, L., and Griesel, E.: Nursing homes: a citizen's action guide. How to organize, plan and achieve nursing home reform in your community, Boston, 1977, Beacon Press.

and area agencies on aging. Over 120 legal service for the elderly projects now exist nationwide, many funded under Title III. Others are financed by Title XX of the Social Security Act, the Housing and Community Development Act, revenue sharing, funds resulting from filing fee legislation, United Way, or private foundations.

The Office of Economic Opportunity (OEO) established the National Senior Citizens Law Center in 1972 in Los Angeles[55] to pay special attention to the legal problems of older people.

The paralegal movement, which started in the late 1960s with the public interest effort to make legal services more available to the poor, has been helpful to older people in dealing with the bureaucratic confusion of federal benefit programs. Paralegals in various settings, with the approval of federal law, can help older people get Food Stamps and Social Security payments as well as Medicare, Medicaid, and unemployment checks.

The American Bar Association in 1978 created a 15-member interdisciplinary Commission on Legal Problems of the Elderly.[56] Its initial priorities were four: the delivery of legal services to older persons, age discrimination, simplification and coordination of administrative procedures and regulations affecting the elderly, and the rights of persons subject to the process of institutionalization. We list references describing further legal issues in old age.[57]

Consumer fraud and quackery. Consumer fraud and quackery are serious legal problems because older people are especially vulnerable.[58]

Many have chronic ailments that seem never to get better. Hard-earned savings may be lost to exploitative medical fakers, land salespeople, hearing aid salespeople, and others. In 1966 the U.S. Senate Special Committee on Aging published a report on "frauds and misinterpretations affecting the elderly."

The human desire for magic cures and salvation runs deep. In late life, additional factors, ranging from brain damage to grief, add to the vulnerability. Public consumer education is not sufficient. Direct advice and discussion by the various service professions and vocations—mental health workers to physicians—carry considerable weight. But legislation, more than we presently have, is necessary, and its strict enforcement is mandatory. An example of such legislation is the Interstate Land Sales Full Disclosure Act.

Credit discrimination. The Equal Credit Opportunity Act Amendment of 1976[59] prohibits discrimination in credit transactions, making it unlawful for a creditor to discriminate against any credit applicant on the basis of "race, color, religion, national origin, sex or marital status, or age (provided the applicant has the capacity to contract)."

Consultative services

Consultative services should be standard to agencies, homes, and religious and other organizations. The following list includes the major users of consultation regarding the problems of older people.

---

[55] The Center is currently funded through the Legal Services Corporation, with offices at 1636 W. 8th St., Los Angeles, Calif. 90017, and at 1424 14th St., N.W., Washington, D.C. 20036.

[56] Commission on Legal Problems of the Elderly, American Bar Association, 1800 M St., N.W., Washington, D.C. 20036.

[57] Brown, R.N., Allo, C.D., Freeman, A.D., and Netzorg, G.W.: The rights of older persons: an ACLU handbook, New York, 1979, Avon Books ($2.50). This comprehensive guide for older persons, their families, their lawyers, and members of nonlaw professions, such as social workers and nurses, incorporates the latest changes in the Social Security Act, the Internal Revenue Code, and the Pension Reform Law; The law and aging manual, 1976, Legal Research Services for the

Elderly, 1511 K St., N.W., Washington, D.C. 20005 ($3.00). The manual provides a thorough introduction to legal services development for older persons. It is intended to introduce the legal community to the aging network and vice versa, describing groups and governmental programs active in each area; and A handbook of model state statutes, Legal Research and Services for the Elderly, 1511 K St., N.W., Washington, D.C. 20005 (free). The handbook includes model statutes benefiting older persons, with commentary covering a range of topics from nursing homes to hearing aids to guardianship.

[58] See Butler, R.N.: Why are older consumers to susceptible? Geriatrics **23**:83-88, 1968.

[59] P.L. 92-239 amending 15 U.S.C. 1691 et. seq.

1. Nursing homes
2. Homes for the aged
3. Nonpsychiatrist physicians
4. General hospital inpatient and outpatient sections
5. Boarding homes, public housing for the aged, and similar residential concentrations
6. Public assistance departments, including their sections for protective service for older persons
7. Members of the clergy
8. Senior citizen centers
9. Industry and government
10. Homemaker and home health aide agencies
11. Visiting nurses and public health nurses
12. Planning bodies, such as model cities boards, senior citizen councils, commissions on aging, housing authorities

Generally speaking, consultative relationships to such institutions and agencies provide evaluation and recommendations concerning the institution itself, its staff, or those it serves. The following list further delineates this general observation and offers some models of consultation.

1. *Administrative consultation.* The center consultant meets with the home administrator, usually to discuss staff problems, but sometimes family or financial problems. The focus is on organization and decision-making.
2. *Staff (milieu) consultation.* The center consultant meets with staff groups to discuss and interpret the psychological importance of events in the home which affect staff and patient group behavior.
3. *Client-centered case consultation.* The center consultant discusses a specific case with a staff group or individual. Focus is on the patient.
4. *Consultee-centered consultation.* The focus of discussion is the patient, but the center consultant keeps the staff members' countertransference in mind during the discussion.
5. *Didactic meetings.* These allow for an organized presentation of basic psychological principles. Many staff have a keen interest in such learning.[60]

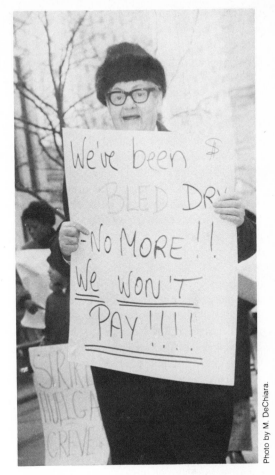

Self-respect follows self-assertion.

The politics of age

The beginning rumblings of "politics of age" are stirring controversy along with some study[61] and political attention. Binstock has written of the

---

[60] From Group for the Advancement of Psychiatry: The aged and community mental health: a guide to program development, vol. 8, no. 81, Nov. 1971. Formulated by the Committee on Aging.

[61] A few studies are appearing. One relates to the question of the alleged development of greater conservatism with age, (Rule, W.I.B.: Political alienation and voting attitudes among the elderly generation, The Gerontologist **17**[5]:400-404, 1977). Another discusses the question of why minority group elderly have a lower rate of political activity (Torres-Gill, F., and Becerra, F.M.: The political behavior of the Mexican-American elderly, The Gerontologist **17**[5]:392-399, 1977).

weaknesses of using older age as a political rallying point. Others see it as positive and inevitable. Already there is talk of a "backlash" by the younger generations.[62]

Several states have annual Governors' Conferences on Aging (for example, Indiana, North Carolina, and Ohio), and others have special days for older people (for example, "Older Vermonters' Day"). Florida, Michigan, Georgia, Missouri, and Utah have what has been called "silver-haired legislatures"—quasi-official groups of older citizens who meet and draft legislation that is then passed on to the state legislators.

Having some sense of power and political participation is therapeutic; the active seeking of objectives may not always be successful, but the process itself can be a source of satisfaction and increased self-esteem. Older people are beginning to be more active politically and may soon vote more consistently as a power block (they constitute 17% of the vote). The National Council of Senior Citizens and the American Association of Retired Persons (the two largest organizations for older people) have lobbied for more favorable Social Security benefits, Medicare, housing, and other areas of concern. The Gray Panthers are a much smaller but more activist group. In addition to their many other advocate activities, the Gray Panthers have created two manuals covering issues such as shared housing and health care.[63]

---

[62] Ragan, P.: Another look at the politicizing of old age: can we expect a backlash effect? Urban and Social Change Review **10**(2):6-13, 1977.

[63] For copies of The Gray Panther manual, vol. I, 1978, and vol. 2, 1979, contact the Gray Panthers, 3635 Chestnut St., Philadelphia, Pa. 19104.

REFERENCES

Brown, R.N.: The rights of older persons: the basic ACSW guide to an older person's rights, New York, 1979, Avon Books.

Burnside, I.M., editor: Working with the elderly: group processes and techniques, North Scituate, Mass., 1978, Duxbury Press.

Cohen, E.S.: Legal research issues on aging, The Gerontologist **14**:263-267, 1974.

Estes, C.L.: The aging enterprise: a critical examination of social policies and services for the aged, San Francisco, 1979, Jossey-Bass, Inc., Publishers.

Gellhorn, W.: Ombudsmen and elderly citizens' protection in nine countries, Cambridge, Mass., 1966, Harvard University Press.

Knight, B.: Psychotherapy and behavior change with the non-institutionalized aged, International Journal of Aging and Human Development **9**:221-236, 1979.

Martin, L.J.: A handbook for old age counselors, San Francisco, 1944, Geertz Printing Co.

Rechtschaffen, A.: Psychotherapy with geriatric patients: a review of the literature, Journal of Gerontology **14**:73-84, 1959.

Sparacino, J.: Individual psychotherapy with the aged: a selective review, International Journal of Aging and Human Development **9**:197-220, 1979.

13

Drug and electroshock therapy

Although older people make up 11% of the population, they consume 25% of all medications prescribed in the United States—as well as massive amounts of over-the-counter medications, which do not require prescriptions. The single largest out-of-pocket health care expense for older persons is the payment for out-of-hospital drugs, yet Congress did not include this benefit under Medicare. Medical and nursing education does not yet focus adequately on pharmacology and clinical pharmacy as it relates to old age. And research studies have seldom included the old in their observations. We know little about the changes in absorption, distribution, metabolism, and excretion of medications (called pharmacokinetics) and the actions and side effects (pharmacodynamics) that occur with aging—an exciting and important territory for research with obviously practical application.

Drugs, judiciously employed, can be of supportive value in the treatment of anxiety, severe agitation, and depression in old age. They should not, however, represent the sole form of treatment given to any older person. When possible, other approaches to the amelioration of symptoms should be tried first: various forms of psychotherapy, social activities, and physical exercise. If drugs are nonetheless deemed necessary, they should be administered only as one component of an organized treatment plan.[1]

There is considerable evidence to support the view that we have an "overmedicated society." Much concern, of course, is voiced about use of drugs in the youth culture and about barbiturate,[2] tranquilizer, and alcohol consumption among the middle-aged. But old age has its own drug problems, resulting from high usages of tranquilizers, antidepressants, sedatives, and hypnotics. To some degree these medications reflect the greater anxiety, depression, and insomnia found in older people. But they also point to the anxiety of doctors and other health personnel, their impatience with older people (to whom they would rather give a pill than listen), and their own need for instant gratification (treatment results). Unfortunately, drugs reinforce some of the slowing observed in older people, aggravate a sense of aging and depression, and can contribute to or directly cause acute and chronic brain syndromes. The Food and Drug Administration does not require

[1]Group for the Advancement of Psychiatry: Pharmacotherapy and psychotherapy: paradoxes, problems and progress 9:93, 1975.

[2]Solomon, F., White, C.C., Parron, D.C., and Mendelson, W.B.: Sleeping pills, insomnia and medical practice, New England Journal of Medicine 300:803-808, 1979.

345

Table 13-1. Drugs used in psychiatry

Generic names	Trade names (examples)
Antianxiety drugs	
Benzodiazepine derivatives	
Chlordiazepoxide	Librium
Diazepam	Valium
Oxazepam	Serax
Sedative types	
Barbiturates (numerous types)	Numerous brands
Meprobamate	Equanil, Miltown
Antidepressants	
Tricyclic derivatives	
Amitriptyline	Elavil
Desipramine	Norpramin, Pertofrane
Doxepin	Sinequan, Adapin
Imipramine	Imavate, SK-Pramine, Tofranil
Nortriptyline	Aventyl
Protriptyline	Vivactil
Hydrazide MAO inhibitors	
Isocarboxazid	Marplan
Phenelzine	Nardil
Nonhydrazide MAO inhibitors	
Tranylcypromine	Parnate
Stimulants	
Methylphenidate	Ritalin
Antimanic drugs	
Chlorpromazine	Thorazine
Haloperidol	Haldol
Lithium carbonate	Eskalith, Lithane, Lithonate
Reserpine	Numerous brands
Antipsychotic drugs (neuroleptics)	
Phenothiazine derivatives	
Aliphatic	
Chlorpromazine	Thorazine
Butyrophenone	
Haloperidol	Haldol
Piperidine	
Thioridazine	Mellaril

Modified from American Psychiatric Association: A psychiatric glossary, ed. 5, New York, 1980, Basic Books, Inc., Publishers.

that aging be considered a factor when new drugs are tested for psychoactivity or potential abuse.[3] As a consequence there is limited testing of psychoactive medications in older persons through well-designed studies. We emphasize some of the untoward side effects and complications of drug therapy while acknowledging the legitimate use of medications in a carefully thought out and monitored treatment plan. But, in general, we submit that the medical profession's penchant for chemotherapy with older persons should be restrained.

It should be understood that we are referring specifically to the present-day pharmacopoeia available for the treatment of anxiety, depression, insomnia, etc. The striking new advances in neurobiology, including the biochemical theories of depression and senile dementia, promise important and, one would hope, safer therapeutic agents in the near future.

Table 13-1 classifies by generic and trade names the drugs most frequently prescribed in psychiatry. For the older age group there are unfortunately no precise methods for measuring blood levels of various drugs or their breakdown products in the body (metabolites) to help ensure the maintenance of the effective blood levels. Thus plasma levels are not reliable indicators for decisions regarding dosage.

DRUG TREATMENT
Antidepressants

Antidepressants include the tricyclic compounds and the monoamine oxidase inhibitors (MAOIs). We recommend against the use of the monoamine oxidase[4] inhibitors. These mood elevators have profound side effects, including orthostatic hypotension (fall in blood pressure when standing erect), inhibition of ejaculation, weakness, and hypertensive crisis associated with the concurrent intake of certain food substances such as cheese. The MAOIs include isocarboxazid (Marplan), nialamide (Niamid), phenelzine sulfate (Nardil), and tranylcypromine (Parnate).[5]

The other group, the dibenzazepine derivatives (tricyclic compounds), mix badly with the MAOIs. Their antidepressant effects are not remarkable but are regarded as established. The most popular are amitriptyline (Elavil) and imipramine (Tofranil). Ten days of amitriptyline at 150 mg daily in divided doses is probably an adequate course. With amitriptyline the patient may feel worse, rather than better, for the first 2 to 5 days. Once he or she has become stabilized on amitriptyline, it is possible for the patient to change from taking divided doses to taking all the medication in one single dose at bedtime.[6] The advantages to this are that side effects such as dryness of mouth occur during sleep, and also the patient is less likely to forget to take the drug. Moreover, there is the sedative effect, which aids sleep.

Strokes and myocardial infarctions ("coronaries") have been reported with the tricyclic compounds. Thus, great caution is recommended in using tricyclic antidepressants with heart patients. These compounds should not be given within 2 weeks after discontinuing an MAOI, since hyperpyretic (high-fever) crises and deaths have occurred. They must be used cautiously in patients with a history of urinary retention or with narrow-angle glaucoma or increased intraocular pressure. They can cause anticholinergic-induced confusional states. Physical and mental performance, as in driving an automobile or operating machinery, may be affected.

---

[3] Animal testing of all drugs before they are marketed is done on very young animals; even "chronic toxicity" experiments are usually done on young puppies. A major reason for this is that older animals are much more expensive to use in testing. They must be maintained in highly controlled settings over the course of their young and middle years. But even in human studies, older people often are not "factored in," a practice that has little to do with economy and much to do with disinterest and disregard for the old.

[4] An important central nervous system enzyme that breaks down norepinephrine.

[5] We first give the generic name for purposes of prescription. Because advertising has been so successful in introducing people to drugs, we also give the most common trade name(s) in parentheses.

[6] Because the plasma half-life is about 24 hours or more.

It is also important to understand the patient's life history and defenses before prescribing antidepressant drugs. Suppression of a symptom—be it depression or anxiety—may be undesirable. For instance, in a depression viewed as a maladaptive expression of grief, the release of suppressed grief will have a more enduring value than drug-suppressed depression. No drug can substitute for a lost loved one as therapeutic counseling and the forging of new relationships can.

Included among the tricyclic compounds is desipramine (Norpramin, Pertofrane). The mechanisms of its established effects against depression are not known. Desipramine is supposed to be a metabolite of imipramine (Tofranil) and was therefore presumed to act more quickly. This has not proved to be so.

A therapeutic trial with tricyclic antidepressants may demonstrate that an apparent case of senile dementia is actually a depression. However experience has shown that unless a patient with dementia has signs and symptoms of depression, it is rarely beneficial to try tricyclic compounds. Furthermore, a person with dementia who is obviously in good spirits runs a significant risk of at least a temporarily worsening cognitive dysfunction with the use of tricyclic compounds because of their central anticholinergic effects. There may also be impairment of mental condition through peripheral anticholinergic effects or orthostatic hypotension. Older persons taking medications with these effects should be advised to get up from chair or bed slowly and carefully.

Amitriptyline (Elavil) has a tranquilizing component and so is especially indicated in anxious depression. The antidepressant effect of this agent may be apparent in 4 days or perhaps not before 3 or 4 weeks. For mild depressions in older persons, the dosage is 25 mg three times daily to 25 mg twice daily and 50 mg at bedtime. Begin at 10 mg three times daily and 20 mg at bedtime. For severe depressions, rapidly build up to 150 to 200 mg daily. As much as 250 mg can be given to a heavily built person.

With *imipramine* (Tofranil) the dosage is 30 to 100 mg daily, in divided doses, and should start at 10 mg three times daily and be increased gradually. From 4 to 8 weeks is a reasonable trial; most patients who are going to respond do so in the first 2 weeks.

Still other tricyclic compounds are nortriptyline (Aventyl) and protriptyline (Vivactil).

Methylphenidate (Ritalin) is a mild central nervous system stimulant that counteracts physical and mental fatigue while having only slight effect on blood pressure and respiration. Its potency is intermediate between amphetamines and caffeine. It is useful only in mild depression and then only in a limited number of cases. We have found it useful in some instances of mild early chronic brain syndromes. It is sometimes helpful in counteracting drug-induced lethargy resulting from barbiturates, tranquilizers, antihistamines, and anticonvulsants. There is reported effectiveness against "apathetic or withdrawn senile behavior." There is little evidence of improvement of cognition.[7] One must be wary of using this drug, however, since it may aggravate anxiety and tension. Glaucoma is a contraindication. Begin with 10 to 15 mg daily in divided doses, preferably taken 30 to 45 minutes before meals; 20 to 30 mg is the maximum for older persons.

Lithium carbonate (Eskalith, Lithane, Lithonate) has been an effective agent in the treatment of patients of all ages with manic-depressive illness. Among older persons, one encounters hypomanic states that often respond to lithium with much smaller amounts than would ordinarily be anticipated. Effective dosages may be as low as 300 mg once daily to 600 mg twice daily. Hypomanic states and bipolar depressions are most susceptible to lithium therapy, and improvement can be dramatic. However older people must be monitored more closely than younger persons. For example, if one doctor prescribes lithium and another diuretics, without collaboration between them, the patient may have dangerous elevation in his or her serum lithium level.

---

[7] Crook, T., et al.: Psychopharmacology **82**:251-255, 1977.

Evidence for the treatment of depressive states is less impressive. One must be certain there is adequate kidney excretion because of the small margin between the therapeutic and toxic doses.[8] With older people on low-sodium diets and on diuretics, the need for caution is increased. Roose et al., at the Lithium Clinic of the New York State Psychiatric Institute, reported that patients over 60 are more prone to develop lithium toxicity and that these episodes can "fulminate more rapidly and at lower levels than those seen in younger lithium-treated patients."[9] Whether this results from increased sensitivity to lithium, decreased renal clearance, or other factors is unknown. Older patients should be kept at somewhat lower maintenance levels (0.6 to 0.7 mEq/L) than younger patients and should be monitored with routine physical examinations, ECGs, blood chemistry tests, and evaluation of kidney and thyroid functions.

Clinical signs of toxicity include diarrhea, vomiting, tremor, mild ataxia, drowsiness, thirst, polyuria (increased urination), muscular weakness, slurred speech, and confusion. The tremor and polyuria may persist for a time after reduction of the dose.

Tranquilizers

Theoretically, tranquilizers are regarded as an improvement over sedatives by virtue of alleviating anxiety with less mental impairment. Physical addiction is not a serious problem, but emotional dependence on tranquilizers is not uncommon.

There is an overprescribing of tranquilizers. Moreover, higher and higher dosages may be given because of developing tolerances and frustration over results. Such practices are dangerous, for the patient may suffer unnecessary complications and untoward side effects. The drugs are also expensive for the older person.

Tranquilizers often serve the provider of service, especially in nursing homes, rather than those served.[10] Zombies are created by the phenothiazines in particular, such as chlorpromazine (Thorazine) and thioridazine (Mellaril). These drugs slow people so markedly that physical activity is greatly reduced, with resultant muscle atrophy. Tranquilizers adversely affecting the libido include chlordiazepoxide (Librium) (sexual desire) and thioridazine (capacity).

We should also point out that not infrequently an older person is given a number of drugs simultaneously, for example, tranquilizers *and* antidepressants. This can be a dangerous practice.

Major tranquilizers

For older persons, the agent of choice among the major tranquilizers is *thioridazine* (Mellaril). It appears to be as effective as chlorpromazine, but it produces less extrapyramidal effect and only moderate sedative and hypotensive effects. It is useful in alleviating the anxiety associated with depression, but one must beware of its possible depressive effects. Its anticholinergic effects can result in toxic delirium. (The phenothiazines chlorpromazine and thioridazine and the tricyclic antidepressants have anticholinergic side effects and can cause a syndrome characterized by anxiety, agitation, delirium, and hallucinations, in addition to urinary retention and cardiac arrhythmias.) Ejaculatory impotence is another possible side effect. In dosages over 800 mg daily, the major danger in prolonged use is retinitis pigmentosa (pro-

[8] Van Der Velde, C.D.: Toxicity of lithium carbonate in elderly patients, American Journal of Psychiatry **127**:1075-1077, 1971.

[9] Roose, S.P., Bone, S., Haidorfer, C., Dunner, D.L., and Fieve, R.R.: Lithium treatment in older patients, American Journal of Psychiatry **136**:843-844, 1979.

[10] The American Pharmaceutical Association has produced a guide for long-term care facilities: Monitoring drug therapy in the long-term care facility: an APHA self study program for pharmacists, 1978. This guide is available from the American Pharmaceutical Association, 2215 Constitution Ave., N.W., Washington, D.C. 20037. Studies of actual prescription usage are possible via the National Prescription Audit (NPA), which audits retail pharmacy prescriptions, and the National Disease and Therapeutic Index (NDTI), which audits physicians' uses of drugs in office settings.

gressive loss of retinal response, retinal atrophy, clumping of the pigment, and contraction of the field of vision). Thioridazine is active against so-called senile (usually nocturnal) agitation and valuable against intractable pain. The dosage is 10 mg two times a day to 100 mg three times a day; usual dosage is 30 to 150 mg daily.

All phenothiazines may potentiate central nervous system depressants (for example, anesthetics, opiates, alcohol). Another danger of phenothiazines is that leukopenia can occur, so routine blood follow-up is indicated. Female patients seem to have a greater susceptibility to orthostatic hypotension. There are many side effects, of varying possible severity: dryness of the mouth, blurred vision, drowsiness, altered libido, and hypothermia (lowered body temperature).[11] The phenothiazines often produce extrapyramidal symptoms.

Haloperidol (Haldol) is the best known of a series of major tranquilizers, the butyrophenones.[12] The patient must be warned of decreased thirst so that he or she can compensate. Fatal cases of bronchopneumonia have been reported following use of all major tranquilizers including haloperidol. The mechanism is thought to be decreased thirst caused by central nervous system inhibition, followed by dehydration, hemoconcentration, and reduced pulmonary ventilation. The patient must be told not to drink alcohol and not to operate machinery or drive a car. The butyrophenones must not be prescribed along with anticoagulants. Parkinsonian symptoms can occur. (Haloperidol should not be used with persons who already have Parkinson's disease.)

---

[11] Accidental, spontaneous, or hidden hypothermia is one of the winter hazards of age. Risk factors include the phenothiazines, tricyclic antidepressants, diseases that diminish physical activity and thus decrease heat production such as dementia and parkinsonism, and increased heat loss such as alcohol-induced vasodilation.

[12] Tsuang, M.M., Lu, L.M., Stotsky, B.A., and Cole, J.O.: Haloperidol versus thioridazine for hospitalized psycho-geriatric patients: double-blind study, Journal of the American Geriatrics Society **19**:593-600, 1971.

Be sure to explain the potential dosages and side effects of drugs to patients. Spell out the possible depressive and retarding effects of the phenothiazines and the likely occurrence of annoying symptoms such as dryness of the mouth. Forewarn the patient about hypotension and extrapyramidal symptoms. Indicate that antiparkinsonian agents are available.

Special caution must be exercised in using drugs with potentially suicidal patients, who may take large quantities and mixtures of tranquilizers and sedatives. Certain drugs should not be prescribed at all for a suicidal patient. For example, glutethimide (Doriden) has a very low therapeutic-lethal ratio.

Minor tranquilizers

There are three widely used agents of the benzodiazepine series: chlordiazepoxide, diazepam, and oxazepam. The first two are widely used.

Chlordiazepoxide (Librium) is of some value in the relief of anxiety and tension. It can be useful for preoperative apprehension. In elderly and especially debilitated patients, begin with minimal dosage to preclude ataxia or oversedation. Begin with 5 mg up to twice daily (10 mg) and do not exceed 5 mg four times daily (20 mg total dosage). Beware of potentiation by the phenothiazines and MAOIs. Both increased and decreased libido have been reported.

Diazepam (Valium) is somewhat useful in tension and anxiety states, particularly when muscular tension is notable. Because of its ability to relieve skeletal muscle spasm related to local inflammation of joints and muscles, it is advantageous for some older persons with arthritis. Lower doses in the range of 2 to 5 mg for the elderly and debilitated are indicated. Begin with 2 to 2.5 mg once or twice daily. Increase gradually only as needed. One should be cautious of potentiation by the phenothiazines, narcotics, barbiturates, MAOIs, and other antidepressants as well as alcohol. Patients should be warned about driving and hazardous tasks that require balance (for example, putting shingles on the roof). Because of withdrawal symptoms, an abrupt discontinuation should not be undertaken.

Beware also of such side effects as excessive drowsiness,[13] fatigue, ataxia, confusion, depression, hypotension, urinary retention, and decreases in libido. The drug is contraindicated in the presence of acute narrow-angle (congestive) glaucoma.

Both chlordiazepoxide and diazepam persist in the body because of a complex degradation process producing many active metabolites. With diazepam, for example, drug detoxification can take up to 40 to 90 hours. *Oxazepam* (Serax) is shorter acting, therefore safer, and is effective for older persons. The initial dosage is 10 mg three times daily. Any increases should be given with caution and should not exceed 15 mg three to four times daily.

The benzodiazepine derivatives are not of demonstrable superiority over the barbiturate series of sedatives. Phenobarbital, however, may provoke paradoxical excitatory reactions in some older patients and thus has to be tried carefully. The long-acting effects and accumulation of benzodiazepines in tissues may produce delayed drug intoxication.

Meprobamate (Equanil, Miltown) is given for tension and anxiety but is probably no more effective than old-fashioned phenobarbital. Physical dependence can occur with either. Begin in the older age group with 200 to 400 mg three to four times daily.

Other drugs

Cerebral vasodilators,[14] cerebral stimulants, hormones, and anticoagulants are among other classes of drugs that have been recommended and sold for depressed, "senile," or deteriorated older people. They are of little clinical use and may be dangerous in some instances.

The antihistamines have not been of demonstrated value. Pentylenetetrazol (Metrazol)[15] and monosodium glutamate seem relatively safe but of uncertain efficiency. Nylidrin (Arlidin) and papaverine, like alcohol, may increase cerebral blood flow, but that is no guarantee of clinical effectiveness.

Vitamins are useful when there are deficiencies. Hypovitaminosis must be carefully evaluated. Victims of pellagra should receive 500 mg of nicotinic acid orally up to three times daily, as necessary. For older people, a basic vitamin-mineral combination may be given to offset effects of the processing of foods, poor dietary habits, and low appetite related to loneliness and grief.

Gerovital H_3 is the controversial drug developed by Dr. Ana Aslan in Romania. It is a long-acting form of procaine hydrochloride that purports to be effective against arthritis, memory loss, rheumatism, heart disease, gray hair, impotency, high blood pressure, wrinkled skin, depression, and Parkinson's disease. The most thorough U.S. review and evaluation of the world literature on the systemic use of procaine in the treatment of the aging process and the common chronic diseases of later life was commissioned by the National Insti-

---

[13] Boston Collaborative Drug Surveillance Program: Clinical depression of the central nervous system due to diazepam and chlordiazepoxide in relation to cigarette smoking and age, New England Journal of Medicine **228**:277-280, 1973.

[14] In 1976 and 1977, the Massachusetts Medicaid program initiated a "Dose-Effectiveness Project" designed to encourage physicians not to prescribe goods or services of dubious value to Medicaid recipients. One major focus was the practice of prescribing peripheral/cerebral vasodilators for older persons. Educational letters were sent to all Medicaid physi-

cians, followed up by "guidelines" and later by more directive communications to recalcitrant physicians, urging them not to use this class of drugs. The communications were prepared by Mark Smith under the supervision of David Danielson and Jerry Avorn and are available from the Harvard University School of Public Health.

[15] See Stotsky, B.A., Cole, J.O., Lu, L.M., and Sniffen, C.M.: A controlled study of the efficacy of pentylenetetrazol (Metrazol) with hard-core hospitalized psychogeriatric patients, American Journal of Psychiatry **129**:387-391, 1972.

tute on Aging of the National Institutes of Health.[16] Included are data from 285 articles and books, describing treatment in more than 100,000 patients in the past 25 years. Except for a possible antidepressant effect, there is no convincing evidence that procaine (or Gerovital, of which procaine is the major component) has any value in the treatment of disease in older patients. However, the large clinical experience of Aslan in Romania deserves thoughtful review.[17]

There is a continuing search for drugs to assist memory. The efficiency of ribonucleic acid in aiding memory has not been established. There are no specific drugs to prevent the brain damage of organic disorders. Hydergine is widely used for what pharmaceutical advertisements describe as "confusion, mood-depression, and dizziness," but it has not proved to be of established significant clinical value in organic brain disorders. It should never be used in place of a careful investigation into the causes of the symptoms it purports to alleviate, especially the treatable causes of organic dementia and functional depression. In 13 of 14 fairly well-designed studies of the drug, investigators noted a very slight but consistent improvement in cognitive functioning. However it is still unclear what exact disorder the drug is treating and whether better results could have been obtained with other treatments, such as antidepressants.

Laxatives

Reference to laxatives in a book on mental health may seem strange, but bowel complaints, especially constipation, in both mental disorders (for example, depression) and physical conditions, are frequent and provoke anxiety in older people.

Laxatives are all too commonly used by or *on*

older people in and out of institutions. Drastic laxatives such as cascara, saline cathartics, and milk of magnesia can cause severe electrolyte imbalances. They may also create "imaginary constipation," or a "laxative-dependency constipation" by so thoroughly "cleaning out" the bowels that time must pass before a bowel movement is possible. Mineral oil can wash away vitamin K (plentiful in vegetables), necessary to normal blood coagulation and perhaps to maintenance of bone integrity (as a prevention of osteoporosis). The best and safest laxatives are bulk diets (vegetables, bran), regular exercise, natural food laxatives (such as prunes and prune juice), and bulk laxatives.

Alcohol as therapy

Wine has been widely recommended in geriatric medicine and in convalescent care. It is the world's oldest tranquilizer. It gives pleasure, helps one sleep (valuable for use against insomnia), and reduces pain. Galen, the great Greek physician, called wine "the nurse of old age." Among the dessert wines, 2 to 3 ounces of port is useful for sleep.

One must beware, however, of the unfortunate potentiating or synergistic action of alcohol on other sedatives, tranquilizers, or narcotics. Many commonly prescribed drugs have altered therapeutic and/or adverse medical effects when taken with alcohol. These drugs include not only sedatives, hypnotics, narcotics, antidepressants, and tranquilizers but also certain antihistamines, analgesics, anticoagulants, and antiinfective agents. Alcohol use in combination with other drugs accounts for approximately 20% of the total number of accidental or suicidal deaths per year that are drug-related.

Sherry appears to stimulate the appetite and digestive processes, and its virtue in increasing sociability has been emphasized by Kastenbaum[18] in his study at Cushing Hospital, Framingham,

[16] Ostfeld, A., Smith, C.M., and Stotsky, B.A.: The systemic use of procaine in the treatment of the elderly: a review, Journal of the American Geriatrics Society **25**:1-19, 1977.

[17] See Aslan, A.: Longitudinal study in the National Institute of Gerontology and Geriatrics of Rumania. In Recent advances in gerontology, proceedings of the XI International Congress of Gerontology, Tokyo, August 20-25, 1978, Amsterdam, 1979, Excerpta Medica, pp. 533-537.

[18] Kastenbaum, R.: Wine and fellowship in aging: an exploratory ACTION program, Journal of Human Relations **13**: 266-271, 1965.

Massachusetts. Alcohol may also be useful for patients suffering from cerebral arteriosclerosis. However, it must be remembered that tolerance for alcohol decreases with old age; mental confusion and poor coordination can combine with alcohol to increase the risk of falling. In addition alcohol adversely influences sexual potency. Of course, anyone with alcoholic tendencies should not be encouraged to drink.

TREATMENT OF INSOMNIA

Sleep medications, both over-the-counter and prescription drugs, are unfortunately widely but not always wisely used among older people. Many older people become anxious simply because they notice a change in sleep patterns with age and fear the beginning of insomnia. They may turn to over-the-counter medications or persuade their doctors to prescribe a drug. The abuse of sleeping pills and tranquilizers in nursing homes is widely recognized; it is easier to have patients sedated or asleep than wandering about. (Of course drugs may also make it possible to avoid physical restraints or even psychiatric hospitalization for wandering, restless patients.)

Insomnia, or the actual inability to sleep (as opposed to changes in sleep patterns with age), may be caused by many emotional reactions—grief, anxiety, anger, depression. It can be a consequence of sexual deprivation, urinary frequency, or simply sleeping in a new place when visiting or traveling. Prescription and over-the-counter medications can lead to insomnia; for example, decongestants used in cold preparations are nervous system stimulants and may keep people awake at night. Finally, insomnia may be a symptom of physical disorders—for example, an early and unrecognized signal of congestive heart failure, an early dementia, drug intoxication, or any pain.

After careful diagnosis for its underlying causes, insomnia should be treated first by the simplest measures. (See Chapter 14.) Drugs for sleep (hypnotics) include barbiturates, which should generally be avoided in treating older people because of the occasions of paradoxical stimulation. Barbiturates can interact badly with corticosteroids, tetracyclines, and certain heart drugs derived from digitalis. They can reduce the effectiveness of warfarin (Coumadin), an anticoagulant. Phenobarbital, pentobarbital (Nembutol), and secobarbital (Seconal) are three popular barbiturates. A number of contemporary older persons have taken barbiturate hypnotics for years and may have "drug-dependency insomnia" after having become habituated and addicted to pentobarbital or secobarbital. An individualized approach rather than automatic withdrawal is recommended in order to ease the older person off the dependency with a minimum of emotional or physical trauma. Fast withdrawal may produce a "drug-withdrawal insomnia," with an increase in dreaming time and a period of disturbing and intense dreams and nightmares.

The ancient drug, chloral hydrate, is still one of the best and safest sleeping medications, with fewer side effects and disturbances of sleep patterns than barbiturates. It is inexpensive as well. Possible problems include gastric irritation, especially if taken on an empty stomach, and the development of tolerance and physical dependence. Physicians like Libow, Besdine, and Butler who have worked with older insomniac patients begin trials of chloral hydrate at 500 to 1,000 mg and even as high as 1.5 gm nightly before trying another agent.

Other nonbarbiturates include glutethimide (Doriden), methyprylon (Noludar), methaqualone (Quaalude), and ethchlorvynol (Placidyl); but tolerance, habituation, addiction, and, indeed, suicide can be the end results of excessive use of these nonbarbiturates as well. Dosages of common nonbarbiturate hypnotics are listed below.

Chloral hydrate	250 to 500 mg (available in syrup as well as capsules)
Ethchlorvynol	500 mg
Flurazepam	15 mg
Glutethimide	250 to 500 mg
Methaqualone	150 mg is preferred dosage; 300 mg may be necessary
Methprylon	300 mg

Glutethimide has a small safety margin between hypnosis and acute overdosage. It is the least preferred of the nonbarbiturate hypnotics in old age.

Mild tranquilizers such as diphenhydramine (Benadryl) (in 25 to 50 mg dosages) may be useful and produce little or no hangover effect in the morning. Meprobamate is not recommended. The benzodiazepines, including flurazepam (Dalmane) and the tranquilizers diazepam (Valium) and chlorodiazepoxide (Librium), have a wider safety margin than barbiturates, with fewer changes in sleep patterns, milder withdrawal effects, and less interference with other drugs the older person may be taking. But they can depress respiration if taken with alcohol. Chlorodiazepoxide (10 to 20 mg) is probably the safest, while diazepam tends to produce ataxia and dysarthria in some older persons.

Such side effects as dizziness, drowsiness, and light-headedness from some hypnotics are seen in older or debilitated persons. Therefore the initial dosage of flurazepam (Dalmane), to cite one example, should be 15 mg rather than the usual adult dosage of 30 mg. Flurazepam is presumed to be valuable because it does not suppress the period of rapid eye movement (REM) sleep as certain other sleep medications do (although this value has not been conclusively proved). It may also potentiate anticoagulants.

A recent study by the Institute of Medicine (IOM)[19] on sedative-hypnotic drugs found an increasing shift from barbiturates to benzodiazepines. (Barbiturates made up 47% of hypnotic prescriptions in 1971 and 17% in 1977.) Flurazepam, a benzodiazepine first marketed in 1970, accounted for 53% of hypnotic prescriptions in 1977. The shift from barbiturates is apparently a result of growing concern about abuse, accidental death, or suicide, as well as the information that barbiturates suppress REM sleep while benzodiazepines do not.

The IOM report questions whether benzodiazepine hypnotics are safer and more effective than barbiturates. Hazards include the fact that the benzodiazepines are longer lasting. (Metabolites of flurazepam, for example, have a half-life of 50 to 100 hours, as compared to the average half-lives of 14 to 42 hours for the most commonly used barbiturates.) Also they suppress stages 3 and 4 of sleep, even though they leave the REM stage of sleep undisturbed.

Recommendations from the IOM include restricting use of any hypnotic drugs for insomnia to short-term treatment, since most of them lose their sleep-promoting properties within 3 to 14 days of continuous use. Hypnotics should be avoided for persons with respiratory problems, depression, or alcohol and drug dependencies.

Over-the-counter drugs sold as sleep aids or sedatives, like Sominex, Nytal, and Sleep-Eze, are of questionable value, containing unsafe levels of antihistamines developed for the treatment of allergies. They may also contain scopolamine in levels for sleep induction that can cause outbursts of uncontrolled behavior and a variety of adverse physical effects. Bromides have been used in the past in over-the-counter medications and are considered unsafe. As of 1977, Nervine (made by Miles Laboratories) no longer contains bromide salts, and other over-the-counter bromide preparations have been removed from the market as well. Nonetheless, some of these preparations purchased before 1977 are in home medicine cabinets; moreover one can still obtain a prescription for Carbrital (a combination of pentobarbital and carbromal) which contains bromide. It is important to make certain that the older person's medicine cabinet is cleared of these preparations.

DANGERS AND SAFEGUARDS IN DRUG USE WITH OLDER PERSONS[20]

The ancient rule of medicine, *primun non nocere* (first do no harm), applies particularly to

---

[19] National Academy of Sciences: Sleeping pills, insomnia, and medical practice, Washington, D.C., 1979, The Academy.

[20] Judge, T.G., and Caird, F.I.: Drug treatment of the elderly patient, Kent, England, 1978, Pitman Medical Publishing Co., Ltd.; and Crooks, J., and Stevenson, I.H.: Drugs and the elderly: perspectives in geriatric clinical pharmacology, Baltimore, 1979, University Park Press.

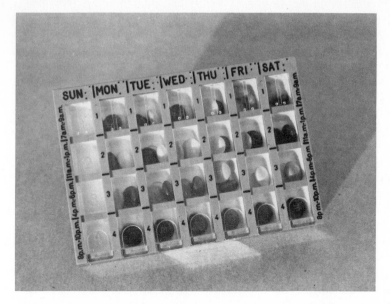

A pill box designed as a memory aid for older people who are required to take
multiple medications. Because of the difficulty in locating such
pill box aids we include the address of the distributor:
Mediset, Keystone Health Systems,
18708 John Rd., Detroit, Mich. 48203.

prescribing medication for older persons. Drugs should be used *only* when necessary, with as few used simultaneously as possible. The average older person is taking several medications (called polypharmacy) at any one time.[21]

In a random sample of 288 long-term care facilities participating in Medicare-Medicaid programs, a 1974 HEW survey of 3,458 residents (78% of whom were 65 years of age or older) found the following.

1. The average number of prescriptions per patient was 6.1.

2. Sixty percent of all patients received cathartics, 51.3% received analgesics, 46.9% tranquilizers, 26% thioridazine, 23% chlordiazepoxide, and 18% diazepam.

3. Aspirin, magnesium hydroxide, multiple vitamins, digoxin (Lanoxin), and propoxyphene (Darvon) were the five most frequently prescribed drugs in skilled nursing facilities; thioridazine was sixth, chlordiazepoxide was tenth, and diazepam was twelfth.

It is currently believed that about two thirds of all nursing home patients receive psychotropic drugs, yet only about 20% have psychiatric diagnoses. Insufficient staffing is perhaps the primary reason for overmedicating older persons into more manageable quietude. Other reasons are the concealment of a psychiatric diagnosis to get an older person into a nursing home, the failure of the doctors who service nursing homes to keep apprised of

---

[21] In nursing homes, the average is six medications at a time and 13 prescriptions per year (some of them repeats). See Physician's drug prescribing patterns in the skilled nursing facilities: long-term facility campaign, Monograph No. 2, Pub. No. (HEW) 76-50050, Washington, D.C., 1976, U.S. Government Printing Office.

the dangers of overmedication, and the fact that some states use Medicaid to pay for drugs but not for careful psychiatric diagnosis and forms of treatment other than drugs.

Drug administration in institutions is marked by special problems of its own.

1. Much medication is prescribed by doctors over the phone, based only on symptoms described by nursing personnel. Errors in diagnosis are therefore common, as well as a tendency to prescribe based on the needs of the institution rather than simply in the patient's best interest.

2. Errors in drug administration occur because medication is often given by untrained or poorly trained aides and orderlies.

3. The possibilities for errors in drug administration are compounded by the number of medications (an average of 5 to 7) each patient receives at once, often in varying combinations of multiple daily doses.

4. Staff shortages lead to less physical exercise for patients, more use of physical restraints, overuse of catheters, lack of an individualized enough diet, less personalized warmth and support, and an unstimulating environment. This results in a higher incidence of urinary tract infections, respiratory and circulatory disorders leading to pneumonia and bedsores, and a rise in mental depression and agitation, to name a few conditions. All of these are typically treated with drugs when they might have been prevented.

Before prescribing any drugs for noninstitutionalized patients, the physician should ask the older person to bring in all his or her present medications, including over-the-counter medications and old, empty bottles. The patient should be asked if he or she tends to ''self-medicate'' and, if so, how much and for what purpose. The physician should check with the patient's other doctors to learn if previously prescribed drugs should still be taken. Older persons experience three times as many adverse reactions as younger persons. The possible adverse interactions of one drug with another

should be anticipated and avoided.[22] Medications should be introduced one at a time when possible in order to monitor their individual effects. The dosage schedule should be kept simple and easily understandable. All medication orders should have automatic discontinuation dates; renewal requires valuable reassessment and averts prolonged, inappropriate, harmful, and useless administration of drugs.

The *sedating effects* of 12 of the 20 most commonly used medications in persons over 65 (for example, flurazepam, chlordiazepoxide, and phenobarbital) can cause serious problems, as we have stated. Older people who are experiencing a physical slowing of speed and coordination find these features exacerbated by a number of drugs. Some persons react with fear and depression, thinking they are failing fast or even dying. In fact, various psychoactive agents have caused deaths in older people through adverse reactions or overdoses.

Drug metabolism is another factor since the liver may have reduced blood flow in older people, and thus the rate of drug detoxification may be slowed. Moreover, older people have a lower general bodily metabolism rate, prolonging drug action or creating exaggerated drug reactions. Kidney impairment can also affect excretion of the drug. The older population has a relatively greater accumulation of drugs in body fat as compared to younger people; therefore drug effects may be prolonged. In general, drug effects are determined by dosage, absorption (quality and rate), distribution in the body (dependent on factors of body composition such as body fluid, organ blood flow, and cardiac output), hepatic metabolism and renal excretion, nutritional status, and personal habits (for

---

[22] See American Pharmaceutical Association: Evaluation of drug interaction, Washington, D.C., 1973, The Association; and Long, J.W.: The essential guide to prescription drugs; what you need to know for safe drug use, ed. 2, New York, 1980, Harper & Row, Publishers, Inc. The latter includes two tables of great importance to older persons: Table 12—Drugs and the elderly (over 60 years of age) and Table 13—Your drugs and sexual activity.

SOME FACTORS AFFECTING DRUG RESPONSE WITH AGE

1. Absorption
   Stomach
      Transit time
      Hydrochloric acid
2. Distribution
   Proteins in blood
   Body composition (lean body mass, fat)
   Tissue sensitivity
   Receptors
3. Metabolism
   Liver enzymes
4. Excretion
   Kidney
      Blood flow
      Glomerular filtration rate
5. Multiple drug use (polypharmacy)
6. Overdose (purposive or accidental)
7. Patient compliance (omission, commission)
8. Physician failure to give complete instructions

---

example, smoking and alcohol intake). Older people have qualitative and quantitative differences from younger people in absorption, distribution, metabolism, and excretion of drugs. See the box above for factors affecting drug response with age.

Iatrogenic brain disorders are not uncommon. Doctors unwittingly produce reversible and often unrecognized irreversible brain disorders. Tranquilizers and hypnotics are the most likely causes of such conditions, but steroids used in arthritis can cause organic brain disorders as well as hypomania and/or depression.

Finally, *tardive dyskinesia* is an affliction often associated with drug treatment. This condition appears more likely to occur in the aged, although it is found at all ages. It is a serious malady that seems to be an end result of phenothiazine therapy and is often irreversible once it occurs.[23]

Of those persons prone to dyskinesia, some may develop it while taking phenothiazines, others

if the dose is increased or decreased, and still others only after the drug has been discontinued. It is estimated that 8% to 24% (more women than men) of persons taking phenothiazines develop tardive dyskinesia. Of these, 15% do so within 1 year. As many as 40% of older persons may develop dyskinesia. Persons with parkinsonism or extrapyramidal syndrome are more likely to develop tardive dyskinesia.

The condition is characterized by slow, rhythmic, involuntary movements of the face and extremities. An abnormal tongue movement may be the first evidence of the syndrome. One may see chewing or gyrating of the jaws, grinning, lip-pursing, eye-blinking, "fly catcher" tongue, difficulty in swallowing, and/or spastic neck-stiffening. Winkleman and others[24] believe it is more commonly seen in the brain-damaged; thus it is a reason for limiting use of the phenothiazines in older people with brain syndromes. Some persons also seem more sensitive to drugs than others. Antiparkinsonian agents such as benztropine mesylate (Cogentin) and procyclidine (Kemadrin) increase dyskinesia.

Many treatments have been evaluated, but none is satisfactory. The condition may improve on its own if what appears to be the offending drug is removed or replaced, especially early in the disorder. The use of antipsychotic drugs at all must be carefully evaluated against the risk factor of tardive dyskinesia. Chronic schizophrenia is the

---

[23] Degenerative brain changes have also been held responsible.

[24] Dr. George Crane of the Spring Grove State Hospital of Maryland early on emphasized the dangers of the phenothiazines—especially the danger of tardive dyskinesia. See Crane, G.E.: Tardive dyskinesia in patients treated with major neuroleptics, American Journal of Psychiatry **124**(supp): 40-48, 1968; Crane, G.E.: Persistence of neurological symptoms due to neuroleptic drugs, American Journal of Psychiatry **127**:1407-1410, 1971; Crane G.E., and Gardner, R., Jr.: Psychotrophic drugs and dysfunctions of the basal ganglia; a multidisciplinary workshop, National Institute of Mental Health, Pub. No. (PHS) 1938, 1969; and Crane, G.F., and Smeets, R.A.: Tardive dyskinesia and drug therapy in geriatric patients, Archives of General Psychiatry **30**:341-343, 1974.

major condition for which such drugs may be scientifically justified on a long-term basis. Meanwhile there is a search for new antipsychotic drugs that will not put the patient at such risk neurologically.[25] A diagnostic point to note with older people is that certain involuntary movements they may have are not always related to tardive dyskinesia.

We do not believe tranquilizers should be used in high dosages, and we recommend that they be prescribed only for brief periods, related to specific symptoms such as anxiety. They should *not* be continued over extended periods. They should *not* be employed for the benefit of the therapist or the quiet serenity of the institution.

In general, it is wise to administer all drugs with caution in old age, beginning with low dosages and increasing gradually in a stepwise, progressive fashion when a higher dosage is definitely indicated. The patient must be under continuous clinical and laboratory surveillance. The basic workup will have afforded baseline data. Complete blood counts should be repeated weekly for 10 weeks and after that at least monthly. With use of the phenothiazines, liver tests such as alkaline phosphatase and bilirubin should also be routinely made.

The potential dangers, complications, and side effects should be carefully and fully explained to patients—both the annoying symptoms like dryness of the mouth, for instance, and the dangerous symptoms such as hypotension (low blood pressure and possible fainting) and extrapyramidal symptoms (parkinsonism).[26] Antiparkinsonian agents are available, with benztropine mesylate (Cogentin) and procyclidine (Kemadrin) most commonly used.[27]

It is exceedingly valuable for patients when doctors fill out a written sheet on each new drug prescribed so the older person can refer to it later. An example is included here.

Medication: _____

Who prescribed it: _____

Date: _____

For what: _____

Dosage: _____

Schedule: _____

Duration: _____

What to avoid:

    Other drugs: _____

    Alcohol: _____

    Food: _____

    Use of machinery: _____

    Driving: _____

    Other: _____

Minor side effects that often occur and what to do about them: _____

_____

_____

_____

Major side effects that can occur and require a call to the doctor: _____

_____

Drugs can affect sexuality in varying manner and degree from individual to individual, especially after the age of 50. See Table 13-2 for a list of drugs and their possible effects on sexuality. Most of the drugs are used for nervous or circulatory system disorders. When sexual problems occur, the doctor may be able to change to another drug.

One of the important reasons for informing older people about the drugs they are taking is to help them distinguish side effects from other bodily changes. As we mentioned previously, we have found that older people may misinterpret the retarding effects of the tranquilizers as signs of aging. Doctors remain all too secretive in preparing patients for drug effects, partly because they fear the development of symptoms in suggestible persons. Many also simply do not wish to take the

---

[25] See Task Force on Late Neurologic Effects of Anti-Psychotic Drugs: Tardive dyskinesia: summary of a task force report of the American Psychiatric Association, American Journal of Psychiatry **137**(10):1163-1172, 1980.

[26] An estimated 1 million Americans (probably an underestimate) of all ages suffer untoward drug reactions yearly, and 30,000 die.

[27] These agents do not appear to ameliorate tardive dyskinesia.

Table 13-2. Drugs and sexual activity

Drug name or family	Possible effects
Alcohol	Reduced potency in men, delayed orgasm in women
Amphetamine	Reduced libido and potency
Bethanidine	Impaired ejaculation
Clonidine	Reduced libido
Debrisoquin	Reduced potency, impaired ejaculation
Dextroamphetamine	Reduced libido and potency
Disulfiram	Reduced potency
Guanethidine	Reduced potency, impaired ejaculation
Haloperidol	Reduced potency
Levodopa	Increased libido (in some men and women)
Lithium	Reduced potency
Methyldopa	Reduced libido and potency
Oral contraceptives	Reduced libido (in some women)
Phenothiazines	Reduced libido and potency, impaired ejaculation (occasionally)
Phenoxybenzamine	Impaired ejaculation
Primidone	Reduced libido and potency
Reserpine	Reduced libido and potency
Sedative and sleep-inducing drugs (hypnotics) when used on a regular basis	Reduced libido and potency
Thiazide diuretics	Reduced libido (occasionally, in some men)
Tranquilizers (mild)	Reduced libido and potency
Tricyclic antidepressants	Reduced libido and potency

Abridged from Table 13, "Your Drugs and Sexual Activity" (p. 809) in The essential guide to prescription drugs, new and revised edition by James W. Long, M.D. Copyright © 1980 by James W. Long, M.D. Reprinted by permission of Harper & Row, Publishers, Inc.

time. It is archaic to assume that "what the patient doesn't know won't hurt him," because often it does. Full disclosure is now imperative for both medical and legal reasons. One must help patients overcome fears of medications while simultaneously encouraging them to respect effects and dangers. Patients also have the legal right to refuse medications or medical procedures.

Older people may have impairments that inter-fere with hearing and/or understanding the doctor's orders regarding drugs, seeing labels well enough to take the correct medicine and the correct dose, or having a steady enough hand to handle fluids, tiny pills, or "child-proof" (and thus more difficult to open) drug bottles. Impairment of intellect (especially with senile dementia) may cause errors in judgment or lapses in memory with regard to drugs. Consequently the older person's capacity for the self-administration of drugs needs to be evaluated as carefully as his or her medical need for drugs. It has been estimated that half of all older people who take drugs do not take them as prescribed, and one fourth make errors serious enough to create drug-induced illnesses. Older people comprise about half of all hospital admissions for drug intoxication.

MENTAL HEALTH THERAPIST'S INVOLVEMENT IN DRUG THERAPY

The mental health therapist's own attitudes toward the use of drugs may influence their effects on older people. If the therapist is philosophically against drugs (feeling that people should resolve issues for themselves)[28] or is anxious about their side effects and potential complications, he or she is likely to convey these concerns to the older person, even when not stating them explicitly. Ideally, the therapist would be open enough to appreciate the value of drugs that are judiciously employed. There are people who need the *immediate* support of the magical/real expectations of medicine and the "medicine man" (the power of the physician as well as the actual, chemically active drug effects). One rational way of reconciling negative feeling about drugs with occasions when people need them is to note that therapy is a *process,* an experience over time. At various points, drugs might maintain working men or women on their jobs or help parents with their parenthood. But in most therapeutic efforts, drugs should be only part of the total treatment ef-

[28] Klerman calls this "pharmacological Calvinism" (Klerman, G., personal communication, 1977).

fort, although a very important part in many instances.

However, even if the therapist is totally opposed to drugs, he or she should not deny the client/patient their usefulness but should collaborate with a physician who will evaluate the usefulness of drugs in situations where they have been found to be helpful for others. Having separate ''talking'' and ''drug'' therapists may provoke some divided reactions in the person being treated, with manipulations in some instances, but such behavior can become a part of the treatment process. At the Chestnut Lodge Sanitarium (Rockville, Maryland), patients were regularly assigned two doctors: the administrative physician, who made decisions about home visits, drugs, etc., and the therapeutic physician.[29]

Nonphysician mental health personnel should know what drugs an older person is taking, whether for physical or mental conditions. The *Physicians' Desk Reference,* although not ideal, is a source of information about the side effects and complications of all drugs. Long's excellent *The Essential Guide to Prescription Drugs* provides a wealth of information. The *Merck Manual* also may be useful. *The United States Pharmacopeia* is the Medicare-designated compendium. Psychoactive drugs are classified into five categories (schedules) under the Controlled Substances Act of 1970.

All mental health personnel should be familiar with prescriptions and know how to interpret them. Nurses especially may be called on to prepare prescriptions for the signature of the physician in some circumstances. Included on this page is a sample prescription form.

Prescription terms

1. Weights (amounts are usually expressed in milligrams, grams, or grains):

   milligram One thousandth of a gram, roughly equivalent to 1/65th grain. It is usually abbreviated mg.

---

[29]See Stanton, A.H., and Schwartz, M.S.: The mental hospital, New York, 1954, Basic Books, Inc., Publishers.

JAMES R. DOE, M.D.
1000 Henry Street, N.W.
Waco, Texas

Phone: 211-2111
BND No: ABb3208036*

℞ (treatment)

Medicine   Amount
  (generic proposed)   (per tablet, capsule, etc.)

Number

Sig. (directions):
Label in full as to contents
Rep: 0-1-2-3-4-5-PRN

_____ , M.D.
(signature)

*Note the BND (Bureau of Narcotics and Dangerous Drugs) number. Some medications, including narcotics, hypnotics, and some tranquilizers, are under such controls.

gram Unit of weight in the metric system. It is usually abbreviated g, gm, or Gm. It is equivalent to about 15.43 gr.

grain Unit of weight in the avoirdupois system. It is usually abbreviated gr. It is equivalent to 1/480 ounce and to 0.065 gm.

ounce One twelfth of a pound avoirdupois and equivalent to 31.1 gm. The abbreviation for ounce is oz.

teaspoonful Four to five milliliters (ml).

The metric system is preferred and the old English system is slowly being phased out.

2. Latin abbreviations:

℞ ''Recipe.''
Sig. To write. It means the directions for taking the drugs.
b.i.d. Bis in die, two times a day.
t.i.d. Ter in die, three times a day.
q.i.d. Quater in die, four times a day.
a.c. Antecibum, before meals.
p.c. Post cibum, after meals.
h.s. Hora somni, before sleep.
p.r.n. Pro re nata, according to circumstances, rather than routine schedule.

s.o.s. Si opus sit, if necessary, if occasion requires.
Rep. Repeat.
q.h. Quaque hora, every hour.
q.2h. Quaque secunda hora, every second hour, etc.

Telephone prescriptions should always be checked later and countersigned. One must also be careful about pronunciation. The names of a number of drugs sound alike (for example, the trade names Haldol and Halodrin, Elavil and Aldoril, Mebaral and Mallaren, Ritalin and Ismelin).

To *label in full* is a sound practice. In the Americas, except for the United States, and in most of Europe, the law requires manufacturers to label all medicines with brand name, ingredients, and dosage as well as what the medicine is for, its side effects, full dosage range, and expiration date (if there is one). Until we have such laws in the United States, the doctor should label in full (in large letters) and instruct the druggist on the prescription to do so. This is valuable for all ages and especially for older people with confusion and defects in memory.

There is another safety factor in adequate labeling. When the doctor cannot be reached or the pharmacist's records are in error, good labeling makes it possible to check on medications if allergic or other untoward reactions occur. The older person or another family member, often a child, may unwittingly take an overdose of a drug or take the wrong drug.

The pharmacist should be instructed to package drugs in easy-to-open containers for older persons. Older patients should be warned not to take medicines in the dark or to keep them on the bedside table (there are exceptions, of course, such as nitroglycerine) since sleepiness can cause errors in judgment. When necessary, supervision of drug taking should be arranged with relatives, friends, or neighbors.

COST OF DRUGS

One should always think of cost in prescribing drugs for older persons. Medicare does not cover out-of-hospital prescription drugs, the largest single personal expenditure that the elderly must now meet almost entirely from their own resources.

Generic prescriptions help the pocketbooks of all patients, especially older persons'. For example, in 1971, reserpine,[30] which is the generic name of an antihypertensive drug, sold for $10 per 1,000 tablets, whereas Serpasil (reserpine by one brand name) sold for $49.

Evidence exists that many older people will not accept a low-priced generic substitute for a brand name just on a pharmacists' advice. Most want their doctor's approval first. Of use are lists of generic drugs such as can be found in the index of Long's *The Essential Guide to Prescription Drugs*.

Discount drugs can be obtained by way of the National Council of Senior Citizens,[31] the American Association of Retired Persons,[32] and some other organizations.

Drug packaging is another issue for older people. It would be useful if drug companies routinely used some special device in packaging drugs for older people, as they do with the clever calendar dispensers of the "pill," which aid younger women in remembering to take contraceptives. Such an aid is invaluable in coping with the memory problems of late life.

DRUG RESEARCH

There are shockingly few well-designed pharmacological studies of any length of time, including psychopharmacological studies that include older persons. For instance, there has not been a single report of a hypnotic drug trial studying older persons, yet more than one half of barbiturate prescribing alone is for this age group. Information from the Food and Drug Administration reveals that in developing new drugs that will be used by older persons there is no requirement (1) that clinical trials of new compounds be conducted on any specific age range of people, (2) that new com-

---

[30] Beware of reserpine, for it is depressogenic. When you see a depressed person, check whether he or she is receiving reserpine for high blood pressure.

[31] Pastors Pharmacy, 126 S. York Rd., Hatboro, Pa. 19040.

[32] 1750 K. St., N.W., Suite 1190, Washington, D.C. 20006.

pounds be tested on a long-term basis, and (3) that clinical tests be included in which new drugs are examined in combination with other drugs likely to be used by older persons. More definitive research on the use of drugs in the treatment of emotional and mental disorders of older persons is indicated, especially on the subjects of polypharmacy; drug-age, drug-drug, and drug-nutrient interactions; overmedication; drug effects on sexual and cognitive abilities; and patient compliance in the use of drugs. Double-blind studies should be done, with carefully selected control groups. A double-blind study is one in which one or more drugs and a placebo[33] are compared in such a way that neither the patient nor the persons directly or indirectly involved in the study know which preparation is being administered. Results of a control group are contrasted to those of an experimental group to counter the possibility that the experimental results might have occurred spontaneously during the course of time, regardless of the experimental manipulation. Control groups are usually matched to experimental groups in terms of age, sex, and other characteristics that might be relevant.

Another type of important drug research is represented by the Boston Collaborative Drug Surveillance Program, in which drug effects in hospitalized patients are monitored for clinical efficacy and toxicity. Herschel Jick is the originator of this unique project. The analysis and interpretation of the data in terms of older persons have been a very valuable contribution. Finally, fundamental pharmacological research is required to understand the relevant mechanisms affected by phenomena of aging.

Research on the blood-brain barrier is an example of work that could eventually benefit older people. The blood-brain barrier separates the brain and its cerebrospinal fluid from the body's blood and acts as a regulatory system to restrict the intercellular diffusion of water-soluble drugs and proteins between body and brain. (The regulatory system consists of three tissue sites—the cerebrovasculature, the choroid plexus, and the arachnoid membrane. Each site has specific transport mechanisms to help regulate the ionic and water content of the brain and to assist in the processes of metabolism.) Rapoport has conducted promising studies on experimental opening of the barrier.[34] This could become a major therapeutic tool—for example, to increase the uptake of drugs, such as methotrexate, which are used in treating brain tumors.

OTHER FORMS OF PHYSICAL TREATMENT
Electroshock therapy

Ugo Cerletti, an Italian psychiatrist, in 1938 developed the use of electroshock to induce convulsion and loss of consciousness by placement of electrodes on the temporal areas of the skull.

If antidepressants in the context of a comprehensive psychotherapeutic plan are contraindicated for medical reasons, or they have received an adequate trial without results, electroshock therapy (EST) is indicated in a severe, refractory depression.[35] Cases of clearly exogenous reactive depressions should not ordinarily be treated by EST. Psychometric tests (of intellectual function and memory) should be considered before the administering of EST, especially when organic brain damage is suspected. Radiographic studies of the spine are advisable because the possibility of osteoporosis could lead to bone breakage during shock therapy. The following are conditions that require evaluation before prescribing EST.

---

[33] Originally, a placebo was an inactive substance such as a "bread pill" given to placate a patient demanding unnecessary medication. It is useful in research and practice because of its potential psychological effect, which may be neutral, therapeutic, or noxious, depending on suggestion by the therapist or experimenter and the patient's own expectations, faith, fear, apprehension, or hostility. In British usage a placebo is sometimes called a dummy. (See American Psychiatric Association: A psychiatric glossary, ed. 5, New York, 1980, Basic Books, Inc., Publishers.)

[34] Rapoport, S.: Blood-brain barrier in physiology and medicine, New York, 1976, Raven Press.

[35] Of course, drugs can be given concurrently.

1. Cardiac arrhythmias
2. Recent myocardial infarction
3. Recent fracture
4. Organic brain syndrome
5. Glaucoma

After comprehensive evaluation with full patient consent and under careful conditions, including the use of preshock sedation and muscle relaxants (such as succinylcholine chloride) to avoid fractures, electroshock therapy can be quite effective against the depressions of old age. Radiographs of the spine, the pelvis, and the hips will help somewhat to assess osteoporosis. Effects on memory must be continually assessed, and the number of treatments should be minimal.[36] Respiratory and cardiovascular complications may occur; neurological complications are rare. Care is strongly advised in instances of coronary occlusion, since fatalities have been reported.

Wayne writes of his experience in treating older persons with EST,

Manifestly, age in itself is no contraindication to treatment. Specific physical conditions, however, might increase the risk. The only absolute contraindications for me have been space-occupying intracranial tumors, recent cardiac or brain infarcts of six weeks or less, moderate to severe cardiac failure and markedly advanced cases of general inanition.[37]

Wayne has treated older patients with cardiac pacemakers in situ without complication and comments on this and other conditions:

At the time of [EST] treatment the patient is anesthetized with a quick-acting barbiturate, preferably Brevital (methohexital sodium) in a minimal effective dose to avoid respiratory depression. This is given along with an adequate amount of Robinul [glycopyrrolate], which is an atropine-like substance that does not cross the blood brain barrier. Atropine crosses the blood brain barrier, is anticholinergic, and is capable of causing

confusion. Robinul averts this from happening, however, and does cut down on nasopharyngeal secretions and vaso-vagal irregularities.

Anectine [succinylcholine chloride] is given in a separate syringe in an amount that appreciably softens or eliminates the muscular movements associated with the brain seizure. This removes practically all danger of muscle, tendon, bone, or joint injury that in the past resulted from unmodified violent epileptiform movements. I always have a pseudo-cholinesterase test or dibucaine test done to be sure that the patient has the enzymes necessary to quickly neutralize the muscle paralyzing effect of Anectine. The effect of Anectine also limits the blood pressure increase with treatment.

Each patient is hyperoxygenated pre- and postictally from one to three minutes or as much as is required to prevent anoxia. The patient always looks pink using this technique, which avoids the frequent cyanotic periods of yesteryear.

If the patient has a tendency to retch or vomit, five mg. of Compazine [prochlorperazine] intramuscularly postictally prevents this complication.

Unilateral, nondominant electrode placement has become routine for me except in those few patients who respond poorly. In such patients I use the standard bitemporal placement, but there is always more postictal confusion and memory impairment than with unilateral placement.

In the presence of truly serious suicidal risk (for example, past suicidal attempts), it is not advisable to wait out drug trials. EST can often bring about prompt relief with a limited series of four to eight treatments. In severe and suicidal situations, even a history of cerebrovascular accidents and/or myocardial infarctions is not a contraindication per se.

Unfortunately, patients who have received EST often hesitate and resist returning to the doctor even years later if once again they develop serious depression. Fear and distaste of EST are commonplace and understandable since it is an intimidating if often effective treatment. Some states have passed laws strengthening the patients' right to refuse treatments like EST; but regardless of law, patients must fully understand the treatment offered and be given the right to accept or refuse it.

---

[36] The possible persistence of memory loss after EST remains controversial.

[37] Wayne, G.J.: Electroconvulsive treatment in the elderly, Journal of the National Association of Private Psychiatric Hospitals **11**:25-27, 1980.

Hyperbaric oxygenation

Claims of improvement in chronic brain disorders by hyperbaric oxygenation (oxygen administered under high pressure) are disputed.[38] Goldfarb, experienced in the assessment of older people, found no "improvement . . . in intellectual or social performance," and an "increase in physical activity, restlessness and aggressivity."[39]

---

[38] Jacobs, E.A., Winter, P.M., Alvis, H.A., and Small, S.M.: Hyperoxygenation effect on cognitive functioning in the aged, New England Journal of Medicine **281:**753-757, 1969; and Thompson, L.W., Davis, G.C., Obrist, W.D., and Heyman, A.: Effects of hyperbaric oxygen on behavioral and physiological measures in elderly demented patients, Journal of Gerontology **31:**23-28, 1976.

[39] Goldfarb, A.I., Hochstadt, N.J., Jacobson, J.H., II, and Weinstein, E.A.: Hyperbaric oxygen treatment of organic brain syndrome in aged persons, Journal of Gerontology **27:**212-217, 1972.

REFERENCES

American Pharmaceutical Association: Evaluation of drug interactions, 1973, Washington, D.C., The Association.

Cole, J.O.: Methods for evaluating drug efficacy in geriatric-psychiatric disorders. In Levine, J., Schiels, B.C., and Bouthilet, L., editors: Principles and problems in establishing the efficacy of psychotropic agents, Pub. No. (PHS) 2138, Washington, D.C., 1971, U.S. Government Printing Office.

Crooks, J., and Stevenson, I.H.: Drugs and the elderly: perspectives in geriatric clinical pharmacology, Baltimore, 1979, University Park Press.

Davison, W.: The hazards of drug treatment in old age. In Brocklehurst, J.D., editor: The textbook of geriatric medicine and gerontology, ed. 2, Edinburgh, 1978, Churchill Livingstone.

Eisdorfer, C., and Fann, W., editors: Psychopharmacology and aging, New York, 1973, Plenum Press.

Fink, M.: Convulsive therapy: theory and practice, New York, 1979, Raven Press.

Gallinek, A.: Electric convulsive therapy in geriatrics, New Jersey State Journal of Medicine **47:**1233-1241, 1947.

Judge, T.G., and Caird, F.I.: Drug treatment of the elderly patient, Kent, England, 1978, Pitman Medical Publishing Co., Ltd.

Klawans, H.L., Goetz, C.G., and Perlik, S.: Tardive dyskinesia: review and update, American Journal of Psychiatry **137:**900-908, 1980.

Lamy, P.P., and Vestal, R.F.: Drug prescribing for the elderly, Hospital Practice **11:**111-118, 1976.

Long, J.W.: The essential guide to prescription drugs: what you need to know for safe drug use, New York, 1980, Harper & Row, Publishers, Inc.

The Merck manual of diagnosis and therapy, ed. 13, Rahway, N.J., 1977, Merck, Sharp and Dohme Research Laboratories.

Miller, R.R., and Greenblatt, D.J., editors: Drug effects in hospitalized patients. Experiences of the Boston Collaborative Drug Surveillance Program 1966-1975, New York, 1976, John Wiley & Sons, Inc.

Ostfeld, A., Smith, D., and Stotsky, B.: A systemic use of procaine in the treatment of the elderly: a review, Journal of the American Geriatrics Society **15:**1-19, 1977.

Physicians' desk reference to pharmaceutical specialties and biologicals, Oradell, N.J., 1981, Medical Economics Inc.

Physicians' drug prescribing patterns in the skilled nursing facilities: long-term facility campaign, Monograph No. 2, Pub. No. (HEW) 76-50050, Washington, D.C., 1976, U.S. Government Printing Office.

Prien, R.F.: A survey of psychoactive drug use in the aged at Veterans Administration hospitals. In Gershon and Raskin, editors: Aging, vol. 2, New York, 1975. Raven Press.

Prout, C.T., and Hamilton, D.M.: Results of electroshock therapy in patients over 60 years of age, Bulletin of the New York Academy of Medicine **28:**454-461, 1952.

Ray, O.S.: Tranquilizers and mood modifiers. In Ray, O.S., editor: Drugs, society and human behavior, ed. 2, St. Louis, 1978, The C.V. Mosby Co.

Shader, R.I., and DiMascio, A.: Psychotropic drug side effects, Baltimore, 1970, Williams & Wilkins Co.

Squire, L.: ECT and memory loss, American Journal of Psychiatry **134:**997-1001, 1977.

Task Force on Late Neurological Effects of Anti-Psychotic Drugs: Tardive dyskinesia: summary of a task force report of the American Psychiatric Association, American Journal of Psychiatry **137**(10):1163-1172, 1980.

Yesavage, J.: Vasodilators in senile dementia: a review of the literature, Archives of Geriatric Psychiatry **36:**220-223, 1979.

Zaeadski, R.T., Glazer, G.B., and Lurie, E.: Psychotropic drug use among institutionalized and non-institutionalized Medicaid aged in California, Journal of Gerontology **33:**825-834, 1978.

14

Treatment of specific conditions

Some of the mental and emotional conditions that have been previously described are so crucial to mental health care in old age that we focus specifically on them in this chapter, summing up as succinctly as possible the major treatment points. Of special concern are the all-too-frequent organic brain syndromes, grief and depression, and paranoid states. Once again we emphasize the absolute necessity of diagnosing those conditions that are subject to improvement, especially the reversible brain syndromes (many deliriums and some dementia) and functional states. We also touch briefly on the treatment aspects of insomnia, parkinsonism, stroke and hypertension, deafness, blindness, and emotional effects of retirement.

ORGANIC BRAIN SYNDROMES
Delirium

Many workers, such as Cosin[1] in Britain, have demonstrated the treatability of acute confusional states in older persons. The work of Simon and his colleagues in the United States is a highly significant affirmation of the possibilities for the psychiatric care of older people. The 1959 Langley Porter studies provided information "quite different from that gathered in institutions for the chronically ill, and our results are more pertinent for the family physician or psychiatrist who deals first with the mentally disturbed aged patient."[2]

Sound diagnosis is of the essence. Persons suffering from delirium must have early active treatment to enhance their likelihood of recovery. Whether the syndrome stands alone or is superimposed on a dementia, it is imperative that there be immediate treatment of the acute pathophysiological disturbance. (One may have to send someone to look in the person's medicine chest to determine whether any drugs are responsible—for example, an antihistamine sold without prescription can be a culprit. Nitrogen retention following urinary tract infection may be causative. See Chapter 5 for other possible contributory factors and Chapter 9 for diagnostic points.) Thorough diagnosis requires a comprehensive evaluation and treatment center. Will an older person get an appropriate workup in a state hospital, a general hospital, or a community mental health center? Will an evaluation be done at all in a nursing home situation? In many cases the answer is no.

Treatment of delirium includes maintenance of adequate fluid and caloric intake. Intravenous flu-

[1]Cosin, L.Z., Mort, M., Post, F., Westropp, C., and Williams, M.: Experimental treatment of persistent senile confusion, The International Journal of Social Psychiatry **4**:24-42, 1958.

[2]Simon, A., and Cahan, R.B.: The acute brain syndrome in geriatric patients. In Mandell, W.M., and Epstein, L.J., editors: Acute psychotic reaction. Psychiatric research reports of the American Psychiatric Association, Washington, D.C., 1966, American Psychiatric Association, p. 9.

ids (sodium chloride or dextrose) and tube feedings may be required. Oxygen inhalation may be necessary. Tranquilization, judiciously prescribed, can be most valuable; but this should not be continued beyond the immediate need. It must be remembered that tranquilizers can actually be the cause of or reinforce the condition. Preferred hypnotics are nonbarbiturates and chloral hydrate. Fever or constipation to the point of impaction can cause delirium, as can drastic cathartics. (As previously mentioned, cascara, saline cathartics, and milk of magnesia can cause severe electrolyte imbalances. Thus bulk laxatives are the best and safest.) The patient's accompanying anxiety and agitation caused by the awareness of confusion must be treated by maintaining the presence of familiar surroundings and people. In general, with prompt and active treatment, 50% of patients with potentially reversible conditions survive and can return home.

Advances in internal medicine and surgery aid in the prevention and treatment of reversible brain syndromes. To take just one example, the "black patch syndrome" (cataract delirium) after eye surgery has been reduced through careful preoperative preparation and efforts toward continuing orientation, using the presence of familiar persons and objects, throughout the postoperative recovery period. "Sundown syndrome," the mental confusion that can occur in the dark because of loss of visual orientation, is another example. This syndrome can often be abated through the simple use of a night light and the provision of familiar objects around the older person.

Dementia of old age

With our present knowledge there is no definitive treatment that can reverse or arrest the causes of the two major brain diseases of old age, senile dementia of the Alzheimer type and multiinfarct dementia. However, much can be done for the patient by suitably adjusting the environment. Structuring of a medically and socially prosthetic milieu, whether at home or in an institution, is important. Simplification, order, the balancing of care versus self-care, the moderation of stimuli (avoiding the Goldstein catastrophic reaction), the provision of recreation and occupational therapy, and the utilization of objects, personnel, and techniques to preserve orientation are among general procedures of value.

Treating what has been called "excess disabilities" (that is, functional defects without explanation on a somatic basis) can enhance the functioning of even severely demented patients.[3] Home care services oriented toward patients with dementia can be excellent when available. Supportive individual and/or group psychotherapy for the patient and his or her family is often advisable.

Psychotherapy is most effective when heavily oriented toward affect—the experiencing of warmth and enhanced self-esteem. Smiles, hugs, handholding, and a warm supportive manner are communications to which even the most severely demented person may respond. Much repetition and little "new material" distinguish the psychotherapeutic process in treating dementia. See the box opposite.

Sensitivity to the level of mental and emotional functioning is crucial. We learned of one older man who refused to be bathed unless he was wearing his cap. A sensitive nurse learned that he was remembering from his past a caution by his mother that he would catch cold if his head was wet. The nurse wisely let the man wear his cap in the bathtub—a form of security that comforted him in the often frightening world of mental confusion.

When agitation is present, one should first try the minor tranquilizers; then thioridazine (Mellaril) is the agent of choice (Chapter 13). We present elsewhere principles of home care (Chapter 10) and institutional care (Chapter 11).

Senile dementia is a major cause of incontinence in late life. But no one need suffer from incontinence of urine or feces. Much can be done to treat

---

[3] Brody, E.M., Kleban, M.H., Lawton, M.P., and Silverman, H.: Excess disabilities of mentally impaired aged: impact of individualized treatment, The Gerontologist **11**:124-133, 1971.

TREATMENT OF SENILE DEMENTIA OF THE ALZHEIMER TYPE

1. The treatment of the basic cause is presently unknown, but one possible example of treatment in the future might be the replacement of certain significant enzymes of the cholinergic system. Another possible future treatment is the development of chemicals that would help in reestablishing circuitry of healthy brain cells to make up for those that are damaged or dead.
2. Direct treatment of primary symptoms such as disorientation and confusion is possible through the provision of memory aids and orientation procedures such as the utilization of cues, calendars, and clocks.
3. The treatment of the common secondary symptoms of patients with Alzheimer's disease is obviously desirable. These symptoms derive from patients' self-incapacity and their reactions to this incapacity. Such symptoms include the following.
   a. Painful self-awareness—patient reactions to psychological and motor symptoms such as agitation, anxiety, depression, and hostility. Treatment includes counseling of patient and family to provide emotional support and the learning of skills to deal with the patient's hostility, anxiety, agitation, and depression. The judicious use of medications (mild to major tranquilizers, antidepressants) may be in order. Agitation and restlessness can often be lessened through exercise.
   b. Self-incapacitation—symptoms directly arising from physical and mental incapacitation, including malnutrition, falling, leaving the stove on, making mistakes in taking medicine, and confused wandering. The provision of proper nutrition and a secure environment are indicated.
   c. Stimulation-threshold problems—symptoms reflecting overstimulation by the environment, that is, stimulation beyond capacity of the patient. Examples are (1) the Goldstein catastrophic reaction with anxiety and (2) irritability. The development of simple routines and techniques for stress reduction are helpful.

In summary, until more is known about senile dementia, the goal in treatment is to preserve functioning (to keep what one has) and even to enhance functioning when this is possible.

---

it, if not cure it. There are artificial sphincters, cleaner, more effective methods of catheterization, and higher quality absorbent material as well as surgical, mechanical, and pharmacological forms of therapy. Relatively simple efforts such as careful organization of the environment can facilitate toileting.

Family education and involvement are of great help to the older person with dementia.[4] As an example, Eisdorfer and Reifler at the University of Washington have developed a clinic for impaired older mental patients and their families.[5] Psychiatric, medical, nursing, social, and architectural evaluations and recommendations are made for older persons along with support and practical advice to the families. An excellent guidebook for families, *Coping with Senility*,[6] has been prepared by the Chronic Organic Brain Syndrome Society of Pennsylvania, one of the network of

---

[4] See M.D. Blumenthal's descriptive paper on families: Mental deterioration and family burden: some theoretical perspectives, presented at the Annual Meeting of the Gerontological Society, San Diego, Nov. 1980.

[5] Reifler, B.U., and Eisdorfer, C.: A clinic for the impaired elderly and their families, American Journal of Psychiatry **137**(11):1399-1403, 1980.

[6] Keene, E.E., editor: Coping with senility. Available from the Chronic Organic Brain Syndrome Society of Pennsylvania, 15th Floor, Arrott Building, Wood St. and 4th Ave., Pittsburgh, Pa. 15222.

self-help groups organizing around the country to help families cope with dementia.

The new Alzheimer's Disease and Related Disorders Association, formed in 1979, is a national federation of groups from such cities as Seattle, Minneapolis, New York, and Boston.[7] The Association's goals include (1) public and professional education on dementia, (2) the building of family support groups for families with one or more members suffering from dementia, and (3) the fostering of research on dementia.

GRIEF AND DEPRESSION
Depressive reactions

One of the treatment problems with depressed people is that they tend toward negativism and withdrawal—making it difficult to locate and stay in contact with them. The Greek biographer, Plutarch, wrote of such a man, "The physician, the consoling friend, are driven away. 'Leave me,' says the wretched man, 'me the impious, the accursed, hated of the gods, to suffer my punishment.'"

It is also dismaying at times how refractory the depressions of late life can be. Nonetheless, depending on the type, the degree, and the duration, considerable relief is possible. With milder depressions associated with a sense of personal insignificance ("over the hill," "out to pasture"), the therapist must help the older person find a role, a place, an activity of authentic interest. Treatment may include no more than talking about problems and providing common-sense advice and support. Physical exercise is often antidepressive.

With the more serious depressions (death of loved one, serious illness, other loss), psychotherapy, drugs, and/or electroconvulsive therapy may be employed. The person is likely to be preoccupied by painful thoughts and feelings, so the help of another, a professional therapist or a friend, through open discussion can be very liberating. The psychotherapeutic approach may not always be oriented toward insight if insight is unbearable. On the other hand, one must not conclude that supportive psychotherapy is the method of choice with older people. Particularly valuable is the release of anger, grief, and guilt. As with the milder depressive states, attention must also be given to the personal and social context. The possibility of suicide must be carefully weighed, particularly in the older man.

The masking of depression by traits subsumed under the wastebasket term "senility" has long been recognized. Psychotherapeutic intervention and electroshock therapy have demonstrated the "organic" simulation of depression.[8] Anxiety is also masked by seemingly organic symptoms such as rigidity.

Anger, considered a crucial element in most depressions, is not a diagnostic entity, yet it perhaps should be. It seems to be a reflection of Western civilization that anxiety and depression are considered diagnostic entities, but anger is not. There are many manifestations of anger—violence, cold hostility, sarcasm, defiance, tantalizing and teasing, sneering, passive obstructiveness (either dependent or aggressive), gossip, withdrawal, and of course self-destructive behavior to the point of suicide. We stress anger for several reasons in our therapeutic work. Anger must be confronted and expressed. However, the expression of anger is not enough and, contrary to popular cant, is not a magical cure-all. Anger can be a cover for deeper problems that may be centered, for instance, around the need for intimacy and a

---

[7] Alzheimer's Disease and Related Disorders Association, 32 Broadway, New York, N.Y. 10004. The formation of the Association was expedited by a meeting called by the National Institute on Aging and the National Institute of Neurological and Communicative Disorders and Stroke in October 1979.

[8] The pioneering papers in this area are Clow, H.E.: Psychiatric factors in the rehabilitation of the aging, Mental Hygiene **34:** 592-599, 1950; Clow, H.E., and Allen, E.B.: A study of depressive states in the aging, Geriatrics **4:**11-17, 1949; Kaufman, M.R.: Old age and aging: the psychoanalytic point of view, American Journal of Orthopsychiatry **10:**73-79, 1940; and Ehrenberg, R., and Gullingsrud, M.J.: Electroconvulsive therapy in elderly patients, American Journal of Psychiatry **11:**743-747, 1955.

profound sense of deprivation. These underlying problems must be brought out. Direct confrontation may be necessary.

Helping the dying person
Psychotherapy and physical care

Dr. Melvin J. Krant, professor at Tufts University Medical School in Boston and director of a cancer unit, has written an article, "The Organized Care of the Dying Patient,"[9] containing ideas that could be adopted by other hospitals. He observed, "Helping someone die well should be conceived as a positive part of health care. . . ." Krant's medical unit moved beyond the walls of the hospital, including home visits. Fundamentally, Krant and his co-workers and others who have contributed to the field concentrate on the elimination of camouflage from the care of the dying and the support of the dying person and his/her family.

Dr. Cicely Saunders' innovations in the care of the dying have evoked widespread interest. The modern hospice concept began in 1843 when Catholic widows in Lyons, France, established a hospice for poor women with incurable cancer.[10] In 1967 Saunders opened St. Christopher's Hospice in London for patients in the final stages of fatal disease.

A modern hospice was planned, built, and staffed under the guidance of Dr. Cicely Saunders to enable patients who are in the last stages of their illness to have a peaceful and above all, a tranquil closure to life and to be supportive to the patients' relatives and friends in their bereavement. "Contrary to common belief, patients in the proper atmosphere, and helped by modern medicine and nursing, can be maintained in an alert and peaceful frame of mind to the last. . . ."[11]

Family and friends are actively involved in care, a homelike atmosphere is encouraged with flowers, colors, and even visiting pets, and the patient often goes back and forth between hospice and home. Saunders' ideas are now providing a model for a number of hospices (perhaps some 200) in the United States. Most notable is the New Haven Hospice, where an inpatient 44-bed facility and a 170-patient home care program are already operating. Both the design of the building and the care offered are chosen on the basis of what is most humane and comforting at each point in the dying person's life.

The National Cancer Institute, the National Institute on Aging, the National Institute on Mental Health, the Administration on Aging, and the Veterans Administration, among other federal agencies, are supporting various studies and demonstrations of hospice care.[12] The federal government began paying for care for dying Medicaid and Medicare patients in 26 hospices as part of a 2-year demonstration project, 1980 to 1982. This involves covering the costs of pain-controlling drugs at home for dying patients as well as easing financial limitations on the number of home visits by physicians, nurses, and other health personnel.

Concern is arising that hospices will become a commercial venture similar to the nursing home industry.[13] Many feel instead that hospice concepts should become automatic components of standard health care for the dying in any setting where they are located rather than requiring new buildings and new systems of reimbursement. The concepts and practices central to the care of the dying are:

1. Physical care of the dying person, easing pain and other discomforts, giving emotional support, and assisting people to put their lives in order through use of the life review and other psychological therapies.

---

[9] Krant, M.J.: The organized care of the dying patient, Hospital Practice **7:**101-108, 1972.

[10] In the Middle Ages, hospices were run by monks for anyone who needed help: the poor, the sick and dying, or travelers and pilgrims going to the Holy Land during the Crusades.

[11] From St. Christopher's Hospice (editorial), London Nursing Times, July 28, 1967. See also Saunders, C.: Care of the dying, London, 1959, Macmillan Publishers Ltd.

[12] For further information on hospices, contact the National Hospice Organization, 765 Prospect St., New Haven, Conn. 06511; and the Hospice Office, Secretary of HEW, 200 Independence Ave., S.W., Washington, D.C. 20201.

[13] Butler, R.N.: The need for quality hospice care, QRB/Quality Review Bulletin **5:**207, 1979.

2. Helping people to die in their home when possible, since this is the preferred location for most people.
3. Helping support the surviving loved ones who are at risk for morbidity and mortality.
4. Educating health and social care providers and the public.[14]

The two major fears of older people with whom we have worked are (1) fear of pain, indignity, loneliness, and depersonalization during dying and the possibility of dying alone, and (2) worry about burdening survivors with the expenses of dying and burial.

In her work, Elisabeth Kübler-Ross delineated five psychological stages occurring during the process of dying, as well as a therapeutic approach to assist persons with terminal illnesses. As we discuss in Chapter 3, many investigators and clinicians, eventually including Kübler-Ross herself, found the stage theory too rigid and arbitrary in describing what really happens when a person dies. The reality is more like a jumble of conflicting or alternating reactions running the gamut from denial to acceptance, with a tremendous variation affected by age, sex, race, ethnic group, social setting, and personality. Kübler-Ross' work brought tremendous attention, sympathy, and interest to the process of dying. Her pioneering work is now being expanded on by others in the effort to help the dying in a more humane and psychologically sound manner.[15]

Analgesics are obviously important, but the intractable pain and anxiety that often accompany dying must be aided also through personal help. Some have advocated mind-expanding drugs such as LSD and also heroin, but these are not available for use in the United States. Cecily Saunders in England uses Brompton's mixture—a formula containing morphine, cocaine, alcohol, syrup, and chloroform water—with good results. Patient alertness is maintained, and pain and fear of pain are avoided by providing medication *before* it is needed.

The active chemical tetrahydrocannabinol (THC), found in marijuana, has proved highly effective in relieving the nausea and discomfort of cancer chemotherapy. Given in proper doses several hours before chemotherapy, THC has proved more effective than prochlorperazine (Compazine), the main antinausea drug used today. This is especially true in younger patients, many of whom have had some experience with marijuana, but it is not always the case for older patients who object to an intoxicant or to disorientation. It is also speculated that THC may affect older people differently than younger persons. Marijuana in both cigarette and pill form was provided free of charge by the federal government to thousands of cancer victims beginning in Fall 1980. The distribution program is being conducted by the National Cancer Institute.

We do not agree with claims that "the time is short, too short for an attempt to start another life and to try out alternate roads to integrity." We find that the fundamental issues in life and consequently in psychotherapy—love, guilt and atonement, separation and integration—can be dealt with to the very end of life itself. It is imperative to encourage the life review and thus aid in the resolution of old as well as recent conflicts. Each person should have the opportunity to live as fully as possible up to the moment of death. It is unthinking and cruel to write off as untreatable those people who have no dependable "future" as long as they have a "present" existence.

Allowing death (the "right to die")

There are medicolegal considerations that go beyond psychotherapeutic efforts with the dying. Technical knowledge has made it possible to preserve life in persons who would have died in the past—and in the absence of apparent consciousness—by artificial support of circulation, respiration, and nutrition.

---

[14] See the Forum for Death Education and Counseling, P.O. Box 1226, Arlington, Va. 22210.

[15] For an example of investigation into the psychology of death, see Cartwright, A., Hockey, L., and Anderson, J.L.: Life before death, London, 1973, Routledge and Kegan Paul.

Among many others, Alvarez[16] has outlined the case for "passive euthanasia," letting people die who are suffering and beyond help. Pope Pius XII stated that when a person is in coma and is beyond recovery, there is no need to employ "extraordinary means" to keep him alive. An Episcopal priest has said, "The Christian obligation of everyone involved is primarily to administer to the person, not to the disease. I personally would like to see euthanasia available to those who want it. If the doctor is too dedicated to fighting the disease, he may forget the person." A Miami physician, Dr. Walter Sackett, who is also a member of Florida's legislature, introduced a "death with dignity bill," but the state of California was the first to pass such a bill in 1976.

Who is to make the decision to allow someone to die? Ideally, there should be a panel to help make the decision when the patient cannot. The patient's family, advisors, doctor, theologian or clergyman, and perhaps his or her social worker may be involved, as well as a second independent doctor and an independent lawyer. It is not simply a matter of taking a vote but making a thoughtful decision. There is a document called "A Living Will,"[17] which persons can sign requesting that if they are unable to make decisions, doctors will not prolong their life.

The mental health specialist can help by individual or collective discussions and fact finding with all pertinent participants in the decision making. The true feelings of the patient if he or she is at all conscious must be ascertained as clearly as possible. One must check to see if the individual's personal affairs are in order and if appropriate arrangements have been made in the interest of the person, his or her family, and the "natural objects of his or her affection." The patient may wish to live only to complete certain personal and tax arrangements. Some persons or their families may want to sustain life until after a granddaughter is born, for example, or a favored grandson has married. The family should not be put into the difficult position of finally deciding, for the doctor has the ultimate responsibility. But the decision must derive from hard data, in the context of moral and legal situations.

Much trepidation exists around the concept of the right to die. Many feel it is impossible to predict death, that persons have recovered from comas, that tampering with death is sacrilegious, or that death itself is such an insult and tragedy that any compliance with it is inhuman. The doctor may have personal religious or moral concerns or be fearful about future litigation; malpractice suits have skyrocketed. Medical training is appropriately directed toward the prolongation of life, and it may be wise indeed for society to sustain that commitment in the medical profession. The debate over the "right to die with dignity" continues, in the attempt to be both humane *and* scrupulous about human rights.

"Laws have to be very carefully written, otherwise you'll end up with human guinea pigs like in Nazi Germany," warns Dr. Angelo D'Agostino, who is both a psychiatrist and a Jesuit priest. A recent legal case[18] illustrates what can begin to happen if the patient's rights are not carefully monitored.

■ A 78-year-old man's relatives obtained a court order terminating his life-sustaining kidney dialysis treatments, claiming he was "mentally incompetent." Their judgment was based on his lack of coherent response to them. Yet the old man was fully conscious and told nurses and a doctor that he did not wish to die. A Massachusetts appeals court judge reversed the lower court decision and ordered the resumption of treatments for the man.

It is currently fashionable to regard medical technology as cruel when it is used to keep alive

[16] Alvarez, W.C.: The old man who wanted to die (editorial), Geriatrics **26**:57, 1971.

[17] One can write to the Concern for Dying (formerly the Euthanasia Educational Fund), 250 W. 57th St., New York, N.Y. 10017, for free copies of "A Living Will."

[18] "Judge orders life support in 'death-with-dignity' case," The Washington Post, Jan. 24, 1980.

patients who will die soon anyway. At times this argument is valid. But it is extremely easy to go one step further and regard the use of such technology wasteful when it is used on older people. The powerful devaluation of the old is thereby given new credibility under the guise of "death with dignity." Each patient is different and should receive individual consideration. Medical procedures that may be an unnecessary ordeal for some (for example, major surgery for a close-to-death cancer patient) may be life-prolonging and life-enhancing for others (like surgery to increase mobility for a cancer patient who still has some time to live).

Funeral arrangements

It is generally accepted that the American funeral system, with the "good funeral" and its obsequies, is outrageously expensive and offers little in the way of meaningful psychological support to mourners.[19] Families are vulnerable to entrenched customs, the dubious approaches of some funeral directors, and the sense that they must "do right by" the deceased. The shock and grief of death are rapidly surcharged with guilt. In 1978 the average American funeral cost $2,300, including cemetery costs. According to a 1978 Federal Trade Commission report, the following are average funeral costs.

Funeral home charges	$1,393
Interment receptacle	142
Obituary notice	19
Clergy honorarium	35
Death certificates	14
Cemetery expenses	555
Flowers	150
TOTAL	$2,308

The funeral industry is in control of state regulatory bodies. Twenty-four thousand morticians share the profits from some 2 million annual U.S. deaths. The churches have not taken great leadership in protection of consumers. This amount of

money may bring comfort to funeral directors but does little to comfort those who may have already outstripped their resources on care of the person while he or she was alive.

Questionable practices of the funeral industry include:

1. Inadequate presentation of lower cost alternatives, such as cremation and the use of memorial societies.
2. Misinformation regarding embalming. (Embalming will not prevent decomposing.) Undertakers embalm without first obtaining survivors' permission. Only some states require embalming and only under certain circumstances, yet the public is led to believe embalming is required.
3. Unavailability of price information to the public and thus reduction in competition within the "funeral industry."
4. Claims of airtight and watertight caskets that mislead consumers to believe these features help prevent decomposition of the body.[20]

Nonprofit memorial societies offer simple, dignified, and economical funeral arrangements, often for less than $500.[21] They tend to make life easier for survivors and give the deceased some control over his or her own demise. These societies are organized as nonprofit organizations, democratically controlled by the members.[22] The first was created in Seattle, Washington, in 1939. They are usually initiated by a church or a ministerial association and occasionally by labor, civic, or educational groups. Most have lifetime mem-

---

[19] Mitford, 1963. See also Consumer Reports Books: Funerals: consumers' last rights, New York, 1979, Consumers' Union.

[20] Information on pine coffins is available by writing to The St. Francis Burial and Counseling Society, Inc., 1768 Church St., N.W., Washington, D.C. 20036.

[21] Social Security provides a lump-sum death benefit. This is a variable amount, which may be as much as three times the monthly benefit the deceased worker would have received if he or she had lived to retirement age.

[22] Ernest Morgan's *A manual of death education and simple burial,* ed. 9, describes memorial societies in detail. It can be obtained from the Continental Association of Funeral and Memorial Societies, 1828 L St., N.W., Washington, D.C. 20036. In Canada write to the Memorial Society Association of Canada, Box 96, Weston, Ontario M9N 3M6.

bership fees of rarely more than $20, plus a $5 records charge at the time of death. There are memorial societies in more than 190 cities in the United States and Canada, with about 1 million members. (These societies do not sell funerals or cemetery lots in advance.)

Memorial services can offer valid "psychotherapy" for survivors. "In a funeral the center of attention is the dead body; the emphasis is on death. In a memorial service the center of concern is the personality of the individual who has died. . . ."[22a] An honest appraisal of the deceased—with both liabilities and assets—can help the survivors work through their own complicated feelings, sometimes cast in an excessive idealization that may actually prolong grief.

In addition to earth burial and cremation, bequeathal to a medical school performs a valuable service[23] and saves expense. Only the Orthodox Jewish faith objects to bequeathal of one's body or of organs for transplant. With changing religious attitudes and the desire to spare survivors soaring funeral costs, there are now more bodies donated than needed by medical schools in some parts of the country. Some people—status conscious to the

---

[22a] Morgan, E.: A manual of death education and simple burial, ed. 9, Washington, D.C., 1980, Continental Association of Funeral and Memorial Societies.

[23] Eye and temporal bone banks and the National Kidney Foundation also give the person a sense of valued legacy. Usually only the corneas of older people are acceptable, however. There is now a Uniform Anatomical Gift Act or its equivalent in every state and in most Canadian provinces. A Uniform Donor's Card filled out and signed by the donor and two witnesses (three in Florida) constitutes a legal document. (See Department of Health, Education and Welfare: How to donate the body and its organs for transplantation, Medical Education and Research, Pub. No. [NIH] 77-776, 1979.) The person now has final say over the disposition of his or her body. However, if a family strongly objects, most institutions will not go against their wishes. France, England, and West Germany have adopted the "Universal Donor Principle," whereby anyone who dies anywhere in these countries is available as a donor of organs or tissues provided he or she has *not* previously specified otherwise. When the problem of transplantation rejection is fully solved, the opportunities to help others through donation of body parts will escalate strikingly.

end—want to leave their bodies to prestige schools like Harvard.

Mourning[24]

Geoffrey Gorer observed that the majority of the people today are "without adequate guidance as to how to treat death and bereavement and without social help in coming to terms with grief and mourning."[25] He describes three distinct stages: the first, a short period of shock lasting for a few days; the second, a time of intense grief, during which the mourner suffers psychological changes such as listlessness, disturbed sleep, failure of appetite, and loss of weight; and the third, a gradual reawakening to an interest in life. Gorer emphasizes that during the second phase, lasting 6 to 12 weeks, "the mourner is in more need of social support and assistance than at any time since infancy and early childhood."

It might be said, "Where depression is, let grief be." If grief is denied outlet, a depression is one of the possibilities. Insulation or denial of grief is not the sole cause of depression, of course, since ambivalence toward the deceased (that is, anger and conflict) complicates the usual course of grief. It is the task of therapy to help open up the grief process. For example, widows or widowers should be encouraged to discuss whether they felt they did all that could be done. It is the goal of prevention to see that grief is never suppressed to begin with.

The impact of bereavement cannot be minimized. Rees and Lutkins[26] were some of the first to show a greater mortality of survivors within 6 months of a loss than among controls of similar age. Data on 4,486 widowers 55 years of age and older were collected for a 9-year period following

---

[24] See also Chapter 4.

[25] Gorer, G.: Death, grief and mourning in contemporary Britain, London, 1965, Cresset Press. He believes that only the Orthodox Jew through formal ritual patterns of religious observance receives the comfort and discipline required to resolve grief.

[26] See the early paper of Rees, W.D., and Lutkins, S.G.: Mortality of bereavement, British Medical Journal **4:**13-16, 1967.

the death of their wives in 1957.[27] Of these, 213 died during the first 6 months of bereavement, 40% above the expected rate for married men of the same age. Thereafter, mortality fell gradually to that of married men and remained at about the same level. The greatest increase in mortality during the first 6 months was found in the widowers dying from coronary thrombosis and other arteriosclerotic and degenerative heart disease. There was also evidence of a true increase in mortality from other diseases, although the numbers of individual categories were too small for statistical analysis. In the first 6 months, 22.5% of the deaths were from the same diagnostic group as the wife's death.

Perhaps even more painful to the older person than the death of a spouse is the loss of a grown child. This experience is more likely to occur the longer the person lives. Many people consider such deaths to be against the laws of nature, and feelings can be extremely difficult to resolve.

Plight of the surviving spouse

The surviving spouse faces practical as well as emotional problems associated with the loss of a mate—relationships with in-laws, children, financial matters, governmental benefits, and unwanted callers who read the death announcement in the papers. Some decisions, such as selling one's home and moving to a completely new location, are best delayed until part of the mourning period is past and the person has greater perspective and energy at hand.

Adjusting to the loss of a spouse, as a process, is often an emotional journey of a year or longer as one moves in fresh and painful memory through all the anniversaries and holidays that may have meant so much, even in conflict as well as in warmth. Often at least 1 year of anniversaries—birthdays, Thanksgiving, the Christmas season,

Fourth of July, etc.—must be experienced nostalgically and sadly before one is ready to again take up life wholeheartedly. The oldest and youngest spouses may need even longer. Consolation is difficult and indeed may not be accepted at all. In therapy the task is to open up grief, uncover any complicating anger, help the person face his or her envy of married friends, develop new relationships, and find activities and meaning. A comfortable standard of living (so often absent) helps in the struggle against apathy and isolation. Because of social and cultural attitudes that have prevented previous experience with finances, some widowed women often need considerable help, not only in obtaining but also in managing finances. (See Chapter 6.)

The widower may also have special problems. He may be totally unprepared to cook for himself, sew on buttons, etc. and will need concrete assistance in learning how to do things for himself.

Socially, the surviving spouses (especially women) may have a difficult time of it. They are often left out by old and good friends, for they are now "fifth wheels." If widows are attractive, others' wives may shun them; if dreary and mournful, everyone will stay away. Self-pity and outrage at one's fate are futile, and action of a constructive sort must be encouraged to get the person back into contact with understanding, but not patronizing, people.

The Widow-to-Widow program was established in the Boston area as an experimental mental health program of preventive intervention directed at new widows and staffed by other widows. It is based on the premise that the best helper of a widow at the time of grief is another widow. Silverman wrote, "Since statistics indicate a higher risk of emotional and psychiatric disturbances among younger widowed women than is to be expected from the population at large, this program was established to find ways of reaching those women (all recently widowed and under the age of 60) to determine what services would ease their distress and grief and, thereby, lessen the possi-

---

[27] Parkes, C.M., Benjamin, B., and Fitzgerald, R.G.: Broken heart: a statistical study of increased mortality among widowers, British Medical Journal **1:**740-743, 1969.

bility of their developing a psychiatric disorder."[28] The idea proved promising and has been set up in various communities,[29] applying the concept to men as well as to women, and for all ages.

Alcoholics Anonymous (for survivors who develop or who have had drinking problems) and Parents Without Partners are also self-help organizations that have been very useful. It is important to have professional skills on hand without at the same time downplaying or interfering with the "natural" talents of the nonprofessionals. Voluntarism, however valuable, must not be misused as a substitute for necessary professional services.

Silverman makes a good point, valuable as a significant rationale for life-crisis group psychotherapy.

Most mental health agencies serve those suffering from a defined psychiatric disorder, such as depression, rather than those in need of preventive services as they pass through a life crisis. This may be because most people suffering from the "hazard of living" that occurs with the death of a spouse do not consult with such agencies unless a prior contact has been established.[30]

Post-Cana is the Catholic lay association for widows and widowers set up to "assist and promote the solution of those spiritual, parental, psychological, financial, social, and other problems arising directly or indirectly from the untimely death of a husband or wife."

Widowhood illustrates well the significance to mental health of employment counseling and work placement. For both practical reasons (income reduction through widowhood) and the appropriate need for activity, work may be needed. There exist in some communities "Over-60 Counseling and Employment Services." The U.S. Employ-ment Service should also be pressured to serve older persons. Low-income elderly may be eligible to participate in various programs (which, however, only operate in some areas): Green Thumb and Green Light, Senior Aides, Foster Grandparents. Other federal programs such as VISTA and the Peace Corps (under ACTION) are not really set up to help poor older people; but they are useful in any case and particularly to skilled people who, out of need to contribute or because of loneliness, may be interested. Indeed, older people are increasingly serving in the Peace Corps.

In some measure, so long as the work ethic is so influential, older people are likely to seek "something to do" even when financial as well as other psychological and interpersonal considerations are not so crucial.

Therapy of body losses

Our efforts with respect to grief and restitution do not apply only to helping the dying in their grief and the survivors in theirs, but they offer help in dealing with the loss of one's body parts, organs, and functions. Help with feelings about limb amputation,[31] mastectomy, and disfiguration is important. The loss of internal organs has still other psychological meanings and requires special help, as does the loss of sensory capacities—blindness and deafness. Losses of sexual capacities are especially poignant. About 15 million persons over 65 suffer from serious chronic diseases, all of which involve some kind of body loss.

Suicide

Suicide cannot be treated, only prevented—or can it? Suicide Prevention Centers have not had the impact of reducing suicide hoped for by Shneidman, Farberow, and others. The National Institute of Mental Health even closed down its Center for Studies of Suicide Prevention in 1972

---

[28] Silverman, P.R.: The Widow-to-Widow program, Archives of the Foundation of Thanatology **2:**133-135, 1970.

[29] The American Association of Retired Persons is conducting Widow-to-Widow programs in selected cities.

[30] Silverman, P.R.: The Widow-to-Widow program, Archives of the Foundation of Thanatology **2:**133-135, 1970.

[31] The "phantom limb" is a phenomenon frequently experienced by amputees in which sensations, often painful, appear to originate in the amputated extremity.

(established in 1966). Older people did call the centers, but that mechanism has not been demonstrated to be a means of averting suicide. Telephone therapy, by which most suicide centers operate, may help people in other emotional crises but not reduce suicide.

Immediate and supportive treatment when suicide has been attempted is of course indicated. For example, barbiturate poisoning, regardless of the dose taken, need not be fatal. Tracheotomy, peritoneal dialysis, active physiological treatment, and psychological support can save lives.

Should suicide always be prevented in old age? This is a difficult question; we already considered the "right to die" issue. In older persons the desire for death may be refractory, persuasive, rational, and deliberate rather than irrational and precipitous. The absence of euthanasia may force some individuals to suicide.

We more fully discuss potential suicide, including treatment, in Chapter 4 but wish to emphasize once again that depression-based suicide is perhaps the most preventable through treatment. There are a number of other motivations for self-destruction, which may not be easily amenable to psychotherapy and instead require societal changes —as in those suicides related to despair over profound poverty or racism.

PARANOID STATES

Many paranoid individuals survive in the community throughout their lives. The situation of some paranoid patients worsens with age as a result of the continuing contraction of their lives— further isolation through deaths of loved ones and acquaintances, with whom there may have been few contacts to begin with. When hostile paranoid feelings and/or delusions are specifically directed against other persons, hospitalization may be necessary, if only briefly. (This is the basis of the laws regarding the mentally ill in which reference is made to "danger to others.")

It is an absolute necessity—and we purposely emphasize *absolute*—to be scrupulously honest with paranoid patients; one should be so with all

patients, but the paranoid person cannot accept our usual lapses.

■ A 70-year-old man retired after a long and successful career with the government.[32] Soon after his retirement, he was hospitalized for evaluation of symptoms of frequent and painful urination. A cystoscopic examination was planned as a part of his evaluation. However, the patient was not told that he would undergo this examination. He therefore did not know what to expect. When he was sent from the operating room to the recovery room, he became agitated and delusional, shouting, "Watch out, they're going to kill all of us!" He was transferred to the psychiatric service, where he received a series of 23 electroconvulsive treatments. He appeared to have made a complete recovery and returned home.

Five years later he experienced a recurrence of his urinary symptoms, and an evaluation, including cystoscopy, was recommended by the same urologist. The patient's son reminded the urologist of the psychosis that seemed to have been precipitated by the cystoscopy 5 years earlier. He also told the physician that his father seemed more agitated and upset. According to the patient's son, the urologist seemed uninterested in this historical information. In fact, he did not report this information to his associate who did cystoscopic examination. For the second time the patient was neither told about the cystoscopic examination nor prepared for it.

The patient's response was markedly similar to the one 5 years before. In the recovery room he shouted, "They're going to kill us—get out!" Although he underwent another extensive series of electroconvulsive treatments, he remained severely depressed 7 months after his hospitalization.

The psychotherapist must be attentive, make reasonable suggestions, and be firm, combining warmth with detachment. The therapist must *not* "be nice," give out reassurances, or accept everything that is said. Nothing offends paranoid people more than to think they are being "buttered up." At various points there must be frank disagreements. If patient and therapist never disagree, that, too spells trouble. The therapist has to take is-

---

[32] This case was contributed by Dr. Steven Steury, Washington, D.C.

sue with the patient or the latter ceases to believe in him. The therapist must have self-confidence and know what he or she is talking about (having listened long and hard) and must be innovative when necessary. For example, one paranoid man was helped to overcome his fear of being poisoned by having a member of his family taste all his food before he did. It is difficult to sustain a therapeutic relationship of trust with the paranoid patient; rapport is slow in building; work may be long term.

Paranoid persons, having been deeply emotionally deprived, yearn for closeness and will not spurn it. They desire love despite their outward appearance of, for instance, withdrawn hostility. He or she has had years of "training" at recognizing phony talk. Irony and humor—referring to the universalities of the human condition—are valuable. The therapist must seek to get "behind the defenses" and understand the underlying anxiety. If the therapist can obtain knowledge of when the symptom developed, he or she may be able to alter the equilibrium or eliminate the need for the symptom effectively without ever discussing the delusional systems. Environmental manipulation may be therapeutic but should be done openly.

Work with the family or contact with the person's medical doctor can help only when the paranoid person is present to hear what is being said. The therapist must help the older paranoid person with hearing impairments by obtaining hearing aids. Tranquilizers, judiciously employed, may help somewhat when agitation is present.

RETIREMENT SYNDROME

A retired editor wrote, "Retirement will soon be the largest occupation in America." Many American men, reared in obeisance to the ethic of useful, lifelong, productive labor, find it painful to discover that they are not indispensable to their work or organization; then they must discover that work is not indispensable for their survival and happiness. They may need to find either new forms of "work" or new means of enjoying idleness.

There is undoubtedly much mythology in the notion of a "retirement syndrome." People who retire do not automatically develop declining mental and physical health. Streib and Schneider's[33] studies, like others, indicate any such generalization to be a fallacy. On the other hand, social scientists may inadvertently overlook those individuals for whom retirement is pathogenic. Reconciliation of clinical experience and social science data is often difficult because the individual gets buried within the larger data. Thus, although there may be no general retirement syndrome, clinical indications are that some individuals are badly affected. Causes are economics, personality, and general health—in short, the range of factors affecting an individual.

In 1971, 105,000 federal workers who could retire chose not to do so. Streib and Schneider found that "both men and women of higher income levels, higher educational attainments, and higher levels of occupational structure tend to work longer than their counterparts with lower socioeconomic status."

On the other hand, some groups cannot retire fast enough, usually those holding tedious, assembly line– or heavy labor–type jobs. The latter, by the way, show some improvement, not decline, in health as a result of retirement, which is not so surprising. But this again illustrates how difficult it is to generalize from either the clinical or the social science perspective. What becomes clear, in our judgment, is the need for continuing specificity of research with careful, detailed studies of various categories (and not only socioeconomic classes and occupations) of people.

There is some evidence that with the changing laws requiring mandatory retirement, coupled with continuing inflation, more people are staying in the work force out of both choice and necessity. The 1980s may see more second and third careers, phase-out retirement, job sharing, parttime work, and other work arrangements.

---

[33] Streib, G.F., and Schneider, C.J.: Retirement in American society; impact and process, Ithaca, N.Y., 1971, Cornell University Press.

INSOMNIA

The amount of sleep that individuals need varies considerably, and each person must find the amount that works best for him or her. From 8 to 9 hours seems to remain the average needed in old age, unless the person is ill. Many older persons experience chronic or semichronic sleep problems. The person may miss part of his or her sleep, most of it, or have "poor sleep" with many awakenings and with feelings of exhaustion the next morning.

Certain sleep changes are common in later life and should not be confused with insomnia. In general, older people sleep less long and less deeply and awaken more easily and earlier. They have a greater tendency to waken throughout the night and to experience less "dreaming sleep" (stage 4 or rapid eye movement |REM| sleep). Deep sleep (called delta sleep), the period of dreamless oblivion, lessens and may vanish in old age. Moreover, REM periods decline in the presence of chronic brain disorders.[34] There is growing suspicion that some of these changes may be caused by age-related changes in biological rhythms, although they can of course also be influenced by environmental factors. Many older persons retire early because of fatigue, waken at 3 or 4 AM, and then fear they have insomnia, when they may in fact have had an adequate 6 to 7 hours or more of sleep.

There are contradictory opinions about the nature of normal sleep with aging. Several early studies showed that sleep characteristics of older people were not very different from those of other ages.[35] But research is becoming more sophisticated. There are now 16 accredited centers for the study of sleep disorders, whose function is to establish the norm for biological sleep rhythms, to clarify the effects of physiological functions on sleep, and to study sleep disturbance. The box opposite lists the members of the American Association of Sleep Disorders Clinics. The sleep centers have not dealt specifically with the pervasive problems of sleep in middle and old age, but they may eventually provide a valuable alternative to drug therapy with older persons. For example, the Montefiiore Center, which has older people among its subjects, found that subjects tended to move to a 25-hour day if removed from social and temporal cues. They progressively began going to bed later and rising earlier. This may be a tendency for older retired persons with no required time for rising or retiring. Chronotherapy, a method for resetting the biological clock to improve sleep, is being evaluated but has not yet been tested in older persons.

Some researchers insist that people need less sleep as they grow older. However, what may seem like a need for less sleep may be the result of illness, anxiety, depression, or simply the need for more exercise and activity during the day. For example, early morning awakening is more common among the inactive who go to bed early and take catnaps (sometimes leading toward serious day-night sleep reversal). It can also be a sign of depression. This is not to say that a daily nap is not valuable; if not too long or too frequent, naps may relax the person and thus contribute to better sleep at night. Older people often need more sleep,[36] not less, if they suffer from illnesses and degenerative diseases that create fatigue, headache, gastrointestinal complaints, aches, and pains. Sleep in these cases is a vital restorative.

Physiological causes of insomnia include noc-

---

[34] Feinberg, I., Koresko, R.L., and Schaffner, I.R.: Sleep electroencephalographic and eye-movement patterns in patients with chronic brain syndrome, Journal of Psychiatric Research **3:**11-26, 1965.

[35] Feinberg, I.: The ontogenesis of human sleep and the relationship of sleep variables to intellectual function in the aged, Comprehensive Psychiatry **9:**138-147, 1968; and Kahn, E., and Fisher, C.: The sleep characteristic of the normal aged male, Journal of Nervous and Mental Disease **148:**477-494, 1969.

[36] Weitzman, E.D.: Sleep and aging. In Katzman, R., and Terry, R., editors: Neurology of aging, New York, 1981, F.A. Davis Co.; and Tiller, P.M.: Bedrest, sleep and symptoms: study of older persons, Annals of International Medicine **61:**98-105, 1964.

turnal myoclonus (leg twitching) and disruption of body rhythms. Insomnia can be produced or exacerbated by an institutional environment such as nursing homes or hospitals where the patient has little control over the lights or the timing of medication or meals. Nocturnal cardiac arrhythmias and nocturnal shortness of breath from congestive heart failure may cause sleeplessness. Sleep apnea (periods of cessation of breathing) may relate to mental deterioration or circulatory disease and is suspected as a cause of sudden nocturnal death.

Increased mortality is associated with too little (less than 4 hours) and too much (more than 10 hours) sleep. These sleep-associated "major mortality-risk predictors" emerge from a new look by Kripke at a 20-year-old survey of health habits of nearly 1 million adult Americans.[37] It has been speculated that sleep apnea syndrome may be one potentially fatal disorder underlying unduly short or long sleep duration.

Persons with sleep difficulties related to psychological problems may fear sleep itself. In sleep their defenses against anxiety (including fear of death), anger, and other emotions are down—de-

[37]What makes the study provocative despite its subjective nature is its size: 366,493 men and 456,572 women completed detailed questionnaires in 1959 and 1960 for the American Cancer Society as to their health-related life-styles, and 98.4% of this vast cohort were followed up 6 years later. See Kripke, D.F., Simons, R.N., Garfinkel, L., and Hammond, E.C.: Short and long sleep and sleeping pills, Archives of General Psychiatry **36:**103-116, 1979.

fenses that may function poorly enough while they are awake. The activities that protect them from anxiety during the day are gone. Psychotherapy can help in clarifying and resolving the individual's basis for insomnia.

Other treatment for insomnia includes the establishment of simple rituals and routines that are followed regularly—perhaps warm baths, a well-made bed, bed boards for support, back massage, eye shields to stop the light, bedtime reading or soft music, or any other comfort mechanisms that suggest protection and relaxation. Mild uses of alcohol such as a small amount of wine or warm saki (Japanese rice beer) as a nighttime relaxer may be tried if the older person does not show a history of vulnerability to alcohol dependency. Perhaps even more useful and harmless is a glass of warm milk, which contains the amino acid L-tryptophan, a probable factor in encouraging sleep.

Other natural factors that may help sleep are the following.

1. Avoidance of daytime napping, particularly the after-dinner snooze
2. A regular program schedule of activities for each day
3. Daily exercise
4. Avoidance of caffeine-containing beverages like coffee and cola, especially in the afternoon and evening
5. No heavy meals after 7:00 P.M.
6. Evening emphasis on relaxation
7. Sexual activity, when possible, including masturbation
8. A regular bedtime hour
9. Getting out of bed if insomnia occurs, rather than tossing and turning (The psychological association with bed should be sleep, and the older person with insomnia should avoid bed unless sleepy.)

Because they create abnormal sleep and may be dangerous, drugs should be tried only as a last resort, reevaluated routinely (no ''standing orders'' for hypnotics, for example), and given only to break up sleepless patterns rather than continued on a long-term basis.

In 1979 the National Institute on Aging brought together the key researchers in sleep to consider the neglected area of sleep and aging. Problem areas for future research were identified as sleep pathologic conditions in older persons, drugs (including hypnotics) used for therapy, and basic mechanisms of sleep and biological rhythms.[38]

PARKINSONISM (PARALYSIS AGITANS, THE SHAKING PALSY)

Persons who suffered with the 1919-1924 influenza may develop parkinsonism in late life. But other causes are not fully understood (''idiopathic'' is the term often used by physicians when that is the case). It is known, however, that there is a deficiency of dopamine in the caudate nucleus and putamen of the brain and a loss of cells in the substantia nigra and locus ceruleus. Arteriosclerosis is no longer believed to play a major role. Of course, the phenothiazines, haloperidol, and reserpine are often responsible for parkinsonlike symptoms.

The course of the disease is slow, characterized by rigidity of the whole body, ''resting tremor,'' and slowness of movement (bradykinesia). The tremor is notable for a ''pill-rolling'' movement of the fingers, accompanied by shaking head and shuffling gait (all of which are often a source of embarrassment). The posture is usually stooped, with the head forward and elbows flexed. The facial expression is masked, lacking emotional expression, but the person is usually depressed. The disease affects men twice as frequently as women and rarely begins before age 40 or after 65.

Emotional excitement and fatigue do appear to augment the tremor. A calm existence, if possible, is advisable—but not inactivity. A measured life is the desideratum. Prescribed exercises are useful. Massage and passive movement may help the rigidity. Drugs are invaluable.

---

[38]See Special report, report planning workshop on sleep and aging, sleep I, 1979, pp. 219-220; and Dement, W.C., and Miles, L.E.: A comprehensive review of the existing literature, Sleep, May 1981.

In a major breakthrough, Cotzias firmly established the clinical usefulness of levodopa (L-3,4-dihydroxyphenylalanine) in the treatment of parkinsonism. Levodopa, or L-dopa, is the metabolic precursor of dopamine. It helps relieve the rigidity and akinesia (lack of voluntary movement) but has less effect on the tremor. Side effects are dose-related and may include hallucinations, persistent vomiting, hypotension, depression, and confusion. The concurrent use of carbidopa (a sister medication) makes it possible to reduce the dosage of levodopa by about 75% and thus reduce the potential for adverse side effects. Levodopa works best early in the disease.[39] Listed below are three classes of important antiparkinsonian agents.

Anticholinergics
  Trihexyphenidyl (Artane)
  Amantadine (Symmetrel)
Antihistamines
  Diphenhydramine (Benadryl)
Dopaminergics
  Levodopa (Sinemet)

The treatment of mild parkinsonism is begun with the anticholinergics or amantadine—alone or in combination.

It is important for the therapist to deal with embarrassment and depression, to help in establishing a meaningful life, and to familiarize him- or herself with the drugs the patient is taking so as to not misinterpret symptoms.

STROKE AND HYPERTENSION

Strokes are an interference with the blood supply to the brain that can result in death or disablement. If the stroke victim survives but the blood supply is interfered with for approximately 5 minutes or more, brain cells invariably die and function is impaired, either temporarily or permanently, in movement, thought, memory, speech, or

Table 14-1. Prevalence of hypertension among men and women, black and white, age 65-74

Black women	58.8%
Black men	50.1%
White women	42.3%
White men	35.3%

Data from Health and Nutrition Examination Survey (HANES), 1971-1974. In Department of Health, Education and Welfare: Vital and health statistics, Series 11, No. 203, Blood pressure levels of persons 60-74 years, United States, 1971-1974, National Center for Health Statistics, Sept. 1977.

sensation. Transient ischemic attacks (TIAs)[40] are sudden episodes of neurologic deficits (''little strokes'') that may be precursors of a major stroke.

Almost 10% of all deaths are caused by stroke (about 500,000 persons in the United States each year have strokes, fatal and nonfatal). Although up to one half of persons who develop strokes do not have high blood pressure, an elevated blood pressure is a major risk factor in stroke. About 40% of older white persons and more than 50% of older black persons (over 65) have either isolated systolic hypertension or systolic-diastolic hypertension. (See Table 14-1.) Although there is no universally accepted definition of hypertension among older people, the following definitions are usually followed.

1. *Systolic-diastolic hypertension.* This involves a systolic blood pressure greater than 160

---

[39]Cotzias, G.C., Van Woert, M.H., and Schiffer, I.M.: Aromatic amino acids and modifications of parkinsonism, New England Journal of Medicine **276:**374-379, 1967.

[40]To be labeled a TIA, symptoms must include one or more of the following: (1) total or partial loss of vision in one eye, (2) an aphasic disorder, and (3) weakness or numbness in an arm or leg, which may lead to a ''drop attack'' in which the person falls down. Most symptoms last 2 to 5 minutes and all signs and symptoms disappear within 24 hours. Anything longer is probably a small stroke. A 1978 Canadian study found aspirin (1,300 mg a day) effective in reducing the risk of recurrent transient ischemic attacks or stroke for men (not for women, for reasons that are not understood) who have had transient ischemia of the brain caused by fibrin platelet emboli. See the Canadian Cooperative Study Group: A randomized trial of aspirin and sulfinpyrazone in threatened stroke, New England Journal of Medicine **299:** 53-59, 1978.

mm Hg with a diastolic greater than 95 mm Hg. In older persons, as in younger, these elevations represent primary hypertension in the majority of cases.

2. *Isolated systolic hypertension.* This type of hypertension is indicated by a systolic blood pressure greater than 160 mm Hg with a diastolic greater than 80 mm Hg. This is the more common form of hypertension in older people, affecting 23% of men and 35% of women over age 60, and usually reflects atherosclerosis of the aorta. Many physicians hesitate to treat older persons for this condition because of dangers resulting from a sudden decrease in blood pressure (for example, decreased blood flow to vital organs). When treatment is undertaken, the goal of therapy, at least in the beginning, is to bring the systolic pressure into an acceptable range (140 to 160 mm Hg) rather than to normal limits (less than 140 mm Hg). The value of treating isolated systolic hypertension at all among older persons is now being studied by the National Heart, Lung and Blood Institute and the National Institute on Aging.

Active treatment of even mild hypertension (a diastolic range of 90 mm Hg to 104 mm Hg) is now recommended by the National Heart, Lung and Blood Institute as a result of a 5-year study of close to 11,000 people begun in 1973, which showed a lowered death rate from heart attack and stroke after treatment.

Antihypertensive treatment in older persons may first involve simple management of the diet (salt and calorie, that is, weight, control). This regimen, along with as much exercise as possible, may bring the pressure under control. If not, an oral diuretic may be the only additional agent needed. But if drugs are warranted, they can often be given with a minimum of negative side effects if they are chosen carefully and dosage is increased over a period of weeks rather than days. The following should be noted.

1. Side effects from antihypertensive therapy occur more frequently in older patients than in younger.

2. Because of the significant orthostatic decrease in blood pressure seen in some older persons, blood pressure should be measured in both sitting and standing positions.

3. Because the systolic blood pressure fluctuates widely in older persons with rigid, atherosclerotic aortas, a number of blood pressure measurements are needed to determine blood pressure.

4. People over 65 frequently have low blood volume and a reduction in baroreceptor (pressure) reflex activity. This may increase their responsiveness to antihypertensive drugs.

5. An inadequate diet can make older people more susceptible to the hypokalemic (potassium-lowering) effects of an oral diuretic. Dietary changes and perhaps a potassium supplement need to be considered in these cases. Salt substitutes with a high potassium content may be helpful.

6. The presence of congestive heart failure, symptomatic atherosclerotic heart disease, or cerebrovascular disease make the reduction of high blood pressure even more imperative in older persons. Data from the Framingham, Massachusetts, study indicate that hypertension, either systolic or diastolic, is a risk factor in cardiovascular and renal disease and stroke in both old and young. Hypertension greater than 160/95 mm Hg doubles the risk of death in men and increases the risk in women 2½ times.

7. Side effects from medication such as drowsiness or mental confusion can usually be handled by changes in diet and/or drug program rather than stopping antihypertensive treatment.

If a stroke has already occurred, the CAT scanner (computerized axial tomography—see p. 233) is valuable in differentiating a stroke caused by a blood clot from one resulting from a cerebral hemorrhage. This differential diagnosis is important because although the symptoms appear to be the same, the treatment is different.

Cerebral revascularization through microsurgery (the extracranial/intracranial bypass) has shown some limited success in restoring function lost through an ischemic stroke—but only if brain damage is quite limited and the impairment minor. The surgery is also used on a limited basis to avert strokes after TIAs. A study supported by the National Institute of Communicative Disorders and Stroke is now underway to further evaluate the effectiveness of this surgery.

Coinciding with a recent overall decline in deaths caused by cardiovascular disease, the stroke death rate (when adjusted for age changes in the population) has declined 36% since 1962, with more than two thirds of that drop occurring since 1972. Factors in the decline are (1) better treatment for TIAs, the ''little strokes,'' (2) a steadily improving quality of general medical care as well as a greater emphasis by the public on prevention of illness through better self-care, physical conditioning, and diet control, and (3) improved detection and control of high blood pressure, a leading cause of stroke. In 1972 a major nationwide campaign, the National High Blood Pressure Education Program (sponsored by the National Heart, Lung and Blood Institute of the National Institutes of Health), was begun for the early detection and treatment of high blood pressure.

The control of salt in the diet seems to be a factor in controlling hypertension.[41] Exercise and weight reduction are factors as well. Older persons should restrict their salt intake as much as possible, including caution with sodium-containing medicine like analgesics and antacids. Regular exercise such as walking briskly for 2 miles a day or swimming are recommended, with special exercises worked out for the disabled. All of these measures should be initiated before medication is considered.[42]

Unfortunately little of the decline in stroke can be attributed to striking improvements in stroke treatment itself. Equally unfortunate, the declining death rate from stroke probably means an increasing number of disabled survivors who experience not only loss of function but great medical expense and sometimes years of physical and emotional stress. Approximately two thirds of those who survive a stroke (about 2.5 million persons) are permanently disabled to some degree.

Some medical schools have developed innovative stroke rehabilitation programs.[43] The National Institute of Neurological, Communicative Disorders and Stroke supports 12 cerebrovascular clinical research centers and three comprehensive stroke centers where research findings can be evaluated in community settings. These centers are involved in testing various techniques to prevent stroke, in rehabilitating stroke patients, and in educating health care personnel and the public about stroke.

It is pitiful indeed when poststroke older patients who potentially can be rehabilitated are left dormant and bedridden. As many as 75% have been estimated to have the capacity to ambulate successfully with the assistance of a wheelchair, crutches, canes, braces, or walkers and even without assistance. Staff must be trained to go beyond the provision of basic physical care. They must work against patient apathy by stimulating motivation, helping the person face the disability but not di-

---

[41] Epidemiological population studies suggest a low sodium intake might explain the low prevalence of hypertension in Greenland Eskimos, Australian Aborigines, and other groups, and the high prevalence in Japan, which has the highest documented rate of stroke in the world. In terms of mechanisms, we know very little about the interaction of salt and water with other physiological mechanisms, especially the renin-angiotensin and adrenergic nervous systems. See Fries, E.D.: Salt, volume and the prevention of hypertension, Circulation **53:**589-594, 1976.

[42] Useful books for those with high blood pressure are Margie, J.D., and Hunt, J.C.: Living with high blood pressure, Radnor, Pa., 1979, Chilton Book Co.; and Payne, A., and Callahan, D.: The fat and sodium control cookbook, New York, 1975, Little, Brown & Co.

[43] The work of Howard Rusk at New York University–Bellevue is outstanding. There is also the Burke Rehabilitation Center, White Plains, N.Y., one of the best stroke rehabilitation centers in the country, associated with Cornell Medical School. It is for short-term rehabilitation (45 to 50 days).

rectly or subtly encouraging him or her to give up.[44]

Patients who have been discharged from occupational and/or physical therapy as "having received maximum benefit" should not then be neglected and allowed to relapse into inactivity. Staff members may do irreparable harm by "overnursing," providing full body care, grooming, bathing, and dressing, while the patient's previous gains in therapy disappear. Restoration of such functions as bowel training are essential to the total care of the stroke patient. Nursing can help reestablish regular bowel patterns that match closely with the prestroke status.[45]

Psychologically, the stroke patient must come to some terms with the disability, and his or her inevitable depression must be treated. The difficult struggle of the person is sometimes interpreted as irritability and cantankerousness. Individual therapy is indicated if available, but group techniques can be quite useful.[46] Socialization can be coupled with exercise (for example, use of exercise pulley for arms and access to parallel bars), games (such as throwing darts), and exercise to music. Patients are also encouraged to eat and chat together. Reading and discussion are valuable. Patient participation in the planning of therapy is beneficial. It is encouraging that in 1975 the first decline in the death rate from strokes occurred, the result of research and better care.

HEARING AND VISUAL IMPAIRMENTS

Perceptual impairments, especially hearing loss, are of great import to older people.[47] As we have stated repeatedly, comprehensive evaluation is crucial.[48] When perceptual deficiencies are found, the mental health worker must consult with appropriate specialists in an endeavor to provide prosthetic help. Institutionalized older patients in mental hospitals and nursing homes are likely to be neglected in these respects. The attitude may be that "it hardly matters." Burnside[49] recommends "blindwalks" for sensitizing treatment personnel to the experience of visual deficits. Staff members are blindfolded and then led through various tasks. Cotton in their ears gives them an added experience of hearing loss.

Those who are hard of hearing are often embarrassed, depressed, isolated, and suspicious—sometimes to the point of being paranoid. These feelings, trends, or states must be dealt with. The deaf person is also frequently embarrassed over the hearing aid, and this concern, too, must be resolved.

Both the hard-of-hearing and those with visual problems[50] benefit from individual and group therapy. A sense of active aid and the elimination of isolation are key components in the care of those with perceptual deficits. There are special efforts that can be made such as the teaching of Braille to the totally blind and the provision of large-type newspapers (for example, *The New York Times*) and cookbooks for the visually impaired. Volunteer readers should be available, and "talking books" recorded on records or tape are useful.[51]

---

[48] Testing should be obtained at a local hearing society or be done by a specialist in otolaryngology or audiology. The American Speech and Hearing Association has 3,600 audiologist members. One must be careful of "testing" by hearing aid salespeople; fraud is all too common. Both hearing and the hearing aid must be periodically checked. It must be remembered that hearing aids do not fully restore natural hearing, and it takes time to accommodate to an aid because of the background noise, etc.

[49] For a sensitive and practical article on blindness and aging, see Burnside, I.M.: A nurse's perspective: blindness in long-term care facilities. In New outlook for the blind, New York, 1974, American Foundation for the Blind, pp. 145-150.

[50] The American Foundation for the Blind, Inc., 15 W. 16th St., New York, N.Y. 10011, draws attention to needs and stimulates research and action nationally and locally in behalf of the older blind person.

[51] For information on talking books, contact the National Library Service, Library of Congress, Washington, D.C. 20540, toll-free telephone (800)424-9100.

---

[44] Adams, G.F., and Hurwitz, L.J.: Mental barriers to recovery from strokes, Lancet **2:**533-537, 1963.

[45] O'Brien, M.T., and Pallett, P.J.: Total care of the stroke patient, Boston, 1978, Little, Brown & Co.

[46] Bier, R.: The nurse's management of the aged dependent patient, ANA Regional Clinical Conference **6:**16-23, 1965.

[47] Schow, R.L., Christenson, J.M., Hutchinson, J.M., and Nerbonne, M.A.: Communication disorders of the aged, Baltimore, 1978, University Park Press.

A new technology is being perfected by which record grooves can be imprinted on a printed page. The blind reader will then be able to pass a microphonograph across a page and hear the voice of the person whose quotation he or she is reading. Seeing-eye dogs and walking canes are available for the visually impaired.

The hard-of-hearing may take courses in lipreading at schools such as the Institute of Lifetime Learning of the American Association of Retired Persons–National Retired Teachers Association. Sometimes older people themselves find ingenious solutions to their hearing problems. Dr. J.J. Groen, a distinguished internist from the Netherlands, visited the National Institute on Aging in 1977, demonstrating the large apparatus that he had assembled to compensate for the severe hearing impairment that he had developed at about age 65. He noted that expecting excellent results from a miniaturized hearing aid is as unrealistic as anticipating fine reception from a tiny transistor radio. Groen's apparatus—which resembles that used in some schools for the deaf—includes an excellent and prominent set of earphones, a hand-held microphone that can be positioned as needed, and an adjustable high-quality amplifier. Groen gives the appearance of an aggressive television interviewer as he engages people in conversation in his enthusiastic and forthright manner. He stated that his bulky but effective apparatus totally corrects his hearing defect in most situations.

Perhaps only 45% of the hearing impaired can benefit from hearing aids, although hearing aid salespeople frequently indicate a higher likelihood of response. About 3 million Americans use hearing aids of the more conventional kind, choosing from about 1,200 different available models. Hearing aids, long associated with a dismal record of usefulness and even outright fraud, are now regulated under the Medical Devices Amendments to the Food, Drug and Cosmetic Act (Public Law 494-295). As of August 15, 1977, under regulations of the Food and Drug Administration, hearing aids may be sold only to people who have had a medical evaluation of their hearing loss unless the examination is specifically waived by the purchaser. The evaluation must have taken place within 6 months before the purchase of the hearing aid.

The high price of hearing aids is less easy to regulate. The Department of Health, Education and Welfare's Task Force on Hearing Aids reported that in 1980 the costs of parts and labor for a hearing aid selling for $350 retail were $75. This represents a 200% to 300% markup for the dealer, over the $80 to $140 he pays the manufacturer.

New prosthetic developments are occurring that will be useful to older persons; for example, a hearing aid ear mold designed with an attached handle to make it more manageable for persons with limited finger dexterity.[52] As another example, the American Humane Society is now training dogs to serve as "hearing dogs," analogous to seeing-eye dogs.[53] These animals signal to their owners to indicate such events as a sounding alarm, a ringing telephone or doorbell, an alarm clock, or a honking car.[54] Hearing dogs are not a good idea in a household where some persons can hear, since hearing persons will invariably do the tasks that the hearing dog is trained to perform.

PAIN

Chronic pain, a physical, psychological, and social state, is conventionally defined as having persisted 6 months or more. It is distinguished from acute pain, which is nature's warning system. The discovery of opiate-binding sites (receptors) in the brain in 1973 and of endorphins (morphine-like substances manufactured by the brain) in 1975 has moved forward fundamental research in both pain and neurobiology. The emergence of pain clinics, 295 in 1979, to help deal with the complex common problem of chronic pain has also been welcome and long overdue. (There is now an American Pain Society.) At such clinics various therapies—acupuncture, transcutaneous electrical

---

[52] Navarro, M.R.: An earmold for the geriatric patient, Journal of Speech and Hearing Disorders 42:44-46, 1977.

[53] For information, contact Hearing Dogs, Inc., 5901 E. 89th Ave., Henderson, Colo. 80640, telephone (303) 287-3277.

[54] Crowley, S.: Man's best friend provides an ear to the world for the deaf, The Washington Post, Feb. 8, 1979.

stimulation, exercise, psychotherapy, family counseling, and hypnosis—are applied rather than pharmacological approaches alone, which, like surgical interventions, have been disappointing. Experimental efforts to lessen pain include insertion of electrodes into the patient's brain to stimulate the secretion of enkephalins or endorphins, the brain's own "opiates." Nerve blocks, neurosurgery, and new drugs are other techniques. For older people, and especially those who are in the very last days of life, it is important to provide effective, prompt relief of pain and any other discomforts without excessive preoccupation with the potentiality of addiction. Nonetheless the search for an effective nonaddictive analgesic continues.

In addition to its own suffering, pain brings with it anxiety and frequently depression. Chronic malignant pain often requires strong analgesics and certainly consistent emotional and physical support and comfort. Both chronic malignant and benign pain sufferers may also find relief through the use of psychotropic drugs—especially the benzodiazepines and other antianxiety drugs, the phenothiazines, and the tricyclic antidepressants. We described some of the benefits, hazards, and indications for these drugs earlier.

The wise management of chronic pain requires an understanding not only of the effects of pain itself but of the psychological conditioning that can result from the way pain is handled by the patient and by medical personnel. If the patient receives medication only when pain becomes pronounced, he or she begins to learn that only the presence of intense pain will bring relief. If a physician sees the patient only when pain is prominent, then attention from the doctor becomes a reward for experiencing pain. To avoid such learned behavior, and to "decondition" those who have already learned it, Fordyce[55] and others recommend the following.

1. Pain medication should be given on a schedule rather than "as needed." Dosage can be reduced whenever the patient or doctor feels it is viable—but keeping on a regular schedule helps encourage the patient to concentrate on something other than "am I feeling enough pain to ask for medication?"

2. Contacts with the doctor and other staff should be on a regular basis rather than in direct response to pain. Contact should not stop when the patient begins to feel less pain. Discussions between patient and staff should focus on subjects other than the pain.

3. Activity, including work, should be encouraged as an antidote to depression, anxiety, and even pain itself. But rest periods should not come just before an upsurge in pain is anticipated, so rest does not become equated with pain.

4. Patients should be encouraged to move away from focusing on pain as quickly and as often as possible. Some benefit from keeping progress charts of their "up" periods as opposed to "down" periods.

5. Finally the expression "Pain is drug-sensitive; suffering is not,"[56] reminds us that attention and care for the patient's feelings and state of mind mark the work of a truly fine physician and other mental health personnel when pain is the focus of treatment.

THOUGHTS ON NUTRITION

The most common causes of nutritional inadequacy in older people are poor dietary habits, poverty, and complications of underlying disease states, including alcoholism and depression; such disease states are an especially frequent contributor to malnutrition. Other diseases or changes associated with aging that may affect nutrition and thus contribute to malnutrition include decreased gastric acidity, biliary tract and pancreatic diseases, fevers (especially if prolonged), and cancer.

Calorie needs become less as one ages because of decreased activity, changes in the body's metab-

---

[55]Fordyce, W.E.: An operant conditioning method for managing chronic pain, Postgraduate Medicine **57**:123, 1973.

[56]Stead, E.A., Jr., and Stead, N.W.: Problems and challenges in the treatment of the aging patient, Disease-a-Month **26** (11), 1980.

olism that cause it to require less energy, and a decrease in cell mass, mostly because of a slow replacement of muscle tissue by fat. But actual nutrient needs for vitamins, minerals, and proteins have not yet been demonstrated to drop along with the lessening caloric need. The present Recommended Dietary Allowances (the government's standards for daily nutritional requirements) for persons age 50 and beyond are extrapolated from those for younger adults.[57] It may be that older people have to be more careful about their food in order to get the same amount of nutrients in a lesser amount of food. The need for protein is at least as great in the elderly as it is in younger age groups.

In fact, since older people experience a decline in digestive secretions, in intestinal absorption of calcium and perhaps of other minerals and vitamins, and in the activity of some enzymes, *more* protein, vitamins, and minerals—not less or the same amount—may be necessary.

Osteoporosis and periodontal disease (loose teeth) may in part be caused by a faulty calcium and phosphorus balance. (Carbonated soft drinks should be avoided because of their high phosphoric acid content.) One gram of calcium a day is recommended. Iron deficiency anemia is common, and 18 mg of iron daily in ferrous (absorbable) form are recommended. Fortified cereals and red meat are good sources. The use of cast-iron cookware will add iron to the daily diet. Drinking a high-acid beverage like orange juice while eating iron-rich food or taking iron supplements will increase the body's absorption of iron.

Vitamin B deficiencies affect the nervous system and may cause a certain amount of mental confusion in some older people. A balanced diet rich in whole grains and low-fat dairy products provides these nutrients. An inexpensive supplement in the form of brewers' yeast or special yeasts grown for human consumption may be taken.

Deficiencies of the fat-soluble vitamins A, D, and E are frequently a result of eating a diet very low in fat and high in soft foods, such as buns, pastry, cereals, and baby foods.

In dealing with older patients, the physician will have to work with complex dietary prescriptions for various medical problems. He or she needs to know the practical limits of compliance by the patient, including how well motivated the patient is and the patient's ability to shop for and prepare a special diet. Vitamins, calcium, and iron supplements may be necessary for persons on low incomes or with chronically poor eating habits.

Much remains to be learned about nutrition for people of every age. It is not enough for medical science to content itself with teaching the "basic four foods" to the public. A good deal of research needs to be done on the short- and long-term effects (both therapeutic and detrimental) of the many food substances and food elements on the human body and its health and its diseases.

It must be remembered that in spite of much medical reassurance to the contrary, many mature adults are improperly nourished—whether out of necessity (inadequate income, etc.), habit, or lack

---

FOODS WITH HIGH SODIUM CONTENT*

Soups, dried and canned
Condiments
   Ketchup
   Soy sauce
Processed foods
   Canned vegetables
   American cheese
   Tomato juice
Dill pickles
Others (but lesser in amounts)
   Breads
   Cookies
   Cakes
   Breakfast cereals
   Ice cream

---

[57] There are no recommended daily allowances of nutrients specifically for persons over 65 and no data base on which to make such recommendations.

*Sodium is added not only as table salt but also as preservatives such as sodium benzoate, flavor enhancers such as monosodium glutamate, and leavening agents such as sodium bicarbonate.

of information. Cultural food habits (snack foods and "junk" foods, to name a few), chemical additives (preservatives, plant and animal growth stimulators, insecticides, pesticides, and herbicides), and food preparation (overcooking, overspicing— especially with salt [see the box on p. 387]—and the refining of flours and sugars) all contribute to a questionable national diet. An abundance of food should not be mistaken for high-quality food.

Scientists at the new federal laboratory at Tufts University, in cooperation with the National Institute on Aging, will be studying nutrition and aging. Studies will include examining the relationship of various nutrients in diets to length of life, using both anatomical and biochemical measurements. The elasticity of collagen, the relationship of rancidity of foods to gastric cancer, and the role of dietary fiber in the metabolism of foods, of dietary fat in helping produce cancer of the breast and colon and in producing atherosclerosis, and of salt in producing hypertension will be subjects for study.[58]

---

[58] The first and probably largest indepth national survey on health and nutrition was the Health and Nutrition Examination Survey (HANES I) conducted from 1971-1974 under the auspices of the National Center for Health Statistics. This was an extension of the Health Examination Surveys done throughout the late 1950s and the 1960s. Under HANES I, participants filled out an extensive questionnaire including nutrition and health history as well as taking part in a physical examination that included laboratory studies of blood levels of vitamins and minerals and a full battery of routine medical, radiographic, and laboratory procedures. About 21,000 persons received the medical history and nutrition questionnaire, while subsamples of this group received a detailed medical examination for specific diseases.

REFERENCES

Bartrop, R.W., Luckhurst, E., Lazarus, L., Kiloh, L.G., and Penny, R.: Depressed lymphocyte function after bereavement, Lancet **1:**834-836, 1977.

Berezin, M.A., and Cath, S.H., editors: Geriatric psychiatry: grief, loss and emotional disorders in the aging process, New York, 1965, International Universities Press.

Blumenthal, M.D.: Mental deterioration and family burden: some theoretical perspectives, paper presented at the Annual Meeting of the Gerontological Society, San Diego, Nov. 1980.

Cameron, D.E.: Studies in senile nocturnal delirium, Psychiatric Quarterly **15:**47-53, 1941.

Carp, F., editor: Retirement, New York, 1972, Behavioral Publishers, Inc.

Elias, M.F., and Streeten, D.H., editors: Hypertension and cognition processes, Mount Desert, Me., 1980, Beech Hill Publishing Co.

Gerber, I., Rusalem, R., Hannon, N., Battin, D., and Arkin, A.: Anticipatory grief and aged widows and widowers, Journal of Gerontology **30:**225-229, 1975.

Glasser, B.G., and Strauss, A.: Awareness of dying, Chicago, 1965, Aldine Publishing Co.

Gorer, G.: Death, grief and mourning in contemporary Britain, London, 1965, Cresset Press.

Jacobs, S.C., and Ostfeld, A.M.: The effects of illness and death of one family member on other family members: a review with some recommendations for research and medical practice, Yale University School of Medicine, Departments of Psychiatry and Epidemiology and Public Health, New Haven, Conn., 1979, commissioned by the National Institute on Aging.

Kastenbaum, R., and Aisenberg, R.B.: The psychology of death, New York, 1972, Springer Publishing Co., Inc.

Lopata, H.: Widowhood in an American city, Cambridge, Mass., 1973, Schenkman Publishing Co., Inc.

Mitford, J.: The American way of death, New York, 1963, Simon & Schuster, Inc.

Patterson, R.D., Abrahams, R., and Baker, F.: Preventing self-destructive behavior, Geriatrics **29:**115-121, 1974.

Policoff, L.D.: The philosophy of stroke rehabilitation, Geriatrics **25:**99-107, 1970.

Saunders, C.: Care of the dying, London, 1959, Macmillan Publishers, Ltd.

Sheps, J.: Paranoid mechanisms in the aged, Psychiatry **21:** 399-404, 1958.

Tichener, J., Zeverling, I., Gottschalk, L., and Levine, M.: Psychological reactions of the aged in surgery, Archives of Neurology and Psychiatry **79:**63-73, 1958.

Tolstoi, L.: The death of Ivan Ilych and other stories, New York, 1969, The New American Library of World Literature.

Weg, R.B.: Nutrition and the later years, Los Angeles, 1978, The University of Southern California Press.

Weitzman, E.D.: Sleep and aging. In Katzman, R., and Terry, R., editors: Neurology of aging, New York, 1981, F.A. Davis Co.

15

Old age and the future

The 1981 White House Conference on Aging and the 1982 United Nation's World Assembly on Aging indicate the increasing public concern for older people, not only for those currently growing older but also for those who will grow older in the future.

Anyone who faces with older people, especially those older people with disabilities, the frequent and often intense struggles of their daily lives wonders how so many of them keep alive the sense that new and good things can still happen. More remarkably, a number of older persons maintain a capacity for creativity until very late in life, in spite of physical and emotional vicissitudes. Goya, who was deaf, is an example.

The longer he lived the more frightful did that world seem—the more frightful, that is to say, in the eyes of his rational self; for his animal high spirits went on bubbling up irrepressibly, whenever his body was free from pain or sickness, to the very end. As a young man in good health, with money and reputation, a fine position and as many women as he wanted, he had found the world a very agreeable place. Absurd, of course, and with enough of folly and roguery to furnish subject matter for innumerable satirical drawings, but eminently worth living in. Then all of a sudden came deafness; and, after the joyful dawn of the Revolution, Napoleon and French Imperialism and the atrocities of war; and when Napoleon's hordes were gone, the unspeakable Ferdinand VII and clerical reaction and the spectacle of Spaniards fighting among themselves; and all the time, like the drone of a bagpipe accompanying the louder noises of what is officially called history, the enormous stupidity of average men and women, the chronic squalor of their superstitions, the bestiality of their occasional violences and orgies.

Realistically or in fantastic allegories, with a technical mastery that only increased as he grew older, Goya recorded it all. Not only the agonies endured by his people at the hands of the invaders, but also the follies and crimes committed by these same people in their dealings with one another. The great canvases of the Madrid massacres and executions, the incomparable etchings of War's Disasters, fill us with an indignant compassion.[1]

Goya once drew a picture of an ancient man tottering along under the burden of years, but with the accompanying caption, 'I'm still learning.' That old man was himself. To the end of a long life, he went on learning. As a very young man he paints like the feeble eclectics who were his masters. The first signs of power and freshness and originality appear in the cartoons for the tapestries of which the earliest were executed when he was thirty. As a portraitist, however, he achieves nothing of outstanding interest until he is almost forty. But by that time he really knows what he's after, and during the second forty years of his life he moves steadily forward towards the consummate technical achievements, in oils, of the *Pinturas Negras,* and in etching, of the *Desastres* and the *Disparates*. Goya's is a stylistic growth away from restraint and into freedom, away from timidity and into expressive boldness.[2]

---

[1] Huxley, A.: Foreword. In The complete etchings of Goya, New York, 1943, Crown Publishers, p. 10.
[2] Huxley, A.: Ibid, pp. 14-15.

Personal creativity is a little-understood but greatly admired (if recognized) phenomenon. But even though we do not know how to "produce" creative people or to provide "specific" conditions to nuture them, we are aware of the general amalgam of biology, personality, and culture that allows creativity to thrive. Goya, for example, was able to work in spite of his deafness, but we can say with a high degree of surety that dementia would have brought even his genius and determination to a halt. All humans, geniuses included, sustain themselves through tragedy, pain, and disabilities with varying but eventually limited degrees of success. There are individual threshold points beyond which persons can no longer function effectively and the accumulated losses of old age begin to take their toll. It is recognized that there can be great variations in personal reactions to any change, loss, or disability, but if the impact of these events is severe, long-lasting, or chronic enough, individuality is erased and a fairly predictable response occurs.

Consequently, the problem we are most interested in is not how to produce creative older people but rather how not to inhibit them. And our concern is not merely with genius but with the creative potential in each human being for a meaningful and satisfying life.

ABKHASIA—A SHANGRI-LA FOR OLDER PERSONS?

We have available to us a few existent cultures that appear to have created conditions favorable for a desirable and extended old age. Natives in the village of Tamish and elsewhere in the Soviet Republic of Abkhasia are reported to live unusually long lives, in good health and with enjoyment. Abkhasia is a subtropical land on its coast along the Black Sea and alpine up to the main range of the Caucasus Mountains. The 100,000 Abkhasians, most of whom are farmers, have ancestors going back 1,000 years on the same soil. Various studies support the general claim of greater longevity, lower prevalence of arteriosclerosis, and little cancer among Abkhasians.

Abkhasians do not use euphemisms for the elderly (they are simply called long living); nor do they "retire." One does what one is capable of doing until the end, and that is often a surprising amount. Most work regularly and have good eyesight, good teeth, and an erect posture. Sexual potency and libido is retained by many of the men after age 70, and a number of the women menstruate until age 55. The Abkhasians exercise regularly, taking long walks and swimming in mountain streams. Work and diet are believed to be key elements in their good health; they eat slowly, have a low caloric intake, eat relatively little meat and rarely eggs, salt, or sugar. Few smoke tobacco, and alcohol consumption is modest.

Benet[3] was impressed by "the high degree of integration in their lives, the sense of group identity that gives each individual an unshaken feeling of personal security and continuity. The sense of continuity in both their personal and national lives is what anthropologists would call their spatial and temporal integration. . . . Their spatial integration is in their kinship structure. . . ." Older people are valued for their transmission of traditions, mediation of disputes, and knowledge of farming, among other things; and with increasing age comes increasing prestige, so much so that people are inclined to exaggerate their age.

The rural existence of Abkhasia appears like a flower under glass, protected by geography and circumstance from industrialization and change. But in the United States there are pockets of cultures where older people live well and proudly. Guttman describes the older Navajo men from the remote Rainbow Plateau and Navajo Mountain regions.

I found many Navajo of great ego integrity. . . . Typically, we found these men still on horseback, herding sheep and dryfarming their cornfields. Their faces are relatively unlined, their bodies tend to be lean, their manner is open and expansive and they tend to deny

---

[3] Benet, S.: Abkhasians: the long living people of the Caucasus, New York, 1974, Holt, Rinehart & Winston. See also Benet, S.: How to live to be 100, New York, 1976, The Dial Press. For a contrasting view see Soviet dissident and scientist Zhores Medvedev: Caucasus and Altay longevity: a biological or social problem? The Gerontologist **14:**381-387, 1974.

Three generations of women in a Guatemalan family.

Photo by Robert N. Butler.

physical limitations. They often have much younger wives, and father children with them. . . . Longevity seems to go hand in hand with Navajo traditionalism and with . . . defiant refusal to accept a victim's fate. . . . The remote traditional society seems to breed a high proportion of these ageless veterans.[4]

Other significant anthropological studies involving old age include Leo Simmons' examination of 71 different primitive cultures, Margaret Clark and Barbara Andersons' efforts, and D.W. Plath on Japan.[5]

Important historical studies shed light on the status of older people from the colonial beginnings of the United States and include books by Fischer, Achenbaum, and Harevan. There is disagreement over the extent of ageism in the early life of America, Fischer[6] reports that older persons enjoyed a higher status; Achenbaum[7] suggests this was not true of the masses.

Transcultural studies can teach both the universal aspects of the aging experience and the variations experienced by the elders of each group. Already, in comparing the American national attitudes with the Abkhasian and Navajo cultures, it is clear that we have not yet established roles of substance and purpose for the old. We isolate the realities of aging and death and deny ourselves the opportunity to build up the joyful, creative, and gen-

[4] Guttman, D.L.: The country of old men: cross-cultural studies of the psychology of later life, Occasional Papers in Gerontology, vol. 5, Institute of Gerontology, Ann Arbor, 1969, The University of Michigan–Wayne State University Press.

[5] Clark, M., and Anderson, B.: Culture and aging, Springfield, Ill., 1967, Charles C Thomas, Publisher; Plate, D.W.: Ecstasy years—old age in Japan, Pacific Years **46:**421-428, 1973; and Plath, D.W.: The after years. In Cowgill, D.O., and Holmes, L.D., editors: Aging and modernization, New York, 1972, Appleton-Century-Crofts, pp. 133-150.

[6] Fischer, D.H.: Growing old in America, New York, 1977, Oxford University Press.

[7] Achenbaum, W.A.: Old age in a new land: the American experience since 1790, Baltimore, 1978, The Johns Hopkins University Press. On a related point, there has been a discussion for some years concerning whether the elderly constitute a minority group or subculture. See Baron, M.L.: Minority group characteristics of the aged in American society, Journal of Gerontology **8:**477-482, 1953; Rose, A., and Peterson, W.: Older people and their social world, Philadelphia, 1965, F.A. Davis Co., and Streib, G.: Are the aged a minority group? In Neugarten, B., editor: Middle age and aging, Chicago, 1968, University of Chicago Press.

erative aspects of human existence. A major step forward would be the enhancement of age awareness—the creation of a sensibility that we are all enmeshed together in a complex life process with death as its end but with the potential for "life" all along the way.

PROBLEM OF HUMAN OBSOLESCENCE

The American social and economic system conspires to rigidify human status and function in life. People are programed and fixed early, and with advancing age—which means 45 on—they face the possibilities of technological, intellectual, and social obsolescence, if not extinction. Bold moves are in order so that our society can create a new flexibility within the individual and within the milieu in which he or she operates. People must be able to change and grow throughout the course of their lives, especially to keep pace with the rapidly changing twentieth century.

Retirement

Our present retirement practices emphasize the need for broad new socioeconomic arrangements. The cost of retirement, measured in dollars and cents alone, is enormous. In 1981 it is estimated that we paid out nearly $136.8 billion through Social Security and $16.7 billion to federal Civil Service retirees. This is only part of the total retirement bill of the United States. The human cost, in terms of personal indignity and loss of vital relatedness to one's community, is immeasurable. Retirement is still too often based arbitrarily on age rather than competence, health,[8] or desire to retire.

Social practices are often introduced into a society in response to emergency conditions; but when the emergency is over, the practice continues. For example, in connection with the severe job scarcity of the thirties, pressure was exerted on workers for earlier and earlier retirement[9] to open up jobs for younger workers with families to support. Thus early retirement, a practice begun with good intent, evolved into one easily abused, to the detriment of older workers. Social practices are frequently inaugurated without an understanding of their long-range human consequences.

There should be a radical reshuffling of education, work, and leisure throughout the course of the life cycle. At present these activities are concentrated in three distinct periods, during childhood, middle life, and later life. Existing financial supports should be reallocated as required. Taking both ends of the life cycle as examples, youth could be given more job opportunities in coordination with their education, and older people could be given greater access to both education and jobs. The important and productive middle-aged group would especially benefit from continuing education and increased opportunities for leisure, relieving them of the pressures of constant work.

Although trends in these directions are already evident, they clearly do not yet go far enough. In small ways the world of education, from public schools to universities, has moved beyond its traditional responsibilities to youth. Continuing education for professional people and for women in mid-life are two examples. Senior universities have been proposed for older people.[10] New train-

---

[8] Efforts to design functional measures of aging include Comfort, A.: Test battery to measure aging in man, Lancet **11:** 1411-1414, 1969; Koyl, L.F.: A technique for measuring functional criteria in placement and retirement practices. In Sheppard, H.L., editor: Towards an industrial society, Cambridge, Mass., 1970, Schenkman Publishing Co., Inc.; and Borkan, G.A., and Norris, A.H.: Assessment of biological age using a profile of physical parameters, Journal of Gerontology **35:**177-184, 1980.

[9] A review of the legal history of mandatory retirement can be found in Botelho, B.M., Cain, L.D., and Friedman, S.M.: Mandatory retirement: the law, the courts, and the broader social context, Willamette Law Journal **2**(3):398-416, 1975.

[10] Community colleges also are beginning to serve older people. Contact the American Association of Community and Junior Colleges, Dupont Circle, N.W., Washington, D.C. 20036. Some community colleges offer programs for second careers such as 2-year associated programs in gerontology, nursing home administration, human services, and mental health technology. Another interesting development is the founding of the Fromm Institute for Lifelong Learning, a "college" in the University of San Franciso, where retired persons attend seminars and lectures given by retired professors.

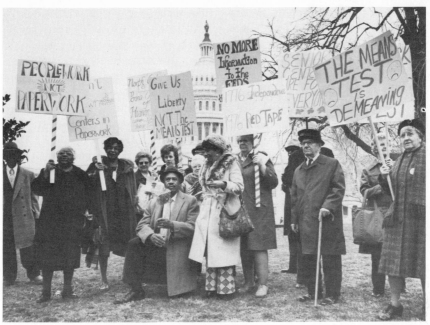

Photo by Patricia and William Oriol.

Protest by older persons against the "means test" in the social services program of Title XX of the Social Security Law.

ing and retraining for "middle starts" and "late starts" have been supported in some small measure under various state and federal laws.

With respect to work and retirement, we are beginning to see shorter work weeks, 2½- and 3-day weekends, and expanded annual vacation periods. In 1978, Congress passed amendments to the Age Discrimination in Employment Act of 1967, ending arbitrary retirement in the federal service and raising it in the private sector to 70, with a few exceptions. In part this was the result of the "civil rights" component of the "aging movement," in part a response to the growing public concern over the costs of Social Security and federal pensions. This gives older people much greater control over the timing of their retirement. But the enormous problems of technological and personal obsolescence and the desire of many for a changed and less rigid life-style remain largely unaddressed by industry, government, or the universities.

Preparation for retirement

Postretirement seminars and counseling are often more crucial than preretirement preparation. It is after being sent home with the gold watch that reality takes hold. The scheduled life is over. Income is halved. Husband and wife are together for the first time (other than on vacations) on a 24-hour basis. This *is* retirement—whether arbitrary, voluntary, or forced by illness, plant shutdown, company merger, or reorganization. The work "grind" is over, but the retirement "void" now begins. Many individuals have not been taught to use their time on their own. Leisure is not one of the major subjects in school, since art, music, and physical education are considered "soft" rather than substantial subjects.[11]

---

[11] An interesting example of retirement counseling can be found in Wolfe, B.R., and Wolfe, G.: Exploring retirement in a small group, Social Work **24**(6):481-484, 1975.

Some return to paid fulltime, parttime, or seasonal work, either in the same line of work they were engaged in previously or in a new area of interest. However, there are few available training programs for "new careers." Others do volunteer work but, unfortunately, there are no guarantees that such work will be commensurate with one's abilities. The entire area of preretirement and postretirement preparation is ripe for development into a much more sophisticated analysis of what older people want and what options are open to them, whether in education, leisure, or volunteer or paid work.

Poverty

It is incredible to speak of retirement roles and activities until basic subsistence needs are met. Poverty in old age is extreme in America.[12] First, to enjoy "leisurely retirement" one must have money, and some 50% of older people in 1979 had available $77 or *less* per week (often far less). So the monies needed to pursue hobbies, to travel, to visit children and grandchildren or exotic places are limited. Second, if the retiree does work, he or she will be penalized if more is earned than is "allowed" under the Social Security retirement "means test." (Those who clip coupons are not punished, for investment dividends do not count as earned income.)

Poverty breeds mental illness in old age. It can cause the malnutrition and anemia that directly result in mental impairments, which, often unrecognized, become fixed. Poverty erodes the spirit. It makes visiting, jobs, and voluntary work difficult or impossible through lack of transportation.

A compulsory national security system financed through general revenues, utilizing a graduated income tax (with no loopholes) as well as earnings-related payroll taxes, should be one component of a retirement system. Built-in escalator clauses of

two types should exist, one related to cost of living and the second to the general economic productivity of the nation. Supplementary to this should be a voluntary national personal-security system that is financed individually. For example, in 1962 the Self-Employed Individuals Retirement Plan (Keogh Plan) was passed. This permitted self-employed physicians, lawyers, businesspeople, and others to set aside up to $7,500 a year (in later amendments). Later, Individual Retirement Accounts (IRA) were open to all. Of course, there are other possibilities for individual savings. Thus collective and indivdiual providence would characterize income maintenance for the final period of life.

In early 1972 Senator Frank Church called on the Congress and the Administration to seize a "historic opportunity to translate the recommendations of the White House Conference on Aging into action—immediate and long-range." The Chairman of the U.S. Senate Special Committee on Aging, Senator Church, noted a few cost estimates on reforms that would help older Americans.

We could abolish poverty among the elderly for what it costs to run the war in Southeast Asia for just three months.

We could broaden Medicare coverage to include out-of-hospital prescription drugs for what we now spend for an aircraft carrier.

We could establish a comprehensive manpower program for older workers for the cost of one submarine.

Much, in fact too much, has been made of the concept of "the graying of America" as it has been applied to projections about the American economy. Public discussion of problems with Social Security, for example, have led to fears about the integrity of the Social Security system (rather than to imaginative, rational solutions to funding problems), to ardent discussion of the "dependency ratio" (the number of old and young who are dependent on the middle-aged), and to a general conviction that large numbers of older people will be a "burden." This frightens both young and old, leading to unnecessary intergenerational conflicts and to reinforcement of stereotypes about

---

[12] "The golden years—the tarnished myth" was the result of one study called Project FIND. This was sponsored by the National Council on Aging (NCOA), funded by the Office of Economic Opportunities (OEO), and conceived and directed by Jack Ossofsky, now NCOA Director.

the old. We might instead take pride in this new triumph of survivorship and see the new age distribution of our population—a new blending of the generations—as a challenge that may lead to a more mature society.

RESEARCH ON THE QUALITY AND LENGTH OF HUMAN LIFE

Simply extending human life for more and more years is folly and even inhumane unless the quality of late life can be improved. Yet until recently very little research in the United States concentrated either on the fundamental biological processes of aging or on the social and psychological supports for old age. Through 1975 less than 1% of all the research monies of the National Institutes of Health (NIH) had been spent on research in aging. However, the National Institute on Aging (NIA), one of the National Institutes of Health, was established by Congress in 1974 for the "conduct and support of biomedical, social and behavioral research and training related to the aging process and the diseases and other special problems and needs of the aged." NIA has emphasized extending the healthy middle years of life and increasing the quality of life. A major impetus for the establishment of NIA was the striking increase in both proportion and total number of older persons in this country.[13] (A recent study points to an acceleration in the number of extreme elderly.[14]) From fiscal year (FY) 1977 to FY 1981 the NIA budget has expanded from $15 million to $70 million and is now about 2% of the overall NIH budget. Moreover, NIA has advanced the field of aging in collaboration with other institutes at NIH and by encouraging geriatric medicine in medical schools.

Numerous contemporary theories of aging represent the continuing efforts of humans to discover and retard the mysterious decline of the body over a span of years. Will one of these theories produce a significant clue? Collagen cross-linking? Errors in protein synthesis? Autoimmunity? Gradual loss of information in the deoxynucleic acid (DNA) molecule? Decline in cell division? Free radical disruption of cell membrane structure and enzyme activity, with resulting formation of lipofuscin (the "age pigment")? Failure of hypothalamus in regulation of normal body rhythms and functions?

Progeria, an extraordinary rare disease that mimics in children some of the characteristics of aging, presents a compressed time-lapse motion picture of aging, which may give us clues.

The lipid (fat) peroxidation theory of aging is advocated by some: the unstable lipid portions of lipoprotein cell membranes are continuously undergoing spontaneous peroxidation through cosmic ray bombardment. Presumably, antioxidants such as the normally present antioxidant alphatocopherol or vitamin E retard peroxidation. Thus synthetic antioxidants are suggested as retardants to aging.

Research on specific diseases that affect older persons also shows signs of promise. As Seneca said, "Man doesn't die. He kills himself." Aging has yet to prove fatal, for humans find "natural diseases" to die from. The most common is arteriosclerosis, which in old age causes brain disorders and strokes as well as affecting such vital organs as the heart and kidneys.

Evidence implicating smoking as a factor in lung cancer, heart disease, and emphysema has been accumulating. There are data showing that heavy smoking is associated with skin wrinkling, probably because nicotine in cigarette smoke contracts small blood vessels in the skin.

In general, people of all ages should follow certain simple steps as a preventive measure against disease.

---

[13] As stipulated by Congress, one of the Institute's initial activities was the establishment of a research plan on aging for the U.S. Department of Health, Education and Welfare (now Health and Human Services). This plan, entitled *Our Future Selves,* was based on reports submitted by three panels of experts on biomedical research, on behavioral and social sciences research, and on service delivery research.

[14] Rosenwaike, I., Yaffe, N., and Sagi, P.C.: The recent decline in mortality of the extreme aged: an analysis of statistical data, American Journal of Public Health **70:**1074-1080, 1980.

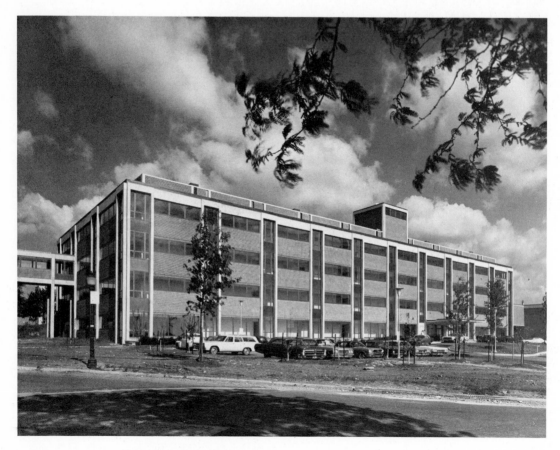

The nation's leading research center on aging—the National
Institute on Aging, Gerontology Research Center, Baltimore, Md.

Courtesy National Institute on Aging.

Research study of identical twins at ages 5, 20, 55, and 86 years.

Courtesy Lissy F. Jarvik, M.D.

1. Eat foods low in saturated fats and cholesterol
2. Stop smoking cigarettes
3. Reduce if overweight
4. Exercise moderately, regularly
5. Control high blood pressure
6. Have a medical checkup periodically
7. Keep alcohol intake moderate
8. Use medications only when necessary
9. Keep stress at moderate levels[15]
10. Eat a balanced diet
11. Learn and use health self-care principles[16]
12. Try to prevent accidents

---

[15] An interdisciplinary study that followed more than 204 men for almost 4 decades concluded that good mental health retards mid-life deterioration in physical health. Vaillant states, "People who cope with stress gracefully are still in good health at age 55." See Vaillant, G.E.: Natural history of male psychologic health: effects of mental health on physical health, New England Jounral of Medicine **301:**1249-1254, 1979; and Vaillant, G.E.: Adaptation to life, Boston, 1977, Little, Brown & Co.

[16] Belloc, N.B., and Breslow, L.: Relationship of physical health status and health practices, Preventive Medicine **1:** 409-421, 1972.

Present research will bring both technological and social changes in the future. The following examples are illustrative.

■ One happy spinoff from the National Aeronautics and Space Administration (NASA) is the application of technology to prosthetics development. NASA's knowledge is useful in many areas, from the telemetry of human physiology across previous barriers of distance to the powering of robot arms for the limbless or paralyzed. (In the United States some 400,000 persons are permanently disabled by trauma and 519,000 are partially or totally paralyzed by stroke.)

■ Religious thinkers joined social and physical scientists and physicians in the world's first institute organized to conduct research into the ethical and scientific aspects of human reproduction and development. The Joseph and Rose Kennedy Institute for the Study of Human Reproduction and Bioethics is located at Georgetown University Medical Center. One of the questions to which the staff devotes attention, pertinent to gerontology, is whether the physician is obliged to keep an aged person alive when his or her condition is hopeless.

Much is being learned about neurotransmitters in the brain by a technique called microiontophoresis, involving use of multiple-barreled electrodes that can be inserted deeply within the brain. Four fine tubes are used to deliver a chemical to a single cell, while a fifth tube records the cell's response as an electrical activity.

NEW LIFE-STYLES AND LIVING ARRANGEMENTS

■ Supreme Court Justice John Marshall Harlan insisted on constitutional and legal safeguards against intrusions on the home and the person to preserve "that spontaneity—reflected in frivolous, impetuous, sacrilegious and defiant discourse—that liberated daily life."

Older people need just such liberation in view of what one hears when one listens to them tell of their lives.[17] One senses immediately that much of human behavior is maladaptive. No one explains to the child that his life is the one and only life he has, that it is tender and short, that it must be carefully nutured, that it is easy to "blow it." No one tells the child that he is a unique possibility, that no one else will ever duplicate him. No one helps prepare him to be resilient and resourceful. People enter friendships, marriages, and work essentially unguided and, once entered into, these "choices" tend to be fixed. Yet one's life need not be traced out with an indelible pencil. Too many lives have been wasteful in comparison to what they could be.

---

[17] There are many programs that tape record the lives of older persons regardless of how well known such persons are. Such materials enrich knowledge and sense of history. As Emerson said, history is collected biography. As an example see Wigginton, E., editor: The foxfire books, Garden City, N.Y., 1972, Doubleday & Co., Inc. The material was collected and put together by Wigginton's high school students. The books are about hog dressing, log cabin building, mountain crafts and foods, snake lore, moonshining, and "other affairs of plain living" in the mountain communities of Appalachia. Wigginton wrote, "Daily our grandparents are moving out of our lives, taking with them, irreparably, the kind of information contained in this book, they are taking it, not because they want to, but because they think we don't care." See also Blythe, R.: The view in winter: reflections on old age, New York, 1979, Harcourt Brace Jovanovich, Inc. Blythe listened to the lives of villagers in Akenfield, England.

Newspaper reporters are fond of asking this question: "Would you like to live your life over?" Most older persons asked say no. Why do they say this? Is it that, as H.L. Mencken said, "No show is so good that it should last forever"? Is it too unbearable to consider seriously that one might have lived out one's life in another way(s)? Is it that, in many cases and even in the best of cases, no one wants to relive his life as it was lived? And, indeed, should anyone be content with his life?

It is striking to observe, in hearing older persons speak, that those who have led open, evolving, and changing lives are few. Rather, people lead lives of fixed roles and enforced identities. They also try to escape. Many lives have an infrastructure—hidden, secret, parallel *infralives* — maintained often with enormous expenditures of energy. Underground living may be seen in the weekday bourgeois who becomes a weekend hippie. Some hold close a secret self that, because it is revealed to no one, leads to the elaboration of a richly fantasied other life. For some, extramarital relationship(s) may be more crucial than marriage, the avocation more salient than the vocation, the lives of one's children more highly valued than one's own.

A second form of escape is through *pseudolives* —barren, stark, empty, nonprogressive lives with retreats from danger and risks. The identity is fraudulent. It is acting, role-playing. These are not even "lives of quiet desperation." The people who deny their sexual feelings, the people who continue to do what they no longer believe in, and those who pretend in order to preserve status and income are illustrative.

Third are those who do lead *"lives of quiet desperation,"* who usually do not have infralives, and who may be too honest or aware to allow themselves pseudolives.

Fourth are those who *disappear*. Some 100,000 middle-aged persons are said to disappear annually, not all permanently. Some try to start anew; some simply drop out. And some elderly people disappear too.

To obviate the necessity for these rather drastic

means of escape, there must be greater freedom over and against identity—freedom to rebel against the freeze. Today, to leave or switch careers in mid-life or to prefer not to climb the career ladder is regarded as suspect. At the same time, however, there are experimenters—individuals who are playing with change and are likely to represent life-styles of the future. Similarly, there are new, stable organizational forms and also anarchic, scattered, unstable forms. It is surprising how punitive society can be toward those who try out new life-styles. It is almost as though they threaten society itself; in reality they lend stability, as an outlet for frustration and creativity. Some older people, like young people, are living in communes or out of wedlock. Some are simply lifelong rebels grown old.

■ January 1972 found Jeannette Rankin of Missoula, Montana, 91, lifelong pacifist and activist, the first woman to win membership in the U.S. House of Representatives, living in a house with a dirt floor in her living room. She gave her money to the peace movement. She demonstrated what Emerson said of Thoreau, that he made himself rich by making his wants few. In 1968 at 87 she led the Jeanette Rankin Brigade of 5,000 women to Washington to protest the Vietnam war. She was quoted (*New York Times,* Jan. 1972) as saying that if she had her life to relive, "I'd be nastier."

Grandparentage: part of an ethic toward the future.

Photo by Myrna I. Lewis.

The idea of humans and technology as partners, not enemies, is important. Humans must change at rates similar to their technology. They invented it, after all. We need not inhibit or destroy technology or oppose scientific development. However, we can respond more rationally by controlling such development. One notes human beings' apparent inability to be decent housekeepers, to clean up after themselves, and to leave the planet the way it was when they came—even if they cannot improve it. There is humans' inability to feed and dress themselves adequately. They cannot control their needs; they greedily devour their environment at the expense of their fellow humans. They have not learned to limit their aggressiveness, their rapacity, and their violence. Nor have humans regulated their sexual drive and their re-

production. A new kind of education, continuing throughout life, is necessary to keep pace with change and provide a humane and life-centered focus. A new kind of ethic—to the future, to posterity—is necessary to help, however weakly, to rectify the balance against individuals' exploitation of their brief visit on this planet.

Inevitable social and technological changes—sometimes euphorically called progress—have brought greater possibilities of choice, diversification of living styles, and options. People—old, young, and middle-aged—have suffered long enough from knowing all too well who they are and being afraid to change.

REFERENCES

Binstock, R.H.: Interest-group liberalism and the politics of aging, The Gerontologist **12:**265-280, 1972.

Borkan, G.A., and Norris, A.H.: Assessment of biological age using a profile of physical parameters, Journal of Gerontology **35:**177-184, 1980.

Butler, R.N.: Toward a psychiatry of the life cycle. Implications of socio-psychological studies of the aging process for policy in and practice of psychotherapy. In Simon, A., and Epstein, L.J., editors: Aging in modern society—psychosocial and medical aspects, Washington, D.C., 1968, American Psychiatric Association.

Butler, R.N.: Why survive? Being old in America, New York, 1975, Harper & Row, Publishers, Inc.

Cain, L.D., Jr.: Age status and generational phenomena: the new old people in contemporary America, The Gerontologist **7:**83-92, 1967.

Carp, F., editor: The retirement process, Pub. No. (PHS) 1778, Washington, D.C., 1968, U.S. Government Printing Office.

Carp, F., editor: Retirement, New York, 1972, Behavioral Publications, Inc.

Clark, M., and Anderson, B.: Culture and aging, Springfield, Ill., 1967, Charles C Thomas, Publisher.

DeGrazia, S.: Of time, work and leisure, New York, 1964, Doubleday & Co., Inc.

Estes, C.L.: The aging enterprise, San Francisco, 1979, Jossey-Bass, Inc., Publishers.

Fries, J.F.: Aging: natural death and the comparison of morbidity, New England Journal of Medicine **303:**130-135, 1980.

Gruenberg, E.M.: The failure of success, Millbank Memorial Fund Quarterly: Health and Society **55**(1):63-64, 1977.

Gruman, G.J.: Cultural origins of present-day ''age-ism'': the modernization of the life cycle. In Spicker, S.F., Woodward, K.M., and VanTassel, D.D., editors: Aging and the elderly: human perspectives in gerontology, Atlantic Highlands, N.J., 1978, Humanities Press.

Harris, L., et al.: The myth and reality of aging in America. A study for the National Council on the Aging, Washington, D.C., Jan. 1975.

Havighurst, R.J.: Social change: the status, needs, and wants of the future elderly. In Herzog, B.R., editor: Aging and income, New York, 1978, Human Services Press.

Havighurst, R.J., Munnichs, J.M.A., Neugarten, B.L., and Thomae, H., editors: Adjustment to retirement: a cross-national study, Assen, Netherlands, 1969, Humanities Press, Inc.

Jung, C.G.: The stages of life. In Modern man in search of a soul, New York, 1933, Harcourt, Brace and World, Inc.

Kreps, J.M.: Lifetime allocation of work and income—essays in the economics of aging, Durham, N.C., 1971, Duke University Press.

Lehman, H.C.: Age and achievement, Princeton, N.J., 1953, Princeton University Press.

Levin, S., and Kahana, R., editors: Psychodynamic studies on aging: creativity, reminiscing and dying, New York, 1967, International Universities Press, Inc.

Maduro, R.: Artistic creativity and aging in India, International Journal of Aging and Human Development **5:**303-329, 1974.

National Institute on Aging: Our future selves; a research plan toward understanding aging, Washington, D.C., 1976-1977, U.S. Government Printing Office.

National Journal: The economics of aging: the economic, political and social implications of growing old in America. A National Journal Issues Book, 1978.

National Journal: Aging: agenda for the eighties. A National Journal Issues Book, 1979.

Neugarten, B.L.: The aged in the year 2025. In Aging in America's future: 2023 AD, 2024 AD, 2025 AD, Somerville, N.J., 1976, Hoechst-Roussel Pharmaceuticals, Inc.

Neugarten, B.L., and Havighurst, R.J., editors: Extending the human life span: social policy and social ethics, Washington, D.C., 1977, U.S. Government Printing Office.

Neugarten, B.L., Havighurst, R.J., and Tobin, S.S.: The measurement of life satisfaction, Journal of Gerontology **16:**134-143, 1961.

Palmore, E., and Jeffers, F.C.: Prediction of life span, Lexington, Mass., 1971, D.C. Heath & Co.

Randall, O.: Some historical developments of social welfare aspects of aging, The Gerontologist **5:**40-49, 1965.

Rosenfeld, A.: Prolongevity, New York, 1976, Alfred A. Knopf, Inc.

Saveth, E.: Utilization of older scientific and professional personnel, New York, 1961, National Council on Aging.

Scientific American on the brain (special issue), Scientific American **241**(3), 1979.

Shanas, E., Townsend, P., Wedderburn, D., Fritis, H., Milhoj, P., and Stehouwer, J.: Old people in three industrial societies, New York, 1968, Lieber-Atherton, Inc.

Simmons, L.W.: The role of the aged in primitive society, New Haven, Conn., 1945, Yale University Press.

Social Security Administration: Social Security programs throughout the world, 1971, Washington, D.C., 1972, U.S. Government Printing Office.

Spicker, S.F., Woodward, K.M., and VanTassel, D.D., editors: Aging and the elderly: humanistic perspectives in gerontology, Atlantic Highlands, N.J., 1978, Humanities Press.

Sunderland, J.T.: Older Americans and the arts, Washington, D.C., 1972, National Council on the Aging.

Tibbitts, C.: Aging in the modern world: a book of readings, Ann Arbor, 1957, The University of Michigan Press.

U.S. Senate Special Committee on Aging: Hearings (December 5-6, 1967), long-range program and research needs in aging and related fields, I. Survey, Washington, D.C., 1968, U.S. Government Printing Office.

VanGennep, A.: The rites of passage, Chicago, 1960, University of Chicago Press.

Veatch, R.M., editor: Lifespan: values and life-extending techniques, New York, 1979, Harper & Row, Publishers, Inc.

APPENDIXES

A

Sources of gerontological and geriatric literature

GENERAL BOOKS

Birren, J.E., editor: Handbooks: the biology of aging, the psychology of aging, and aging and the social sciences, New York, 1976, Van Nostrand Reinhold Co.

Birren, J.E., and Sloane, R.B., editors: Handbook of mental health and aging, Englewood Cliffs, N.J., 1980, Prentice-Hall, Inc.

Busse, E.W., and Blazer, D.G., editors: Handbook of geriatric psychiatry, New York, 1980, Van Nostrand Reinhold Co.

Eisdorfer, C., and Lawton, M.P., editors: The psychology of adult development and aging, Washington, D.C., 1973, American Psychological Association.

National Council on the Aging: Current literature on aging, published quarterly, Washington, D.C.

Poon, L.W., editor: Aging in the 1980's, Washington, D.C., 1980, American Psychological Association.

Riley, M.W., and Foner, A.: Aging and society, vol. I, An inventory of research findings, 1968; vol. II, Aging and the professions, 1969; vol. III, A sociology of age stratification, 1972, New York, Russell Sage Foundation.

Shock, N.W.: A classified bibliography of gerontology and geriatrics, vol. I, 1900-1948; vol. II, 1949-1955; vol. III, 1956-1961, Stanford, Calif., 1951, 1957, and 1963, respectively, Stanford University Press.

Shock, N.W.: Index to current periodical literature, published quarterly in the Journal of Gerontology through 1980.

MEDICAL AND NURSING BOOKS

Anderson, W.F.: Practical management of the elderly, ed. 2, Oxford, 1971, Blackwell Scientific Publications, Ltd.

Brocklehurst, J.C., editor: Textbook of geriatric medicine and gerontology, Edinburgh, 1978, Churchill Livingstone.

Burnside, I.M.: Nursing and the aged, New York, 1976, McGraw-Hill Book Co.

Exton-Smith, A.N., and Overstall, P.W.: Geriatrics, Baltimore, 1979, University Park Press.

Libow, L.S., and Sherman, F.: The core of geriatric medicine: a guide for students and practitioners, St. Louis, 1980, The C.V. Mosby Co.

Reinhardt, A.M., and Quinn, M.D., editors: Current practice in gerontological nursing, vol. I, St. Louis, 1979, The C.V. Mosby Co.

Rossman, I., editor: Clinical geriatrics, ed. 2, Philadelphia, 1979, J.B. Lippincott Co.

Steinberg, F.U., editor: Cowdry's the care of the geriatric patient, ed. 5, St. Louis, 1976, The C.V. Mosby Co.

PERIODICALS

AAGE Newsletter. Association for Anthropology and Gerontology, Department of Anthropology, University of Denver.

Age and Ageing. British Geriatrics Society and British Society for Research of Ageing, Williams & Wilkins Co., Baltimore.

Aging. Department of Health, Education and Welfare, Administration on Aging, Washington, D.C.

Aging and Work; A Journal on Age, Work and Retirement (formerly Industrial Gerontology), National Council on the Aging, Washington, D.C.

Aging International. International Federation on Aging, Washington, D.C.

American Journal of Nursing. American Nursing Association Co., New York.

American Journal of Public Health. American Public Health Association, Washington, D.C.

Concern in Care of the Aging. American Association of Homes for the Aging, Putnam, N.J.

Contemporary Administrator; the Long-term Health Care Magazine. Contemporary Administrator, Inc., Murfreesboro, Tenn.

Developmental Psychology. American Psychological Association, Inc., Washington, D.C.

Educational Gerontology. Hemisphere Publishing Corp., Washington, D.C.

Geriatric Focus. G.F. Publications, New York (discontinued).

Geriatric Nursing. American Journal of Nursing Co., New York.

Geriatrics. Lancet Publications, Inc., Minneapolis.

The Gerontologist. Gerontological Society, St. Louis.

Human Development (formerly Vita Humana). S. Karger, Basel, Switzerland.

International Journal of Aging and Human Development. Baywood Journals, Farmingdale, N.Y.

Journal of the American Geriatrics Society. American Geriatrics Society, New York.

Journal of the American Health Care Association. American Health Care Association, Washington, D.C.

Journal of Chronic Diseases. Pergamon Press, Ltd., Oxford, England.

Journal of Geriatric Psychiatry. International University Press, New York.

Journal of Gerontological Nursing. Charles B. Slack, Inc., Thorofare, N.J.

Journal of Gerontological Social Work. Haworth Press, New York.

Journal of Gerontology. Gerontological Society, St. Louis.

Journal of Long-term Care Administration. American College of Nursing Home Administrators, Silver Spring, Md.

Journal of Minority Aging (formerly Black Aging). National Council on Black Aging, Inc., and the North Carolina Citizen's Federation Inc., Durham, N.C.

Journal of Nutrition for the Elderly. Hayworth Press, New York.

Life-Span Development and Behavior. Academic Press, Inc., New York.

Maturitas. Elsevier North-Holland, Inc., New York.

Modern Health Care. Crain Communications, Inc., Chicago.

Modern Maturity. American Association of Retired Persons, Long Beach, Calif.

Modern Nursing Homes. American Nursing Home Association, Heightstown, N.J.

National Retired Teachers Association Journal. National Retired Teachers Association (NRTA), Washington, D.C.

The Network. Gray Panthers, Philadelphia.

Neurobiology of Aging: Experimental and Clinical Research. Ankho International, Inc., Fayetteville, N.Y.

NSCLC Washington Weekly. National Senior Citizens Law Center, Washington, D.C.

Nursing Care. Duaal Publishing Co., New York.

Nursing Homes. American Nursing Home Association, Lake Forest, Ill.

Nursing Outlook. National League for Nursing, New York.

Occasional Papers in Gerontology. Institute of Gerontology, The University of Michigan–Wayne State University, Ann Arbor, Mich.

Omega, Journal of Death and Dying. Baywood Journals, Farmingdale, N.Y.

Perspectives on Aging. National Council on the Aging, Washington, D.C.

Prime Time. 1700 Broadway, New York, N.Y. 10019.

Research on Aging; A Quarterly of Social Gerontology. Sage Publications, Inc., Beverly Hills, Calif.

Retirement Life. National Association of Retired Federal Employees, Washington, D.C.

Senior Citizens News. National Council of Senior Citizens (NCSC), Washington, D.C.

Social Casework. Family Service Association of America, New York.

Social Work. National Association of Social Workers, New York.

Therapeutic Recreation Journal. National Therapeutic Society (a branch of the National Recreation and Park Association), Washington, D.C.

Today's Nursing Home. McKnight Medical Communications, Inc., Northfield, Ill.

PAMPHLETS, BULLETINS, REPORTS, ETC.

Ciompi, L.: A comprehensive review of gerontopsychiatric literature in the postwar period: a review of the literature to January 1, 1965, Pub. No. (PHS) 1811, Washington, D.C., 1969, National Clearinghouse for Mental Health Information.

National Institute of Child Health and Human Development: International directory of gerontology, Washington, D.C., 1968, U.S. Government Printing Office. (Includes a list of persons specializing in geriatrics and gerontology by geographic area.)

Social Security Administration: Social Security bulletin, Washington, D.C.

U.S. Health, Education and Welfare Department: Directory, Medicare providers and suppliers of service, U.S. Government Printing Office, Washington, D.C. 20402.

U.S. House of Representatives Select Committee on Aging: Hearings and reports, Washington, D.C.

U.S. Senate Special Committee on Aging: Hearings and task force reports, Washington, D.C.

B

Organizations pertaining to the elderly

GENERAL ORGANIZATIONS

AFL/CIO Social Security Department*
815 16th St., N.W.
Washington, D.C. 20006

American Academy of Geriatric Dentistry
2 N. Riverside Plaza
Chicago, Ill. 60603

American Aging Association
University of Nebraska Medical Center
Omaha, Nebraska
Made up of scientists, it seeks to promote research in aging.

American Art Therapy Association
P.O. Box 11604
Pittsburgh, Pa. 15228

American Association for Geriatric Psychiatry
230 N. Michigan Ave., Suite 2400
Chicago, Ill. 60601

American Association of Homes for the Aging*
1050 17th St., N.W., Suite 770
Washington, D.C. 20036
AAHA represents the nonprofit homes for the aging— religious, municipal, trust, fraternal.

American Association of Retired Persons†
1909 K St., N.W.
Washington, D.C. 20006
Age 55 or above, retired to still employed.

American Coalition of Citizens with Disabilities, Inc.
1200 15th St., N.W., Suite 201
Washington, D.C. 20005

American College of Nursing Home Administrators
4650 East-West Highway
Washington, D.C. 20014

American Dance Therapy Association
2000 Century Plaza, Suite 230
Columbia, Md. 21044

American Foundation for the Blind, Inc.
15 West 16th St.
New York, N.Y. 10011

The American Geriatrics Society
10 Columbus Circle
New York, N.Y. 10019
The American Geriatrics Society, made up of physicians, has an annual meeting.

---

*Denotes steering committee members of the Leadership Council

†Denotes General Members of the Leadership Council of Aging Organizations, 1980-1981.

American Nurses' Association, Inc.
Council of Nursing Home Nurses
Division on Gerontological Nursing Practice
2420 Pershing Rd.
Kansas City, Mo. 64108

American Occupational Therapy Association
6000 Executive Blvd.
Rockville, Md. 20853

American Osteopathic Association
212 E. Ohio St.
Chicago, Ill. 60611

American Personnel and Guidance Association
2 Skyline Pl., Suite 400
Falls Church, Va. 22041

American Physical Therapy Association
1740 Broadway
New York, N.Y. 10019
   and
1156 15th St., N.W.
Washington, D.C. 20005

American Psychiatric Association
Council on Aging
1700 18th St., N.W.
Washington, D.C. 20009

American Psychological Association
Division of Adult Development and Aging (formerly Division of Maturity and Old Age)
1200 17th St., N.W.
Washington, D.C. 20036

American Public Health Association
Section of Gerontological Health
1015 18th St., N.W.
Washington, D.C. 20036

American Public Welfare Association
1125 15th St., N.W., Suite 300
Washington, D.C. 20005

American Speech and Hearing Association
10801 Rockville Pike
Rockville, Md. 20852
   3,600 audiologist members.

Asian and Pacific Coalition on Aging
1851 S.W. Moreland Ave.
Los Angeles, Calif. 90006

Asociación Nacional Pro Personas Mayores†
1730 W. Olympic Blvd., Suite 401
Los Angeles, Calif. 90015
   and
1801 K St., N.W., Suite 1021
Washington, D.C. 20005
   For Spanish-speaking elderly.

Association for Gerontology in Higher Education†
1835 K St., N.W.
Washington, D.C. 20006

Association for Humanistic Gerontology
1711 Solano Ave.
Berkeley, Calif. 94707

Canadian Association on Gerontology/Association Canadienne de Gérontologie
722 16th Ave., N.E.
Calgary, Alberta, T2E 6V7

Canadian Psychiatric Association
225 Lisgar St., Suite 103
Ottawa, Ontario K2P 0C6

Commission on Legal Problems of the Elderly
American Bar Association
1800 M St., N.W.
Washington, D.C. 20036

Committee to Combat Huntington's Disease
250 W. 57th St.
New York, N.Y. 10010

Concerned Seniors for Better Government†
1346 Connecticut Ave., N.W., Suite 1213
Washington, D.C. 20036

Continental Association of Funeral and Memorial Societies
1828 L St., N.W.
Washington, D.C. 20036

Council of Home Health Agencies and Community Health Services
National League for Nursing
10 Columbus Circle
New York, N.Y. 10019

*Denotes steering committee members of the Leadership Council of Aging Organizations, 1980-1981.
†Denotes General Members of the Leadership Council of Aging Organizations, 1980-1981.

The Forum for Professionals and Executives
c/o The Washington School of Psychiatry
1610 New Hampshire Ave., N.W.
Washington, D.C. 20009
The interests of this group have ranged from contemplation to active examination of public issues, including those affecting the elderly.

The Gerontological Society of America*
1835 K St., N.W., Suite 305
Washington, D.C. 20006
This professional society has an annual meeting and an international meeting every 3 years. It is made up of four components–biological sciences, clinical medicine, psychological and social sciences and social research, and planning and practice.

Gray Panthers†
3700 Chestnut St.
Philadelphia, Pa. 19104
Activistic group of older people who resent "stereotyping."

Group for the Advancement of Psychiatry, Inc.
Committee on Aging
c/o Mental Health Materials Center
419 Park Ave., S.
New York, N.Y. 10016

Home Health Services Association
407 N St., N.W.
Washington, D.C. 20024

The Institute of Retired Professionals
The New School of Social Research
60 W. 12th St.
New York, N.Y. 10011
This pioneering school also led the way in providing intellectual activities for retired professional people.

The Institutes of Lifetime Learning
These are educational services of the National Retired Teachers Association and the American Association of Retired Persons.

International Center for Social Gerontology
425 13th St., N.W., Suite 840
Washington, D.C. 20004

The International Federation on Aging
1909 K St., N.W.
Washington, D.C. 20006
Confederation of aging organizations of various nations.

International Senior Citizens Association, Inc.
11753 Wilshire Blvd.
Los Angeles, Calif. 90025
Endeavors to reflect older people of many nations.

Memorial Society Association of Canada
Box 96
Weston, Ontario M9N 3M6

National Association of Area Agencies on Aging†
1828 L St., N.W., Suite 404
Washington, D.C. 20036

National Association of Black Social Workers, Inc.
2008 Madison Ave.
New York, N.Y. 10035

National Association of Counties
Aging Program
1735 New York Ave., N.W.
Washington, D.C. 20006

National Association of Home Health Agencies
426 C St., N.E.
Washington, D.C. 20002

National Association of Mature People†
918 16th St., N.W.
Washington, D.C. 20006

National Association of Meals Programs, Inc.
924 14th St., N.W.
Washington, D.C. 20005

National Association for Music Therapy, Inc.
P.O. Box 610
901 Kentucky St.
Lawrence, Kan. 66044

National Association of Retired Federal Employees†
1533 New Hampshire Ave., N.W.
Washington, D.C. 20036
Represents and lobbies for needs of retired civil servants.

---

*Denotes steering committee members of the Leadership Council of Aging Organizations, 1980-1981.
†Denotes General Members of the Leadership Council of Aging Organizations, 1980-1981.

†Denotes General Members of the Leadership Council of Aging Organizations, 1980-1981.

National Association of Social Workers
1425 H St., N.W.
Washington, D.C. 20005

National Association of Spanish-Speaking (Hispanic) Elderly
National Executive Offices
1730 W. Olympic Blvd., Suite 401
Los Angeles, Calif. 90015
  Research Center
  1801 K St., N.W., Suite 1021
  Washington, D.C. 20006
    There are also regional centers in Miami and New York.

National Association of State Units on Aging*
1828 L St., N.W., Suite 505
Washington, D.C. 20036
  Information resources on state policies on aging. Represents and lobbies for state agencies at the federal level.

National Caucus of the Black Aged
1424 K St., N.W., Suite 500
Washington, D.C. 20005
  Advocates improving the quality of life for the black aged.

The National Center on Black Aged*
1424 K St., N.W., Suite 500
Washington, D.C. 20005
  Provides comprehensive program of coordination, information, and consultative services to meet needs of black aged.

National Citizens' Coalition for Nursing Home Reform
1424 16th St., N.W., Suite 204
Washington, D.C. 20036

National Committee on Careers for Older Americans
1414 22nd St., N.W., Room 602
Washington, D.C. 20037

National Conference of State Legislatures
444 N. Capital St., N.W.
Washington, D.C. 20001

National Council on the Aging*
1828 L St., N.W., Suite 504
Washington, D.C. 20036
  Research and services regarding the elderly.

National Council of Health Care Services
1200 15th St., N.W., Suite 402
Washington, D.C. 20005
  Represents commercial nursing home chains.

National Council for Homemaker–Home Health Aide Services
67 Irving Pl.
New York, N.Y. 10003

National Council of Senior Citizens*
1511 K St., N.W.
Washington, D.C. 20005
  Represents and lobbies for needs of the elderly. Membership at any age.

National Federation of Licensed Practical Nurses
250 W. 57th St.
New York, N.Y. 10019
  Educational foundation.

National Geriatrics Society
212 W. Wisconsin Ave.
Milwaukee, Wis. 53203

National Hospice Organization
1331A Dolley Madison Blvd.
McLean, Va. 22101

National Indian Council on Aging, Inc.†
P.O. Box 2088
Alburquerque, N.M. 87103

National Institute of Senior Centers
1828 L St., N.W.
Washington, D.C. 20036

National Interfaith Coalition on Aging
P.O. Box 1904
Athens, Ga. 30603
  Coordinates the involvement of religious groups in meeting the needs of the elderly.

---

*Denotes steering committee members of the Leadership Council of Aging Organizations, 1980-1981.

*Denotes steering committee members of the Leadership Council of Aging Organizations, 1980-1981.
†Denotes General Members of the Leadership Council of Aging Organizations, 1980-1981.

National Pacific/Asian Resource Center on Aging
The Alaska Bldg., Suite 423
618 Second Ave.
Seattle, Wash. 98104
    and
927 15th St., N.W., Room 812
Washington, D.C. 20005

National Retired Teachers Association (NRTA)*
1909 K St., N.W.
Washington, D.C. 20006
    Members once active in an educational system, public or private.

National Tenants Organization, Inc.
425 13th St., N.W., Suite 548
Washington, D.C. 20004
    Represents older people, among others, in public housing.

National Therapeutic Recreation Society
National Recreation and Park Association
1601 N. Kent St.
Arlington, Va. 22209

National Voluntary Organizations for Independent Living for the Aging (NVOILA)
National Council on Aging
1828 L St., N.W.
Washington, D.C. 20036

The Oliver Wendell Holmes Association
381 Park Ave., S.
New York, N.Y. 10016
    This group is interested in the expansion of the intellectual horizons of older people.

Retired Officers Association
1625 I St., N.W.
Washington, D.C. 20006
    Represents needs of retired military officers of the United States.

Retired Professionals Action Group
200 P St., N.W., Suite 711
Washington, D.C. 20001
    This action group was organized through Ralph Nader. Its efforts include investigative reports and class-action cases.

Senior Action in a Gay Environment, Inc.
Serving the Older Gay Community
487A Hudson St.
New York, N.Y. 10014

Sex Information and Education Council of the United States (SIECUS)
84 Fifth Ave., Suite 407
New York, N.Y. 10011
    Part of its program is to provide sex information to older people.

Southern Gerontological Society
c/o Gerontology Center
Georgia State University
Atlanta, Ga. 30303

United Auto Workers/Retired Members Department
8731 E. Jefferson St.
Detroit, Mich. 48214

Urban Elderly Coalition
1828 L St., N.W.
Washington, D.C. 20036
    Effort of municipal authorities to obtain funds for the urban elderly poor.

U.S. Conference on Mayors
Task Force on Aging
1620 I St., N.W.
Washington, D.C. 20006

Western Gerontological Society†
785 Market St., Room 1114
San Francisco, Calif. 94114
    Works to promote the well-being of older Americans.

ORGANIZATIONS CONCERNED WITH OLDER WOMEN

The Gray Panther's National Task Force on Older Women
6407 Maiden Lane
Bethesda, Md. 20034

National Action Forum for Older Women
2000 P St., N.W., Suite 508
Washington, D.C. 20036

National Organization for Women
425 13th St., N.W.
Washington, D.C. 20004

The National Women's Political Caucus
1411 K St., N.W.
Washington, D.C. 20005

Older Women's League
3800 Harrison St.
Oakland, Calif. 94611

Women's Equity Action League
805 15th St., N.W.
Washington, D.C. 20005

Women's Studies Program and Policy Center
George Washington University
2025 I St., N.W.
Washington, D.C. 20052
Has formed a coalition with the Congressional Women's Caucus to draft and promote legislation to benefit older women.

LEGAL RESOURCES FOR THE ELDERLY

National Senior Citizens Law Center (NSCLC)
1200 15th St., N.W.
Washington, D.C. 20005
and
1636 W. 8th St.
Los Angeles, Calif. 90017
The NSCLC is a national support center, specializing in the legal problems of the elderly poor, and is funded by the Legal Services Corporation, the Administration on Aging of the Department of Health and Human Services; and the Community Services Administration. Its principal function is to provide support services to legal service attorneys, and other publicly funded programs providing legal assistance to older persons, on the legal problems of their elderly clients.

ALZHEIMER'S DISEASE AND RELATED DISORDERS ASSOCIATION
32 Broadway
New York, N.Y. 10004
Purposes of the organization include coordination, education, family support, research/prevention, public policy, advocacy, and organizational development.

Alzheimer Disease Association
31 Meadow Park Ave.
Columbus, Ohio 43209

Alzheimer Disease Society
Wollin Associates
560 Sylvan Ave.
Englewood Cliffs, N.J. 07632

Alzheimer Support, Information, and Service Team (ASIST)
c/o University of Washington
RP-10
Seattle, Wash. 98195

Association for Alzheimer's and Related Diseases
5000 W. 109th St.
Bloomington, Minn. 55437

Chronic Organic Brain Syndrome Society
17th Floor, Allegheny Bldg.
429 Forbes Ave.
Pittsburgh, Pa. 15219

Family Survival Project
c/o Mental Health Association of San Francisco
1745 Van Ness Ave.
San Francisco, Calif. 94109

Massachusetts Society Against Senility
Dept. of Biochemistry
Boston University Medical Center
80 E. Concord St.
Boston, Mass. 02118

Societe Alzheimer
2 Surrey Pl.
Toronto, Ontario
M5S 2C2

NATIONAL CITIZENS' COALITION FOR NURSING HOME REFORM

Membership information, May 14, 1980: the Coalition has 73 membership groups in 25 different states.

California
ACLU Medical Complaint Center, Pacoima
Citizens for Better Nursing Home Care, Oakland
Citizens Who Care, Davis
Gray Panthers of the East Bay, Berkeley
Ombudsman Inc., Riverside
United Neighbors in Action Research Association, Oakland

Colorado

Concerned Relatives and Friends of Residents, Ft. Collins

Organization for Nursing Home Improvement, Ft. Collins

District of Columbia

Christian Communities Committed to Change

Washington Home Residents' Council

Florida

Nursing Home Hotline/Patrol, St. Petersburg

Illinois

Illinois Citizens for Better Care, Chicago

Lake View Evangelical Fellowship, Chicago

Indiana

Byron Health Care Center, Residents' Council, Fort Wayne

United Senior Action, Indiana Center for Urban Encounter, Indianapolis

Maryland

Maryland Advocates for the Aging, Baltimore

Massachusetts

Age Center of Worcester Area, Inc., Worcester

Cambridge and Summerville Legal Services, Cambridge

Cape Cod Nursing Home Council, Hyannis

Central Massachusetts Legal Services, Worcester

Consumer Advocates for Better Care, Leominster

Life is for the Elderly (LIFE), Boston

Massachusetts Health Care Coalition, Boston

Nursing Home Advocacy and Assistance Project, Holyoke

West Surburban Ministries, Newton

Michigan

Citizens for Better care (statewide); chapters: Big Rapids, Flint, Grand Rapids, Lansing, metropolitan Detroit, Port Huron, Traverse City, and Upper Peninsula

Citizens for Better Care Institute, Detroit

Metro Consumer Co-op, Detroit

United Auto Workers Retired and Older Workers Dept., Detroit

Minnesota

Friends and Relatives of Nursing Home Residents, Minneapolis

Minnesota Senior Federation, St. Paul

Nursing Home Residents Advisory Council, Minneapolis

Nursing Home Residents Advocates, Minneapolis

Mississippi

Jackson Gray Panthers, Jackson

Mississippi Mental Health Project, Jackson

Missouri

Kansas City Gray Panther Network, Kansas City

St. Louis Nursing Home Ombudsman Program, St. Louis

New York

Caring Community, New York

Coalition of Institutionalized Aged and Disabled, Bronx

Community Council of Greater New York, Ombudsman Program, New York

Friends and Relatives of the Institutionalized Aged, New York

State Communities Aid Association, Buffalo

North Carolina

Friends of Nursing Home Patients, Chapel Hill

Ohio

Lutheran Metropolitan Ministry Nursing Home Ombudsman Program, Cleveland

Toledo Area Council of Churches Metropolitan Mission, Toledo

Oregon

Benton County Nursing Home Task Force, Corvallis

Gray Panthers, Portland

Gray Panthers, Salem

Northwest Portland Gray Panthers, Portland

Pennsylvania

Coalition of Advocates for the Rights of the Infirm Elderly, Philadelphia

Community Concern for Nursing Home Residents, Mechanicsburg

Interfaith Friends, Wilkes-Barre

National Gray Panthers, Philadelphia

Northwest Interfaith Movement, Philadelphia

Pennsylvania Advocates for Better Care, Harrisburg

Rhode Island

RIsource, Providence

Tennessee

SAGA—Social Action Group on Aging, Nashville

UTAH

Citizens for Quality Care in Bountiful, Lake City

Virginia

Friends and Relatives of Nursing Home Residents, Richmond

Washington

Citizens for the Improvement of Nursing Homes, Seattle

Citizens for the Improvement of Nursing Homes, Spokane

Wisconsin

Nursing Home Consumers Who Care, Madison

Nursing Home Ombudsman Program, Madison

Wyoming

Advocates for the Care of the Elderly, Laramie

Concerned Citizens for Quality Nursing Home Care, Casper

C

Government programs for the elderly

Volunteer employment programs	Sponsor	Purpose	Address
RSVP (Retired Senior Volunteer Program)	ACTION	Funds for volunteer programs in public and nonprofit institutions; volunteers reimbursed for travel and meal expenses	ACTION* 806 Connecticut Ave., N.W. Washington, D.C. 20525
SCORE (Service Corps of Retired Executives)	ACTION, administered by Small Business Administration	Retired businesspersons advising novices in business	ACTION 806 Connecticut Ave., N.W. Washington, D.C. 20525
VISTA (Volunteers in Service to America)	ACTION	Volunteers for 1 to 2 years in community projects in United States with small salary to cover living expenses	ACTION 806 Connecticut Ave., N.W. Washington, D.C. 20525
Peace Corps	ACTION	Overseas service	ACTION 806 Connecticut Ave., N.W. Washington, D.C. 20525
Senior Environmental Employment Program	Administration on Aging and Environmental Protection Agency	Protection of the environment	Senior Environmental Employment Program 1909 K St., N.W. Washington, D.C. 22049
Senior Community Service Employment Program (SCSEP) "Project Agenda"	National Association for Spanish-Speaking Elderly	Community service	Senior Community Service Employment Program 1801 K St., N.W., Suite 1021 Washington, D.C. 20006
IESC (International Executive Service Corps)	An independent organization supported by government and nongovernment funds	Overseas service by executives	International Executive Service Corps 545 Madison Ave. New York, N.Y. 10022

*ACTION's toll-free number is (800)424-8580.

Continued.

413

Low-income elderly programs*	Sponsor	Purpose	Address
Foster Grandparent Program	ACTION	Provide relationship and care to orphans and mentally retarded, physically handicapped, or troubled children and teenagers in institutions for 20 hours per week at $1.60 per hour	ACTION 806 Connecticut Ave., N.W. Washington, D.C. 20525
SOS (Senior Opportunities and Services programs) Operation Mainstream programs	Office of Economic Opportunity	Service in programs to meet needs of older people: nutrition, consumer education, outreach, employment, information, and referral	Office of Economic Opportunity 1200 19th St., N.W. Washington, D.C. 20506
1. Green Thumb	National Farmers Union Green Thumb 1012 14th St., N.W. Washington, D.C. 20005	Conservation and landscape	Write sponsor or Department of Labor Washington, D.C.
2. Senior AIDES	National Council of Senior Citizens 1511 K St., N.W. Washington, D.C. 20005	Community service	Write sponsor
3. Senior Community Service Program	National Council on the Aging 600 Maryland Ave S.W. Washington, D.C. 20024	Community service	Write sponsor
4. Senior Community Service Aides	National Retired Teachers Association Senior Community Service Aides Project 1909 K St., N.W. Washington, D.C. 20006	Community service	Write sponsor

*Only persons over 60 with incomes below OEO (Office of Economic Opportunities) guidelines are eligible.

FEDERAL CONGRESSIONAL AND EXECUTIVE INVOLVEMENT WITH THE ELDERLY*

U.S. Senate Special Committee on Aging

U.S. Senate Subcommittee on Aging of the Committee of Labor and Public Welfare

U.S. House of Representatives

U.S. House of Representatives Select Committee on Aging

U.S. Department of Health and Human Services

Administration on Aging
Washington, D.C. 20201

The Administration on Aging (AOA), in the Office of Human Development Services, was created by the Older Americans Act (OAA) in 1965. The Act has been amended seven times in the period between 1965 and 1978. As first enacted it authorized funding under its Title III to support a state agency on aging in each state. Title III also provided funds for each state agency to initiate local community projects to provide social services to older persons.

In 1972, a new Title VII was enacted, which authorized funds for local community projects to provide nutrition services to the elderly. Emphasis was placed on serving older persons with the greatest economic need and on reducing the isolation of old age.

A second major change occurred in 1973. The amendments revised the Title III state grant program in order to provide for better oganization at state and local levels and to authorize the targeting of limited resources to priority services. The state agency was directed to divide the entire state into planning and service areas, determine for which areas an area plan would be developed, and designate an area agency on aging to develop and administer the plan in each area. The 1973 amendments also added a new Title V to the Act, which authorized the Commissioner to make grants directly to local community agencies to pay part of the cost of the acquisition, renovation, alteration, or initial staffing of facilities for use as multipurpose senior centers.

The 1975 amendments specified four priority services to be provided under state plans: transportation, home services, legal services, and residential repair and renovations.

The 1978 amendments contained renewed emphasis on the concept of a single focal point for service delivery within each community and on the expectation that each area agency, in carrying out its plan, would ensure that nutrition services and social services were fully integrated with each other. The 1978 amendments also enacted a new Title VI, Grants for Indian Tribes, which authorized a new program of direct grants from the Commissioner on Aging to Indian tribal organizations.

The legislative history of the Act has consistently stressed prohibition of means testing. For example, the Senate report on the 1973 amendments stated, "The Older Americans Act was never intended to operate as a welfare program in the sense that it does not contain a means test and its services are not restricted to those with incomes below the poverty line." The 1978 Conference Report emphasized that inclusion of a preference for those with the greatest economic or social need was not to be interpreted as a first step toward requiring a means test for programs under the Act.

Implementation of the OAA has produced the following pattern of organization:

1. The state agency on aging has responsibility for (a) developing a state plan, (b) coordinating activities with other state agencies, and (c) acting as advocate for older people. There are 52 state agencies on aging.*

2. The state agency is responsible for dividing the state into planning and service areas (PSAs). There are 612 PSAs.

3. Within the PSAs, territory is divided into area agencies on aging (AAAs). These agencies have operational responsibilities similar to state agencies, and in addition they may offer services directly or indirectly. For example, they

---

*See pamphlet of charts compiled by the Congressional Research Service of the Library of Congress for the House of Representatives Select Committee on Aging: Federal responsibility to the elderly (executive programs and legislative jurisdiction), Washington, D.C., 1979, U.S. Government Printing Office.

---

*See The emerging aging network: a directory of state and area agencies on aging, compiled by the U.S. House of Representatives Select Committee on Aging. The directory lists 52 state-operated units on aging and 599 area agencies. It may be obtained from the Superintendent of Documents, U.S. Government Printing Office, Washington, D.C. 20402. The price is $3.

may operate a service such as an information and referral service, or they may fund a new or existing agency to provide this service. AAAs may be a local city or town, a multicounty or multiregional organization, or a single state such as Rhode Island. There are 573 AAAs.

Research is an integral part of the OAA. The Administration on Aging accepts grant applications from two categories of organizations: (1) national associations of officers of state, substate, or municipal offices responsible for programs supported under the OAA, and (2) national organizations representing elderly members of the following minority groups: American Indian/Alaskan Native, Asian/Pacific, Black, and Hispanic. Areas of research include (1) needs assessment, (2) evaluation of programs, (3) mission-related policy research, (4) information gathering, (5) demonstrations, and (6) service programs.

Social Security Administration
Baltimore, Md. 21235
The Social Security Administration provides services through district and branch offices and teleservice centers. Contact any office for free publications on Social Security, Supplemental Security Income, and Medicare.

National Institute on Aging
National Institutes of Health
Bethesda, Md. 20205

Alcohol, Drug Abuse, and Mental Health
Administration (ADAMHA)
A government agency within the U.S. Department of Health and Human Services responsible for administering federal grant programs to advance and support research, training, and service programs in the areas of alcoholism, drug abuse, and mental health.
Center for Studies of the Mental Health of the Aging
   National Institute of Mental Health
   National Institutes of Health
   Rockville, Md. 20857

National Institute on Alcohol Abuse and Alcoholism
An institute within ADAMHA responsible for programs dealing with alcohol abuse and alcoholism.
National Institute on Drug Abuse
An institute within ADAMHA responsible for programs dealing with narcotic and drug abuse.

Federal Information Centers

With the federal government comprised of 125 different departments and agencies and with 132 different federal programs directly affecting older people, locating the correct source of assistance is difficult. Federal Information Centers (FIC) have been created to help. There are 38 FICs operating in major metropolitan areas throughout the country, and toll-free telephone connections to the nearest FIC are available in 47 other cities. In areas without local FIC access, long-distance calls or letters to the nearest FIC are welcomed. If the local telephone directory (under U.S. Government) has no listing for an area FIC, contact the Federal Information Center Program, General Services Administration, 18th and F Streets, N.W., Room 6034, Washington, D.C. 21415, for a list of FICs and toll-free telephone numbers.

Other federal government agencies involved with the elderly

Administration for Native Americans
Hubert Humphrey Blvd., Room 357G
Washington, D.C. 20201

Community Services Administration
Room 556
1200 19th St., N.W.
Washington, D.C. 20506

Farmers Home Administration
U.S. Department of Agriculture
South Bldg., Room 5420
Washington, D.C. 20250

Federal Council on Aging

Washington, D.C. 20201
The Federal Council on the Aging was established by the 1973 Amendments to the Older Americans Act of 1965 (P.L. 93-29, 42 U.S.C. 3015) for the purpose of advising the President, the Secretary of Health and Human Services, the Commissioner on Aging, and the Congress on matters relating to the special needs of older Americans.

Health Care Financing Administration

Project Grants Branch
Room 4200-C, Mary E. Switzer Bldg.
330 C St., S.W.
Washington, D.C. 20201

Internal Revenue Service
1111 Constitution Ave., N.W.
Office of Public Affairs
Washington, D.C. 20224
(202)566-4743
For a determination of whether a private pension plan meets minimum government requirements, local IRS offices can be contacted.

National Center for Health Services Research
Grants Review Branch
Room 7-50A
3700 East-West Highway
Hyattsville, Md. 20782

Office of Personnel Management
(formerly Civil Service Commission)
Retirement Bureau
Washington, D.C. 20415
(202)632-7700
The Retirement Information Office of the Office of Personnel Management gives general benefit information on civil service retirement and makes referrals to appropriate offices.

Pension Benefit Guaranty Corporation
202 K St., N.W.
Washington, D.C. 20006
(202)254-4817
If a pension plan is terminated or is about to be terminated, questions regarding payment of benefits can be obtained from the Pension Benefit Guaranty Corporation at the above address.

Railroad Retirement Board
844 Rush St.
Chicago, Ill. 60611
The Railroad Retirement Board has 80 district offices to provide information and to develop and process railroad retirement claims.

Veterans Administration
Central Office
Washington, D.C. 20420
(202)389-2356
There are over 500 regional offices nationwide to provide information related to veterans. Veterans Benefit Counselors can be called toll-free.

STATE AND LOCAL GOVERNMENT INVOLVEMENT WITH THE ELDERLY

National Association of Counties
1735 New York Ave., N.W., Suite 500
Washington, D.C. 20006

U.S. Conference of Mayors
1620 I St., N.W.
Washington, D.C. 20006

D

Grant programs and social services*

NATIONAL INSTITUTE OF MENTAL HEALTH GRANT PROGRAMS†

Hospital staff development

The hospital staff development program is designed to improve the quality of patient care in public mental health hospitals included in state systems of care, through inservice training for personnel. It encourages hospitals to provide staff development programs at the subprofessional and professional levels through a variety of courses such as orientation, refresher, and continuation training as well as through special courses for those who conduct the training.

Hospital improvement program

The hospital improvement program is directed toward improving the treatment, care, and rehabilitation of the mentally ill in the 302 eligible state-supported mental hospitals throughout the United States. It is specifically focused on use of current knowledge, in demonstrating improved services for patients, stimulation of the process of change, and development of relationships, with community mental health programs.

Research

The National Institute of Mental Health (NIMH) program of research in aging has the following goals: the development of knowledge about human behavior and adjustment to the aging process; the increase of knowledge necessary for the understanding, treatment, and rehabilitation of the aged; and the evaluation of services resources designed to care for the aged. Within this context many subsidiary objectives are included, such as exploring the effects of environmental conditions on aging in hospitals, nursing homes, and other settings and the effects of retirement; psychosocial studies of adjustment to aging; studies of the terminal stages of life; and experimentation with and evaluation of new methods of serving the aged in the community and in institutional settings. Through the support of basic behavioral science research, the program in aging encompasses studies in neuropsychology, personality and motivation, cognition and learning, and cultural variables that affect the aging process; these studies include such areas as tissue deterioration, biochemical change, perception, memory, and intelligence. Within the program of psychopharmacological research, studies are concerned with the use of psychoactive drugs with the aged and their effects on performance and memory. The program of clinical research supports studies relevant to aging.

Training

At present the major portion of NIMH training funds for aging is being used in support of training grants, including teaching costs and trainee stipends, fellowships, and research development awards. There is continued interest in the curricula of the mental health profession and in training new types of workers to care for the aged and provide preventive mental health services.

* For an overview on sources for funds in aging, see Cohen, L., Oppedisano-Reich, M., and Gerardi, K.H.: Funding in aging: public, private and voluntary, ed. 3, Garden City, N.Y., 1979, Adelphi University Press (originally a national guide to governmental and foundation funding sources in the field of aging, 1977).
†5600 Fishers Lane, Rockville, Md. 20852.

NATIONAL INSTITUTE ON AGING*

Individual research project and program project grants for support of research in the biomedical, behavioral, and social science aspects of aging. Training funds are available.

The National Institute on Aging (NIA) supports investigator-initiated research rather than directed research. However NIA does catalyze research program development in various promising areas of science through workshops and conferences and through program announcements that indicate areas where research is viable and needed.† The following are examples of titles of program announcements.

Pharmacology program

Behavioral studies related to diabetes mellitus

Nutrition in relation to health of the aged and the aging processes

Minority aging

Retirement and aging

Aging and bereavement

Geriatric medicine academic award (for which departments of psychiatry can apply)

---

*Bethesda, Md. 20014. The National Institute on Aging was established by the "Research on Aging Act of 1974." Congress declared that (1) the study of the aging process, the one biological condition common to all, has not received research support commensurate with its effects on the lives of every individual; (2) in addition to the physical infirmities resulting from advanced age, the economic, social, and psychological factors associated with aging operate to exclude millions of older Americans from the full life and the place in our society to which their years of service and experience entitle them; (3) recent research efforts point the way toward alleviation of the problems of old age by extending the healthy middle years of life; (4) there is no American institution that has undertaken comprehensive systematic and intensive studies of the biomedical and behavioral aspects of aging and the related training of necessary personnel; and (5) the establishment of a National Institute on Aging within the National Institutes of Health will meet the need for such an institution.

†See Summary of active program announcements, NIH guide for grants and contracts **8**(13), 1979. (Announcements appear in issues of the *NIH Guide,* available in the administrative offices of institutions of higher education.)

Senile dementia is a key priority of the NIA. The NIA also has intramural training programs, one of which is a psychiatric residency program in association with the Johns Hopkins University Medical School.

SOCIAL SERVICES: SOCIAL SECURITY AUTHORIZATIONS

Under *Titles I, IV, X, XIV,* and *XVI* of the Social Security Act:

The National Council on the Aging: Funding social services in model cities. A guide to Title IV, Part A of the Social Security Act, 1971.

The National Council on the Aging, Community Development, National League of Cities—U.S. Conference of Mayors (J.E. Bloom and R.H. Cohen) Social Services for the Elderly. Funding Projects in Model Cities through Titles I and XVI of the Social Security Act, 1972.

Title XX—See Burr, J.J.: Delineating the ramifications of Title XX, Perspective on Aging **4:**14-19, 1975. Title XX, short hand for Part A of the 1974 Amendments to the Social Security Act, a new law (P.L. 93-647), "grants to States for Services," that took the place of older legislation. The latter, "Grants to States for Services to Aged, Blind, or Disabled," was repealed, as were parts of Title IV-A, "Grants to States for Aid and Services to Needy Families with Children." The service program continues, as under previous legislation, to be essentially a grant-in-aid program, administered by states with federal matching funding of three federal dollars for each state dollar (75% federal, 25% state) with an annual federal ceiling of $2.5 billion.

Research under the Social Security Act

The Social Security Administration cooperates with the Social and Rehabilitation Service in administering research grant funds authorized by Section 1110 of the Social Security Act.

E

Training and education
in gerontology and geriatrics

EDUCATIONAL ASSOCIATIONS

American Association of Community and Junior Colleges—Programs in Gerontology
1 Dupont Circle, N.W.
Washington, D.C. 20036

Association for Gerontology in Higher Education*

An alliance of 80 colleges and universities that has compiled a national directory of educational programs in gerontology and geriatrics. Sponsored by the Administration on Aging. For information write to the Gerontological Society, 1 Dupont Circle, Washington, D.C. 20036; or Administration on Aging, Department of Health and Human Services, Washington, D.C. 20201

CENTERS AND INSTITUTES ON GERONTOLOGY (SELECTED LIST)

Alabama

Jacksonville State University
Research Institute for Longevity
Jacksonville, Ala. 36265

University of Alabama
Center for the Study of Aging
Tuscaloosa, Ala. 35486

*For information on schools offering course work in gerontology see The national directory of educational programs in gerontology, ed. 2, 1978, Association for Gerontology in Higher Education, 1835 K St., N.W., Suite 305, Washington, D.C. 20006.

California

Ethel Percy Andrus Gerontology Center
University of Southern California
Los Angeles, Calif. 94143

San Diego State University
Center on Aging
San Diego, Calif. 92115

Connecticut

University of Bridgeport
Center for the Study of Aging
Bridgeport, Conn. 06602

District of Columbia

Federal City College/University of District of
  Columbia
Institute of Gerontology
Washington, D.C. 20001

Florida

Eckerd College
Center for Studies on Aging
St. Petersburg, Fla. 33733

University of Florida
Center for Gerontological Studies, Programs
Gainesville, Fla. 32611

University of Miami
Institute for the Study of Aging
Miami, Fla. 33124

Illinois

University of Chicago
Committee on Human Development
Department of Behavioral Sciences
Chicago, Ill. 60637

Indiana

Ball State University
Institute of Gerontology
Muncie, Ind. 47306

Kansas

Kansas State University
Center for Aging
Manhattan, Kan. 66506

Kentucky

University of Kentucky
Sanders-Brown Research Center of Aging
Lexington, Ky. 40506

Maryland

University of Maryland, Baltimore
Task Force on Aging
Baltimore, Md. 21201

University of Maryland, College Park
Center on Aging
College Park, Md. 20742

Massachusetts

Boston University
Gerontology Center
Boston, Mass. 02215

Michigan

University of Michigan
Institute of Gerontology
Ann Arbor, Mich. 48109

Wayne State University
Institute on Gerontology
Detroit, Mich. 48202

Missouri

St. Louis University
Institute of Applied Gerontology
St. Louis, Mo. 63103

University of Missouri
Center for Aging Studies
Columbia, Mo. 65201

New York

Malloy College
Institute on Gerontology
Rockville Center, N.Y. 11570

New York State Psychiatric Institute
Geriatric Research Unit
722 W. 168th St.
New York, N.Y. 10032

SUNY at Albany
Institute of Gerontology
Albany, N.Y. 12222

SUNY at Buffalo
Multidisciplinary Center for the Study of Aging
Buffalo, N.Y. 14260

Syracuse University
All-University Gerontology Center
Syracuse, N.Y. 13210

North Carolina

Duke University
Center for the Study of Aging and Human Development
Durham, N.C. 27710

Ohio

The Benjamin Rush Institute
Applied Gerontology Research Center
636 Rose Bldg.
Cleveland, Ohio 44115

Miami University
Scripps Foundation Gerontology Center
Oxford, Ohio 45056

University of Akron
Institute for Lifespan Development and Gerontology
Akron, Ohio 44325

University of Toledo
Center for Studies in Aging
Toledo, Ohio 43606

Oklahoma

East Central University
Gerontological Institute
Ada, Okla. 74280

Oregon

Oregon State University
Program on Gerontology
Family Life Department
Corvallis, Ore. 97331

Portland State University
Institute on Aging
Portland, Ore. 97207

University of Oregon
Oregon Center for Gerontology
Eugene, Ore. 97403

Pennsylvania

Pennsylvania State University
Gerontology Center
University Park, Pa. 16802

Philadelphia Geriatric Center
5301 Old York Road
Philadelphia, Pa. 19141

Temple University
Aging Research Center
Philadelphia, Pa. 19140

Tennessee

University of Tennessee/Nashville
Center on Aging
Nashville, Tenn. 37203

Texas

North Texas State University
Center for Studies in Aging
Denton, Tex. 76203

Tarleton State University
Institute on Gerontology
Stephenville, Tex. 76402

Utah

Rocky Mountain Gerontology Center, Joint Program University of Utah
Brigham Young University, Provo, Utah 84602
Southern Utah University, Cedar City, Utah 84720

University of Utah, Salt Lake City, Utah 84112
Utah State University, Logan, Utah 84321
Weber State College, Ogden, Utah 84403

Wisconsin

University of Wisconsin
Faye McBeath Institute on Aging, Adult Life
Madison, Wis. 53707

FAMILY PRACTICE PROGRAMS INVOLVED IN TEACHING GERIATRIC COMPONENTS (PARTIAL LIST)

Center for the Study of Aging in collaboration
with Department of Family Practice
Duke University Medical Center
Durham, N.C. 27706

Department of Family, Community and Emergency
Medicine
University of New Mexico
Albuquerque, N.M. 87131

Department of Family and Community Health
University of Arizona
Tucson, Ariz. 85721

Department of Family and Community Medicine
University of Missouri—Columbia
Columbia, Mo. 65211

Department of Family and Community Medicine
University of Nevada—Reno
Reno, Nev. 89557

Department of Family and Community Medicine
University of Utah
Salt Lake City, Utah 84112

Department of Family Practice
College of Human Medicine
Michigan State University
East Lansing, Mich. 48825

Department of Family Practice
Division of Geriatrics
Southern Illinois University School of Medicine
Springfield, Ill. 62708

Department of Family Practice
Fayetteville Area Health Education Foundation
Fayetteville, N.C. 28302

Department of Family Practice
Louisiana State University
New Orleans, La. 70153

Department of Family Practice
Medical College of Georgia
Augusta, Ga. 30912

Department of Family Practice
Medical College of Wisconsin
Milwaukee, Wis. 53201

Department of Family Practice
Medical Unversity of South Carolina
Charleston, S.C. 29401

Department of Family Practice
University of Iowa
Iowa City, Iowa 52242

Department of Family Practice
University of South Carolina
Columbia, S.C. 29208

Family and Community Medicine
Milton S. Hershey Medical Center
Pennsylvania State University
Hershey, Pa. 17033

Family Medicine Program
University of Baltimore
Baltimore, Md. 21201

Family Practice Residency Program
Illinois Masonic Medical Center
Chicago, Ill. 60680

Geriatric Center
Family Practice Center
MacNeal Memorial Hospital
Berwyn, Ill. 60402

Geriatric Program
St. Joseph's Hospital and Nursing Home
Yonkers, N.Y. 10701

Program in Gerontology
Department of Family Practice and Community
 Health
University of Minnesota
Minneapolis, Minn. 55455

Texas Tech University
Lubbock, Tex. 79406

GERIATRIC PSYCHIATRY TRAINING PROGRAMS*

Comprehensive Gero-Psychiatry Training Program
Duke University Medical Center
Box 3812
Durham, N.C. 27710

Fellowship in Geriatric Psychiatry
Section on Geriatric Psychiatry
The University of Texas Health Science Center
Houston Medical School
6431 Fannin
Houston, Tex. 77030

Geriatric Training in Psychiatry and Psychology
Texas Research Institute of Mental Science (TRIMS)
1300 Moursund Ave.
Houston, Tex. 77030

Inter-disciplinary Training Program in Mental Health and Aging
Wayne State University
Detroit, Mich. 48202

McLean Hospital
Geriatric Department
115 Mill St.
Belmont, Mass. 02178

Post-residency Training in Psychogeriatrics
University of Pittsburgh
Western Psychiatric Institute
3811 O'Hara St.
Pittsburgh, Pa. 15261

Psychosocial Medical and Psychiatry for the Elderly
Illinois State Psychiatric Institute
1601 W. Taylor St.
Chicago, Ill. 60612

Tampa V.A. Medical Center
University of Southern Florida College of Medicine
Department of Psychiatry
13000 N. 30th St.
Tampa, Fla. 33612

---

*For most of these programs funds from the National Institute of Mental Health are provided for teaching costs and post-doctoral/postpsychiatric general residency stipends. Contact National Institute of Mental Health, Center for Studies of the Mental Health of the Aging, 5600 Fishers Lane, Room 18-95, Rockville, Md. 20857.

University of Washington School of Medicine
Department of Psychiatry
Seattle, Wash. 98195

GERIATRIC RESEARCH, EDUCATION AND CLINICAL CENTERS

There are eight Veterans Administration Geriatric Research, Education and Clinical Centers, five of which conduct research in areas related to mental health.

Centers	Research areas
American Lake/Seattle, Wash.	Senile dementia and related disorders
	Affective disorders in older persons
Boston/Bedford Division, Mass.	Mental performance and aging
	Anatomy and biochemistry of the aging brain
Minneapolis, Minn.	Neuroendocrinology and aging
	Psychological aspects of aging brain function
Palo Alto, Calif.	Psychophysiological studies of cognitive functioning
Sepulveda, Calif.	Mechanisms of memory formation and processing in the elderly

PREDOCTORAL AND POSTDOCTORAL STIPENDS RELATED TO THE BEHAVIORAL AND SOCIAL SCIENCES—THE NATIONAL INSTITUTE ON AGING

Dr. Jack Botwinick
Aging and Development Program
Department of Psychology
Washington University
St. Louis, Mo. 63130
Psychology—aging and development

Dr. Marjorie Fiske*
Department of Psychology
University of California
San Francisco, Calif. 94143
Human development and aging

Dr. Bernice Neugarten
Adult Development and Aging Program
University of Chicago
5730 S. Woodlawn Ave.
Chicago, Ill. 60637
Behavioral and social sciences—adult development and aging

Dr. Charles Parrish
Institute of Gerontology
Wayne State University
203 Library Ct.
Detroit, Mich. 48202
Social policy and aging

Dr. Warren Peterson
Institute for Community Studies
University of Missouri
Kansas City, Mo. 64110
Adult development and aging—social-behavioral sciences

Dr. K.W. Schaie
Ethel Percy Andrus Gerontology Center
University of Southern California
Los Angeles, Calif. 90007
Multidisciplinary—social, behavioral, and biological sciences

Dr. Charles Taylor
College of Human Development
Pennsylvania State University
S-102 Human Development Bldg.
University Park, Pa. 16802
Multidisciplinary—social and behavioral sciences

Dr. Harry Todd, Jr.
Department of Epidemiology
University of California
1320 Third Ave.
San Francisco, Calif. 94143
Anthropological gerontology

POSTDOCTORAL STIPENDS RELATED TO SENILE DEMENTIA—THE NATIONAL INSTITUTE ON AGING

Dr. Stanley Appel
Department of Neurology
Baylor College of Medicine
1200 Moursund Ave.
Houston, Tex. 77030
Biological approaches to senile dementia

Dr. Ivan Diamond
Department of Neurology
University of California
Third and Parnassus Streets
San Francisco, Calif. 94143
Molecular studies of aging in the nervous system

---

*Predoctoral stipends only.

Dr. Robert Terry
Department of Pathology
Albert Einstein College of Medicine
1300 Morris Park Ave.
Bronx, N.Y. 10461
Senile dementia —biomedical and behavioral aspects

Dr. F. Stephen Vogel
Department of Pathology
P.O. Box 3712
Duke University Medical Center
Durham, N.C. 27710
Senile dementia —biological approaches

RESIDENCIES IN GERIATRIC MEDICINE

Jewish Institute for Geriatric Care
Long Island Jewish Hospital
271-11 76th Ave.
New Hyde Park, N.Y. 11040

OTHER SOURCES OF INFORMATION ON CLINICAL GERIATRIC TRAINING OPPORTUNITIES

Clinical Geriatrics Training Sites Directory
American Medical Students Association
Task Force on Aging
P.O. Box 131
14640 Lee Rd.
Chantilly, Va. 22021

Geropsychiatry Training Program
National Institute of Mental Health
Center for Studies of the Mental Health of the Aging
5600 Fishers Lane, Room 18-95
Rockville, Md. 20857

V.A. Geriatric Fellowship Program
Medical/Dental Division (141 B)
Veterans Administration
Washington, D.C. 20420
(202)389-5171

Staff inservice education material for work with older people

RECOMMENDED FICTION (concerning later life, memory, time, aging, disease, and death)

In James Hilton's *Goodbye, Mr. Chips* (1934) the elderly protagonist reminisces in his room across from the school where he taught three generations of English boys.

Aldous Huxley's *After Many a Summer Dies the Swan* (1939) is a satirical novel. The hero is a California multimillionaire terrified of death. His physician is working on a theory of longevity. The novel ends in horror.

Georges Simenon's *The Bells of Bicetre* (English title: *The Patient*) portrays a powerful French newspaper owner who has a stroke that leaves him speechless and paralyzed. At first he is passive, with no wish to recover. His mind is clear; he views his wife, his doctor, and his own life with detachment. As his memories flow through his mind and he begins to recover his speech and movement, his mental attitude changes favorably.

In Muriel Spark's *Momento Mori* (1959) a woman's death and an anonymous phone caller who says "remember you must die" provoke a series of humorous adventures for a group of elderly English aristocrats.

Leo Tolstoi, in *The Death of Ivan Ilych* (1884), describes a Russian judge who learns that his wealth, status, and power are useless to him when he becomes ill. His painful disease and his death are merely inconveniences to his family and lifelong friends. A young peasant servant is his only comfort.

In John Updike's *The Poorhouse Fair* (1959) residents of an old folks' home put on their annual fair despite the well-intentioned mistakes of the new administrators and poor weather.

OTHER FICTION

Adams, S.H.: Grandfather stories, New York, 1947, Random House, Inc. (paperback).

Ashton-Warner, S.: Spinster (1959), New York, 1961, Bantam Books, Inc. (paperback).

Beckett, S.: Krapp's last tape (a drama) (1957), New York, 1958, Grove Press, Inc. (paperback).

Bromfield, L.: Mrs. Parkington, New York, 1949, Harper & Brothers.

Cary, J.: To be a pilgrim, London, 1942, Michael Joseph, Ltd.

Cervantes, M.: Don Quixote, part I, 1605; part II, 1615, New York, 1957, New American Library.

Chekov, A.: Uncle Vanya in four great plays, New York, 1958, Bantam Books, Inc.

Durrenmatt, F.: The visit of the old lady, 1956.

Hansberry, L.: A raisin in the sun, New York 1961, Random House, Inc.

Hemingway, E.: The old man and the sea, New York, 1952, Charles Scribner's Sons.

Ibsen, H.: The master builders. In Eleven plays of Henrik Ibsen, New York, Random House, Inc.

James, H.: The beast in the jungle (1903). In Fadiman, C., editor: The short stories of Henry James, New York, 1945, Random House, Inc. pp. 548-602.

Kaufman, G., and Hart, M.: You can't take it with you, New York, 1937, Simon & Schuster, Inc.

Lampedusa, G. di: The leopard, New York, 1960, Pantheon Books, Inc.

Mann, T.: The black swan, New York, 1954, Alfred A. Knopf, Inc.

Miller, A.: Death of a salesman, New York, 1949, The Viking Press.

Porter, K.A.: The jilting of Granny Weatherall. In Flowering Judas, New York, 1930, Harcourt, Brace & World, Inc.

Proust, M.: Remembrance of things past (1913-1922), New York, 1934, Random House (two volumes).

Richter, C.: The waters of Kronos, New York, 1960, Alfred A. Knopf, Inc.

Romains, J.: The death of a nobody (1911), New York, 1961, Signet Book (paperback).

Shakespeare, W.: King Lear (1608), Cambridge, England, 1960, Cambridge University Press (paperback).

Shaw, G.B.: Back to Methuselah. Collection of five linked plays: In the beginning; The gospel of the brothers Barnabas; The thing happens; The tragedy of an elderly gentleman; and As far as thought can reach, New York, 1947, Oxford University Press.

Trollope, A.: The fixed period, Tauchnitz editions of English authors, 1882, Leipzig.

Van Velde, J.: The big ward, New York, 1960, Simon & Schuster, Inc.

Waugh, E.: The loved one, Boston, 1948, Little, Brown & Co.

Wilde, O.: Picture of Dorian Gray (1906), New York, 1956, Dell Books (paperback).

ARTICLES ON FICTION

Loughman, C.: Novels of senescence. A new naturalism, The Gerontologist **17**:79-84, 1977.

Sohngren, M.: The experience of old age as depicted in contemporary novels, The Gerontologist **17**:70-78, 1977.

CURRENT PULITZER PRIZE–WINNING PLAYS

Coburn, D.L.: The gin game.

Cristofer, M.: The shadow box.

RECOMMENDED FILMS

Films are very important. Teaching films focus on diagnosis.* Certain movie films offer the subjective, human side of aging.

Feature films	Director	Year
The Last Laugh	F.W. Murnau	1924

The story of an old doorman demoted to washroom attendant. 60 minutes.

Goodbye, Mr. Chips	Sam Wood	1939

114 minutes.

Sunset Boulevard	Billy Wilder	1950

108 minutes

Ikiru (To Live)	Akira Kurosawa	1952

140 minutes.

Umberto D.	Vittorio de Sica	1952

Concerns an aging impoverished pensioner who considers suicide. 89 minutes.

Tokyo Story	Yasujiro Ozu	1955

The story of an elderly couple's last visit to their children, its disappointments, its sadness.

Wild Strawberries	Ingmar Bergman	1957

Concerns a 76-year-old physician who learns to love on the brink of eternity.

*Miller, P.R., and Tupin, J.P.: Multimedia teaching of introductory psychiatry, American Journal of Psychiatry **128**:1219-1222, 1972.

The Leopard	Luchino Visconti	1965

Story of an aging Sicilian prince who realizes, "If one wants things to stay as they are, things have to change."

The Two of Us	Claude Berri	1968

About a 75-year-old man and a 9-year-old boy. 86 minutes.

The Shameless Old Lady	Rene Allio	1969

Story of a 70-year-old French widow who, having spent her life serving others, serves herself in the last 18 months of her life. 94 minutes.

I Never Sang for My Father	Gilbert Cates	1970

92 minutes.

Harold and Maude	Hal Ashby	1971

92 minutes.

The Autobiography of Miss Jane Pittman	John Forty	1974

116 minutes.

Harry and Tonto	Paul Mazursky	1974
Sendakan 8	Kei Kumai	1975

Documentary Films

Antonia: A Portrait of the Woman. 58 minutes, color, 1974. Directors: Judy Collins and Jill Godmilow. Distributor: Rocky Mountain Productions.

Bubby. 5 minutes, B&W, 1966. Director: Murray Kramer. Distributor: Youth Film Distribution Center.

Don't Count the Candles: An essay by Lord Snowdon. 60 minutes, B&W, 1968. "CBS News Special." Director: Wilbein K. McClure. Distributor: CBS Television.

Home for Life. 58 or 86 minutes (2 versions), B&W, 1967. Director: Gerald Temaner. Distributor: Films, Inc.

I.F. Stone's Weekly. 62 minutes, B&W, 1973. Director: Jerry Bruck, Jr., Distributor: I.F. Stone Project.

Imogen Cunningham, Photographer. 20 minutes, color, 1970. Director: John Korty. Distributor: Time-Life Films.

Nana: Un Portrait. 25 minutes, color, 1973. Director and Distributor: Jamil Simon.

Number Our Days. 30 minutes, color, 1976. Directors: Lynn Littman and Barbara Meyerhoff. (Academy Award, Best Documentary—Short, 1976.)

Peege. 28 minutes, color, 1973. Director: Randal Kleiser. Distributor: Phoenix Films.

Sex After Sixty. 10 minutes, color, 1974. CBS Magazine. Director: Irina Posner. Distributor: CBS Television.

Three Grandmothers. 28 minutes, B&W, 1963. Directors: Julian Biggs and John Howe. Distributor: McGraw-Hill Films and New York University Film Library.

When Parents Grow Old. 15 minutes, color, 1973. Producer and Distributor: Learning Corporation of America.

When You Reach December. 50 minutes, color, 1970. Director: Richard Hubert. Distributor: Westinghouse Broadcasting Corporation.

You'll Get Yours When You're 65. 40 minutes, color or B&W, 1973. Director: Gene DePoris. Distributor: Carousel Films.

FILM CATALOGS

Trojan, J.: Aging, a filmography, Educational Film Library Association, 17 W. 60th St., New York, N.Y. 10023, Summer 1974.

Ethel Percy Andrus Gerontology Center: About aging: a catalog of films, revised, University of Southern California, 1975.

COMMERCIAL TELEVISION

In the New York City area: *The Prime of Your Life.* (Joe Michaels, Lucia Suarez, producer) NBC Television.

In the Boston Area: *Prime Time.* (Barbara Brilliant, producer) Westinghouse Broadcasting Corporation.

There is a great interest in *Over Easy,* the Public Broadcasting System daily program on aging developed through KQED, San Francisco, and hosted by Hugh Downs (producer, Joles Power). It has a weekly audience estimated at approximately 7 million, one third of whom are under 30. Its goal is to provide information to improve the quality of life in the later years and to provide a positive and constructive image of aging. The program began in 1977 and received the Peabody Award in 1978.

SELECTED HISTORICAL REFERENCES

Achenbaum, W.A.: Old age in the new land: the American experience since 1790, Baltimore, 1978, The Johns Hopkins University Press.

Altmeyer, A.J.: The formative years of social security, Madison, 1966, University of Wisconsin Press.

Aries, P.: Centuries of childhood, New York, 1962, Random House, Inc.

Charcot, J.-M.: Clinical lectures on the diseases of old age (Lecons cliniques sur les maladies les vieillard et les maladies chroniques [1867]), Hunt, L., translator, New York, 1881, William Wood.

Cicero, M.T.: De senectute, Copley, F.D., translator, Ann Arbor, 1967, The University of Michigan Press.

Elder, G.: Children of the Depression, Chicago, 1975, The University of Chicago Press.

Emerson, R.W.: Old age, Atlantic Monthly **9:**134-138, 1862.

Fischer, D.H.: Growing old in America, New York, 1977, Oxford University Press.

Gruman, G.J.: A history of ideas about the prolongation of life: the evolution of prolongevity hypotheses to 1800, Philadelphia, 1966, The American Philosophical Society.

Hall, G.S.: Senescence: the last half of life, New York, 1922, D. Appleton and Co.

Hareven, T.K.: The last stage: historical adulthood and old age, DAEDALUS **105:**20, 1976.

Metchnikoff, E.: The prolongation of life, New York, 1908, G.P. Putnam's Sons.

Minot, C.S.: Senility. In Buck, A.H., editor: Reference handbook of medical science, vol. 6, New York, 1885, William Wood, p. 388.

Nascher, I.L.: Geriatrics, Philadelphia, 1914, P. Blakiston's Son and Co.

Rush, B.: An account of the state of the mind and body in old age. In Medical inquiries and observations, 4 vol., 1793 (reprinted Philadelphia, 1797, Thomas Dobson).

Stearns, P.N.: Old age in European society: the case in France, New York, 1976, Holmes and Meier Publishers, Inc.

Stone, L.: Walking over grandma, New York Review of Books, May 12, 1977.

Zeman, F.D.: Life's later years: studies in the medical history of old age (series), Journal of Mt. Sinai Hospital, 1944-1947.

LIFE REVIEWS: ORAL HISTORY

Blythe, R.: Akenfield: portrait of an English village, New York, 1979, Pantheon Books Inc.

Hareven, T.K., and Langenbach, R.: Amoskeag: life and work in an American factory city, New York, 1978, Pantheon Books, Inc.

PHOTOGRAPHY AND DRAWINGS OF OLD AGE

Jacques, M.: Images of age, Cambridge, Mass., 1980, ABT Books.

Martine, F.: Le temps de vieillir, Paris, France, 1980, Editions Filipacchi.

GLOSSARIES

General glossary*

adaptation Fitting or conforming to the environment, typically by means of a combination of autoplastic maneuvers (which involve a change in the self) and alloplastic maneuvers (which involve alteration of the external environment). The end result of successful adaptation is termed "adjustment." "Maladjustment" refers to unsuccessful attempts at adaptation.

affect A person's emotional feeling tone and its outward manifestations. Affect and *emotion* are commonly used interchangeably.

aggression A forceful physical, verbal, or symbolic action. May be appropriate and self-protective, including healthful self-assertiveness, or inappropriate. Also may be directed outward toward the environment, as in explosive personality, or inward toward the self, as in depression.

ambivalence The coexistence of two opposing drives, desires, feelings, or emotions toward the same person, object, or goal. These may be conscious or partly conscious, or one side of the feelings may be *unconscious*. An example is love and hate toward the same person.

anomie Apathy, alienation, and personal distress resulting from the loss of goals previously valued. Durkheim popularized this term when he listed it as one of the principal reasons for suicide.

anxiety Apprehension, tension, or uneasiness that stems from the anticipation of danger, the source of which is largely unknown or unrecognized. Primarily of intraphysic origin, in contrast to fear, which is the emotional response to a consciously recognized and usually external threat or danger. Anxiety and fear are accompanied by similar physiological changes. May be regarded as pathological when present to such extent as to interfere with effectiveness in living, achievement of desired goals or satisfactions, or reasonable emotional comfort.

autonomic nervous system The part of the nervous system that innervates the cardiovascular, digestive, reproductive, and respiratory organs. It operates outside consciousness and controls basic life-sustaining functions such as the heart rate, digestion, and breathing. It includes the sympathetic nervous system and the parasympathetic nervous system.

behavior therapy (behavior modification, conditioning therapy) Any treatment approach designed to modify the patient's behavior directly rather than correct the dynamic causation. Behavior therapy is derived from laboratory investigations of learning and focuses on modifying observable and, at least in principle, quantifiable behavior by means of systematic manipulation of the environmental and behavioral variables thought to be functionally related to the behavior. Some of the many techniques included within behavior therapy are operant conditioning, shaping, token economy, systematic desensitization, assertive training, flooding, implosion. See also BIOFEEDBACK.

assertive training A form of behavior therapy in which patients are taught appropriate interpersonal responses, involving frank, honest, and direct expression of their feelings, both positive and negative.

*Modified from American Psychiatric Association: A psychiatric glossary, ed. 4, New York, 1975, Basic Books, Inc., Publishers.

aversion therapy A behavior therapy treatment based on respondent conditioning. Stimuli associated with undesirable behavior are paired with a painful or unpleasant sensation, resulting in the suppression of the undesirable behavior. For example, the look, smell, and taste of alcoholic beverages may be paired with nausea induced by emetics so that the patient feels conditioned nausea in the presence of alcoholic beverages, thus discouraging his or her drinking of them.

conditioning (learning) A more or less permanent change in an individual's behavior that occurs as a result of experience and practice. Conditioning is employed clinically in behavior therapy. There are generally considered to be two types of conditioning, operant conditioning and respondent conditioning.

operant conditioning (instrumental conditioning) A process by which the environmental events (reinforcers) following the individual's behavior determine whether the behavior is more or less likely to occur in the future. Through shaping, the individual learns to make new responses. Through differential reinforcement, the individual learns to make some responses more frequently, others less. This process of extinction results in the behavior returning to its preconditioning level. These principles and related procedures are used in behavior therapy to teach patients new, appropriate behavior and to eliminate undesirable behavior.

biofeedback Provision of information to the subject by measuring one or more of his or her physiological processes such as brain wave activity or blood pressure, often as an essential element in visceral learning, or learning to control physiological processes even though they produce no consciously perceived sensations (also known as physiological self-regulation).

The work of experimental psychologist Neal E. Miller and his associates, however, has shown that visceral reactions, reflexes, and similar processes that are under *autonomic nervous system* control are also subject to learning (learned autonomic control), even though not conscious and not under the control of the somatic nervous system. Instrumental or operant conditioning refers to the fact that immediate rewards influence subsequent behavior, that patterns of behavior instrumental in satisfying needs and relieving pain or stress tend to be repeated. Because vital functions such as blood pressure are never maintained at an absolutely constant level, their fluctuations can be treated as responses and reinforced appropriately (rewarded) so that the subject can learn to control internal organ function, even though he or she may not consciously understand how such learning has been achieved (operant autonomic conditioning).

Alpha brain waves (7.5 to 13.5 cps) characterize relaxed and peaceful wakefulness, which is accordingly known as the alpha state. Alpha biofeedback training attempts to teach the subject to achieve a state of relaxation by giving the subject information on his or her EEG. In one technique an acoustic tone sounds in the absence of alpha waves; when the subject produces alpha waves, the tone disappears.

Similar results in relaxation training and control of states of consciousness are achieved with transcendental meditation. In this technique the subject repeats a mantra (a Sanskrit syllable or word) over and over until he or she is so relaxed that even the mantra disappears from consciousness. If the subject starts to have disturbing thoughts, the subject begins again to repeat the mantra until he or she is relaxed. The subject usually continues in that state for 15 to 20 minutes.

These techniques have excited interest because of their possible application to large groups of psychiatric patients as antianxiety agents that are under control of patients and as ways of affecting physiological processes that have psychological and emotional analogues (for example, psychosomatic disorders).

catchment area Used in psychiatry to define a geographical area for which a mental health facility has responsibility. See COMMUNITY PSYCHIATRY.

catharsis The healthful (therapeutic) release of ideas through a "talking out" of conscious material accompanied by the appropriate emotional reaction. Also, the release into awareness of repressed (that is, "forgotten") material from the unconscious.

cathexis Attachment, conscious or unconscious, of emotional feeling and significance to an idea or object, most commonly a person.

character The sum of the relatively fixed personality traits and habitual modes of response of an individual.

cognitive Referring to the mental process of comprehension, judgment, memory, and reasoning, as contrasted with emotional and volitional processes.

commitment A legal process for admitting a mentally ill person to a mental hospital. The legal definition and procedure vary from state to state. Usually requires a court or judicial procedure, although not in all states. Sometimes the commitment may be entirely voluntary.

community mental health center A health service delivery system first authorized by the federal Mental Retardation Facilities and Community Mental Health Centers Construction Act of 1963 to provide a coordinated program of continuing mental health care to a specific population. The CMHC is typically a community or neighborhood facility or a network of affiliated agencies that serves as a locus for the delivery of the various services included in the concept of *community psychiatry*. Emphasis is on provision of a comprehensive range of services and continuity of care that are readily accessible to the population served. Since 1964 regulations governing federally supported centers have required that they offer at least five services: inpatient, outpatient, partial hospitalization, emergency services, and consultation and education for community agencies. It is also considered desirable that the center provide diagnostic, rehabilitative, precare and aftercare, training, research, and public education services.

The form and style of a center and the specific programs it provides are largely determined by the needs of the population it serves. Since emotional and mental health needs are so closely interwoven with broader social and political issues, centers serving different populations develop different ways of functioning. In some, for example, the emphasis may be on support services such as welfare, legal aid, placement, and homemaker services. In others the emphasis may be on alternatives to 24-hour inpatient care such as day, night, or weekend hospital care or day-care programs, drop-in lounges or outreach and home visits. Still others may lean heavily on sociotherapy with peer group interaction, indigenous workers and community caregivers in a storefront or similar non-clinical setting, or community socialization opportunities.

community psychiatry That branch of psychiatry concerned with the provision and delivery of a coordinated program of mental health care to a specified population (usually all residents of a designated geographical area termed the *"catchment area"*). Implicit in the concept of community psychiatry is acceptance of continuing responsibility for all the mental health needs of the community—diagnosis, treatment, rehabilitation (tertiary *prevention*) and after-care, and, equally important, early case-finding (secondary prevention), and promoting mental health and preventing psychosocial disorder (primary prevention). The organizational nucleus for such services is typically the *community mental health center*. The body of knowledge and theory on which methods and techniques of community psychiatry are based is often called *social psychiatry*. See also PREVENTION.

complex A group of associated ideas that have a common strong emotional tone. These are largely unconscious and significantly influence attitudes and associations.

conflict A mental struggle that arises from the simultaneous operation of opposing impulses, drives, or external (environmental) or internal demands; termed *"intrapsychic"* when the conflict is between forces within the personality, "extrapsychic" when it is between the self and the environment.

counterphobia The desire or seeking out of experiences that are consciously or unconsciously feared.

countertransference The psychiatrist's partly conscious or unconscious emotional reaction to a patient. See also TRANSFERENCE.

defense mechanism Unconscious intrapsychic processes serving to provide relief from emotional conflict and anxiety. Conscious efforts are frequently made for the same reasons, but true defense mechanisms are unconscious. Some of the common defense mechanisms are compensation, conversion, denial, displacement, dissociation, idealization, identification, incorporating, introjection, projection, rationalization, reaction formation, regression, sublimation, substitution, symbolization, undoing.

delusion A firm, fixed idea not amenable to rational explanation, maintained despite logical argument and objective, contradictory evidence.

denial A *defense mechanism,* operating unconsciously, used to resolve emotional *conflict* and allay *anxiety* by disavowing thoughts, feelings, wishes, needs, or external reality factors that are consciously intolerable.

dependency needs Vital needs for mothering, love, affection, shelter, protection, security, food, and warmth. May be a manifestation of regression when they appear openly in adults.

displacement A *defense mechanism,* operating unconsciously, in which an emotion is transferred from its original object to a more acceptable substitute used to allay *anxiety.*

dissociation A *defense mechanism,* operating unconsciously, through which emotional significance and *affect* are separated and detached from an idea, situation, or object. Dissociation may defer or postpone experiencing some emotional impact as, for example, in selective amnesia.

drug holiday Discontinuing the administration of a drug for a limited period of time in order to evaluate baseline behavior and to control the dosage of psychoactive drugs and side effects.

drug interaction The effects of two or more drugs being taken simultaneously producing an alteration in the usual effects of either drug taken alone. The interacting drugs may have a potentiating or additive effect, and serious side effects may result. An example of drug interaction is alcohol and sedative drugs taken together and causing additive central nervous system depression.

DSM-I Abbreviation for the first edition of the American Psychiatric Association's *Diagnostic and Statistical Manual of Mental Disorders,* published in 1952.

DSM-II Abbreviation for *Diagnostic and Statistical Manual of Mental Disorders,* second edition (1968).

DSM-III Abbreviation for *Diagnostic and Statistical Manual of Mental Disorders,* third edition (1980).

dynamic psychiatry Refers to the study of emotional processes, their origins, and the mental mechanisms as distinguished from descriptive psychiatry. Implies the study of the active, energy laden, and changing factors in human behavior and their motivation. Dynamic principles convey the concepts of change, or evolution, and of progression or regression.

ego In psychoanalytic theory, one of the three major divisions in the model of the psychic apparatus, the others being the *id* and *superego.* The ego represents the sum of certain mental mechanisms such as perception and memory and specific *defense mechanisms.* The ego serves to mediate between the demands of primitive instinctual drives (the *id*), of internalized parental and social prohibitions (the *superego*), and of reality. The compromises between these forces achieved by the ego tend to resolve intrapsychic *conflict* and serve an adaptive and executive function. Psychiatric usage of the term should not be confused with common usage, which connotes ''self-love'' or ''selfishness.''

ego ideal The part of the personality that comprises the aims and goals of the self; usually refers to the conscious or unconscious emulation of significant figures with whom the person has identified. The ego ideal emphasizes what one should be or do in contrast to what one should not be or do.

electroencephalogram (EEG) A graphic (voltage versus time) depiction of the brain's electrical potentials recorded by scalp electrodes. It is used for diagnosis in neurological and neuropsychiatric disorders and in neurophysiological research. Sometimes used interchangeably with electrocorticogram and depth record, in which the electrodes are in direct contact with brain tissue.

empathy An objective and insightful awareness of the feelings, emotions, and behavior of another person, their meaning and significance; usually subjective and noncritical.

encounter group A sensitivity group stressing emotional rather than intellectual insight. It is oriented to the here and now, with emphasis on developing awareness through confrontation to improve coping behavior.

epidemiology The study of the incidence, distribution, prevalence, and control of mental disorders in a given population. Common terms used in epidemiology are the following:

endemic Describes a disorder that is native to or restricted to a particular area.

epidemic Describes a disorder or the outbreak of a disorder that affects significant numbers of persons in a given population at any time.

pandemic Describes a disorder that occurs over a very wide area, or in many countries, or even universally.

extrapyramidal syndrome A variety of signs and symptoms, including muscular rigidity, tremors, drooling, restlessness, peculiar involuntary movements and postures, shuffling gait, protrusion of the tongue, chewing movements, blurred vision, and many other neurological disturbances. Results from dysfunction of the *extrapyramidal system.* May occur as a reversible side effect of certain psychotropic drugs, particularly the phenothiazines. Compare with Parkinson's disease.

extrapyramidal system The portion of the central nervous system responsible for coordinating and integrating various aspects of motor behavior or bodily movements.

fantasy An imagined sequence of events or mental images (for example, daydreams). Serves to express *unconscious conflicts,* to gratify unconscious or conscious wishes, or to prepare for anticipated future events.

fear Emotional and physiological response to recognized sources of danger, to be distinguished from *anxiety*.

health maintenance organization (HMO) A form of group practice by physicians and supporting personnel that provides comprehensive health services to an enrolled group of subscribers who pay a fixed premium to belong. The emphasis is on maintaining the health of the enrollees as well as treating their illnesses. HMOs should and often do include psychiatric services among their benefits.

hot line Telephone assistance for people in need of crisis intervention (for example, suicide prevention), staffed by trained lay people with mental health professionals used in an advisory or back-up capacity; also serves a preventive function and as a line of communication between different community services. Most hot lines operate 24 hours a day, 7 days a week.

hyperactivity (hyperkinesis) Increased or excessive muscular activity seen in diverse neurological and psychiatric disorders.

hyperventilation Overbreathing associated with *anxiety* and marked by reduction of blood carbon dioxide, subjective complaints of light-headedness, faintness, tingling of the extremities, palpitations, and respiratory distress.

iatrogenic illness An illness unwittingly precipitated, aggravated, or induced by the physician's attitude, examination, comments, or treatment.

id In freudian theory, the part of the personality structure that harbors the *unconscious instinctual* desires and strivings of the individual. See also EGO.

idealization A mental mechanism, operating consciously or unconsciously, in which the individual overestimates an admired aspect or attribute of another person.

ideas of reference Incorrect interpretation of casual incidents and external events as having direct reference to oneself. May reach sufficient intensity to constitute *delusions*.

identity crisis A loss of the sense of the sameness and historical continuity of oneself and inability to accept or adopt the role that one perceives as being expected of oneself by society; often expressed by isolation, withdrawal, extremism, rebelliousness, and negativity and typically triggered by a combination of sudden increase in the strength of instinctual drives

and the milieu or rapid social evolution and technological change.

insight Self-understanding. The extent of the individual's understanding of the origin, nature, and mechanisms of his or her attitudes and behavior. More superficially, recognition by a patient that he or she is ill.

instinct An inborn drive. The primary human instincts include self-preservation and sexuality and—for some proponents—aggression, the ego instincts, and the ''herd'' and ''social'' instincts. Freud also postulated a death instinct (thanatos).

intellectualization The utilization of reasoning as a defense against confrontation with *unconscious conflicts* and their stressful emotions.

International Classification of Diseases (ICD) The official list of disease categories issued by the World Health Organization, subscribed to by all WHO member nations, which may assign their own terms to each ICD category. ICDA *(International Classification of Diseases, Adapted for Use in the United States),* prepared by the U.S. Public Health Service, represents the official list of diagnostic terms to be used for each ICD category in this country. *DSM-III* is based on the ninth revision of the *International Classification of Diseases (ICS-9)* prepared in 1966.

interpretation The process by which the therapist communicates to the patient understanding of a particular aspect of the patient's problems or behavior.

intrapsychic That which takes place within the *psyche* or mind.

introjection A *defense mechanism,* operating unconsciously, whereby loved or hated external objects are taken within oneself symbolically. The converse of *projection.* May serve as a defense against conscious recognition of intolerable hostile impulses. For example, in severe depression, the individual may unconsciously direct unacceptable hatred or *aggression* toward himself (that is, toward the introjected object within himself). Related to the more primitive mechanism of incorporation.

isolation A *defense mechanism,* operating unconsciously, in which an unacceptable impulse, idea, or act is separated from its original memory source, thereby removing the emotional charge associated with the original memory.

malingering Deliberate simulation or exaggeration of an illness or disability that, in fact, is nonexistent or minor in order to avoid an unpleasant situation or to obtain some type of personal gain. See SECONDARY GAIN.

masochism Pleasure derived from physical or psychological pain inflicted either by oneself or by others. When it is consciously sought as a part of the sexual act or as a prerequisite to sexual gratification, it is classifiable as a sexual deviation. It is the converse of *sadism,* and the two tend to coexist in the same individual.

narcissism (narcism) From Narcissus, figure in Greek mythology who fell in love with his own reflected image. Self-love, as opposed to object-love (love of another person). In psychoanalytic theory, cathexis (investment) or the psychic representation of the self with libido (sexual interest and energy). Some degree of narcissism is considered healthy and normal, but an excess interferes with relations with others. To be distinguished from egotism, which carries the connotation of self-centeredness, selfishness, and conceit. Egotism is but one expression of narcissism.

Oedipus complex Attachment of the child to the parent of the opposite sex, accompanied by envious and *aggressive* feelings toward the parent of the same sex. These feelings are largely repressed (that is, made unconscious) because of the fear of displeasure or punishment by the parent of the same sex. In its original use the term applied only to the boy or man.

overcompensation A conscious or unconscious process in which a real or imagined physical or psychological deficit inspires exaggerated correction. Introduced by Adler.

passive-dependent personality A personality disorder manifested by marked indecisiveness, emotional dependency, and lack of self-confidence. For diagnostic purposes, considered to be a subtype of *passive-aggressive* personality.

placebo Originally, an inactive substance such as a ''bread pill'' given to placate a patient demanding unnecessary medication. Useful in research and practice because of its potential psychological effect, which may be neutral, therapeutic, or noxious, depending on suggestion by the therapist or experimenter and the patient's own expectations, faith, fear, apprehension, or hostility. In British usage a placebo is sometimes called a dummy.

prevention (preventive psychiatry) In traditional medical usage, the prevention or prophylaxis of a disorder. The modern trend, particularly in *community psychiatry,* is to broaden the meaning of prevention to encompass also the amelioration, control, and limitation of disease. Prevention is often categorized as follows:

primary prevention Measures to prevent a mental disorder (for example, by nutrition, substitute parents).

secondary prevention Measures to limit a disease process (for example, through early case finding and treatment).

tertiary prevention Measures to reduce impairment or disability following a disorder (for example, through *rehabilitation* programs).

primary gain The relief from emotional *conflict* and the freedom from *anxiety* achieved by a *defense mechanism.* The concept is that mental states, both normal and pathological, develop defensively in largely unconscious attempts to cope with or to resolve unconscious conflicts. All mental mechanisms operate in the service of primary gain, and the need for such gain may be thought of as responsible for the initiation of an emotional illness. To be distinguished from *secondary gain.*

problem-oriented record A simple conceptual framework to expedite and improve the medical record. The record is structured to contain four logically sequenced sections: (1) the data base, (2) the problem list, (3) the plans, and (4) the follow-up. The data base provides the information required for each patient, regardless of diagnosis or presenting problems. The problem list is the list of numbered problems characterizing the patient to be treated. The plans specify what is to be done with regard to each problem, including what further needs to be done to identify and delineate the problem, what treatments are to be enacted for each problem, and what education of the patient and family is to be conducted regarding the problems. Plans are specified for each problem separately. The follow-up includes progress notes and often flow sheets. Progress notes are titled by problem and numbered according to their number on the problem list. Each progress note is subdivided into a data section (differentiated by data source—subjective and objective), assessments of the data entered concerning the problem, and plans for the problem as it has been assessed.

Professional Standards Review Organization (PSRO) An organization of physicians (or, in some cases, allied health professionals) in a designated region, state, or community that reviews the quality of health care services. A basic intent is to ensure that health care services rendered are "medically necessary," particularly in the case of inpatient hospital services that on review might be adjudged more effectively rendered on an ambulatory basis or in another health care facility. Specifically required by federal law (P.L. 92-603, Social Security Amendments of 1972) in relation to hospital care under Medicare and Medicaid but may later be extended to out-of-hospital care.

psychodynamics The systematized knowledge and theory of human behavior and its motivation, the study of which depends largely on the functional significance of emotion. Psychodynamics recognizes the role of unconscious motivation in human behavior. It is a predictive science, based on the assumption that a person's total makeup and probable reactions at any given moment are the products of past interactions between his or her specific genetic endowment and the environment in which the person has lived since conception.

rationalization A *defense mechanism* operating unconsciously, in which the individual attempts to justify or make consciously tolerable, by plausible means, feelings, behavior, and motives that would otherwise be intolerable. Not to be confused with conscious evasion or dissimulation.

reaction formation A *defense mechanism* operating unconsciously, wherein attitudes and behavior are adopted that are the opposites of impulses the individual harbors either consciously or unconsciously (for example, excessive moral zeal may be a reaction to strong but *repressed* asocial impulses).

reality principle In psychoanalytic theory, the concept that the *pleasure principle,* which represents the claims of *instinctual* wishes, is normally modified by the inescapable demands and requirements of the external world. In fact, the reality principle may even work in behalf of the pleasure principle; but it reflects compromises in the nature of the gratification and allows for the postponement of gratification to a more appropriate time. The reality principle usually becomes more prominent in the course of development but may be weak in certain psychiatric illnesses and undergo strengthening during treatment.

reality testing The ability to evaluate the external world objectively and to differentiate adequately between it and the internal world, between self and nonself. Falsification of reality, as with massive *denial* or projection, indicates a severe disturbance of *ego* functioning and/or the perceptual and memory processes on which the ego is partly based.

rehabilitation The methods and techniques used in a program that seeks to achieve maximal function and optimal adjustment for the identified patient and to prevent relapses or recurrences of his or her condition (because of the latter, sometimes termed *"tertiary prevention"*). The focus in rehabilitation is on the patient's assets and recoverable functions rather than on the liabilities engendered by the patient's pathologic condition or the complications of disuse and social deterioration that formerly were often mistakenly considered to be part of the underlying disease process. Includes individual and group psychotherapy, directed socialization, vocational retraining, education. See COMMUNITY PSYCHIATRY.

remotivation A group treatment technique administered by nursing service personnel in a mental hospital; of particular value to long-term, withdrawn patients because it stimulates their communication skills and interest in their environment.

repression A *defense mechanism,* operating unconsciously, that banishes unacceptable ideas, *affects,* or impulses from consciousness or that keeps out of consciousness what has never been conscious. Although not subject to voluntary recall, the repressed material may emerge in disguised form. Often confused with the conscious mechanisms of suppression.

sadism Pleasure derived from inflicting physical or psychological pain or abuse on others. The sexual significance of sadistic wishes or behavior may be conscious or unconscious. When necessary for sexual gratification, classifiable as a sexual deviation.

secondary gain The external benefits derived from any illness, including personal attention and service, monetary gains, disability benefits, and release from unpleasant responsibility. See PRIMARY GAIN.

sensory deprivation The experience of being cut off from usual external stimuli and the opportunity for perception. May occur experimentally or accidentally in various ways such as through loss of hearing or eyesight, by becoming marooned, by solitary confinement, or assignment to a remote service post, or by travelling in space. May lead to disorganized thinking, depression, panic, *delusions,* and hallucinations.

sleep The recurring periods of relative physical and psychological disengagement from one's environment that are accompanied by characteristic EEG *(elec-*

troencephalogram) findings and are divisible into two categories: nonrapid eye movement (NREM) sleep, also known as orthodox or synchronized (S) sleep; and rapid eye movement (REM) sleep, also referred to as paradoxical or desynchronized (D) sleep. Dreaming sleep is another, less accurate term used for REM sleep.

There are four stages of NREM sleep based on EEG findings. Stage 1 occurs immediately after sleep beings and has a pattern of low amplitude and fast frequency. Stage 2 has characteristic waves of 12 to 16 cycles per second known as sleep spindles. Stages 3 and 4 have progressive slowing of frequency and increase in amplitude of the wave forms. During a period of about 1½ hours after the beginning of sleep, a person progresses through the four stages of NREM sleep and emerges from them into the first period of REM sleep. REM sleep is associated with dreaming, and brief cycles (20 to 30 minutes) of this sleep occur about every 90 minutes throughout the night. Coordinated rapid eye movements give this type of sleep its name. Sleep patterns vary with age, state of health, medication, and psychological state.

social breakdown syndrome The concept that some of the mental patient's symptomatology is a result of treatment conditions and facilities and not a part of the primary illness. Factors bringing about this condition are social labeling, learning the chronic sick role, atrophy of work and social skills, and identification with the sick. See REHABILITATION.

social psychiatry The field of psychiatry concerned with the cultural, ecological, and sociological factors that engender, precipitate, intensify, prolong, or otherwise complicate maladaptive patterns of behavior and their treatment; sometimes used synonymously with *community psychiatry,* although the latter term should be limited to practical or clinical applications of social psychiatry. Important in social psychiatry is the ecological approach to maladaptive behavior, which is viewed not only as a deviation of an individual but also as a reflection of deviation in the social systems in which he or she lives.

sublimation A *defense mechanism,* operating unconsciously, by which instinctual drives, consciously unacceptable, are diverted into personally and socially acceptable channels.

transference The *unconscious* assignment to others of feelings and attitudes that were originally associated with important figures (parents, siblings, etc.) in one's early life. The transference relationship follows the pattern of its prototype. The psychiatrist utilizes this phenomenon as a therapeutic tool to help the patient understand his or her emotional problems and their origins. In the patient-physician relationship the transference may be negative (hostile) or positive (affectionate). See COUNTERTRANSFERENCE.

transient situational disturbance A transient disorder of any severity (including psychosis) that represents an acute reaction to overwhelming stress such as the severe crying spells, loss of appetite, and social withdrawal of a child separated from its mother or, in an adult, a reaction to an unwanted pregnancy manifested by suicidal gestures and hostile complaints. The symptoms generally recede as the stress diminishes.

unconscious That part of the mind or mental functioning of which the content is only rarely subject to awareness. The unconscious is a repository for data that have never been conscious (primary *repression*) or that may have become conscious briefly and were later repressed (secondary repression).

undoing A *defense mechanism,* operating unconsciously, in which something unacceptable and already done is symbolically acted out in reverse, usually repetitiously, in the hope of relieving *anxiety.*

Glossary on aging

age cohort Groups of similar age moving through time; or all those who grew up in the same time period.

age grading Age used for the assignment of roles and opportunities for people in the society.

age norms Role expectations at various age levels.

ageism Aversion, hatred, and prejudice toward the aged and their manifestation in the form of discrimination on the basis of age.

androgen Any one of a number of male sex hormones.

arteriosclerosis The loss of elasticity or the hardening of the walls of the arteries.

atheroma A fatty plaque or deposit on the inner wall surface (intima) of blood vessels (usually arteries).

atherosclerosis A fibrous thickening of the inner walls (intima) of blood vessels, accompanied by the accumulation of soft, pasty, acellular fatty material.

autoimmunity Attack response by the immune system of the body to its own tissues as a result of the production of antibodies against such antigens.

cross-sectional study Research focusing on many different persons at the same period of time.

demography The statistical study of the incidence or distribution within populations of births, deaths, marriages, diseases, etc.

estrogen The generic term for the hormonal substance involved in the female monthly cycle or estrus; the female sex hormone.

geriatrics The practice of medicine concerned with the diseases associated with old age.

gerontocracy Governmental rule by older persons.

gerontology That branch of science concerned with aging.

gerontophilia Exhalting and/or venerating the aged.

gerontophobia Fear and aversion of aging.

involution The return to a former, more primitive condition or previous form (for example, the involution of the uterus after birth); also, a degenerative change.

life expectancy The statistical prediction of how long an organism will live beyond a given initial age.

lipofuscin Brown pigment granules representing lipid-containing residues of lysosomal digestion, usually occurring with increased incidence with advancing age in certain tissues.

longitudinal study Research that focuses on the same persons over many years of time.

neuroplasticity The reestablishment of nerve connections in the central nervous system. Nerve receptors denervated because of death of neurons or brain cells may be reinervated by unaffected neurons. The terms ''recircuitry'' and ''reactive symptogenesis'' have been used.

osteoarthritis Inflammation of the articular extremities of bone resulting from structural changes in the cartilage and degeneration of the bones with osteophytic growths (bony outgrowths).

osteoporosis A gradual resorption of bone such that the tissue becomes unusually porous and fragile.

prolongevity Defined by Gruman in 1955 as ''the belief that it is possible and desirable to extend significantly the length of life by human action.'' Another definition is ''the significant extension of the length of life by human action.''

transcription (genetic) The transfer of genetic information from the DNA in the nucleus to RNA, the substance ultimately responsible for protein synthesis in the cytoplasm.

translation (genetic) The synthesis of amino acid chains and proteins by messenger RNA carrying the specific genetic information for such syntheses.

Author index

Subject index